AMERICAN PRESIDENTS

YEAR BY YEAR

VOLUME 2 • 1861-1932

LYLE EMERSON NELSON

SHARPE REFERENCE

an imprint of M.E. Sharpe, Inc.

SHARPE REFERENCE

Sharpe Reference is an imprint of M.E. Sharpe INC.

M.E. Sharpe INC.
80 Business Park Drive
Armonk, NY 10504

© 2004 by Lyle Emerson Nelson and New England Publishing Associates, Inc.

Produced by New England Publishing Associates, Inc.

Editors: Edward W. Knappman and Ron Formica
Production and Design: Ron Formica
Photo Researcher: Victoria Harlow
Editorial Assistant: Caitlin E. Cushman
Copyediting: Jody Thum and Gail Battles of Miccinello Associates
Proofreading: Sue Paruch, Gail Battles, and Lois Chamberlain of Miccinello Associates
Indexing: Darilee Penrod and Angela Miccinello of Miccinello Associates

Library of Congress Cataloging-in-Publication Data

Nelson, Lyle Emerson, 1924–
    American presidents : year by year / Lyle Emerson Nelson.
      p. cm
    Includes bibliographical references and index.
    Contents: v. 1. 1732–1860 — v. 2. 1861–1932 — v. 3. 1933–2000.
    ISBN 0-7656-8046-7 (set : alk. paper)
      1. Presidents—United States—Biography. 2. Presidents—United States—History—Chronology. 3. United States—Politics and government—Chronology. 4. United States—History—Chronology. I. Title.

E176.1.N44 2002
973'.09'9—dc21
[B]
                                             2002030898

Printed and bound in the United States of America

The paper used in this publication meets the minimum requirements of American National Standard for Information Sciences--Permanence of Paper for Printed Library Materials,
ANSI Z 39.48.1984.

BM (c) 10 9 8 7 6 5 4 3 2 1

CONTENTS

PREFACE

Pursuit of power, usually associated with ambition, drove most of the men who became President of the United States. Theodore Roosevelt led America onto the world stage, and Franklin D. Roosevelt shared world domination with Joseph Stalin. Since the implosion of the Soviet Union, the U.S. President, starting with George Herbert Walker Bush, has been alone at the center of world political power.

Few of these men, however ambitious, aspired to the presidency and its enormous power before they were well into middle age. George Washington, at Valley Forge, could not possibly have known that the presidency of an uncreated nation later would be his, any more than Harry S Truman, at 27, walking behind a horse in western Missouri, could have foreseen making the decision to drop the atomic bomb on Hiroshima. (Theodore Roosevelt, at 27, incidentally was the Republican candidate for mayor of New York City, quite a contrast with Truman.)

What I am showing, in a sense, is a unique vertical and horizontal view of future and former presidents at the same time—snapshots frozen in time—when one old man in retirement and a baby in his mother's arms were contemporaries.

The vertical perspective shows us Washington was on his death bed at Mount Vernon in December, 1799, while Millard Fillmore was in the womb in a scene of rural poverty on the Finger Lakes frontier of upstate New York. Closer to our time, Bill Clinton was not born when Hiroshima was crushed like an eggshell, but George W. Bush was a month old.

The horizontal pairings trace the paths each of these men took to the White House with all the paths not taken and detours along the way. Thus the 27-year-old Theodore Roosevelt can be juxtaposed with Truman. At the same age, Richard M. Nixon was studying oranges and trying to determine the technology needed to create frozen juice to make himself rich, while at 27 Franklin D. Roosevelt is an unknown lawyer in Manhattan and U.S. Grant an obscure soldier stationed in a backwater base on the banks of Lake Ontario.

But achieving power, in most cases, involved goal-oriented resolve, as shown by James Buchanan and Lyndon B. Johnson. In John F. Kennedy's case it was a father who pushed. Yet Andrew Jackson, Andrew Johnson, Rutherford B. Hayes, James Garfield, Herbert Hoover, and Bill Clinton had no fathers to push them.

Few Presidents were reluctant to accept power: William Howard Taft was pushed by his wife, and in 1952 Truman, who hadn't wanted the office in the first place, pushing a reluctant Adlai Stevenson to face a reluctant Dwight D. Eisenhower. That's a rare circumstance.

Most presidents were in the right place at the right time to seek political promotion. Luck, therefore was a factor. Dumb luck is a better way to put it when looking at John Tyler, our first "accidental" President, or Gerald R. Ford.

But positioning themselves for political gain was a game most played with skill and enthusiasm. When Desert Storm made George Herbert Walker Bush a hero, top Democratic contenders Mario Cuomo, Bill Bradley, Sam Nunn and others backed off, unwilling to face what looked like sure defeat. But by the 1992 Democratic convention, Bush's popularity had nosedived bringing forth Clinton from out of nowhere—along with such previous long shots as Jerry Brown and Paul Tsongas—along with independent H. Ross Perot.

For every reluctant Taft or Truman, there were endless men like Buchanan, Abraham Lincoln, and Lyndon Johnson consumed by ambition.

Throughout history, past and future presidents often knew each other, and these relationships have ranged from affection and hero-worship (James Monroe for Thomas Jefferson) to bitter hostility or condescension (Franklin D. Roosevelt for Herbert Hoover).

Reading Richard Hofstadter's *American Political Traditions* (1948) was a major influence on my pursuit of this subject in this way. He was discussing American political traditions, political philosophy, and thus included John C. Calhoun who was never president. But his chapter on Hoover caught my attention: the young engineer, an orphan, wealthy before he was 30, walking across Mongolia followed by an army of fascinated Chinese peasants mumbling to each other that here was a man, a geologist, who could walk across terrain and "see" gold under the ground. And Hoover was literally escorted by a Chinese Army on horseback there to keep away marauding predators, ruthless bandits. Now there's an experience Calvin Coolidge and Bill Clinton never had, nor the rest of us. No doubt, Hoover must have looked back with fondness on the hardships of Mongolia amidst the misery of his Depression-besieged presidency.

With my thanks to Adam A. "Bud" Smyser, Margaret Owen, Harold Morse, and Arlene Nelson.

Lyle Emerson Nelson
Honolulu, Hawaii
July 2003

AMERICAN PRESIDENTS: YEAR BY YEAR

1861 – 1932

1861
James Buchanan

President Buchanan's last 2 months of his single-term presidency found him trying everything to prevent the ship of state from capsizing before Lincoln could take the helm.

January: On January 1, South Carolina excluded U.S. ships from Charleston Harbor and cut off mail to Fort Sumter. At a cabinet meeting the next day, General Winfield Scott (who was included in the meeting) recommended that all forts in the South be reinforced. The president agreed. On the same day, South Carolina forces seized the vacant Fort Johnson in Charleston Harbor.

During the first week of January, Southern states began to prepare to secede. Georgia assembled a pro-secession convention, and the governor seized Fort Pulaski at Savannah. Florida and Alabama seized federal property and planned secession conventions. Meanwhile, Southern senators in Washington made plans to create a confederation of Southern states and make it *fait accompli* before Buchanan left office. At the same time, Southern congressmen began to withdraw from Washington and head back to their home states.

On January 5, Buchanan secretly directed Scott to send troops to Fort Sumter aboard the merchant ship *Star of the West*. As the ship approached Charleston Harbor on January 9, South Carolina troops opened fire on it. The captain of the *Star of the West* turned the ship around and headed back to New York.

In a special message to Congress on January 8, Buchanan stated, "The prospect of a bloodless settlement [in South Carolina] fades away." He added: "We are in the midst of a great revolution ... action, prompt action is required.... The Union must and shall be preserved by all constitutional means ... the right and duty to use military force defensively against those who resist the federal officers is clear and undeniable."

On January 9, South Carolina governor Francis Pickens demanded the surrender of Fort Sumter. Major Robert Anderson stalled and referred the request to Washington. Pickens then sent an emissary, Isaac W. Hayne, the state's attorney general, to see Buchanan on January 12. But Southern senators wanted Hayne to delay negotiating with the president until the foundations for a Confederacy could be built.

Buchanan still had hopes for a constitutional convention, but the Senate, on January 16, took it up for consideration only to have Republicans vote against even debating the question. The Republicans were firm in their policy of keeping Congress inactive. They voted down every Buchanan plan: extension of the Missouri Compromise line, new customs collectors for Charleston, and a force bill that would enable the president to mobilize troops.

The cabinet discussed the reinforcing of Fort Sumter during the last 2 weeks of January, and Secretary of State Jeremiah Black wrote to the president on January 22: "I solemnly believe that you can hold this revolution in check ... it will subside after a time into peace and harmony."

In the middle of the secessionist crisis, Kansas embraced statehood on January 29.

On January 31, Hayne presented Pickens's plan to Buchanan. Pickens said that South Carolina was willing to buy Fort Sumter. Otherwise it would "seize the fort" by force. The president refused the deal.

February: Delegates from the seven states that had seceded (South Carolina, Mississippi, Florida, Alabama, Georgia, Louisiana, and Texas) met in Montgomery, Alabama, on February 4 to frame a constitution for the Confederate States of America. On the same day, a peace convention with delegates from twenty-one states (but none of the seceding states) met in Washington to try to reach a compromise. Former president John Tyler presided over the convention.

On February 16, Jefferson Davis was inaugurated as president of the Confederate States of America, with Alexander H. Stephens of Georgia as vice president.

Buchanan's cabinet spent much of February discussing the matter of how to reinforce Fort Sumter without provoking a war. General Scott and others wanted to use naval units for reinforcement at night. The president wanted to wait until Anderson asked for help. Anderson appeared willing to stall on the reinforcement question until the problem could be dumped on Lincoln. Anderson and Buchanan agreed that any effort to reinforce Sumter would bring war.

Lincoln made his first visit to the White House on February 24 to meet with Buchanan. The meeting was a courtesy meeting with nothing of significance discussed.

March: Clerks and foreign ministers paid courtesy calls on the president in the final days, and he was busy signing congressional bills until noon on March 4 when Secretary of

War Joseph Holt brought him news from Major Anderson that 20,000 men were needed to reinforce Fort Sumter. With no time to act on the request, the president took his carriage to pick up Lincoln. They rode in a procession from the Willard Hotel to the Capitol and chatted amiably to the surprise of many.

On March 5, Buchanan, still shocked by Anderson's request, held a final cabinet meeting at the War Department to tie up loose ends. Buchanan then directed Holt to turn over all correspondence regarding Fort Sumter to Lincoln. The next day, Buchanan left Washington for his Wheatland estate in Lancaster.

April: When South Carolina opened fire on Fort Sumter on April 12, Buchanan wrote to J. B. Henry: "The Confederate States have deliberately commenced the civil war, and God knows where it may end."

May–September: Buchanan's first months in retirement were plagued by accusations and attacks against his administration. Southern newspapers called him a traitor and a liar. The Republican press blamed his inaction for starting the war. Buchanan was hurt by the attacks but remained firmly behind the Union. He encouraged volunteers and wrote to William B. Rose in September: "If I were a young man I should be there myself."

฿ఌ

ABRAHAM LINCOLN's first year in office featured diverse adversaries: a major Confederate military victory, problems relative to Union army leadership, a hostile Great Britain, and problems with mobilization. Lincoln had 5 weeks of uneasy peace before the Civil War started. His critics saw him as indecisive, ill prepared for the crisis, and without a plan or strategy to meet the greatest challenge ever to the American democracy.

January–February: During the months before his inauguration, Lincoln was besieged by office seekers as well as the well meaning. The Lincolns received numerous guests at their home on Eighth Street. At the end of January, Lincoln went to Charleston, Illinois, to visit his stepmother and to visit the grave of his father.

Lincoln made his final visit to his law office on February 10. Sprawled on a couch, he talked to partner Billy Herndon and told him: "Let it [their law shingle] hang there undisturbed. Give our clients to understand that the election of a President makes no change in the firm of Lincoln and Herndon. If I live I'm coming back … we'll go right on practicing law as if nothing had ever happened." Lincoln left for Washington the next day. At the train station, he said: "I now leave, not knowing when, or whether ever, I may return, with a task before me greater than that which rested upon Washington."

Detective Allan Pinkerton warned Lincoln that assassination plots were brewing in Baltimore. As a result, Lincoln was sneaked through Baltimore from Harrisburg in the middle of the night.

On his first day in Washington on February 24, Lincoln met with President Buchanan. He also met with his opponents in the presidential race: John Breckinridge, John Bell, and Stephen Douglas.

March: On March 4, Lincoln rode to his inaugural in an open carriage with Buchanan. Soldiers all along the route stood guard against trouble. Douglas sat on the platform close to Lincoln. Chief Justice Roger Taney administered the oath of office.

In his inaugural address, Lincoln said he had no plan to interfere with slavery. "No state, upon its own mere motion, can lawfully get out of the Union.… I shall take care … that the laws of the Union be faithfully executed in all the states." He said that "there will be no invasion—no using of force against, or among the people anywhere.… In your hands, my dissatisfied fellow countrymen and not in mine, is the momentous issue of civil war.… The government will not assault you."

Lincoln had selected his cabinet before leaving Illinois but kept his choices to himself in order to avoid friction and second-guessing. The cabinet was not announced until after his inauguration. For the top two cabinet posts, Lincoln selected William Seward for secretary of state and Salmon Chase of Ohio for secretary of Treasury. To complete his cabinet, Lincoln selected Edward Bates of Missouri for attorney general, Montgomery Blair of Maryland for postmaster general, Gideon Welles of Connecticut for secretary of the navy, Caleb B. Smith of Indiana for interior secretary, and Simon Cameron of Pennsylvania for secretary of war.

From the beginning, Lincoln had to deal with Fort Sumter. Major Anderson informed Lincoln on March 5 that he could only hold out another 6 weeks at Fort Sumter without provisions. Lincoln asked his cabinet and General Scott for written opinions on the question of supplying Anderson. All but Blair advised letting Sumter go.

Meanwhile, the Confederate states adopted their constitution on March 11. It was very similar to the U.S. Constitution—with small but significant differences. Instead of a union, the new nation was a confederacy of independent states. Also, the constitution specifically guaranteed the rights of citizens to own slaves.

On March 29, Lincoln announced that he would be sending food to resupply Fort Sumter but not troops.

April: Seward, in a memorandum to Lincoln, complained on April 1 that Lincoln still had no policy toward the South and that Sumter was still U.S. property. On April 8, three U.S. ships left New York to resupply Fort Sumter. On April 10, Confederate Secretary of War Leroy Walker ordered General P. T. Beauregard, the commander of Confederate forces in Charleston, to demand the surrender of Fort Sumter or to take it by force. On April 11, Beauregard demanded Major Anderson's surrender. Anderson answered that unless supplies reached him by April 15, he would be forced to evacu-

The Confederate bombardment of Fort Sumter on April 12, 1861, the opening conflict of the American Civil War.

ate the force. Beauregard regarded this as a refusal and did not want to chance that supplies would reach the fort before April 15.

Before dawn on the morning of April 12, Confederate batteries opened fire on Fort Sumter. Anderson surrendered the fort on April 14 after 2 days and nights of bombardment.

Lincoln met with his cabinet the next day and called for the mobilization of 75,000 men for service tours of 3 months. The North responded enthusiastically to Lincoln's proclamation; there were soon more volunteers than guns available. Southern unionists turned against the president, believing that Lincoln had betrayed them by abandoning his conciliatory stance.

On April 18, Lincoln offered Robert E. Lee the command of the Union forces. Lee declined the offer. "Though opposed to secession and deprecating war, I could take no part in an invasion of the southern states," he said.

The next day, Lincoln ordered the blockade of all Southern ports. Although the U.S. Navy did not have the capabilities to blockade all of the ports, the order set in motion a huge expansion of the navy.

Based on an opinion by Attorney General Bates, on April 22, Lincoln suspended the privilege of habeas corpus—the right of anyone arrested to appear before a court to appeal detention.

May: On May 6, Jefferson Davis signed a bill declaring that a state of war existed between the United States and the Confederate states. The next day, Arkansas, North Carolina, and Tennessee joined the Confederacy. Governor Beriah Magoffin of Kentucky wired Lincoln, "Kentucky will furnish no troops for the wicked purpose of subduing her sister southern states." The Kentucky legislature declared neutrality on May 16.

June: After Fort Sumter, there were several minor skirmishes between Northern and Southern forces. In what many histo-

rians consider the first significant skirmish of the Civil War, on June 3, Union forces under General George B. McClellan routed a band of 1,500 Confederates at Philippi in western Virginia.

Lincoln and his cabinet discussed strategy on June 29 and decided on a frontal assault into Virginia. Scott preferred a blockade of the Mississippi.

July: At the opening of the special session of Congress on July 4, Lincoln told the Congress, "This is essentially a people's contest. Our popular government [is] an experiment."

The first major battle of the Civil War took place on July 21 near Manassas, Virginia. General Irvin McDowell headed a motley Northern army of 30,000 south. Confederate Generals P. T. Beauregard and Joseph E. Johnston established a Confederate line of defense at Manassas Junction, about 20 miles from the Potomac River. The Confederates won the First Battle of Bull Run when McDowell made a hasty retreat. However, casualties on both sides were stunning. The Union suffered more than 2,600 killed, wounded, or missing; and the Confederates suffered approximately 2,000 killed, wounded, or missing.

The South celebrated the victory, while the North was disheartened by the defeat. Many in the South believed that their victory at Bull Run would lead to a quick end of the war.

The day after Bull Run, Lincoln removed McDowell from command and named General George B. McClellan commander of the Army of the Potomac. Lincoln also named John C. Fremont commander of the Army of the West with headquarters in St. Louis.

August: Forces under Union general Nathaniel Lyon were defeated by Confederate forces on August 10 at the Battle of Wilson's Creek in Missouri. Each side suffered more than 1,000 casualties.

September: Kentucky's neutrality was tested on September 4 when Confederate troops moved into southeastern Kentucky in Columbus on the Mississippi River to prevent a possible Union move to take the state. Union troops soon occupied Louisville and Covington in northern Kentucky. The Kentucky legislature on September 12 abandoned its neutrality because of the Confederate army's occupation of southeastern Kentucky. As a result, Governor Magoffin resigned and was replaced by the pro-Union James F. Robinson.

October–November: Lincoln, dissatisfied with the command of Fremont in Missouri after the defeat at Wilson's Creek, relieved him of his command on October 24. On Octo-

Abraham Lincoln and his first cabinet. From left to right: Attorney General Edward Bates; Secretary of the Navy Gideon Welles; (seated) Secretary of State William Seward; (standing) Postmaster General Montgomery Blair; (seated) Secretary of the Treasury Salmon Chase; President Lincoln; General Winfield Scott; Secretary of the Interior Caleb Smith; and Secretary of War Simon Cameron.

ber 31, Winfield Scott, tired of his battles with younger officers, offered his resignation. Lincoln accepted the resignation on November 1 and appointed McClellan to replace Scott as commander of the Union forces.

On November 8, the USS *San Jacinto* stopped the British mail steamer *Trent* off the coast of Havana, Cuba, and removed two Confederate commissioners bound for England—James Mason and John Slidell. Mason and Slidell were later brought to Boston and held captive. The incident touched off a diplomatic crisis between the United States and Great Britain. The British foreign secretary, Lord John Russell, demanded an apology from the United States for the incident and the immediate release of Mason and Slidell.

December: The *Trent* incident came to a boil during the month, nearly plunging the United States and Great Britain into a war. On December 4, the British announced a ban on shipments of war supplies to the United States. A solution was reached on December 26 when Seward said that the captain of the *San Jacinto*, Charles Wilkes, had acted on his own in capturing Slidell and Mason. On December 30, the two were released and allowed to continue their journey to England.

Former Presidents

MARTIN VAN BUREN declined an invitation from Pierce to chair a meeting of former presidents at Philadelphia for the purpose of devising a plan that might save the nation from fighting a war.

Pierce's letter of April 16 stated that because Van Buren was the senior living president of the five, he should call the meeting. Van Buren replied on April 20: "I regret ... after the

most careful consideration ... serious doubts ... to the practicability of making a volunteer movement of that description." Rather than himself, Van Buren suggested that Buchanan be the chairman because he was the most recent White House occupant. Van Buren said he would attend such a conference, if Pierce desired it, even though the Kinderhook, New York, retiree doubted much could be accomplished at such a late hour.

&oc&

JOHN TYLER played a major role in a futile peace conference held in Washington that delegates hoped might avert war. When the effort failed, Tyler turned bitter against the United States and was later elected to the Confederate House.

January–February: The Virginia legislature passed a joint resolution on January 19 calling for a peace conference in Washington on February 4 "to consider and, if practical, agree upon some suitable adjustment." The legislature also recommended certain resolutions to preserve the Union. Five commissioners were selected, including Tyler and William C. Rives.

Tyler was anxious to serve the cause and hurried to Washington to present the Virginia resolutions to Buchanan. Buchanan said he would present them to Congress but complained that the South was guilty of hostile acts by seizing the forts of Charleston. In the end, Congress ignored the Virginia resolutions.

Tyler received a unanimous vote from delegates to preside as president of the peace convention that opened on February 4. Tyler accompanied delegates to the White House on February 7 to meet Buchanan. Tyler told the president that if troops at Fort Sumter were reduced in number, Tyler would try to keep the forts from being fired at. Buchanan replied that if he did that he would be hanged in effigy in the North. The peace conference made these points:

No slavery above 36°30' slavery would continue south of this line and any disputes in territories south of the line would be settled by federal courts; and new states on either side of the line would be admitted with or without slavery, depending on the constitution of each.

Tyler presented the peace convention resolutions to Congress on February 27, and John Crittenden's special committee agreed to submit the package of ideas to the states as constitutional amendments. The Senate rejected the resolutions, voting 28 to 7. Now Tyler returned to Virginia with quite a different attitude. He gave up on the Union and decided Virginia needed to present a solid secession front. He reasoned that if Virginia took a united stance there would be no war.

March: Tyler took his seat at the Virginia state convention on March 1. George W. Summers gave a speech opposing secession and suggested that Virginia await further attempts in Washington to find peaceful solutions. Tyler replied on March 13 or 14. He said he was "an old man wearied overmuch with a long course of public service." Tyler, who would be 71 in 2 weeks, was weak from illness. He added that there was no hope of settlement and advocated secession or adoption of resolutions, insisting on obtaining status quo agreements from the federal government.

April: The convention finally ended, and Tyler voted for secession on April 17.

June–July: In June, Tyler was nominated for a seat in the Provisional Congress of the Confederacy slated to meet on July 20.

October–November: Through a notice in the *Richmond Daily Examiner* on October 5, Tyler notified voters in his area that he was willing to accept a draft to serve in the Confederate Congress once the Confederate Constitution took effect in February 1862. Later in October, Charles City County endorsed Tyler for a seat. Tyler won his Confederate House seat on November 7.

&)(&

MILLARD FILLMORE supported the North, hosted Lincoln at his Buffalo, New York, home, lost his old southern political friends, and then organized a home guard militia for elderly men.

Fillmore, 61, early in the year, was willing to take part in the parley for former presidents promoted by Pierce. Editorial attacks soon killed the idea however.

Lincoln, en route to Washington, arrived in Buffalo on February 16. Fillmore, as Buffalo's first citizen, entertained the president-elect.

&)(&

FRANKLIN PIERCE'S long association with Southern causes and politicians caused problems for him when Union sentiment burst forth in Concord, New Hampshire. The retired Pierce took a major role in the idea of the five living former presidents pooling their prestige in an effort to meet and work out a formula to stop the conflict.

When he first heard about the peace meeting idea involving the former presidents, Pierce said that he saw no hope for such an idea. Besides, he said, he had a cold. After the fall of Fort Sumter in April, Pierce reconsidered the idea and wrote Van Buren suggesting that as the senior retiree he should call the five together in Philadelphia in a last-ditch move to quiet the public clamor for war. Van Buren turned him down and suggested that Pierce call such a meeting with Buchanan at the head. In the end, the peace meeting of the former presidents never took place.

Meanwhile, a committee in Concord demanded that Pierce make public his position on the national crisis. Pierce gave a speech outside a newspaper office and said he opposed secession and coercion and Southern talk of attacking Washington. He then endorsed a patriotic resolution, saying he hoped "so long as the fratricidal strife is not more fully developed than at present, that some event, some power" would intervene.

Future Presidents

ANDREW JOHNSON defiantly opposed Tennessee's secessionists. Now a hero in the North, a Unionist in many strong speeches, Johnson became friendly with Lincoln and was even considered for a cabinet post. By year's end his concern was for his family in isolated eastern Tennessee, a pocket of Union sympathy and resistance to Confederate occupation.

January–February: Early in the year, Johnson felt that Tennessee might still remain in the Union. Johnson wrote to John Trimble on January 13: "If Tennessee will stand firm in the end she can and will act ... in bringing back the seceding states." The Tennessee legislature in January ordered an election on the secession question, and on February 9 the state voted against secession. In reaction, Governor Isham G. Harris ordered another election and joined forces with the Confederacy to raise 55,000 troops.

Johnson took the offensive against the secessionists in a Senate speech on February 5. He attacked Jefferson Davis and Joseph Lane. Said Johnson: "There are two parties in this country that want to break up the government ... the nullifiers of the South [and] some bad men in the North." Texas senator Louis Wigfall called Johnson a "black Republican" and "renegade southerner."

April–June: Governor Harris in April ordered another election on secession for Tennessee, and Johnson decided to return home for the event. On the train at Lynchburg, Virginia, a man assaulted Johnson. Others on the station platform wanted to hang him. At Bristol a mob surrounded the train, again planning to lynch the senator, but the train did not stop, reportedly on the orders of Jefferson Davis.

On May 30, Johnson's sons Robert and Charles attended a convention in Knoxville called to consider the organization of a new state out of eastern Tennessee, a rekindling of feelings for the old stillborn state of "Franklin." However, Confederate pressure blocked this move.

In June, Tennessee voted to secede, although most voters in eastern Tennessee voted to stay in the Union.

July: When the special session of Congress opened on July 4, Johnson was the lone senator from a state that had seceded. From his Senate seat on July 27, he defended Lincoln's call for troops, saying, "It is not Lincoln but Davis who is overthrowing our government and making of it a despotism.... We will triumph, we must triumph. Right is with us."

December: Johnson was put on a joint select "Committee on the Conduct of the War." Johnson's two oldest sons were now in the Union army.

ഇരുൻ

ULYSSES S. GRANT found himself the only professional soldier in Galena, Illinois, as the Civil War took shape. In the chaos of the early days of the war, with its political intrigue and infighting for favors, Grant became a colonel and was even mentioned as a major general prospect before the year was out.

April–May: On April 16, the day after news reached Galena of Fort Sumter's fall, a mass meeting was held and Grant attended. There was an address by the Republican congressman for the district, Elihu B. Washburne. After the meeting Grant told his brother Orvil, "I think I ought to go into the service." Two nights later a second meeting was held to discuss recruiting. Being the only former army man around, Grant chaired the meeting.

Grant traveled with the other Galena recruits to Camp Yates at Springfield. Camp Yates was named after the governor of Illinois, Richard Yates. Grant drilled volunteers and awaited a commissioning, by brevet. Considering his West Point education, Grant expected to be commissioned a colonel. Grant complained to this father, Jesse, on May 6 that he would not engage in political wire-pulling to obtain a position in the army. He also wrote to Julia on May 6 that in his opinion, "this war will be but of short duration."

June: Grant received his commission from Governor Yates as a colonel. He was assigned on June 16 to the Twenty-First Illinois, whose colonel was a drunken buffoon.

July–August: The Twenty-First Illinois moved into Missouri through Quincy, Illinois. The Missouri campaign aimed at keeping the state in the Union. At Salt River, beyond Palmyra, Grant's force faced Confederate Colonel Thomas Harris and soon forced him to retreat.

On reaching Mexico, Missouri, Grant learned that he was being considered for brigadier general and he wrote to his father on August 3: "This is certainly very complimentary ... particularly as I have never asked a friend to intercede in my behalf." On August 7, Lincoln commissioned Grant a brigadier general.

September: Grant was ordered to Cape Girardeau, Missouri, on September 1 and 3 days later to Cairo, Illinois. On September 5, Grant informed the speaker of the Kentucky house that Confederates were invading the southeastern portion of the state. On September 6, Grant took Paducah, Kentucky, without a fight to set up a Union position in the state.

On September 13, Grant's brother Samuel Simpson died.

November: Grant launched maneuvers in Kentucky on November 1 to keep Confederates troops in that state off balance. With more than 3,000 troops, he moved south by river from Cairo, Illinois, to Columbus, Kentucky, to threaten the position of Confederate General Leonidas Polk. On November 6, Grant, acting on a report of Confederate troops moving from Kentucky into Missouri, decided to attack Belmont, Missouri. On the morning of November 7, Grant's troops arrived near Belmont. Pushing through thick woods, his forces drove the Confederates from the camps to the riverbank. While Grant's men looted the abandoned camps, Polk ferried his men across the Mississippi River to organize a maneuver to cut off Grant. Seeing the threat, Grant beat a hasty but successful retreat. Grant felt that the raid was a success and a victory, but Polk held Belmont and Grant's forces had suffered nearly 600 killed, wounded, or missing.

ഇരുൻ

RUTHERFORD B. HAYES, like Grant, entered the war as an army officer and saw action in the mountains of western Virginia. Hayes was the city solicitor for Cincinnati when war clouds approached.

April: Anxious to soldier, Hayes wrapped up his work as city solicitor and resigned.

June–August: Ohio governor William Dennison on June 27 offered Hayes a spot in the Twenty-Third Ohio Regiment from Cincinnati as a major, on the recommendation of Lieutenant Colonel Stanley Matthews. The colonel for the regiment was William S. Rosecrans. Two days later Hayes was in a military camp in Columbus.

The summer campaign in the mountains went poorly for the South. Men died of measles, and Robert E. Lee was unable to defeat Rosecrans. The South often operated like guerrillas, making quick attacks on wagon trains.

At the end of August, the regiment was ordered to Suttonsville and camped at Cheal Mountain Pass. There were 3,000 Confederates close at hand when Hayes took four companies and charged a hill through a cornfield overlooking the Gauley River. The attack was unnecessary, as Hayes found that the Confederates had slipped away, leaving behind tents, ammunition, and battle flags.

September–December: On September 19, Hayes received an appointment as a judge advocate to hear court-martials. Next Hayes was assigned to intercept Confederate recruits seeking to link up with Virginia governor and Brigadier General Henry A. Wise, the Confederate commander. Hayes wrote that he was in the saddle for 19 hours, without sleep for 36 hours.

Hayes then went to Camp Tompkins for his duties as judge advocate and tried twenty cases.

Hayes was promoted to lieutenant colonel on October 24, just 3 weeks after he turned 39. He returned to his regiment and wrote to his wife, Lucy, in November, "I confess to … preferring … to be called colonel to being styled major."

The regiment spent the winter 16 miles from the Kanawha River. Hayes now was depressed by the boredom of no action. Back in Cincinnati, Lucy gave birth to a son, Joseph, on December 21.

ᑕᎧᏌᏌ

JAMES A. GARFIELD, after a number of false starts and more soul-searching and obstacles, entered the army as an officer. By the end of the year he was in command of green troops in the mountains of eastern Kentucky.

January: On January 5, Garfield, the Ohio state senator wrote that only the "miracle of God" could prevent a civil war. Garfield thought such a war would "doom" slavery. As conservative elements in both the Republican and Democratic Parties sought a compromise, Garfield wrote on January 26: "Now I am resolved to fight these fellows to the bitter end."

April: Garfield was sitting in the Ohio senate chambers on April 12 when a senator burst in with a telegram that Sumter was under attack. Garfield wrote to J. H. Rhodes on April 14: "I hope we will never stop short of complete subjugation.… The war will soon assume the shape of slavery and freedom. The world will so understand it."

Garfield offered himself to the governor and believed he was entitled to be a colonel or maybe even a brigadier general. When someone suggested that he enlist as a private, Garfield replied, "buncombe." Ohio received a quota of thirteen regiments. Enough men for twenty-three volunteered, but there were no uniforms or places to put them.

Garfield helped raise the Seventh Regiment of Ohio volunteers but was not on hand to promote his own case for a colonelcy. Instead, Dennison sent him on a secret mission to Illinois to buy muskets and convince the governors of Illinois and Indiana to allow Major General George McClellan of Ohio to direct a consolidated force.

June–September: Dennison offered Garfield a lieutenant colonel billet in the Twenty-Fourth Ohio. Garfield, still believing he was entitled to be a full colonel, turned it down, saying "personal affairs" kept him home.

Garfield spent July reading the Federalist Papers and Alexis de Tocqueville. Then he made a trip to western Virginia to visit Bethany College. Next he took Lucretia to Princeton, Illinois, to visit her brother John. Garfield, now alone, took the train to Byron, Michigan, east of Lansing, to visit the Boynton uncles. He then kept Lucretia waiting in Illinois while he met secretly with Maria and Rebecca again in Port Austin, at the tip of the Michigan thumb.

When Garfield returned to Ohio, Dennison again offered a lieutenant colonelcy, this time in the Forty-Second Ohio.

Garfield took it only to quickly learn there was no Forty-Second Ohio; he was the whole outfit because it existed only on paper. Garfield went to Hiram in his new uniform to recruit. In a week he had filled most spaces with eager young men who wanted to serve under someone they knew personally. Within a few weeks Dennison made Garfield a full colonel.

October–December: Garfield spent the fall drilling and training his new recruits. On December 14, the Forty-Second Ohio was ordered to Kentucky. Confederate General Humphrey Marshall had driven Union troops out of Sandy Valley in eastern Kentucky. The Forty-Second Ohio, ordered to retake it, moved by steamer from Cincinnati to Cattlesburg, Kentucky, at the mouth of the Sandy River. Garfield went on to Louisville to confer with General Don Carlos Buell. Garfield impressed Buell, who quickly put Garfield in command of the Eighteenth Brigade and told him to work out his own plan of operations.

ᑕᎧᏌᏌ

CHESTER ALAN ARTHUR also became an army officer but with a different mission—to equip men in New York City for combat and send them on their way. The job led to a friendship with the governor. Arthur's family was divided, however: By marrying Ellen Herndon, he had married into southern aristocracy. Many of Ellen's cousins fought for the Confederacy.

January: On January 1, Arthur was commissioned an engineer-in-chief on Governor Edwin Morgan's staff. But the job was a social, unpaid post in which he was to attend the governor's functions wearing an expensive uniform. Initially, Arthur didn't even know Morgan, but they quickly became good friends.

April: After the attack on Fort Sumter, the New York legislature ordered up 30,000 troops. Arthur received orders the day after Sumter's fall to report to the quartermaster general's office in New York City with a rank of brigadier general. His task: to figure out ways to feed, house, clothe, and equip new soldiers. He also was to handle the logistics of all troops from New England passing through New York en route to the war zone. Soon Governor Morgan was impressed with Arthur's work and by late April promoted him to acting assistant quartermaster general.

June–August: By the end of July, Arthur had worked to process thirty-eight regiments at the front. Arthur arranged temporary housing for new soldiers on Long Island, Riker's Island, and Staten Island and in Central Park. Morgan was a driven taskmaster, and Arthur said later he had to get by on only 3 hours of sleep per night.

September–December: In the fall, Governor Morgan promoted Arthur to major general in charge of all independent military organizations in New York. Thus Arthur reached this rank before either Grant or Hayes did.

On December 22, Arthur was made chairman of a committee to devise a plan for the defending New York Harbor after the *Trent* affair on the high seas threatened war with England (see **Abraham Lincoln**, page 284).

ഇൻറ

GROVER CLEVELAND, age 24 and a lawyer in Buffalo, New York, lacked the military spirit. He was not the type to rush off and enlist. His brothers did, however. On May 15, his brother Lewis Fred enlisted in the Thirty-Second New York Volunteers in New York City and saw fighting with the Army of the Potomac. His brother Richard C. joined the Twenty-Fourth Indiana at Bedford and was mustered in at Vincennes on July 31.

ഇൻറ

BENJAMIN HARRISON, the Indiana Supreme Court reporter, published his first volume of supreme court decisions and worked with such intensity in his regular legal practice that he neglected his family and his health.

The Harrison house was bulging with a pregnant wife, two children, younger brother John from North Bend, nephew Harry Eaton from Cincinnati, and Carrie's brother Henry Scott from Oxford. The baby was stillborn, but Harrison, now making more money than he had anticipated, moved into a larger house before the end of the year.

Late in the year, Harrison dissolved his partnership with William Wallace and took in a new law partner, William P. Fishback. The men hung out their shingle on December 11.

ഇൻറ

WILLIAM MCKINLEY, 18, volunteered for the army out of a patriotic sense of duty and soon was in a minor skirmish in western Virginia while serving with Major Rutherford B. Hayes in the Twenty-Third Ohio Regiment. Things back home had turned grim. William McKinley Sr. had creditors knocking at the door. His employees at furnaces in Pennsylvania had not been paid and his brother Benjamin had left for California with many horses that William had purchased "on time."

January–May: At the beginning of the year, McKinley took two jobs to help support the family. He was a schoolteacher at the Kerr District School and clerked at the post office after school.

June–December: In June, McKinley attended a patriotic mass meeting and the oratory overwhelmed him. Volunteers were stepping forward for 3-month enlistments. McKinley and his cousin, William McKinley Osborne, talked it over and decided to enlist on June 11. The young men were sent to Camp Jackson, renamed Chase, in Columbus. There they learned that the quota for 3-month enlistments had been filled and that they had to accept 3 years or the duration. John Fremont swore them in.

McKinley was with E Company of the Twenty-Third, and the regiment started south into western Virginia on July 25. William S. Rosecrans was the brigadier general. The Twenty-Third went into battle on September 10 at Carnifex Ferry and won the engagement, which gave the men more confidence.

Illness felled many troops, but McKinley never got sick. Winter quarters stretching from September until April 1862 meant endless drill and no fighting.

ഇൻറ

THEODORE ROOSEVELT, 3 in October, lived in New York City where a minor civil war developed inside his home: His father favored the North; his mother favored the South.
September 17: Theodore's sister, Corinne, was born.

ഇൻറ

WILLIAM HOWARD TAFT, now 4, lived in Cincinnati.
December 28: A brother, Horace Dutton, was born.

ഇൻറ

WOODROW WILSON lived in Augusta, Georgia, as the Civil War broke out. He turned 5 in December.

1862
Abraham Lincoln

The president's troubles multiplied as he hired and fired generals in a futile effort to improve the performance of Northern military forces. The relatively minor skirmishes of 1861 gave way to major battles in 1862. Lincoln was appalled at the horrendous number of casualties. His problems also included the death of a son.

January: Congress was becoming increasingly agitated with the lack of progress made by the Union army. Representatives Ben Wade and Zachariah Chandler and Senator Andrew Johnson led a joint "Committee on the Conduct of the War," which criticized the mistakes made at Bull Run the previous summer. Wade was especially tough on McClellan. On January 6, he demanded his war plans and hinted that the general might have Southern sympathies.

The Wade committee also unearthed graft in the War Department, where Secretary Simon Cameron was a sloppy administrator. Cameron resigned on January 11, and Lincoln put Edwin M. Stanton in charge on January 13.

On January 27, Lincoln issued General War Order Number 1, calling for a frontal assault on Richmond. McClellan argued for a peninsular campaign via the York and James Rivers.

February: In the West there was combat. Brigadier General Ulysses S. Grant captured Fort Henry on February 6 and a week later Fort Donelson on the Tennessee River near the Kentucky border in northwest Tennessee. Lincoln now began to watch Grant closely and promoted him to major general on February 16.

Willie Lincoln fell ill and died on February 20. He was only 11 years old. Mary Lincoln was hysterical with grief over the death of her son.

March: Lincoln yielded to pressure and ordered an army shakeup on March 8. The plan involved creating five army corps headed by Generals Irvin McDowell, Edwin Sumner, Samuel Heintzelman, Erasmus Keyes, and Nathaniel P. Banks. The effect was to weaken McClellan's position and to improve Stanton's. Henceforth McClellan was commander of the Army of the Potomac only. Control at the top consisted of Lincoln, Stanton, and General Ethan A. Hitchcock.

Panic hit the White House on March 9 when Lincoln learned that the Confederate ironclad *Merrimac* at Hampton Roads, Virginia, had rammed two federal ships and forced a third aground. The fear was that the *Merrimac* would sail up the Potomac and shell Washington. When the federal ironclad *Monitor* later fought the *Merrimac* to a draw, the immediate threat to Washington was lessened.

Meanwhile, Lincoln reluctantly approved McClellan's idea of a peninsular campaign. On March 17, McClellan began

On February 13, 1862, Union troops captured Fort Donelson on the Tennessee River near the Kentucky border.

moving twelve divisions by water to Fort Monroe at the tip of the Virginia peninsula.

April: McClellan began his advance toward Richmond on April 4, but the next day he halted the march when he encountered a small Confederate position along the Warwick River near Yorktown. McClellan's forces outnumbered the Confederates by nearly four to one, yet the general's siege on Yorktown was slow and methodical, lasting nearly a month.

The first major battle of 1862 was fought at Shiloh in Tennessee not far from the Mississippi border on April 6 to 7. The casualties were staggering: over 13,000 Union soldiers killed, wounded, or missing; and nearly 10,700 Confederates killed, wounded, or missing (see **Ulysses S. Grant**, page 292).

Other Union victories followed in April: General John Pope took an island on the Mississippi River, while Commodores David G. Farragut and David D. Porter entered the mouth of the Mississippi to land General B. F. Butler's troops at New Orleans.

May–July: McClellan moved up the peninsula and finally took Yorktown on May 4, a day after the Confederates abandoned their positions in the city. McClellan's slow actions at Yorktown enabled Confederate General Joseph E. Johnston to strengthen Confederate positions just outside of Richmond. On May 5, Johnston's rear guard engaged advance elements of the Army of the Potomac and inflicted nearly 2,000 casualties. Although a small portion of Johnston's troops was engaged in this battle, the bulk of his army reached Richmond.

For the remainder of the month, Union troops slowly made their way to Richmond. On May 31, Johnston struck

McClellan's left wing, cut off from the rest of the Army of the Potomac just south of the Chickahominy River. The 2-day battle, known as the Battle of Fair Oaks/Seven Pines, stalled the advance of the Army of the Potomac but cost General Johnston his life.

On June 1, Robert E. Lee replaced Johnston and prepared his counter-offensive. McClellan failed to counterattack north of the Chickahominy River at Richmond. McClellan wrote to Lincoln: "Lee is too cautious and weak … wanting in moral firmness … likely to be timid and irresolute in action."

Lee attacked White House Landing and, in a 7-day battle at Mechanicsville and Gaines Mills, defeated McClellan's forces, although at a high cost. Known as the Battles of Seven Days, the battle began on June 25 and lasted until July 1. Casualties were enormous. For the "victorious" Confederacy, the number of killed, wounded, or missing nearly reached 20,000. The Army of the Potomac suffered 16,000 casualties.

Harsh criticism of McClellan surfaced all over the country. Lincoln asked for 300,000 volunteers, while McClellan on July 1 asked for an additional 50,000 men. Lincoln told him the soldiers were not available.

Lincoln visited Harrison's Landing on July 8 to review the troops because heat was again mounting that McClellan be replaced. Lincoln then went to West Point to consult retired general Winfield Scott, and on July 11 appointed General Henry Halleck as supreme commander.

August: Halleck visited McClellan and saw that much of the Army of the Potomac was sick. On August 3 he ordered McClellan to leave the peninsula and take up a new position at Aquia Greek near Bull Run. McClellan protested: "It is here on the James … that the fate of the Union should be decided." Halleck replied on August 7: "Hurry along this movement…. Your reputation as well as mine may be involved in its rapid execution."

Successes in the western theater had led to the promotion of Union General John Pope to the command of the newly formed Army of Virginia in July. Late in July, Pope began a slow march toward Gordonsville, Virginia. By late August, General Lee maneuvered his men in an attempt to destroy Pope's army before McClellan could reach him. Lee assigned this task to Generals James Longstreet and Thomas "Stonewall" Jackson. Jackson destroyed a federal supply depot in Manassas in the rear of Pope's army. Jackson set up positions just 2 miles from the site of the First Battle of Bull Run and waited for Lee's army to arrive.

On August 28, Jackson attempted to lure Pope into a battle. Known as the Battle of Groveton, the daylong battle lasted well into the night. Pope then ordered a full attack on Jackson for the following morning. The Second Battle of Bull Run began with Union frontal assaults on Jackson's positions. Heavily outnumbered, Jackson managed to hold the lines, ending the first day of battle in a draw. General Longstreet had arrived in the late afternoon but did not participate in the battle during that first day.

During the night, Jackson pulled his troops back to a stronger position. Mistaking the move for a retreat, Pope sent word to Washington of his "victory." When Pope renewed his attack on August 30, he met heavy resistance. While Pope attacked Jackson, Longstreet launched an attack on Pope's left flank. The Union troops began to pull back and were able to retreat toward Washington.

September: Lincoln decided on September 1 that the army was demoralized and that Pope must go. He put McClellan in command of the defense of Washington. On September 17, McClellan was victorious at the Battle of Antietam. Lincoln wired McClellan: "God bless you and all with you. Destroy the rebel army if possible."

At a cabinet meeting on September 22, Lincoln told his cabinet that he had decided to issue the Emancipation Proclamation declaring that all slaves in any state still in rebellion as of January 1, 1863, were free.

October: Lincoln's earlier praise of McClellan again turned to annoyance. Lincoln asked McClellan to attack Lee in the Shenandoah Valley. McClellan delayed, and Lincoln wrote

asking what the delay was. McClellan replied that his horses were tired. McClellan did not cross the Potomac until October 26. By this time, Lincoln had lost all confidence in him.

November: Lincoln replaced McClellan with General Ambrose E. Burnside on November 7. Burnside reorganized the Army of the Potomac and put the army in motion on November 15 for Fredericksburg, Virginia, midway between Richmond and Washington, D.C. Burnside hoped to make a dash for Richmond from Fredericksburg. However, delays in getting pontoons across the Rappahannock River hampered Burnside in getting his men into position, and the attack did not take place until December.

December: Burnside attacked, crossing the Rappahannock on December 13, but the entrenched Confederates slaughtered the Union troops. Over the next 2 days, Union casualties ran to more than 10,000 killed, wounded, or missing.

Former Presidents

MARTIN VAN BUREN was in bed through January suffering from a cough and having troubles breathing. He went to New York City in March to have his asthma condition treated.

Throughout June, he was confined to his room, and in mid-July, son Smith summoned his brothers John and Abraham. Van Buren bid good-bye to his three boys. A 3-day coma at his Lindenwald estate preceded death from asthma on July 24 at the age of 79. Van Buren was buried in the Kinderhook Cemetery not far from the Hudson River.

୫୦୯ଓ

JOHN TYLER was in Richmond meeting with members of the Confederate Provisional Congress on January 10 when his wife joined him. Tyler became suddenly ill on January 12, fainted, but recovered. Doctors called it a combination of biliousness and bronchitis. Tyler was confined to his room but received callers.

On January 17, Tyler turned seriously ill, probably from a stroke, and died shortly after midnight on January 18 at the age of 71. His last words were, "Doctor, I am going." The Confederate Congress adjourned, and the body was placed on view in the House of Delegates. President Jefferson Davis and his cabinet, the governor of Virginia, and members of the Confederate Congress took part in the funeral procession. No announcement of the death was made in the United States Congress, nor did the U.S. government make any statement. Tyler was survived by eleven of his fifteen children.

୫୦୯ଓ

MILLARD FILLMORE, retired in Buffalo, New York, found much of his time involved in civic duties as unofficial first citizen of Buffalo.

Confederate troops fleeing Union troops across the bridge over Antietam Creek in Maryland on September 17, 1862.

April–May: In April, Fillmore was chairman of the meeting that organized the Buffalo Historical Society. He became its first president by unanimous vote on May 20.

November: Fillmore contributed money to the new Buffalo Fine Arts Academy and was made a director of it, although he was not well versed in fine art.

༄

FRANKLIN PIERCE, retired in New Hampshire, became a critic of Lincoln administration policy and was rumored to be disloyal to the Union cause.

The Emancipation Proclamation late in the year turned Pierce into a bigger critic. He was against it and said the object of the war now was to wipe out "property" (i.e., slaves). He said he could not see why people would "butcher" the white race for the sake of "inflicting" emancipation on Blacks, who would be incapable of profiting from their freedom.

༄

JAMES BUCHANAN was under constant Republican attack, charged with bungling his administration. He counterattacked but believed his major defense would have to await publication until after the war ended.

February: Buchanan, retired at Wheatland in Lancaster, Pennsylvania, wrote to John A. Parker on February 3 that he thought Lincoln was an "honest and patriotic man."

Thurlow Weed published an article in the *London Observer* on February 9 that pictured Buchanan as helpless and unwilling to accept Secretary of War John Buchanan Floyd's resignation at a cabinet meeting on December 29, 1860. The story received wide circulation. Buchanan called Weed's story a "tissue of falsehood."

October–December: Late in the year, Buchanan finished his book *Mr. Buchanan's Administration on the Eve of the Rebellion*, but it was not published until 1866 so as not to embarrass Lincoln nor hurt the war effort.

Senator Garrett Davis of Kentucky submitted a resolution on December 15: "Resolved, [that with war imminent] James Buchanan, then President, from sympathy with the conspirators … failed to take necessary and proper measures to prevent it; therefore he should receive the censure and condemnation of the Senate and the American people." The resolution did not pass, and Buchanan wrote, "If two years after a presidential term has expired the Senate can go back, try, condemn, and execute ... who would accept the office?"

Future Presidents

ANDREW JOHNSON was appointed military governor of Tennessee by Lincoln. The Confederate army had held Nashville for 6 months prior to Johnson's arrival and also controlled eastern Tennessee, where Mrs. Johnson remained near her home.

February–March: The Confederates evacuated Nashville in late February after Grant's victories at Fort Henry and Fort Donelson. When General Don Carlos Buell occupied Nashville, Governor Harris moved the state government to Memphis. Lincoln wanted to restore civilian government to Tennessee and reestablish federal relations; therefore, on March 4 he named Johnson military governor with the rank of brigadier general.

Secessionists in Tennessee were furious over the appointment and plotted to ambush Johnson's train. Buell warned Johnson that Nashville, being pro-Confederate, would be hostile. Johnson reached Nashville safely on March 12.

༄

ULYSSES S. GRANT made an aggressive move into western Tennessee, won two important battles at Forts Henry and Donelson, then directed Union forces at Shiloh, the greatest battle ever fought in North America to date. By year's end, Grant was the commanding general of the Department of Tennessee and was on the offensive over wide areas of northern Mississippi.

January: Grant, at Cairo, Illinois, worried that he might lose his command. He wrote to his sister that he now had more men under his command than Scott had in Mexico.

Grant went to St. Louis to see General Halleck and suggest a drive into Tennessee and Alabama by river routes and in coordination with naval units. Halleck was cool to the idea and said no. But naval officer Andrew H. Foote told Halleck on January 28 that a combined services drive on Fort Henry would work. Foote had seven gunboats, and Grant had 17,000 men.

February: Grant attacked Fort Henry on February 6, and the Confederate force of 2,500 under Colonel Lloyd Tilghman retreated 11 miles to Fort Donelson on the Cumberland River.

McClellan was happy with the victory, but Halleck congratulated Foote, not Grant.

Grant then held his only council of war, choosing the ladies cabin of a boat. He heard various opinions, then immediately said he would attack Donelson.

Confederate guns routed Foote's gunboats on February 14, and Confederate ground forces attacked troops led by Grant's deputy, General John A. McClernand, and chewed them up, causing a retreat. While McClernand and General Lew Wallace conferred, Grant rode up and ordered an immediate attack to prevent the Confederates from escaping to Clarksville and Nashville. Grant's forces counterattacked, and Confederate General John B. Floyd, former secretary of war under Buchanan, escaped by boat.

When Grant attacked, his old friend Confederate General Simon Bolivar Buckner asked on February 16 for a truce and conditions. Grant demanded unconditional surrender. Buckner accepted the "ungenerous and unchivalrous terms" and surrendered 11,500 men. The North rejoiced in its greatest victory, and Grant became a household name. Lincoln promoted him to major general on February 16.

March: Grant made his headquarters at Savannah, Tennessee, with Generals Lew Wallace and William T. Sherman both at Pittsburg Landing. Sherman informed Grant that he was ready to attack the Confederates at Corinth, Mississippi, about 19 miles to the southwest. Albert Sidney Johnston and G. T. Beauregard had 40,000 men; Grant had 38,000 men.

April–June: The Confederates attacked at dawn at Shiloh on April 6 and surprised the Union, which had no picket screen. Confederates under General Albert S. Johnston burst through the lines and sent hundreds of Union troops toward the Tennessee River. The Union drove the Confederates from the field on April 7, when General Don Carlos Buell came to Grant's aid. General Johnston was killed. The casualties were staggering: over 13,000 Union soldiers killed, wounded, or missing; and nearly 10,700 Confederates killed wounded or missing. Grant's reputation was damaged by Shiloh, but Lincoln backed him, saying, "I can't spare this man. He fights."

Halleck cautiously moved a huge force slowly toward Corinth, digging defenses all along the way. Grant was now second in command of the western armies but without duties. The Confederates pulled out of Corinth, leaving nothing behind for Halleck. There

Confederate General Robert E. Lee

were rumors at Corinth that Grant, bored, would be leaving the command. Sherman went to Grant's camp and asked where he was going. Grant said, "St. Louis." Sherman convinced him to stay, saying something lucky might happen.

July–September: Halleck was promoted to a Washington post in July. After Pope took Memphis 80 miles directly west of Corinth, Grant moved his headquarters there.

October–December: Grant was given command of the Department of Tennessee on October 25.

In November, Grant attacked Holly Springs, Mississippi, south of Corinth, and then took Oxford as Confederate General John C. Pemberton retreated. That put Grant 200 miles from Vicksburg. He ordered Sherman to the Yazoo River, 12 miles northwest of Vicksburg. Sherman's goal was Chickasaw Bluffs.

On December 20, the Confederates attacked Grant's supply base at Holly Springs and captured a garrison of 1,500 men. The Confederate thrust almost captured Julia Grant, who was headed for Oxford.

છાલ્ફ

RUTHERFORD B. HAYES, a lieutenant colonel in the Union army, was transferred from western Virginia to Maryland.

April–June: Hayes's outfit, the Twenty-Third Ohio, in the spring had a 20-minute skirmish with Confederate forces at Princeton, near Bluefield and close to the Virginia border. He had a chance to talk to the prisoners of war, who seemed "grateful for the kindness which I always gave them." The

Twenty-Third Ohio barely escaped bumping into a Confederate force of 3,000. Hayes felt lucky and wrote to Lucy, "I shall come safely out of the war."

There was little fighting in western Virginia amid rumors of great victories by McClellan before Richmond. Hayes thought this would be a short war.

July 23: Hayes was offered a colonelcy with the Seventy-Ninth Ohio but turned it down to remain with the Twenty-Third.

August–September: In August the Twenty-Third was removed from the mountains and sent to Washington, then south on August 30 into Virginia at Upton. Hearing cannon fire, Hayes said, "If we suffer it is in the place where decisive acts are going on."

Hayes led a charge up a hill at South Mountain in Maryland before the Battle of Antietam on September 14 and fell wounded when hit below the left elbow. Hayes was almost left on the field in the confusion. He shouted, "Twenty-third men, are you going to leave your colonel here for the enemy?" Later Hayes had to walk a half-mile to an ambulance.

October–December: Hayes was bored with his long convalescence at Middletown, Maryland, until Lucy arrived there. Hayes's brother-in-law, Dr. Joe Webb, was there to treat him.

Lucy and the children visited several times. Hayes, 40 in October, recovered rather quickly and once walked Lucy back over the battlefield.

Hayes received a home leave and then returned East to the army's winter quarters.

છાલ્ફ

JAMES A. GARFIELD began the year an obscure colonel in eastern Kentucky. By year's end, he was in the glitter of Washington leadership and society. Garfield was elected to Congress, promoted to brigadier general, and sat on court-martial boards.

January: At the start of the year, Garfield had the duty of working out a strategy to defeat a Confederate force under General Humphrey Marshall. Although inexperienced, Garfield overruled his staff and divided his force. A clever faint, however, made Marshall panic and he went into retreat. Garfield took Paintsville on January 7 without firing a shot.

Garfield then made a cold, icy 13-mile march to a Confederate cavalry camp at Jenny's Creek only to find that the rebels had vanished. Garfield's grumbling men, on returning to camp, were fired upon by their own pickets.

On January 9, Garfield made contact with Marshall on

Middle Creek. Garfield marched some troops back and forth on a slope to make Marshall think he had a much larger force.

In the nick of time, Colonel Sheldon arrived with reinforcements after Garfield had advanced slowly all day, taking few casualties. The Confederates were green and scared.

Marshall moved into Virginia, and Garfield now controlled eastern Kentucky, an area that had given aid to the Confederates. There was no law and order left except for that furnished by Garfield. Garfield issued a "proclamation" for Kentuckians: "I have come among you to restore the honor of the Union." He promised amnesty to those who had taken up arms against the government. At this point, Garfield favored leniency and conservative treatment of the South.

February: Rations were low and the Sandy River swollen by rain when Garfield returned to Catlettsburg, took over a steamer, and acting as riverboat captain made a dangerous voyage to Paintsville. When he reached Piketon (now Pikeville) on February 18, a flood had inundated the town. Garfield spent 2 weeks sick with camp fever. The epidemic that hit his camp killed fifty soldiers, many of them recruited by Garfield himself. He was tormented by guilt.

Garfield was promoted to brigadier general.

March: On March 14, Garfield began a drive toward Pound Gap on the Kentucky–Virginia border. During a snowfall the Confederates were routed. His men burned a Confederate camp and then returned to Piketon. Never again would Garfield lead troops in battle.

Fremont sent for Garfield because Buell was looking for someone to lead an assault on the Cumberland Gap, 90 miles to the southwest. Two days later Buell changed his mind and ordered the Forty-Second back to Louisville.

On reaching Louisville, Garfield learned Buell had left behind instructions to hurry to Pittsburg Landing in Tennessee where Grant was prepared to smash into Mississippi. The Forty-Second was not to follow. This news, according to Garfield, was the "severest trial I have suffered."

April: Garfield caught up with Buell outside Nashville on April 4. There Garfield was introduced to the Twentieth Brigade, his new outfit, made up of green men from Ohio, Michigan, and Indiana. It made Garfield "gloomy."

Garfield was at Turkey Creek, far from Shiloh, when Johnston opened the battle. The Twentieth Brigade marched through thunderstorms and mud and finally reached Savannah, Tennessee. They boarded a steamboat with the decks bloody from the dying and wounded, and headed for the front, arriving at Pittsburg Landing, 5 miles from the battlefield.

Garfield's men advanced on the retreating Confederates through fields of dead and dying. Garfield pushed his troops recklessly and drew some fire. As the fresh brigade appeared ready to fight, a cheer went up from the tired Union veterans of Shiloh. The rebels had gone south, and Shiloh was over just as Garfield prepared for combat.

May: Garfield's new outfit was attached to Halleck's slow move toward Corinth. Camp fever was common due to exposure.

July–August: Throughout the spring, Garfield's friend Harmon Austin wrote asking Garfield to run for Congress. Garfield wrote to Lucretia that he would "rather be in Congress than in the army," citing the dullness of camp life. Meanwhile, Garfield's health took a sharp decline. He came down with jaundice and diarrhea. In August, Garfield was shipped home to Hiram on sick leave.

September: Despite Garfield's illness, his friends continued their political work. The nominating convention on September 2 nominated Garfield for the House. Fully recovered, Garfield was ordered to Washington to receive his next assignment. During his time in Washington, he met with Secretary of War Edwin Stanton and Secretary of Treasury Salmon Chase. Chase and Garfield soon became good friends.

October: Garfield won the congressional seat in a landslide. He would not have to take his seat in Congress until the December 1863 session.

November–December: Garfield, still in Washington, finally received his next assignment from the army. On November 7, he was assigned deputy to General David Hunter in a campaign against Charleston, South Carolina. But when yellow fever hit the Carolina coast, the campaign was canceled.

Garfield was then selected to sit on the court-martial of General Fitz-John Porter, who was charged with disobedience in carrying out orders at the Second Battle of Bull Run. The court-martial began in November and dragged on into January 1863.

ଔଷ

CHESTER ALAN ARTHUR changed titles from inspector general to quartermaster general for the State of New York. The closest Arthur ever got to seeing combat was a field trip to Virginia to see how soldiers from New York were being taken care of.

February 10: The title of inspector general was conferred on Arthur.

March–April: Arthur ventured into Virginia in the spring to inspect New York troops. He reached Fredericksburg and the Chickahominy River before being ordered home by Governor Edwin Morgan.

July: Arthur became quartermaster general for the State of New York on July 10. His responsibilities included inspecting forts and defenses all over the state. After his promotion, Arthur had to enlist and prepare a New York quota of 120,000 men. Arthur established his headquarters in New York City. More than 200 temporary barracks were constructed.

December: A Democratic governor was to take office on January 1, 1863, which meant that the Republican Arthur would be replaced as quartermaster. Arthur ended the year by compiling a summary of quartermaster work, and he served on two auditing boards. He reported that the state sent sixty-eight regiments to the war and noted the "untiring zeal, exhaustless energy" of Governor Morgan in the war effort.

ℰℭ

GROVER CLEVELAND, 25, blossomed as a young Buffalo, New York, trial lawyer interested in a political career. He was nominated and elected a ward supervisor in Buffalo and soon moved up to assistant district attorney, where he handled most of the courtroom caseload.

Cleveland was a delegate to a party convention on October 23 with recent Buffalo Mayor Timothy T. Lockwood presiding. Cleveland represented the Second Ward. At a caucus on October 30, Cleveland was nominated ward supervisor and in the November election received 509 votes. Cyrenius C. Torrance was elected district attorney and soon announced that Cleveland would be his assistant.

The *Buffalo Courier* said on December 24: "Mr. Cleveland is one of the most promising of the younger members of the bar, is a thoroughly read lawyer, and possesses talents of a high order." The newspaper went on to predict higher posts ahead for Cleveland.

Cleveland worked in the Erie County Courthouse doing much of the work because of Torrance's infirmities. The job required Cleveland to watch city government for corruption and prosecute those cheating the government.

ℰℭ

BENJAMIN HARRISON went to war as a captain and later became a colonel and commander of the Seventieth Indiana Regiment, which he had recruited. The unit drove across Kentucky into Tennessee by year's end, while experiencing one minor skirmish and many of the hardships common to army life. While Harrison was gone, the Democrats back in Indiana wrested his job as state supreme reporter away from the temporary replacement that Harrison had appointed.

April: Recruiting had been stopped, although Governor Oliver Morton opposed Lincoln's decision on this. As it was, neighboring Ohio had provided more men in the first quota call than all of New England.

June–August: Over the summer, apathy hit Indiana, as the war was not going well in the East and General Braxton Bragg was threatening Ohio with a potential attack through Kentucky. Lincoln again called for more men, and Governor Morton led the call in Indiana. When Indiana did not respond, Morton asked for Harrison's help. He told Harrison to raise a regiment and that someone would be found to lead it. Harrison declined, adding that if he raised a regiment he would be its leader. Still, Harrison hesitated because of his lack of military experience. Morton held off making Harrison a colonel and instead made him a second lieutenant for recruiting purposes.

A rally was held at the Masonic Hall on July 12, but the hall was soon so packed that the meeting was moved to the statehouse grove. Governor Morton and Harrison both made speeches. Recruiting books were opened at the end of the rally. Harrison made several recruiting speeches, but after July 20, Confederate victories resulted in dampened enthusiasm. After 2 weeks, Harrison had eighty-five men. Morton commissioned him on July 22 as a captain of the Seventieth Regiment. The regiment set up camp at the state fairgrounds, and Harrison himself recruited and paid a drillmaster from Chicago.

August–October: By August the Seventieth Regiment had a surplus of 250 men, and on August 8, Harrison was commissioned a colonel. The regiment's first task was to escort Confederate prisoners of war on a train. But for the most part, daily life for the regiment consisted of endless drilling and training.

Late in August, Harrison received orders to rush to Bowling Green, more than 100 miles to the southwest. Confederate Colonel John H. Morgan had captured Gallatin, Tennessee, and was headed toward Bowling Green to destroy railroad tracks. Rumors reached Indianapolis that Morgan had routed and captured Harrison, but Benjamin wrote to his wife, Carrie, that they had arrived safely in Bowling Green and that Morgan's closeness helped the men to drill better.

The Confederates in the area moved to Russellville, about 30 miles southwest of Bowling Green, on September 30—just as Harrison received orders to advance to Russellville. On October 3, Harrison surrounded Russellville and caught the Confederates by surprise in a minor skirmish. Only one Union soldier was killed, compared with thirty-three Confederates.

November–December: General William Rosecrans reorganized the Seventieth Regiment in November and made it a part of the Fourteenth Corps. He then moved the corps to Scottsville, Kentucky, and then on to Gallatin, Tennessee, by November 24.

In early December, Rosecrans sent the Seventieth Regiment to Drake's Creek to guard 26 miles of railroad between Gallatin and Nashville. This order upset Harrison because it meant he would not be able to return to Carrie and the children for Christmas.

ℰℭ

WILLIAM MCKINLEY showed heroism at Antietam as a commissary supply man who brought hot food and coffee to soldiers manning forward positions in the firing line. At the start of 1862, McKinley was a private; he finished the year a second lieutenant.

April: Lieutenant Colonel Rutherford B. Hayes led the Twenty-Third Ohio to Princeton near what would later be the West Virginia–Virginia border on April 22. Also in April, McKinley was promoted to commissary sergeant.

May 8: A Confederate attack at Flat Top Mountain led to a retreat by the Twenty-Third Ohio.

August–September: On August 15, there was a forced march to Camp Piatt on the Great Kanawha River, and the Twenty-Third Ohio arrived on August 18, doing 104 miles in

3 days. Then they boarded transports for Parkersburg and finally to the Washington and Potomac area.

The Twenty-Third Ohio drove the Confederates from Frederick and then reached Middletown on September 13. The next day the Battle of South Mountain took place. During these engagements, McKinley's job was to keep the troops supplied with provisions.

At Antietam on September 17, McKinley drove a mule train into the thick of the battle.

On reaching the troops under fire, McKinley received a cheer for bringing the meals. He had been in the rear earlier in the battle. Hayes was very impressed and later said that the young soldier showed "unusual and unsurpassed capacity, especially for a boy his age."

On September 23, he was promoted to second lieutenant.

∞∞

THEODORE ROOSEVELT, at 4, had serious health problems. The lad was always sick: nausea, colds, diarrhea, fever, coughs, and asthma. The asthma was the worst problem, causing breathing problems that made it necessary to prop him up in bed to sleep or to sometimes sleep in a chair.

∞∞

WILLIAM HOWARD TAFT, 5 in September, lived in Cincinnati, Ohio.

∞∞

WOODROW WILSON, 6 in December, lived in Augusta, Georgia, then part of the Confederate States of America.

1863
Abraham Lincoln

The president experienced another fearful year of trial and failure, changing generals, rising war resistance from Copper-heads, conscription and riots, and more private anguish in the White House. As in the prior year, 1863 was a year of marching armies everywhere and the ebb and flow of strategy, fate, lost opportunities, and enormous mounting sacrifice.

January: On January 1, Lincoln signed the Emancipation Proclamation, which freed all slaves in all parts of the United States still in rebellion. For the majority of Southern slaves, however, true freedom would not come until the end of the war more than 2 years later.

The year opened militarily with the Battle of Stones River at Murfreesboro, Tennessee, between Confederate General Braxton Bragg and Union General William Rosecrans. The battle had opened on the last day of 1862 but continued on January 2 when Bragg attacked Union positions east of the Stones River. Union artillery successfully broke up the Con-

federate attack. Rosecrans held his positions, and Bragg withdrew his forces during the night of January 3.

Burnside met with Lincoln early in January and asked for approval to strike at Fredericksburg again. However, Burnside's commanders warned the president that the army was in no mood for a repeat of Burnside's fiasco at the same place in 1862. Burnside opened an offensive over the Rappahannock River on January 20, but was bogged down in the mud and returned to winter quarters on January 23. It was obvious to Lincoln that Burnside had lost the army's confidence; therefore, he replaced Burnside with General Joseph Hooker for the Potomac command on January 26.

This illustration celebrates the Emancipation Proclamation issued by President Abraham Lincoln on January 1, 1863. (Library of Congress)

March 3: Congress passed the Enrollment Act, which called for 3-year draft of all able-bodied males between the ages of 20 and 45.

April–May: In early April the 54-year-old president and son Tad visited the army, which was within sight of Fredericksburg. They spent 6 days at the camp.

Hooker took the offensive on April 30, crossed the Rapidan and Rappahannock Rivers, and stopped at Chancellotsville. Confederate General "Stonewall" Jackson struck Hooker's right on May 2 in a surprise thrust, while Confederate General Robert E. Lee battled Union General John Sedgwick on May 3. A lack of coordination between Hooker and Sedgwick helped cause another Union defeat as the North withdrew across the Rappahannock. During the battle, Jackson was accidentally shot by one of his own sentries during a night reconnaissance. He died on May 10.

In the West, Grant moved his army south in April along the bayous of the Mississippi to a point 50 miles south of Vicksburg. Rear Admiral David D. Porter, on April 16, ran gunboats past the Confederate guns despite heavy fire from Vicksburg. Porter then ferried Grant's army to the eastern bank of the Mississippi. From May 11 to 25, Grant moved around Vicksburg, won five battles in 3 weeks against General Joseph E. Johnston, captured Jackson (Mississippi), and drove General John C. Pemberton behind Vicksburg's defenses (see **Ulysses S. Grant**, page 298).

June–July: On June 5, Hooker told Lincoln that Lee had broken camp at Fredericksburg. Now Hooker wanted permission to drive on Richmond. The president told him to forget Richmond and to destroy Lee. By June 14 there were rumors that Lee was moving north. Lee's army of 70,000 moved north through the Blue Ridge passes and up the Shenandoah Valley to the Potomac River. The Army of the Potomac moved north with him. Halleck and Hooker argued over details of the movement, and Hooker asked to resign. Lincoln told his cabinet on June 28 that after consulting only Secretary of State Seward and Secretary of War Stanton, Lincoln had de-cided to re-place Hooker with General George Meade.

Meanwhile, on June 19, West Virginia was admitted to the Union. The western part of Virginia had remained loyal to the Union and had not voted in favor of secession.

The armies collided at Gettysburg, Pennsylvania, by accident on July

This engraving portrays Pickett's charge at Gettysburg on July 3, 1863. Pickett lost over 3,000 men during the charge, and on July 4, the Confederates retreated.

1. At first the Union was overmatched and retreated to a defensive line on Cemetery Ridge. Confederate General James Longstreet attacked on July 2, while Lincoln spent most of the day at the War Department. On July 3, Lee, against Longstreet's judgment, decided on a frontal assault from Seminary Ridge. Meade decided to hold his ground. The South attacked with 9,000 men in the first wave and 6,000 men in support. Confederate General George Pickett's charge faltered and fell back. On July 4, Lincoln received word that Lee was in retreat. Union losses at the Battle of Gettysburg numbered 23,000, and Confederate losses numbered 30,000.

On July 8, Meade reported that Lee was stopped at the Potomac by high water, but Meade said, "I do not desire [to] assault a position where the chances are greatly against success." On the same day, Lincoln heard the news that Vicksburg had surrendered to Grant on July 4 along with 31,600 prisoners and 172 guns. Lincoln wired Meade this news and said, "Now, if [you] can complete … work so gloriously prosecuted thus far, by … destruction of Lee's army, the rebellion will be over." Lincoln and Halleck urged Meade to attack Lee, but on July 13 they received word that Lee had crossed the river at night and that Meade had congratulated

his army for "driving the enemy from our soil." Lincoln complained, "This is a dreadful reminiscence of McClellan."

Meanwhile, rioters in New York attacked the draft offices on July 13. New York officials had drawn the first names of draftees under the Enrollment Act on July 11. The names of 1,200 conscripts were published in newspapers on July 12, the same day many newspapers listed the names of the dead from Gettysburg. By the evening of July 13, an angry mob of 50,000 stormed an armory and an orphanage for African American children. Rioting lasted for days before 4,000 Union troops arrived on July 16 and began to restore order. In all, nearly 120 people died in the rioting.

September: On September 15, Lincoln again urged Meade to attack Lee. The goal again was to destroy Lee's army, not Richmond. Then, the president was summoned on the night of September 20 to go to the War Department where Stanton had word of a defeat at Chickamauga in Georgia at the hands of Confederate General Braxton Bragg. At first Rosecrans warned of a "serious disaster." Later, General Thomas repulsed a Confederate attack on the right wing. Lincoln was upset further when Burnside was slow coming to Rosecrans's assistance. Hooker then was dispatched from Washington to Chattanooga with 30,000 men.

The Confederates occupied Missionary Ridge and Lookout Mountain at Chattanooga. Lincoln told John Hay, his personal secretary, that Rosecrans acted "stunned, like a duck hit on the head." However, Bragg's victory at Chickamauga proved worthless because he failed to follow up the advantage. Confederate losses at Chickamauga totaled 2,300 killed and 18,000 wounded, whereas Union losses totaled 1,600 killed and 16,000 wounded.

October: Grant was in Cairo, Illinois, on October 17 when he received orders to go to Louisville and then to Indianapolis, where he met Stanton for the first time. Stanton handed him Lincoln's orders to take command in the West, including military districts on the Mississippi, Ohio, Cumberland, and Tennessee Rivers with the option to replace Rosecrans with Thomas.

Grant accepted and ordered Thomas to hold Chattanooga at all costs.

November: Lincoln gave the brief Gettysburg Address on November 19 at the dedication of the cemetery there. His address followed lengthy oratory by Edward Everett. Lincoln said, in part, "It is rather for us to be here dedicated to the great task remaining before us—that from these honored dead we take increased devotion to that cause for which they here gave the last full devotion—that we here highly resolve that these dead shall not have died in vain, that this nation under God shall have a new birth of freedom, and that government of the people, by the people, for the people, shall not perish from the earth." The brief message was at the time ridiculed by many newspapers across the country.

On November 25, Lincoln heard from Grant that he and General William T. Sherman had defeated Bragg and had driven the Confederates off Lookout Mountain and Missionary Ridge.

December: In his message to Congress on December 8, Lincoln offered reconciliation for the South and promised no vengeful military rule. He added that most men would be pardoned for the rebellion and that full rights, with the exception of slavery, would be restored to the South.

Former Presidents

MILLARD FILLMORE, 63, despite the impact of the Civil War, nationally showed more interest in the history of and well-being of Buffalo.

January: Fillmore leased rooms for use by the Buffalo Historical Society, an organization that interested him more than any other civic activity in which he was involved.

March 28: Fillmore's father, Nathaniel, died at the age of 91.

May: His interest in enlarging the canal in Buffalo led to a trip to Chicago to represent the Buffalo Board of Trade at the National Canal Convention.

৪০৫৪

FRANKLIN PIERCE'S criticism of the Civil War isolated him from the "patriotic" element in his native New Hampshire. It was not a good year for the retired President, who also lost his wife.

January: Pierce had little use for Lincoln and none for the Emancipation Proclamation. Pierce said it showed that the abolitionists ruled through Lincoln, a man of "limited ability and narrow intelligence [who was responsible for] all the degradation, all the atrocity, all the desolation and ruin" in the country.

June–August: Because Pierce noticed a coolness toward him in Concord, he took to spending more time in Andover or Hillsborough. Pierce, however, was the principal orator at a Democratic rally on July 4. He once again took the opportunity to attack Lincoln.

Not long after the July 4 speech, a Union soldier found an 1860 Pierce letter to Jefferson Davis. It was lithographed to accompany a biting attack on the Pierce administration, which claimed that Pierce sold out Kansas to the South and likened Pierce to Benedict Arnold. This work helped to create a further climate of bitterness toward Pierce in New Hampshire.

President Abraham Lincoln as he delivers the Gettysburg Address on November 19, 1863. (Library of Congress)

November–December: Pierce turned 59 on November 23.

On December 2, Pierce's wife Jane died at Andover, Massachusetts, at the age of 57.

৪০৫৪

JAMES BUCHANAN, age 72 when the Battle of Gettysburg shaped up near Wheatland, his Lancaster, Pennsylvania, home, was urged by friends to flee his retirement home. He decided to stay put, however, and the Confederate Army came within 10 miles of Wheatland. Buchanan also had to deal with various health problems: gout, indigestion and diarrhea, and swollen joints.

Future Presidents

ANDREW JOHNSON, by the end of the year, was nearly in control of all of Tennessee in his post as military governor.

April 4: Johnson's son Charles, an army surgeon, was killed when he was thrown from a horse in Nashville.

September–December: By late summer, Bragg evacuated Chattanooga, and Lincoln wired Johnson, "All Tennessee is now clear of armed insurrectionists … it is the nick of time for reinaugurating the loyal state government. Not a moment should be lost."

When Bragg beat Rosecrans at Chickamauga in late September and Longstreet laid siege to Knoxville and drove into eastern Tennessee, Johnson's plans for controlling the entire state went on hold. In November, however, Bragg was routed from Lookout Mountain and Missionary Ridge, and Johnson again began the process of bringing Tennessee back into the Union.

❧❧

ULYSSES S. GRANT scored two smashing victories at Vicksburg and Chattanooga that made him the North's military hero.

January–April: At the start of the year, Grant was in Mississippi closing the noose on Vicksburg, the key to the Confederate supply line on the Mississippi River. There was pressure on Grant to produce a victory. He felt that if the Vicksburg campaign faltered, Lincoln would seek another general for the theater.

Endless rain hampered operations, and attempts to create a canal passage for ships to points near Vicksburg also had to be abandoned.

Grant's strategy to break Vicksburg was to move the army to a point south of Vicksburg on the west side of the river, then cross over and move north on Vicksburg before attacking from the east. Another idea was to link up with General Nathaniel P. Banks, then in New Orleans, to accomplish the same thing. Of the generals, only McClernand thought the idea would work. Banks had been attacking northward toward Port Hudson, Louisiana, the Confederate supply link with Vicksburg.

On the night of April 16, Union Admiral David Porter's gunboats ran the bluffs going south, despite many hits, and Grant now had the river transportation he wanted. Grant occupied Port Gibson, 25 miles below Vicksburg, while General William T. Sherman was active to the north of the city in order to confuse General John Pemberton, the Confederate defender.

May–July: Grant then marched to Jackson to the northeast. His moves were based on speed and deception. After taking the Mississippi capital of Jackson on May 14, Grant handed Pemberton a defeat at Champion's Hill on May 16.

Grant and Sherman differed on how to attack Vicksburg, with Grant wanting the southern approach. Confederate General Joseph E. Johnston, always in the vicinity of Jackson and Vicksburg, was a threat to Grant. Johnston had 60,000 men to Grant's 33,000.

Grant stormed Pemberton at Stockade Redan, one of Vicksburg's strongest points, on May 22. The frontal assault was a failure, costing 3,000 Union casualties.

Grant then decided on a "siege" strategy to take Vicksburg. The main components of this strategy called for artillery bombardment, construction of trenches, and starving the enemy before a final assault. The siege began on May 23.

On June 15 the *Memphis Evening Bulletin* carried General McClernand's cry that his men were ready to take Vicksburg.

General Ulysses S. Grant

Generals Blair and Sherman were disgusted, and Grant fired McClernand. The Union army spent June building trenches and earthworks as Grant's ranks swelled to 75,000 men.

The siege of Vicksburg ended on July 4 when Pemberton surrendered even though he still had an ample supply of ammunition.

August–December: Grant had emerged as the North's hero. Grant's new strategy was to march to Mobile and then attack General Braxton Bragg from below, but General Halleck said no to this.

Grant ordered Sherman to pass through Mississippi in an orderly manner, "They should try to create as favorable an impression as possible upon the people."

On October 10, Grant was summoned to Cairo, Illinois, then to Indianapolis where he had his first meeting with Secretary of War Edwin Stanton. In the new command alignment Stanton talked about, Grant would head the Military Division of the Mississippi over both Rosecrans's Army of Cumberland and Burnside's Army of the Ohio. Stanton gave Grant a choice to keep Rosecrans or replace him with George H. Thomas. Grant took Thomas. It appeared Halleck was to have no veto power over Grant's decisions.

Grant arrived in Chattanooga on October 23. By October 30, he was able to break the Confederate siege, and soon supplies were flowing into Chattanooga. Sherman arrived in November, and Grant began to plan his offensive against Bragg on Missionary Ridge.

Grant attacked Missionary Ridge and Lookout Mountain on November 24, and General Thomas broke the Confederate lines on Missionary Ridge the next day. With this victory, Grant's reputation rose even further.

Grant moved his headquarters to Nashville in early December. Late in December, he inspected the supply line through the Cumberland Gap. He did this in preparation for an assault on Atlanta.

❧❧

RUTHERFORD B. HAYES recovered from his wounds in Maryland and returned to his earlier theater, the mountains of southern West Virginia.

Hayes's son Joseph died on June 24. The boy was only 1 year old.

Hayes received orders in July to send two regiments to attack John Morgan, the Confederate raider, who was riding all over southern Ohio. A minor engagement occurred at Gallipolis on the Ohio River.

Next Hayes took over George Crook's first brigade, which consisted of the Twenty-Third and Thirty-Sixth Ohio and two regiments from western Virginia. The brigade moved south from Fayetteville in south-central West Virginia to Poplar Hill, 45 miles due west of Roanoke, Virginia, by way of Princeton, West Virginia, near the border. Hayes won a small engagement at Cloyd Mountain but lost twenty-five men.

෨෬

JAMES A. GARFIELD began this year as he ended the prior year, sitting on the court-martial of General Fitz-John Porter. By the end of the year, the brigadier general was back in Washington as a member of Congress.

January: The court-martial of General Porter wrapped up on January 10. Porter was found not guilty on several charges, but on the most serious, disobedience and misconduct, he was found guilty. Porter was cashiered out of the army.

Garfield had been in Washington for 4 months when he finally received orders in mid-January to report to General Rosecrans, since the Army of the Cumberland needed a general. Rosecrans was a bundle of restless energy. Before long Garfield and Rosecrans were close friends.

February–March: Back in Ohio, there was political trouble. John Hutchins, the man Garfield defeated for the House seat, claimed that Garfield had to resign his commission by March 4 or lose his seat in Congress. Garfield asked for opinions from Samuel Chase, Ben Wade, and Attorney General Edward Bates, all of whom said he could stay in the army.

Rosecrans made Garfield chief of staff. His predecessor had died in the Battle of Murfreesboro. Headquarters were in a southern mansion. Garfield was the communications link between Rosecrans and his army, although most of the business was routine.

May: Rosecrans's excessive demands on Washington for men, supplies, and horses angered Stanton and Halleck. Lincoln was impatient with his inaction. Garfield, earlier in the year a strong supporter of Rosecrans, agreed. Garfield was unable to soften Rosecrans's list of complaints to Stanton, and he expressed his disgust to his wife, Lucretia.

June–July: Garfield told Rosecrans that the War Department thought the army should move, that "[the] country is anxiously hoping for it." Rosecrans moved south on June 24 in the Tullahoma campaign and hinted that it was Garfield's idea. Confederate General Braxton Bragg panicked and fell back as Rosecrans used cavalry behind Confederate lines. Both armies were trying to reach Tullahoma first. Too many baggage trains and torrential rains bogged down Rosecrans.

When Rosecrans reached Tullahoma on July 3, Bragg fled. Halleck and Whitelaw Reid lauded the campaign, but national attention was riveted on Vicksburg and Gettysburg. Garfield advised an attack but his advice was ignored. Halleck had warned Rosecrans on July 24 to get moving.

August–September: The army crossed the Tennessee River on August 29, and Bragg was slow to see that he had been outflanked. Rosecrans thought Bragg was retreating to Rome, Georgia.

Bragg left Chattanooga on September 8. The mountains in this area hid the armies from each other. Garfield wired Halleck on September 9, "Chattanooga is ours without a struggle and eastern Tennessee is free." Crittenden moved southward rapidly as Rosecrans, in Chattanooga, told Charles A. Dana that he felt something was amiss, his army was spread out over 50 miles.

The Battle of Chickamauga began on September 19 with Union General George Thomas guarding the road to Chattanooga. Fighting was in clumps of thicket, and Rosecrans was unable to see clearly what was happening. On the morning of September 20, Rosecrans ordered General Thomas J. Wood to fill an apparent gap in the lines on the right, which in actuality was not there. Confederate General James Longstreet took advantage of this and launched an attack into the gap created by the movement of Wood's troops. Longstreet's men encountered light resistance and advanced a full mile into the Union's rear lines. Union troops broke their lines and ran. Rosecrans's headquarters were abandoned, and the general along with Garfield headed toward Chattanooga.

As they made their way through the chaos, Garfield could still hear the guns of General Thomas still firing. Garfield urged Rosecrans to help. He gave Garfield grudging permission to check on Thomas.

Garfield's ride to check on Thomas, much debated years later, turned him into a hero. He galloped across Missionary Ridge and down Dry Valley Road, Confederate soldiers in all directions. At one point, he rode into a Confederate ambush, surviving the attack while several of his escorts were killed. Eventually, Garfield found Thomas and saw that he was holding the left line. Later, Rosecrans claimed that he knew Thomas was holding the line and that Garfield's ride served no purpose.

Although the Union suffered a defeat at Chickamauga, Thomas held his ground for hours and prevented Longstreet from reaching Chattanooga.

The Union forces reformed at Chattanooga but were trapped by the Confederates. On September 23, Garfield sent a telegram to Chase saying that the troops could hold out for only 10 days. Lincoln discussed the telegram with Halleck, Seward, Stanton, and Chase, and decided to send 20,000 fresh troops.

October: Before the troops arrived, Garfield was ordered to report to Washington. Rosecrans was sorry to see Garfield go. General Thomas said to Garfield before he left: "You know the injustice of all these attacks on Rosecrans. Make it your business to set these matters right."

Stanton met Garfield in Louisville and grilled him about Chattanooga. Garfield confirmed the bad reports on Rosecrans but later wrote to Rosecrans that he had defended him.

Meanwhile, on October 11, Garfield's wife, Lucretia, gave birth to a son named Harry.

November–December: Garfield arrived in Washington and met with Lincoln at the White House. The president informed him that he had been promoted to major general. After spending a few weeks in Washington attending meetings and addressing several Republican Party meetings, Garfield returned home to Hiram in December, when he learned that his daughter Eliza had the died. The little girl died on December 3 at the age of 3.

Garfield was back in Washington on December 5, still in uniform, to take his seat in Congress. He resigned his commission later that day.

෨෬

CHESTER ALAN ARTHUR returned to his law practice in New York City.

January: Arthur lost his commission at the start of the year but did not enlist although he could have. He decided to wait to see if the Republicans could regain control in the elections, which would have opened up another top military post for him.

July 8: Arthur's son William Lewis Herndon Arthur died in Englewood, New Jersey, at the age of 2. Arthur wrote to his brother, "We have lost our darling boy … from convulsions, brought on by some affection of the brain."

෨෬

GROVER CLEVELAND, 26, managed to avoid combat by purchasing a substitute to take his place, a common practice in the Civil War.

The Enrollment Act of March 3 made Cleveland eligible for service, and his name was drawn in July. His options were to find a substitute or pay $300. Cleveland's brother Lewis had been mustered out of the army on June 9 after 2 years of combat, yet he offered to take Grover's place. "Fred has done enough," Cleveland said, "I have my man." Cleveland's substitute was an illiterate man named George Brinske (or Benninsky), age 32.

෨෬

BENJAMIN HARRISON, 30 in August, spent a tedious year in noncombat garrison duty in Tennessee, first at Gallatin, then Nashville. Harrison, a colonel in the Union Army, fought the boredom by reading novels and studying military manuals and history in an attempt to make up for his deficiencies in knowledge about military matters.

The Indiana Seventieth was ordered to Gallatin in February, and there it sat for 4 months. During this period of ennui, Harrison took to novels and military works. He tried to make the best of the garrison duty.

The Indiana Seventieth moved to Nashville on August 19 to guard trains bound for Chattanooga. Harrison called this "scavenger" duty. Harrison's wife, Carrie, visited his camp in May and again in September.

In October, Harrison attended a brigade school after a major told him a promotion might be in the works.

෨෬

WILLIAM MCKINLEY, 20, and the Twenty-Third Ohio Regiment remained at the Falls of the Great Kanawha in western Virginia until July.

In February, McKinley was promoted to first lieutenant and made an aide-de-camp on Rutherford B. Hayes's staff. Hayes described McKinley as "a handsome bright, gallant boy, one of the bravest and finest officers in the army."

In July, Hayes ordered a force to go into Ohio and find John Hunt Morgan, the Confederate raider. Morgan's surrender followed in July near West Point, Ohio.

෨෬

THEODORE ROOSEVELT, 5 in October, lived in New York City.

෨෬

WILLIAM HOWARD TAFT, who turned 6 in September, attended Sunday school at the Western Unit Conference Church with his brothers. His father, Alphonso, had rebelled against the family's Baptist heritage and become a Unitarian. William followed suit in later years but never had much interest in religion.

෨෬

WOODROW WILSON, 7 in December, saw Union prisoners of war and wounded Yankees in the churchyard of his father's church in Augusta, Georgia. After Chickamauga, Joseph Wilson's Presbyterian Church served as a hospital for Union wounded. The war isolated Joseph Wilson from the rest of his family. Two of his brothers became generals in the Union army. But after the war he managed to renew contact with his northern clan.

1864
Abraham Lincoln

President Lincoln, in the fourth year of his term, managed to survive revolts within his own ranks, resisted a "peace" movement, and despite Ulysses S. Grant's bloody tactics managed to win reelection, the first incumbent to do so since Andrew Jackson in 1832. The military frustrations of 1863 slowly gave way to steady success in 1864 as Confederate forces were ground down.

February: In the only battle of the Civil War fought in Florida, Confederate general Joseph Finegan defeated Union troops under General Truman Seymour on February 20 near Jacksonville.

On February 22, Congress approved a bill creating the rank of lieutenant general, and Lincoln decided that he would name Grant supreme commander of the army.

March: Lincoln officially nominated Grant as the supreme commander of the army on March 1, and the Senate confirmed the appointment the next day. Grant arrived in Washington on March 8, and Lincoln introduced him as the new commander at a White House reception.

Grant considered an invasion of North Carolina, but Lincoln opposed this idea. Instead, Lincoln wanted Grant to wipe out Lee's army in Virginia while General William T. Sherman, now senior commander of the Armies of the West, struck at Georgia.

Reconstruction proceeded in two Southern states, Louisiana and Arkansas. On March 15, Union military authorities in Louisiana transferred power to a civilian government. On March 18 a pro-Union convention in Arkansas ratified a new constitution that abolished slavery.

April: On April 8 the Senate passed the Thirteenth Amendment, which prohibited slavery throughout all of the United States.

May: The Battle of the Wilderness in Virginia began on May 5, with Grant's force of 120,000 men clashing with Robert E. Lee's army of 62,000. After 2 days of fierce fighting, the Union army pulled away from Lee's forces. Although viewed as a retreat and a defeat for Grant, he continued to push south.

On seeing the wounded from this battle straggling back into Washington, Lincoln said, "I cannot bear it. This suffering, this loss of life is dreadful."

Grant's army reached Spotsylvania Court House, Virginia, on May 8 almost at the same time as Lee's army. For the next 12 days, Grant and Lee took turns attacking one another. Some time after May 20, Grant's army left Spotsylvania and began a series of operations along the North Anna River in Virginia before reaching Cold Harbor on May 31.

Secretary of the Treasury and future Chief Justice of the Supreme Court Salmon P. Chase. Relations between Lincoln and Chase grew so strained that Chase resigned his cabinet post in 1864.

June: The huge forces of Grant and Lee faced one another over a line of trenches at Cold Harbor. Grant tried to outflank Lee with an assault on June 3. The assault was a hopeless failure, and the Union suffered over 7,000 casualties.

Republicans met at Baltimore on June 7 to 9 and renominated Lincoln as their presidential candidate on the first ballot. Missouri, however, gave its 22 votes to Grant as delegates were unhappy with the president. Republicans nominated Andrew Johnson for vice president (see **Andrew Johnson**, page 302). Lincoln later wrote that his renomination was as a result of the country believing that "it is -not best to swap horses while crossing the river."

Grant tried to sweep around Richmond, Virginia, to Petersburg to the south. The Petersburg assaults began on June 15 with the Union army swiftly overrunning more than a mile of Confederate trenches. However, Union general William F. Smith was too cautious and broke off the battle. Confederate general P. T. Beauregard later said that Smith could have

walked into Petersburg practically unopposed. Instead, Smith's inaction led to Grant's decision to lay siege to Petersburg. The siege would last until the end of the war in April 1865 (see **Ulysses S. Grant**, pages 303 and 309).

Meanwhile, relations between Lincoln and his secretary of Treasury, Salmon Chase, continued to be cool. The two had become so estranged by the beginning of June that they did not speak to one another except through memos. The rift occurred earlier in the year as a result of the so-called Pomeroy Circular, a radical Republican proposal to replace Lincoln with Chase as the Republican nominee. Although Chase was not directly involved in the proposal, Lincoln felt betrayed. On June 30, Chase resigned from the cabinet, replaced by William Pitt Fessenden. (Later, in December, Lincoln appointed Chase to the Supreme Court.)

July: Lincoln visited the Virginia front with his son Tad. Against the advice of some of his cabinet members, Lincoln called for a 500,000-man draft on July 19. In view of Grant's losses, a great public outcry arose against this call.

At the same time, the Confederates were marching toward Washington, D.C. On July 5, Confederate general Jubal Early headed north with 10,000 men and crossed the Potomac River. On July 9, Early routed a Union force of 6,000 men under General Lew Wallace. Early reached Silver Spring, just on the outskirts of Washington, on July 11. Grant sent a detachment of men for protection of the city and Early soon abandoned the idea of pushing into Washington.

In Georgia, Union general William T. Sherman began his Atlanta campaign.

August 29–31: Democrats met in Chicago and nominated George B. McClellan for president and George Hunt Pendleton of Ohio for vice president.

September: Sherman, after 10 weeks of fighting in Georgia, completed the occupation of Atlanta on September 8. He telegraphed Washington: "Atlanta is ours, and fairly won."

Meanwhile, Early's forces in the Shenandoah valley withstood an attack by General Philip Sheridan at Winchester, Virginia, on September 19. Early retreated to the south, with Sheridan's cavalry in pursuit. Sheridan attacked again on September 22 at Fisher's Hill, this time breaking through and routing Early.

October: Early surprised Union forces by regrouping and attacking them at Cedar Creek, Virginia, on October 19. Sheridan, 20 miles away, returned in time to turn a rout into a Union victory.

November–December: Lincoln, with 2,203,831 votes to McClellan's 1,797,019, was reelected on November 8. In the Electoral College, Lincoln took 212 votes to McClellan's 21.

With the election over, the president could refocus his attention on the war. Sherman blew up the arsenals and depots of Atlanta on November 16 and his army of 62,000 began the march to the sea, traveling 15 miles per day. On December 12, Sherman was on the verge of his siege of Savannah, Georgia. While Sherman prepared to attack, Savannah's garrison of 10,000 men slipped out of the city; on December 21, Union troops moved into Savannah without a fight. Sherman wired Lincoln on December 24: "I beg to present to you as a Christmas gift the city of Savannah."

Former Presidents

MILLARD FILLMORE, 64, turned against Lincoln and opened himself up to charges that he had become a Copperhead.

February: The Great Central Fair, sponsored by the Ladies Christian Committee, had Fillmore as the main speaker. In his speech, Fillmore said: "Three years of civil war have desolated the fairest portion of our land, loaded

General George B. McClellan was Abraham Lincoln's Democratic opponent in the 1864 presidential election. (Library of Congress)

the country with enormous debt … arrayed brother against brother, father against son." The blame should go, he said, to Lincoln and the Republicans: "It is no time now to inquire whether [the war] might have been avoided.… Nor are we now to criticize the conduct of those who control it. Let impartial historians [look into] partisan prejudice, petty jealousies … intriguing, selfish ambition. Before lasting peace much must be forgiven, if not forgotten. [After the Northern victory] let us show our magnanimity by winning back the deluded multitude who have been seduced into this rebellion … by restoring them to all their rights."

୫୦ଓ

FRANKLIN PIERCE, in the wake of his wife's death in December 1863, lost interest in the Congregational church that he had been attending with her for many years.

In the spring, Pierce traveled to the White Mountains with his old Bowdoin classmate, Nathaniel Hawthorne. The author was gravely ill and died soon after in May at Plymouth, New Hampshire.

Despite the political climate in New Hampshire, some of Pierce's friends recommended that the former president come out of retirement and run as the Democratic candidate for president, although he had now been out of the White House for 8 years. Pierce refused to consider the idea.

୫୦ଓ

JAMES BUCHANAN, 73, although he had been a Democratic president, would not support Democrat McClellan's candidacy.

After Lincoln's victory, Buchanan wrote Dr. J. B. Blake on November 21: "Now would be the time for conciliation on the part of Mr. Lincoln. A frank and manly offer to the Confederates that they might return to the Union just as they were before … might possibly be accepted."

Future Presidents

ANDREW JOHNSON was nominated for vice president on the Republican ticket in the middle of the year. Early on, Johnson's state was still on the firing line. Trying to govern Tennessee under such difficult conditions was a challenge for him.

January: On January 21, Johnson announced in Nashville his plans for creating a new state government that would consist of Loyalists only. Rebels would not be able to take part in government, he said, and voters would be required to take a loyalty oath promising to support the Constitution. He said that Tennessee had never been out of the Union, only that the state's federal processes had been temporarily paralyzed. On January 26, Johnson set the state election for March 5. Conservative Unionists complained to Lincoln that Johnson had gone too far, but Lincoln supported him.

March: Voter turnout on March 5 was low (only about 50,000), and many counties did not hold an election at all. Johnson's prestige dropped over the loyalty oath issue. Both ex-Confederates and some Unionists resented its imposition.

June: On June 6, Lincoln told Simon Cameron, S. Newton Pettis, and Alexander K. McClure that Andrew Johnson was his choice to replace Hannibal Hamlin, who was now too closely identified with the radical wing of the Republicans. Lincoln believed that Europe should know that a man from a state like Tennessee could remain loyal to the Union, and that the ticket needed a Loyalist not connected with the Republican Party.

The New York delegation to the Republican National Convention in Baltimore June 7 to 8 initially favored New Yorker Daniel S. Dickinson for vice president, then switched to Hamlin. It was Thurlow Weed who finally swung the delegation to support Johnson.

C. M. Allen of Indiana officially nominated Johnson. Representative Horace Maynard of Tennessee seconded. Johnson was nominated on the first ballot.

July–November: Johnson was urged to hit the campaign trail; but he spent most of his time in Nashville, writing campaign tracts and wiring Lincoln on various matters pertaining to the governing of Tennessee.

Nathaniel P. Sawyer of Pittsburgh wrote Johnson in August that he wished Johnson had been nominated for president rather than Lincoln.

On November 8, Lincoln was reelected and Johnson became the vice president–elect.

ℰℭ

ULYSSES S. GRANT became commander in chief of the Union army and exerted a bulldog grip in Virginia. Defeats early in the year and the huge number of Union casualties for a time caused many to lose faith in Grant's leadership. In the end, Grant owed much of his military success to Sherman and Sheridan.

January–March: On January 13, Grant returned to his Nashville headquarters from Knoxville, then went to St. Louis because his son Fred was very ill with dysentery there.

Sherman, moving south through Mississippi, occupied Meridian on February 14.

Grant wrote Sherman on March 4 that Grant had been ordered to Washington, D.C., where Congress had revived the three-star rank of lieutenant general. Lincoln had nominated Grant for the supreme command of the army on March 1, and the Senate approved the appointment the next day. Grant arrived in Washington on March 8 and was introduced as the supreme commander of the army by Lincoln at a White House reception.

Grant returned to St. Louis to get his family and arrived back in Washington, D.C., on March 23.

May: On May 2, Grant wrote his wife, Julia, about the upcoming Wilderness campaign: "[Soon] the army will be in motion. I know the greatest anxiety is now felt in the North.... I feel well myself."

The Union army crossed the Rapidan River on May 3. Grant had 120,000 men, and Lee had 62,000. Close fighting in the woods began May 5 at a site about 15 miles from Chancellorsville. Two days of fierce fighting ensued, and when the battle ended on May 7, Union losses were staggering: more than 17,000 Union troops were killed, wounded, or missing. Casualties for the Confederates numbered about 7,700. During the night of May 7, Grant gave the order to move out. However, Grant's order was not to retreat north, but to continue south toward Spotsylvania Court House, Virginia. Union soldiers cheered Grant when his army moved south toward Spotsylvania instead of making a turn northward in retreat.

Grant's army reached Spotsylvania on May 8. Confederate reconnaissance tipped off Lee about Grant's southern march.

Advance units of Lee's Army of Northern Virginia reached Spotsylvania just ahead of Grant's. The Confederates managed to withstand Grant's attack on that first day. Over the next 12 days, Grant and Lee launched several attacks and counterattacks. The endless assaults ended on May 20 when Grant pulled his army out of Spotsylvania. During the next 10 days, Grant tried to turn Lee's flank with a series of skirmishes along the North Anna River in Virginia, but Lee proved to be resilient. By May 31 the leading elements of Grant's army reached Cold Harbor, Virginia, with Lee arriving almost at the same time.

June: The armies of Grant and Lee faced one another in opposing trenches stretching a length of several miles. Before dawn on June 3, Grant began his assault. In charge after charge the Union troops were turned back by the Confederates. Grant ended the attacks by noon, but not before the Union army had suffered over 7,000 killed, wounded, or missing.

Using pontoon bridges, Grant moved his soldiers southeast across the James River on June 14 to attack Petersburg, 23 miles south of Richmond. The idea was to attack Lee from the rear. However, a breakdown in communications between the commanders in the field occurred. The Petersburg assaults began on June 15 with portions of the Union army quickly overrunning more than a mile of Confederate trenches. Union general William F. Smith found a weak point in Lee's lines near Petersburg but hesitated to attack, and the advantage was soon lost.

During the night of June 16, General P. T. Beauregard moved the Confederate position back a mile, shortening and strengthening the lines. The Union troops, beginning their assault on June 17 on the Confederates' original position, found only empty trenches. Union general George G. Meade was confused by the Confederate retreat and wasted valuable time deciding on his next move. Finally, Meade ordered an assault on the new Confederate positions; however, the Confederates easily repelled the Union attack. Grant finally decided that Petersburg could not be taken by frontal attacks. Instead he ordered a siege to starve the Confederates into submission. The siege of Petersburg would last until the end of the war in April 1865.

July: Confederate general Jubal Early attacked areas near Washington, D.C., early in the month, forcing Grant to send a detachment of troops to the capital. By July 13, however, Early had abandoned the idea of invading Washington.

As the siege of Petersburg continued, a Union officer from Pennsylvania, Lieutenant Colonel Henry Pleasants, came up with an idea to break the Confederates: he proposed tunneling under the Confederate lines and rigging a mine to blow a huge hole through which the Union infantry could enter and attack. General Ambrose E. Burnside endorsed the project and assigned a specially trained division of African-American troops to lead the advance. Grant approved the plan but nixed the idea of having that division lead the attack.

The explosion at 4:44 A.M. on July 30 blew a huge crater in the Confederate line. The assault was a debacle from the beginning. Awestruck attackers wasted valuable time by gazing into the crater, which measured 200 feet wide, 60 feet across, and 10 to 30 feet deep. Union troops moved into the crater in a confused manner and were soon cut down by Confederate fire. The Union suffered nearly 4,000 casualties in the attempt.

August–September: In August, Grant put General Philip Sheridan in charge of the Shenandoah valley offensive, which was to be based on a "scorched-earth" policy of burning and smashing property to prevent the planting of crops. He gave a similar order to General William T. Sherman, whose forces were now nearing Atlanta.

Grant announced to his commanders in early September that Sherman had taken Atlanta. On September 22, Sheridan defeated Early at Fisher's Hill, Virginia.

October: Sheridan turned a defeat into a victory on October 19 in the Shenandoah after Early led a surprise attack on Union troops at Cedar Creek. Sheridan, 20 miles away at the start of the attack, arrived just in time to prevent a Confederate victory. Sheridan and his staff reformed the Union lines and made a counterattack that completely routed the Confederates.

November–December: For Grant and the Union army the year ended with more victories. Sherman blew up the arsenals and depots of Atlanta on March 16 and began his march to the sea. In early December, Sherman began his preparations for the siege of Savannah, Georgia. Sherman's troops moved into Savannah on December 21 and took the abandoned city without firing a shot.

శాలు

Rutherford B. Hayes saw considerable action, mostly in the Shenandoah Valley, and had a few close calls. By year's end he had been promoted to brigadier general and elected to Congress as a representative from Ohio.

May: Hayes's brigade, consisting mainly of soldiers from his native Ohio, moved into the valley of Virginia through Salt Sulphur Springs, near Blacksburg. -He deplored the burning of the Virginia Military Institute by Union troops.

July: On July 8, Hayes was ordered to Parkersburg, West Virginia, on the Ohio River, then to Martinsburg near Hagerstown, Maryland, before spending a week with his family in Chillicothe, Ohio.

Back in Cincinnati the talk making the rounds was a boom for Hayes for Congress. On hearing about it, he wrote his uncle Sardis Birchard on July 30: "I care nothing about it … easier to let the thing take its own course than to get up a letter declining to run."

August: Hayes was in Sheridan's camp on August 24 when he wrote William H. Smith, "I cared very little for being a candidate … but having consented to the use of my name I preferred to succeed." When Smith recommended that Hayes

return to Ohio to campaign, Hayes responded that anyone doing that in wartime "ought to be scalped."

September: Hayes was in the second battle of Winchester in Virginia on September 19, about which he wrote: "My brigade led the attack on the left…." Hayes attributed the success of this battle to General George Crook, but when Crook was wounded in the assault Hayes took over the division.

Hayes saw action again at Fisher's Hill on September 22, and again led a division in battle but gave credit to Crook: "My division led again [but] Crook is the brains of the army."

On September 29, Lucy Hayes gave birth to a boy. The couple named him George Crook in honor of General Crook.

October: On October 17, Hayes was elected to the U.S. House of Representatives from the Second District in Ohio (Cincinnati). His Democratic opponent was Joseph C. Butler, a banker. Hayes remained with the army. He was now an acting colonel and brevet brigadier general of volunteers.

Two days later, at Cedar Creek, Confederate general Jubal Early beat Crook and took 1,500 prisoners before General Philip Sheridan arrived to save the day (see **Ulysses S. Grant**, opposite column). During this battle Hayes's horse was shot out from under him and rolled down into a ravine, knocked out. For a time his troops thought he had been killed in action.

Hayes received his commission as brigadier general for bravery in the field on October 19, after his last battle and 2 weeks after his forty-second birthday. "I know full well that the honor has been conferred on all sorts of small people and so cheapened shamefully," he wrote about the promotion.

శాలు

James A. Garfield worked himself to exhaustion in the House.

January–March: Garfield established his "lone wolf" ways early. On January 6, he stood alone in the House vote on paying bounties for reenlistments, feeling it would be too costly for the government. In March he voted in opposition to the restoration of the rank of lieutenant general. He also made no secret of his dislike for Lincoln.

Garfield worked on his committee assignments to exhaustion. He was on the Military Affairs Committee and the importance of this committee at this time brought prominence to Garfield. The chairman of the committee, Robert Schenck, asked Garfield to revise conscription laws and get the measure through Congress. Garfield opposed the use of substitutes to serve in the army and commutation. However, the Military Affairs Committee did not support Garfield on commutation, and the bill was shot down by James G. Blaine, who himself had hired a substitute.

April: As a radical, Garfield opposed every idea favoring a negotiated peace to end the war. He wanted to confiscate rebel estates and give them to loyal men. He said Southern leaders "must be executed or banished. Let the republic drive from its soil the traitors."

On April 8, Alexander Long, an Ohio Democrat, gave a speech calling for an end to the war and recognition of the Confederacy. Garfield launched a glib, spontaneous reply that at times became a personal attack on Long.

June 18: Garfield wrote William Cooper Howells that he favored equal pay for African American soldiers: "I have never been anything else than radical on all these questions of freedom and slavery, rebellion and the war. I have had neither inclination nor motive to be otherwise."

September–December: In the fall, Garfield won a lopsided victory for reelection to the House.

In November, Garfield, now 33, returned to Hiram, Ohio, to rest and see his wife, Lucretia. She pointed out that the couple, after nearly 5 years of marriage, had lived together exactly 20 weeks. Taking the hint, on his return to Washington, D.C., Garfield rented rooms for the entire family.

ഇരുന്നു

CHESTER ALAN ARTHUR often lobbied for clients in Washington, D.C., was disappointed when he failed to land a political job with the state of New York, and attended the convention that renominated Lincoln. He also moved up in political circles.

June 7–8: Arthur attended the Republican Party convention in Baltimore and reluctantly went along with Lincoln's renomination. For vice president, Arthur supported Andrew Johnson.

July 25: A second son, Chester Alan Arthur III, was born.

November: In the fall election a Republican radical, Reuben Fenton, became governor of New York. Arthur applied for the job of inspector general, but in a disappointing turn of events, didn't land the post.

ഇരുന്നു

GROVER CLEVELAND, 27, was narrowly defeated for re-election as a ward supervisor in the fall election. Cleveland always liked Lincoln, and family members were certain that he voted against McClellan in the presidential election. Cleveland once said that Lincoln was "a supremely great and good man."

ഇരുന്നു

BENJAMIN HARRISON fought a succession of battles in northern Georgia with displays of courage and leadership that inspired his soldiers. Colonel Harrison fought more battles in a month's time than his grandfather, William Henry Harrison, did in a lifetime of frontier fighting.

January–February: In an army reorganization on January 2, Harrison took command of a brigade in a division under General William Thomas Ward, in a corps under General Joseph Hooker, part of General William T. Sherman's Mississippi command.

On February 11, Major General Daniel Butterfield, Hooker's chief of staff, arrived from Nashville to find out why Ward's forces were still sitting in place when Grant wanted them rushed to the front. Harrison's men left Nashville on February 24. Harrison was upset when Ward marched his men into a mountain pass and lost his way. The men had to turn around and retreat for several miles. Harrison blamed Ward's heavy drinking habits for the blunder.

Without his knowledge, Republicans in Indiana had nominated Harrison for his old post of reporter for the Indiana Supreme Court.

March: On the road from Bridgeport, Alabama, to Wauhatchie, Tennessee, Harrison reported seeing dead horses and mules everywhere. He was appointed commandant of the Wauhatchie camp.

April–May: General Otis Howard, Harrison's commander, was transferred in April and Harrison was now under General Hooker. Ward took command of Harrison's brigade.

Harrison accepted the supreme court reporter's nomination on April 27 but made it clear that he would not be available until after his service in the army was complete.

The Seventieth Regiment crossed the Chickamauga battlefield on May 1 to Lee and Gordon's Mills, and after a minor skirmish marched to a point 6 miles from Dalton, Georgia. Hooker went into action on May 9 to 10 at Tunnell Hill, holding the Seventieth, of which Harrison was a part, in reserve. Sherman planned to outflank Joe Johnston at Resaca, Georgia, and Harrison was second in the line in the May 13 attack. The Confederates were in an excellent defensive horseshoe and when Sherman opened with a frontal assault, the Seventieth stormed a hill. Harrison got down flat as fire knocked sand on his head. He scrambled up the hill and later wrote his wife, "sharpshooters did not fail to pay their compliments to me all the way up."

The next day the Seventieth Regiment, under fire, advanced down a valley. Harrison waved them on to a 12-pound Napoleon gun emplacement where they bayoneted some Confederate gunners. With sword and revolver in hand Harrison led the assault on troops under General J. B. Hood and into the Confederates' breastworks. Harrison's men mistakenly went into retreat when they heard the Confederate command, "Retreat, they are flanking us." Harrison tried to rally his men when he heard that General Ward had been wounded in the arm. Harrison took over the brigade and asked permission to recapture a position held earlier, but General Butterfield gave orders for Harrison to support Brigadier General John Coburn's nearby brigade. The Confederates made a charge, but approaching nightfall halted the action. Johnston then retreated across the Oostanaula River, and the Union army took Resaca.

Harrison received a promotion and became chief of the brigade on May 29.

July: Sherman was 10 miles from Atlanta on July 7 when Harrison wrote his wife, "We can see the steeples of the churches in Atlanta…. We had a sharp artillery fight on the Marietta road on Sunday … lost several men killed. I had several very narrow escapes."

September: On September 2, Harrison gleefully wrote his wife that "Atlanta is ours…." Harrison received orders on September 4 to report to Governor Oliver Morton in Indianapolis. Arriving on September 20, Morton gave Harrison a double assignment: to campaign for Lincoln and recruit more soldiers.

October–December: Harrison spent the beginning of October campaigning for the supreme court reporter post. In mid-October he was won by nearly 20,000 votes. For the rest of October and into November, Harrison campaigned for Lincoln throughout Indiana.

Harrison hoped to be able to stay in Indiana to assume the reporter job immediately, but he was ordered back to his regiment. His brigade was ordered to Nashville to reinforce General George Thomas. The Battle of Nashville began on December 15. Harrison positioned his troops on the right to move against General Benjamin Franklin Cheatham. Harrison charged against a Confederate battery without success. The next day, Confederate general John Bell Hood shortened his lines but was soon rolled backward in a rout. When General Thomas ordered a pursuit of Hood, Harrison was directed to Murfreesboro, Tennessee, to try and reach the Tennessee River before Hood to cut him off. Harrison's infantry could not move fast enough because of ice and mud, and Hood reached Tennessee first. Harrison never caught up with Hood.

✍ଔ

WILLIAM MCKINLEY, 21 in January, participated in battle after battle in the Shenandoah valley of Virginia. As a first lieutenant he risked his life several times and was promoted to captain before the end of the year.

April–May: McKinley's Twenty-third Regiment (from Ohio) received orders on April 29 to join General George Crook for a raid on the Virginia and Tennessee Railroad. Fighting in the mountains was difficult, McKinley later reported, as the soldiers crossed deep ravines and moved through dense forests. They had little rest or food.

The Twenty-Third made a successful charge on a Confederate position in the Battle of Cloyd Mountain on May 9. Confederate artillery pieces were within 10 paces of Union forces.

June–September: McKinley's E Company reached Staunton, Virginia, on June 8 and joined General David Hunter, then moved to Brownsburg and Lexington. By June 14 they were close to Lynchburg for another battle. The Twenty-Third marched until June 27, when the hungry men reached a supply train at Big Sewall Mountain.

From July 20 until September 3, McKinley's Twenty-third Regiment engaged in continuous marching and skirmishes with Southern forces. While camped in Charleston on July 1 the twenty-third received orders to move into the Shenandoah valley to stop the raids by Confederate general Jubal Early.

From Parkersburg the Twenty-Third reached Martinsburg on July 14, then Cabletown, 10 miles from Harper's Ferry, on

July 18. Early quickly surrounded the regiment but the Union soldiers managed to cut their way out and rejoin Crook at Winchester on July 22. Two days later the army was resting when it received word that Early was approaching again, even though Early was greatly outnumbered by Crook's force. The Union army formed a line at Kernstown, 4 miles south of Winchester.

Colonel William Brown's regiment, situated in an orchard, was in danger of being smashed by rebel forces. Colonel Rutherford B. Hayes selected McKinley to carry an order to Brown to retreat. McKinley made a wild ride through Confederate fire and exploding artillery shells, gave Brown the message, and returned without a scratch.

In September, McKinley was promoted to captain.

October: McKinley was with the Twenty-third Regiment when they were surprised by a Confederate attack at Cedar Creek on October 19 (see **Ulysses S. Grant**, page 304).

✍ଔ

THEODORE ROOSEVELT, 6 years old in October, lived in New York City.

✍ଔ

WILLIAM HOWARD TAFT, age 7 in September, attended the Sixteenth District School at Mt. Auburn on the outskirts of Cincinnati.

✍ଔ

WOODROW WILSON, 8 in December, lived in Augusta, Georgia, as the Civil War brought severe shortages to the people of the South.

1865
Abraham Lincoln

President Lincoln, although exhausted by 4 years of strain, made visits to the military front and spoke against any policy of vindictive indemnity toward the South as the Civil War rushed to a conclusion. He hoped for the North and South to come together as a nation without recrimination by Northern leaders. Lincoln would be shot down by an assassin's bullet before he could help guide a postwar reunited nation to reconciliation.

January: In an effort to push the military advantage, Lincoln ordered another draft of 300,000 men.

On January 16, Admiral David Porter, with 60 ships, and General Alfred H. Terry, with 8,500 men, took Fort Fisher outside Wilmington, North Carolina. This move left Galveston, Texas, as the only remaining open port for Confederate blockade runners.

The Confederate situation bordered on desperation. Lee's men stationed around Richmond, Virginia, suffered from a shortage of blankets and food. Desertions occurred rampantly. Peace overtures surfaced, especially in North Carolina, as the Confederacy neared collapse. Congressman Francis Blair of Missouri returned to Washington from his trip to Richmond with word that Jefferson Davis was willing to talk of a peace settlement between "the two countries." Lincoln, realizing that Davis still dreamed of independence, replied that he would talk peace for "the people of our one common country."

On January 31 the Thirteenth Amendment to abolish slavery nationwide came up for a vote in the House. It had passed in the Senate nearly a year earlier. The House approved the amendment by a 119-to-56 vote, only 3 votes above the required minimum.

February: Davis assigned Vice President Alexander H. Stephens, Judge John A. Campbell, and R. M. T. Hunter as peace commissioners. The three Confederate peace negotiators met on February 3 at Hampton Roads with Lincoln and Secretary of State William Seward. The talks quickly failed; the Southern delegation sought an armistice first, with discussions of reunion to come later. Lincoln balked at this notion.

General William T. Sherman reached Columbia, South Carolina, on February 17 and burned the city the next day. Confederate forces abandoned Charleston on February 19.

March: By early March, General Robert E. Lee, foreseeing the inevitable, sought to draw General Ulysses S. Grant into negotiations. Lincoln told Secretary of War Edwin Stanton to reply to Grant, "[H]ave no conference with General Lee unless it be for the capitulation of General Lee's army … you are not to decide, discuss, or confer upon any political question. [Y]ou are to press … your military advantages."

On March 4, Lincoln was sworn in for his second term. Chief Justice Salmon Chase administered the oath. For security reasons Lincoln did not ride in the customary procession to the Capitol.

Lincoln said in his address, "The progress of our arms, upon which all else chiefly depends, is … well known … it is … reasonably satisfactory and encouraging to all.… Neither party expected the magnitude, or the duration.… Neither anticipated that the cause of the conflict might cease with, or even before, the conflict itself should cease.… [W]ith malice toward none, with charity for all, with firmness in the fight, as God gives us to see the right, let us strive on to finish the work … to bind up the nation's wounds."

On March 25, Lee attacked Fort Steadman but was repulsed. Lincoln inspected the battlefield from a railroad coach soon afterward.

Sherman arrived on March 27 and conferred with Lincoln. Lincoln was tired of the war and hoped to avoid the last bloody battle that Grant said was necessary. Lincoln's wish was to have Confederate troops return to their farms in time for spring planting.

April: Grant telegraphed Lincoln on April 1 that General Philip Sheridan was routing Confederate forces at Five Forks,

an important road junction covering the South Side Railroad in Virginia. Lee moved west from Petersburg, Virginia, that same night and Grant entered Petersburg on April 2, finally ending the long siege of that city. Grant asked Lincoln to join him, and Lincoln and his son Tad arrived by horse.

On April 3, Union troops entered the city of Richmond. The following day, Lincoln arrived at Richmond, a city in ruins, with his son Tad. While walking the streets, newly freed slaves crowded around the president to catch a glimpse of the man.

Meanwhile, Lee headed for Danville, Virginia (south of Richmond), to link up with Joe Johnston, but when Sheridan's cavalry reached the town first, Lee veered westward toward Lynchburg.

Sheridan caught up with General Richard S. Ewell's corps at Sayler's Creek on April 6 and wiped out almost half of Lee's army and most of his wagon train. Sheridan telegraphed Grant, "If the thing is pressed, I think that Lee will surrender." Lincoln agreed and sent a wire on April 7 stating, "Let the thing be pressed."

Lincoln hurried back to Washington on April 9 after hearing that Secretary of State Seward had suffered a broken jaw after being thrown from his carriage. That night Lincoln received Grant's message that Lee had surrendered at Appomattox Court House.

Booming salutes in celebration of war's end resounded in Washington, D.C., on April 10, and Lincoln requested that a band play "Dixie." He gave a speech at the White House the next day, saying he was tired and distressed by some in the Republican Party who sought revenge, and he argued that it would be better to consider the Southern states as never having left the Union.

On April 14, Lincoln met with his cabinet and General Grant. The president told them that he had dreamed that word of a great victory would be forthcoming from General William T. Sherman. Lincoln also spoke highly of Lee and his Confederate soldiers, and said that there had been enough bloodletting.

That evening Lincoln went to Ford's Theater to see Laura Keene star in *Our American Cousin*. He invited Grant to join him, but the general said he preferred to visit his sons who were then staying at Long Branch, New Jersey. During the play, actor John Wilkes Booth, 26, sympathetic to the cause of the South, sneaked into Lincoln's box. He shot the president in the back of the head with a derringer. He then jumped to the stage below, breaking a leg, and made a limping escape through the back of the theater after yelling Virginia's motto: "*Sic semper tyrannis!*" [Thus be it ever to tyrants!].

Lincoln was carried across the street to the home of William Peterson, a tailor. Lincoln, who never regained consciousness, died at 7:22 the following morning, April 15. He was 56.

Lincoln's funeral service took place in the East Room of the White House on April 19. Afterward, his body was placed in a black-draped train for the trip to his final resting place in Springfield, Illinois. It took 12 days to reach Springfield, with stops en route at Baltimore, New York City, Albany, Cleveland, Indianapolis, and Chicago. Burial at Oak Ridge Cemetery in Springfield took place on May 4.

ഇൗൽ

ANDREW JOHNSON began the year as the vice president–elect, still trying to get Tennessee back into the Union. In a few short months he would have to take over a country in need of reunion and healing after a long and bloody war.

January: Johnson was in Nashville tying up loose ends as military governor of Tennessee when he became sick with typhoid fever. Confined to bed, he asked if he could take his oath of office for the vice presidency in Nashville. Lincoln talked the matter over with his cabinet and on January 24 replied, "It is unsafe for you not to be here on the 4th of March."

March: Johnson reached Washington, D.C., on March 1 and took quarters at the Kirkwood House Hotel. Johnson's lengthy illness in Tennessee and overindulgence at a party the night before his inauguration led to a traumatic and embarrassing event for the new vice president on March 4. He rode in the inaugural parade down Pennsylvania Avenue with the outgoing vice president, Hannibal Hamlin. On reaching the Senate, Johnson told Hamlin that he felt weak from a recent fever and asked Hamlin if he had any whiskey. Johnson took several slugs in the warm, crowded room and then, after some delays, gave a rambling speech that mortified his friends and stunned everyone else.

April: On Lincoln's invitation, Johnson joined the president in Richmond on April 5.

On the night of April 14, Johnson went to bed early. L. I. Farwell (the former governor of Wisconsin) had been at Ford's Theater and he woke the vice president in the night with the news that Lincoln had been shot.

Johnson insisted on going to see Lincoln and arrived at the Peterson home at 2 A.M. He remained half an hour, then returned to Kirkwood House. In the morning General Henry Halleck stopped by the hotel and informed Johnson that he was not to go anywhere without a guard, an indirect way of saying that Lincoln had not survived. Chief Justice Salmon Chase arrived at Kirkwood House soon thereafter. Chase administered the oath of office to Johnson about 10 A.M.

The cabinet talked of offering resignations, but Johnson wanted no immediate changes in his staff. The radicals moved quickly, sensing that Lincoln's death might have opened the possibility to their hopes for a postwar policy based on no reconciliation toward the South.

The assassination of President Abraham Lincoln at the hands of John Wilkes Booth on April 14, 1865, at Ford's Theater in Washington, D.C.

General Joseph Johnston surrendered all Confederate armies to Sherman on April 18 on the following terms dictated by Sherman: (1) armies were to disband and put down their arms, (2) Southern states would be recognized providing their leaders took the oath to support the U.S. Constitution, (3) the U.S. Supreme Court would decide between any rival claimants to state government leadership, (4) federal courts would be reestablished in the South, and (5) the people of the South would be guaranteed political rights.

The cabinet met that night and disapproved of Sherman's terms. Johnson decided to inform Sherman that the terms were not acceptable and to resume the war. Sherman accepted Johnson's orders on April 26 at Durham, North Carolina, and forced General Johnston to surrender on the basis of the terms Lee had accepted at Appomattox.

May: In a formal announcement on May 10, Johnson declared the war to be "virtually at an end." That same day, Confederate president Jefferson Davis was captured by Union cavalry near Irwinville, Georgia.

The last battle of the Civil War was fought on May 13 at Palmitto Ranch near Brownsville, Texas.

Johnson issued an amnesty proclamation on May 29, "to all persons [who] participated in the existing rebellion … with the restoration of all rights of property." Pardons were given (with 14 exceptions) to Confederate civil and military leaders and to persons whose property was worth more than $20,000.

June–August: Johnson and his cabinet debated all summer about what to do with Jefferson Davis. Most favored a military trial on the charge of treason. In the end, Davis was never tried—he was released from prison 2 years after his arrest.

The cabinet also discussed the issue of Black suffrage. Radicals in Congress strongly favored granting freed male slaves the right to vote. Johnson believed that the matter should be decided by the individual states.

September–December: In the last months of the year ordinances of secession were repealed in the Southern states and slavery was fully abolished in every state. Confederate state debts were repudiated, and the extension of Black suffrage was left to each individual state to decide.

Johnson's message to Congress on December 5 exuded a conciliatory spirit. He said he was against military governors and favored the restoration of the federal courts in Southern states. He urged the races to "live side by side in a state of mutual benefit and goodwill."

On December 6, after ratification by twenty-seven states, the Thirteenth Amendment formally abolishing slavery throughout the United States went into effect.

Radical Republican Congressman Thaddeus Stevens said in a speech on December 18, the "Republican Party and it alone can save the Union." He called for turning Southern states into territories, and urged that every African-American in the South be given a homestead and suffrage.

House and Senate leaders created the Joint Committee on Reconstruction, with Stevens appointed the House chair of the committee. Stevens would become a major thorn in Johnson's side during the next year.

Former Presidents

MILLARD FILLMORE, 65, retired, and living in Buffalo, New York, was out of town because of an illness in the family on the night of Lincoln's assassination. When a passerby saw that there was no black crepe on Fillmore's front door the house was vandalized with a smear of black ink. Fillmore's Copperhead views on the war had created a climate in which this desecration was possible. He returned home in time to organize and lead a committee that escorted Lincoln's funeral train between Batavia and Buffalo.

ജ

FRANKLIN PIERCE, like Fillmore, endured the wrath of his neighbors in Concord, New Hampshire, at the time of Lincoln's assassination. A crowd rushed to Pierce's house during rumors that the retired president displayed no mourning crepe on his door. Pierce, deeply shocked by news of the assassination, came to the front door carrying a small American flag and made a speech denouncing the violence.

Pierce took to drinking heavily again this year. A bad cough, along with the liquor he consumed, made him very ill in February and June, and he was near death in the fall. When he managed to pull through this third illness he renounced "sin" and the "devil," and on December 3 was baptized at St. Paul's Episcopal Church. Pierce turned 61 on November 23.

ജ

JAMES BUCHANAN, retired and living in Pennsylvania, responded to Lincoln's assassination by writing Horatio King:

"I feel the assassination ... to be a terrible misfortune.... My intercourse with [Lincoln] convinced me [Lincoln had a] kindly and benevolent heart and [was] of plain, sincere and frank manners. I felt for him much personal regard."

Turning 74 in April, Buchanan entertained frequently at his Wheatland estate in Lancaster, especially during good weather.

Future Presidents

ULYSSES S. GRANT'S victorious command of Union forces opened political doors to a man who, just 4 years earlier, had been a poor farmer. Grant gave serious thought to seeking the presidency.

January: At the beginning of the year, defeat for Lee and the Confederate army was obviously near. In Petersburg, Lee had fewer then 60,000 undernourished and ill-equipped men, compared with Grant's well-fed and heavily equipped force of nearly 125,000.

March: With spring approaching, Confederate president Jefferson Davis ordered Lee to try and break the Petersburg siege. Lee chose Fort Stedman, east of Petersburg, as the place to try the breakout. The initial assault on Fort Stedman began on March 25, surprising the Union defenders. The Union was able to regroup after the surprise attack and put together a counterattack that repelled the Confederates.

April: The long siege of Petersburg finally came to an end at the beginning of April. Sheridan routed Confederate forces at Five Forks, Virginia, on April 1, forcing Lee to move west from Petersburg. Before dawn on April 2, Grant opened his attack on Petersburg. The small band of Confederates held off the Union army long enough to enable Lee to escape from the city. Also on April 2 the Confederates abandoned Richmond, allowing Union forces to take the city without a fight on April 3.

Grant asked for surrender on April 7, to which Lee responded, "Though not entertaining the opinion you express on the hopelessness of further resistance.... I reciprocate your desire to avoid useless effusion of blood....[I] ask the terms." Grant replied, "Peace being my great desire ... [Confederate forces should] be disqualified [from fighting against the United States again]."

Lee attempted one last effort to break free of the pursuing Union army. When this attempt failed on April 9, Lee decided to come to terms with Grant. The two met at one o'clock at the home of Wilmer McLean at Appomattox Court House, Virginia. Grant's terms for surrender included (1) that Confederate officers would sign paroles for their men in exchange for not fighting anymore; (2) turning over all equipment to the Union army except for sidearms, private horses, and private baggage; and (3) that Confederate soldiers would be allowed to go home. Lee asked if the soldiers could take other horses home with them to be able to plow crops and

Grant agreed. Lee also asked for rations, and Grant offered 3 days' worth to Lee's starving army.

Grant attended a cabinet meeting on April 14, during which Lincoln invited Grant to join him in attending Ford's Theater. Julia Grant invented an excuse about going to New Jersey to see the children and Grant was supposed to go with her. He long wondered what would have happened had he been sitting next to Lincoln at Ford's Theater that fateful evening.

May: A large, 2-day, Union army parade was held on May 23 to 24 in Washington, D.C. Grant was the most popular

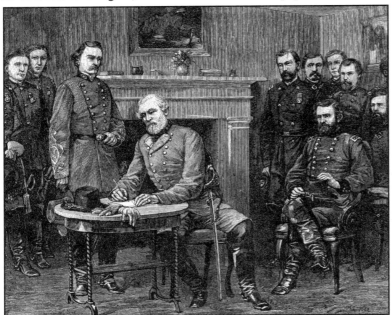

Confederate general Robert E. Lee (seated, left) formally surrenders his forces to Union general Ulysses S. Grant (seated, right) on April 9, 1865, at Appomattox Court House, Virginia.

attraction at the parade celebrating the end of the war, receiving admiration and praise from the cheering crowds.

At the end of May, Grant and Julia traveled to Burlington, New Jersey, to see their children.

June–August: Grant combined his duties as commander of the army with speaking engagements he undertook in several cities. He was a big hit during a Johnson rally held at Cooper Union Hall in New York City in June. Grant visited West Point during the same month, and spoke at a July 4 celebration in Albany. During the months of July and August, Grant visited Boston, New Hampshire, Vermont, and Saratoga, New York, before finally returning home to Galena, Illinois, on August 18.

October–December: Grant and Julia returned to Washington on October 8. Almost as soon as he arrived, President Johnson sent him on a 5-day fact-finding mission throughout the South. Grant visited Raleigh, Charleston, Savannah, and Augusta and took time to visit Julia's sister in Richmond, Virginia. On December 15 he presented to Johnson the report about his trip, in which he supported the

Freedmen's Bureau (an agency set up to assist African Americans throughout the South) but implied that its agents were corrupt. Grant also believed in the wisdom of stationing army garrisons in the South as a precaution but was against posting African American troops in the Southern states because they were resented there. Grant's report coincided more with Johnson's more moderate views than with those of the radicals in Congress.

ഇ *ഇ*

RUTHERFORD B. HAYES, wounded five times in the Civil War, was promoted to major general before returning to the political wars as a member of the U.S. House of Representative from Ohio.

January–March: Hayes went into winter quarters at Cumberland, Maryland, at the start of the year. On March 3 he was promoted to brevet major general of volunteers "for gallant and distinguished services."

June–July: Hayes resigned his commission on June 8 and traveled to Cincinnati. In July he joined the law office of Stephenson and Noyes.

November–December: Hayes was 43 when he became a member of the Thirty-ninth Congress in November, representing Ohio's Second District. Thaddeus Stevens controlled the House agenda with a vengeance, and Hayes decided to say little to avoid conflict. When General Robert Schenck demanded that Black suffrage be approved, Hayes offered an amendment proposing an educational test for the right to vote even though few African Americans could read. Hayes avoided the passion aired on the floor over Reconstruction issues and always voted with the majority.

ഇ *ഇ*

JAMES A. GARFIELD faced multiple options in 1865: should he be a college president again, practice law in California, campaign for a U.S. Senate seat or the governorship of Ohio, rush into oil speculation or concentrate on real estate deals, or slip away from radical influence to remain friends with Andrew Johnson?

January–April: Early in the year, Garfield was asked about heading a new Disciple of Christ college in Pennsylvania. The deal fell through.

Despite Garfield's flimsy law experience, Jeremiah S. Black offered him a partnership in which Garfield would head the California office of the firm. In April they signed papers and Garfield was quite happy with the idea; however, that deal also soon fell apart.

At this same time, William Bascom suggested that Garfield could become governor of Ohio if he so chose. However, the position paid less than his congressional salary, and Hayes already had his eyes on a Senate seat that would soon be opening up.

Meanwhile, Ralph Plumb, formerly part of Garfield's army staff, came up with a scheme of buying allegedly oil-rich land in Sandy Valley, Kentucky, cheaply and making big profits by reselling to wealthy insiders regardless of whether oil was actually discovered. Garfield attached his name to the plan, which was little short of a swindle. He went to Detroit to sell the parcels, but nothing came from the dealings, and the land eventually was sold for taxes.

Garfield learned of Lincoln's assassination while he was in the Exchange Building on Wall Street. Outside, a mob was ready to lynch suspected Southerners and was on the verge of smashing the offices of the Copperhead-leaning *New York World*. Garfield went to the balcony of the customhouse and cried out, "Fellow Citizens!… Clouds and darkness are round about Him.…Justice and judgment are the establishment of His throne!… God reigns, and the government at Washington still lives!" The spontaneous speech hushed the crowd, purportedly, and people wondered who it was that offered this speech. It became part of the Garfield legend; however, its authenticity is uncertain.

July: Publicly, Garfield favored giving the vote to African Americans. On July 4, he asked what freedom for African Americans really meant. "Is it the bare privilege of not being chained?" He said that if there must be an educational test to be able to vote, it should be the same for African Americans as well as all immigrants: "Let us not [believe] absurd and senseless dogma that the color of the skin shall be the basis of suffrage."

October 17: Another son, James Randolph, was born.

ഇൽ

CHESTER ALAN ARTHUR, 36 in October, was an assessment collector along with Tom Murphy for U.S. Senator Edwin Morgan of New York. Morgan headed a Union Party committee that collected assessments for postmasters. As a result of Arthur's help, Morgan obtained a place for Arthur and his wife at Lincoln's inaugural ceremony.

ഇൽ

GROVER CLEVELAND, 28, ran for district attorney of Buffalo and lost. He was defeated by his own roommate, Lyman K. Bass, although Cleveland had the support of the *Buffalo Courier*. While both were campaigning, Cleveland and Bass would go to a saloon together and drink their fill of beer. Cleveland did well in Buffalo, but Bass's support was great enough in the outer districts to carry the day. The defeat momentarily ended Cleveland's political career.

ഇൽ

BENJAMIN HARRISON covered considerable ground (and water) early in the year before the war ended. His rail and steamship trips contrasted sharply with his immovable garrison duty of 1863.

January–April: On January 16, General George Thomas ordered Harrison to report to his old regiment, which was then stationed in Savannah, Georgia. The orders soon changed, however, and Harrison was first to have a furlough in Indianapolis. From there he was to take a train to New York, and then a steamer to Savannah.

On leaving Chattanooga, Brigadier General Charles Cruft wrote the War Department to recommend Harrison for promotion to brigadier general. In February, Harrison was notified that he had made brevet brigadier general and that Senate confirmation would follow.

Harrison brought his family to New York, stopping in Honesdale, Pennsylvania, to visit his wife Caroline's sister. While in Pennsylvania, Harrison contracted scarlet fever. He and his family had to be quarantined for 30 days as soon as they arrived in New York.

Still feeling ill and against a doctor's advice, on February 26 Harrison sailed on the *Fulton* for Hilton Head to rejoin his unit and arrived on March 2. He busied himself for most of the month by training new recruits.

In April, Harrison and his troops boarded a steamer to join General Sherman in North Carolina. Sherman had already left North Carolina by the time Harrison arrived, and on April 10, Harrison sailed for Wilmington. When he arrived there, he was informed of Lee's surrender. On April 19, he arrived in Raleigh, where he learned of Lincoln's assassination.

May: For much of May, Harrison pushed his troops to arrive in Washington, D.C., in time for the celebratory parades on May 23 to 24. By the time they got there, his men were dirty, hot, and thirsty.

June: Harrison received his discharge from the army on June 8. He traveled home to Indiana with his regiment by train, and once there was welcomed by receptions and parties in his honor.

July–December: Harrison was soon aligned with the radical elements of the Republican Party. He also returned to his post as reporter for the Indiana Supreme Court.

ഇൽ

WILLIAM MCKINLEY, a 22-year-old captain in the Union army, returned to Ohio after the war and found his parents wanted him to pursue the ministry and not a military career. Instead, McKinley selected law because he already envisioned a future in politics.

On March 13, McKinley was promoted to brevet major for gallantry in the Shenandoah valley. He participated in the parades in Washington, D.C., on May 23 to 24 and was mustered out of the army on July 26 at Cumberland, Maryland.

McKinley soon began his law career. He entered the law office of Charles E. Glidden, 30, a Mahoning County lawyer who was elected a judge that year. McKinley wrote Russell Hastings on August 28: "I am at times … flighty … wrapped in the mysteries of law."

ഇൽ

THEODORE ROOSEVELT, 7, and his younger brother Elliott on April 25 watched the Lincoln funeral procession as it passed down Broadway from the second-story window of the home of their grandfather Cornelius.

Theodore Jr., fighting almost constant illness, decided to become a naturalist. His strong interest in zoology became kindled while he was walking up Broadway one day and saw a dead seal on a slab at a market. Theodore asked questions about it, then measured it, and accumulated other information.

୫୦୯ଓ

WILLIAM HOWARD TAFT 8, lived in Cincinnati.

July 18: Taft's sister Frances Louise was born.

୫୦୯ଓ

WOODROW WILSON, 9 in December, lived in Augusta, Georgia, and after the war ended witnessed Union soldiers guarding Jefferson Davis.

୫୦୯ଓ

WARREN G. HARDING was born November 2 in Blooming Grove, Ohio. His father was George Tyron Harding; his mother was Phoebe Elizabeth Dickerson Harding.

George Harding, called Tyron, was born on June 12, 1844, in a log cabin built by his great-grandfather Amos in Blooming Grove. Tyron was the only surviving boy in the family. His five sisters, Phoebe, Sophia, Lydia, Margaret, and Sarah, lived long lives. Tyron entered Iberia College, 7 miles from Blooming Grove, in 1858 and graduated with a bachelor of arts degree in June 1860. The Presbyterian college was then only 4 years old. Tyron taught at Mount Gilead, then enrolled in the Ontario Academy, 6 miles to the north.

Phoebe Dickerson, born near Blooming Grove on December 21, 1843, was a student at Mount Gilead.

Tyron enlisted as a fifer in Company C of the Ninety-Sixth Ohio Volunteer Infantry, but developed pleurisy and was mustered out. Regaining his health, he reenlisted on May 3, 1864, as a drummer boy with the 136th Regulars of the Ohio National Guard at Camp Chase. He asked Phoebe to marry him before he left for the war.

Phoebe and Tyron were married on May 7. Tyron left his bride 4 days later and shipped to Fairfax, Virginia, and then to Washington, D.C., where the outfit took up garrison duty at Fort Williams with an assignment to protect the city. Tyron later came down with typhoid fever and was discharged from the army on August 29.

Warren Harding was named after his aunt Malvina Dickerson's husband, Warren Gamaliel Bancroft, a Methodist prison chaplain from Wisconsin. Harding's ancestors were Puritans who sailed from England to Braintree, Massachusetts, in 1623. The Hardings were of English, Irish, and Scotch ancestry.

1866
Andrew Johnson

The president's conflict with Republican radicals over the methods of reincorporating the secessionist states back under a national umbrella rushed toward a climax by the end of

1866. Throughout the year, Johnson sought ways to rid his cabinet of radicals, especially Secretary of War Edwin Stanton. One idea was to replace Stanton with General William T. Sherman.

January–February: Senator Lyman Trumbull of Illinois sponsored the creation of the Freedmen's Bureau, an agency whose aim was to assist Blacks in each county of the South. Penalties (fines or imprisonment) awaited those violating the civil rights of the former slave population. The bill passed in the Senate by a 27-to-10 vote, and in the House by a 136-to-33 vote.

On January 22, Thaddeus Stevens's House committee on Reconstruction submitted a constitutional amendment (the Fourteenth) that would strip the South of representation unless every Black in the population was counted. A long debate followed. In early February, Stevens and Senator Charles Sumner enlisted the support of a delegation of Blacks, led by Frederick Douglass, to confront the president about his foot-dragging and nonsupport.

Johnson told Douglass he was against a policy that would "end in a contest between the races … if persisted it will result in the extermination of one or the other."

The president vetoed the Freedmen's Bureau legislation on February 19, and the radicals were unable to raise the two-thirds votes necessary to override the veto.

April: Congress passed a Civil Rights Act to protect African Americans from Southern codes restricting their freedom. The act made African Americans citizens of the United States and precluded states from enacting laws that would restrict their rights. Johnson vetoed the bill, saying that it was a mistake to grant immediate citizenship to African Americans. His argument was that they needed to go through a period of "probation" before being granted citizenship. On April 9 the House and Senate successfully overrode Johnson's veto.

May: Johnson's relationship with his secretary of war grew more strained; by May Johnson was convinced that Stanton was on the side of the radicals. Johnson opposed the Fourteenth Amendment then before Congress and held a cabinet meeting on May 1 to discuss it and see where everyone stood on the issue. Stanton, however, managed to keep his views private and his ties to the radicals hidden.

June: Congress ratified the Fourteenth Amendment on June 8. Its five sections called for (1) equality for all persons born or naturalized in the United States; (2) congressional representation based on counting the actual African American population, or a reduction in representation proportionate to the number of African Americans denied civil rights; (3) denial of the franchise to those who supported secession until 1870; (4) prohibition of payment of the Confederate debt; and (5) congressional control over enforcement powers.

July: Several radical Republicans in Johnson's cabinet resigned. Postmaster General William Dennison resigned on

July 11 and was replaced by Alexander Williams Randall. Attorney General Joshua Speed resigned a few days after Dennison and was replaced by Henry Stanbery. Interior Secretary James Harlan would not quit, so Johnson asked him to resign on July 27. Orville Hickman Browning of Illinois replaced Harlan. However, Secretary of War Edwin Stanton, whom Johnson wanted to resign, remained at his post.

August–October: The national convention of the National Union Party opened in Philadelphia on August 14. North–South harmony prevailed for those representing 36 states. All the delegates, most of whom were Democrats, supported Johnson. They passed resolutions concerning the abolition of slavery, saying that former slaves had rights, and proposed that every state should have a vote on constitutional questions regarding voting rights.

A convention resolution was presented to Johnson on August 18 with Ulysses S. Grant attending the event. Johnson responded by saying he sought "to restore the Union, to heal the breach," but that "we found a disturbing and warring element opposing us." He added that the radicals controlled a U.S. Congress that did not represent all the states.

President Johnson decided to take his case directly to the American people by stumping in his old Tennessee style. He started west on August 28, traveling from Baltimore to New York, then on to Albany, Buffalo, Cleveland, Detroit, Chicago, Springfield, St. Louis, Indianapolis, Cincinnati, Pittsburgh, and back to Washington, D.C. Tremendous crowds greeted him at all his stops, but as the tour went on, radicals planted hecklers in the crowds to harass the president.

November–December: In spite of the efforts of the National Union Party and Johnson's tour, radical Republicans gained even more seats in Congress in the November election.

In his December message to Congress, Johnson asked that Southern congressmen be allowed to be seated in Congress again. Eleven states still had no representation in Congress. "[N]o people ought to bear the burden of taxation yet be denied the right of representation," Johnson declared. "Each state shall have at least one representative...."

On December 17, Representative James M. Ashley of Ohio introduced a resolution calling for Johnson's impeachment, but the measure failed to receive the necessary two-thirds majority vote.

Former Presidents

MILLARD FILLMORE resumed his status as Buffalo's first citizen while the animosities of the war years, including memories of his Copperhead proclivities, faded. Politically, Fillmore now allied himself with Johnson's Reconstruction policy, although the retired president did not get involved in congressional races in his western New York district. Mrs. Fillmore had become a chronic invalid, and in an attempt to improve her health the couple spent the winter months in Europe, mostly in Madrid and Paris.

∞∞

FRANKLIN PIERCE, no longer drinking, was confirmed in the Episcopal faith in the spring, and by summer the retired president's health had improved enough that he took frequent walks along Main Street in Concord, New Hampshire.

∞∞

JAMES BUCHANAN was a proud witness in January to the marriage of his niece (and former hostess of his White House), Harriet Lane, to Henry E. Johnson, a Baltimore banker, at the Wheatland estate. When she became orphaned at the age of 9, Harriet had chosen Buchanan as her guardian.

Buchanan's own book, written in defense of his administration soon after the war began, was finally published. However, only 5,000 copies were sold.

Andrew Johnson assumed the presidency after the assassination of Abraham Lincoln and oversaw the beginning of Reconstruction (Library of Congress)

Future Presidents

ULYSSES S. GRANT had to step lightly through a web of political intrigue as President Johnson attempted to use Sherman as a shield against the radical Republican drive to force through their postwar policy.

February: Talk of Grant as a presidential candidate began early in the year. The *New York Herald* endorsed him for president in the 1868 election.

May: Congress voted to make Grant, now 44, a full general. The four-star appointment took effect on July 25.

August–October: Grant spent much time touring the country with President Johnson as the latter pushed for his Reconstruction policies. Grant only did so because he could not find an excuse to avoid it.

∞∞

RUTHERFORD B. HAYES, the U.S. representative from Ohio, received renomination by acclamation from the Republican Party. In the general election his victory margin of 2,556 was a gain of more than 100 votes over his first election.

May 24: Hayes's son, George Crook Hayes, died in Chillicothe, Ohio. He was 1 year old.

October 30: Hayes's mother, Sophia, died in Columbus at the age of 74.

ഔരു

JAMES A. GARFIELD began his legal career at the top, arguing a case before the U.S. Supreme Court.

February: Garfield delivered a major speech on Reconstruction to Congress on February 1, trying to moderate the conflict between President Johnson and the radicals. In the speech, Garfield stated that Southern states needed to show themselves fit to return to the congressional scene. The best way to do that, he argued, would be to allow Black suffrage.

With Johnson's veto of the Freedmen's Bureau bill on February 19, Garfield rejoined the radical camp—forced back there, he said, by Johnson himself.

April: The Supreme Court case that Garfield argued came his way through Jeremiah S. Black, former president James Buchanan's attorney general. In *Ex Parte Milligan*, several Indiana Copperheads had been convicted and sentenced to hang by a military court in 1864. Black needed a radical Republican lawyer who knew Chief Justice Salmon Chase to try the case.

Garfield prepared for 4 days and nights. On April 3 he presented his case before the Court for 2 hours. The Court did not hand down a decision until December.

October–November: Garfield was opposed for reelection in Ohio even though constituents generally approved of his radical Reconstruction policies. Gradually Garfield's Republican opposition fell by the wayside, and Garfield won renomination for a third term by acclamation.

Garfield's campaign took the form of denouncing President Johnson and his followers as the "unwashed, unanointed, unforgiven, unrepentant and unhung Rebels." Garfield defeated Coolman, the Democrat, 18,362 to 7,376.

December 17: The Supreme Court decision in the *Milligan* case was announced. A great storm of protest unseen since the *Dred Scott* case arose against the decision because of the potential impact on military Reconstruction policy in the South. The U.S. Supreme Court ruled that the military trial of 1864, which resulted in the death penalty for the Indiana Copperheads, had been unlawful.

ഔരു

CHESTER ALAN ARTHUR continued to work with prominent New Yorkers as friends and allies to gain higher positions. Arthur desired a high-paying job in the Office of the Collector for the Port of New York, a major source for patronage plums. He traveled to Washington to lobby for the job and was aided in his quest by Thurlow Weed. In the end, the appointment did not come through. Arthur was now alone in his law firm because his partner, Henry Gardiner, had died.

During this period Arthur, who turned 37 in October, increased his list of prominent friends to include State Senator Charles Folger, lawyer Richard Crowley, and General George H. Sharpe.

ഔരു

GROVER CLEVELAND practiced law with Major Isaac K. Vanderpoel, who had been state treasurer of New York from 1858 to 1859. Cleveland, 29, did a fine job for his clients and often refused payment.

ഔരു

BENJAMIN HARRISON went back to working long hours again as the reporter for the Indiana Supreme Court. He turned 33 in August.

ഔരു

WILLIAM MCKINLEY, 23, entered law school in Albany, New York, against the advice of his Civil War commander, Congressman Rutherford B. Hayes. In the fall, McKinley wrote to Hayes to tell him of his decision.

Hayes replied on November 6: "With your business capacity and experience I would have preferred railroading or some commercial business. A man in any of our western towns with half your wit ought to be independent at forty in business. As a lawyer, a man sacrifices independence to ambition which is a bad bargain at the best."

McKinley kept the letter but did not heed its advice.

ഔരു

THEODORE ROOSEVELT, 8, lived in New York City.

ഔരു

WILLIAM HOWARD TAFT, 9, was seriously injured in a fall. A runaway horse threw the boy on the slopes of Sycamore Street in Cincinnati, Ohio, and he was cut on the head and suffered a slight skull fracture. Some people later believed the fall dented his skull sufficiently to affect the pituitary gland, which perhaps later resulted in his great size as an adult.

ഔരു

WOODROW WILSON, 10 in December, lived in Augusta, Georgia, where Union soldiers occupied his father's Presbyterian church. Woodrow's brother Joseph R. Wilson Jr. was born some time during the year. (The exact date is not known.)

Woodrow briefly attended a school operated by Joseph T. Derry, a former Confederate army officer.

ഔരു

WARREN G. HARDING was a baby living in Blooming Grove, Ohio. He turned 1 year old in November.

1867
Andrew Johnson

President Johnson's fight with the radicals in Congress became shriller as they discussed and voted on impeachment proceedings. Meanwhile, a new Reconstruction system that split the South into five military districts served to reduce the power normally wielded by the executive branch.

January: On January 7, Johnson vetoed Senator Charles Sumner's bill authorizing African-American voting in the District of Columbia. Congress overrode the veto the next day.

Talk of impeachment proceedings was in the air. Sumner gave a 3-day speech to the Senate in mid-January, the theme of which was "Protection against the President." He gave it during debate on the Tenure-of-Office Act, legislation designed to strip the president of appointive powers and to make it impossible for him to remove even his own cabinet appointees. Sumner argued that during the time of the first Congress the founding fathers had not had problems when it came to a president's appointment powers because "there was no President of the United States who had become an enemy to his country." However, Senator John Sherman, brother of General William T. Sherman, supported Johnson and the legislation was watered down in House action.

February–March: The House Committee on Reconstruction, chaired by Thaddeus Stevens, produced the military bill, which carved the South into five military districts governed by five generals. The bill passed the House on February 6, but Senate amendments restored power to the president to select the military governors. James G. Blaine offered an amendment that any Southern state could leave the military district once it adopted the Fourteenth Amendment and changed its state constitution to accept Black suffrage. Stevens helped to ensure that the Blaine effort was voted down.

Johnson placed the military bill before the cabinet on February 22. Edwin Stanton suggested the cabinet support the bill.

On March 2, Johnson vetoed the military bill and the Tenure-of-Office Act, collectively known as the Reconstruction Acts. The military measure, he said, would deprive Americans of the right of habeas corpus, and would put ten Southern states "under the absolute domination of military rulers…. Everything is a crime which he [the military governor] chooses to call."

Congress quietly listened to Johnson's veto message, then overrode his vetoes. The Reconstruction Acts established martial law in the South, and stripped Johnson of the traditional role of commander in chief of American military forces. To end military rule, the former Confederate states would have to establish new state constitutions guaranteeing African Americans the right to vote. They would also have to ratify the Fourteenth Amendment.

Congressman James M. Ashley of Ohio again introduced a resolution for impeachment, which was referred to the judiciary committee. Ashley charged Johnson with "high crimes and misdemeanors" and "usurpation of power and violation of law." Ashley went so far as to try to coerce John H. Surratt, one of the plotters in the assassination of Abraham Lincoln,

to implicate Johnson in the assassination. By mid-March, however, it was apparent that Ashley lacked enough evidence to proceed with impeachment.

On March 12, Johnson and Stanton conferred on the issue of which five to appoint as leaders of the military districts. They settled on John M. Schofield, Daniel E. Sickles, E. O. C. Ord, Philip Sheridan, and George H. Thomas.

In March, Congress passed a supplemental Military Reconstruction Acts bill which permitted the military governors to establish the steps necessary to bring their states back into the Union. At this point, no Southerners held office in Congress. Johnson vetoed this measure on March 26, but Congress quickly overrode his veto.

On March 30 a treaty with Russia finalized the sale of the territory of Alaska.

April: Two provisional governments, one in Mississippi and the other in Georgia, on April 5 tried to place the Military Reconstruction Acts before the Supreme Court to prevent Johnson from carrying them out. Ten days later the Court denied jurisdiction. Almost immediately, Philip Sheridan, the commander of the military district of Louisiana and Texas, removed several top state officials in Louisiana, including the governor, by invoking his power to do so. Similar trouble brewed in Alabama and Georgia.

June–July: Soon after Sheridan removed the governor of Louisiana, Johnson asked his attorney general, Henry Stanbery, for an opinion on the Military Reconstruction Acts. The military governors had asked for the same thing. The entire cabinet discussed the issue on June 18 and every member, except Stanton, agreed that military commanders in the South did not have unlimited powers "to abolish, modify, control or supersede the laws of the state."

Radicals, alarmed by the direction Johnson was heading, demanded a July session of Congress. The House passed a bill allowing the military governors to remove any Southern officeholder or "disloyal persons." Johnson vetoed this bill on July 19, pointing out that Congress was stripping the executive office of its powers by putting the military governors above the president, and the general of the army above the Senate. Once again, Congress overrode the Predident's veto.

August: On August 1, Johnson told Ulysses S. Grant that Stanton would be fired and that Grant was the desired replacement as secretary of war. Grant replied that removing Stanton would be "impolitic." That same day, Johnson told the cabinet he was prepared to fire Sheridan, even if it meant increasing his chances of being impeached.

On August 2, Johnson asked Stanton to resign. Stanton refused and Johnson decided to suspend Stanton and appoint Grant on an interim basis. The president informed Grant of his decision. Grant had no personal conflicts with Johnson, but did not agree with the president on the issue of the Reconstruction Acts.

Johnson notified Stanton on August 12 of his suspension. Stanton replied that he was submitting only "under protest to the superior force of the President."

October–December: Some time in October Johnson asked Grant what he would do if an effort were made by Stanton to regain the helm of the War Department. Grant assured Johnson that he would advise the latter in advance if he were to quit so that the president would have sufficient time to find an interim appointee.

Conservative Republicans scored victories over radical candidates in the November elections. Johnson was pleased by the election results, but talk of his impeachment continued.

The House Judiciary Committee gave their majority report to the full House on November 27. Included within it was a recommendation for Johnson's impeachment. The chairman of the committee presented a dissenting recommendation, noting that most of the testimony for impeachment was "of no value whatever.... Much of it is mere hearsay." In the end, the House voted against impeachment proceedings.

Johnson turned 59 at the end of the year.

Andrew Johnson's firing of Secretary of War Edwin Stanton, pictured here, in August 1867 added momentum to the growing mood in Congress for Johnson's impeachment. (Library of Congress)

Former Presidents

MILLARD FILLMORE, 67, continued to build on his reputation as Buffalo's chief do-gooder. The retired president served as vice president of the Buffalo Society for the Prevention of Cruelty to Animals. He helped found the exclusive Buffalo Club, a social organization, and served as its first president. He also became chairman of the Buffalo Historical Society.

၈၀ ၄၃

FRANKLIN PIERCE, 63, was in retirement and lived in New Hampshire.

၈၀ ၄၃

JAMES BUCHANAN, retired and residing in Lancaster, Pennsylvania, did not approve of giving the vote to African Americans. Now 76 years old, he wrote Augustus Schell on November 9: "Emancipation is now a constitutional fact, but to prescribe the right and privilege of suffrage belongs exclusively to the states."

Future Presidents

ULYSSES S. GRANT was being touted for president from many corners. In a surprising move, President Johnson made Grant interim secretary of war.

January–June: John W. Forney, the editor of the *Washington Daily Chronicle* who had pushed James Buchanan for president before the Civil War, now lent his support to Grant. John Rawlins, a friend of Grant's, informed Forney: "General Grant does not [necessarily] want to be President [but feels the] Republican Party may need him, and he believes, as their candidate, he can be elected and reelected." Forney decided to write a Grant-for-president story. Before publishing it, Forney asked Rawlins to ask Grant to read it. Grant didn't object to the editorial and Forney subsequently published it.

July–August: Grant had now become the major pawn in the Johnson–radical Republican struggle over the nature of Reconstruction. Grant was enjoying New Jersey's seashore when the president called him to Washington, D.C., in July and offered him the position of secretary of war.

Grant hesitated at first. On August 1, Grant responded to Johnson with a letter stating the appointment would be in violation of the Tenure-of-Office Act. He added that Philip Sheridan, because of his popularity, should not be removed as military governor. Johnson, however, wanted Sheridan removed as military governor in Louisiana.

Johnson, in a tactical move, decided to appoint Grant secretary of war ad interim while Congress was not in session. Grant accepted the post and wrote his wife, Julia, on August 5 to expect "a startling piece of news." Grant had now moved from the military sphere into the realm of politics while still retaining the rank of general.

၈၀ ၄၃

RUTHERFORD B. HAYES, tired of the congressional battlefield in Washington, D.C., won the governorship of Ohio in a close race in which his war service probably helped him to be elected.

February: As rumors made the rounds that Hayes would be a candidate for governor of Ohio, he wrote his uncle Sardis to say that he was tired of political life in the nation's capital: "I have no ambition for congressional reputation and influence.... If the [governor] nomination is pretty likely, it would get me out of this scrape, and after that I am out of political life decently."

June–September: Hayes was one of three gubernatorial candidates the Republicans were considering, but the only war veteran. In June he received the nomination on the first ballot. He subsequently resigned his congressional seat on the adjournment of Congress.

Judge Allen G. Thurman, Hayes's Democratic opponent, also enjoyed popular support in Ohio. Hayes made 81 speeches in a campaign that drew national interest because of the major issue: suffrage for all males—Hayes favored it, whereas Thurman was opposed. Republicans in a few cities wanted Hayes to soft-pedal the idea of Black suffrage. But Hayes answered that "color ought to have no more to do with voting than size."

On September 2, Lucy Hayes gave birth to the couple's first daughter, Fanny.

November: Hayes won in a close election, beating Thurman by 3,000 votes to become governor of Ohio. Despite Hayes's success, Democrats won most of the elections in the state including the Second District congressional seat Hayes had given up. The Democratic legislature then sent Thurman to the U.S. Senate. Voters also defeated a state constitutional amendment for Black suffrage.

ଔଔ

JAMES A. GARFIELD made the grand tour of Europe with his wife Lucretia in what amounted to a long-delayed honeymoon.

January–March: Garfield's second daughter, Mary ("Molly"), was born on January 16.

President Johnson's policy of mild conciliation toward the South was, Garfield said, "a complete and disastrous failure." However, any move to impeach Johnson, Garfield reasoned, would be "ruinous" to both country and party.

In March, Garfield voted for the Tenure-of-Office Act in the belief that the Constitution vested power of removal with the Senate rather than the president.

June–November: At the beginning of the summer Garfield complained of being "dizzy and stupid sick" from overwork. He sought a doctor's advice, who recommended travel as a remedy to his ills.

The Garfields decided on a European vacation and booked passage on the *City of London*. On July 13 they embarked on a 17-week vacation without their children. Their stops in Europe included England, Scotland, the Rhine, Switzerland, Florence, Milan, Venice, Rome, and Paris. They returned to the United States in November.

ଔଔ

CHESTER ALAN ARTHUR, noticed by the upcoming New York political powerhouse Roscoe Conkling, gravitated toward the Republican Party elite of New York City.

Arthur was still tied to the older Edwin Morgan and his considerable connections; Conkling, however, was a new influence in state politics and was the same age as Arthur, who turned 38 in October. Andrew White, the president of Cornell, once said, "Conkling seemed to consider all men who differed with him as enemies of the human race."

Arthur sat on the city's executive committee as a representative of the Eighteenth Assembly District. The committee chose Republican candidates within a district.

ଔଔ

GROVER CLEVELAND was a 30-year-old lawyer living in Buffalo, New York, where he frequented the city's German saloons. Noted for both working in his office far into the night and for staying out all night, Cleveland liked to gamble on euchre or poker.

ଔଔ

BENJAMIN HARRISON'S collapse from overwork mirrored Garfield's similar affliction. Instead of Europe and the cathedrals of Italy, however, Harrison's recovery required the quiet solitude of the isolated lakes and woods of Minnesota.

Harrison collapsed in April after winning a notable victory in a court case. As a result he decided to lead a less arduous lifestyle and declined to stand for reelection for the Indiana State Supreme Court reporter's post in 1868. Convalescence consisted of 3 months of relaxed hunting and fishing in Minnesota. Harrison, who turned 34 in August, returned to work in the fall feeling rejuvenated.

Once back at work he hired two clerks to help with the mundane tasks: his brother-in-law Henry Scott and Howard Cale. With the added help, Harrison had more time to hunt ducks and fish for bass.

ଔଔ

WILLIAM MCKINLEY, 24, became a lawyer; moved to Canton, Ohio; and at a picnic first met beautiful, young Ida Saxton, his future wife.

McKinley did not finish his law studies in Albany, New York, and upon returning to Ohio, first went to Canton in the spring to visit his sister Anna, 12 years his senior, who was a principal of a grammar school there. While visiting with his sister he met people in the community, liked what he saw, and decided to settle there. He passed the bar in Warren and moved to Canton armed with a letter of introduction to Judge George W. Belden. McKinley asked Belden to take him in as a partner. Belden gave McKinley a case to try even though the young man protested that he had never tried a case before. However, McKinley won the case and Judge Belden later paid him $25 and took him in. Within a year the elderly judge died and McKinley embarked on his legal career.

McKinley, who enjoyed debating, joined the Masonic Lodge in Canton, became president of the YMCA's literary club, and became a member of the Republican Party in town. His rapid acceptance in the community was partly due to his oratorical skills.

ଔଔ

THEODORE ROOSEVELT, now 9, wrote his first book, a zoology opus he called the *Natural History on Insects*. Describing each in detail, he wrote that "All the insects ... inhabbit [*sic*] North America."

Theodore Jr.'s childhood in New York City was a happy one despite his continued illness. For a while he attended school at "Professor McMullen's" on 20th Street.

ဢ‌ဢ

WILLIAM HOWARD TAFT, 10, lived in Cincinnati.

ဢ‌ဢ

WOODROW WILSON learned how to read in 1867 when he was 10 years old. He turned 11 at the end of December. The Southern educational system was a shambles following the Civil War and children were taught in the home. Wilson lived in Augusta, Georgia, where his father, Pastor Joseph Wilson, engaged in parish work much of the time.

ဢ‌ဢ

WARREN G. HARDING was badly scalded on the shoulders and chest from hot water that had been accidentally spilled on him. His aunt Elizabeth Ann wrote that the child's skin came off in pieces "as big as … [a] hand." Harding turned 2 years old in November.

February: The Harding family moved into a new house in Blooming Grove, Ohio.

March 1: Harding's sister Charity was born.

June: Warren and Charity, called "Chat," contracted whooping cough.

1868
Andrew Johnson

President Johnson, in his fourth year in the White House, came within 1 vote of being impeached by a vindictive group of Republican radicals intent on tight military control of Southern states. Johnson's impeachment was one of the major challenges to American democracy in the 19th century.

January: On January 10, Johnson heard from the Senate Committee on Military Affairs that it had rejected his explanation of why he had fired Edwin Stanton in 1867 as secretary of war. The next day, interim Secretary of War Ulysses S. Grant told Johnson that he had decided it would be best to step down. Johnson agreed. On January 13 the Senate ruled that Stanton had been illegally removed and ordered him reinstated. The next day Stanton returned as secretary of war and Grant resumed his army duties.

Johnson, opposing the Senate ruling, then sent for Grant and confronted him with his earlier promise to quit only after giving the president adequate time to locate a replacement. Grant replied that in doing so he would suffer a penalty under the Tenure-of-Office Act. Johnson was furious at what he considered Grant's duplicity in not keeping his word.

General William T. Sherman later joined Grant in conferring with the president, and the two generals agreed with Johnson that Stanton should resign. This time, however, Stanton would not step down.

Johnson asked Sherman to take over the War Department, but the latter declined. Johnson also ordered Grant not to follow any directives from Stanton. On January 28, Grant wrote President Johnson that he needed written instructions

because of "the many and gross misrepresentations affecting my personal honor … purporting to come from the President." Grant added that he would indeed take orders from Stanton and denied that he had told the president he would give Johnson time to name a replacement if he quit the cabinet.

February: The reading of the Johnson–Grant correspondence in the House caused a sensation. Republican congressman Thaddeus Stevens reportedly was eager to initiate impeachment proceedings and said it was probable that both Johnson and Grant lied. On February 17 the president decided to replace Stanton with John Potts, chief clerk of the War Department. Potts asked not to be put in such a hot spot, and 4 days later the president chose General Lorenzo Thomas, the adjutant general, to replace Stanton.

Thomas went to the War Department and presented his orders to Stanton, with Grant as an observer. Stanton hedged on obeying Thomas's orders and Senator Charles Summer sent Stanton a one-word memo: "Stick." Stanton wrote Senate supporters that he would hold on until evicted by force. House radicals now screamed for Johnson's impeachment.

Stanton had been living at the War Department for several weeks and ordered Grant to put guards on his doors. On February 22, Thomas boasted to a friend that if necessary, he would use force to break down the doors to remove Stanton. Stanton thereupon ordered Thomas's arrest on the grounds that a forcible removal would be in violation of the Tenure-of-Office Act.

Thomas, under arrest, was accompanied by marshals to the White House, where he informed Johnson what had occurred. Thomas posted bail, returned to the War Department, and ordered Stanton out. Stanton thereupon ordered Thomas to vacate the premises and to return to his adjutant general's office. The tension finally broke when Thomas and Stanton shared a couple of shots of whisky. Thomas then returned to the White House to tell Johnson what happened. Johnson then sent the Senate yet another nominee for secretary of war, Thomas Ewing.

The House of Representatives initiated impeachment proceedings on February 22 with a short resolution that stated: "Resolved: that Andrew Johnson, President of the United States, be impeached for high crimes and misdemeanors."

Thaddeus Stevens made an impassioned presentation of his case for impeachment on February 24, and the House was in favor by a vote of 126 to 47. Every radical lined up behind Stevens, who announced the vote to the Senate.

Radical senators and Chief Justice Salmon Chase met on February 26 to plan the trial. Eventually, they brought ten charges against Johnson and reported these to the House on February 29. The charges included usurpation of the law, corrupt use of the veto power, interference at elections, and several misdemeanors.

March–May: A House caucus of radicals agreed on seven

congressmen to serve as "managers of impeachment": Thaddeus Stevens, John A. Bingham, Benjamin F. Butler, Henry Wilson, George Boutwell, Thomas Williams, and John A. Logan. (In impeachment proceedings, the House acts as grand jury and the Senate conducts the trial; a two-thirds vote of the Senate is required for removal.)

The trial formally began on March 13, with Associate Supreme Court Justice Samuel Nelson administering the oath to Chase, who then gave the same oath to the senators who would vote.

The cabinet, deeply saddened by the turn of events, agreed on Attorney General Henry Stanbery as President Johnson's chief counsel, assisted by Benjamin R. Curtis of Boston, a former Supreme Court justice; Jeremiah S. Black from Buchanan's cabinet; William M. Evarts; and Judge T. A. R. Nelson of Greeneville, Tennessee. Stanbery resigned as attorney general to avoid a conflict of interest.

The House opened its case against Johnson on March 30 with Benjamin F. Butler as its leadoff speaker. It took 23 days for the House managers to present their case. They attempted to show that by opposing the Tenure-of-Office Act, Johnson had violated the Constitution. They also attacked Johnson's character, bringing up allegations of excessive drinking.

Judge Nelson led off for the defense by calling Johnson a strict constitutionalist in the same mold as Thomas Jefferson. William S. Groesbeck, who had replaced Jeremiah Black on

Thaddeus Stevens delivers the closing speech during President Andrew Johnson's impeachment trial. (Library of Congress)

the defense team, argued that "no good can come" of conviction and that the Senate can "maintain its ancient dignity and high character in the midst of storm and passion and strife" by acquittal.

William Evarts handled the majority of Johnson's defense because Stanbery was ill during much of the trial. Evarts made a brilliant summation and defended Johnson's behavior before the cabinet, saying that through endless abuse the president had "stood firm as a rock."

The radicals needed 36 votes for the necessary two-thirds for conviction. They huddled regularly to strategize about how they could sway those on the fence. On May 26 the final Senate vote took place—35 to 19 in favor of impeachment, 1 vote short of the necessary two-thirds majority. Johnson was acquitted.

June–July: Johnson's hopes for the Democratic presidential nomination were all but dashed because of his impeach-

ment. Johnson backers spent the month of June trying to drum up support for the president, but the Democrats knew that Johnson had little chance of defeating the Republican candidate, Ulysses S. Grant, who had been nominated in May by the Republicans (see **Ulysses S. Grant,** page 320.)

The Democrats met in New York on July 4 to 9. On the twenty-second ballot they nominated Horatio Seymour, the former governor of New York, as the presidential candidate. Congressman Francis Blair was nominated as the vice presidential candidate.

On July 28, Congress ratified the Fourteenth Amendment to the Constitution.

December: In his annual message to Congress on December 8, Johnson condemned Reconstruction policy in the South; discussed financial matters concerning war debts; and urged amendments to the Constitution relating to the popular vote for president, senators, and federal judges.

On Christmas Day, Johnson issued a proclamation of amnesty without condition for all Confederates.

Former Presidents

MILLARD FILLMORE, 68 in January, was retired and living in Buffalo, New York.

ജര

FRANKLIN PIERCE, who turned 64 in November, was in retirement in Concord, New Hampshire.

ജര

JAMES BUCHANAN became seriously ill in May with a cold, rheumatic gout, and the complications of old age. He died at 8:30 A.M. on June 1. He was 77. Buchanan had asked for a quiet funeral without pomp and circumstance. Nevertheless, 20,000 people attended the services on June 4. Burial was at Woodward Hill Cemetery in Lancaster, Pennsylvania.

Future Presidents

ULYSSES S. GRANT, in a near coronation atmosphere, was the unanimous choice of the Republican convention and was an easy winner in the presidential race. The nation rewarded and honored the general a little more than three years after his victory at Appomattox.

January–February: Grant began the year as Johnson's secretary of war. Johnson wanted a promise from Grant that the latter would stay on the job a few days before Stanton was due to reclaim the office so that Johnson could name a replacement. On January 11, Grant informed the president that he had decided it was best to resign as secretary of war and to return to his old post as commander of the army. Johnson agreed to this decision.

During a cabinet meeting on January 14, Johnson gave Grant a dressing-down for resigning before Johnson could find a replacement. This led to a serious rift between the two in which each claimed the other was lying. Grant said that he had never promised to remain at the War Department long enough to allow Johnson to find a replacement. By February the rift between Grant and Johnson became fodder for House leaders looking for additional reasons to impeach the president (see **Andrew Johnson,** page 318).

March: In March, Grant wrote his friend Charles W. Ford that impeachment "will give peace to the country." Grant, however, remained aloof during the impeachment proceedings.

May: The Republican Party National convention was held May 20 to 21 at the Crosby Opera House in Chicago. After General John A. Logan nominated Grant, a curtain was lifted to reveal large pictures of Grant and the Goddess of Liberty. Grant, now 46 years old, received all 650 delegate votes on the first ballot. Speaker of the House Schuyler Colfax of Indiana was the choice for vice president.

July–November: Grant did not formally campaign but did visit several cities and towns across the country. General William T. Sherman congratulated Grant on his nomination but remained publicly neutral. Grant then toured the Great Plains with Sherman and General Philip Sheridan. Grant offered no speeches and only appeared before the crowds on hotel balconies with the other two generals.

Grant established his campaign headquarters in the DeSato House in Galena, Illinois, where he read reports from his campaign staff in the field. The *New York Times* complimented Grant for his campaign of silence.

Election day on November 3 went the way most expected—for Grant. The election results gave Grant 3,012,833 votes to Seymour's 2,703,249. Grant earned 214 electoral votes to Seymour's 80.

ഔയ

Rutherford B. Hayes entered the Ohio governor's office with optimism, despite facing a Democratic-controlled state legislature.

Hayes was inaugurated on January 13 and gave a short address. He implied that Ohio's importance was such that any governor of the state should be presumed to be of presidential timber.

Hayes filled his cabinet and offices with the best-qualified people, including Democrats, which caused some criticism. His was a nonpartisan government but conservative in financial matters.

Hayes, who turned 46 on October 4, was an enthusiastic supporter for Grant and denounced Seymour for taking a "soft" stand on the South.

ഔയ

James A. Garfield returned from Europe with high hopes for the chairmanship of the House Ways and Means Committee. His goal was to help solve the nation's financial problems. Instead, the radical leadership gave him the chair of the Military Affairs Committee. He was disappointed.

Garfield, although in favor of it, voted against impeachment, partly because he didn't think the effort to impeach Johnson would succeed. He did not feel the House committee had made a strong enough case and noted, "I did not believe the attempt was likely to be successful."

During the congressional race that year, rumors circulated that Garfield had gone to Europe to be cured of a disease. Garfield made 66 speeches in his district and easily won re-election to the House.

ഔയ

Chester Alan Arthur became less active in his law practice in New York City and more involved in Republican politics. Arthur, who was chair of the Central Grant Club of New York, worked on a state committee as a fund collector and also became chair of the city executive committee for the Eighteenth Assembly District.

In the presidential race, Horatio Seymour carried New York by 10,000 votes, partly because of massive fraud, which included 50,000 illegal votes, on the part of the Tammany Society and "Boss" William Tweed.

ഔയ

Grover Cleveland, 31, went to Albany as a delegate to the State Democratic convention, where he was a member of the platform committee. He had increased his ties to and interest in Democratic politics. The convention nominated New York City mayor John T. Hoffman to run for governor. Hoffman subsequently won the governorship in the New York Democratic victory that was helped by "Boss" Tweed's fraud.

ഔയ

Benjamin Harrison played a minor role in Grant's presidential campaign because Indianapolis residents at the time were preoccupied by a double-murder case. The September 13 homicide, which occurred at Cold Springs on the White River, was the most celebrated in Marion County annals. Killed were a businessman and his wife. Mrs. Nancy Clem was indicted for the crime, with John T. Dye, a former associate of Harrison's, leading the prosecution.

Harrison did not participate in the trial because he was still working as the Indiana Supreme Court reporter. At the time, he was finishing Volume 28 of the Indiana court reports and also worked on a Bar Association committee to study problems in the Indianapolis court system.

Harrison, who turned 35 in August, made two speeches for Grant. As a result of Schuyler Colfax of South Bend being elected vice president, Harrison was now considered a major Indiana politician.

ഔയ

WILLIAM MCKINLEY, 25, became chairman of the Republican Central Committee for Stark County, Ohio; organized Grant clubs in the townships; staged demonstrations; and made speeches.

McKinley shared the stump on one occasion with a veteran politician, Charles Manderson, who later became a senator from Nebraska. McKinley had done his homework, whereas Manderson was unprepared. Manderson asked McKinley what he was going to talk about, and McKinley made the mistake of telling him everything. Manderson, who spoke first, gave McKinley's speech and even asked for the younger man's notes to be able to cite the facts McKinley had prepared. McKinley was left with nothing to say but also wiser for the lesson he had learned.

&⊃CR

THEODORE ROOSEVELT, a 10-year-old naturalist, spent the summer at a retreat in the Catskills, his family's attempt to give him some relief from his asthma. He got none. The location, Barrytown-on-Hudson, was about 10 miles north of Hyde Park and across the river from Kingston, New Jersey. Theodore was now reading all the time and noted in his diary on August 10 that he was reading the life of George Washington.

&⊃CR

WILLIAM HOWARD TAFT, 11 years old and living in Cincinnati, quite often spent the summer with his grandfather Torrey in Millbury, Massachusetts. The Taft boys were afraid of the old man, a retired Boston merchant, who was a much tougher disciplinarian than their father.

&⊃CR

WOODROW WILSON, who turned 12 in December, lived in Augusta, Georgia. The religious nature of his home life meant daily devotions, Bible reading, and prayer. On Sundays the family went to church to hear Woodrow's father, Joseph Wilson, preach; afterwards the children attended Sunday school.

&⊃CR

WARREN G. HARDING, who was 3 in November, lived in Blooming Grove, Ohio, situated in the north central part of the state.

April 26: Warren's sister Mary Clarissa was born. She had malfunctioning eyes.

1869
Andrew Johnson

President Johnson intended to return to Tennessee to retire, but the smoldering fires of his political ambition and anger directed at the radicals prompted him to seek a U.S. Senate seat.

January–March: President Johnson was startled when Benjamin F. Butler, one of Johnson's prosecutors at his impeachment, showed up at a White House reception on New Year's Day. On January 11, at Butler's suggestion, the House repealed the Tenure-of-Office Act.

On February 10 a woman named Annie O'Neil was discovered in a White House corridor with an unloaded pistol. She said that God had sent her to kill Johnson.

On February 26, Congress passed the Fifteenth Amendment, which gave the vote to all men, including former slaves. The amendment stated the right "to vote shall not be denied … on account of race, color, or previous condition of servitude." An attempt to add suffrage for women was killed.

On the morning of March 4, Johnson, in conference with his cabinet, continued signing papers and remained undecided about whether to attend Grant's inauguration. The cabinet discussed the issue and Secretary of State William Seward then asked if everyone was leaving for the ceremony. Seward and Secretary of Treasury Hugh McCulloch favored going "for appearance sake." Johnson said, "I think … we will finish up our work here by ourselves." At noon, Johnson shook hands all around and rode in his carriage to the home of John Coyle.

A week later in Baltimore, Johnson received a parade and banquet in his honor. During the banquet he said, "My deliverance has been the greatest case of emancipation since the rebellion commenced."

Johnson left for Greeneville, Tennessee, on March 18. The traveling party included his wife; their daughter Martha (Patterson) and her husband David, whose term as a senator had expired; and son Robert and his children.

April: Johnson, because of his frugal financial habits, was now worth about $150,000. He decided to invest in a large commercial building. The Johnsons had not lived in their Greeneville home with any regularity for 18 years. They undertook extensive renovations including a second story, new closets, fireplaces, and new stoves.

On April 22, Johnson's son Robert, 35 years old and an alcoholic, killed himself at Greeneville.

June–August: In early summer the retired president boarded a special train for a tour of Tennessee. In numerous speeches Johnson said he wasn't necessarily against Black suffrage but that it was a question for the states to decide, not a federal matter.

Johnson returned to Washington, D.C., in the summer to see his son Andrew, who attended school in Georgetown.

September–December: On his return to Tennessee, Johnson continued to speak frequently and campaigned for the reelection of Governor D. W. C. Senter, a conservative Republican running against a radical challenger.

During the summer the idea of having Johnson run for the Senate began to surface. By the fall the idea intrigued Johnson, whereas radicals in Washington, D.C., were not overjoyed by the prospect. When the Tennessee legislature met on October 19, Johnson's former secretary Edmund Cooper offered Johnson's name in nomination for the U.S. Senate, saying that the retired president was a "statesman ... of incomparable integrity and unflinching courage." On the first ballot Johnson received the votes of eleven of twenty-five senators and thirty-two of eighty-one house members. By the eighth ballot, Johnson was short of victory by only 2 votes. He was up against Henry Cooper, Edmund's brother. Upon being told that these 2 votes had been bought, Johnson refused to make any further effort to remain in the contest. On October 22, Henry Cooper received 55 votes (to Johnson's 51) and won the Senate seat. Even though Edmund had nominated him, Johnson's defeat made him become bitter toward the Cooper brothers. He turned 61 years old at the end of the year.

ಶಾ

ULYSSES S. GRANT entered the White House less than a decade removed from his days as a dirt-poor farmer. Almost from the start the Grant administration was plagued with problems, beginning with his cabinet choices. In addition to his military friends, one of Grant's closest political advisers was the New York radical Roscoe Conkling. Conkling, along with Simon Cameron and James G. Blaine, grew in political power and had much influence in Grant's administration. The death of John Rawlins—Grant's closest confidant from the early days of the Civil War—in the first year of his administration created a vacuum Grant never managed to fill.

January–February: Grant accepted many formal dinner invitations from foreign consulates. He did not seek advice on cabinet positions and speculation ran high as to whom he would tap. Grant remained mum as to his choices through the first 2 months of the year.

March: On March 4, African American citizens lined the route to the Capitol, where Grant witnessed the swearing in of 45-year-old Vice President Schuyler Colfax.

After a twenty-two-gun salute, Chief Justice Salmon P. Chase administered the oath of office to 46-year-old Grant, who thereupon became the eighteenth president of the United States. In his address, Grant

Less than a decade after struggling as a poor farmer, Ulysses S. Grant became president of the United States on March 4, 1869.

said he took office "without mental reservation.... The responsibilities of the position I feel, but accept them without fear." He said he would not hesitate to express his opinions but would execute the laws passed by Congress "whether they meet my approval or not." He disavowed increasing the amount of greenback currency in circulation and said that every dollar in government indebtedness would be paid in gold, including the $400 million war debt. He called on the

states to ratify the Fifteenth Amendment and for the "proper treatment" of the Indians, a remark that surprised many.

Speculation on who would be part of Grant's cabinet ended a few days after the inauguration when Rawlins handed the list of cabinet appointees to the Senate for confirmation. Grant had chosen Elihu B. Washburne of Illinois for secretary of state, Alexander T. Stewart for secretary of Treasury, John M. Schofield to remain as secretary of war, Adolph E. Borie of Pennsylvania for secretary of the navy, General Jacob D. Cox of Ohio for secretary of the Interior, Ebenezer R. Hoar of Massachusetts for attorney general, and John A. J. Creswell of Maryland for postmaster general.

Grant's naming of Washburne as secretary of state seemed odd as Washburne had instead wanted to be the minister to France; six days later Grant assigned him to Paris and named Hamilton Fish secretary of state. Fish declined the job, but Grant had already sent his name to the Senate for confirmation. The two men didn't know each other, but Grant's wife Julia had befriended Fish's wife during a visit to West Point in 1865. Grant's personal secretary, Orville Babcock, talked Fish into taking the job, and Grant quickly took a liking to Fish.

A week after his appointment, Stewart resigned from the cabinet to avoid a possible conflict of interest that concerned his running a successful retail store in New York. A lawyer for Senator Charles Sumner pointed out two obscure laws that prevented a person from being active in trade and commerce while serving as Treasury secretary. Although Stewart had served as secretary of Treasury during Andrew Johnson's administration, the Senate would not waive the law to allow Stewart to continue in the post. Grant selected George Boutwell of Massachusetts to replace Stewart.

The final replacement in Grant's cabinet came on March 11 when John A. Rawlins replaced Schofield as secretary of war.

April: On April 10, Congress passed legislation creating the Board of Indian Commissioners. Grant named Ely S. Parker, a Seneca, as commissioner of Indian affairs. Grant soon established a peace policy toward Native Americans based on an end to the treaty system, the establishment of reservations, and the education of Native Americans to allow them to become citizens of the United States.

June: The Grants visited the Corbins in New York City on June 15. While in the city, Grant met with financier Jay Gould.

The following day, Grant took a ship to Fall River, Massachusetts, accompanied by Gould and Gould's friend Jim Fisk, where they discussed Grant's monetary policy. The two men decided that Grant was a monetary contractionists, that is, against increasing the money supply or the selling of gold.

Gould had been telling Corbin to let Grant know that the government should not sell its gold reserves. Indeed, soon Gould believed that Grant should be buying gold. However, Gould was not necessarily interested in restoring sound financial policy in the United States. Rather, he was secretly selling gold while Fisk was buying it. Both Gould and Fisk were interested in planting someone in the Treasury Department who could tip them off in advance whenever the government planned to sell its gold.

On June 25, Secretary of the Navy Borie resigned. New Jerseyan George M. Robeson replaced him.

September: Grant was in Saratoga, New York, with Roscoe Conkling on September 5 when he received word that his best friend, Secretary of War John Rawlins, was dying. Grant rushed back to Washington, D.C., but arrived to be by Rawlins's side an hour too late.

General William T. Sherman replaced Rawlins as secretary of war on September 11.

On September 23, Grant met with Boutwell and agreed with his Treasury secretary that there was too much speculation in the gold market. They decided that the government would need to sell $4 million of its gold to lower the price. When news of this reached the gold markets the next day, the price of gold dropped from $160 an ounce to $140. The drop in price caused the Black Friday financial panic. A congressional committee headed by James Garfield would later look into the matter. There was much talk about Julia Grant's role as a speculator in the gold market, particularly by the Democrats.

Former Presidents

Millard Fillmore, 69, remained active in politics and commerce. He appointed a commission to visit Russia with the idea of attracting trade and capital to Buffalo, New York. On October 11, Fillmore presided over the Southern Commercial Convention that met in Louisville, Kentucky.

এওগ্র

Franklin Pierce, living in retirement in Concord, New Hampshire, went to Baltimore in May to attend a convention of the Order of the Cincinnatus. He traveled to his cottage at Little Boar's Head in New Hampshire on the Atlantic for the summer.

Suffering from dropsy, Pierce had difficulty returning to Concord. He became bedridden from an inflamed stomach in September. He died before dawn on October 8 at the age of 64.

Future Presidents

Rutherford B. Hayes, a supporter of the Fifteenth Amendment, won reelection as governor of Ohio based largely on this issue.

The Democrats nominated George H. Pendleton, who opposed ratification and the paying of interest on the war debt with greenbacks instead of coin. The Republicans renominated Hayes in June by acclamation. Hayes, 47, won reelection by 7,500 votes and emerged as a national political figure.

এওগ্র

James A. Garfield, 38 in November, had a brief falling out with Speaker of the House James Blaine over committee assignments but eventually received what he wanted: chairman of the Banking and Currency Committee. Blaine and Garfield were friends when, at the end of 1868, Blaine sought Garfield's help to become the Speaker over another aspirant, Henry Dawes. In return, Garfield wanted the chairmanship of the House Ways and Means Committee. Trouble developed when Blaine suggested that there had been no quid pro quo. The feud spilled over into 1869.

Blaine avoided Garfield, who wrote Blaine on March 11: "This disavowal of my right to see you has filled me with sorrow and amazement … [while preferring Ways and Means to Military Affairs] I shall regard [losing] chairmanship as a personal and official degradation to which you have no right to subject me.…" Blaine replied that no slight had been intended and assigned him to the House Rules Committee, whereupon Garfield must have grumbled sufficiently to be switched to the chairmanship of Banking and Currency, closer to what he wanted.

Later in the year, as a result of the September Black Friday crisis, Garfield headed a committee to look into the Wall Street manipulations of Gould and Fisk.

এওগ্র

Chester Alan Arthur, by staying close to New York City power brokers, landed the high-paying job of counsel to the city's tax commission. Because tax fraud was a common occurrence in the days of Tammany Hall and "Boss" Tweed, Arthur later avoided talking about this part of his past.

January: Arthur was very disappointed when his old friend Senator Edwin Morgan lost his seat. Morgan, despite the backing of Roscoe Conkling, Secretary of War Edwin Stanton, and Senator Charles Sumner, lost on the first ballot to fellow Republican, Governor Reuben Fenton. Arthur's disappointment came from the hope that through Morgan he could land a job at the New York Customhouse.

Arthur's mother, Malvina, died on January 16 in Newtonville, New York, just outside Albany, with three of her children present. Arthur arrived from New York City in the evening.

May: Arthur rushed to Fredericksburg, Virginia, on learning that his son Alan was seriously ill with dysentery. Mrs.

Arthur had taken the boy to visit her old home and family. The boy eventually recovered.

October 5: Arthur celebrated his fortieth birthday.

℘ℭ

GROVER CLEVELAND, a lawyer in Buffalo, New York, formed a new partnership with Albert P. Laning and Oscar Folsom. Laning had moved to Buffalo about the same time as Cleveland, whereas Folsom, a graduate of the University of Rochester, had been admitted to the bar in Buffalo in 1861. Laning, an orator, was active in Democratic Party politics and later became an attorney for New York Central and other railroads. Cleveland was drawn to Folsom's high spirits and popularity.

Cleveland did not like criminal law and avoided representing anyone he believed was guilty. He often prepared civil cases in the office, whereas one of the partners would make the courtroom presentation.

Cleveland, who turned 36 in March, lived for his work. Although he also enjoyed socializing in saloons, Joseph Warren, editor of the *Buffalo Courier*, predicted a political future for Cleveland.

℘ℭ

BENJAMIN HARRISON gave up the Indiana Supreme Court reporter job and turned to prosecuting the famous White River double-murder case, which he had observed with interest in 1868. Mrs. Nancy Clem had been acquitted in the first trial. Harrison spent countless hours going over the transcript, while her defense attorneys tried to prevent him from bringing the case.

During the second trial, Harrison proved that Mrs. Clem had bribed witnesses, and after his eight-hour summation he won a conviction. Mrs. Clem received a life sentence, but the Indiana Supreme Court soon reversed the conviction and moved the third trial to Boone County.

James Garfield with his young daughter Mollie. *(Library of Congress)*

Harrison retried the case and again won a conviction, but this decision also was reversed by the Indiana Supreme Court. Eleven years later, Clem was convicted of perjury on another case and served 4 years in jail.

Harrison turned 36 in August.

℘ℭ

WILLIAM MCKINLEY, 26 in January, entered political life as the prosecuting attorney for Stark County in northeast Ohio. His family moved from Poland, Ohio, to Canton to be near the young lawyer and his sister Anna, who also lived in Canton.

McKinley received the Republican nomination for prosecuting attorney in July, and in the fall defeated the Democratic candidate, William A. Lynch.

℘ℭ

THEODORE ROOSEVELT took a tour of Europe with his family that lasted nearly a year. The main purpose of the trip was to see if Theodore Jr. could find relief from his asthma.

The family left aboard the *Scotia* on May 12 bound for Liverpool, which they reached on May 21. They stopped at nine countries, including the Netherlands, France, Italy, Switzerland, and Austria. Theodore, who turned 11 in October, kept a detailed journal documenting his trip. Much of it was spent suffering from asthma. The Roosevelts returned home the following year.

℘ℭ

WILLIAM HOWARD TAFT, 12 years old in September, lived in Cincinnati and spent the summer at home while his parents and older brothers toured Europe. Both political parties nominated his father, Alphonso Taft, to remain as judge on the superior court. Judge Taft earned $5,000 a year in this post.

℘ℭ

WOODROW WILSON, 13 in December, lived in Augusta, Georgia, and now attended a "classical" school under the leadership of Charles H. Barnwell.

℘ℭ

WARREN G. HARDING's father was restless. Tyron Harding was tired of teaching in Blooming Grove, Ohio, and started moving his family from house to house on the outskirts of town, but always in either Morrow County or nearby Marion. He was often in debt.

Tyron decided to become a doctor. He visited with Dr. Joseph McFarland to study medical books. His wife, Phoebe, worked as a practical nurse and midwife to augment their meager income. Phoebe also taught Warren, who turned 4 in November, the alphabet.

1870
Ulysses S. Grant

President Grant's passion for bringing the Dominican Republic under the American flag as a major Reconstruction program led to an open conflict with Senator Charles Sumner and a scandal involving Orville Babcock, the president's new right-hand man.

January: It was on January 2 that Grant misread Sumner. Grant, along with two newsmen, including John W. Forney, walked over to Sumner's house that night for dinner. Grant thought he had Sumner's support for making the former Spanish colony of Santo Domingo a home for Southern ex-slaves. Sumner's interest, however, was African American equality in the United States, not in acquiring a Caribbean possession for the country. Secretary of State Hamilton Fish, with reluctance, supported Grant on this issue.

Senator Carl Schurz exposed corruption involving Babcock and Ingalls in Santo Domingo, where they had received gifts of real estate. Schurz's criticism of Grant's personal secretary was a humiliation for the president. Grant viewed the attack on Babcock as an attack on himself and subsequently made Babcock the strong man of the White House, giving him the power to decide who would see the president.

February 18: Grant appointed William Strong of Pennsylvania to the Supreme Court.

March 21: Grant appointed New Jerseyan Joseph P. Bradley to the Supreme Court.

June: Grant abruptly fired Attorney General Ebenezer Hoar on June 16 because the president needed a Southern Republican in the post to carry out his Reconstruction aims. Interior Secretary Jacob Cox later said that Grant had told Hoar there was a need to "carry out his purposes, of securing support in the Senate from Southern Republicans who demanded that the cabinet place should be filled from the South."

Amos T. Akerman of Georgia replaced Hoar. Akerman was a Dartmouth graduate born in New Hampshire who had lived in Georgia since 1842.

On June 22, Congress established the Department of Justice and the office of solicitor general. The solicitor general would argue the federal government's position in all cases before the Supreme Court.

The Senate rejected the treaty to annex Santo Domingo on June 30. The next day, Grant told the cabinet, "I will not allow Mr. Sumner to ride over me."

October–November: Cox followed Hoar out of the cabinet on October 5. Upon Cox's departure, Grant said: "Cox thought the Interior Department was the whole government, and that Cox was the Interior Department." Columbus Delano became secretary of the Interior on November 1.

December: On December 5, Grant delivered his message to Congress, making a strong plea for the annexation of Santo Domingo. Grant called Santo Domingo a "weak power … one of [the] richest territories under the sun." Grant envisioned Santo Domingo as a Black American frontier, a country that would "become a large consumer of the products of Northern farms and manufactures."

However, Sumner, who was chairman of the Senate Foreign Relations Committee, put forth the argument that in annexing Santo Domingo the United States would launch an "imperial system" that would lead to a "dance of blood." It was Sumner's opinion that Grant, instead of having noble goals, was merely a bully.

Former Presidents

MILLARD FILLMORE, 70 years old and living in western New York, became president of the board of trustees of Buffalo General Hospital. He also became president of the Grosvenor Library Board after helping relocate the library to its new quarters.

❧❧

ANDREW JOHNSON was retired from the presidency and living in the eastern part of Tennessee. Supporters urged him to run for governor, but he declined because he still harbored an ambition to return to the U.S. Senate. For the most part the former president remained in his hometown of Greeneville, meeting friends, reading newspapers, and writing a defense of his administration. Johnson turned 62 in December.

Future Presidents

RUTHERFORD B. HAYES, now in his second term as governor of Ohio, decided to refuse the enticement of a third term and instead followed George Washington's precedent of two terms.

January: In his second inaugural address, Hayes urged the legislature to ratify the Fifteenth Amendment. He also stated his opposition to increases in municipal debt and taxes, and asked for better conditions for prisoners and the insane.

April: Just 1 vote in the Ohio Senate and 2 in the Ohio House tipped the balance in favor of ratifying the Fifteenth Amendment

October 4: Hayes celebrated his 48th birthday.

❧❧

JAMES A. GARFIELD was urged by Governor Rutherford B. Hayes to run for governor of Ohio but declined to do so. Garfield became annoyed by the efforts of Hayes to make him his successor in Columbus. "My tastes do not lead me in that direction," he wrote. Voters instead reelected him to the House of Representatives.

Garfield's wife, Lucretia, was back in Hiram, Ohio, when she gave birth to their son Irvin McDowell on August 3.

Garfield chaired the House committee looking into the Black Friday panic of September 1869. He concluded that Grant probably was tainted by what went on. As he investigated the incident, Garfield resolved to "let chips fly as they may," even though he suspected the Grant family's involvement. In his report, however, Garfield cleared Grant but not General Corbin, and placed most of the blame on Jay Gould.

Garfield defeated Howard, the Democrat, in the fall House election by a vote of 13,538 to 7,263. Congressman Robert Schenck, chairman of the Ways and Means Committee, lost in his Ohio district and blamed Garfield for not helping him. Garfield had turned down a speaking request to stump for Schenck believing that Schenck did not need his help.

With Schenck out of Congress, Garfield held renewed hope that Speaker of the House James Blaine would name him chairman of the Ways and Means Committee.

Garfield was 39 years old on November 19.

✂ᑫ

CHESTER ALAN ARTHUR by this time was not only a close friend of Tom Murphy, the new head of the customhouse in New York City, he also was a "lieutenant" in Roscoe Conkling's Republican army of eager spoilsmen. Both Murphy and Conkling were close to Grant. Arthur, who turned 41 in October, returned to his law practice late in the year while he continued with his political maneuvering.

✂ᑫ

GROVER CLEVELAND was elected sheriff of Buffalo, New York, which launched his political career. The Democratic convention held on September 28 had nominated William Williams, a railroad manager, to run for Congress. To balance the ticket, it was decided that a young lawyer was needed for sheriff.

Cleveland's campaign speeches—three given in Buffalo and one each in Tonawanda and Williamsville—were unimpressive; however, he won by 303 votes.

Buffalo was noted as a town of crime and rowdyism. Many assaults and murders occurred. Within a 3-year period, 673 saloons had opened. This was the situation Cleveland stepped into.

✂ᑫ

BENJAMIN HARRISON mostly avoided politics and spent more time with his family.

Harrison's law partner, William P. Fishback, resigned from the firm in June to become editor of the *Indianapolis Journal*. A former circuit court judge, Cyrus C. Hines, replaced Fishback.

Harrison, 37, avoided the Republican state convention and had no plans to campaign for anyone. In August, however, Lew Wallace, who was running for Congress, asked for Harrison's help. Harrison agreed and on September 13 he

U.S. Senator Charles Sumner opposed Grant's plans to establish Santo Domingo as a home for ex-slaves and wanted African-American equality in the United States. He introduced the bill that became the Civil Rights Act of 1875 that would be overturned by the Supreme Court in 1883.
(Library of Congress)

made a speech in support of Wallace. Wallace eventually lost the election by 393 votes.

After giving the speech, Harrison took his family on their first real vacation since the war. They traveled first to Niagara Falls and then on to New England and visited relatives in New York and Pennsylvania.

✂ᑫ

WILLIAM MCKINLEY took office as prosecuting attorney for Stark County, Ohio, on January 1. By the end of the year he planned to marry Ida Saxton.

Ida was the daughter of James A. Saxton, a prosperous banker in Canton, who had put her to work as a teller. Her mother was Kate Dewalt.

McKinley, who turned 27 in January, fell for Ida's beauty and charm. The two would arrange to meet between Sunday school sessions, and soon the town was gossiping about their relationship. McKinley proposed to her during a carriage ride while they sat atop a hill overlooking the view of Canton. She accepted without hesitation.

✂ᑫ

THEODORE ROOSEVELT returned to New York City in May from his European trip with his family. They wrapped up the grand tour with 6 weeks in Rome, 7 weeks in Paris, and a week in London.

Theodore's sister Bamie also had health problems and she had been left behind to attend a French finishing school while the family was traveling.

Theodore suffered three bad asthma attacks during the summer, and the family returned to the Catskills. He turned 12 in October.

✂ᑫ

WILLIAM HOWARD TAFT, 13 in September, entered Woodward High School in downtown Cincinnati. There he studied Latin, elocution, history, Greek, mathematics, and literature.

✂ᑫ

WOODROW WILSON, along with his family, moved in the fall from Augusta, Georgia, to Columbia, South Carolina. His father, Joseph, in addition to being minister of the First Presbyterian Church, was elected by a wide margin to a professorship of "pastoral and evangelical theology and sacred rhetoric" at the local seminary. Woodrow was 14 in December.

✂ᑫ

WARREN G. HARDING, 5 in November, made his school debut at the Buckhorn Tavern School in Blooming Grove, Ohio.

Near the end of the year, Warren's father, Tyron, went to Cleveland to study for a term at the Western College of Homeopathy. The Northwest Medical Society subsequently issued Tyron a certificate to practice.

1871
Ulysses S. Grant

The President had several critical issues to contend with during his third year in office. Chief among them was a revolt by liberal Republicans, led by U.S. Senator Carl Schurz, who were interested in reform and in removing Grant from office. The ongoing dilemma of how to deal with the Ku Klux Klan (KKK) while also enforcing the Fourteenth Amendment was a major concern as well. Additionally, Grant had to face bringing the South back into the nation while avoiding military despotism.

March: Congress passed the Appropriation Act of 1872 on March 3. A portion of the act established major restrictions for Native Americans: "Hereafter, no Indian nation or tribe within the territory of the United States shall be acknowledged or recognized as an independent nation."

Another piece of legislation Congress worked on was the force bill, which would empower the army to enforce the Fourteenth Amendment. On March 23, Grant told Secretary of Treasury George Boutwell that he was prepared to explain to Congress why he didn't want the army carrying out this policy. Boutwell talked him out of doing this, and Grant's subsequent message to Congress endorsed the action.

April–May: Secretary of State Hamilton Fish and British ambassador John Rose handled British–American negotiations regarding Great Britain's alliance with the Confederacy during the Civil War. Senator Charles Sumner felt that Britain had violated the Monroe Doctrine and should therefore abandon all its interests in the hemisphere, including Canada.

Fish and Rose reached a settlement in which the United States agreed not to pursue the issue of British interests in Canada, while the British made an "expression of regret" for "misdeeds" during the Civil War. The Treaty of Washington agreement was reached on May 8.

On April 20, Congress passed the Ku Klux Klan Act to be able to enforce the Fourteenth Amendment. The act gave Grant the power to declare martial law and to suspend the writ of habeas corpus. Congress established a joint committee to investigate the KKK on the same day.

August: Several serious attacks against African Americans occurred in Louisiana, but Attorney General Amos Akerman was pleased that in parts of North Carolina prosecution by district attorneys against White perpetrators was driving other members into the woods to avoid prosecution.

Grant, 49, returned to Washington, D.C., from Long Branch, New Jersey, to confer on the Klan problem. He didn't want to appear to be a military despot, and he was worried that there weren't enough jails to hold all those convicted of threatening African Americans. Grant also wanted to avoid martial law and creating the impression of another invasion by the North.

Terrorists ran wild in South Carolina during Akerman's fact-finding trip through the South. As a result, Grant suspended habeas corpus in nine counties. Akerman remained in South Carolina to campaign against Klan influence.

December: Fish told Grant that he believed Akerman was pushing the Klan too hard. Fish thought a better plan to reduce the violence would be to show leniency toward the KKK. Grant subsequently fired Akerman on December 12, and the attorney general, without bitterness or regret, returned to his law practice in Georgia.

Former Presidents

Millard Fillmore, 71, was in retirement in Buffalo, New York. In February, as a result of a request from the Buffalo Historical Society, he began sketching an outline for an autobiography.

℘℃ℛ

Andrew Johnson, 63 in December, lived in retirement in Greeneville, Tennessee.

Future Presidents

Rutherford B. Hayes turned aside pleas to run for a third term as governor of Ohio.

February 8: Lucy Hayes gave birth to a son, Scott.

June: Hayes said that if he were renominated for governor he would have his name withdrawn.

This engraving depicts an attack by the Ku Klux Klan on an unsuspecting African American family.

Instead, General Edward F. Noyes, a distant relative, received the Republican nomination.

November: Aided somewhat by Hayes's campaigning for him, Noyes was elected governor.

ജറ

JAMES A. GARFIELD, who turned 40 in November, received the runaround from Speaker of the House James G. Blaine for the second time, and turned down a job offer from Northern Pacific Railroad.

Democrats at the time were interested in possibly joining ranks with liberal Republicans to elect a reform-minded Speaker of the House. Key reformers wanted Garfield to head the Ways and Means Committee, but many congressmen believed he had an understanding with Blaine. By November, however, Jacob Cox was of the opinion that Blaine "is wholly given to intrigue," and Garfield publicly stated, "If Mr. Blaine does not appoint me … he is the basest of men."

Henry L. Dawes was the rumored choice for the House Ways and Means Committee, but he wrote Blaine on December 3 that he didn't want the job, and if forced to take it, "I shall surely fail." Even so, at the opening of the session in December, Dawes was made chairman of Ways and Means and Garfield received the chair of the Appropriations Committee.

Late in the year, Jay Gould, at the Northern Pacific Railroad, asked Garfield to accept a position as railroad land commissioner at a salary of $8,000 a year plus $100,000 worth of stock. The job entailed being supervisor of their coast-to-coast land interests. Garfield declined the offer. The project went bankrupt by 1873.

ജറ

CHESTER ALAN ARTHUR, after fraud and corruption charges caught up with the administration of Tom Murphy, took over the customhouse in New York City in December. Grant appointed him at both Roscoe Conkling and Murphy's suggestion. Arthur's annual income soon reached $50,000, comparable to the president's.

Murphy's running of the customhouse caused Horace Greeley to write in the *New York Tribune* on September 22: "This shoddy contractor, swollen with robberies from our soldiers, and backed by the power of an Administration that has honestly trusted him, has had his clutch on the throat of the Republican Party in New York long enough."

Conkling, having control of the Republican Party, initiated an "investigation" of Murphy that put Murphy in a positive light. The Democratic minority report, however, revealed Murphy to be a ruthless spoilsman. Grant accepted Murphy's resignation in November but also let Murphy select his own successor. Conkling's faction urged Arthur as a replacement.

The New York Customhouse had jurisdiction over the seas and shores of New York, as well as two counties in New Jersey. About 75 percent of all U.S. customs receipts were collected in New York.

Arthur, 42, took over the customhouse on December 1. Many critics assumed he had to take his orders from Conkling. On the same day Arthur took the job, his daughter Ellen Herndon was born.

ജറ

GROVER CLEVELAND took office as Buffalo's sheriff on January 1 and retained W. L. G. Smith as his undersheriff. Smith knew all details of the office, and Grant believed he would be valuable.

Cleveland, 34 in March, began cutting down on petty thievery in his department. He soon became unpopular with some associates and had his troubles with ward politicians.

ജറ

BENJAMIN HARRISON by now was now considered a potential candidate for governor of Indiana by state Republican leaders. They viewed him as a good party soldier, a popular war veteran, a relentless prosecutor, and a skillful defense attorney.

Harrison became involved in another high-visibility court case during this year. President Grant appointed Harrison defense counsel for General Salvin P. Hovey, ex-governor of Indiana Oliver Morton, and others in a suit brought by Democrat Lambdin P. Milligan, an Indiana lawyer convicted of treason in 1864. (Milligan had been sentenced to hang, but President Johnson commuted the sentence to life after Governor Morton urged a stay of execution.)

In 1868, Milligan sued for damages, claiming that his civil rights had been infringed by military action. Harrison, for the defense, intended to show that there were mitigating circumstances during the war. He wanted to send a message to the Democrats and reduce the $100,000 damages Milligan sought.

On May 29, Harrison described the case to the jury as the "legacy of war … [it was a time of] struggle for national life." Harrison enraptured the jury with his appeal. They decided in favor of Milligan, but awarded him only $5.

In the aftermath of the case, Republican political leaders began to view Harrison as an ideal candidate for governor. But Harrison's father, John Scott, wrote his son on June 21, advising him to temporarily refuse to seek or accept any public office until he had sufficient worldly goods so that he could avoid the "crooked and devious ways of politics."

ജറ

WILLIAM MCKINLEY married early in the year, but by the end of 1871 had lost his post as prosecuting attorney for Stark County, Ohio.

January: McKinley married Ida Saxton on January 24 at the new Presbyterian church in Canton, Ohio. He was 5 days short of his 28th birthday; Ida was 23.

July: The Republican Party renominated McKinley for prosecutor.

November: McKinley lost the prosecutor's job to Democrat William A. Lynch by only 143 votes.

಄ଓ

THEODORE ROOSEVELT, who turned 13 in October, spent his first summer in the Adirondacks. With the help of a private tutor, he improved in English, German, French, and Latin.

಄ଓ

WILLIAM HOWARD TAFT, 14, was a schoolboy living in Cincinnati.

಄ଓ

WOODROW WILSON, 15 in December, lived in Columbia, South Carolina, where his father was a Presbyterian minister and seminary lecturer.

಄ଓ

WARREN G. HARDING turned 6 in November. He lived in Blooming Grove, Ohio, where he attended school.

1872
Ulysses S. Grant

President Grant stood above the crowd, somewhat untouched by rumbles of corruption affecting others and easily won renomination and reelection. Throughout the year, Grant and several members of Congress had to fend off allegations of wrongdoing as a result of what came to be known as the Credit Mobilier scandal.

January: The Civil Service Act went into effect on January 1. The act was meant to combat the rampant spoils system that had plagued the U.S. government since the 1820s.

George Henry Williams of Oregon became attorney general on January 10.

April: Rumblings and rumors about Credit Mobilier became more prevalent. Investors seeking to profit from the construction of railroads established Credit Mobilier. They felt there was more money to be made in constructing railroads than in operating them. The heads of the firm either gave outright or sold shares of stock below value to congressmen to prevent congressional investigation of certain railroad companies. It was rumored that the bribery recipients included Vice President Schuyler Colfax, but the public would not know about what was happening at Credit Mobilier until the fall.

To avoid a possible scandal, Republicans decided to drop Colfax from the presidential ticket in the upcoming election.

May: A Republican splinter group unhappy with Grant formed its own party, the Liberal Republican Party, and held a convention in Cincinnati. They nominated newspaper editor Horace

Horace Greeley, the 1872 Democratic presidential nominee and one of the most influential journalists in American history.

Greeley for president.

June: Republicans held their national convention on June 5 and 6 at the Academy of Music in Philadelphia. They unanimously renominated Grant on the first ballot and chose Henry Wilson, a senator from Massachusetts, to replace Colfax as the vice presidential candidate. Wilson, an orphan, once operated a shoe factory and wrote a history of the Civil War. In his book he blamed the war on the slaveholding families of the South.

July: The Democrats also nominated Horace Greeley at their national convention held July 9 and 10 at Ford's Opera House in Baltimore. They chose Benjamin G. Brown of Missouri as Greeley's running mate.

September: The Credit Mobilier scandal went public when the *New York Sun* published articles about the bribery scheme. The article revealed that Colfax had accepted stock from Congressman Oakes Ames, one of the founders of Credit Mobilier. Colfax was allowed to finish out his term, but his political career was finished.

November–December: Grant defeated Greeley in the presidential election on November 5. Grant earned 3,597,132 votes, and Greeley earned 2,834,079. Greeley died 3 weeks after the election, however, and when it came time for the Electoral College to cast its votes, those for Greeley were split among several candidates. Grant received 286 electoral votes. Greeley's electoral votes were split as follows: Thomas A. Hendricks of Indiana 42, Benjamin Brown 18, Charles J. Jenkins of Georgia 2, David Davis of Illinois 1.

Grant appointed Ward Hunt of New York to the Supreme Court on December 11.

Former Presidents

MILLARD FILLMORE, 72, lived in retirement in Buffalo, New York, continuing to be very active in society there.

಄ଓ

ANDREW JOHNSON, after repeatedly saying that his great desire was to return to his Senate seat, surprisingly ran for a new, at-large U.S. House seat that became available through redistricting. In a three-man race for the office, however, Johnson finished a poor third.

The other candidates were Horace Maynard, a former House member and close friend of Johnson's during the war years, and former Confederate general Benjamin Franklin Cheatham, the nominee put forth at the state Democratic convention.

Maynard won with 80,000 votes. Cheatham received 63,000 votes, and Johnson received 37,000 votes.

Johnson, who lived in Greeneville, Tennessee, turned 64 at the end of the year.

Future Presidents

RUTHERFORD B. HAYES completed his second term as governor of Ohio. Political friends wanted him to run for a U.S. Senate seat, which he refused. But when a House seat later opened up, he reluctantly agreed to run.

January: As his term came to an end, Hayes wrote a friend, "I am looking forward to a release [from office] as hopefully as a schoolboy to his coming vacation ... I shall make no attempt to go higher."

Liberals believed that Hayes could beat incumbent John Sherman in the Senate race if Republicans unhappy with Sherman formed a coalition with Democrats to support Hayes. However, on January 4, Hayes published a statement in the *Ohio State Journal* saying he would not seek Sherman's seat.

In his parting message to constituents on January 8, Hayes said that Ohio was free of the corruption found in other states. He stressed the importance of continuing to pursue a policy of "economy, efficiency and purity."

May: Hayes and his wife, Lucy, attended the Liberal Republican convention held in Cincinnati, but remained on the sidelines. Hayes preferred Charles Francis Adams as a presidential candidate and was disappointed when the Liberal Republican Party chose Horace Greeley.

June: Hayes was a delegate to the Republican national convention on June 5 and 6 in Philadelphia and served on the platform committee. He was pleased with Grant's renomination and found the delegates to be "united, harmonious and the most enthusiastic any of us ever saw."

July–August: Two hundred Republican "stalwart" signatories to a petition supporting Grant asked Hayes to run for the Second Ohio congressional district seat, which he had held in the years immediately after the Civil War. Hayes declined the offer, but was nominated anyway at a convention held on August 6. A friend wired him, "We assured the party that General Hayes never retreated when ordered to advance." Hayes reluctantly decided to accept the nomination.

October: Hayes, 50, lost by 1,500 votes in the congressional election, which was held a month before Grant's presidential victory.

November: President Grant offered Hayes the position of assistant U.S. treasurer for the Cincinnati district. Hayes felt this was an inferior post for an ex-governor. He wrote in his diary, "That office I would not take except as a means of keeping hunger from the door. After what I have been (and done) it would be small potatoes to grasp this crumb."

୨୦୯୨

JAMES A. GARFIELD, the workaholic congressman, enjoyed his position as chairman of the House Appropriations Committee. At times the demands of the office required him to make upwards of forty speeches in a single day to promote or explain legislation. Garfield contemplated a run for the Senate against John Sherman but instead stood for reelection for his House seat.

May: Garfield considered supporting the Liberal Republicans but decided against it when they nominated Greeley for president. Still, he was reluctant to give full support to Grant, saying, "Grant is not fit to be nominated [and] Greeley is not fit to be elected."

July–August: The Republicans renominated Garfield for his House seat. He himself did not campaign. After the nomination he took his first trip west of the Mississippi, an adventure that he had been eagerly anticipating.

Oakes Ames, the Congressman from Massachusetts and director of the Union Pacific Railroad, had given Garfield a free railroad pass in 1870. Garfield used the pass while getting himself appointed to a commission to negotiate with the Flathead Indians. The Flathead Indians were situated at Fort Owens, Montana.

September: Reading an article in the *New York Sun* published several days earlier, Garfield first saw his name linked to the Credit Mobilier scandal. According to the article, Credit Mobilier, a railroad construction company, had distributed stock to many congressmen. Garfield's name was on the list of recipients.

In response to the public accusation, Garfield on September 16 sought out a friendly reporter from the *Cincinnati Gazette* to make a statement claiming he had never subscribed to, had never received, and indeed had never even seen a share of the company's stock. His statement, however, avoided mentioning Congressman Ames's name.

Garfield's old friend Jeremiah Black advised him to leave well enough alone. Black assured Garfield that he was guilty of nothing more than being an innocent victim deceived in a fraud. This defense, however, portrayed Garfield as gullible and greedy. Garfield ignored Black's advice and decided to shoulder his own defense.

November: Garfield, who turned 41 this month, defeated Liberal Republican lawyer Milton Sutliff by a vote of 19,189 to 8,254 in the election to retain his House seat.

On November 21, Lucretia gave birth to the Garfields' son, Abram.

୨୦୯୨

CHESTER ALAN ARTHUR, 43, collector of the port of New York, was now the prime patronage mover and shaker in the city and often attended top-level state political strategy huddles with Roscoe Conkling and others loyal to Grant. Although Arthur had instructions from Grant to "reform" the system, he was now in a position to hand out plums to those he chose, including his own kin. Arthur sought government jobs for his relatives, such as his brother-in-law Henry Haynesworth and Dabney Herndon.

Arthur was a firm supporter of Grant and at the custom-house he "requested" that his employees make "voluntary contributions" to Grant's campaign. The contributions, however, were actually an assessment deducted from each employee's salary. How much was contributed through these assessments is unknown.

On October 11 the chairman of the Civil Service Commission asked Arthur about the assessments. Arthur replied that until recently he had known nothing about them. He added, "I have not thought it either my duty or my right to interfere" with "voluntary" giving by subordinates.

§)(ß

GROVER CLEVELAND, 35, had a traumatic year: he lost two brothers during a fire at sea and was the hangman at an execution.

Cleveland's younger brother Lewis, known as Fred, obtained a lease on a nice winter retreat, the Royal Victoria Hotel, in Nassau in the Bahamas. On October 17, Fred and his older brother Richard, who was called Cecil, sailed from New York City on the steamer *Missouri*. Cecil came along to help manage the hotel. On October 22 a fire broke out about 25 miles off the coast of Great Abaco in the Bahamas. The fire killed eighty people, including Cleveland's brothers. Fred was 31, Cecil 37.

Cleveland's job as sheriff included being the hangman. His first execution was of a drunkard who had knifed his mother to death. Anguished, Cleveland sought his mother's advice. She suggested that he delegate the task of pulling the lever to a deputy. But Cleveland refused to have someone else do what he thought was his duty, however unpleasant, and spent several sleepless nights before the event.

On the day of the hanging, Cleveland did away with the circus atmosphere of previous executions: he banned spectators, covered the jail yard with canvas so people could not watch the event from their housetops, and set as solemn a tone as he could. Cleveland sprung the trap himself from a position where he could not see the victim.

§)(ß

BENJAMIN HARRISON, 39, was coerced by friends into seeking the Republican nomination for governor of Indiana but the reluctant future president lost the election. His subsequent foray into political thickets, however, began with courtroom dynamite.

January: Harrison's former law partner, William P. Fishback, had been charged by the Democratic attorney general with defrauding the state of $30,000 while doing the printing for the state. Governor Oliver Morton's brother-in-law also was charged. Harrison and Porter defended Fishback, and after 2 days of questioning by Harrison, the judge dismissed the case for lack of evidence.

February: An angry Fishback countered with suits against

the owner of other newspapers, and Harrison again acted as his attorney. The jury found the defendant not guilty.

The state Republican convention was held on February 22. The *Cincinnati Commercial* reported that the contest for governor in Indiana was between Harrison and General Thomas McLean Browne, the U.S. attorney for Indiana. Harrison remained quiet about his possible nomination and busied himself with his law practice. Still, he took the time to seek the advice of his father, John Scott Harrison. The elder Harrison advised his son not to enter the race unless he could win, even if only by a small margin. He pointed out that Democratic Governor Conrad Baker had won in 1868 by only 961 votes.

Harrison reluctantly threw his hat into the ring for the Republican nomination but did not campaign. Harrison, Thomas McLean Browne, and Godlove S. Orth were the top three contenders for the gubernatorial nomination at the Republican convention. Browne was nominated on the second ballot.

July–November: Busy practicing law in July, Harrison refused to endorse a petition that called for him to run for Congress.

Early on, Harrison actively campaigned for the Republican candidates: Grant for president and Browne for governor. He gave a speech on July 19 in which he condemned Greeley. As the elections drew closer, however, Harrison spent less time campaigning.

Browne lost the governor's race, but Grant carried Indiana by 22,000 votes.

§)(ß

WILLIAM McKINLEY, 29, spent one of the happiest years of his life with his new wife and their baby, a girl named Katherine born on January 25. He campaigned for Grant and became president of the YMCA branch in Canton, Ohio, leading young men in song and prayer.

§)(ß

THEODORE ROOSEVELT, along with his family, embarked on a second tour of Europe, this one more grand than the one taken 3 years earlier. The tour included a stop in Egypt.

Theodore Sr. had been appointed American commissioner to the Vienna Exposition, which was scheduled to open early in 1873. The family left for Liverpool on October 16, a few days before Theodore's fourteenth birthday. From England the Roosevelts traveled to Belgium, Paris, and Bonn, and then on to Switzerland.

Writing in his diary, Theodore noted that Paris still showed its scars from the war of 1870 in that many buildings were burned. He was critical of the various European political systems, considering them inferior to and less efficient than America's.

They reached Alexandria, Egypt, on November 28, and the youngster immediately started studying the birds he saw upon arriving in Cairo. On December 12 the Roosevelt family began a 2-month cruise on the Nile.

WILLIAM HOWARD TAFT, 15, mostly experienced a good childhood free of stress or want in Cincinnati, Ohio, where his father was a prominent judge. His father, Alphonso Taft, wrote his friend S. D. Torrey on October 15 that Will was "the foremost [of his children] and I am inclined to think he will always be so."

≈≈≈

WOODROW WILSON witnessed the construction of the family's new home at 1705 Hampton Street in Columbia, South Carolina. It was the only home the family ever owned.

Woodrow's father was shattered when members of the Presbyterian church of which he was pastor insisted on having a full-time pastor and forced him to resign in July. He had been teaching in his spare time and upon being fired from his pastorship, suffered a loss in income. Woodrow, who was16 in December, later recalled life in Columbia as an otherwise happy time.

≈≈≈

WARREN G. HARDING was a boy living in Blooming Grove, Ohio. His father returned home from Cleveland, and began his medical career, again traveling with Dr. McFarland. Warren's school was a one-room building constructed by his grandfather.

November 11: Warren's sister Eleanor Priscilla was born, 9 days after his seventh birthday.

≈≈≈

CALVIN COOLIDGE was born on July 4 in the drab, five-room family quarters in back of an adjoining store in Plymouth Notch, Vermont. Maple trees shaded the house and kept it cold and dark. His father was John Calvin Coolidge, 27; his mother was Victoria Josephine Moor Coolidge, 26. They named the baby John Calvin, but from infancy family members called him Calvin.

John Calvin Sr. was born on March 31, 1845, in Plymouth, Vermont. A wheelwright, mason, bricklayer, and carriage maker, he was a handyman capable of doing every task around the Notch. Each spring and fall he traveled to Boston to buy merchandise for the store. His interest in politics led him to serve three terms in the state house of representatives and one term as a state senator. He also held offices as township superintendent of schools, selectman, tax collector, road commissioner, deputy sheriff, and notary public.

Victoria Moor was born on March 14, 1846, also in Plymouth. Her father owned a large farm and a house originally built as a hotel. It was located across the road from the Coolidge store. Her father was Hiram D. Moor and her mother was Abigail Franklin Moor.

The Coolidges were wed in 1868. Victoria became a chronic invalid soon after the marriage.

Calvin's great-great grandfather, Captain John Coolidge, came to Plymouth Notch from Lancaster, Massachusetts, in 1781. Captain John had been a private stationed at Lexington, Massachusetts, at the start of the Revolutionary War but was promoted to captain by war's end.

Of Puritan stock, the original John Coolidge, at the time about 26 years old, sailed from England around 1630 and settled in Watertown, Massachusetts. Many of his Massachusetts descendants prospered. They included diplomats, Harvard graduates, architects, and a U.S. senator.

1873
Ulysses S. Grant

The president's fifth year in the White House was a tumultuous one, filled with personal tragedies, political battles, and rough economic times. He was 51 this year.

February: Congress stopped using silver as a monetary standard, causing its value to drop.

March: A major snowstorm and near-zero temperatures marred Grant's second inaugural ceremony on March 4. Chief Justice Salmon Chase administered the oath. It was so cold at the inaugural ball that dancers had to wear their coats.

Grant made one change in his cabinet at the start of his second term. George Sewall Boutwell, the secretary of Treasury had been elected to the Senate from Massachusetts. Grant replaced him with William Adams Richardson of Massachusetts.

April: After they killed General E. R. S. Canby and a Methodist minister during peace talks, General William T. Sherman declared total war on the Modoc Indians in Oregon. Sherman did this without consulting Grant.

May: Chief Justice Chase died on May 7. Grant and his wife, Julia, rode to the funeral with Roscoe Conkling. Julia told Conkling that if the decision were left to her, he would be chosen to replace Chase. After she told Grant what she had said to Conkling, Grant named Conkling to the Supreme Court. Conkling, however, declined to accept the post. Grant then named Senator Timothy Howe of Wisconsin as his next choice, but he, too, declined.

June–August: Jesse Grant, 79, died in Covington, Kentucky, on June 29. The president attended the funeral. Afterward, Grant retired to Long Branch, New Jersey, for the summer, as speculation on a replacement for Chase increased. Associate Justice Noah H. Swayne, 69, lobbied for promotion to chief justice, tied to the idea of adding Benjamin Bristow to the Court. Swayne had the backing of fellow Ohioan James Garfield.

Grant sat on the issue all summer, while Julia continued to promote Conkling and then William M. Evarts.

September: A major economic collapse occurred on September 18 when Jay Cooke was unable to sell Northern Pacific Railroad securities. As a consequence Northern Pacific went bankrupt, followed soon thereafter by several more companies. Wall Street suspended trading on September 20. The cause of the crash and business failures was a combination of uncontrolled credit, inflation, speculation, and over-expansion. The panic of 1873 was the deepest and longest yet in the nation's history and would linger for nearly 6 years.

Grant and his new secretary of Treasury, William A. Richardson, traveled to Wall Street to try and sort out the nation's financial mess. Grant agreed to the government's making bond purchases, but Secretary of State Hamilton Fish advised against taking any inflationary measures. Richardson eventually reissued $26 million in greenbacks.

October–December: By the fall, Grant offered the job of chief justice to Fish, who declined on the grounds that he had been away from the law business for 20 years.

Caleb Cushing, although 73 years old, also briefly came under consideration. When Grant finally named Attorney General George Henry Williams as chief justice, Benjamin Bristow was selected to replace him as attorney general. But Williams's confirmation was not a sure thing. It was soon discovered that Williams's wife's carriage was more elegant than the president's, equipped with coachmen and footmen, and all paid for out of Justice Department funds. Confirmation of Williams seemed unlikely by the end of the year.

Julia's father, Frederick Dent, died on December 15. He was 87 years old. Grant took Dent's remains to St. Louis for the funeral. Grant still owned his old farm outside St. Louis, but with her father's death, Julia inherited additional land.

Secretary of the Treasury William A. Richardson was faced with major economic collapse on Wall Street shortly after his appointment by Ulysses S. Grant.

Former Presidents

MILLARD FILLMORE, now 73, lived in western New York. He recommended that former presidents should receive a pension of $12,000 per year, writing, "It is a national disgrace that our Presidents should be cast adrift, and perhaps be compelled to keep a corner grocery for subsistence.... We expect [a president] to be honest, to give up a lucrative profession [and later] let him go into seclusion and perhaps poverty."

ॐ

ANDREW JOHNSON nearly died during a cholera epidemic that spread to eastern Tennessee, where he lived in retirement in Greeneville. During his illness he said, "Approaching death to me is a mere shadow of God's protecting wing.... I will rest in quiet and peace beyond the reach of calumny's poisoned shaft."

Although Johnson eventually rallied, his health was not what it had been. He turned 65 on December 29.

Future Presidents

RUTHERFORD B. HAYES, at 51 years old, was something of the country squire lawyer at Spiegel Grove in Fremont, Ohio.

April: Work progressed to increase the size of his estate. The lands Hayes owned near Toledo were valued at $143,000.

August: Another son, Manning, was born.

September: Hayes wrote a friend, "I am now chiefly interested in providing a good estate for myself and family."

November: One of the fallouts of the economic crisis was the defeat of Hayes's friend Governor Edward Noyes by Democrat William Allen of Chillicothe, a man Hayes also admired.

ॐ

JAMES A. GARFIELD suffered through the most troubling year of his public career as the Credit Mobilier scandal and the issue of a congressional pay raise led to demands in Ohio for resignation from his House seat.

January–May: On January 14, Garfield was called before the Poland committee to testify about Credit Mobilier. Speaker of the House James Blaine had pushed for an investigation of the company.

Testimony revealed that Congressman Oakes Ames had offered Garfield 10 shares of Credit Mobilier stock for $1,000 near the end of 1868. At the time Garfield didn't have the money to buy it, so Ames said he would hold the stock in Garfield's name. A year later Garfield told Ames that he was not interested in the deal, but accepted a $300 loan from Ames. Later, Ames changed his testimony and said Garfield had wanted the stock.

Garfield refused to refute Ames's account of events. He explained his silence on the issue by saying, "If the people will believe the testimony of a man blackened all over with contradictions and fraud as against my statement I cannot help it."

The Poland report, however, treated Garfield kindly. It also condemned Ames for making bribes but exonerated the congressmen who took them. Although the House censured him, Ames was not expelled. Attempts to censure Garfield were ruled out of order by Blaine.

On February 24, Benjamin Butler introduced an amendment to the appropriations bill that would have increased salaries for the president and congressmen, retroactive to 1871. Garfield felt this was a bad idea coming upon the heels of the Credit Mobilier scandal. Many congressmen were happy with the bill, however, and Grant confided to Garfield that he could use the money. The situation was tense in the conference committee as Garfield fought against the measure for 6 hours. Eventually Garfield was outnumbered and the bill passed, although he did manage to cut the travel mileage reimbursement, which saved the taxpayers $200,000.

In the belief that Butler was preparing to hold an extra session, Garfield, tired and overworked, signed the conference report and voted for it. Even though he had fought strenuously against it, much of the public subsequently blamed Garfield for the bill's passage rather than Butler.

Back home in Ohio, Garfield was universally condemned and he wrote, "My constituents are hunting for ropes to hang me with." At the March convention held in Warren, Ohio, Republicans demanded Garfield's resignation. In a show of principle he returned $4,548—the amount he had received in retroactive pay—to the Treasury. Garfield then wrote a pamphlet on the Credit Mobilier scandal and an open letter to Republican voters in his district explaining his position. Both helped to win back many of his detractors.

July–August: Garfield continued in his efforts to rebuild constituent support in Ohio. By August he believed the tide was turning in his favor.

December: Garfield, 42, reported to the December session of Congress, at which it was rumored that Blaine would penalize everyone touched by the Credit Mobilier business. Friends urged Garfield to stand up to Blaine, but this turned out to be unnecessary as the Speaker not only returned Garfield to his committee, he also assigned Garfield to the Rules Committee. The Forty-third Congress immediately repealed the pay hike approved earlier.

Ѕଠଔ

CHESTER ALAN ARTHUR, 44 years old, was riding high as a key member of the Grant–Conkling Republican political machine in New York and had influence on public policy beyond municipal and state levels. Arthur's machinations were private, subtle, and conducted out of sight in backrooms and away from press scrutiny.

Because the city was heavily Democratic and Tammany had influence in Democratic circles, Arthur often made deals with Tammany to get his men in certain positions. "Honest John" Kelly had succeeded "Boss" William Tweed, and Kelly often did business with Arthur.

Ѕଠଔ

GROVER CLEVELAND, 36, completed the second (and final) year of his term as sheriff of Buffalo, New York, with a second hanging.

Early in the year a young saloon keeper shot and killed a man during a card game in a quarrel over the stakes. Lyman K. Bass defended the man by claiming the defendant was insane, although in fact he was not. The case was delayed while Cleveland impaneled a jury to determine if the defendant was indeed insane. When the jury found him of sound

mind and hence guilty of the crime, it fell to Cleveland to again pull the lever as hangman. As before he anguished about it, even more than the first time because the condemned man had a wife and children.

Cleveland proved to be conscientious, worked well with prosecutors, ran an orderly jail, and served writs promptly. Friends said the office was good for him because it broadened his stature in Buffalo. His term ended on December 31.

Ѕଠଔ

BENJAMIN HARRISON, who turned 40 this year, was a prosperous lawyer in Indianapolis, Indiana. His firm made $26,322 during the calendar year, of which Harrison's share was $8,777.

The panic of 1873 kept Harrison's law firm busy with defaults, mortgage foreclosures, and bankruptcies. The firm grossed $12,000 from this type of work alone. Although business was generally down in Indianapolis, Harrison himself did not feel the pinch.

Ѕଠଔ

WILLIAM McKINLEY, 30, a lawyer in Canton, Ohio, had to face his wife, Ida's, sudden illness this year.

Ida's mother died just before Ida gave birth to the McKinleys' second child on April 1. Ida was in shock and grief over her mother's death when she went into a difficult labor resulting in the birth of a daughter, also named Ida. The baby died of cholera on August 22.

The two deaths had a major impact on Ida's life. She became very ill following the birth and developed a phlebitis condition that made walking difficult. Worse, she went into convulsions, fell into a severe depression, and often would sit in the dark for hours on end, weeping and holding her daughter, Katie, in her lap. Rumors began to circulate in town that Ida was prone to "fits," and nerve specialists were called in. It turned out that Ida was epileptic.

Ѕଠଔ

THEODORE ROOSEVELT, who turned 15 in October, spent most of the year overseas, living for a time with a family in Dresden, Germany. He continued the travels started the previous year and began the year in Egypt with his family on the Nile, living on their private riverboat. While in Egypt, Theodore climbed one of the Pyramids.

The Roosevelts' tour of the Middle East included stops at Jericho, Jerusalem, Jordan, the Dead Sea, and Bethlehem. Syria, Turkey, and Greece were also explored before the family traveled back to Vienna in April. While in Vienna, Theodore Sr. completed his business concerning the forthcoming exposition and returned alone to the United States to oversee the building of the family's new home in New York.

Theodore's mother, Martha's, main concern was that the children were not getting a normal education. She wanted them to learn German. As a consequence, Theodore and his brother Elliot found themselves living in the Dresden home of Dr. Minckwitz, a member of the German Reichstag; their

334

sister Corinne went to live in the home of Professor Wackernagel. It wasn't long, however, before 11-year-old Corinne could not handle the loneliness and she moved in with her brothers.

In October, Theodore and his family began the return trip to the United States. They arrived in New York on November 5 and settled into their new mansion at 6 West 57th Street near Central Park.

∽◯∼

WILLIAM HOWARD TAFT, 16 in September, during his senior year had the second-highest grade point average at Woodward High School in Cincinnati, Ohio. His father, Alphonso, later recounted how one of Will's teachers, W. H. Pabodie, had told him the schoolboy had the best head in school but might be too lazy to really achieve success in life.

∽◯∼

WOODROW WILSON, who wouldn't turn 17 until the end of December, entered Davidson College in North Carolina, a Presbyterian school, for the fall term. While there he befriended Frank J. Brooke, a student of religion from Columbia, South Carolina. Both boys had it in mind to enter the ministry.

Woodrow's father, Dr. Joseph Wilson, was a trustee at Davidson, which was located north of Charlotte about 100 miles from Columbia. Although Woodrow received high marks in composition, he struggled in mathematics. Overall, however, he was an outstanding student.

∽◯∼

WARREN G. HARDING and his family moved to Caledonia, Ohio, located in Marion County 14 miles west of Blooming Grove, early in the year. At the time, Caldeonia was a small town with a population of only 700. Not until spring did Warren's father, Tyron, return to Cleveland to finish the required two terms at the homeopathic college. On moving back to Caledonia he put out his M.D. shingle but often had to take foodstuffs in lieu of payment.

Warren turned 8 in November.

∽◯∼

CALVIN COOLIDGE was an infant living in Plymouth Notch, Vermont. He celebrated his first birthday in July.

1874
Ulysses S. Grant

President Grant, because of the expanding corruption being revealed in the Treasury Department and the comic opera aspects of naming a new chief justice, appeared rudderless in the White House without a trusted adviser to consult.

January: Grant withdrew Attorney General George Williams's name for the Court and again suggested the 73-year-old statesman Caleb Cushing, for which he was chas-

tised by opponents. He withdrew Cushing's name and on January 18 put forth Morrison R. Waite of Ohio. Two days later Waite was confirmed as chief justice.

March–April: The nation's economic difficulties led Congress to debate all spring the feasibility of going to a gold and silver standard. Passage of the so-called inflation bill meant that the Treasury Department would issue additional greenbacks and specie currency totaling $64 million. The bill had the support of western politicians, eastern businessmen, farmers, and factory workers.

The bill reached Grant's desk in April, but he didn't fully understand the workings of the economy and didn't know if he should sign it or not. Boston banker William Gray visited the White House and received a chilly reception. Gray urged Grant to veto the bill.

Grant finally decided to veto the bill and Secretary of State Hamilton Fish helped write the veto message, which came as a surprise to most moneymen. Conservatives had won the day; Grant had taken the "safe" position, and as a consequence workingmen began to feel estranged from Republican Party policy.

May: Grant's daughter Nellie was 18 years old when she married Englishman Algernon C. F. Sartoris at the White House on May 21. The president gave the bride away but behaved as if he was attending a funeral. Throughout the event he looked down at the floor and wept. Few approved of the match. Afterward, the couple left to live in England.

June: The president fired Secretary of Treasury William Richardson because of a scandal involving a contractor obtaining information on delinquent taxpayers. Richardson had signed a contract allowing John D. Sanborn to be an informant against delinquent taxpayers and to receive as a reward 50 percent of what the government recovered. Sanborn later told a congressional investigatory committee that he made $213,500 doing this. The practice dated back to 1872 when Benjamin Butler attached a rider to a bill making an exception for Sanborn's type of work. On June 2, Grant replaced Richardson with Benjamin Bristow.

July 7: Grant appointed James W. Marshall of Virginia to be postmaster general.

September–December: On September 1, Grant replaced James W. Marshall with Marshall Jewell.

In the South, African Americans continued to be murdered. Grant, 52, feared that the situation would worsen when white supremacists won fall elections in Texas and Arkansas. On being told that African American voters in Arkansas had been terrorized, Grant asked Congress to do something. He also ordered General Philip Sheridan to use the army to prevent further killings in Louisiana.

On October 20, Grant's son Fred married Ida M. Honore in Chicago.

In December, Grant informed Carlin, his property caretaker in St. Louis, that he could no longer afford to pay him $12,000 a year to look after the property. The farm was not bringing in enough money to support Carlin's salary.

Former Presidents

MILLARD FILLMORE was invited in early January by W. W. Corcoran to Washington, D.C., to have dinner with the men who had served in his cabinet. Fillmore never made it. He asked Corcoran for a postponement until April, writing on January 7 (coincidentally Fillmore's seventy-fourth birthday): "My health is perfect. I eat, drink and sleep as well as ever, take a deep but silent interest in public affairs, and if Mrs. Fillmore's health can be restored, I should feel that I was in the enjoyment of an earthly paradise."

Fillmore made his last public appearance in February to speak on the subject of the 1853 Oliver Perry expedition to Japan.

Fillmore was shaving when he suffered a stroke on February 13, which resulted in paralysis to his left side and a limp left arm. By February 22 he had recovered sufficiently to be able to walk around his house for the next 3 days.

Following a second stroke Fillmore died at his home at 11:10 P.M. on March 8. He was buried at Forest Lawn Cemetery in Buffalo, New York, 3 days later. President Grant, the governor of New York, and a delegation of congressmen were in attendance at the funeral

ഇൻ

ANDREW JOHNSON, 66, rejoined the political wars in pursuit of his goal of returning to the U.S. Senate.

In the fall of 1874, Johnson began his Senate campaign by sending out friends to gather information about the public's preferences. Parson Brownlow had decided to vacate his Senate seat. It was Johnson's estimation that the major candidates for the office, Tennessee Governor Neil Brown and General W. C. Bate, would cancel each other out, leaving Johnson as a viable alternative. The voting was scheduled to take place in the Tennessee legislature in January 1875.

Future Presidents

RUTHERFORD B. HAYES inherited a fortune and 50 acres of land when his uncle and longtime mentor, Sardis Birchard, died in January. Sardis had been the guiding hand in Hayes's life from the time he had been an infant.

Hayes continued to enjoy his retirement and wrote of leading "a life of leisure and book … no longer troubled [by politics]." He studied the history of the Sandusky valley, was active in local civic affairs, and managed his real estate investments.

Hayes's son Manning, only 1 year old, died in Fremont, Ohio, on August 28. Hayes turned 52 in October.

ഇൻ

JAMES A. GARFIELD, 43 this year, was accused of influence peddling in a District of Columbia street improvement scandal. He survived the negative publicity, as he had that of the

Credit Mobilier scandal in 1873, and easily won reelection to his House seat against divided opposition.

April–May: In the spring, Garfield's name became linked to yet another scandal. The De Golyer McClelland Company of Chicago was to pave Washington, D.C.'s dirt roads with wooden paving blocks. It later came to light that De Golyer had made make payoffs to get the contract; Garfield had received $5,000 as payment for legal advice. Garfield's critics viewed this as Garfield selling influence. Garfield, however, argued that he should be free to counsel any clients he saw fit.

June–August: Garfield's health was again a concern, and Irvin McDowell warned the congressman that he was headed for a breakdown. Doctors diagnosed the haggard-looking Garfield as having "neuralgic dyspepsia" and suggested that he eat raw beef and bread and drink only milk.

Several politicians in Garfield's Ohio district believed he was a "dead duck" as a result of the De Golyer scandal. However, his old friend Harmon Austin, who vowed to campaign with vigor, recommended hiring Dr. Lewis Pinkerton to write anonymous but effective letters to the newspapers on Garfield's behalf. By June, Garfield's popularity in Ohio had improved, and his renomination appeared certain.

Garfield won an easy nomination at the state Republican convention on August 8 as the opposition melted away. After surviving the scandals of the past few years, he called it the "greatest political victory of my life."

September–November: Garfield had no taste for campaigning, especially because he had been put on the defensive during the contest for Republican nomination. Still, he hit the road, realizing that he needed to campaign to retain his House seat and made speeches in small towns throughout Ohio.

Garfield was reelected in the November elections, but Democrats won six congressional seats in Ohio and Garfield suddenly found himself in the minority party.

Disappointed, he traveled to Cleveland the day after the election to look into the price of real estate on Euclid Avenue and to consider establishing a law practice there.

December 25: Garfield's sixth child, Edward ("Neddie"), was born.

ഇൻ

CHESTER ALAN ARTHUR, 45 in October, had to tread lightly after copper king William E. Dodge screamed that he had been wrongly accused of undervaluing cargo.

Dodge had been charged with undervaluing cargo, the purpose of which was to avoid publicity. After Arthur received his $21,906 cut, Dodge learned in a letter from U.S. District Attorney George Bliss that the under evaluation totaled only $6,658. Dodge exploded, saying, "We paid the money in ignorance.… We were fools." His complaints led to a congressional investigation.

Arthur initially escaped being identified with the fraud by claiming he knew nothing about it. Arthur told Bliss that he didn't want to testify before Congress and he wasn't called.

Judge Noah Davis's testimony described a meeting of customhouse people, including Arthur, Cornell, and Roscoe Conkling, during which they considered suing Dodge for $1,750,000—the sum the government legally had a right to collect. Davis talked them out of doing this, saying that if a jury knew the true amount owed the government, they would have received nothing. The $271,017 fine they decided Dodge should pay appeared to be an arbitrarily chosen amount.

In June, Congress repealed the moiety system of turning over fines such as these to the customhouse. As a consequence, Arthur's income plummeted.

Arthur's political influence appeared to be plummeting as well when Democrats won key positions in the fall elections: Samuel Tilden beat John Dix for governor, the Democrats took over the assembly in Albany, and Senator Edwin D. Morgan, Arthur's earliest benefactor, lost to Francis Kernan.

∞∞

GROVER CLEVELAND, 37, was a very successful lawyer. He had saved an estimated $40,000 from his salary as sheriff and had time for extra legal study that he felt he needed.

He joined a new law firm established with Lyman K. Bass and Wilson S. Bissell. John G. Milburn was the office clerk for the firm. Because Bass as a congressman spent most of his time in Washington, D.C., Cleveland ran the office, which was located in downtown Buffalo. Bass had been a friend for years, and Bissell eventually became a longtime associate.

∞∞

BENJAMIN HARRISON, now 41, built a new home in Indianapolis and gained a new law partner.

John F. Hill made Harrison an offer of $7,000 to buy the latter's house for Hill's daughter, Mrs. Neal. Harrison agreed to sell and in the fall built a new house on North Delaware Street, where in 1857 he had bought a double lot for $4,200. The red brick, two-story house with sixteen rooms and a spacious library cost him $21,123.

In April, William Henry Harrison Miller of Fort Wayne joined Harrison's law firm. Harrison had noticed the man's skill in federal court in Indianapolis. They soon became close friends and agreed on everything: politics, religion, personal matters, and legal issues. Within a short period their firm was considered one of the best in the state.

∞∞

WILLIAM MCKINLEY, 31, was a lawyer living in Canton, Ohio. He spent much of his time adjusting to living with his wife Ida, who was by now an invalid and still depressed over the death of their baby daughter the previous year.

∞∞

THEODORE ROOSEVELT, who turned 16 in October, spent much of the year preparing to enter Harvard. The family had rented a house on Long Island's Oyster Bay and moved in during the spring. Edith Carow, Theodore's future wife whom he met while living in Oyster Bay and the Roosevelt children's close friend from Manhattan, spent every summer there.

During the year, Theodore joined the Dutch Reformed Church.

∞∞

WILLIAM HOWARD TAFT, 17, entered Yale for the fall term. Yale was then led by President Noah Porter, who had established a scientific school, a school of fine arts, and a graduate school on campus. Taft's most stimulating teacher was Professor William G. Sumner. He also liked his rhetoric professor, Cyrus Northrup, who later became president of the University of Minnesota.

Taft was known as a big, friendly student who had strict morals. He roomed at Farnham Hall with George Edwards of Kentucky.

∞∞

WOODROW WILSON, who turned 18 in December, completed only 1 year at Davidson College. He left primarily because of a split between his father and the school. Afterward, he joined his family, who were living in their new home in Wilmington, North Carolina, on the coast in the southeast corner of the state.

The Reverend Joseph Wilson's troubles at Davidson stemmed from his insistence 2 years earlier that seminary students attend chapel at the same time the Presbyterian church was holding services. Reverend Wilson, who was a trustee of the school, could not effectively defend himself on the chapel issue. When the assembly voted for voluntary chapel attendance for students, Joseph Wilson resigned shortly thereafter. The reverend landed on his feet by taking a job at the First Presbyterian Church in Wilmington.

While at Davidson, Woodrow was disciplined a few times for "improper conduct" and "talking." He also played second base on the freshman baseball team. His father's problems at Davidson appeared to shake his confidence and perhaps made him less sure of himself.

Woodrow completed his examinations at Davidson in May and went home to Wilmington assuming he would return to Davidson for the fall term. Instead, he would remain in Wilmington for a year before entering Princeton in the fall of 1875.

∞∞

WARREN G. HARDING, 9 in November, lived with his family in Caledonia, Ohio.

April 8: Warren's brother Charles Alexander was born.

∞∞

CALVIN COOLIDGE lived in rural Vermont and turned 2 on the Fourth of July.

∞∞

HERBERT CLARK HOOVER was born near midnight on August 10 in West Branch, Iowa, in a three-room, wooden house on

Wapsinonoc Creek. His father was Jesse Hoover, 28; his mother was 26-year-old Huldah Minthorn Hoover. The Hoovers' simple house was close to Jesse's blacksmith shop. The Hoovers were Quakers.

The Hoover clan had arrived in West Branch by prairie schooner in 1854. The Minthorns arrived there in 1861. Jesse Hoover was born on September 2, 1846, in West Milton, Miami County, Ohio, 20 miles northwest of Dayton. Huldah was born on May 4, 1848, in Norwich, near Burgessville, Oxford County, Ontario, Canada. Jesse and Huldah were married on March 12, 1870.

Jesse's Swiss ancestors had migrated first to Germany and then to Lancaster County, Pennsylvania, in the 18th century. The original spelling of the name was "Huber."

Jesse's grandfather was born in 1800 on the Uwharrie River, Randolph County, North Carolina. His grandmother, Rebecca, born in 1801, was a true pioneer who raised nineteen children in addition to her own. She still lived in West Branch when Herbert was born in 1874. The Quakers traveled in groups, and a strong belief in freedom for slaves caused them to leave North Carolina. West Branch, with about 400 people, was a completely Quaker community inhabited mostly by Hoovers.

The Minthorns, of French Huguenot ancestry, came to New England from England in the 1630s. They lived as farmers in Massachusetts and Connecticut before moving to Ontario. From there they relocated by wagon to Detroit. In Iowa the Minthorns settled between West Branch and Springdale.

Herbert's older brother, Theodore, known as Tad, had been born 3 years earlier, in 1871.

1875
Ulysses S. Grant

President Grant protected the scoundrels in his administration as best he could this year, while the Whiskey Ring scandal implicated Orville Babcock, the president's right-hand man since the death of John Rawlins. The year also was marred by further Democratic gains in the fall elections and the death of the vice president.

January: Racial segregation in the South grew more pronounced with each passing year of Grant's presidency. African Americans and Republicans were steadily pushed out of positions of power by white supremacist Democrats. In his message to Congress in January, Grant read from a report by a judge in a Louisiana murder case. The case involved the systematic killing of 37 African Americans, who had been hiding under a courthouse. The victims had been taken away two by two and shot in the back of the head.

In his address, Grant condemned the murders but added that not everyone in Louisiana was guilty of the crime. Grant

had not given federal agents in the South any encouragement nor had he given them any specific plan of action for enforcing federal laws protecting African Americans. He told Congress that he did not want to use the U.S. Army for "domestic concerns" in Louisiana, or any other Southern state for that matter, to put down actions by white Southern agitators.

February: On February 11 the editor of the *St. Louis Democrat* tipped off Secretary of Treasury Benjamin Bristow that he knew a man who could break up the Whiskey Ring. The man he named was Myron Colony, an investigative reporter. Bristow was determined to break the ring, and to do so he had to use outside investigators who had no connections with the conspirators.

After the Civil War, the federal government placed a high tax on liquor. Distillers bribed government officials to be able to keep the tax proceeds normally collected for liquor. The distillers used the tax money they kept to bribe government officials for other purposes, including financing political activities, curtailing possible investigations, and silencing newspaper editors. The Whiskey Ring conspiracy originated in St. Louis in 1870 and soon spread to Wisconsin, Illinois, Ohio, Louisiana, and Washington, D.C.

The trail soon led to an old friend of Grant's, General John McDonald, the collector of internal revenue for St. Louis. Bristow called in McDonald for questioning, whereupon the latter broke down and confessed. Bluford Wilson, solicitor for the Treasury Department, said had it been his decision, he would have fired McDonald on the spot. McDonald implicated Grant in the conspiracy by claiming he went to Grant urging that the evidence against McDonald be burned, and that Grant replied that the evidence would be sealed.

April 26: Edward Pierrepont of New York was named attorney general, effective May 15.

May: On May 7, Bristow and Bluford Wilson met with Grant, now 53, to inform him of what McDonald had told them. Grant replied that McDonald had "grievously betrayed, not only [his] friendship, but the public."

On May 13, 350 men working for the government or in the distillery business were arrested. Bristow felt that McDonald "was the … center of the frauds." McDonald eventually was indicted, convicted, and jailed for his involvment.

Bristow convinced Grant's friend General James H. Wilson to go to Grant and tell him that Orville Babcock was involved in the fraud. Bristow feared that Grant would dissolve the cabinet, or at the very least fire Bristow and Bluford Wilson, to protect his friend Babcock.

General Wilson outlined the situation to Grant, who refused to believe the allegations against Babcock. As a result of Wilson being the message bearer, the friendship between Grant and Wilson ended. Wilson later said that Grant had tried to shield Babcock as much as he could and that the president "was a deeply affectionate man, and was surrounded by mean, low hangers-on."

June–August: In June, Grant met with Red Cloud, chief of the Red Face band of Oglalas, and other Native Americans to ask them to accept $25,000 for the hunting rights on the Platte River. Red Cloud refused.

Grant went to Long Branch for the summer. While there, Secretary of State Hamilton Fish and Attorney General Pierrepont told him that Babcock was guilty. When Grant asked Babcock about the charges, Babcock countered by saying that the investigation of him was really an attack on the president.

September: The power of the Reconstruction acts was tested in Mississippi. Near Jackson, Mississippi, several men fired into a crowd of Republicans holding a barbeque, killing two women and two children. African Americans trying to flee the scene were also attacked.

On September 2, Governor Adelbert Ames, a Northerner who had moved to and become governor of Mississippi wrote to his wife, Blanche, in Lowell, Massachusetts: "The old rebel armies are too much for our party and the colored man [does] not dare to organize even when they know their liberty is at stake." Ames informed President Grant that he was unable to stop the intimidation of African Americans and that Republican leaders in Mississippi were powerless to do anything.

Ames finally called for federal troops on September 7, with an appeal to Grant that the Constitution required the government to protect its citizens. Democrats, however, wrote Grant to tell him that it was not necessary to send troops. Ames's request was denied.

While Grant tried to decide what to do about the unrest in the South, during cabinet meetings Bristow and Pierrepont revealed telegrams implicating Babcock. Grant, however, remained satisfied with Babcock's denials of guilt. Eventually, Babcock asked for and received an army trial and was acquitted of the charges.

October: In mid-October, Benjamin Butler went to Grant to request federal troops to assist Ames, who was Butler's brother-in-law, in quelling the unrest in Mississippi. Ames believed that African Americans had been forced to return to serfdom and, in fact, that "[a] second slavery" era was beginning. Grant, who wanted no part of a race war and believed that Whites would support other Whites across regional lines, often was angry during cabinet meetings when hearing about reports of violence in the South. However, he

could not mount an effective program of law enforcement to end the terrorism there.

November–December: Elections across the nation resulted in Democrats making key gains, including the majority in the House of Representatives. Republicans were routed in the election in Mississippi.

On November 22, Vice President Henry Wilson died in Washington, D.C., at the age of 63.

The Democratic majority in the Forty-fourth Congress met on December 6 and selected Michael C. Kerr of Indiana as Speaker and began an investigation into the scandals of the Grant administration. Before the Democrats were finished, they had investigated every department in the cabinet, including Fish's.

Secretary of the Treasury Benjamin Bristow used investigators from outside the Treasury Department to break the Whiskey Ring scandal, where distillers bribed government officials in order to retain liquor taxes.

Former Presidents

ANDREW JOHNSON, after two previous unsuccessful attempts, was finally elected to the U.S. Senate. However, he would die soon after taking his seat in the Forty-fourth Congress.

January: Johnson was in attendance at the Tennessee legislature in Nashville to watch the voting on January 19 for the U.S. Senate seat Parson Brownslow had vacated. At the end of the first ballot Johnson had 10 more votes than any of the seven other candidates, but not enough to win the seat. Still, he was confident on winning when he retired to his quarters at the Maxwell House for the night.

The next day a battle for the nomination between Governor Neil Brown and General W. C. Bate, a former Confederate general, lasted through the forty-fourth ballot before Brown withdrew. The contest then was down to Bate and Johnson. On the forty-fifth ballot, Bate garnered 48 votes—only 1 vote shy of election; Johnson had 42.

Said Johnson of the long and grueling process, "I may not be elected but Bate never will be" and referred to Bate as a "one-horse general." Johnson got so nervous awaiting the results of the voting that he got drunk on brandy.

The next day Bate withdrew and Brown reentered the race. Johnson was finally elected on the fifty-fourth ballot—by 1 vote. The *St. Louis Republican* called Johnson's election the "most magnificent personal triumph which the history of American politics can show."

March: When President Grant called a special session of the Senate on March 4, Johnson arrived to large applause as he took his seat. Radicals who had previously voted for his impeachment were embarrassed. Of the thirty-five men who had voted for his impeachment in 1868, thirteen still remained in the Senate.

Vice President Henry Wilson, who 7 years earlier had voted for conviction and for disqualifying Johnson from holding office, now escorted Johnson to the oath taking.

Future Presidents

RUTHERFORD B. HAYES's happy retirement at Spiegal Grove, Ohio, was short lived. Without his authorization, a Republican caucus selected him for a third term as governor of Ohio.

March: The political fires caught Hayes unprepared. He was happy living in retirement, working on his library, garden, and house. It came as a surprise to Hayes when, on March 25, a caucus in Columbus, Ohio, unanimously picked him to oppose Democratic Governor William Allen.

Hayes was against making another run for governor. He was not in sympathy with national party leaders, didn't like the strong policy in the South, and didn't approve of the spoils system. Nevertheless, he wrote, "I wouldn't hesitate to fight a losing battle if the cause was … clearly good."

April–May: Hayes wavered about accepting the nomination, but then declined. Some took this as Hayes's final word. His inaction led to Judge Alphonso Taft, father of William Howard Taft, being chosen as the Republican gubernatorial candidate.

Judge Taft was a friend of Hayes. For the sake of party unity, Hayes refused the nomination again, but noted in his diary on May 31: "If Judge Taft should withdraw, and the convention … insisted on my candidacy, I shall not refuse. This is not likely to happen." Taft, however, remained in the race.

June: At this time Roman Catholicism was a major issue. A Vatican Council had recently espoused the doctrine of papal infallibility. As a consequence, British Prime Minister William Gladstone had publicly declared that the Catholics were seeking world domination.

Judge Taft had tilted toward a group of Catholics in an education case that came before his court. Friends of Hayes suggested him as a candidate, not to do combat with the Grant element in the party, but to make America safe from "Catholic domination" as they believed that Taft was a Catholic sympathizer or worse.

On June 2 convention delegates voted 396 to 151 in favor of Hayes. Taft withdrew and his son Charles P. Taft moved that Hayes's nomination be made unanimous by acclamation.

September: Hayes campaigned daily throughout Ohio. On his return home he wrote in his diary that if he won, he realized he would be pushed to become a presidential candidate and that any happy retirement in Spiegal Grove would be an illusion. By late September, however, Hayes believed that he would lose the gubernatorial race, "perhaps badly."

November: Hayes defeated Allen by 5,544 votes. The day after the election, 53-year-old Hayes received a letter from Judge Manning Force of Cincinnati confirming Hayes's earlier prediction: "It is natural that you should now be spoken of for the presidency."

Ten newspapers in Ohio endorsed Hayes for president, and George W. Curtis, writing in *Harper's Weekly,* noted that Hayes's victory showed that when Republicans were united in supporting reform, Democrats lost.

ೞ೦೪

JAMES A. GARFIELD became convinced that Grant was inimical to the Republican Party's hopes. Garfield saw the administration as having botched Reconstruction policies in the South.

January 4: Garfield wrote Hinsdale that after fighting many political wars, he had lost his "cheerful spirit … [I am] less genial."

February: Garfield was disillusioned with the current administration and considered making an open break with Grant. He also was unhappy about having to serve in the first Democratic Congress since 1859. He was put on the Ways and Means Committee and the Pacific Railroad Committee, but scoffed at the Democratic chairmen of the committees.

March: The Democrats proposed amnesty to some former Confederate rebels. Speaker of the House James Blaine disagreed with the idea, but his attack was so overblown that he lost much of his support. Garfield took the floor and did his best to salvage the debate. Garfield said he had not seen such "passion and excitement" in the House in 10 years, yet his thrust was the same as Blaine's, to indict Jefferson Davis for conditions at Andersonville prisoner camp during the Civil War.

April–June: Garfield decided to accept an offer from Jay Gould, made nearly 6 years earlier, to travel to California. Gould put a private car at Garfield's disposal but his wife and children remained home. Garfield enclosed a map with his letters home to help the children learn geography.

Garfield left Cleveland on April 19. He visited Yosemite and Belmont, California, and the Comstock Lode in Virginia City, Nevada. Garfield returned to Washington, D.C., 18 pounds lighter after 3 weeks on the road. The rough rides brought back his hemorrhoid troubles, and later surgery revealed he had a rectal ulcer.

July–August: Garfield spent much of the summer in bed in Washington, D.C., recuperating from surgery.

November: Garfield, at 44, was no longer as orthodox in religious matters as he once had been. He wrote, "I have come to wonder at those happy mortals who know the whole counsels of God and have no doubts. Are religions, past and present, false, except that of Christ?"

ℰℛ

CHESTER ALAN ARTHUR survived his 4-year term of office as collector of the port of New York, the first man in 25 years to do so. The Conkling-controlled U.S. Senate subsequently reconfirmed him without objection.

Arthur held onto his patronage plum because he ran an efficient operation and was popular with merchants, importers, his subordinates, Grant, and Republicans in Congress. Arthur followed orders, discreetly ignored civil service rules, did favors for and hired his friends, raised funds for the party, and was not tied to many scandals.

In the fall, Arthur's father became ill in Newtonville, New York, possibly from stomach cancer. Chester and his sister Annie were sent for, and their father was very pleased to see them. Arthur, 46 on October 5, returned to New York City after the visit. His father died on October 27 at the age of 78.

ℰℛ

GROVER CLEVELAND, 38 in March, was a lawyer in Buffalo, New York. Tragedy struck on July 23 when his law partner, Oscar Folsom, riding in a buggy with Warren F. Miller, was thrown out and killed. Folsom had left no will and Cleveland took over administration of his estate for Mrs. Folsom.

ℰℛ

BENJAMIN HARRISON, a well-known 42-year-old trial lawyer in Indianapolis, by the end of the year was touted in a few newspapers in Indiana and Ohio as presidential timber for 1876. Earlier, Republican Party leaders had wanted him to run for governor of Indiana. Harrison declined the offer, citing his legal load, church duties, and involvement with veteran affairs and reunions.

In November the Republican state convention met in Indianapolis. On November 25, L. M. Campbell, a friend of Harrison's, wrote that the "entire Republican party … earnestly desire your nomination and election [as governor]." Harrison didn't respond for 2 weeks and then turned down the request for the gubernatorial nomination with regret.

Harrison's friends whispered that his decision to decline the state race left him free to accept the Republican nomination for president in 1876. The *Cincinnati Commercial* began the campaign to promote Harrison for president. As more requests that he run for the presidency surfaced, he would turn them down, finally saying on December 29, "there is no public necessity for my services."

ℰℛ

WILLIAM MCKINLEY, 32, lost a second child, his older daughter, in 1875, which further aggravated his wife's precarious health. He also supported Hayes's run for governor of Ohio and gave thought to seeking a congressional seat.

Katie McKinley, 4, died of either diphtheria or typhoid on June 25. Ida Hayes believed that God was punishing her and she became increasingly possessive over her husband's time,

to the point of obsession. McKinley gave up taking walks and riding to be with her.

McKinley never got over the loss of his two children. His buoyancy of old turned into a personality both guarded and reticent.

Ida's health fluctuated for most of the year. She suffered from blinding headaches, heavy colds, and digestive problems. McKinley became resourceful in helping her to walk, anticipating her seizures, or massaging her temples. He was tactful, soft voiced, always supportive, and patient. He refused to discuss her condition with others.

ℰℛ

THEODORE ROOSEVELT, who turned 17 in October, continued studying to prepare for entering Harvard but found time for hikes in the Adirondacks and Maine. He took preliminary exams for Harvard and passed all eight subjects.

On his breaks from studying, Theodore continued to collect specimens in the woods of upstate New York and New Jersey. He had long talks with his father on the subject of becoming a naturalist. Theodore Sr. gave his blessing but warned his son that a naturalist's life would mean a modest standard of living.

ℰℛ

WILLIAM HOWARD TAFT, 18, was a student at Yale. His father, Judge Alphonso Taft, made a run for the Republican gubernatorial nomination but lost to Rutherford B. Hayes.

ℰℛ

WOODROW WILSON entered Princeton in September as a freshman despite having spent a year at Davidson. He turned 19 at the end of the year.

Wilson spent most of 1875 in Wilmington, North Carolina, studying hard in preparation for entering Princeton. He also mastered shorthand. Once at Princeton, he did well from the start despite early difficulties with Greek and mathematics. Other students soon began to view him as a superior, well-focused scholar.

ℰℛ

WARREN G. HARDING, who would turn 10 in November, became a printer's devil (apprentice) after his father, Tyron, purchased the *Caledonia Argus* in their small town in north-central Ohio. Editor Will Warner, a man with courtly manners, had put out the newspaper periodically and remained on after Tyron took ownership. As printer's devil, Warren swept the floors, ran errands, and learned to return the type to the bins.

After 2 months, Tyron turned his interest in the paper back over to Warner, who gave the young Warren a steel makeup rule, which he would keep for the rest of his life.

May 31: Warren's sister Abigail Victoria was born. She was the sixth Harding child.

ℰℛ

CALVIN COOLIDGE, a child of 3, welcomed a sister also named Abigail to the family on April 15. Calvin had two adventures during 1875: he fell from a horse and broke his arm, and his grandfather took him and his mother to Montpelier, Vermont, to watch his father at work in the legislature.

ℰℭℛ

Herbert Hoover, 1, almost died from croup, a breathing difficulty. He lived in a small Quaker community in Iowa with his family.

1876
Ulysses S. Grant

President Grant saw his second administration come to a disgraceful end featuring an impeachment, forced resignations, and a few other crimes against public decency. His wife, Julia, however, loved the White House so much that after 8 years she privately hoped somehow for a third term.

January: The Whiskey Ring scandal was still in the news. Newspapers during the month ran whiskey fraud stories about Orville Babcock and implicated Grant's brother, Orvil, and his eldest son, Fred.

February: Grant told his cabinet at a meeting on February 6 that he was under attack from all quarters but was confident that Babcock was innocent.

Grant had wanted to take the witness chair during the Babcock's grand jury hearing in St. Louis, but Secretary of State Hamilton Fish advised him that a sitting president could not do that. Instead a deposition was taken in the White House with Babcock's lawyer present for cross-examination as evidence was presented.

Babcock was acquitted on February 28.

March: When Babcock casually reported at the next cabinet session after his acquittal, Fish was appalled. Finally Grant agreed to Babcock's departure and replaced him as private secretary with his son, Buck Grant.

More troubles shook Grant's cabinet. Secretary of War William Belknap had confessed to Grant on March 2 that Belknap's second wife, Carrie Belknap, and the sister of his third wife had made a trading post deal in Oklahoma in which they would receive $6,000 a year. The deal had been arranged in 1870, and Carrie Belknap died that same year. The *New York Tribune* said Belknap profited from the trading post at the expense of Native Americans who shopped there. A House special committee had heard Belknap's testimony on February 29, and news of the evidence was taken to Secretary of Treasury Benjamin Bristow. Bristow told Grant on March 2, the same day Belknap showed up weeping for his confession. Grant asked for Belknap's resignation, and the secretary of war complied.

Alphonso B Taft, father of William Howard Taft, replaced Belknap on March 11.

June: Taft remained secretary of war only briefly, until he was made attorney general on June 1. On the same day, J. D. Cameron became secretary of war.

The battle of Little Big Horn in eastern Montana took place on June 25. Colonel George Custer had attacked the Sioux and Cheyenne Indians but was killed along with all 265 of his troops. General Philip Sheridan said Custer had a superabundance of courage.

July–August: An attack on African Americans at Hamburg, South Carolina, on July 8 caused Republican Governor Daniel H. Chamberlain to seek Grant's help. At the time of this request Grant was not in Washington, and Fish and Attorney General Taft turned Chamberlain down without consulting the President. It was not until July 22 that Grant saw Chamberlain's message. The president said he was powerless to act.

At the Belknap impeachment, evidence showed that the former secretary of war and his third wife, Amanda, were paid $20,000 over several years. Belknap was paid in banknotes or by cash in person. Amanda had held many gala receptions and was a social rival of Julia Grant.

During impeachment proceedings, Grant showed a short temper with reporters. Testimony soon showed that Indian trading centers had been sold for profit by Babcock's brother and also by Julia's brother, John C. Dent.

In the end, the Senate voted to acquit on August 1. There were 23 guilty votes but not the two-thirds necessary.

November: On election night, Grant, 54, was at the home of George W. Childs of Philadelphia and went to bed thinking he would have to congratulate Samuel Tilden in the morning. But before he could write such a statement, several prominent Republicans appeared and asked to look over the returns again. It seemed that a winner could not yet be determined.

"Custer's Last Stand" at the Battle of Little Big Horn on June 25, 1876.

December: Grant's final message to Congress on December 5 discussed his long years in the army. He said that his judgment errors were in making appointments of men he had not known very long. All presidents after Washington made mistakes, Grant said, "But I leave comparisons to history." He said he tried to stand behind Reconstruction measures rather than throw control of Southern state governments back to the people who had tried to destroy the United States.

Grant was also critical of those who broke Native American treaties and the poor behavior of miners in the Black Hills of South Dakota. He closed by saying, "My official life terminates."

Future Presidents

RUTHERFORD B. HAYES was inaugurated for a third term as governor of Ohio but then became the surprise compromise reform presidential candidate endorsed at the Republican National Convention. He ended the year not knowing if he had won the presidency.

January: Hayes's third gubernatorial inauguration in Columbus, Ohio, was held on January 10. In his speech, Hayes said Ohio faced "questions of national concern." He named reducing the debt, collecting fewer taxes, taking care of the unfortunate, reforming the criminal system, and reforming civil service as his prime objectives.

February–April: Almost immediately the presidential buzz began. He received letters and callers interested only in the upcoming presidential race. His old friend Guy Bryan wrote from Texas that Hayes would be "desirable" as a presidential nominee. Hayes replied: "The result you desire is a possibility, but, as I see it, not at all probable."

The Republican state convention met on March 29 and unanimously passed a resolution asking Ohio delegates to the national convention to try hard to nominate Hayes.

Although Hayes acted a bit reluctant, in April he told one Ohio delegate who planned to vote for James Blaine, "If I am to be voted for at all, may I not reasonably expect the solid vote of Ohio?"

May: Hayes wrote in his diary on May 19 that Blaine had a large lead in the upcoming Republican nomination but that if Blaine were to fail, Blaine's managers would dictate who the nominee would be. "This would not be in my favor. My independent position aloof from the bargaining puts me outside the list from which the managers will select."

June: As the Republicans gathered in Cincinnati June 14 to 16 to nominate their presidential candidate, contenders were Blaine, Benjamin Bristow of Kentucky, Roscoe Conkling of New York, and Oliver Perry Morton of Indiana.

Blaine was vulnerable because of claims he was involved in graft in the Union Pacific Railroad case. Press leaks claimed that Blaine received $64,000 from Union Pacific for some nearly worthless railroad bonds.

Bristow had uncovered the Whiskey Ring and was riding a wave of popularity. Conkling was seen as Grant's choice but was also closely identified with machine politics. Morton was governor of Indiana during the Civil War and later supported Johnson's policy. He was considered the mildest of Republican candidates in the eyes of southern voters. But Morton had health problems.

As the convention neared, Republican leaders had begun to woo Hayes as a vice presidential candidate. Hayes, however, was not considered a likely running mate on a Blaine ticket.

The convention opened on June 14 at Exposition Hall. Former governor of Ohio Edward Noyes introduced the Hayes candidacy, saying that although he had nothing bad to say about the other candidates, "I only wish to say that General Hayes is the peer of these gentlemen in integrity, in character, in ability."

The first ballot was held on the third day, with 378 votes needed for the nomination. Blaine received 285 votes, Morton 125 votes, Bristow 113 votes, Conkling 99 votes, and Hayes 61 votes. By the fifth ballot Hayes had climbed from fifth to third with 104 votes. On the sixth ballot Blaine had 308 votes and Hayes had 113 votes. Conkling and Morton realized that the only way to stop Blaine from receiving the nomination was to switch to Hayes. On the seventh ballot, Hayes had 384 votes, five more than needed, to Blaine's 351 votes. William P. Frye of Maine moved that the Hayes nomination be made unanimous. The convention approved.

Congressman William Wheeler of New York was the choice for vice president.

The Democrats met in St. Louis, Missouri, on June 27 to 29 and chose Samuel J. Tilden of New York as their presidential candidate and Thomas Andrews Hendricks of Indiana as their vice presidential candidate.

July–September: As was then traditional, Hayes and Tilden sat on the sidelines while their friends and supporters campaigned for the two candidates. Zachariah Chandler, former secretary of the Interior for President Grant, ran Hayes's campaign. The Michigan man was chairman of the Republican National Executive Committee. Chandler had switched support from Blaine to Hayes on the fifth ballot, which was viewed as a signal of Grant's approval of Hayes. Hayes, however, was not happy with the way Chandler ran the campaign.

Shortly after he was nominated, Hayes said he would not accept a second term if elected. Some saw this pledge as a slight to Grant, who earlier had considered seeking a third term. Hayes wrote the president to assure him that he did not intend it as such.

Mud-slinging was the order of the day. Democrats tried to tie Hayes with the corruption of the Grant administration. Republicans stressed Hayes's war record and Tilden's lack of one.

October: The bitter summer campaign led Hayes, 54, to write Lucy in Chillicothe, "I wish I was a private citizen again. But it will be so if we are beaten. I almost hope we shall be."

November–December: Republican leaders gathered at the Fifth Avenue Hotel in New York on Election Day, November 7, but went to bed facing the nightmare of defeat. The same went for candidate Hayes in Columbus.

The *New York Times* edition at 6:30 the next morning said Tilden had 184 electoral votes, 1 vote short of the necessary 185. The *New York Tribune*, however, confidently said Tilden was elected. Later in the morning, Zachariah Chandler sent out a dispatch saying, "Hayes has 185 electoral votes and is elected."

Nearly every Republican newspaper conceded to Tilden. Tilden received 4,300,590 popular votes to Hayes's 4,036,298 votes. Tilden's 184 electoral votes were balanced by Hayes's 165 votes, with 20 votes in four states—Louisiana, Florida, South Carolina, and Oregon—in dispute. The three southern states were the last still controlled by Republicans.

A dispute in Oregon led to different election counts. There were three different tallies coming from Florida, first favoring Hayes, then Tilden, and then Hayes again. In Louisiana, Republicans managed to throw out the Democratic majority. South Carolina also had different tallies, supporting both Hayes and Tilden. Charges of fraud were leveled against each side. There was no precedent for resolving this situation. The year ended without the election being resolved. It would be in the hands of the Congress at the start of 1877.

୨୦୦୧

JAMES A. GARFIELD, seeing the need for a reform candidate, supported Benjamin Bristow as the best and logical nominee for president but acknowledged that Hayes was a spotless candidate.

March–April: Garfield favored Bristow early in the year and wrote to his wife, Lucretia, on March 10, "Bristow is a higher type of man." Garfield felt Blaine was not a statesman, just a man with a "magnetic" personality. Garfield worried about Roscoe Conkling or Oliver Perry Morton winning the nomination. Hayes, Garfield believed, was fortunate to be free of scandal. Hayes was "born lucky on that score," Garfield wrote.

May–June: Garfield, dreaming of retirement, vowed that his upcoming House race would be his last campaign for office. If the Republicans could retake the House, Garfield felt he stood a chance to become Speaker of the House.

July: Garfield won unanimous renomination. His opponent would be reformer General John S. Casement.

October: While campaigning for Hayes in New Jersey, Garfield received a telegraph that his 2-year-old boy Neddie was ill with whooping cough. The boy was unconscious when Garfield arrived home, and he died on October 25.

The next day Garfield was escorted through town in a torch-light parade leading up to a speech for Hayes. "It was hard," he admitted later, "but it seemed to be a duty."

On October 31, Garfield bought 120 acres of farmland at Mentor from James Dickey and later obtained an additional 40 acres, all for $17,500. He began to fix-up the place and soon named the farm "Lawnfield."

November–December: On election night on November 7, Garfield saw a Democratic sweep, but a possible Hayes victory. He retained his House seat by a 2-to-1 margin.

Soon after the election, President Grant sent Garfield to Louisiana to help investigate and observe what was happening in that disputed state. Garfield soon decided Hayes won the state and wrote to J. H. Rhodes on November 18 that Louisiana was a "different world from ours … in many respects, un-American and un-Republican."

Garfield was assigned to the West Feliciana Parish, where the Democrats had won by 471 votes. He noticed this vote differed from past elections in which Republicans won and attributed the change to "rifle clubs" and bullying at the polls. The returning board then threw out the Democratic ballots, putting the Republicans in front by 386 votes. Democrats cried fraud.

୨୦୦୧

CHESTER ALAN ARTHUR attended the Republican National Convention in Cincinnati as a floor manager for Roscoe Conkling, but not as a delegate from New York. When the Conkling boom burst, Arthur returned home and campaigned very little for Hayes but through the customhouse "donations" tradition saw that $72,000 was coughed up for Hayes.

Arthur was far more concerned with New York politics and doing Conkling's bidding than he was with the big picture. He supported old friend Edwin Morgan for governor again and controlled the nomination process in New York City's 18th district. In November, Morgan lost and so did all of Arthur's men.

୨୦୦୧

GROVER CLEVELAND, 39, was a lawyer in Buffalo, New York. A Democrat, he never liked Samuel Tilden and was a spectator during this election. He wanted the Democrats to choose Senator Thomas F. Bayard of Delaware.

୨୦୦୧

BENJAMIN HARRISON lost a late-hour bid to be Indiana's governor but gained national stature through the publicity the race received in the press. Early in the year, he had some support for the Republican presidential nomination.

January–February: The *Indianapolis Evening News*, an independent voice under editor John H. Holliday, opened a Harrison-for-president campaign in January by opposing Grant's administration as filled with greed, the self-seeking, loose morals, and so forth. The *Indianapolis Sentinel,* a Democratic paper, said that once Oliver Perry Morton was stopped, Harrison would be the Republican choice. Both newspapers suggested that Harrison could carry Indiana, whereas Morton could not.

When Indiana Republicans met in February, Harrison stayed on the sidelines and Morton was chosen as Indiana's presidential representative. Godlove S. Orth was chosen as the Republican candidate for governor.

July: Orth quit the race for governor when he was linked to a scandal known as the Venezuela Ring. Meanwhile the Democrats nominated "Uncle Jimmy Blue Jeans" James Douglas Williams for governor.

August: The Republican central committee met in Indianapolis on August 4 and selected Harrison to replace Orth as their candidate. At the time, Harrison was in Michigan on a fishing trip. Harrison received word of his nomination when his train reached Ft. Wayne, and a welcoming committee traveled to Muncie to escort him to Indianapolis. There were thousands at the station to meet him.

In a speech at the train station, Harrison said he would "seriously consider the matter" but did not immediately accept the nomination. Later Harrison said it was his friends who tilted him into accepting the nomination.

Harrison opened his campaign at Danville, west of Indianapolis, on August 18, two days before his 43rd birthday. His train left amid a rousing demonstration.

October: After a long campaign, Harrison lost the election to Williams by just 5,000 votes.

November–December: On November 11, Harrison received a telegram from President Grant asking if he would visit New Orleans to witness the vote count. Harrison declined because Lew Wallace and John Coburn were there. Later Zachariah Chandler asked Harrison to go to South Carolina, and he declined this offer as well.

❦

WILLIAM MCKINLEY, 33 and a lawyer in Canton, Ohio, won a seat in Congress despite the high costs of Ida's illness.

When McKinley announced his candidacy, he faced opposition from Congressman L. D. Woodworth, Judge Joseph Frease, and Dr. Josiah Hartzell, editor of the *Canton Repository*, for the Republican nomination. McKinley won the nomination on the first ballot.

McKinley made a vigorous campaign against Democrat Leslie L. Sanborn. He held strategy talks with Rutherford B. Hayes and formed Hayes clubs in the Canton area. McKinley's strong effort worked, and he won by 3,300 votes.

❦

THEODORE ROOSEVELT, 18 in October, entered Harvard in the fall focused on leading an Audubon-type career. Right off, other students saw him as a bit eccentric.

Roosevelt passed the second round of Harvard examinations in the spring with no trouble and was admitted on July 3. Charles W. Eliot had been president of Harvard since 1869, the cause of much interest there. Dr. Oliver Wendell Holmes wrote a friend in 1871 that Eliot had turned "the whole university over like a flapjack." Roosevelt soon disliked Eliot, a widespread feeling in Cambridge. He also disliked the rigidity of the class format and later said he learned little at Harvard. His lust for a career as an outdoorsman was dampened by laboratory work, causing him to reconsider his goals.

Roosevelt did not conform in appearance, manner, or views. He was often excited about everything, and he was astonished that many students had little interest in getting an education. Some students found him so eccentric that he was "a good deal of a Joke," one said later. He soon found a kindred spirit—biology student Henry D. Minot of West Roxbury. They would go into the countryside collecting specimens.

❦

WILLIAM HOWARD TAFT, 19 in September, was a student at Yale while his father became a member of President Grant's cabinet. Judge Alphonso Taft was secretary of war from March until May and attorney general for the rest of the year.

❦

WOODROW WILSON, in his 2nd year at Princeton, decided law, maybe even politics, lay ahead. And he became a published essayist.

On June 21 the Reverend Joseph Wilson became editor of Wilmington's *North Carolina Presbyterian*, which enabled him to express his opinions. Woodrow wrote an essay for his father's paper, entitled *Life is a Work Day*, which called service to God a daily need, "not for a parade one day every week, but for constant use in warding off the attacks of the evil one." In a second essay, entitled *Christ's Army*, he discussed warfare against the devil—a battle that offered "no middle course, no neutrality."

Another essay followed in August, *The Bible*. In it, the young author called the Bible "the most perfect rule of life," and said that no nation could prosper unless its laws were founded on biblical principles.

At the start of the September school term, Woodrow decided to pursue a law career. In his essay *The Christian Statesman*, he expressed his view of politics as a divine vocation, writing that Christian faith was "the first requisite for a statesman." He added that a statesman, if not advocating truth, "advocates error."

Wilson turned 20 on December 29.

❦

WARREN G. HARDING, not 11 until November, practiced with his cornet and joined the Caledonia Aeolian Band. He lived in a small north-central Ohio town.

❦

CALVIN COOLIDGE, 4 in July, moved across the street from his birthplace in Plymouth Notch, Vermont, when his father bought a house for $375. The sale included several sheds, a blacksmith's shop, barns, and several acres.

❦

HERBERT HOOVER, 2, lived in Iowa.

September 1: Herbert's sister May was born.

1877
Ulysses S. Grant

President Grant completed his 8 years in office and almost immediately set off on a grand tour of Europe, during which thousands greeted him as a world-class hero.

January–March: The year started with Washington tense as the presidential election dispute dragged toward Inauguration Day. Hayes supporters worried that Grant might be led by Roscoe Conkling, angry at not getting the Republican nomination, into favoring a compromise that would put Tilden in the White House.

At a White House dinner in January, Republican senators talked about an independent election commission, but Grant told George W. Childs, "You see the feeling here. I find them almost universally opposed to anything like an electoral commission." Still, Childs arranged for Grant to meet with Samuel J. Randall, Speaker of the House, and General Robert Patterson, 85, a friend of Andrew Jackson, with influence among southern Democrats. Grant also called in Conkling and Senator Oliver P. Morton to discuss the electoral commission idea.

In the Senate, the Democrats favored the electoral commission bill by a vote of 26 to 1, and the Republicans favored it by a narrower majority of 21 to 16. In the House, the Democratic majority carried the bill with half the Republicans against it.

Grant hesitated, then signed the bill at the urging of Childs. The electoral commission began the count on February 1, and on March 2 announced Hayes the winner. Congress accepted this decision (see **Rutherford B. Hayes** in the opposite column).

Hayes arrived in Washington on March 2 and rushed to the White House to grasp Grant's hands. Grant said, "Governor Hayes, I am glad to welcome you." Hayes took the oath of office in a private ceremony on March 3. The formal inauguration was held on Monday, March 5, because March 4 fell on a Sunday (see **Rutherford B. Hayes**, page 347).

Julia Grant had declined to attend the inauguration and instead gave a luncheon for Hayes after the ceremony. The Grants then said goodbye to the servants, and the Hayes party came out under the portico to wave good-bye.

The Grants stayed at the Hamilton Fish residence in Washington until March 17 when daughter Nellie, who had been visiting the White House, gave birth to Algernon E. V. Sartoris.

May–December: The Grants sailed from Philadelphia for their European tour aboard the *Indiana* on May 17. Banker A. J. Drexel and Wall Street executive Ferdinand Ward financed the trip. Julia was seasick and Grant smoked cigars constantly. The trip to Liverpool took 11 days, and the couple arrived on May 28.

Grant treated the grand tour as a vacation adventure with no fixed schedules. John Russell Young, a reporter for the *New York Herald*, covered the Grants during the trip and eventually published a two-volume work, *Around the World with General Grant.*

From Liverpool, the Grants visited Manchester and London where Grant met the Prince of Wales. In late June the Grants spent a week with Nellie and the baby at her home on the south coast of England. The Grants then moved on to Belgium, Germany, Switzerland, Italy, then backtracked to Copenhagen, Antwerp, and London again, then to Edinburgh, Paris, and a Mediterranean cruise. They spent Christmas in Palermo.

☙❧

RUTHERFORD B. HAYES began his presidency under a cloud of doubt concerning his legitimacy as Democrats charged that the office had been stolen from Tilden by subterfuge and sinister machinations. It took a special, innovative electoral commission to break the deadlock and end the anarchy. Events leading up to the inauguration were unprecedented in America history.

January–March: After weeks of jockeying by Republicans and Democrats, both houses of Congress finally voted for a plan to end the presidential impasse. The idea passed the Senate, 47 to 17, and the House, 191 to 60. Grant signed the measure on January 29.

The plan called for a commission of fifteen men—seven Democrats, seven Republicans, and one "independent." Two Democrats and three Republicans from the Senate, three Democrats and two Republicans from the House, two Republican justices and two Democratic justices, and one "independent" justice were chosen. The designated independent justice was David Davis. Davis declined to serve on the electoral commission, however, because he had just been elected to the Senate from Illinois. Justice Joseph Bradley, a Republican, was substituted as the independent justice.

The electoral commission began counting the votes on February 1. When it reviewed the returns from Florida, Louisiana, South Carolina and Oregon, Bradley voted with the Republicans each time. This process, with Bradley's crucial votes, gave Hayes an 8-to-7 margin in each state dispute, thus ensuring a Hayes victory.

The count was not completed until March 2, when at 4:10 A.M. President of the Senate Thomas White Ferry proclaimed Hayes the winner of the electoral vote, 185 to 184. (Most historians agree that Democrats went along with the results only in return for a Republican promise that federal troops would be withdrawn from all southern states, ending Reconstruction governments in the South and handing control of the South over to the Democrats. The election of Hayes, in essence, signaled the end of Reconstruction and the beginning of white, Democratic domination of the South.)

Hayes, 54, received the news by telegram while aboard a train at Marysville, Pennsylvania. There were 2,000 at the station in Washington when Hayes arrived later in the day. Hayes met with Grant shortly after arriving and later that night attended a state dinner at the White House. After the dinner Hayes was secretly sworn in by Chief Justice Morrison Waite in the Red Room of the White House. This was Grant's idea; he worried that Tilden's men might try to pull off some surprise at the last moment.

On Monday, March 5, at noon Hayes took the oath again from Waite standing on the East Portico before about 30,000 people. Vice President William A. Wheeler was sworn in earlier.

In his address, Hayes pledged to follow the party platform including reform in the patronage system, even though Conkling and Blaine could be heard muttering while the new president was talking. The address covered five topics: the South, civil service reform, monetary policy, foreign affairs, and the disputed election.

Once in office, Hayes announced his cabinet selections: William Evarts of New York as secretary of state, John Sherman of Ohio as secretary of Treasury, George Washington McCrary of Iowa as secretary of war, Charles Devens of Massachusetts as attorney general, David Key of Tennessee as postmaster general, Richard Wig-ginton Thompson of Indiana as secretary of the navy, and Carl Schurz of Missouri as secretary of the Interior.

April: Hayes felt that having federal troops in southern states had become counterproductive to the well-being of African Americans. By executive order on April 3, Hayes told McCrary to remove Union soldiers from the statehouse in Columbia,

The inauguration of Rutherford B. Hayes on March 5, 1877. Hayes's election signaled the end of Reconstruction in the South. (Library of Congress)

South Carolina, and confine them to their encampment area. On April 24, Hayes withdrew troops from New Orleans.

May 6: Chief Crazy Horse and several hundred of his warriors surrendered to army officials at Camp Robinson in Nebraska.

July: Labor unrest erupted in several U.S. cities. On July 14 workers for the Baltimore & Ohio Railroad went on strike. On July 21 militia troops in Philadelphia clashed with railroad strikers in Pittsburgh. On July 26 police and mounted troops attacked a crowd of strikers.

October 15: A 4-month-long pursuit of Chief Joseph ended with his surrender in Montana to General Oliver Howard. "I am tired of fighting," said the Nez Perce chief.

Future Presidents

James A. Garfield was a member of the electoral commission set up early in the year to decide the presidency. He wanted to be Speaker of the House but lost this fight to the Democrats. Later, he wanted to enter the Senate as John Sherman's replacement but was unable or unwilling to promote himself for the office.

January–February: Garfield was at first opposed to the idea of an electoral commission. He talked against the idea on the House floor but reversed himself when he was appointed to the commission.

He wrote to Harmon Austin on February 16 about the commission meetings: "You can hardly imagine the strength of passion which seethes and hisses in this city." In the final votes, Garfield cast his lot with Hayes.

March: Garfield lost his bid for Speaker of the House by just 6 votes. Although now a favorite for John Sherman's Senate seat, Garfield made little effort to go after the seat, instead sitting back and waiting for it to come to him. He wrote in his diary, "I shall [seek] nothing and [let] events take care of themselves."

Hayes wanted to put his friend Stanley Matthews in Sherman's Senate seat; therefore, Hayes wanted Garfield to remain in the House and available to become Speaker when the opportunity arrived again. Garfield was somewhat annoyed by the president's action and on March 11 sent regrets to friends in Columbus who had supported him.

November: Garfield learned from Matthews that he had turned down the president's offer. Hayes asked Garfield to run for the seat, but Garfield told the president it was too late and that he would stay in the House. Relations between the two men now cooled.

&❧

Chester Alan Arthur was asked to resign as collector of the port of New York by President Hayes on the recommendation of Secretary of Treasury John Sherman and the cabinet. This came after a special investigation committee held hearings on customhouse fraud in six major port cities.

April–May: On April 9 the *New York Tribune* revealed that Hayes would investigate the customhouses in New York, New Orleans, Baltimore, Boston, Philadelphia, and San Francisco.

Sherman called Arthur to Washington on April 14 and told him the objectives of the investigation. Three men—two from private life—would investigate each city. Arthur was allowed to pick the third investigator in the case of the New York probe. He selected New York merchant Lawrence Turnure. John Jay, grandson of the jurist, was chairman. J. H. Robinson of the Treasury Department was the third member.

The New York state chamber of commerce had created a committee on custom revenue reform back in October 1876. Arthur was the first witness, appearing on April 23. After the first two sessions Sherman opened proceedings to the press and the public. There were twenty-four open sessions plus several others held in private at the request of witnesses. Ninety men testified. Arthur was somewhat evasive in answering questions on corruption.

The findings were released at the end of May. The committee found gross overstaffing, suggesting that a 10-percent cut could easily be made. Some workers agreed that cuts would lead to more efficient work, and some division leaders said that new workers sent to them often were incapable of doing the work. Accounting errors ran to $1.5 million per year. Many clerks avoided work. Bribery and corruption were everywhere.

The committee recommended a 20-percent manpower slash along with the abolition of some positions. Sherman worried that the report would splinter the party, and he himself had sought favors from Arthur. Arthur said he could cut only 12 percent of his workers. President Hayes was happy with the report, and Sherman ordered a 20-percent cut but said nothing about political influence and left it to Arthur to trim the excess baggage.

The New York state chamber, however, believed the Jay report to be mild and called for a much larger overhaul of the system, suggesting that Arthur could not make the reforms. Arthur offered a written reply, belittling the testimony, and said most complaints concerned events that happened prior to his term in office. Sherman gave Arthur until the end of June to shape things up.

June: Arthur took no hand in the distasteful details of firing workers and complained bitterly to the press about events. Eight deputy collectors were fired.

On June 22, Hayes ordered federal workers to stop taking part in political organizations.

July: Jay issued a second report on July 4 criticizing the top officials of the customhouse and citing great "carelessness" by these managers. The reformers told Hayes that Arthur had to go. Sherman told Hayes on July 5 that he had met with Arthur, who needed assurances from the president that he could stay on the job.

September–December: President Hayes advised Sherman that he wanted Arthur's resignation and that the public would benefit from a wholesale change in the customhouse.

Sherman called Arthur to Washington on September 6 but inexplicably made Hayes's private decision on the question public before Arthur could be officially notified by mail.

Arthur gave Sherman a tart reply by letter, saying that he had read all about it in the newspapers. Arthur then stalled a week before going to Washington.

The press then broke the story that Theodore Roosevelt, Sr. would become the Collector. A special session of Congress was called in October to consider new presidential nominations. Before Roosevelt's name was put before Congress, Sherman again asked Arthur to resign. Arthur refused and President Hayes sent Roosevelt's nomination to the Senate on October 24.

Senator Roscoe Conkling, Arthur's friend and supporter, was chairman of the key commerce committee which would pass nominations to the full senate. On November 15, Conkling asked Hayes for all evidence concerning Arthur's removal. Arthur then sent Conkling a written rebuttal to the charges on November 27.

On November 30 the commerce committee of the senate unanimously rejected Roosevelt's nomination.

Arthur was elated and wrote Conkling on December 13: "I cannot tell you how gratified I am at the splendid victory you have won."

ഇൻ

GROVER CLEVELAND, at 40, was a bachelor lawyer in Buffalo, New York. He was instrumental in starting a summer sports club on Beaver Island on the Niagara River. Members would fish from the clubhouse and take a steam launch back to the city. Being a bachelor, Cleveland for practical purposes acted as club manager. Cleveland's law partner Lyman K. Bass came down with tuberculosis and moved to Colorado Springs.

ഇൻ

BENJAMIN HARRISON'S reputation was enhanced as a result of several events. President Hayes briefly considered him for a cabinet position. Harrison's quick handling of volunteers to prevent a railroad strike from turning violent in Indianapolis was praised. The death of Senator Oliver Perry Morton, the leading Republican in Indiana, helped increase Harrison's stature as Indiana's brightest political star.

January–March: A place in Hayes's cabinet seemed a possibility for Harrison. Hayes wrote in his diary on January 17 that Harrison rated a cabinet spot, perhaps secretary of the navy. Murat Halstead, editor of the *Cincinnati Commercial*, told Harrison the job was his if Morton approved. Harrison, however, admitted he was not a follower of Morton. Instead, Morton pressed for Richard W. Thompson for the position, and Hayes agreed to the selection in March.

June–July: In June the Harrisons went to the White House to meet with President Hayes. When Harrison returned home on July 13 the railroad strikes that were brewing across the country hit Indiana.

The worry in Indianapolis was that only 13 soldiers were available to guard the U.S. arsenal there.

The strike reached Indianapolis on July 23 as Harrison and other lawyers met to discuss the issue. The governor decided a hands-off policy was best. A volunteer citizen group calling themselves the Committee of Public Safety was established to help keep control of the strikers. Harrison wired Washington that he had 200 men ready to protect government property.

Harrison and Albert Porter met with the strikers all day on July 25 and agreed that wages were too low. Harrison managed to cool hotheads who wanted to send the militia against the strikers. "I don't propose to go out and shoot down my neighbors," Harrison said.

Harrison once made the strikers angry by asking, "Have you a right, while you are breaking the law, to appear before a committee of law-abiding citizens." Then Harrison cooled their anger by adding that he would try to get a pay raise if the men went back to work.

A committee of mediation issued findings, read by Porter, who said that the grievances had received a public airing and, "This is the only good such a rebellion can accomplish."

Governor Godlove S. Orth was slow to call up the militia. Several strike leaders were arrested, but Harrison appeared for them and asked that they not be punished. The judge discharged the men.

August–December: The strike crisis helped build Harrison's prestige. But Harrison sidestepped the claim that he was running against Morton and added on August 4 that public life "is not attractive."

Morton suffered a stroke in San Francisco and was taken to Richmond, Indiana, where President Hayes paid a visit. The press called Morton old and broken, yet he was only 54. Harrison turned 44 on August 20.

Morton took a turn for the worse and died on November 1. Harrison served on four committees to honor the senator's memory.

℠℗

WILLIAM MCKINLEY, the freshman Congressman from Ohio, moved to Washington, D.C., to take his seat in the House of Representatives. McKinley had an advantage over the other newcomers to Congress—he was a friend of President Hayes.

The McKinleys moved into Ebbitt House where the children of President Hayes were frequent visitors. During the year, Ida McKinley spent 2 weeks in the White House looking after the Hayes children while their parents were out of town.

McKinley, 34 in January, was a friend of James Garfield as well. The Garfield boys were also frequent visitors at Ebbitt House.

℠℗

THEODORE ROOSEVELT, 19, continued with classes at Harvard. He also published, at his own expense, a pamphlet entitled *The Summer Birds of the Adirondacks in Franklin County.*

Theodore was fastidious in dress. Students saw him as different, energetic, curious, and talkative. So talkative in fact that he would interrupt the professors, usually in science class.

Roosevelt went to the Adirondacks in June with Harry Minot to collect bugs and birds. Theodore had an ear for birdcalls. The two then published a pamphlet, which was more like a catalog. Their study area was north of Lake Placid at the northern end of the Adirondack Mountains. The catalog included some fine writing describing birds and nature. Later he wrote *Notes on Some of the Birds of Oyster Bay.*

℠℗

WILLIAM HOWARD TAFT, a student at Yale, was tapped by Skull and Bones, a prestigious secret society founded by his father, Alphonso. The honor normally went to athletes and intellectuals. Taft, 20, felt it was the best aspect of life at Yale, and he attended meetings for years afterwards when possible.

℠℗

WOODROW WILSON, 21 in December, become editor of the campus newspaper at Princeton and gradually became interested in politics. Wilson, as a junior in the fall, became temporary managing editor of the *Princetonian* and before long was unanimously elected editor. He wrote about drama, politics, history, and music.

℠℗

WARREN G. HARDING took a trip to Chicago with the Aeolian Band, his first venture outside of Ohio. The trip was tied to the opening of the Erie Railroad. Warren was 12 in November.

℠℗

CALVIN COOLIDGE started school in December now that he was 5. The schoolhouse in rural Plymouth Notch, Vermont, was a stone building close to the family home. Calvin was one of twenty-five students between the ages of 5 and 18. Study included the usual history, geography, algebra, writing, and reading.

℠℗

HERBERT HOOVER, 3, lived in West Branch, Iowa, which now had two hotels, a dentist, and a doctor but no saloons.

1878
Rutherford B. Hayes

The president spent much of the first part of the year dealing with the situation in New York involving port collector Chester A. Arthur. The legitimacy of Hayes's presidency was also questioned again.

January–February: Secretary of Treasury John Sherman made corruption charges against Arthur and Alphonso B. Cornell during an executive session of the Senate. Senator Roscoe Conkling of New York asked that the charges be kept secret.

Hayes followed up on January 31, charging that the two "made the Customhouse a center of partisan political management. The Customhouses should be a business office." Hayes believed that appointees should not be politically active, as Arthur and Cornell had been. Hayes forbade federal officeholders from becoming involved with managing party politics: "Office holders must attend to the public business and not become organized political machines.... If they participate actively in politics, people resent their interference."

The charges against Arthur were neglect of duties, letting deputies run offices, spending too much money, inefficiency, and retaining on the payroll political hacks who did no work.

At the same time that Sherman was leveling charges against Arthur, he was also asking for favors, seeking jobs for his friends. The secretary of Treasury wrote several letters to Arthur asking for the jobs. Later, Arthur leaked the letters to the press (see **Chester Alan Arthur**, page 351).

Hayes hoped that Arthur and Cornell would resign voluntarily. Neither man did. Under the Tenure of Office Act, Hayes could not fire the two while Congress was in session because the Senate approved both appointments. By this time, Hayes had decided that both would go as soon as Congress adjourned in June.

Hayes decided to replace Arthur with Theodore Roosevelt Sr., but with his death in February, Hayes went with his second choice, Edwin A. Merritt.

With currency values at their lowest point since the Civil War, Congress passed the Bland–Allison Act. The law would require the federal government to make monthly purchases and mint between $2 million and $4 million worth of silver. Hayes vetoed the bill on February 23. He did not think silver could be kept on par with gold: "I cannot consent to a measure which stains our credit." On February 28, Hayes's veto was overridden.

May: Conkling linked up with some Democrats in Congress to reopen the disputed election of 1876. Conkling, upset with Hayes over the charges leveled against Arthur and Cornell, saw this as a way to get back at the president. Clarkston N. Potter of New York was made chairman of the committee to look at election returns from South Carolina and Florida. The plot backfired when Democratic attempts to use corruption to determine vote totals were uncovered.

July: Soon after Congress adjourned, Hayes fired Arthur. He was replaced by Merritt, who took over even though he did not have Senate confirmation. Arthur felt that he might get his job back because the Senate could still reject Merritt's appointment.

November: Democrats made significant gains in the midterm elections, regaining control of the House and the Senate. Cornell, to Hayes's consternation, was elected governor of New York.

President Rutherford B. Hayes *(Library of Congress)*

Hayes's hopes for the future of African Americans in the South were shaken by the election returns. More Democrats were elected from the South. Joseph H. Rainey, an African American congressman from South Carolina, warned Hayes that Whites were resorting to intimidation and violence to prevent Blacks from voting.

Hayes confessed to the *National Republican* newspaper on November 13, "I am reluctantly forced to admit that [his southern policy] was a failure."

December: In his December 2 message to Congress, Hayes talked of "southern outrages" in the treatment of African Americans and said that some winners of the most recent election should not be seated in Congress.

Former Presidents

Ulysses S. Grant's world tour continued, featuring visits with Pope Leo XIII, Otto von Bismarck, Czar Alexander II, and Emperor Franz-Joseph. Grant's tour included stops in Egypt, Jerusalem, Constantinople, Rome, Florence, Venice, Norway, St. Petersburg, Vienna, Madrid, Barcelona, Berlin, and India. Grant, 56, wrote to Elihu Washburne in October: "It is bliss to be out of the U.S. ... at a time when every bad element [is winning]."

Future Presidents

James A. Garfield believed President Hayes was hurting the Republican Party with some of his political decisions and that many in the party were losing faith in the president. Garfield's opinion, expressed on February 28, was that Hayes was "without a friend" in Congress.

In the fall elections, Garfield survived the Democratic surge by retaining his seat in Congress. He did this despite Ohio Democrats gerrymandering his district once again by removing Garfield's home city of Portage from the district.

With the Democrats in control of Congress and all its committees, Garfield's workload lightened significantly. However, his chance of becoming Speaker of the House would have to wait until Republicans could regain control of the House. Garfield, 47, now had time for some simple pleasures, such as reading and the theater.

                                                    ℘©℘

Chester Alan Arthur battled with President Hayes for most of the year in an attempt to retain his position as collector of the port of New York. Arthur refused to resign, even after Hayes had named a new appointee.

January–March: Secretary of Treasury John Sherman, who had pushed for Arthur's ouster in 1877, now badgered Arthur to give his friends jobs. For the first 3 months of the year, Sherman kept asking Arthur for favors. Arthur turned Sherman down on March 2, pointing out that no vacancies existed since reforms went into effect.

Hayes wanted Arthur to resign his position. He charged that Arthur was using his post as "a center of partisan political management" and accused Arthur of neglecting his duties, inefficiency, and overspending. Because Hayes could not fire Arthur while the Senate was in session, he decided to wait and make his move once Congress adjourned. In the meantime, Arthur leaked Sherman's letters to the press, causing great embarrassment to the secretary.

April–May: A special agent of the Treasury Department claimed in April that fraud in the New York Customhouse amounted to $42,000. Arthur was accused of ignoring the corruption going on around him.

The Meredith Investigating Committee started looking at the practice of the New York Customhouse again on May 15 after complaints from merchants.

July: President Hayes moved when Congress was not in session. He fired Arthur on July 11 and named Edwin A. Merritt to be the new collector. Hayes believed Merritt would have time to show an efficient operation of the customhouse before Congress returned in December. Arthur felt that there was a possibility of keeping his job, since Merritt was taking over the office without Senate approval. Until then, Arthur refused to acknowledge Merritt as the new collector.

November–December: In New York, unlike much of the country, Republicans carried the state in the fall elections, winning the governorship and other key posts.

When Congress convened on December 2, the New York Customhouse was the talk of the town. Since July the House Ways and Means Committee had also made an investigation. Sherman was ready to resign his post if the Senate refused to confirm Merritt. Senator Roscoe Conkling, a staunch supporter of Arthur, sat on the nominating committee. Hearings on Merritt's appointment, however, would not be over until early 1879.

෨෬

GROVER CLEVELAND, 41, was a lawyer in Buffalo, New York. Discontent was growing over a ring of corrupt aldermen from both parties then running the city. Cleveland helped elect a new mayor of Buffalo, Solomon Scheu, an honest Democrat and wealthy brewer.

෨෬

BENJAMIN HARRISON's father died, but perhaps just as trying was the theft of his body from his grave. The theft helped bring to light how medical schools used thieves to secure cadavers for research and instruction.

May–June: John Scott Harrison, son of President William Henry Harrison, died suddenly on May 26 of a heart attack at North Bend, Ohio, at the age of 73. He was buried at Congregational Green Cemetery near his wife and his father. The body was put in a metallic casket with marble slabs. A week earlier, body snatchers had stolen the body of Augustus Devin, John Scott's 23-year-old nephew, from a grave in the same cemetery. Because of this, two watchmen were hired to keep an eye on John Scott's grave.

John Harrison, Benjamin's brother, decided to search for Devin and went to the Ohio Medical College in Cincinnati at 3 A.M. with a search warrant and a police officer. Instead he discovered the body of his father hanging from a rope. Newspapers got wind of the finding.

At the same time, Harrison relatives in North Bend discovered the empty grave of John Scott and rushed to Cincinnati. Benjamin's brother Carter, on seeing John, said, "John, they've stolen father's body"—just as John said to Carter, "I've found father's body."

As more details became known, Benjamin's son Russell released them to the press. Carter visited the site of the finding and met with Dr. William W. Seely, professor of clinical ophthalmology and otology, who remarked that the affair "matters little, since it would all be the same on the day of resurrection." This remark angered the Harrisons and the public.

A. Q. Marshall, a janitor at the medical school, was arrested for the theft. He was bailed out of jail by the school's faculty, which further angered the public. Dean Roberts Bartholow issued a statement on June 1: "Under existing circumstances bodies necessary for the instruction of medical students must be stolen."

In an open letter to the citizens of Cincinnati, Harrison admitted the value of anatomical research but claimed the faculty's denial of complicity was "hypocrisy" and described how his father's body had been found "hanging by the neck, like that of a dog, in a pit of a medical college."

John Scott's body was reinterred in a vault at Spring Grove Cemetery near Cincinnati.

Another suspect in the case was Charles O. Morton of Toledo, who, helped by his wife, had a contract with the Ohio Medical College to produce so many bodies per year.

Harrison returned to his own law practice while the Cincinnati newspaper searched for additional facts and kept the story going all through June. The public learned that American medical schools operated with the help of people who robbed graves and that Cincinnati was a shipping center for "dead traffic" to cities as far away as Fort Wayne, Indiana, and Ann Arbor, Michigan. (Augustus Devin's body was later found near Ann Arbor. Eventually, a grand jury indicted both Morton and Marshall. A law was passed in 1880 to help colleges obtain legitimate sources of cadavers.)

August–December: Harrison stumped for Republicans throughout the election season. He began in Richmond, Indiana, on August 10 following a heat wave. History, he said, would show that "the Democratic Party had a stronger instinct for the wrong side of every question than any other political organization the world ever saw." He attacked Senator Daniel W. Voorhees on the issue of liquidating southern war claims. Voorhees had been appointed by Governor James Williams to fill Oliver Perry Morton's seat.

But the Democrats won big in Indiana. Harrison wrote his friend Margaret Peltz in St. Louis, "The Democrats have beaten us again—more badly than before."

ട്ര

WILLIAM MCKINLEY, 35, came to regret his vote for the Bland–Allison Act in opposition to his friend President Hayes. But constituents in Ohio favored this vote that would later prove an embarrassment to him. He never voted for silver again. He later admitted his ignorance on the silver issue at the time he took his stand.

In Congress, McKinley was always the practical politician, willing to compromise and to concede points. He once told a group in Canton, "We cannot always do what is best, but we can do what is practical at the time." McKinley supported labor rather than corporations, favored high moral principles, and favored restrictions on immigration and a protectionist trade policy.

ട്ര

THEODORE ROOSEVELT, 20 in October, was a student at Harvard in Cambridge, Massachusetts, when his father died.

January–February: Theodore Roosevelt Sr. was a player in the feud between President Hayes and Chester A. Arthur. Hayes had selected Roosevelt to take over the New York Customhouse as soon as Arthur was dismissed. However, Theodore Sr. died on February 10 at the age of 46.

Theodore Sr. had a malignant tumor of the bowel that put him in great pain. Theodore Jr. rushed by train to New York but arrived too late. The son wrote in his diary on February 12 of the "terrible three days" leading to the burial. Theodore Jr. felt he owed it to his father "to study well and live like a brave Christian gentleman."

September–December: Theodore returned to Harvard for the fall semester. Theodore's friend Harry Minot moved on to law school, and now Richard Saltonstall became Roosevelt's closest friend at Harvard.

Saltonstall invited Roosevelt to the Saltonstall home in Chestnut Hill in October, soon after the start of his junior year. Next door to the home of Leverett Saltonstall was the home of a Saltonstall cousin, George Cabot Lee. Lee's daughter, Alice Hathaway Lee, 17, was a constant companion of Rose Saltonstall, Richard's sister. One evening Alice came over, and Roosevelt fell in love with her at first sight.

In November, Roosevelt wrote to his sister Corinne that he had "gone out walking with Miss Rose Saltonstall and Miss Alice Lee." In December he escorted Alice around Harvard Yard.

As for his studies, Roosevelt was abandoning the idea of becoming a naturalist because the school was not encouraging and he found there was too much indoor lab work and that there were too few outdoor field trips.

ട്ര

WILLIAM HOWARD TAFT graduated from Yale, took up the study of law, and became a newspaper reporter.

June: As senior class orator, Taft gave a speech on June 25 that he titled "The Professional and Political Prospects of the College Grad." The talk actually dealt largely with corruption in the country and the centralization of government. He said the Republican Party had "lost its grip on the affections of the people" and added, "It is to be an age when there are no political giants because of the absence of emergencies to create them."

Commencement was on June 27; Taft ranked 2nd out of 132 graduates.

July–August: During the summer months Will read law in the office of his father, Alphonso. He told his aunt that legal study wasn't "as pleasant as one's fancy might paint it."

September–December: Taft could have gone to Yale Law School like his father, or to Columbia as brother Charles did and brother Harry was to do. Instead he entered the Cincinnati Law School in September for the fall term. Classes usually ran 2 hours per day, which gave the students time to hold down jobs. Taft landed work as a reporter for Murat Halstead's *Cincinnati Commercial*. He was assigned to the courts.

ട്ര

WOODROW WILSON, 22 in December, was a student at Princeton in New Jersey. By the end of his junior year he had dropped in class standing from 20th to 37th.

As a senior he was selected by the Whig Society to debate Clio Hall, but he refused because he would have had to defend universal suffrage.

As student editor of the campus newspaper, most of what he wrote concerned extracurricular doings. Wilson urged support of athletic teams, was secretary of the football association, and briefly was president of the baseball association.

ട്ര

WARREN G. HARDING lost a brother and sister to jaundice but gained a new brother in this year. Harding's grandfather also died, leaving a small amount of money to Tyron. Harding befriended Sherwood Anderson, the future writer, when the Anderson family moved to Caledonia, Ohio.

March 11: Harding's brother George Tyron was born.

November 9: His brother Charles Alexander and sister Eleanor Priscilla died within hours of each other. The boy was 4, and the girl was 6. Warren turned 13 this month.

ട്ര

CALVIN COOLIDGE, age 6, lost his grandfather, who earlier had deeded 40 acres called Lime Kiln to Calvin and expected the boy eventually to farm the land. Property was also left to

Calvin's father John, increasing his holdings at Plymouth Notch, Vermont.

∽∾

HERBERT HOOVER, 4, moved into a larger house closer to town when his father sold his blacksmith shop, house, and land on May 25.

Earlier in the year Herbert stepped on a hot iron at the blacksmith shop, causing a permanent scar.

His mother became secretary of the Young People's Christian Association.

1879
Rutherford B. Hayes

President Hayes had fairly smooth sailing during his third year in office. Yet he and Lucy sat down one night and agreed that it was indeed fortunate for them that the one-term pledge had been made. Retirement at Spiegal Grove was looking enticing. Politically, with Democrats controlling Congress, a familiar sequence took place several times: Democrats would pass legislation, Hayes would veto it, and Congress would be unable to override.

February–March: Congress passed a bill restricting Chinese immigration. The number of Chinese in the United States had grown dramatically because of the railroads, where they were used as cheap labor.

Curtis wrote to Hayes on February 21 that the Chinese exclusion bill was "an act of bad faith [and a] flagrant breach of the national faith … that the Republican Party should [not] shut the gates of America."

The California Constitutional Convention asked Hayes to sign the bill. He vetoed it on March 1 and was denounced in the West.

In March states rights southerners in Congress tried to repeal the fourth section of the first article of the Constitution, which provided that that Congress could alter regulations regarding the time and place for elections. When Hayes opposed the idea, Congress threatened to refuse appropriations for government functions.

Hayes said he would not be coerced. Hayes saw the issue as a resurrection of pre–Civil War "Ultra" states rights opposition to the central government. The Democrats believed that if they could repeal election laws in order to control the vote in the South, it would become necessary for Republicans to carry New York in order to win any election.

April–May: Congress passed an army appropriations bill with a rider that would have prevented the army from keeping the peace at the polls. In his veto message of April 29, Hayes said that everyone had a right to cast an "unintimidated ballot" and have it "honestly counted." On May 1 the Republicans sustained the veto.

When Hayes vetoed a similar measure on May 12, James

Garfield wrote to him: "No speech or paper" ever "will strike so deep into the heart and minds of American people" as this veto message.

A meeting was held in Paris in May to discuss a canal for Central America. Ferdinand de Lesseps proposed a Panama Canal that could be built by 1892 for $240 million. U.S. Navy representatives attended the meeting but preferred a Nicaragua canal.

November–December: In the November elections Republicans won everywhere except in New York, where the Conkling machine was derailed. This made Hayes, 57, happy.

In a cabinet change, George W. McCrary, secretary of war, was replaced by Alexander Ramsey of Minnesota on December 12.

Also on December 12, Benjamin A. Bidlock, U.S. minister to New Granada (Colombia and Panama), signed a commercial treaty between the governments. The United States received the right of way across the isthmus to build a canal. In return the United States guaranteed the neutrality of the isthmus and the sovereignty of New Granada.

Hayes joined party leaders to talk over presidential prospects for 1880 and on December 26 made a trip to Philadelphia to try to persuade Grant not to run. He was fond of Grant but did not think a third term was a good idea.

Former Presidents

ULYSSES S. GRANT completed his world tour and in the fall returned to the United States where he visited several cities. The seeds of a possible third term as president were probably planted this year.

The Grants began the year in India and Burma, then continued on to Singapore, Bangkok, and Saigon. They saw Canton, Shanghai, Peking, and Tokyo, meeting the emperors of China and Japan.

Unable to get a ship to Australia, they instead returned directly to San Francisco. They reached Yosemite, a park created during the Grant presidency, on November 1. They moved on to Oregon and Vancouver, Washington, where General Oliver Howard greeted them.

In Sacramento, a crowd of 20,000 greeted Grant. A dinner at the Palace Hotel in San Francisco put on by Senator William Sharon featured plates engraved in gold. Grant reached Chicago on November 13 as the Army of the Tennessee held its annual reunion. There he met Samuel L. Clemens, better known as Mark Twain, and thus began a friendship that later took the Grants to Twain's home in Hartford, Connecticut.

Grant reached Philadelphia on December 16 and was treated to a procession on Chestnut Street that lasted 4 hours. His American travels produced welcomes that were a little less enthusiastic than he had received elsewhere. At every turn he saw party leaders and to each he would say, "I am not a candidate for any office."

Future Presidents

JAMES A. GARFIELD was seen as presidential timber by the *Cincinnati Commercial* following a sensational speech on the House floor condemning Democrats over voting procedures in the South. The speech received national attention. Garfield was also "floor manager" for the Hayes administration in defending veto actions by the president, which made Garfield a virtual House spokesman for Hayes.

March: The Democrats had been critical of the use of federal troops at polling places in the South. In Garfield's March 29 speech, "Revolution in Congress," he departed from his usual dignified manner to rush up and down the aisle. He charged the Democrats with a revolution against the Constitution and the government. Well-wishers mobbed Garfield when he was finished, and the House suspended business.

The speech made a hit everywhere. The *Cincinnati Commercial* on March 30 said, "If the entire nation is as completely electrified and aroused as ... here in Cincinnati, it would not be surprising if you [Garfield] would be called upon to accept the nomination in 1880."

May 10: Garfield was proud of the faith Hayes had in him. He wrote his wife, Lucretia: "I spent an hour with the President today on the veto for the new bill which the Democrats have passed, restricting the use of the army. I think I have never had so much intellectual and personal influence over him as now. He is fully in line with his party."

September–November: Hayes had hinted that the way to the presidency was through a governorship first. Garfield did not want to be governor of Ohio. Charles Foster, a millionaire friend from Fostoria, ran for governor on the Republican ticket. He and Garfield crisscrossed the state on a speaking campaign. Foster won the election, and Democratic losses in the legislature meant that the senator replacing Democrat Allen Thurman would be a Republican.

Garfield's Republican rivals for the Senate seat were former governor William Dennison, Alphonso Taft, and Stanley Matthews. Garfield allowed Charles Henry to set up a Senate campaign headquarters in a Columbus hotel but with tight restrictions, especially on liquor. By November, 52 of 90 Republican legislators favored Garfield.

౸౮

CHESTER ALAN ARTHUR'S retirement from the customhouse became permanent after an ugly airing of dirty linen in the Senate, where Roscoe Conkling fought a bitter battle in an attempt to save Arthur's job and embarrass President Hayes.

January: The confirmation hearings for Edwin Merritt began. Secretary of Treasury John Sherman's letter to the Senate outlined the reasons for Arthur's removal from the customhouse. Sherman summed up the findings of two investigative committees. He then pointed out that in the 6 months since Edwin Merritt took over the New York Customhouse, he had saved the government $245,636.15. Sherman added that to put Arthur back in charge would "require this business to be performed by persons in hostility to [the administration]."

Arthur made his formal reply to Sherman on January 27, and it dripped venom. "My suspension [is a] violation of every principle of justice," Arthur said.

Sherman's political life was in the balance when he recited every bit of evidence against Arthur, of "gross abuses ... bribes and gratuities." At an executive session of the Senate, Thomas F. Bayard, a Democratic senator, made the plea that a president must have the right to select his subordinates and that there was cause for Arthur's removal.

Merritt was confirmed, 33 to 24, with 13 Republicans joining 20 Democrats to vote for confirmation.

February–March: In February, Arthur was made permanent president of the Republican Central Committee. He told a meeting of the group that the gubernatorial race in New York would impact the 1880 election.

At this point Arthur returned to his law practice. Friends offered him plenty of work, and he was hardly pressed for funds thanks to the huge income he had raked in during his customhouse days.

June–October: Although Arthur was mentioned in the gubernatorial race, his old customhouse subordinate Alphonso Cornell passionately wanted the office and won the Republican nomination. Arthur was in charge of the Cornell campaign and enjoyed it, talking of being freed from the "drudgery" of the customhouse.

As the campaign heated up in the fall, the Hayes administration reluctantly backed Cornell. In the height of irony, Arthur escorted Sherman on stage at a huge rally in New York City on October 27. Sherman said that the election of Cornell was of the "highest national importance, and if I had a thousand votes ... would all be for him."

Arthur, 50, had his headquarters in the swank Fifth Avenue Hotel, mixing with the wealthy as he had done for 20 years.

In November, Cornell was elected governor of New York.

Secretary of the Treasury John Sherman
(Library of Congress)

ಬಲ

GROVER CLEVELAND, 42, was a lawyer in Buffalo, New York. A prominent member of the Buffalo Bar, he was elected president of the association.

ಬಲ

BENJAMIN HARRISON, the Indianapolis trial lawyer, was nominated for a U.S. Senate seat, but the Indiana legislature voted in favor of Daniel Voorhees. Harrison's legal work ranged from election fraud and railroad law to a murder case.

February: The Indiana legislature selected Voorhees over Harrison for a U.S. Senate seat by a vote of 83 to 60.

June 28: Harrison was working on a murder case when President Hayes picked him to be one of seven members of the new Mississippi River Commission, a body created by Congress to work on problems related to flooding and improved navigation. Harrison declined until he received a private note from Hayes. Harrison would serve on the river commission for 20 months.

July–August: Harrison, while working on railroad cases, began to work on a constitution for the Indiana Bar Association and was appointed a delegate to the national meeting in Saratoga, New York, in August.

The Harrisons left Indianapolis on August 1 for Yonkers. On the way, Harrison met with President Hayes on August 4.

ಬಲ

WILLIAM MCKINLEY supported the president's veto of the appropriations bill on April 18, saying federal supervision of southern elections did not interfere with states rights. McKinley, 36, warned the South against "ballot box stuffing … fraud at the polls, intimidation."

McKinley and Ida often went to the Garfield home for dinner and to play cards. The men became close, and Garfield found McKinley could keep a secret.

ಬಲ

THEODORE ROOSEVELT began a book on the naval war of 1812, climbed Mount Katahdin in Maine, and took a beating in a boxing match that was covered by the *New York Times*. His romance with Alice Lee continued along an uneven course. He proposed to Alice on Class Day, June 20, but she stalled him for the rest of the year.

He was still undecided about a career. Roosevelt, 21 in October, wrote in his diary that he would "either pursue a science course, or else study law preparatory to going into public life." He was concerned that a career as a naturalist might mean an additional 3 years of study in Europe.

Roosevelt was president of Alpha Delta Phi and an honorary member of the glee club. He also was Phi Beta Kappa.

ಬಲ

WILLIAM HOWARD TAFT, still attending Cincinnati Law School, received his introduction to politics while seeking delegates in Cincinnati for his father's unsuccessful bid for governor of Ohio. Charles Foster won the nomination over Alphonso Taft and others. Will believed it was because of "superior" experience, money, and finesse.

In the course of seeking delegates, Will one day administered a beating to the editor of a scandal sheet newspaper that had made malicious comments about Alphonso.

Taft, 22 in September, joined the Literary Club of Cincinnati. For them he prepared a paper: "Crime and Education."

ಬಲ

WOODROW WILSON finished his senior year at Princeton as a class leader, a good writer, a skilled debater, and an orator. For the fall term he entered the University of Virginia Law School.

Before leaving Princeton, Wilson, 22, reached an ambitious "solemn covenant" with his best friend, classmate Charles A. Talcott. Their idea was to obtain knowledge in order to obtain power; become persuasive in order to lead. The covenant was a pledge to a political career, while working toward Christian principles.

Wilson turned 23 at the end of December.

ಬಲ

WARREN G. HARDING, although not 14 until November, had reached a height of 6 feet.

October 21: Once again there were six children in the family living in Caledonia, Ohio, when a sister, Phoebe Caroline, was born. She was always called Caroline because the mother was Phoebe. Later she would change the spelling to Carolyn.

ಬಲ

CALVIN COOLIDGE lived in a quiet rural backwater in south-central Vermont among the Green Mountains. Calvin, 7 in July, would rise before dawn, wash in cold water, keep the wood box filled when fires were needed, lead the cattle to pasture, and feed the chickens.

ಬಲ

HERBERT HOOVER, 5, caused a stir when he put a stick in hot tar causing a great cloud of black smoke that brought the fire department and everyone in town running. The scared boy never confessed his role for 30 years.

The incident on December 23 "caused much excitement among our people," the West Branch, Iowa, newspaper reported.

1880
Rutherford B. Hayes

The President's fourth year in office was generally a peaceful one, leading earlier critics to agree that Hayes's quiet leadership had been good for the country after the turmoil and graft of the Grant era. Hayes also became the first president to tour the Pacific Coast. President Hayes, for the most part, remained on the sidelines during the presidential campaign. His final year in office turned out to be a fairly quiet one.

February: The Panama Canal became an issue early in the year. Hayes was a believer in the Panama Canal, but only if it was built and operated under American control. He wrote in his diary: "The policy [of the United States concerning a canal] is either a canal under American control or no canal at all." Congress agreed but wanted Ferdinand de Lesseps to build it.

Hayes ordered the establishment of naval stations as coaling stations on both the Pacific and Atlantic sides of Nicaragua, a strategic location in light of the canal talks. Congress, however, did not support this plan.

June: Republicans met in Chicago June 2 to 5 and 7 to 8 and nominated James A. Garfield for president and Chester Alan Arthur for vice president (see **James A. Garfield**, page 357, and **Chester Alan Arthur**, page 358).

Hayes said the Garfield nomination was "the best that was possible." He added, "What other convention in all our history can show as much good and as little harm?"

Democrats met in Cincinnati, Ohio, June 22 to 24 and nominated General Winfield Scott Hancock for president and William Hayden English of Indiana for vice president.

August–November: Hayes and Lucy left Washington on August 26. They rested at Spiegal Grove for a week, where they celebrated Lucy's forty-ninth birthday. Aboard the presidential train to California were two sons of the Hayes's, General William T. Sherman, and several other dignitaries.

Hayes gave a major speech on the steps of the capitol in Sacramento. In it he said that California, Oregon, Washington, and Alaska—then with a population of a million and a half—could support 50 million. Touching on the issue of Asian labor, Hayes said all would be well if Whites would "stand on that great principle of equal rights of all men."

The party reached San Francisco in early September, and Oregon by stagecoach later in the month. Lucy wrote in her diary of the "magnificent scenery, grand majestic trees, and luscious fruits." The itinerary included going down the Columbia to Walla Walla, then backtracking to Puget Sound to catch a ship for San Francisco, where they arrived on October 18.

Hayes, 58, visited Yosemite and Los Angeles before returning to Chicago via Tucson, Santa Fe, and Topeka. Before returning to Washington on November 6, Hayes stopped in Fremont, Ohio, to vote on November 1. Garfield defeated Hancock to win the presidency.

December: Hayes's final message to Congress repeated his request to retire greenbacks and stop minting silver coins that were not the equivalent of the gold dollar. Hayes also urged improvements in the army and navy. In addition, Hayes urged Congress to investigate frauds committed against Black voters and asked for more funds for Black schools. He also called for further civil service reform.

Hayes named William Burnham Woods of Georgia to the Supreme Court on December 21.

Former Presidents

Ulysses S. Grant barely missed obtaining a third-term nomination at the Republican national convention. Julia was sorely upset, as she desperately wanted to live in the White House again.

January–March: Grant and Julia spent much time early in the year traveling. They spent most of January in Florida and traveled to Cuba in February. Mexico was the next stop in March.

Thoughts of a third term slowly germinated in Grant. He wrote to Elihi Washburne on February 2: "All that I want is that the government rule should remain in the hands of those who saved the Union until all the questions growing out of the war are forever settled. I would much rather that any one of ten … should be President rather than that I should have it." A month later he qualified the situation a little by saying that he would take the nomination if the Union veterans thought "my chances are better [than others]."

June: Grant, 58, was anxious before the Republican convention began in Chicago. He left all maneuvering and organization to Roscoe Conkling. Grant remained at Galena close to the convention scene in Chicago, where Conkling made a stunning, memorable nomination speech for his hero. On the first ballot, Grant led Blaine, 304 to 284.

At this point, Julia urged her husband to rush to Chicago and make a personal appearance to swing the pendulum. Grant chastised her for suggesting such an aggressive, unprecedented move.

In subsequent voting, Grant's strength flowed between 313 at the top to 302 at the bottom. Grant had 306 votes on the thirty-sixth and final ballot to Garfield's 399. About this time in Galena, Grant said, "My friends have not been honest with me. I can't afford to be defeated. They should not have placed me in nomination unless they felt perfectly sure of my success."

Grant was soon to say, "I felt no disappointment at the result of the Chicago convention. In fact I felt much relieved."

August–October: The Grants went to Colorado in August to inspect some mines with the idea of making investments. At Gunnison on August 5, he received a letter from Garfield suggesting that they campaign together. Grant replied quickly that he would be glad to.

Grant told Garfield that he would be at state fairs in Madison, Wisconsin, and at Rockford and Sterling, in Illinois, and later in New York City and Boston. Grant even suggested, "Could you not join me some place in Ohio, or further west, and go east with me as far as might be convenient to you?" Garfield suggested that they meet the night of September 27 at Mentor, Ohio. Grant replied that he would be in Chicago that day greeting son Jesse and his new bride, Elizabeth Chapman. (The couple had married in San Francisco on September 21.) From Chicago the Grants would be in New York to see Jesse and Elizabeth sail for Europe on a honeymoon. In actuality the meeting and a large welcome for Grant was arranged for Warren, Ohio.

November–December: Grant was happy about Hancock's defeat even though they had served together in Virginia. Grant believed Garfield's victory would cause "dissolution" of the Democratic Party. And he knew Republicans would no longer get the votes of the South but would become a party with a solid northern base.

There was talk of a cabinet post for Grant, or some other mission, but there was "no position within the gift of the President that I would accept," Grant replied.

Future Presidents

JAMES A. GARFIELD stood on the floor of the Republican national convention and gave an impromptu nominating speech for John Sherman. Garfield soon ended up with the prize himself when the Grant–Blaine contest played itself out before exhausted delegates. In November he would be elected president.

January–March: Garfield's future appeared quite different on January 6 when the Republican nominating caucus in Columbus, in quick order and without debate, nominated and approved Garfield for a U.S. Senate seat. It took less than a half-hour.

On January 26, Garfield sent a letter to R. A. Horr that was not entirely an unequivocal endorsement of John Sherman for president. Rather, it said the majority of party members in Ohio favored Sherman.

Several Ohio delegates were not dissuaded by Garfield's support for Sherman and privately backed Garfield. Garfield decided he had to stick with Sherman even if Grant ran, and leave his own prospects in the hands of his managers and fate.

April–May: Garfield wrote in his journal in April, "I like [James] Blaine, always have, and yet there is an element in him which I distrust." Blaine told Garfield on May 23 that Grant's nomination was "quite probable." Garfield agreed. By this point, newspapers talked only of Blaine, Grant, and Sherman as potential Republican nominees. Liberal Republicans lined up behind George Edmunds, the Vermont senator, and Elihu B. Washburne was considered a dark horse.

On the eve of the convention John Sherman told Garfield that he would have to be a delegate-at-large and floor manager, an idea Garfield disliked. Sherman did not notify Garfield that he would be making the nominating speech in Chicago until after Garfield gave his final House speech on May 25.

June: As the Republican convention opened amid chaos on June 2, support for a Garfield nomination was virtually nonexistent. As a Sherman supporter, Garfield now was seen as the floor manager for the anti-Grant forces.

On Saturday evening June 5, the convention was ready to nominate. Roscoe Conkling made a memorable speech for Grant.

Garfield's speech for Sherman was next. Although he had found no time to prepare a speech, he managed a memorable and persuasive address. Convention Speaker George Hoar later called it the "finest" oratory he had ever heard. Still, many felt he came up short underscoring Sherman's qualities.

At the end of the day, most felt that only the speeches by Conkling and Garfield really mattered and that Garfield got the better of this exchange.

On Monday June 7 came the first of twenty-seven ballots taken that day. Grant opened with 304 votes, Blaine 284 votes, Sherman 93 votes, Edmunds 34 votes, Washburne 30 votes, and Windom 10 votes. Garfield polled no votes on the first ballot.

On the second ballot Garfield earned his 1st vote. Garfield received 2 votes on the sixth and seventh ballots, but from the fourteenth to the eighteenth he received none. Garfield asked that the single vote for him go to Sherman since he was not nominated. Garfield's gesture quickly won him more support.

Pressure mounted to nominate Garfield, but he resisted, saying, "I am [a] friend of Sherman and what will he and the world think of me if I am put in nomination? I won't permit it."

Before the thirty-fifth ballot, the Wisconsin delegation was polled and announced 2 votes for Grant, 2 for Blaine, and "sixteen votes for General James A. Garfield." Cheers followed.

Garfield was "pale and dumbfounded" and struggled to his feet to make a point of order. He said he had not given his consent. On the next ballot, Indiana threw 27 votes of 30 to Garfield to give him 50 votes.

On the 36th ballot, Connecticut shifted to Garfield, then 7 votes from Illinois, then all 22 votes from Iowa, and the stampede was on. Nevada's Stalwart Senator Jones appealed to Conkling to throw New York to Blaine. He refused and said he did not have time to poll the delegation. The states fell in line one-by-one amid cheering. Garfield had 399 votes, enough to secure the nomination.

Chester Alan Arthur received the vice presidential nomination (see **Chester Alan Arthur**, page 358).

July–October: Although Garfield was one of the nation's great orators, tradition still called for presidential candidates to sit home and do little or no campaigning. Having no organization of his own, Garfield had to rely on others, such as the Conkling machine in New York. Six biographies of Garfield were turned out by August to help the rest of the country become more familiar with the little-known congressman.

November 2: Garfield defeated Winfield Scott Hancock by fewer than 10,000 votes. Garfield earned 4,454,416 votes to Hancock's 4,444,952 votes. Garfield's electoral margin was

214 to 155. The decisive electoral count prevented grumbling despite the closeness of the popular vote.

December: Garfield, 49, spent the last month of the year contemplating his cabinet.

જાભ્ય

CHESTER ALAN ARTHUR, the personification of the spoilsman of the Gilded Age, was elected vice president of the United States to the dismay of the reformers who had prevented Grant from reclaiming the White House. It was a giant leap for a man who had never held an elective office. The office was far above Arthur's ambitions or dreams and came as a total surprise to him.

January: Arthur was in Albany preparing Republican policy for the next session of the state legislature when he received a telegram that his wife was critically ill. Ellen "Nell" Arthur had caught pneumonia on January 10 after waiting outside for a carriage following a concert. When Arthur reached her she was under morphine and never regained consciousness. She lingered for 24 hours with Arthur at her bedside and died on January 12 at the age of 42. The doctor cited heart disease and double pneumonia.

Arthur had showered Ellen with luxuries but let his political life usurp his home life. She had been lonely and neglected.

February: The New York state Republican convention was held on February 25 in Utica, where Conkling and Arthur arranged to load the New York delegation with Grant voters.

May–June: Arthur arrived in Chicago 5 days before the national Republican convention to sound out strength for Grant and predicted victory on the first ballot.

After Garfield's nomination it seemed obvious that a New Yorker would be considered for the vice presidential post. Before the convention Levi P. Morton had discussed this possibility with New York Governor Alphonso Cornell.

When Dennison approached Conkling on the vice presidential question, Conkling said he had no one in mind but would caucus. The New York people had not discussed the matter.

Steve French and Clint Wheeler overheard Dennison and then ran to tell Arthur to bid for the number-two slot on the ticket. Smarting from the customhouse humiliation, he realized a place on the ticket would be an answer to the charges made by Hayes. Arthur told French and Wheeler that he was all for being number two.

The first ballot for vice president went as follows: Arthur 468 votes, Elihu Washburne 103 votes, and 90 votes for others. Publicly Garfield was satisfied with Arthur; privately he preferred Morton.

November: With Garfield's election, Arthur accepted congratulations the next day at the Fifth Avenue Hotel. Now vice president–elect, Arthur had reached far beyond his dreams. He calculated he could learn quickly how to run the Senate.

જાભ્ય

GROVER CLEVELAND, 43, was a lawyer in Buffalo, New York. Alexander Brush, a conservative Republican and rich manufacturer of bricks, was mayor. The Republican machine in Buffalo had two bills passed in Albany that assured control of the police and fire departments for years to come. When the cost of operating these public services rose dramatically, graft was suspected. The citizens of Buffalo were in the market for a reform mayor.

જાભ્ય

BENJAMIN HARRISON took the stump for Garfield. Although Indiana Republicans were prepared to run Harrison for the Senate, there was speculation that he might land a seat in the cabinet.

March: Still serving on the Mississippi River commission, Harrison and an engineer gave a dissenting opinion on a levee system to control flooding on the Mississippi. When a Louisiana Democrat sought to reduce the size of the commission he was on, Harrison protested in a letter to Garfield.

While on a Mississippi boat trip for the commission, Harrison missed a message from James Blaine's people asking him to give the Blaine nominating speech. (Harrison's whereabouts on the river at the time were unknown.)

June: Harrison headed the Indiana delegation to Chicago for the Republican convention. Observers were uncertain how Indiana would go except that Harrison had shown an anti-Grant tendency in his Indiana speeches. He wrote to Hayes, "Our state has preferences but no pets." Although Harrison asked his people not to put his name before the convention, talk continued that he might make a good vice presidential nominee.

After being put on the committee to notify Garfield and Arthur, Harrison henceforth was an intimate friend and adviser to Garfield.

November: Garfield carried Indiana by 6,642 votes. Harrison wrote to Garfield on November 4, "You must know how sincerely I rejoice over your success.... Indiana has splendidly vindicated the action of her delegation at Chicago." Harrison also said he would be a candidate for the Senate but that four or five others also wanted the seat. "I think I shall succeed," Harrison predicted.

જાભ્ય

WILLIAM MCKINLEY was named to the House Ways and Means Committee by Speaker Samuel Randall on Garfield's recommendation.

McKinley toured Ohio giving speeches for Garfield, who even visited the Saxton House in Canton (where McKinley lived) to make a speech.

McKinley served as an Ohio representative on the Republican National Committee. As temporary chairman of the Ohio Republican convention, he made a speech on April 28 denouncing the disenfranchisement of southern Blacks. McKinley, now 37, pointed out that in one Georgia district the Republican vote had been 9,616 in 1872 but was reduced to 6 by 1878. He said African Americans had been "oppressed, bullied and terrorized, they stand mute and dumb in the exercise of citizenship, politically paralyzed." In this same keynote speech to the convention, he said Ohio would support Sherman.

McKinley gained reelection to the House by a margin of 3,571 votes over Democrat Leroy D. Thoman.

୫୦ଓ

THEODORE ROOSEVELT graduated from Harvard, married Alice Lee, entered Columbia University Law School, and took his first steps into Republican Party politics by starting at the very bottom.

January–February: Alice finally accepted Roosevelt's proposal. On January 25 he wrote, "At last everything is settled.... I am so happy ... it was nearly eight months since I had first proposed."

He rushed to New York to tell his mother. She wrote Alice, who responded on February 3, "I do love Theodore deeply."

March 26: The Harvard physician Dr. Dudley A. Sargeant examined Roosevelt. He had gained 12 pounds since his freshman year. The doctor told the senior that he had a heart problem and now must live a sedentary life. Theodore reacted with defiance. He said he would do just the opposite and that he did not care how short his life might be. He did not pass this information on to either Alice or his diary. He kept this secret from everyone for the next 35 years.

June 30: Roosevelt received his bachelor's degree *magna cum laude*, ranking 21 out of 177.

October 27–28: Alice and Theodore were married at the Unitarian church in Brookline, Massachusetts. He was 22, and she was 19. The wedding reception took place at the Lee mansion in Chestnut Hill, and the couple escaped to a suite at the Massasoit House in Springfield and reached New York City the next day.

November: Theodore registered at Columbia Law School and promised Alice a European trip the following spring. They moved into Theodore Sr.'s home on 57th Street on November 13. New York City now had a population of 1.1 million. Theodore soon took his father's seat at the Newsboys' Lodging House dinner, and functions of the Orthopedic Dispensary and New York Infant Asylum but found that charity work was not his style. He quit these activities after a year.

୫୦ଓ

WILLIAM HOWARD TAFT, 23, turned down a career in journalism and became a political campaigner.

February: Taft had his first date with future wife Helen "Nellie" Herron. In her diary she wrote, "I was surprised immensely ... receiving an invitation from Will Taft. Why he asked me I have wondered.... I know him very slightly though I like him very much." That was the end of the romance apparently until a chance meeting on the street in August.

Taft, on the side, had been covering the courts for Murat Halstead's newspaper; and the editor, impressed with the young man's work, offered him $1,500 per year if he would quit law. Taft passed on this chance.

May: After graduating from Cincinnati Law School, he wasted no time, cramming at his father's law offices, then traveling to Columbus on May 5 to take the bar examination, which he passed.

October 25: Taft was named assistant prosecutor of Hamilton County (Cincinnati). Taft received the appointment because of his friendship with young Miller Outcault, who had been working on an embezzlement case.

୫୦ଓ

WOODROW WILSON, 24 in December, had trouble concentrating on his law studies at the University of Virginia, and his love for his first cousin Hattie led to a health breakdown.

Wilson was missing so many law classes by making trips to Staunton to see Harriet "Hattie" Woodrow that the university sent his father a warning about the situation. Wilson was interested in Harriet for a year and a half, writing her affectionate letters. However, she thought marriage between first cousins was not right.

The romance and frustrations over his legal studies made Wilson sick. He left Charlottesville at the end of the first year in poor health but recovered enough to reenter for the fall term. By December his parents, worried about his health, suggested that he drop out and return home to Wilmington, North Carolina.

୫୦ଓ

WARREN G. HARDING entered college for the fall term before his fifteenth birthday. Iberia College (later Ohio Central) had three professors, sixty students, and tuition of only $7 per term.

At Iberia, Warren and another student boarded with the Reverend A. C. Crist, a professor of math and science. Political excitement impacted Warren's life at Iberia as the Garfield–Hancock race was in full swing.

When the Toledo & Central Railroad recruited young men to do grading and lay track, Harding joined a work gang. He managed to do the lighter work and used a mule team to haul material.

୫୦ଓ

CALVIN COOLIDGE was busy helping with the farming in Vermont, working with sugar, mending fences, and picking fruit. The family could afford a hired man and woman, and Calvin, age 8, often deferred to them.

୫୦ଓ

HERBERT HOOVER's father, Jesse, fell ill and died of typhoid fever on December 10 at the age of 34. Herbert, 6, had only a faint memory of him in later years. His mother moved the three children to Uncle Banajah's farm, and the uncle took over Jesse's farm implement business.

1881
Rutherford B. Hayes

President Hayes left Washington with the sort of public affection and good feeling for a clean administration that James Monroe had experienced 56 years earlier. Once out of office, Hayes worked to build the size of the Birchard Library in Ohio, attended his first Odd Fellow meeting in 33 years, and went to New York City to attend a board meeting of the Peabody Education Fund, which sought to fight illiteracy among poor children.

January: Hayes appointed Nathan Goff Jr. secretary of the navy on January 6. A seat on the Supreme Court opened, and Hayes conferred with president-elect James Garfield on his choice. Hayes and Garfield agreed on Stanley Matthews, even though he had run against Garfield for the Senate in 1877. (The Senate did not confirm Matthews, but Garfield later renewed the nomination and the Senate approved it by a margin of 1 vote.)

February 1: In a special message, Hayes asked Congress to compensate the Ponca Indians for wrongs done them and to let them choose where they wanted to live. Hayes wanted Native Americans to become citizens. Congress later appropriated $165,000 for the Poncas. Hayes also said that the United States must control any canal development in Panama and cited the 1846 treaty with New Granada. He also proposed that the United States subsidize mail steamers to Asia, lay a cable to Hawaii, and expand the navy.

March: A state dinner was given for Garfield on March 3. After the inaugural on March 4, Hayes gave Garfield a lunch and then went to John Sherman's home.

A military troop from Cleveland filled three cars and escorted the Hayes train to Fremont the next day. Near Baltimore, the train collided with another train, throwing Hayes from his seat but not injuring him. Two people were killed in the accident.

April–September: Once back at Spiegal Grove in Ohio, Hayes stayed out of politics and political associations. He spent most of his time increasing the size of the Birchard Library there.

An admirer of President Garfield, he was distraught when the president was shot in July and grieved over his death in September. Hayes rode in the funeral cortege with Grant.

୫୦ର

JAMES A. GARFIELD's presidency would be a short one. He would become the second president to fall to an assassin's bullet, just 16 years after the first.

January–February: In the months leading to his inauguration, Garfield had to deal with office-seekers and the badgering by Roscoe Conkling and James Blaine, both of whom had a slate for Garfield's approval.

On January 12, Blaine published an editorial in the *New York Tribune* in which he denounced the Conkling machine. He said he was "fully authorized" to speak for the president-elect. Garfield had not authorized this but did not speak out against Blaine's editorial.

Most of Garfield's time since his victory in November was spent agonizing over cabinet selections. Things were so bad for him that he was having headaches and nightmares much like Lincoln. Because of this, Garfield had little time to work on his inaugural address.

March: An all-night snow turned Pennsylvania Avenue into slush. Despite a penetrating cold on March 4, 16,000 marched in the parade. Chief Justice Morrison Waite administered the oath. Garfield's mother, Eliza, 79, was the first mother of a president to witness an oath-taking.

Garfield arose and with no introduction began speaking before a crowd estimated at 17,000. He asked for an end to the bitter feelings caused by the Civil War, talked about the role of Blacks in America and the need to protect their right to vote. He praised various groups but denounced the Mormons, a major surprise. Garfield grew hoarse near the end and made remarks about civil service heard only by those on the platform.

The inaugural ball was held in the new National Museum (Smithsonian). Electric lamps were displayed over the entrance.

By March 11, Garfield's cabinet was set: James Blaine as secretary of state; William Windom of Minnesota as secretary of Treasury; Robert Todd Lincoln, the son of Abraham Lincoln, as secretary of war; Wayne McVeagh of Pennsylvania as attorney general; Thomas Lemuel James of New York as postmaster general; William Henry Hunt of Louisiana as secretary of navy; and Samuel Kirkwood of Iowa as secretary of the Interior.

May: Lucretia Garfield took ill with malaria and a fever of 104 on May 4. She almost died, and the staff once found the president on his knees sobbing and praying. Garfield remained at her bedside for days. By the end of May, Lucretia had recovered enough to go to Long Branch.

In other matters, Stanley Matthews of Ohio was confirmed for the Supreme Court on May 12. Earlier when Hayes had nominated Matthews for the Court, the Senate did not confirm him.

June: Garfield visited his wife at Long Branch in late June, then returned to Washington to prepare for his own vacation, which was to feature a return to Williams College in Massachusetts to receive an honorary degree.

July–September: On July 1, Garfield walked over to Blaine's office for a talk without being aware that he was being stalked by Charles J. Guiteau.

Guiteau was born in Freeport, Illinois, and had once stayed in Ann Arbor, Michigan, expecting to get into the University of Michigan. Now he wanted to be the consul general in Paris. Guiteau had long been considered insane. Both parents were either psychotic or unstable. Guiteau had been a preacher, an attorney, a chiseler, and a drifter.

Initially Guiteau asked for a post in Vienna. After he moved to Washington to join the army of office-seekers, he asked for the Paris post. Guiteau bombarded the White House with letters but was forbidden entry because he had become a pest.

Guiteau hung around both the White House and State Department for 2 months. The clerks all knew him. After receiving an upbraiding from Blaine one day, Guiteau got the idea that Garfield needed to be "removed."

Riding in the carriage with Blaine to the train station on July 2, Garfield reviewed his summer plans: a yacht ride provided by millionaire Cyrus Field, then to Williams, then to Blaine's home in Augusta, Maine, then a cutter ride on the Maine Coast, and finally a talk to the New Hampshire legislature. From there Garfield would go to Mentor, Yorktown, and Atlanta for speeches on his southern policies.

In the Baltimore and Potomac train station waiting room at 9:30 A.M. were four cabinet members and their wives, including Robert Lincoln. As Garfield made his way through the waiting room to catch his train, Guiteau fired the first shot from less than a yard away. Garfield's hat flew and his arms went up. "My God! What is this?" he asked. Guiteau stepped forward and fired again as Garfield twisted and fell.

Officer Patrick Kearney of the District of Columbia police arrested Guiteau before he could flee the station.

Garfield was conscious but in shock. One bullet was 4 inches to the right of the spine, the other grazed his arm. His eleventh rib was shattered. He was taken to the White House, where one doctor said, "He is dying, look at his eyes."

Lucretia rushed back from the New Jersey coast. On her arrival, Lucretia vowed she would nurse him back to health.

The next morning Garfield was cheerful and his pulse was normal. By July 13 the doctors turned optimistic, although

Garfield was being treated with morphine. Day by day the nation waited, and Garfield became a folk hero. William Chandler wrote to Blaine on July 18, "This worship will make him all-powerful if he lives." Despite the optimism Garfield slowly slid downhill over the next 80 days.

Doctors were preoccupied with finding the bullet still lodged in Garfield, often poking around the wound with unclean hands. Alexander Graham Bell was brought in with a device like a mine detector to look for the bullet.

The first sign of a deep infection came on July 23 when Garfield suffered chills, tremors, vomiting, and a fever of 104. There was improvement on July 29 when he held a brief cabinet meeting. But doctors ordered no business decisions.

The government continued to run smoothly without a president. Blaine suggested making Arthur the acting president. For this the secretary of state was ridiculed as a ghoulish plotter, and Arthur vetoed the idea.

Garfield's last letter was written August 11 to his mother: "Don't be disturbed by conflicting reports on my condition.... I am gaining every day and need only time and patience to bring me through."

Yet Garfield soon began to weaken. He could not eat or sleep, and his weight dropped from 200 pounds to 135. The parotid gland behind the ear became swollen, indicating blood poisoning, and the right side of his face became paralyzed. He had hallucinations. On August 26 newspapers said death was imminent.

Instead, the gland was lanced, his mind cleared, and he ate solid food again.

Heat and boredom caused Garfield to ask for a change on September 1. Reluctantly the doctors let him go to Elberon on the New Jersey coast. He was transferred to a train on September 6 and managed to wave to a few spectators. The trip of 230 miles took 7 hours.

Soon after arriving in Elberon, Garfield started to sink with chills, fever, vomiting, a cough, and spasms near the heart.

On the morning of September 19 his temperature reached 108.8 and his heart grew unsteady. At 10:35 P.M. the faint heartbeat stopped. Garfield was 49; he had been president for 199 days.

Garfield was buried on September 26 at the Lakeview Cemetery in Cleveland.

(Guiteau's trial began on November 14, 1881. The jury reached a guilty verdict on January 25, 1882. He was hanged on June 20, 1882.)

෪෬

CHESTER ALAN ARTHUR was suddenly thrust into the White House by the cruel fate of an assassin's bullet. He became the third man to serve as president in 1881.

President James Garfield was shot by Charles Guiteau at the Baltimore and Potomac Railway Depot in Washington, D.C., on July 2, 1881.

January–February: Before Hayes left office, vice president–elect Arthur was right back in Albany, wheeling and dealing in New York political battles over the Senate seat that would have gone to him had he not been put on the national ticket. People were appalled at such improprieties.

In the upcoming Senate session, Arthur was to play a big role as vice president. Deadlocked with thirty-seven Republicans, thirty-seven Democrats, and two independents, Vice President Arthur might possibly have to cast the tie-breaking vote on some bills.

March: On inauguration day, March 4, Arthur rode in the second carriage behind Hayes and Garfield. Arthur made a short speech in the Senate and was sworn in. Arthur then administered the oath to the new senators.

Early in the Senate sessions, Arthur's vote was needed to break ties. On March 18, Arthur twice broke ties by voting in favor of the Republican Party, appearing nervous in his new career.

July–September: Arthur and Roscoe Conkling were aboard a steamer on July 2 en route from Albany to Manhattan when they were notified of Garfield's shooting. The vice president returned to his home in New York City and received an optimistic telegram about the president's condition from Secretary of State James Blaine along with a description of the shooting. Arthur replied, "I am profoundly shocked at the dreadful news. The hopes you express relieve somewhat the horror of the first announcement."

Arthur said he would not go to Washington until notified of Garfield's death. Twice in the evening he met with Conkling and other Republicans. At 9:30 P.M., Arthur received a wire suggesting that Garfield's condition had worsened. Blaine suggested Arthur take the midnight train to Washington. Conkling saw him to the depot, and Arthur left with Senator John P. Jones and a government detective.

Arthur and Jones reached Washington at 8 A.M. and went into seclusion at Jones's house near the Capitol. That evening Arthur went to the White House and talked to Mrs. Garfield. Everyone talked of Arthur's agony; he seemed overwhelmed by the prospects. When Garfield seemed to improve, Arthur returned to New York, where he remained in seclusion at his Lexington Avenue home. Arthur now decided to avoid Washington, fearing it might appear to be a grab for power. But plans were established to administer the oath of office in New York City if Garfield died.

On August 16, Arthur met with his closest advisers and friends, including Ulysses S. Grant and Conkling, to discuss the course to take if Garfield died.

Chester Alan Arthur assumed the presidency after the assassination of James Garfield in 1881. (Library of Congress)

On September 1, Arthur received a letter from Attorney General MacVeagh warning that Garfield's condition was critical. Another letter September 10 said there was little hope. The cabinet sent Arthur a telegram on September 19 saying that Garfield's end was near. On September 20, at 12:25 A.M., official notification of Garfield's death came to Arthur from the cabinet. Arthur sent a telegram to MacVeagh at 1 A.M.: "[I am filled] with profound sorrow. Express to Mrs. Garfield my deepest sympathy."

Arthur's friends went looking for a judge. Elihu Root and Daniel Rollins appeared with Judge John R. Brady at 1:50 A.M. Brady administered the oath at 2:15 A.M. Arthur's son kissed him, and others shook hands. On September 22, Arthur was sworn in again in the vice president's room at the Capitol by Chief Justice Morrison Waite.

Arthur gave a brief inaugural address, noting that this was the fourth time the office of president had been vacated by a death.

October–December: As had happened in the past when a president died in office, many expected Garfield's cabinet to resign. Arthur talked to the cabinet about staying on at least until the Congress met in December. William Windom, however, resigned the Treasury post to run for the Senate. Charles J. Folger of New York replaced him on October 27.

With the close of the year, more cabinet resignations came: Attorney General MacVeagh resigned in November, and Benjamin Harris Brewster of Pennsylvania replaced him in late December. Secretary of State Blaine resigned in December, and Frederick T. Frelinghuysen of New Jersey replaced him. Postmaster General James resigned in December, and Timothy Howe of Wisconsin replaced him.

Former Presidents

ULYSSES S. GRANT quickly split with Garfield over an appointments battle and became president of a railroad to Mexico.

January–February: Grant suggested to Garfield on January 26 that John Jacob Astor would be a good secretary of Treasury. As appointments were announced, Grant wrote Garfield on February 6, congratulating him on his selections as they corrected "a grievous mistake of your immediate predecessor." Grant did not think much of Hayes.

March: Grant's purpose in taking the railroad job was to foster free world trade, not to grab land, but others saw the move as necessitated by Grant's need for money. The railroad was incorporated in New York, and Grant and Romero left for Mexico on March 26. Grant obtained the needed concessions from a less than enthusiastic Mexican government.

Grant's sister Virginia died on March 28. She was 49.

April: By April 24, Grant was furious that Garfield named William H. Robertson to the New York Customhouse without first consulting Roscoe Conkling. Robertson had not supported Grant in 1872.

August 5: Grant's brother Orville died. He was 46.

September–December: The Grants visited Galena in the fall, then moved into the Fifth Avenue Hotel in New York. George W. Childs and A. J. Drexel, both of Philadelphia, and J. P. Morgan, kicked in a gift of $100,000 to buy Grant, 59, a mansion at East 66th Street.

Future Presidents

GROVER CLEVELAND was a bachelor quietly practicing courtroom law in Buffalo, New York, when reformist elements in both political parties realized that an honest Democrat was the only hope to rout out the corruption at city hall. Cleveland, they decided, was that man but only after the search committee had actually considered several others. Cleveland was more than reluctant to pick up their broom, but he did so after considerable arm-twisting.

About the same time there was pressure on Cleveland, now 44, of an entirely different sort—to opt for a high-paying job as a railroad lawyer. He turned that deal down in order to retain his independence and very routine lifestyle.

August–October: Scholarly George Sicard, a Hamilton College graduate, was brought into the law firm as a junior partner. Former partner Albert P. Laning died in September. He had been a lawyer for the New York Central railroad. Two other railroad lawyers suggested that they merge with Cleveland's firm.

Cleveland decided against the merger, saying he did not like the frenetic pace Laning endured doing railroad litigation. He preferred his personal independence and, he told his friends, he did not need money.

City Republicans held their convention on October 19 and nominated Milton C. Beebe, president of the Common Council and a political machine man, to be a candidate for mayor. A five-man committee from the Democratic county committee started a search for a reform candidate opponent for Beebe, certain they could win with reform Republican support.

The committee approached several Democrats before getting around to Cleveland. It hit upon Cleveland because he was pugnacious and honest. Cleveland was reluctant at first. He specified that the ticket would have to eliminate a corrupt controller from the First Ward, John C. Sheehan, who was up for reelection. Reformers, headed by Charles W. McCune, editor of the *Buffalo Courier*, agreed with Cleveland's point, and Sheehan was told he was "retiring."

Cleveland was nominated at the Democratic city convention in Tivoli Hall on October 25. The conventioneers adjourned to a saloon to await Cleveland's answer. The committee had just entered the saloon when someone said, "He's accepted, boys, let's have a drink."

The voting returns in November gave Cleveland the victory by a wide margin, 15,120 votes to Beebe's 11,528 votes.

✄♋

BENJAMIN HARRISON was selected a U.S. senator by the Indiana legislature in January despite Garfield's hope that Harrison would accept a cabinet position. On becoming a senator, Harrison resigned his Mississippi River Commission post.

In the Senate, Harrison, 48 in August, was made chairman of the Transportation Committee and put on four others: Indian Affairs, Military, Territories, and Rules.

✄♋

WILLIAM MCKINLEY, 38, continued as a U.S. representative from Ohio. The death of Garfield ended the McKinley connection with the White House that had started with the Hayes presidency.

✄♋

THEODORE ROOSEVELT, at the age of 23 years and 1 day, was nominated by Republicans of the Twenty-first District to be their candidate for the New York Assembly in Albany. Roosevelt also found time to climb the Matterhorn and publish his book, *The Naval War of 1812*.

January–March: Roosevelt spent much of the first part of the year writing. He also enjoyed the social scene, attending several parties with Alice. By March he was more active in Republican politics. He served on an executive committee of Young Republicans.

May–September: Theodore and Alice left for Europe aboard the *Celtic* on May 12 and reached Ireland on May 21. Alice was very seasick during the crossing. They spent 10 days in Ireland before moving on to London. Then it was on to Paris, Venice, and Milan, followed by a 10-day visit to Switzerland.

From Switzerland, it was on to Bavaria, then to The Hague, where Roosevelt spent a month writing more of *The Naval War of 1812*. On September 10, Roosevelt arrived in Liverpool, where he and Alice prepared to leave for America.

October–November: The Roosevelts arrived in New York City on October 2. Soon, Roosevelt was in the thick of Republican Party politics. At the state Republican convention on October 28, Roosevelt was nominated by Joe Murray for for an assembly seat.

Wealthy friends promised money, including Elihu Root. The *New York Times* was laudatory, saying the district was "united upon so admirable a candidate ... Mr. Roosevelt himself is a public-spirited citizen, not an office seeker, but one of the men who should be sought for office."

Roosevelt faced Dr. W. W. Strew, a Democrat recently fired from the Blackwell's Island Lunatic Asylum. Roosevelt won with 3,490 votes to 1,989 votes for Strew. The winner spent Election Day, November 9, at the library working on his book, which he delivered to the publisher as promised on December 3.

୫୦୦୪

WILLIAM HOWARD TAFT took office as an assistant prosecutor of Hamilton County, Ohio, on January 3. His pay was $1,200 per year.

His first case came on January 20 and involved a scrubwoman, Mary Finckler, who had taken $35 from her employer. She admitted her guilt, and Taft asked the court to go easy on her. He also prosecuted murderers, including the case of Nellie Stickley, a slain prostitute. Taft asked for the death penalty for her lover, Joseph J. Payton. But Payton got off on an insanity plea.

୫୦୦୪

WOODROW WILSON, 25 in December, was crushed when first cousin Harriet "Hattie" Woodrow turned down his marriage proposal.

While recuperating from ill health in Wilmington, Wilson worked on his oratory skills and was busy writing essays and poetry. Wilson wrote "Stray Thoughts from the South" and "New Southern Industries," pieces published by the *New York Evening Post*.

Wilson graduated from the University of Virginia Law School in June.

୫୦୦୪

WARREN G. HARDING attended Iberia College in north-central Ohio. He became president of the Philomathic Literary Society. He also worked in the print shop of William Beebe, an editor and owner of the *Union Register*. Harding turned 16 in November.

୫୦୦୪

CALVIN COOLIDGE, 9 in July, was living in south-central Vermont.

୫୦୦୪

HERBERT HOOVER, 7, spent most of the year in Pawhuska, Arkansas, at an Osage Indian reservation near the Mississippi River, where his uncle, Major Laban Miles, was a U.S. Indian agent to the Osage nation. The move was made to cut widow Huldah Hoover's costs. Herbert stayed 8 months and attended the agency school. The adventure made Herbert a lifelong fan of outdoor living.

1882
Chester Alan Arthur

President Arthur produced the most elegant dinner parties in the history of the White House but a lifetime of rich food and drink may have caught up with him when he was diagnosed with Bright's disease. Arthur's periods of indolence and procrastination in working on the business of state may be traced to the onset of his medical problem.

January–March: Although Washington was still in mourning for Garfield, the first big White House reception was held on January 2 for the cabinet, judges, the foreign contingent, and congressmen.

Justice Ward Hunt resigned from the Supreme Court. Arthur offered the seat to Roscoe Conkling in February, who declined. Instead, Arthur appointed Samuel Blatchford of New York on March 22.

Congress passed the Reapportionment Act on February 25, increasing the size of the House of Representatives from 293 members to 325.

In March the first state dinner of the year honored the Grants. Arthur's elegant style was first revealed at the Grant dinner. There were flower bouquets for each lady, many other flowers, elegant decorations, and a Marine band playing operatic selections. The meal included fourteen courses and eight wines.

April: On April 4, Arthur vetoed a Chinese exclusion bill that would have banned Chinese immigrants for 20 years. The next day, Congress failed to override the veto.

More changes were made in Arthur's cabinet. Henry More Teller of Colorado became secretary of the Interior on April 6, and William Eaton Chandler of New Hampshire became secretary of the navy on April 12.

August: Congress passed the Rivers and Harbors Bill, which Arthur vetoed. Congress voted to override on August 2. The new law set aside $18 million for public works.

Arthur signed a revised Chinese exclusion bill on August 5 that reduced the duration of a ban on Chinese immigration to 10 years.

October–September: Arthur took a vacation in September and returned to the White House on October 7, reportedly "improved" in health. Two weeks later he slipped away to the Soldier's Home cottage weary and exhausted.

In early October the Associated Press ran a story that the surgeon general had discovered during the summer that Arthur, 53 on October 5, had Bright's disease, usually a fatal kidney ailment. Rest and relaxation was the prescription for the president.

A friend denied the story "on the authority of the President himself" and added that Arthur had had a mild attack of malaria. A friendly newspaper, the *New York Herald*, on October 21 said the kidney disease story was "pure fiction."

Former Presidents

ULYSSES S. GRANT, 60 in April, was appointed by President Arthur to negotiate a trade agreement with Mexico. It was Grant's fourth visit to Mexico.

Very little progress was made in laying track for his Mexican railroad venture, and he achieved few financial rewards from this business—unlike Jay Gould and others who made fortunes out of railroading.

In October, Grant persuaded President Justo R. Barrios of Guatemala to allow his railroad a 250-mile extension into that country.

೩ೕCಒ

RUTHERFORD B. HAYES, 60 in October, enjoyed his retirement at his Spiegel Grove estate in Fremont, in the northwest corner of Ohio not far from Lake Erie. Spiegal Grove was a bit pretentious with twenty guest rooms, a 25-acre park, large trees, a ravine, and two small lakes.

Future Presidents

GROVER CLEVELAND's rapid rise in politics continued, as he went from mayor of Buffalo to governor of New York in one year.

January: Cleveland took office as Buffalo's mayor on January 1 at the age of 44. In his inaugural address, Cleveland talked about "shameful neglect of duty" in the street department, and "wasting" of people's money. He said public works would go to the low bidder and that the schools needed repairs. He attacked old problems related to street cleaning and sewage disposal with vigor never before seen in the city.

February–June: Cleveland did much of the mayor's job himself, since he knew little about delegating authority. Cleveland was blunt in calling attention to petty abuses. He stopped gifts to developers and closely checked contractor bills to the city.

His work as Buffalo's mayor caught the attention of state Democratic leaders, and by June, talk of him as the Democratic candidate for governor grew.

July: Prior to Cleveland's nomination to head the state Democratic ticket, his mother Anne died on July 19 at the age of 76.

September: The Democratic State Convention was held in Syracuse on September 21. In addition to Cleveland, the major Democratic front-runners were Roswell Flower, a former congressman, and General Henry W. Slocum.

On the first ballot, Slocum had 98 votes, Flower 97, and Cleveland 66, with the remaining votes scattered among five other candidates. On the second ballot, Cleveland took 71 votes. Slowly, Cleveland began to emerge as the favorite. On the last ballot, Cleveland earned 211 votes to Slocum's 156 and Flower's 15.

October–November: Cleveland did not campaign and left campaign strategy to law partner Wilson Bissell.

On November 7, Cleveland defeated Republican Charles J. Folger by nearly 200,000 votes. Cleveland wrote to his brother William that night, "Can I well perform my duties.... I shall spend very little [time] in the purely ornamental part of the office.... I shall have no idea of re-election or any higher political preferment in my head."

೩ೕCಒ

BENJAMIN HARRISON, a U.S. senator from Indiana, started to receive some support for the presidency from his home state. As a senator, Harrison believed that the Treasury surplus might best be passed on to veterans. He was protectionist on the tariff, favored civil service reform, and backed Arthur's views on Chinese immigration. He soon learned that serious Senate business was done in committee, not on the floor. The one thing Harrison disliked about being a senator was the crush of office-seekers.

೩ೕCಒ

WILLIAM MCKINLEY, 39, won reelection to Congress by only 8 votes. The Democrats had gerrymandered his district again. The tally: 16,906 votes for McKinley, and 16,898 votes for Democrat Jonathan H. Wallace. Although Democrats contested the vote, McKinley was certified as the winner in December.

೩ೕCಒ

THEODORE ROOSEVELT, only 23, made a lasting impression from the New York Assembly floor in Albany when he called millionaire Jay Gould and New York Supreme Court Justice T. R. Westbrook "sharks" and "swindlers." He called for and got an investigation into their doings and made headlines in all the newspapers in the state. By year's end political observers thought Theodore had a real shot at taking over the state Republican Party and becoming speaker of the New York Assembly.

Roosevelt was the youngest man in the state legislature when he arrived in Albany at the start of the year. For much of the early part of the year, Roosevelt was frustrated by the blatant corruption of some of the other assemblymen.

On a brighter note for Roosevelt, his first book, *The Naval War of 1812*, was receiving many excellent reviews.

೩ೕCಒ

WILLIAM HOWARD TAFT did not like the job of Collector of Internal Revenue for the first district of Ohio that President Arthur gave him in January. Prior to the appointment Taft was assistant prosecutor for Hamilton County, Ohio. His father was appointed U.S. minister to the Austro-Hungarian Empire in Vienna. More important, Taft fell in love with Helen "Nellie" Herron, age 22.

Taft began escorting Nellie to social functions. The couple played tennis, took boat excursions on the Ohio, and gathered with other young people at the Herron home on Pike Street in downtown Cincinnati. Nellie was the daughter of John Williamson Herron, a lawyer, and Harriet Collins Herron. A graduate of the Cincinnati College of Music, her interests were literature and music.

At the end of the year, the young Taft visited Arthur in the White House to discuss his resignation with the president. Arthur "kindly consented" to Taft's resignation.

೩ೕCಒ

WOODROW WILSON moved from Wilmington, North Carolina, to Atlanta to practice law. He made his political debut in the fall by testifying before a commission studying tariff rates.

Wilson went into partnership with Edward I. Renick, a man he did not know but who was an 1881 University of Virginia Law School graduate. The office was established in August. Renick did the research while Wilson did the courtroom work.

Wilson was admitted to the Georgia bar in October. He handled only a few cases, one of which was his mother's inheritance. The problem was that Wilson did not have his heart in the work. He was much more interested in writing and studying history and politics.

A six-man Tariff Commission that Arthur appointed was studying rates in Atlanta. Walter H. Page, a reporter for the *New York World* and a friend of Renick, persuaded Wilson to testify without pay. Wilson did so on September 23 in a brief argument against the protective tariff as being monopolistic and destructive.

ഔ൭

WARREN G. HARDING was one of only three seniors to graduate from Iberia College in the spring.

Before receiving his bachelor of science degree, he gave the commencement address. Earlier in the year he and student Frank Miller had an idea for a college newspaper, and the first issue of the four-page Iberia *Spectator* came out in February. The paper died after just six issues.

Woodrow Wilson, circa 1882. Wilson practiced law in Wilmington, North Carolina, but was much more interested in pursuing a life in politics.

Warren returned to the Caledonia, Ohio, farm after graduation and on July 1 took his father's mule and set out for Marion.

Harding landed a job in a hardware shop in Crestline, and a few weeks later took the county school board examination for a teaching job. He landed a good job at $20 per month. The school was 2 miles from Marion.

Warren turned 17 on November 2.

ഔ൭

CALVIN COOLIDGE sneezed from allergies and developed hypochondriac tendencies at the age of 10. In rural Vermont his activities included acting in plays, bobsledding, hayrides, fishing, and playing checkers.

ഔ൭

HERBERT HOOVER, 8, took a summer trip to northwest Iowa to visit relatives. Hoover was often involved in hunting and fishing and earned $5 picking strawberries. He now attended the West Branch Free School.

ഔ൭

FRANKLIN DELANO ROOSEVELT was born on January 30 at 8:45 P.M. in an upstairs room at the family estate at Hyde Park, New York, in Duchess County and next to the Hudson River. His father was James Roosevelt, age 53; his mother was Sara (Sallie) Delano Roosevelt, age 27.

The delivery was difficult for both mother and child because Dr. Edward H. Parker used too much chloroform. Both mother and infant turned blue. The doctor gave mouth-to-mouth resuscitation to Franklin to save him.

James met Sara in New York City at the 57th Street home of Theodore Roosevelt, who was away at Harvard that evening. James, born on July 16, 1828 at Hyde Park, had married Rebecca Howland, age 22, in 1853. She died in 1876 at the age of 45, leaving James with a son, James "Rosy" Roosevelt, born in 1854, who was then a senior at Columbia. He later married Helen Astor and served in the U.S. embassy in Vienna during Cleveland's first administration and in London during the second.

Franklin's father, a Democrat, was a friend of Cleveland. The Delanos were Republicans, as were all of the other Roosevelts. James was a country squire, founder of Con-solidated Coal and president of the Southern Railroad Security Company. He owned his own railroad car. He attended New York University briefly, graduated from Union, toured Europe for 3 years, served for a month in Garibaldi's revolutionary army in Italy, graduated from Harvard Law School, and practiced briefly in New York City. Great Grandfather Klas Maertensen van Rosevelt left the Netherlands and settled in New Amsterdam about 1644.

Sara's ancestors included Philippe de la Noye, a French Huguenot in the Netherlands, who reached Plymouth in 1621. She was born on September 21, 1854, at the family estate near Newburgh, New York. Her marriage to James, a sixth cousin, was on October 7, 1880, at Hyde Park. Her father was in the China trade. He was born in Fairhaven, Massachusetts, near New Bedford.

It was 7 weeks before James and Sara named the baby Franklin after a grand uncle, Franklin Hughes Delano. Franklin was related to eleven presidents, including fifth cousin Theodore Roosevelt, and was a seventh cousin to Winston Churchill.

Franklin's ancestry was Dutch and French Huguenot, with a little English, Swedish, and Finn mixed in.

1883
Chester Alan Arthur

President Arthur's deteriorating health was the big development of the year, although the president attempted to keep the public in the dark about his condition. Every presidential trip involved big crowds, receptions, and standing in line for hours to shake hands. The fatigue for him was unending. Arthur was looking older and confessed to his son that he was ill. Often he was unable to work and documents piled up. The president's Bright's disease and heart condition produced kidney ailments, hypertension, high blood pressure, and nausea.

January: Congress passed the Pendleton Act on January 4. The new law, signed by Arthur, reformed the system for hiring and firing federal employees. The act set up the Civil Service Commission, which would administer competitive examinations for federal job applicants.

March: Arthur confided to son Alan that he had been ill since Congress adjourned and had been unable to finish the work piled before him.

Postmaster General Timothy Otis Howe died on March 25. Walter Q. Gresham of Indiana replaced him.

April: As his health worsened the President took fishing trips, steamer trips, and short horseback rides to relieve tension. At the end of the congressional session, Arthur announced he was going to Florida because he had a cold.

Arthur traveled with Secretary of the Navy William Chandler and others plus four reporters reluctantly permitted to tag along. The party left Washington on April 5.

A steamer took them down the St. John's River to Sanford, and a carriage brought them to the orange plantation of Henry S. Sanford, former minister to Belgium. The hot weather made Arthur irritable. The party continued by train to Orlando, and Arthur was displeased when the train made a stop there against his orders. Next came Maitland and Winter Park. The train stopped at Kissimmee, and the party boarded a steamer for a trip south to Lake Tohopekaliga. A camp was established, where the party was overwhelmed with mosquitoes and Arthur caught malaria.

Returning north to St. Augustine, the group was meeting a reception committee headed by General Fred Dent, Ulysses S. Grant's brother-in-law. A ship took the party back to Savannah, Georgia, where Arthur took two long carriage rides in the sun, had lunch, then stood in a reception line for hundreds of handshakes.

The president soon wanted to return to Washington and canceled a planned ocean voyage. The party reached Washington on April 22. On the White House steps he said he never felt better and was heard complaining about the imagination of newsmen.

May: Arthur went to New York for the opening of the Brooklyn Bridge. There were tremendous crowds, and 150 police were needed to surround the Fifth Avenue Hotel when the president, his son, four cabinet members, and Governor Grover Cleveland arrived.

July–August: Arthur began to plan a trip to Yellowstone National Park in July. The trip included riding in wagon trains and on horseback. The president's small party of travelers crossed the Continental Divide three times.

September–October: Arthur returned to the White House tanned and well rested in September. But with the onset of fall, Arthur soon began to feel the effects of his Bright's disease.

Former Presidents

ULYSSES S. GRANT played the role of high financier in New York City without realizing he had no talent for this art.

Grant's son Buck, a partner in the financial firm Grant and Ward (with Ferdinand Ward), was on his way to becoming a millionaire. Grant, 61 in April, invested $100,000 in the business. Grant went to his office at Grant and Ward regularly, signed papers, and took in money from friends wanting to invest. Grant's relatives also put money in the company.

Grant gave Ward railroad bonds, sold his home in Washington for $65,000, and borrowed $45,000 on his New York residence to invest with Ward. Grant told family members he was now worth $2.5 million. He said that Ward was the finest financial mind since Alexander Hamilton.

What Grant did not know was that Ward was involved in illegal loans with another partner, James D. Fish, president of Marine Bank, who in turn was making loans without adequate security. Grant and Buck apparently were oblivious to what was going on. Grant's many friends on Wall Street failed to warn him to exercise caution.

Grant's mother, Hannah, died on May 11 at Jersey City, New Jersey, at the age of 84.

80CR

RUTHERFORD B. HAYES, 61 in October, gradually changed his opinion of the Arthur administration. Originally distrustful of Arthur and upset by reports of "liquor, snobbery, and worse" at the White House, Hayes eventually was pleased by Arthur's policies.

Living in retirement in northwest Ohio, Hayes accepted the presidency of the National Prison Association and would remain its president for life. Prison reform was always his interest.

Future Presidents

GROVER CLEVELAND, as governor of New York, appointed quality men for various tasks and ignored the cries of protest from Tammany Hall. This won him public support. He turned into a workaholic, almost imprisoned in his office. His capacity for staggering hours of work was not lost on the newspapers.

January–February: Cleveland took office in Albany on January 1 on a cold but sunny day. Both Alphonso Cornell and Cleveland spoke in the state senate chamber. In his inaugural address the new governor called for civil service legislation and reform of the tax system. He also discussed problems concerning the Erie Canal, militia, immigration, banking, and harbormasters.

The first thing Cleveland did was to open the doors to all and conduct business in public. Cleveland was soon impressed by Daniel Lamont and made him military secretary and then private secretary.

Democrats, by a margin of 84 to 42, controlled the New York State Assembly. The Senate margin was 18 to 14. There were many factions in both parties. Corruption was rampant in Albany and New York City. One-third of the legislature could be bought for a price.

April–May: Cleveland took aim at dishonesty in the immigration commission and at the uselessness of harbormasters. Cleveland's choice for the immigration job named on April 27 immediately upset Tammany, and the matter was referred to a committee.

Cleveland said later that the pressure was intense to give patronage to various factions in the senate. When Tammany and Republicans blocked Cleveland's man until the last day of the session on May 4, Cleveland sent in his last appointments to the senate; not one was a Tammany favorite. Senator Thomas F. Grady begged Cleveland for favors. Then Grady and others blocked all confirmations.

Cleveland told Lamont, "Give me a sheet of paper, I'll tell the people what a set of damned rascals they have upstairs." In his message he told how immigration offices needed cleaning up and how lobbyists were active.

On appointments, Cleveland picked men of merit. He surprised people by rejecting party hacks and appointing engineers and those with technical qualifications to the new Board of Railroad Commissioners and to superintend public works.

August–September: Cleveland enjoyed the Adirondacks and visited mountain lakes with Dr. S. B. Ward after first visiting his sister Rose in Holland Patent and his brother William in Forestport. The Governor vacationed at White Lake Corners, Woodhull Reservoir, and the Fulton chain of lakes.

Cleveland kept a hand in Buffalo politics, working to get a reform delegation selected for the state convention. He wrote Bissell on September 12 that all the spoilsmen and special interest groups would be on one side and all the "true and earnest men [like himself]" would be on the other.

BENJAMIN HARRISON'S wife, Carrie, was ill from January to March. She had surgery and was under a

Theodore Roosevelt loved the outdoors and the wilderness. As president, Roosevelt set aside more than 230 million acres of wilderness as national forests, preserves, parks, and sanctuaries.

doctor's care in New York. Their son Russell came from his Montana ranch and stayed at the Metropolitan Club to be near his mother.

As a U.S. senator from Indiana, Harrison voted for tariff revisions and stumped the Midwest in the off-year election to preach protectionism, particularly in Iowa as a favor to Senator William B. Allison.

After the Senate session, Harrison took Carrie back to Indiana. In July he took the family to West Baden Springs, a resort in southern Indiana, where Carrie could use the mineral baths.

Harrison, 50 in August, began stumping for protectionism in September in both Ohio and Iowa. In Iowa he made five speeches in 5 days. He told Iowa farmers on October 22: "Every honest and intelligent advocate of free trade must admit that if we abandon our system of protective duties, the wages of labor must be reduced."

WILLIAM MCKINLEY, 40, was involved in many of the key debates in Congress during the year. On January 27 he argued that lowering tariff rates would increase imports and increase revenue.

During a tariff debate on March 3, William Springer of Illinois chided McKinley on his 8-vote victory in 1882. McKinley replied, "My fidelity to my constituents is not measured by the support they give me."

He supported Arthur on the Pendleton Act and favored excluding Chinese immigrants for 10 years.

THEODORE ROOSEVELT was nominated by the Republicans for the speakership, but he became minority leader because the Democrats controlled the state assembly in Albany.

January: The Republicans held a caucus on New Year's Day, and Isaac Hunt recommended Roosevelt for speaker. The party approved. In the vote for speaker, the Democratic candidate won 84 to 41 in a vote along party lines. This made Roosevelt minority leader.

February: Governor Cleveland called Roosevelt and Hunt in to discuss civil service reform, as Roosevelt had already introduced a bill on the subject. Hunt reported that the bill was bogged down in the Judiciary Committee, and they discussed how to dislodge it. Roosevelt enjoyed Cleveland's support.

March: Roosevelt favored a "five-cent fare" elevated railroad bill. Cleveland vetoed it as unconstitutional. Roosevelt changed his position after the governor explained why and then spoke admirably of Cleveland's position.

April–May: Roosevelt took the floor on April 9 in support of a civil service reform bill that Cleveland wanted despite the objections of Tammany. The bill was passed on May 4, the last day of the session.

July–August: Alice was pregnant, and Theodore now turned to planning his new hilltop home at Oyster Bay that he would call Leeholm. He wanted a big piazza, library, huge fireplaces, and a sunroom. Soon asthma and cholera morbus returned, and Roosevelt became very ill. House plans were put on hold, and the family doctor suggested the sulphur springs at Richfield Springs as a cure.

In August, Roosevelt returned to the Leeholm project and on August 20 purchased 95 acres for $20,000 to increase his holdings to 155 acres.

September–October: Roosevelt left for the Dakota Territory alone on September 3, a 2,400-mile trip. When he arrived, he checked into the crude Pyramid Park Hotel, where he was given a cot in an upstairs dormitory where thirteen men were sleeping. He hired Joe Ferris to take him on a buffalo hunt and shot a bison.

☙❧

WILLIAM HOWARD TAFT, 26, quit his job in March, went into law practice with a friend of his father, and visited his parents in Vienna. He found there were too many long hours involved his internal revenue job.

Taft's new law partner was Harlan Page Lloyd, an associate of Alphonso Taft. Lloyd was a Civil War veteran and a Hamilton College graduate. Taft found Lloyd a man of high character, and he was to be the only law partner Taft ever had.

Taft made a summer trip to Europe. Beginning his tour in Ireland, he went on to Scotland and England before staying in Vienna for three weeks. Will did some hiking in Switzerland with a boyhood friend, Rufus Smith, before returning home in October.

☙❧

WOODROW WILSON, 27 at the end of December, decided law was not for him and entered Johns Hopkins University to study history, to write, and to become a professor.

March: Wilson qualified to appear before the federal courts but could not raise the required $10 fee; he had only $5. His father Joseph had been supporting Woodrow for nearly a year and remarked that he "didn't seem to be earning his salt."

April: Unfocused on his future, he wrote to the president of Princeton for opinions on a teaching career.

He wrote to a friend that he needed a job that paid moderately but allowed considerable leisure time to pursue his interest: "What better can I be, therefore, than a professor, a lecturer upon subjects whose study delights me?"

September–December: Wilson decided further study at Johns Hopkins would give him time for "reading and for original work" while being paid. He enrolled in the Baltimore school, founded in 1876, for the fall term in September. He studied under Herbert B. Adams and Richard T. Ely.

Wilson resented Adams's use of him as a research assistant on Adams's own project to find the roots of American political parties in earlier governments in the colonies and England. Wilson found it "very tiresome," digging through "dusty records of old settlements and colonial cities," as his interest was the politics of the present. Finally Wilson went to Adams and told him what he wanted to do, and Adams gave the student free reign.

Wilson studied economic theory under Ely, then prepared a lecture dealing with Adam Smith.

In October, Wilson's uncle, William Woodrow, died in Rome, Georgia. Wilson traveled there to help with estate work. At his uncle's funeral, he met Ellen Axson for the first time. As Wilson was to write on October 11 about first seeing Ellen, "I remember thinking 'what a bright, pretty face; what splendid, mischievous, laughing eyes.'" Ellen was the daughter of Presbyterian minister Samuel E. Axson. Reverend Axson's career had begun under the tutelage of Woodrow's father. Axson's wife died in childbirth, and Ellen had responsibility for two younger brothers.

☙❧

WARREN G. HARDING hated teaching and seemed unable to find his calling as his eighteenth birthday approached. For a time Harding was an idler around the house, while his mother went to Cleveland to learn obstetrics.

On February 12 he wrote to his aunt Sarah Harding Dickerson that, "I am still fighting ignorance with fair success," but that he would quit his teaching job on February 23.

Harding tried his hand at insurance sales, but in late spring his insurance career ended when he underwrote coverage on the Hotel Marion at below established rates and had to return the premium.

☙❧

CALVIN COOLIDGE, 11 on July 4, thought the maple season in April was the most interesting of all the Vermont farm operations. He tapped the trees, set the buckets, and took the sap to the sugarhouse.

☙❧

HERBERT HOOVER, 9, lived in West Branch, Iowa, where he was kept busy with farm chores.

His mother Huldah was still struggling to care for her children. In September, Huldah, who had become a Quaker preacher, went to preach in Kansas, and the children boarded with relatives for several weeks.

☙❧

FRANKLIN D. ROOSEVELT, 1 year old, accompanied his parents to New Brunswick's Bay of Fundy where his father purchased a partially built house at Campobello, within sight of Maine. American business interests were developing the island.

1884
Chester Alan Arthur

The president, despite the secrecy attached to his affliction, ran a strong second on the first ballot at the Republican national convention behind James Blaine—even though the president had discouraged all efforts on his behalf and even asked his cabinet not to attend the convention. Many observers credited Arthur with running a good administration, displaying general competence, and avoiding scandals throughout his term.

January–February: Early in the year, Republicans were jockeying for position in anticipation of the presidential election. Former secretary of state James Blaine was the early favorite.

May: On May 17, a territorial government was established in Alaska.

Arthur had not made clear to the public if he would be seeking the Republican nomination. New York City businessmen, who liked Arthur's conservatism, held a giant rally for the president on May 20.

When Arthur asked his cabinet not to appear in Chicago, Secretary of the Navy William Chandler said, "I was aghast." Chandler warned that if he did not go to Chicago to line up Arthur support, there would be no guiding hand for the second-term effort.

Frank B. Conger was a young Washington, D.C., postmaster and avid backer of Arthur. In May the president asked Conger to abandon his efforts and tell his friends that the president did not "want to be re-elected." Conger politely refused the president, who told the young man to drop by the White House again after the convention.

June: Republicans met in Chicago on June 3 to June 6 to choose their presidential and vice presidential candidates. On the first ballot, Arthur received 278 votes to James Blaine's 334½, impressive considering that little effort was being made on Arthur's behalf. With each successive ballot, Arthur's total slipped. By the fourth ballot, Blaine won the nomination with 541 votes. Arthur took 207 votes on the fourth ballot. John Logan of Illinois was the nominee for vice president.

Two weeks later Frank Conger came by the White House as requested. He was "terribly shocked" when Arthur confided that he was suffering from an advanced case of Bright's disease and had little time left to live, making clear to Conger why Arthur did not want to be renominated. Arthur also told his son Chester his medical prognosis for the first time.

July 8–11: Democrats met in Chicago and nominated Governor Grover Cleveland of New York for president and Thomas A. Hendricks of Indiana for vice president (see **Grover Cleveland**, p. 371).

August–October: Arthur did little to help James Blaine in his campaign for president. There was bad blood between the two, stemming from remarks that Blaine had made 2 years earlier. Blaine, reacting to a suggestion that Arthur would be the nominee in 1884, said "What, this man? This man? Why, he will no more be the candidate than I will fly across the Potomac."

November: Grover Cleveland defeated James Blaine in the presidential election.

December: Unknown to Arthur, a few of his faithful met in a hotel in Albany on December 3 to discuss running the president for the Senate. Conkling's old seat, now occupied by Elbridge G. Lapham, would be open and several men, such as Steve French and George Sharpe, thought Arthur would be perfect.

Later in the month, a treaty was signed with Nicaragua for construction of a canal. The canal was never built.

Former Presidents

Ulysses S. Grant went broke, wiped out by a con artist who skipped the country when his pyramid scheme collapsed. With the failure of Grant and Ward, the firm in which his son was a partner and in which Grant had invested most of his money, the former president lost just about everything. To make matters worse, Grant felt the first signs of the throat cancer that would eventually kill him.

The problems with Grant and Ward began in the spring. Grant, 62, received a visit from Ferdinand Ward on May 4. Ward normally exuded confidence but this time talked of a crisis in the firm. Ward said he was going to put $150,000 into the company, could Grant match it? Grant was able to match it by getting a loan from William Vanderbilt.

Later, when son Buck had the bank vault opened, he found it empty. Ward had operated with double books. The firm had $67,000 instead of the $27 million that Ward had claimed. Grant's poor business sense led, in part, to Ward's duplicity. Grant was too trusting of Ward, who fled the United States but later served a 10-year jail term.

Soon after his financial crash, Grant was diagnosed with throat cancer. He was forced to give up his cigars.

A magazine editor suggested that Grant write about his Civil War experience. Desperate for cash, Grant wrote an article on Shiloh that led to a second piece on Vicksburg for which he was paid $500. Soon Grant was a neophyte author, writing 4 hours per day, 7 days per week, and searching for a book deal. He had a tentative deal that would only pay him a 10-percent royalty rate, hardly enough to bail him out of his debt.

Mark Twain visited New York and told Grant that the former president should find a better deal. Finally Twain promised to publish Grant's war book himself with the general getting 75 percent of the royalties. Grant soon went to work on his book, probably knowing that he had very little time left to finish it.

ৰ০৯

RUTHERFORD B. HAYES, 62 in October, lived in retirement in Fremont, Ohio.

Future Presidents

GROVER CLEVELAND'S quick, sharp political rise was completed when he was elected president just 3 years after winning the Buffalo mayoral race.

January–May: Cleveland's exhilarating ride to Washington began on January 1 when as governor of New York he addressed the legislature in Albany. In the speech, he stayed clear of national issues.

Republicans controlled the New York legislature. During the session, Cleveland signed many bills, including some sponsored by Theodore Roosevelt that gave more power to mayors throughout the state. Cleveland also pushed for banking changes, reforms in state charities, an aqueduct bill for New York City, and preservation of land around Niagara Falls. By the time the legislative session ended on May 16, Cleveland was so busy that he often took meals at his desk while studying proposed bills.

June: Republicans met in Chicago on June 3 to June 6 and nominated James Blaine for president and John Alexander Logan for vice president.

July: Prior to the Democratic national convention, many Democrats were still loyal to the cause of Samuel Tilden, who had lost to Rutherford B. Hayes in 1872. But Tilden was 70, and following a stroke spoke and walked with difficulty. Shortly before the convention, Tilden issued a statement saying he was not interested. That left the field to Thomas Bayard of Delaware, Allen Thurman of Ohio, and Cleveland.

The Democratic convention opened in Chicago on July 8. The first ballot on July 11 gave Cleveland 392 votes, Bayard 168 votes, Thurman 88 votes, and Samuel Jackson Randall of Pennsylvania 78 votes. Cleveland won the nomination on the second ballot, with 683 votes to Thurman's 81½. Cleveland was working in his Albany office when he learned of his nomination. Thomas Andrews Hendricks of Indiana received the nomination for vice president.

Cleveland's candidacy got off to a rocky start. Just 2 weeks after Cleveland won the Democratic nomination, a Buffalo newspaper revealed that the 47-year-old bachelor was the father of an 11-year-old son. Cleveland never denied the accusation, and the Blaine campaign took full advantage to exploit the issue.

Author Samuel Clemens (Mark Twain) was instrumental in convincing former president Ulysses S. Grant to write his memoirs.
(Library of Congress)

August–October: The 1884 presidential campaign was one of the most bitterly fought in the history of the United States. While the Blaine campaign sought every opportunity to remind voters of Cleveland's illegitimate son, they could not escape the fact that Blaine was far from a perfect candidate. It was well known that during the 1870s, while a member of the U.S. House of Representatives, Blaine had accepted stock in a railroad holding company intended to influence his vote on railroad issues. The scandal had hurt his hopes for the Republican nomination in 1876 and still dogged him in 1884, when several prominent Republicans, called "Mugwumps," threw their support to Cleveland.

In late October at the tail end of the campaign, Blaine was further hurt by comments made by a delegation of Protestant clergymen. On October 29 the clergymen met with Blaine. One of them, Samuel Dickinson Burchard, made a speech in which he referred to the Democrats as the party of "rum, Romanism, and rebellion." The remarks were seen as an attack on Catholics, and Blaine did little to disavow this insult. In the end, this may have cost him several thousand votes in New York, which could have swayed the election.

November–December: Cleveland was elected president on November 4 in a close election. In the popular vote, Cleveland polled 4,874,986 votes to Blaine's 4,851,981 votes. In the Electoral College, Cleveland took 219 votes to Blaine's 182 votes.

In his last 2 months as governor of New York, Cleveland continued to work hard for his state.

ৰ০৯

BENJAMIN HARRISON briefly had the support of Indiana's Republican leadership as the state's representative for the Republican presidential nomination. At the last moment, seeing that the support was not nationwide, Indiana Republicans decided not to submit Harrison's name to the convention.

For the 51-year-old U.S. senator from Indiana, the year's highlights were the weddings of his son and daughter. Son Russell married Mary Saunders on January 9. Mary was the daughter of Alvin Saunders, a U.S. senator from Nebraska. Harrison's daughter Mary married James McKee on November 5.

ৰ০৯

WILLIAM MCKINLEY gained national stature with a prominent role at the Republican national convention in Chicago. As a member of the resolutions committee, he made the report on the platform. And during a moment of convention chaos, the exasperated permanent chairman John B.

Henderson called McKinley to the chair. McKinley whacked the gavel and quickly brought about quiet and order to the convention.

Politically, however, McKinley had a strange year. He sat in the House because of his 8-vote victory over Democrat Jonathan Wallace in 1883. But on May 14, before the national convention took place, the House Committee on Elections reported that Wallace had won the contested race in the district. Put to a House vote on May 27, the Democratic majority prevailed and McKinley lost his seat on a party-line vote, 158 to 108. McKinley was stung to silence.

When he returned to Canton he received a hero's welcome and announced that he would be a candidate again. Overcoming another gerrymandering effort in his district, McKinley defeated Democrat D. R. Paige by 2,000 votes to regain his House seat.

❧❧

THEODORE ROOSEVELT was struck with double tragedy when both his wife and his mother died in New York City on the same day in February. The shocked legislator managed to mask his grief with a whirlwind political effort during the spring session of the state assembly in Albany. Later he attended the Republican national convention and made a major effort to block Blaine's nomination.

January–February: Alice was 9 months pregnant and had seen little of her husband for much of 1883. He had been out to Dakota, then had campaigned statewide for the speakership. Having lost that race, he now began the year in Albany as majority floor leader.

With the baby due at any moment, Theodore nevertheless took the train back to Albany to rally forces behind his anti-corruption legislation known as the Roosevelt bill. In Albany, Roosevelt received a telegram on February 12 that Alice had given birth to a girl.

After receiving congratulations all around the assembly, Roosevelt, on the afternoon of February 13, remained to report fourteen other bills out of the Cities Committee, which he controlled.

Theodore's sister Corinne then made a visit to the Roosevelt brownstone, now owned by brother Elliot, where she was greeted at the door by Elliott who said, "There is a curse on this house. Mother is dying and Alice is dying too." A telegram was sent to Albany about the new situation, and Roosevelt rushed for the train. He reached Grand Central Station at 10:30 P.M. Alice was dying of Bright's disease and was semi-comatose. She hardly recognized her husband. Roosevelt's mother had acute typhoid fever. She died at 3 A.M. on February 14. She was 49. Alice died later that day at 2 P.M. She was 22.

Roosevelt scratched a cross through his diary for February 14 and wrote, "The light has gone out of my life."

March–May: To relieve himself of the grief he felt over the death of his wife and the death of his mother, Roosevelt plunged into work during the spring session of the assembly.

In April, Roosevelt, though only 25, took control of the state Republican convention held at Utica, New York. Surprisingly, in May, he announced that he would not be seeking reelection and that he planned to retire from politics.

June 3–6: Roosevelt attended the Republican national convention in Chicago and made a major, yet unsuccessful, attempt to block the nomination of James Blaine.

July–December: Roosevelt spent much of the remainder of the year traveling back and forth to the Dakotas to hunt Buffalo.

❧❧

WILLIAM HOWARD TAFT's father, Alphonso, was transferred by the president from his post as U.S. minister to Austria-Hungary to take over as U.S. minister to Russia.

❧❧

WOODROW WILSON's studies at Johns Hopkins were often interrupted by his unending concern about his fiancée, Ellen Louise Axson. But he did manage to publish his first book and at the end of the year accepted a teaching position at Bryn Mawr, a new school for girls.

Wilson spent much of the year working on *Congressional Government*, a book that Houghton Mifflin accepted for publication. However, the book was somewhat slight and lacking in critical analysis. Wilson did not visit Congress while doing the research, and some glib phrases and generalizations showed a lack of understanding.

Ellen entered the Art Students League in New York City in the fall, and Wilson escorted her to New York. En route in Washington they took a trolley for a look at the White House; and later, when he left for Baltimore and Johns Hopkins, she wept.

For the fall term, Wilson decided that 2 years of graduate work would be enough, and his father discouraged him from going for a doctorate. He wrote to Ellen on November 8 that he felt it was not worth the risk to his health to seek a Ph.D.

Late in the year Wilson, 28 in December, met Martha C. Thomas, dean of Bryn Mawr, a new Quaker school 8 miles northwest of Philadelphia. He was hesitant to teach girls and work under a woman his own age, but it was an opening and he would be given time to lecture at nearby Johns Hopkins. The 2-year contract called for $1,500 a year.

❧❧

WARREN G. HARDING, not yet 19, jumped into the newspaper business at the top—as editor—and mingled with the mighty and prominent national writers at the Republican national convention in Chicago. Almost overnight he had found his two loves—newspaper work and politics—after false starts at teaching and selling.

The Hume brothers, owners of the Ohio newspaper *Marion Star*, sold it to Ben Demster, a friend of Harding, on May 18 just before it was to be auctioned off. Warren's father, Tyron, traded a house lot for a half interest in the paper, and by the end of the month Warren was the editor.

The *Marion Star* had 700 subscribers, but many had not paid. The inventory included four free railway passes that had been given in exchange for running train schedules. The paper had two employees.

Using the free transportation, Warren on June 2 headed for Chicago and the excitement of the Republican convention. He then rushed back to Marion to put his newspaper behind the nominee Blaine, only to find that the paper had folded because of a judgment to satisfy creditors against the house lot his father had used to close the deal.

Undaunted, Warren put on a gray plugged hat, symbol of the Plumed Knight, and at the district schoolhouse in Caledonia made his maiden political speech. Only a dozen people heard his pitch for Blaine.

Harding's only income now came from managing the band and small insurance commissions. His father was worried about Warren's near poverty and asked the owner of the *Mirror* to give his son a job. Warren took the job offered, $5 or less per week to do everything: write the stories, set the type, write the editorials, chase advertising, and even handle deliveries. Despite all this, *Mirror* owner Colonel James H. Vaughan soon fired Harding for "loafing."

The *Marion Star* was revived briefly with Harding's help but ceased publication before the Cleveland–Blaine election. The night of the presidential election, Harding ran into two former members of the Aeolian Band, Jack Warwick and Johnnie Sickle. A brakeman on the railroad, Sickle had inherited $1,600 and was looking for a place to invest the windfall. Sickle suggested that the three of them buy the *Marion Star* and make Harding editor.

In late November the three bought the paper from Demster. The *Marion Star* quickly did show changes. As he had at the *Mirror*, Harding did everything: wrote almost all the stories, sold the ads, and set the type.

୫୦୧୫

CALVIN COOLIDGE was a 12-year-old farmer in south-central Vermont, plowing the fields by himself using oxen. He sold cornballs and apples at town meetings. In the fall he would go to county fairs.

୫୦୧୫

HERBERT HOOVER became an orphan at the age of 9. His mother, Huldah, became ill with typhoid in Springdale, Iowa, and died on February 24 at the age of 35.

Huldah's three children were split up to live with relatives. At first the children went to the home of their grandmother Rebecca Minthorn in Kingsley, Plymouth County, across the state from West Branch. Two months later Herbert, now called Bert, returned home to move in with his uncle Allen Hoover and wife Millie on a farm a mile outside West Branch. Grandmother Minthorn then took sister May, not yet 8. Brother

Theodore went to live with another uncle, Davis Hoover in Hardin County, north of Des Moines.

୫୦୧୫

FRANKLIN ROOSEVELT, 2, in the fall sailed for Europe with his parents and was left in England with a governess. James and Sara then took to the waters in Bavaria.

୫୦୧୫

HARRY S TRUMAN was born on May 8 in the family home in Lamar, Missouri. His father was John A. Truman, age 32; his mother was Martha Ellen Young Truman, age 31.

John Truman was born on December 5, 1851, in Jackson County, near Kansas City. Martha Truman was born on November 25, 1852, on a Jackson County farm. The couple was married on December 28, 1881, in Grandview on the outskirts of Kansas City.

John, mostly self-educated, worked the family farm for 30 years, until he married and moved to Lamar to farm. He was also a horse and mule trader. Martha grew up in a pro-Confederate family that experienced traumatic events during the Civil War.

An ancestor of Harry was Joseph Truman of Nottingham, England, who arrived in New London, Connecticut, in 1666. Later generations moved to Shelby County, Kentucky.

Harry was named after his uncle Harrison Truman. The two grandfathers were A. Shippe Truman and Solomon Young. A Shippe–Solomon name conflict led to Harry taking a simple *S* as his middle name in a family compromise. Truman was a distant relative of President John Tyler and was of English, Irish, and German stock.

1885
Chester Alan Arthur

President Arthur completed his term as president and went into retirement, a wealthy but sick man. On his retirement, he decided to return to his law practice in New York City, strictly as counsel adviser and not as a courtroom participant.

January 29: The Senate rejected the canal treaty between the United States and Nicaragua.

February 21: The Washington Monument was dedicated more than 36 years after the cornerstone was laid. Money problems and the Civil War were among factors contributing to its lengthy construction. Arthur was part of the daylong ceremony to commemorate the event.

February 27: Arthur opened Indian land in the Dakota Territory to White settlers.

March: Arthur's last act as president was to put Ulysses S. Grant on the retired list at full pay. The Grant bill reached the House 3 hours before adjournment of the forty-eighth Congress on March 3.

The next day, Arthur and Grover Cleveland rode side by side to Cleveland's inauguration. After the ceremonies,

Arthur gave a luncheon for Cleveland. That night Arthur and his cabinet attended the inaugural ball.

Two days after leaving office Arthur was unanimously elected an honorary membership in the New York Chamber of Commerce. An official said, "Mr. Arthur has … by his prudent and conservative course … earned the confidence and respect of men of all parties."

April–December: Arthur's health fluctuated for much of the year. At times he felt strong and healthy. At other times he was weak and often in bed. His law partners gave him a salary of $1,000 per month, but he was often too sick to work and had to remain home.

Arthur turned 56 on October 5. He made his last public appearance on December 30 when he presided over a meeting of the Court of Common Pleas, which was honoring Chief Justice Charles P. Daly.

ഇരു

GROVER CLEVELAND, upon his inauguration, was a workhorse of a President. He made cuts in the federal payroll, screened appointments with far more care and attention than his predecessors, and tried to keep efficient men at their desks regardless of party affiliation. Cleveland worked harder and kept long hours but seemed to get little enjoyment from high office. More important to him was doing the right thing as he saw it.

March: Cleveland refused a free train ride from Albany and arrived in Washington on March 2. President Arthur offered the Clevelands the use of the White House, but the president-elect turned him down and went to the Arlington Hotel.

On March 4, Thomas A. Hendricks of Indiana took the vice presidential oath in the Senate. Arthur and Cleveland walked together from the Senate to the Capitol. Cleveland took the oath of office from Chief Justice Morrison Waite. Cleveland then stepped forward without an introduction and gave his inaugural address without notes. He said that the government was for all and that it was time to forget partisan and sectional strife.

Cleveland's cabinet was in place by March 6. Thomas Francis Bayard of Delaware was secretary of state; Daniel Manning of New York was secretary of Treasury; William Endicott of Massachusetts was secretary of war; Augustus Garland of Arkansas was attorney general; William Vilas of Wisconsin was postmaster general; William Collins Whitney of New York was secretary of the navy; and Lucius Lamar of Mississippi was secretary of the Interior.

April–July: On April 17, Cleveland declared Arthur's act

Grover Cleveland, one of the most industrious presidents, gained little enjoyment from the office. (Library of Congress)

of February 27 opening Indian land in the Dakota Territory to settlers "inoperative." Sympathetic to Native Americans, Cleveland sent General Philip Sheridan west to learn the facts about cowboys encroaching on Indian territory.

Sheridan recommended giving ranchers 40-day notices to get out, and Cleveland agreed by decree that he signed on July 23. Cleveland acted too quickly, however, and most cattle died from a severe winter. He later lamented his action.

Meanwhile, on May 17 Apache Chief Geronimo went on the warpath in Arizona and New Mexico. Cleveland suppressed the uprising but pressed for American citizenship for Native Americans.

August–October: In August, Cleveland wrote to Frances Folsom, his ward and the daughter of his deceased law partner. Cleveland proposed to Frances, only 21 at the time.

Cleveland set a goal of reforming the White House administration by laying off workers. Early cabinet meetings dealt largely with reform within departments and the desire to cut deadwood. By August 13 the *New York World* declared that the administration had routed out corruption in the navy, Treasury, Indian bureau, land office, and war department.

Cleveland also had to deal with office-seekers, as did all presidents before him. He told a reporter, "This office-seeking is a disease." He insisted that not all Republicans be removed and that no Democrat be appointed unless competent and honest. Cleveland did not put personal friends in office.

November 25: Vice President Thomas A. Hendricks died.

Former Presidents

ULYSSES S. GRANT was now in a race against death to finish his book that dealt mostly with the Civil War. It was in a way a heroic contest closely followed by the public. On bad days he could not work. On good days he wrote 10,000 words. Grant received endless encouragement from Mark Twain, and even Jefferson Davis sent a sympathy note.

February–March: Grant's throat was worse in February, and he also suffered a pain in the ear. Doctors confirmed the malignancy would prove fatal. His wife, Julia, wrote to a friend, "General Grant is very, very ill. I cannot write how ill—my tears blind me."

On March 3, Congress passed an act restoring Grant to four-star general status with full pay.

April–June: In April, Grant was much better, and the book became a more important project as something that had to be done for the sake of his family. The *New York Tribune* reported on April 19 that Grant would move to the Catskills to complete the book.

W. J. Arkell, a real estate promoter, thought it would help his resort at Balmoral in the Adirondacks if Grant died. Arkell wrote to a friend, "If he should die there, it might make the place a national shrine … and incidentally a success." Grant decided to sell his cottage at Long Branch, New Jersey, and took Arkell up on the offer.

Vanderbilt offered his private railroad car, and on June 16 Grant, suffering even more with a swollen neck, and a party of eight including nurses and valets, left Grand Central Station for Balmoral. The local stations were crowded with people wishing to get a glimpse of Grant.

Once at his new home, Grant faced a stream of visitors including Civil War generals, both Union and Confederate, and politicians. Grant appeared to love it. Any number of Grant's rich friends could have arranged for a sheltered retreat, but Grant seemed to thrive on Arkell's arrangement despite the spectacle atmosphere.

Publishers were eager to see the book now that there was national focus on the dying general. In June the first volume ran in the press, although Grant kept making changes as he edited the material. Grant would bundle up on the porch to work. His prose was very simple, strong, and clear. He said little about the low years for him between the wars and nothing about his presidency.

July–August: By early July, Grant could not talk and communicated with others using notes. He continued working on his memoirs. Grant rallied briefly on July 12 but wrote on July 14, "There is nothing more I should do to it [the memoirs] now and therefore I am not likely to be more ready to go than at this moment."

Grant died at 8 A.M. on July 23 with Julia and the family at his bedside. He was 63 years old.

The funeral ride up Fifth Avenue on August 8 included many generals as well as Presidents Cleveland, Rutherford B. Hayes, and Chester Arthur, and the governors of twenty states. It was one of largest military-civilian pageants in history. Grant was buried in Central Park until being moved in 1897 to Grant's Tomb, Morningside Heights, at Riverside Drive and 122nd Street.

Grant's memoirs were a tremendous success when published later in 1885. The royalties for the book were estimated at $500,000.

ഇൻറ

Rutherford B. Hayes was in retirement at Spiegal Grove, in Fremont, Ohio. Spiegal Grove continued to grow in size. The height of the building was doubled with a new upper floor, and the porch was extended to 80 feet.

In August he went to New York City and rode with Arthur in the 5-hour Grant funeral procession.

Hayes turned 63 on October 4.

Future Presidents

Benjamin Harrison and his wife, Carrie, took a train trip to the Pacific Coast, including Yellowstone, a short second honeymoon. The U.S. senator from Indiana also conducted some Senate business on Indian affairs and visited son Russell, who was now ranching near Helena, Montana.

Harrison spent much of his time working on railroad legislation. Harrison wanted an interstate commerce commission created to stop railroad abuse and said the small man in the towns of America could not be heard because "he is but a pigmy in this contest and he is contending with giants."

When Harrison heard that the Democrats would gerrymander Indiana, he was angry and wanted the *Indianapolis Journal* to stir up "some hot talk" on the issue. The Democrats were lining up Isaac P. Gray to run against Harrison in 1887. Harrison wrote to Nicholas Ensley on February 18, "I could leave the Senate and return … home and to business without any personal regrets.… But … owe it to the Republican Party to make the best fight possible, and shall do so."

ഇൻറ

William McKinley, 42, was back in the U.S. House of Representative and was discussed as a potential governor of Ohio. But Joseph Foraker won the office, and now McKinley promoted his appointment ideas on the new governor.

ഇൻറ

Theodore Roosevelt made two more trips to Dakota Territory to ranch, became engaged to Edith Carow, and kept a hand in New York politics during his "retirement."

April–June: Roosevelt returned to Medora in North Dakota on April 14. His ranch there, Elkhorn Ranch, had eight rooms, a perpetual fire, library, bearskins, and stuffed heads. He bought 1,500 cattle at a cost of $39,000. The herd, under Roosevelt's supervision, arrived in Medora on May 5. The cattle stampeded, forcing Roosevelt and his hands to round up the herd. The cattle reached Box Elder Creek on May 19. Roosevelt returned to New York in late June.

July–September: Roosevelt spent time with his daughter Alice in July before returning to Medora on August 22. Newspapers in the area now suggested Roosevelt for the Senate when statehood came to Dakota, and he was made a deputy sheriff for Billings County.

October–December: Roosevelt headed back for New York and the state Republican convention at Saratoga in October. At the convention, Roosevelt helped draft the party platform.

Early in October he bumped into Edith Carow. Edith was still making regular visits to the Roosevelt home to visit Theodore's sister Corinne, her best friend.

On November 17, Theodore, now 27, proposed marriage, and the 24-year-old accepted. The engagement was kept secret, even from relatives, and on purpose in memory of his first wife, Alice. But soon Theodore and Edith were together all the time, going to dinners and operas.

෨෬

WILLIAM HOWARD TAFT took on a new job and became engaged to Nellie Herron.

January: As of January 1, Taft had a new job as assistant solicitor for Hamilton County, Ohio. He worked under his friend Rufus B. Smith. Taft tried civil cases in the county but because the workload was light, he had tine to practice law privately with his partner Harlan Page Lloyd.

April–May: In April, Taft proposed to Nellie. She rejected him. He wrote to her on May 1, "Oh, Nellie … I believe you could be happy with me." On May 10, he wrote to her, "Do say that you will try to love me. Oh, how I will work and strive to be better and do better." Later in May she accepted.

෨෬

WOODROW WILSON, 29 in December, married Ellen Louise Axson and began his teaching career as Bryn Mawr's only history professor.

He kept up his writing regimen after his first book received favorable reviews.

January–June: Woodrow and Ellen set their wedding for June 24. He wrote to her on April 15, "My heart is given [you] in marriage already.… I don't care a rap for myself, but I do care everything for you." He wrote to her in May about "our love. I can't … tell whether I am sitting still or standing on my head!"

The marriage on June 24 took place in Savannah, Georgia. The service was performed by Wilson's father, Joseph, and her grandfather, Isaac Stockton Keith Axson, both southern Presbyterian ministers.

The honeymoon was at the Arden Park Hotel cottages in North Carolina, a location visited at other times by Wilson and his mother.

July–December: The couple made their first home at Bryn Mawr, close to Philadelphia. The new school had only forty-two students on a campus of two buildings. Wilson taught Greek and Roman history. One student recalled years later, "His lectures were fascinating and held me spellbound."

෨෬

WARREN G. HARDING posted a solid year of achievement in making the *Marion Star* bigger, better, and a factor in the life of a small town in north-central Ohio. At the start of the year the newspaper was close to going broke, but Harding managed to keep it going somehow. He sometimes slept in the office. He installed a telephone over Jack Warwick's objection and bought his partner off by winning a poker hand. Warwick remained with the paper as a salaried worker and eventually became city editor.

On June 14, Harding produced the first *Weekly Star*, a Republican sheet, and a challenge for political advertising for George Crawford's *Marion Independent* as the Republican voice in town.

Two weeks later Harding obtained the Associated Press wire and the boilerplate material on page one was replaced by national and foreign news, stocks, and baseball scores. By July, Harding boasted that his *Marion Star* had twice the circulation of the *Independent* or *Mirror*.

Harding turned 20 in November.

෨෬

CALVIN COOLIDGE was 12 when his mother died on March 14 and was buried in south-central Vermont. She was just 39. "Life was never to seem the same again," Calvin later wrote.

Calvin turned 13 on July 4.

෨෬

HERBERT HOOVER, 11, moved from Iowa to Oregon to live with his mother's brother, Dr. Henry John Minthorn, whose own young boy had died the year before. Hoover left West Branch on November 12 and traveled on a train with Mr. and Mrs. O. T. Hammell, Quaker friends. The train took 7 days to cross the Rockies from Council Bluffs to Portland. Uncle John met the boy and escorted him 20 miles southwest of Portland to Newberg, a new Quaker community of only a few hundred.

Hoover lived in a two-story wooden house at 115 South River Street built in 1881 and purchased by Minthorn in 1884. Minthorn, a doctor and missionary, had asked relatives in Iowa to send him Hoover.

Minthorn had been a government doctor in Indian territory, then in Iowa, before becoming Indian school superintendent at Forest Grove, Oregon. Henry and Laura Minthorn had two daughters, Tennessee, age 11, and Gertrude, age 3.

෨෬

FRANKLIN D. ROOSEVELT, now 3, and his parents returned to New York after a rough Atlantic crossing from England.

The new vacation home at Campobello was finished. The property had 4 acres.

෨෬

HARRY S TRUMAN, 1 year old, and family moved to a farm in Harrisonville, not far south of Kansas City.

1886
Grover Cleveland

The president had a mixed bag of problems on his desk: confrontation with the Senate, a surplus, the tariff, war pension graft, and such labor strife as the nation had never before seen. But on the bright side was the first White House wedding for a sitting president. (John Tyler had married in New York City. (See **John Tyler**, Volume 1, page 228.)

January 19: Congress passed the Presidential Succession Act, under which the secretary of state would take over if both the president and vice president died, resigned, or were incapacitated.

February–March: Republicans, in control of the Senate, decided to renew the old Tenure of Office issue. Senators

George Edmunds and John Sherman wanted more Senate control over dismissals and nominations. In doubtful cases the Senate wanted reasons for Cleveland's dismissals.

Cleveland believed that the Senate was trying to erode his executive discretion. Cleveland ordered department heads to refuse to cooperate. But there was a distinction between *dismissals*, in which the Constitution gave the Senate no authority, and *appointments*. The president was willing to give formal papers but not confidential material.

Cleveland sent a message to the Senate on March 1 which stated that the Constitution gave the president power of suspension or removal, that Congress did not have a constitutional right in the first Tenure of Office law, and that many papers regarding appointments were private and privileged and not official papers. He also said he was upholding the Constitution and that "discontent of party friends" would not change his resolve.

Soon Republican senators fell in line and the revolt instigated by Edmunds collapsed. Many had given secret memos to Cleveland regarding someone they wanted removed. On March 29, Washington and New York newspapers said the Senate would ask for no more information on appointments. The contest was a major defeat for Edmunds.

Secretary of Treasury Daniel Manning, 55, collapsed from overwork on March 23 with a ruptured vessel in the brain. He offered to resign, but Cleveland said Charles Fairchild could take over while Manning recovered. Manning went to England where he gradually recovered.

April–May: Labor unrest had been spreading throughout the United States since the beginning of the year. On April 22, Cleveland proposed that Congress set up a special commission to mediate labor disputes. Many viewed this proposal as a weak attempt to settle the labor problems.

On May 1 more than 100,000 workers across the country left their jobs to show solidarity for labor changes. They protested the long hours as well as the lack of safety in most factories. In Chicago alone, nearly 40,000 walked out on their jobs.

The strike gained momentum from day to day across the country. By May 5 the number of strikers had reached more than 190,000. However, the great strides made by unions were quickly dashed when a bomb exploded in Haymarket Square in Chicago on May 4 where a labor rally was being held. The explosion killed eight policemen and wounded sixty-seven others. In retaliation, the police fired into the crowd, killing and wounding dozens of strikers.

June: Cleveland married Frances Folsom on June 2 to become the first president to marry in the White House. Folsom was the 21-year-old daughter of Cleveland's former law partner, Oscar Folsom. Oscar Folsom died in 1875, and Cleveland had been guardian to Frances since that time.

August 20: Eight anarchists were convicted for the bloody bombing of Haymarket Square on May 4. Seven were sentenced to die. Four of the death sentences were later commuted to life in prison.

September 4: Apache Chief Geronimo surrendered to U.S. General Nelson A. Miles in Arizona. Geronimo and his warriors used terror and killing for 10 years to try to discourage White settlers from moving into Arizona and New Mexico.

December: For much of the year, what to do with the government's $94 million budget surplus was a hot issue. Cleveland discussed the surplus in his December message to Congress. The dilemma was whether or not to keep the Treasury out of the picture or to embark on a public spending spree.

The president also called for lowered tariffs in his December message, adding that there was a popular demand for lower tariffs and this feeling "should be recognized and obeyed." Another House vote, however, again rejected lowering tariffs, 154 to 149. Cleveland was disappointed but not discouraged.

Former Presidents

R<small>UTHERFORD</small> B. H<small>AYES</small>, 64, was in retirement at Fremont, Ohio. His son Birchard married Mary Nancy Sherman in Norwalk, Ohio, on December 30.

80C3

C<small>HESTER</small> A<small>LAN</small> A<small>RTHUR</small> was deathly ill throughout the year. His health turned for the worse early in the year and continued to slide until his death in November.

February: News about his battle with Bright's disease was leaked to the press. For the first time, the public knew just how sick Arthur truly was.

The Haymarket Square riots in Chicago, Illinois, on May 4. The riots began when a bomb exploded at a labor rally, killing and wounding police officers and strikers.

April–August: In April, Arthur was critical, but in June he rallied and was taken from his Lexington Avenue residence in New York City to a cottage at New London, Connecticut, at the suggestion of doctors.

September–November: Rutherford B. Hayes and Chief Justice Morrison Waite visited Arthur in New York in the fall, and Hayes described Arthur as "thin and feeble." Arthur could hardly move when Hayes and Waite visited.

Arthur returned to the city from Connecticut on October 1. He was an invalid, propped up in bed, and despondent.

On November 16, Arthur felt better and received visitors and dictated letters. He told his doctors he had not "felt better in six months."

Arthur asked for his old customhouse friend, Jimmy Smith, and then told Smith to destroy virtually all of Arthur's personal and official papers as his son Alan watched them burn.

At 8 A.M. on November 17, a nurse found him unconscious from a massive cerebral hemorrhage. Arthur died at 5 A.M. on November 18 at the age of 57. Federal offices closed in Washington on November 22. Newspapers were strong in their praise for Arthur's White House years.

A private funeral was held on November 22 at the Church of the Heavenly Rest, his wife's former parish. Among those attending the funeral were Robert Todd Lincoln, General Philip Sheridan, Cornelius Vanderbilt, President Grover Cleveland, and Chief Justice Waite.

Future Presidents

BENJAMIN HARRISON campaigned hard in Indiana for Republican candidates. When Republicans won a narrow victory in Indiana in the fall election, Senator Preston B. Plumb of Kansas wrote to Harrison on November 10 that the victory "puts you in the line of Presidential promotion. It seems to me that you and a good New Yorker would make an invincible team."

Earlier in the year Harrison received national publicity twice. His battle in the U.S. Senate for South Dakota statehood exposed Democratic fears that a new Republican state would tilt the electoral balance in the 1888 election. His statehood measure passed. In the other, Harrison attacked the spoils system in a Senate floor speech that was printed in many newspapers and was aimed at embarrassing Cleveland. In both cases Harrison was perceived as both a party leader and party spokesman of national stature.

ജര

WILLIAM MCKINLEY was re-elected to his House seat from the Canton, Ohio, district. He defeated Wallace H. Phelps by 2,559 votes.

McKinley was a speaker at the dedication of the Garfield Memorial in Cleveland. In a eulogy to Garfield on January 19, McKinley said, "To me he was the strongest, broadest, brav-

est when he spoke for honest money…. He was at his best [arguing sound money]."

ജര

THEODORE ROOSEVELT, incredibly, while still 27 years of age, ran for mayor of New York City. At one stage of the race he was the favorite, but he not only lost—he finished third. He also made two trips to Dakota during this year, and his reputation among cowboys grew. He married for a second time, to Edith Carow, a childhood playmate.

March–June: In early March, Theodore and Edith went on separate trips, Edith to Europe and Theodore to Medora, North Dakota. As he worked on his ranch, Theodore began working on a biography of Thomas Hart Benton. From April 30 to May 21 he wrote 83,000 words on Benton and was nearly finished by the end of June.

July: Roosevelt finished the Benton book on July 2, then left for New York on July 7 and on his arrival spent 3 weeks finalizing it.

August–November: Roosevelt headed back to Medora on August 5. There he received a letter from Edith confirming a London wedding for December 2.

Between August 21 and September 18, Roosevelt went to Idaho with Bill Merrifield to hunt in the Coeur d'Alene Mountains. On returning to Medora, Roosevelt was "savagely irritated" with newspaper gossip that he was engaged to Edith.

New York City Republicans held their convention at the New York Grand Opera House on October 15. Henry George, a radical, was in the race as Labor Party candidate. The Democrats had nominated Congressman Abram S. Hewitt, a wealthy man. Roosevelt told reporters that he was not a candidate and that George's strength was great.

A group of Republicans asked Roosevelt if he would run. He was surprised but agreed "with the most genuine reluctance." Roosevelt was nominated by the Republicans but ran a poor third in the November elections, with Hewitt winning the race.

Roosevelt delayed leaving for England until November 6 in order to see what happened in the New York City mayor's race. With his defeat, he was free to move ahead with his planned wedding in December.

December 2: Theodore and Edith were married in London, England.

ജര

WILLIAM HOWARD TAFT married and took his bride to Europe for a honeymoon. He also had a house built for her.

February: Will borrowed $1,000 to build a two-story wooden house in East Walnut Hills, Ohio, on East McMillan Street. Her father gave them a lot that overlooked the Ohio River.

June–September: Will was 28 years old and Helen "Nellie" Herron was 25 when they married on June 19 in the Herron home at 69 Pike Street in downtown Cincinnati. The Reverend D. N. A. Hoge of Zanesvillle, Ohio, officiated.

The honeymoon trip began at the Albemarle Hotel in Sea Bright, on the New Jersey shore near New York City, where word spread that they were newlyweds. After 4 nights in Sea Bright and 1 night in New York, they boarded a ship for Europe. They spent 3 months in France, England, and Scotland.

October–December: On returning to Cincinnati, Taft learned that a vacancy existed on the Ohio Superior Court because Judge Judson Harmon had wanted to return to private practice. The superior court office was elective except when filling an unexpired term, and Harmon's move would mean a vacancy of 14 months. Will was under consideration for the post.

⁕

WOODROW WILSON, 30 in December, was awarded a Ph.D. by Johns Hopkins University in Baltimore, and Ellen gave birth to the couple's first child. At the time Wilson was lecturing on history at Bryn Mawr University outside of Philadelphia.

April–May: Ellen gave birth to a girl, Margaret, on April 30. Woodrow was a "little disappointed" that the baby was not a boy.

For the spring term Wilson taught English history and special topics in American history, and later he taught French history, the Italian Renaissance, and German Reformation. He emphasized the social causes of the Civil War, and to impress the connecting links, he taught an English history course backward to show what he meant.

June: Wilson was awarded his Ph.D. when Professor Adams at Johns Hopkins received approval for Wilson to get special treatment. Formal oral examinations were replaced by a written examination in five subjects plus an interview before the degree-granting board.

July–September: Wilson wrote reviews that appeared in publications in Chicago and Philadelphia. An article about the need for a new political party for strong men of principle and boldness was published on September 26 in the *Boston Times*.

⁕

WARREN G. HARDING continued to build on his reputation as a competitive editor in rural Ohio. Once again his opponent was George Crawford, owner of the *Independent*. Harding and Crawford were in competition for legal ads and county commission reports.

A depression caused the advertising market to dry up, and on May 24 Harding had to cancel his Associated Press coverage. Now he ran free fillers from the *Chicago Sun* and *Detroit Free Press*. By September things were better, and Harding hired Harry Sheets who had been with the *Pittsburgh Daily Post* and resumed the Associated Press.

Harding was 21 years old in November.

⁕

CALVIN COOLIDGE was 14 when he left home for Ludlow, Vermont, only 12 miles away, to enter a Baptist finishing school, Black River Academy. He was to write later that going to Black River was "one of the greatest events of my life." His father was one of the school's twenty-four trustees.

Both his parents and grandmother Coolidge had gone there. Coolidge arrived in Ludlow in November by sleigh in below freezing weather. The school building was on a bluff above the Black River. The school had 125 students, one principal, and two assistants. Coolidge took grammar, Latin, government, and algebra and got his first look at the United States Constitution. He took a job in a cabinet shop on Saturdays.

⁕

HERBERT HOOVER, 12, lived in Newberg, Oregon. His chores included burning logs, splitting wood, milking and driving cows to pasture, and watering and feeding horses.

⁕

FRANKLIN D. ROOSEVELT, 4, lived at the family Hyde Park estate on New York's Hudson River. His mother continued to keep him in girls' dresses.

⁕

HARRY S TRUMAN, 2, lived in Harrisonville, Missouri.

April 25: Harry's brother John Vivian was born.

1887
Grover Cleveland

President Cleveland ended his third year in office with another White House first—he devoted the entire December annual message to Congress to the tariff issue. It was Cleveland's contention that the growing surplus was unhealthy for business, hurt the workingman, and protected the trusts.

January–March: Cleveland signed the bill to create the Interstate Commerce Commission on February 4, which culminated a long congressional debate over the regulation of railroads. This was the first regulatory effort. The act called for "just and equal" rates for railroads and banned rebates to large customers. The commission and railroads worked well in setting rates and other reforms, but before long corporations began setting secret rates.

Early in the year, party leaders talked about the feasibility of a special message to Congress on the tariff. Many duties were still what they had been in Civil War days, and others had risen.

Secretary of Treasury Daniel Manning, before resigning his office in February, suggested using the surplus to retire all greenbacks, or about $346 million. He wanted to substitute gold or silver coin for every dollar of greenback. The project would take 3½ years to retire all of the greenbacks. There was a sense, however, that the public felt safe with greenbacks.

The tariff issue grew after Congress adjourned on March 3 without solving the problem of the surplus.

Cleveland gained a big victory when Congress repealed the Tenure of Office Act on March 3. By repealing the law, Congress returned to the president the ability to fire federal appointees.

April 1: Charles Stebbins Fairchild of New York was appointed secretary of Treasury.

July–September: Cleveland called a summer meeting at his Oak View retreat to discuss the tariff and with House Speaker John Carlisle and others talked about it for 4 days.

On September 7, Cleveland told the *New York World* that an extra session of Congress was not necessary, and he asked that congressmen discuss the matter with their constituents during the recess. Cleveland's men decided, however, that reducing the tariff was a must.

December: By December 1 the Treasury surplus was more than $55 million and was projected to be $140 by 1888. Cleveland decided to devote his entire December 6 message to Congress on the tariff, a first. Some of his advisers said the message would bring about his defeat. Cleveland replied that he had a duty to reform.

In the tariff message, the president said that the surplus was a danger to business health. He dealt with unjust protection, the burden on the poor, and a system of taxation that hit hardest at the ill-paid workingman—blaming the trusts "which have for their objective the regulation of the supply and price of commodities." These, he said, were selfish schemes.

The protectionist press congratulated Cleveland for being forthright and clearing the air on the issue. The *Philadelphia Press* called the message the "unequivocal avowal of his extreme free trade purposes."

Former Presidents

RUTHERFORD B. HAYES was in retirement at his estate in Fremont, Ohio, in the north-central part of the state near Lake Erie.

Future Presidents

BENJAMIN HARRISON lost his Senate seat, and his presidential hopes were clouded when James Blaine sent mixed signals from Europe about his presidential intentions for 1888. From Europe, Blaine several times said he was out of the race but then answered Cleveland's December message to Congress point by point, acting like a candidate outlining the 1888 platform.

January–March: Harrison's term ended when a fight developed in the Indiana legislature over seating a Republican president pro tempore in the state senate. In mid-January the Indiana legislature met and declared Republican Lieutenant Governor Robert S. Robertson the winner. Alonzo G. Smith, Democrat and president pro tempore of the Indiana senate,

went to court seeking an injunction to forbid Robertson from presiding. Harrison was Robertson's chief counsel.

The issue concerned the status of Robertson. The Indiana constitution called for an election every 4 years for lieutenant governor.

The legislature split in the dispute, which impacted Harrison's status as a senator. Harrison appeared before the Indiana Supreme Court, a group leaning toward the Democrats, to argue for Robertson. Smith's attorneys included David Turpie, likely opponent for Harrison's U.S. Senate seat. The court sustained Smith, a blow to Harrison.

Now came the vote regarding Indiana's U.S. senator. Throughout fifteen ballots neither Harrison nor Turpie were able to obtain a majority because of the votes of four independent Greenbacks in the legislature. Finally on the sixteenth ballot, one lone Democratic Independent Greenback switched to Turpie, and Harrison was defeated.

Harrison returned to Washington to finish his term in March and hoped a review on the legality of his ouster might keep Turpie from taking over. Harrison had information that bribery may have been involved in the vote and urged Michener to seek redress from the Indiana Supreme Court.

Harrison turned his Senate seat over to Turpie on March 3, then wrote railroad tycoon James J. Hill saying he wanted to invest now that he was out of public life,

October–December: Harrison's status as a potential Republican presidential candidate in 1888 remained clouded. Much of this had to do with James Blaine's intentions. On October 11, Blaine wrote to Whitelaw Reid, saying he was "strongly disinclined to run. ... I abhor ... becoming a chronic candidate."

As late as December a friend from New Jersey told Harrison, 54, not to believe the business about Blaine bowing out of the race. This belief was furthered when the *New York Tribune* interviewed Blaine at his hotel in Paris on December 7 in response to Cleveland's address to Congress. Blaine's rebuttal of the president's views were widely published and appeared tantamount to announcing his candidacy, especially because of the prompt manner in which he answered Cleveland's arguments. However, when Blaine reached Venice he said again that he would not be a candidate.

ೞോ

WILLIAM MCKINLEY, in supporting John Sherman for president in 1888, moved closer to Mark Hanna and away from Governor Joseph Foraker as a political adviser. Hanna was a powerful Ohio businessman who had supported Garfield in his quest for the presidency in 1880.

Sherman supporters met quietly in Canton, Ohio, on June 24 to discuss their man's chances at the next Republican national convention. Governor Foraker, now ambitious to become a senator as well as president eventually, was not invited, but newspapers leaked news of the meeting in Canton.

The gathering agreed to support Sherman. Foraker was angry with both Hanna and McKinley for not inviting him. Foraker later endorsed Sherman in a show of party unity, but McKinley resented his attitude.

Still, Foraker was renominated for governor and won the election.

In the U.S. House of Representatives, McKinley, 44, supported the Interstate Commerce Act.

෨෬

THEODORE ROOSEVELT was publicly labeled presidential timber for the first time, although he was not yet 29. Some critics scoffed at the suggestion that he was headed for the White House at such a tender age. After completing his European honeymoon with Edith he saw his book *Thomas Hart Benton* published and started writing another, *Gouverneur Morris*. He also made two more trips to Dakota, where the winter of 1886 to 1887 had devastated his investment in beef.

January–March: Theodore and Edith honeymooned for 15 weeks in England, France, and Italy. The honeymoon started in Paris, moved to Provence, then to the Italian Riviera, Pisa, Florence, Rome, and Naples. Then it was on to Sorrento and Capri before heading back to Rome and Florence. From Florence, Roosevelt wrote to his mother, "I have not theslightest belief in my having any political future." After Milan, Paris, and London the couple sailed from Liverpool on March 19. They arrived back in New York on March 28.

April: When Roosevelt arrived back in the United States, he received word of the brutal winter that had hit the Dakotas. The great blizzard of January 28 was the worst anyone in Dakota could remember. Cattle died everywhere, many frozen like statues. Roosevelt left for Medora on April 4 to personally look at the damage to his investment.

May: The New York Federal Club gave a banquet at Delmonico's on May 11 with Roosevelt as guest of honor. The club consisted of a group of Republican reformers. Roosevelt gave a fighting speech, and Cleveland was one of many targets. Chauncey Depew, the next speaker, said that the remaining speakers would have to submit their speeches first to Roosevelt, "So that when he runs for President no case of Burchard will interfere [a reference to "rum, Romanism, and rebellion," the gaff that helped beat Blaine]."

Depew was the first to link Theodore with presidential ambitions. The Roosevelt speech made headlines nationwide, and the *Harrisburg Telegraph* suggested that Roosevelt be made the vice president on a ticket headed by Joseph Foraker. The *New York Sun* pointed out that Roosevelt, at 28, could not be eligible for the presidency until 1897.

September 13: Edith gave birth to Theodore Jr.

෨෬

WILLIAM HOWARD TAFT left his solicitor's post to become a superior court judge in March while only 29. His father, Alphonso, once held the same chair. Taft turned 30 on September 15.

෨෬

WOODROW WILSON, 31 in December, was tired of teaching women at Bryn Mawr but had to turn down an offer from the University of Michigan because of his contract with Bryn Mawr. Later in the year, he tried to get a job with the U.S. government.

March: Wilson went to Washington and looked up his old law partner, Edward Renick, now in the Treasury Department. Wilson visited Congress for the first time and interviewed a few bureau heads.

April: President James B. Angell of the University of Michigan made a job offer on April 9, but Wilson's Bryn Mawr contract prevented any move.

August 28: Once again Ellen went south to give birth to another daughter, Jessie, in Gainesville, Georgia.

October–November: Wilson was still disappointed with teaching women. He wrote to Ellen on October 8 that lecturing women about current politics was about the same as lecturing stonemasons on the "evolution of fashion in dress."

Wilson on November 7 sought Angell's help to become an assistant secretary of state. Originally Wilson wrote to Angell, "Can you suggest proper dignified means of getting my name mentioned in the proper quarter? Or can you—to be at my boldest—give me in any way your own personal assistance?" Wilson added that he needed a "seat on the inside of government—a seat high enough to command views of the system." In the end, nothing ever came Wilson's way.

෨෬

WARREN G. HARDING was in the middle of cutthroat small-town newspaper wars enlivened when his father armed with a shotgun went after an enemy editor.

George Crawford, honcho of the *Marion Independent*, complained again about whether or not his paper was more "Republican" than Harding's *Marion Star*. Crawford called Harding's paper "almost Republican" and chided Harding on May 16 about how Vaughan of the *Mirror*, the Democratic paper in Marion, endorsed a note for Warren.

Harding, 22, made a political decision during this year by supporting Ohio governor-elect Joseph B. Foraker. Foraker came to Marion in September to campaign, and Harding later wrote an excited account of this political visit.

෨෬

CALVIN COOLIDGE, 15, was a student at the Black River Academy in Ludlow, Vermont. Sometimes he would spend a weekend at the home of Mrs. Sarah Pollard, 46, his mother's elder sister, who lived in Proctorsville, 3 miles away. Calvin enjoyed riding a horse but had no one to accompany him.

Coolidge started Greek in the fall term and also took French, ancient history, geometry, and American history. He was an average student but poor in mathematics. Calvin continued working in the carriage shop, often making toys and baby buggies. His father had him put all of his earned money in the bank.

ഇരുൻ

HERBERT HOOVER, 13, accompanied Dr. Minthorn on long buggy rides to see patients around Newberg, Oregon. The doctor was austere, had great energy, and was an interesting conversationalist. Herbert's older brother Theodore moved from Iowa to Newberg. They had been separated for 2 years. The brothers slept in the academy where they received their schooling.

ഇരുൻ

FRANKLIN D. ROOSEVELT, 5, met President Grover Cleveland in the White House. The Roosevelts spent the winter in Washington. Before returning to Hyde Park, James Roosevelt took his son to meet his friend Cleveland. The harried president said, "My little man, I am making a strange wish for you. It is that you may never be president."

ഇരുൻ

HARRY S TRUMAN, 3, and family moved into the home of his mother's parents in Grandview, close to Kansas City. The two-story house had eight rooms, two barns, a granary, and hog sheds.

1888
Grover Cleveland

President Cleveland won his tariff fight in Congress but lost the election—in part because the Democrats were unable to match the better organized Republican campaign, which displayed nonstop oratory by Benjamin Harrison and James Blaine. In contrast to the 1884 campaign, Cleveland fought this campaign mostly on the tariff issue, not reform of the system.

January: Many industrialists in the East favored the status quo and were against Cleveland's tariff ideas. Cleveland urged that the nation's tariffs be lowered, arguing that protectionism resulted in higher prices. Steel and iron men were against Cleveland, whereas bankers were split.

Cleveland and House Speaker John Carlisle left it to Roger Mills of Texas, the new chairman of the Ways and Means Committee, to write a new tariff schedule. His work made only moderate cuts and appeared to favor southern industries. Critics said it was not real reform.

April–May: Debate on the tariff opened in the House on April 17 with Mills speaking for 2 hours. William McKinley directed the Republican line of attack, claiming that many free items would hurt farmers and lead to competition from Canada. On May 18, McKinley said that Cleveland was using patronage to force passage of the Mills measure.

June: Democrats met in St. Louis, Missouri, on June 5 to June 7 and renominated Cleveland on the first ballot by acclamation. Allan Gransberry Thurman of Ohio received the vice presidential nomination. The president's campaign was put in the hands of William H. Barnum of Connecticut, a protectionist, and Calvin Brice, a millionaire industrialist, who was lukewarm on the tariff.

On June 13 the Department of Labor was established.

July: By July the Democrats had 151 votes but needed 10 more from among 19 Samuel Jackson Randall Democrats. Randall, a former Speaker of the House and once chairman of the Appropriations Committee, proposed refunding taxes to states as a way to cut the surplus. Lobbyists soon favored this idea, but a filibuster led to its defeat.

The Mills Bill passed on July 21, by a vote of 162 to 149. E. L. Godkin stated in the *Washington Evening Post*: "The vote on the Mills Bill in the House will serve as the historical record of the transformation of the Democratic Party which President Cleveland has accomplished."

The president gave a special message to Congress on the status of civil service reform on July 23, in which he said that things were going well, but, "Its importance has frequently been underestimated and the support of good men has thus been lost by their lack of interest in its success. [The] administration [is] still often annoyed and irritated by the disloyalty to the service and the insolence of employees who remain in place as the beneficiaries and the relics and reminders of the vicious [spoils] system."

August–September: Cleveland did not believe in campaign speeches, which he said undermined the dignity of the office. His acceptance letter on September 10 was primarily a rehash of the tariff issue.

In September the health of vice presidential candidate Thurman, 75, broke down, and he was unable to do much for the rest of the campaign. With Cleveland doing little campaigning, the lack of campaigning by Thurman was another blow to the president.

October: Two laws took effect on October 1: The Labor Act of October 1 authorized arbitration in railroad disputes and authorized the president to appoint a commission to investigate any labor conflict. Cleveland also signed the Chinese Exclusion Act (the Scott Act) on October 1, which regulated Chinese laborers by curbing reentry for those who left the country.

November 6: Cleveland beat Republican Benjamin Harrison in the popular vote but was soundly defeated where it mattered—in the Electoral College. Cleveland polled 5, 537,857 votes to Harrison's 5,447,129 votes. In the electoral votes, Harrison took 233 votes to Cleveland's 168 votes.

Former Presidents

RUTHERFORD B. HAYES, 66, and retired in Fremont, Ohio, was in Cincinnati on election night on November 6. Later he heard the first newsboys outside shouting about Benjamin Harrison's victory. Hayes said he rushed outside to buy a paper. "How good, how good," he said on learning of Harrison's victory.

Future Presidents

BENJAMIN HARRISON, running on a protectionist platform, became president in another Gilded Age, paper-thin close contest. Harrison's election came somewhat as a surprise, since he started the year virtually out of politics after losing his Senate seat in 1887.

January–March: At the start of the year, much of the talk for Republicans centered on what plans James Blaine was making for the year. Although Harrison's friends were doubtful about Blaine's plans, Blaine appeared certain to bow out after a letter on January 25 to B. F. Jones, chairman of the Republican National Committee, in which he stated, "My name will not be presented to the national convention."

Also in January the Indiana state party chairman, James Huston, went to New York City to discuss Harrison's possibilities with party brokers. Senator John G. Spooner of Wisconsin said, "Everybody [in the Republican Party] can support" Harrison. After the letter from Blaine was published, Blaine's supporters made it public that Harrison, not John Sherman, was heir to Blaine as nominal party leader.

With Blaine out of the race, the picture changed. William Allison and Sherman were better known than Harrison. Others interested in the nomination included Chauncey M. Depew of New York, Judge Walter Q. Gresham of Indiana, Governor Russell A. Alger of Michigan, Senator Joseph R. Hawley of Connecticut, and William W. Phelps of New Jersey.

Harrison decided he had to blow his own bugle and settled on an invitation from the Michigan Club of Detroit to talk on February 22. "I feel that I am at some disadvantage," Harrison told diners. "I did not approach Detroit from the direction of Washington.… I am a dead statesman but I am a living and a rejuvenated Republican." The speech drew national attention and reporters called his performance in Detroit "one of his greatest."

Next Harrison addressed the Marquette Club of Chicago on March 20. He said that the Republican Party responded with the highest statesmanship during the Civil War. He was also critical of Cleveland's free trade stance.

June–September: Republicans met in Chicago June 19 to 25. John Sherman appeared to be the frontrunner for a time, but Harrison quickly gained momentum as the convention moved on. The first ballot gave Sherman 229 votes to Harrison's 85 votes as eighteen other men were nominated, including Blaine who earned 35 votes on the first ballot. By the fifth ballot the Republican preferences went Sherman, 224 votes; Harrison, 213 votes; Alger, 142 votes; Allison, 99 votes; Gresham, 87 votes; Blaine, 48 votes; and William McKinley, 14 votes.

At this point word came from Scotland, where Blaine was staying with Andrew Carnegie, that Blaine favored Harrison. This began the wave for Harrison. By the eighth ballot,

Harrison had 544 votes and the nomination. Levi Morton of New York was the vice presidential nominee.

After his nomination Harrison gave eighty extemporaneous speeches from his Indianapolis porch to about 300,000 pilgrims who for weeks arrived steadily at the train station, then paraded to the candidate's home. Harrison often gave six talks per day.

November–December: Harrison was elected president on November 6, losing the popular vote by 90,000 votes to President Grover Cleveland but easily winning the electoral contest, with 233 votes to Cleveland's 168 votes.

Harrison spent much of the last 2 months of the year formulating his cabinet.

❧☙

WILLIAM MCKINLEY, 45, now was considered "presidential timber," but the timing wasn't quite right for him as the Republican national convention drama unfolded. This was also a year in which McKinley's wife, Ida, suffered a major epileptic seizure, causing doctors to fear for her life. The illness was serious enough for McKinley to take a rare leave of absence from Congress to be at her bedside. Then, when the wife of McKinley's brother died, her two homeless children went to live with McKinley's mother in Canton, and McKinley became their guardian.

May: McKinley, the champion of protection, made a major address in the House on May 18 in answer to Cleveland's firm position on lowering the tariff. McKinley's message to the House also denounced trusts by saying that they were really free traders. McKinley dismissed foreign markets for agricultural products as "one of the delusions of free trade."

June: At the Republican convention in Chicago, June 19 to 25, McKinley supported John Sherman for the nomination. McKinley himself received 2 votes on the first ballot and 4 votes on the eighth and final ballot.

November: After Harrison's election, McKinley's name surfaced for possible cabinet roles, none of which came to fruition.

❧☙

THEODORE ROOSEVELT spent most of the year researching and writing a new book, *The Winning of the West*. He also made a speaking tour for presidential candidate Benjamin Harrison and went hunting in the northern neck of Idaho.

January–March: Roosevelt wrote to a friend in January, "I shall probably never be in politics again.… My literary work occupies … my time. [I would] like to write some book that would really take rank in the very first class, but I suppose this is a mere dream."

Inspired by reading proofs of James Bryce's *The American Commonwealth*, Roosevelt came up with the idea of writing about American expansion westward starting with Daniel Boone in 1774 and ending with Davy Crockett's death at the Alamo in 1836. Historian Francis Parkman also inspired

Roosevelt. By mid-March Roosevelt had a publishing contract with Putnam to deliver two volumes by the spring of 1889.

April–May: After spending time in the South in April researching his subject, Roosevelt began writing his book at Sagamore Hill in May. He complained of slow going, only a page or two per day.

August–September: At the end of August, Roosevelt took a break from his writing and went hunting in the Kootenai Mountain country of Idaho, where he slept on the ground. En route to New York he visited Medora in Dakota and sold a few of his remaining cattle.

October: Roosevelt returned to Sagamore Hill on October 5 but 2 days later hit the road for Benjamin Harrison on a tour that took him into Illinois, Michigan, and Minnesota. He believed Harrison an excellent candidate and therefore campaigned with zest and was one of the better Republican speakers available.

On October 10, Edith gave birth to the couple's second son, Kermit.

November–December: After campaigning for Harrison, Roosevelt returned to writing with new vigor, as he was falling behind on his book. He finished the first volume just before Christmas.

෧෬

WILLIAM HOWARD TAFT's interim appointment to complete Judge Judson Harmon's term on the superior court bench in Cincinnati, Ohio, ended in April when Taft was elected to the post.

Governor Joseph Foraker warned Taft that he would have to "quit the bench at the end of the term … you will then be of mature age and experience … and so established in the confidence of the people that all other things will come naturally."

Despite troubles with Foraker in the past, Taft, 31 in September, told the governor, "My debt to you is very great."

෧෬

WOODROW WILSON, 32 in December, broke his contract with Bryn Mawr, leaving behind ill will, and moved to the faculty of Wesleyan University in Middletown, Connecticut.

April 15: Wilson's mother, Jessie, died in Tennessee at the age of 61.

June: Wesleyan made an offer for Wilson to be a professor. Despite a contract commitment for 2 years more at Bryn Mawr, Wilson now began negotiations with both schools. Wesleyan offered $2,500 and a lighter teaching load, and Wilson asked Bryn Mawr for $3,000 on condition that he could leave if something better came along. Bryn Mawr trustees believed Wilson broke the contract when he accepted the Wesleyan offer. When he resigned on June 29, the parting was unpleasant.

September–December: Wilson began teaching at Wesleyan for the fall term. He taught European and American history, the history of political institutions, constitutional history, and political economy.

Wilson was asked to teach Sunday school at the Second Congregational Church. He opted in November, instead, for the First Congregational Church. Its pastor, Azel W. Hazen, was to become a lasting influence.

෧෬

WARREN G. HARDING became a delegate to the state Republican convention in this presidential election year as he slowly moved toward political participation. He preferred James Blaine to Benjamin Harrison and wrote in the *Marion Star* that Blaine was "the idol of his party," even though John Sherman made "every Buckeye … proud."

Harding's newspaper in small-town Ohio continued upward and onward as the paper increased in size by one column and in May had a 2,000 copy run. By November, Harding, now 23, reported that the *Marion Star* had gone from a "despised … generally uncertain sheet … to be the real newspaper of Marion."

෧෬

CALVIN COOLIDGE was joined in the fall term at Black River Academy in Vermont by his sister Abigail. Coolidge had been looking forward to her companionship. He developed an interest in classical history owing to the teaching of Principal George Sherman and Miss M. Belle Chelis.

Coolidge turned 16 in July.

෧෬

HERBERT HOOVER, 14, became an office boy and file clerk for his uncle's new business venture in Salem, Oregon, a town of 8,000 people 25 miles south of Newburg. It was in February that Dr. Minthorn decided to move to Salem. Minthorn resigned from the Friends' Pacific Academy and organized the Oregon Land Company with a few other men. The capitalization began at $20,000 and reached $200,000 in 2 years.

Hoover dropped out of school and handled company mailings, advertising, and the hiring of carriages to show clients properties. His salary was $20 per month.

In October, Hoover's sister May and grandmother Minthorn arrived in Salem from Kingsley, Iowa.

෧෬

FRANKLIN D. ROOSEVELT, 6, lived on the family estate at Hyde Park, New York. Being an only child, Franklin was the center of attention.

෧෬

HARRY S TRUMAN, 4, lived in Grandview, Missouri. He liked to go riding with his grandfather.

1889
Grover Cleveland

President Cleveland finished his term and on leaving Washington, selected a New York City brownstone on Madison Avenue and the quiet life of an "adviser" to a law firm. Shortly before leaving the White House, Cleveland escaped a war scare caused by German aggression in Samoa.

January: On January 16, Cleveland sent Congress a message on his efforts to protect American interests in Samoa. He was to write a second message denouncing the German effort to subvert Samoan freedoms but on second thought decided against making it public. (At the end of Cleveland's term, German and U.S. warships were at Apia looking at each other. The issue was settled by a hurricane in late March that sank every ship at the scene except for one British cruiser.)

February: Cleveland visited New York City on February 7 and talked to old friend Francis L. Stetson about a job in his law firm. Cleveland was close to Stetson, a Williams College graduate, whose firm later inherited the legal work for the Morgan house following the death of J. P. Morgan.

On February 11, Cleveland signed the Hatch Act establishing the Department of Agriculture, and he appointed Norman J. Colman of Missouri as its secretary.

On February 22, Cleveland signed the territorial bills that led to statehood for the Dakotas, Montana, and Washington.

March: Following the inauguration ceremonies, the Clevelands, on March 7, checked into the Victoria Hotel at 816 Madison Avenue near 68th Street in New York City. Cleveland, 52, encouraged political friends to visit but discouraged generic callers and accepted few dinner invitations.

April: Cleveland wrote to a friend on April 13, "You cannot imagine the relief [of leaving the presidency. I] feel that I am fast taking the place which I desire to reach—the place of a respectable private citizen."

Cleveland accepted a job offer from Stetson. Cleveland was not a partner; he was "of counsel." He had staffers, was brought into consultations on occasion, wrote few briefs, and made little money.

December: Cleveland talked about ballot reform before the Merchants Association in Boston on December 12. The talk was well received and Cleveland received a big ovation. All who where there realized he was hardly finished as a political figure. Still, for most of the year he refused to criticize President Harrison and talked little about politics.

℘Ↄ℞

BENJAMIN HARRISON entered the White House with the intentions of a reformer. But like many of the men who preceded him, he was swamped by the number of office-seekers. Harrison was tied up with patronage problems in the early days for as much as 4 to 6 hours per day, as he wanted final approval on all 1,700 appointees.

February: Harrison left Indianapolis on February 25 aboard a coach owned by the president of the Pennsylvania Railroad. Harrison's friends and relatives were in a second coach, and the press was in a third. Harrison's secretary, E. W. Halford, said Harrison was "badly broken up" on leaving his home. An emotional Harrison read a statement before he left the city: "I love this city.… It is a city on whose streets the pompous displays of wealth are not seen."

March: Harrison met with President Grover Cleveland on March 2. The two men discussed several issues and were very cordial to each other.

Harrison was inaugurated on March 4 in a driving rain and strong winds. Chief Justice Melville Fuller administered the oath of office. In his inaugural address, Harrison cited his belief in protectionism. He also said that he had no separate southern policy and called for Black voting in the South. In foreign affairs, Harrison said he wanted the Monroe Doctrine used and asked for a larger navy and merchant marine.

The inaugural ball took place at the Pensions Office, and more than 12,000 people attended.

President Benjamin Harrison

By March 7, Harrison's cabinet was in place. James Blaine was named secretary of state; William Windom of Minnesota was named secretary of Treasury; Redfield Proctor of Vermont was named secretary of war; William Henry Harrison Miller of Indiana was named attorney general; John Wanamaker of Pennsylvania was named postmaster general; Benjamin Franklin Tarcy was named secretary of the navy; John W. Noble of Missouri was named secretary of the Interior; and Jeremiah Rusk of Wisconsin was named secretary of agriculture.

April: Indian Territory in the Oklahoma District bordering Texas and Kansas was opened to settlers on April 22. More than 200,000 people flooded the newly opened territory in a mad rush to claim a portion of the more than 2 million acres available.

On April 29 the nation celebrated the 100th anniversary of the inauguration of George Washington, including a ceremony in Washington, D.C., attended by Harrison.

May 31: The flood in Johnstown, Pennsylvania, wiped out the small town in a matter of minutes. The flood killed nearly 2,000 people.

October: The Pan American Conference opened on October 2 in Washington, D.C., with Secretary of State James

Blaine presiding. Every independent country in the Western Hemisphere except the Dominican Republic attended the event. Blaine's goal for the conference was to seek a Latin American policy of solidarity based on "friendship, not force."

November: Four new states were admitted to the Union: North Dakota and South Dakota on November 2, Montana on November 8, and Washington on November 11.

December 18: Harrison named David Josiah Brewer of Kansas to the Supreme Court.

Former Presidents

RUTHERFORD B. HAYES lost his wife, Lucy, not long after the couple returned to Ohio from New York City where they had attended ceremonies surrounding the 100th anniversary of Washington's inauguration.

Lucy suffered a stroke on June 23 while Hayes was in Columbus on business involving Ohio State. He rushed back to their Spiegal Grove estate in Fremont and was at her bedside when she drifted into a coma. Lucy died 2 days later, on June 25, at the age of 57.

After the death of Lucy, Hayes, 67 in October, embraced more religious subjects in his speeches as he became something of a lay preacher.

Future Presidents

WILLIAM MCKINLEY, 46, was a strong contender for Speaker of the House but lost the contest to Thomas B. Reed of Maine.

October 11: McKinley's brother James died (age unknown).

December: The vote for Speaker came in a Republican caucus. Reed received 78 votes on the first ballot; McKinley received 39 votes; and Joe Cannon of Danville, Illinois, received 22 votes. On the second ballot, Reed had 85 votes, McKinley had 38, and Cannon had 19. On the third ballot McKinley moved that the choice be unanimous.

৪০০৪

THEODORE ROOSEVELT, 31 in October, took little time once he moved to Washington to stir things up as the newcomer on the U.S. Civil Service Commission. His new book also created sparks.

January–May: In January, Roosevelt was anxious to finish the second volume of *The Winning of the West* and moved to his mother's place at 689 Madison Avenue while she was in Europe. But to get away from the children, Roosevelt worked at Putnam's office on West 23rd Street. He finished the work on April 1.

Early in the Harrison administration, Roosevelt wrote to Henry Cabot Lodge, "I do hope the President will appoint good Civil Service Commissioners." Roosevelt added, "I would like above all things to go into politics."

Harrison was not eager to hire Roosevelt for anything but finally agreed to give him a post on the Civil Service Commission paying $3,500 a year. Desperate for money, Roosevelt grabbed it. He left Edith in Sagamore Hill, as she was pregnant.

He arrived in Washington on May 13 and moved into Lodge's house on Connecticut Avenue, as Lodge was away on vacation. The Civil Service Commission met at City Hall. The other members were Republican Charles Lyman and former governor of South Carolina, Democrat Hugh S. Thompson.

On May 20, Roosevelt went to New York City and reported a "great laxity" and "positive fraud" in the handling of customhouse examinations and called for the dismissal of three men and the prosecution of one man.

June: Volumes I and II of *The Winning of the West* were published after Roosevelt reached Washington. The *New York Tribune* said, "Many episodes … are written with remarkable dramatic and narrative power." Good reviews from London helped make the book a best seller. However, in the *New York Sun* historian James R. Gilmore said Roosevelt was guilty of plagiarism and doubted he could have written the book so rapidly. Roosevelt ripped Gilmore by name and offered $1,000 to anyone who could prove he used a collaborator as Gilmore claimed.

July 28: Frank Hutton, editor of the *Washington Post* and an enemy of civil service, attacked Roosevelt as a man who bribed his way into New York machine politics. Roosevelt called the charges "falsehoods."

৪০০৪

WILLIAM HOWARD TAFT was amused by efforts to land him a seat on the United States Supreme Court. Taft was 32 in September. A Supreme Court seat was not all that preposterous in that Joseph Story was 32 when appointed to the Court. But Taft certainly lacked credentials.

June 4: Taft's half-brother Peter Rawson Taft, bright but unstable, died in a sanatorium after a breakdown at the age of 44.

July: Taft's interest in a possible appointment to the Court came even though he felt his chances were slim owing to age and inexperience. President Harrison selected Thomas McDougall of Cincinnati for the Court, but he declined to serve. This prompted Taft to write his father, Alphonso, in Russia, on July 20 that jurists in Cincinnati were involved "in the innocent amusement of pushing me."

Harrison, on a visit to Cincinnati, told Governor Joseph Foraker that he knew who Taft was. Taft supported Foraker for a third term as governor and believed that if elected Foraker had a shot at becoming president.

After Harrison's visit to the city, Taft wrote to his father: "Foraker said he put in some good words for me with the President." Taft said Foraker was interested to know if Harrison knew of him. Foraker said Harrison answered, "Oh, yes, what a fine looking man he is." Foraker said he discussed Taft without specifically citing the Supreme Court vacancy.

September: Helen gave birth to the couple's first child, a son named Robert Alphonso, on September 8.

Foraker wrote to Harrison on September 23 and sent a copy to Taft: "His [Taft's] appointment [to the Court] would be satisfactory to an unusually high degree to the Republicans of this state, and no Democrat could justly criticize it." Taft wrote the governor that he was "very grateful" for the "much too complimentary words."

December: Harrison decided against Taft for the Supreme Court but did offer him the solicitor general's office. Taft accepted the post, which would begin the following May.

❧❧

WOODROW WILSON, 33 in December, a professor at Wesleyan University, finished a scholarly textbook on government and expressed interest in returning to Princeton University as a professor of public law. The book, entitled *The State*, was an improvement on *Congressional Government*. But Wilson, who leaned heavily on new German material, came close to plagiarism.

At Wesleyan, Wilson was elected a director of the football association. He helped coach the team, worked on plays, and walked the sidelines during games yelling encouragement.

Woodrow wrote a friend on August 9 that to teach at Princeton would be a real opportunity. Bridges lobbied for Wilson through Francis L. Patton, who had become president of the school, but nothing came of this effort immediately.

A third daughter, Eleanor, was born on October 16 at Middletown, Connecticut. Ellen cried when told the baby was not a boy.

❧❧

WARREN G. HARDING was arrested for criminal libel, was saddened by the defeat of his political favorite, Joseph Foraker, and then collapsed from a nervous breakdown. The Marion, Ohio, newspaper editor was only 24 years old.

Mary Lynn, a farmer's wife, brought the libel action. On July 13 the *Marion Star* said she had eloped with a clergyman. Her husband threatened to "tar and feather" the editor. The *Marion Star* printed a retraction, but Lynn demanded $10,000. On October 24 the newspaper reported the matter was "laid in an early grave by an intelligent, grand jury … [the claim] too silly to be countenanced in court."

After Harding's nervous breakdown the *Marion Star* announced on October 16, that Harding would be working only a half-hour per day. At the urging of his father, Tyron, Harding on November 7 checked into the Battle Creek Sanitarium. The Seventh-Day Adventists sponsored the Michigan facility, and vegetarian Dr. J. P. Kellogg, eventually a cereal magnate, ran it. This was to be the first of five visits to Battle Creek for Harding over the next 12 years.

❧❧

CALVIN COOLIDGE was a 17-year-old student at Black River Academy in Ludlow, Vermont.

❧❧

HERBERT HOOVER, 15, in the fall started class at the Capital Business College. The $60 his guardian sent from Iowa helped.

Teacher Jeannie Gray took an interest in Hoover, cultivated in him an interest in books, introducing him to *Ivanhoe* and *David Copperfield*. She also invited him to Sunday dinner and took him to her Presbyterian Sunday school class.

❧❧

FRANKLIN D. ROOSEVELT, off again on a trip to Europe, was diagnosed with typhoid, possibly caused by an earlier swim in the Hudson River, and was put in the captain's bed.

On landing in Liverpool the 7-year-old was taken by ambulance to the hospital and soon recovered. There was little stress in Roosevelt's childhood. He was protected and surrounded by relatives and cousins, many of them neighbors along the Hudson.

❧❧

HARRY S TRUMAN, 5, was taught to read by his mother.

August 12: Harry's only sister, Mary Jane, was born.

1890
Benjamin Harrison

The President grappled with money matters in his 2nd year in the White House.

January–February: At the start of the year Harrison faced three major problems: the election bill regarding Black voting, the silver issue, and the tariff.

The "silver bloc" of western senators wanted liberalization of the Bland–Allison Act of 1878, under which the government was required to buy and mint $2 million to $4 million in silver each month. Western senators wanted to increase the amount.

On January 15, Walker Blaine, a lawyer and son of Secretary of State James Blaine, died suddenly. Harrison had stopped to see him 20 minutes before he died.

Many mass meetings of African Americans took place around the country, protesting the suppression of Black voting rights in the South. Protesters offered an "Address to the President" on February 3: "Negroes are cowardly lynched and murdered without a hearing [and ride] in filthy and inferior [railroad] cars." The address also discussed the lack of school facilities, the unfair labor system, and the lack of a voice in lawmaking in the South.

With the help of House Speaker Thomas Reed, the lodge bill, or "force bill" as the Democrats called it, was introduced to provide for federal supervision of elections in the South. It passed the House but failed in the Senate.

May 2: Congress created the Territory of Oklahoma, formerly Indian territory. The need for federal recognition came about as a result of lawlessness in the territory since it was opened to White settlers in 1889.

July: The Sherman Antitrust Act passed Congress on July 2. The new law, debated for more than 4 months in both houses, provided new guidelines for dealing with monopolies and sought to strengthen a state's ability to regulate giant corporations whose reach extended beyond state lines. The law was ambiguous, however, when it came to defining exactly what constituted a trust.

Idaho became a state on July 3, and Wyoming was admitted to the Union on July 10.

On July 14, Congress passed the Sherman Silver Purchase Act to replace the Bland–Allison Act of 1878. The Sherman Silver Purchase Act required the Treasury Department to buy 4.5 million ounces of silver each month to be turned into silver coinage.

October–November: Congress passed the McKinley Act. Sponsored by William McKinley, the new act increased tariffs on several imported goods to their highest level in history (see **William McKinley** in opposite column).

In the fall political campaign, Harrison performed a presidential rarity by taking to the stump for the Republican cause in a 2,851-mile swing through the Midwest. Traveling with his wife Carrie, he gave one of his thirty-seven speeches from the back of his train at St. Joseph, Missouri, at 6:30 A.M.

First Lady Caroline ("Carrie") Harrison
(Library of Congress)

December: Sioux Indians at Wounded Knee Creek on the Pine Ridge Reservation in South Dakota were massacred by troops of the U.S. Seventh Cavalry. More than 150 Sioux were killed, half of them women and children. The massacre began when Colonel James Forsyth entered the Sioux camp at Wounded Knee with 500 soldiers and asked for the Sioux's weapons. Tensions between the two sides grew and turned violent. American cannons, positioned on a nearby hill, began firing on the Sioux. In the battle that followed, twenty-five U.S. soldiers died.

Former Presidents

Rutherford B. Hayes lived in retirement at Spiegal Grove in Fremont, Ohio. He kept up correspondence worldwide with people he had met. For a time he was rumored to be engaged to a cousin, Mary Anne Bigelow.

Hayes deplored Harrison's lack of tact and their limited friendship. Hayes wrote in his diary: "Lincoln was for a gov-

ernment of the people. The new tendency is a government of the rich, by the rich, and for the rich."

Hayes was 68 years old in October.

&CR

Grover Cleveland was a private attorney in New York City but feeling rising pressure to make a run for president again in 1892.

March–April: Henry Watterson made a speaking tour and reported to Cleveland that wherever he went he "heard no other name than yours" for president in 1892. But Governor David Hill of New York wanted the prize, and Watterson warned that no man could afford "to stand wholly aloof and alone" and let Hill win.

Cleveland, 53, wrote on April 7, "I do not assume to obtrude my advice [but] I have seen the Republicans getting deeper and deeper into the mire [and we] should let them flounder and throw more dirt in the eyes of the public."

September–November: Cleveland wrote to his former private secretary Daniel Lamont on September 13: "If I had my way … I would now put a stop to the mention of my name in connection with any political office.… Besides my personal repugnance to the atmosphere of politics in their present phase, I am nearly convinced that my nomination again for the Presidency would result in party defeat."

In October, Cleveland appeared before the Supreme Court (the first former president to do so since John Quincy Adams) in a minor case involving a drainage project in New Orleans. He lost the case.

In November, Cleveland went to Columbus for a banquet and gave a ringing denunciation of the McKinley tariff.

On November 8, Cleveland wrote: "Hill and his friends are bent on his nomination for the Presidency, and failing in that they are determined that it shall not come towards me." Watterson wrote to Hill on November 24 and asked Hill to step aside for Cleveland for party harmony, adding that Hill held the key to success in 1892.

Future Presidents

William McKinley was author of the McKinley tariff in the "Billion-Dollar Congress," the name given to Congress because for the first time in history, it appropriated over $1 billion during the fiscal year. However, Ohio Democrats gerrymandered his district again, and he lost his House seat to Lieutenant Governor John G. Warwick by 303 votes.

On the subject of his tariff, McKinley, 47 years old in January, said, "The protective system meets our wants, our conditions, promotes the national design, and will work out our destiny better than any other."

McKinley's tariff bill, introduced to the House in the spring, aimed to reduce revenue on raw sugar and molasses. The revenue tax on tobacco was reduced, but there were high or prohibitive rates on most commodities. McKinley had been against trade agreements, but he no longer opposed them because this was what the Republican Party wanted.

The final bill, with Senate alterations, was passed on October 1. The McKinley Act increased duties on various imported goods by an average of 48.4 percent. Items affected included imported hides, wheat, potatoes, and barley.

In the November elections, the Democrats used the McKinley tariff as a weapon against the Republicans. As a result, along with McKinley losing his seat in the House, the Republicans as a whole lost their majority in the House.

80Q8

THEODORE ROOSEVELT, in his usual aggressive manner, became a one-man commission and wrecking crew on the Civil Service Commission and was thought to be sizing up the White House as a nice place to hang his hat.

Theodore and Edith started the year in the White House by attending a New Year's reception there. In the following months they made the rounds of the Washington social whirl, often eating out five times per week. Roosevelt was popular at these gatherings, with influential hosts attracted to him. He was now friends with the vice president, cabinet members, the Speaker of the House, Supreme Court justices, and many congressmen.

Frank Hatton, a critic of Roosevelt's handling of civil service in 1889, continued to attack, and on January 27 the House Committee on Reform in Civil Service announced an investigation that would be headed by Representative Hamilton G. Ewart of South Carolina with Hatton as his assistant.

80Q8

WILLIAM HOWARD TAFT, the new U.S. Solicitor General, had to learn the ropes in a hurry in Washington and soon found himself standing before the Supreme Court, conferring with the president, and receiving invitations to dinners with the movers and shakers. For a brief time he was acting attorney general when William H. Miller fell ill.

February: Taft was sworn in on February 14. As solicitor general, Taft was counsel to the attorney general, wrote legal opinions for the president, and represented the United States before the Supreme Court. He wrote to his father that the job was "rather overwhelming." Taft had plenty of work to do since his predecessor, Ordow W. Chapman, had died in January. Taft found out he had to digest ten tough cases, write

briefs, and appear before the Supreme Court prior to its June adjournment.

April: Taft wrote to his father in April, "I am gradually getting acquainted with the prominent people here ... no doubt that after one year I shall have a pretty general knowledge of the persons who run things."

Nell and Robert arrived in Washington and took a house at 5 Du Pont Circle.

On April 26, he wrote to his father that his first court appearance left him "a great deal discouraged. [I am not] easy or fluent on my feet.... I have difficulty in holding the attention of the court." He complained that the justices read letters and ate lunch while he was talking.

May: Attorney General Miller turned ill, and Taft had to assume the top job for a few weeks. "The novelty of it wore off in just about a day, and no man will be happier than I shall be when he returns to his desk," Taft wrote to his brother Charles on May 2. Taft consulted with Harrison on judicial appointments in Texas and Oklahoma Territory but felt he could contribute little.

June: Taft began to learn federal procedures and how to look up matters of precedence. The attorney general directed him to determine if Congress could annul an army court-martial, and Taft learned that Congress had no such power. Then he investigated the ruthless timber cutting in Alabama. Yet overall Taft now found this work less interesting than the cases he had seen on the Ohio Superior Court.

September: A doctor warned Taft, 33, to cut his weight or face heart troubles ahead.

80Q8

WOODROW WILSON, 34 in December, returned to his alma mater, Princeton University, as professor of jurisprudence and political economy and vowed never to be dull in the lecture hall. During the year, Woodrow's sister Marion Wilson Kennedy died in Arkansas (the exact date is unknown).

February–March: Princeton made the offer to Wilson in February, and Wesleyan University was willing to grant almost anything to keep him but failed to do so.

Wilson wrote to his father, Joseph, on March 20, "Everybody regards my election to Princeton as a sort of crowning success" but added that he did not consider it any great personal triumph. It was his understanding with Princeton that he would be in charge of developing a law school. He also wanted to keep his job lecturing at Johns Hopkins University.

April–June: While still at Middletown, Connecticut, he was influenced by the appearance of the evangelist Dwight L. Moody. In June he started a popular lecture series entitled "Leaders of Men," in which he emphasized that Christian love was a proper inspiration for leaders: "If nations reject and deride moral law ... penalty will inevitably follow."

September–December: On his return to New Jersey in September, he rented a house on Library Place. He wrote to his father, "My mind cannot give me gratification. I have to rely on my heart, and that craves [the] companionship of those I love."

∽∝

WARREN G. HARDING, 25 in November, returned to Marion, Ohio, from his exile at the Battle Creek, Michigan, spa feeling better and 20 pounds lighter.

In the spring he joined the Young Men's Republican Club and the Elks.

The Saturday *Marion Star* expanded to eight pages, and the Toledo *Blade* called Harding's newspaper "a splendid paper."

In July, Marion changed from village to city status, continuing to expand with a museum and waterworks. The new board of trade included Harding, his newspaper rivals Crawford and Vaughan, and Amos Kling, the richest man in town.

∽∝

CALVIN COOLIDGE'S graduation from Black River Academy in Ludlow, Vermont, was sobered by the unexpected death 2 months earlier of his younger sister Abigail, 14, also a student. The principal of the school, George Sherman, felt that Coolidge should attend Sherman's alma mater—Amherst College in Massachusetts. But Calvin's initial attempt to enter Amherst was a disaster.

March 6: Abigail Coolidge died, probably of appendicitis, with Calvin at her bedside.

May: Graduation for Black River Academy was May 17. The class was made up of only five boys and four girls. Calvin was senior class secretary and delivered one of the speeches. He discussed, in his "Oratory in History," the role of oratory in influencing public opinion during great moments in history.

June–September: Calvin worked on the farm all summer before the 18-year-old left by train alone for Amherst to take the entrance examinations. Black River Academy did not grant entrance certificates to Amherst. The train ride was Calvin's first outside Vermont, and he had a severe head cold at the time. The test was in English, Greek, Latin, and mathematics. He did poorly and returned home to regain his health.

October–December: Calvin helped his father paint the inside of the store at the Notch and in late winter returned to Ludlow for further study.

Now Sherman recommended St. Johnsbury Academy, Vermont's best preparatory school.

∽∝

HERBERT HOOVER, 16, met an engineer from the East Coast and decided to become one himself. Robert Brown told Hoover that mining engineers were rare and in demand and that he should consider it as a career. After Dr. Minthorn offered to pay brother Theodore's tuition to a Quaker college in Iowa, William Penn College, the older Hoover accepted.

Ben Cook later said that Herbert was excellent working in

his uncle's land company in Salem, Oregon. He would locate correspondence quickly, was industrious, knew every facet of the business, and impressed stenographers with how he stayed on top of things. Herbert was earning $35 per month, a good salary for the times.

∽∝

FRANKLIN D. ROOSEVELT, 8, was in London when a new governess was hired. During the year, the young boy also traveled to Paris.

∽∝

HARRY S TRUMAN, 6, found out he had bad eyes when his mother took him to an oculist in Kansas City. From now on he wore thick glasses and had to avoid rough stuff with boys.

The Trumans moved for the fourth time to a house with a large lot and barn in Independence, Missouri, a town of 6,000 east of Kansas City.

Harry attended the Noland grammar school, could quote from the Bible, and attended the Presbyterian church because the minister was kind to the Trumans. Harry first saw Bess Wallace at church, but he was too shy to talk to her.

Before the Civil War, Independence was the starting point for those headed for the Santa Fe or Oregon trails. The Mormons stopped there for a time in the 1840s.

∽∝

DWIGHT D. EISENHOWER was born on October 14 in a rented room near the railroad tracks in Denison, Texas, 5 miles south of the Oklahoma border. His given name was David Dwight.

His father was David Jacob Eisenhower, age 27; his mother was Ida Elizabeth Stover Eisenhower, age 28. His father was a native of Elizabethville, Pennsylvania, located in the mountains north of Harrisburg and near the Susquehanna River, where he was born on September 23, 1863. Ida was born on May 1, 1862, in Mt. Sidney, Virginia, in the Shenandoah Valley 10 miles north of Staunton.

David Eisenhower had moved to Abilene, Kansas, in 1878. He was a gas company manager and mechanic who disliked farming. He studied engineering at Lane University in Kansas but quit to marry Ida in 1885, 2 years after meeting her at her brother's home in Topeka. He had been a partner in a general store in Hope, Kansas, but 3 years later his partner vanished with the cash, leaving Eisenhower humiliated by the bankruptcy and with angry creditors calling at his door. He went to work on the railroad in Texas, then returned to Kansas.

Great-grandfather Hans N. Eisenhauer emigrated from the Palatinate to Philadelphia in 1741 and later farmed in Lebanon County. In the 1878 move, David, his grandfather, and father (now spelled *Eisenhower*) left the East for Abilene.

Although the infant was named David Dwight after his father, he soon became known by his middle name to avoid confusion in the family.

1891
Benjamin Harrison

The president faced the possibility of war with both Italy and Chile. Harrison also took the longest trip in presidential history, a train ride across the continent made possible by the rapid increase in railroad mileage. Harrison made 140 impromptu speeches along a route through Tennessee and Alabama to the Southwest and Pacific Coast, then as far north as Seattle. During this year were also signs of a revolt within the Republican Party against another Harrison term.

January–February: Secretary of Treasury William Windom died on January 29, and Charles Foster of Ohio replaced him on February 24.

March: Tensions between the United States and Italy increased after eleven Italian–Americans were lynched in New Orleans on March 14. The murders stemmed from the assassination of New Orleans Police Chief David C. Hennessey the previous October, allegedly by Italian mafia members. Following a mistrial for nineteen men accused of Hennessey's murder and conspiracy to commit murder a mob broke into the New Orleans prison where the nineteen men were being held and executed eleven of them.

On March 31 the Italian government recalled its ministers to the United States in protest of the murders. Harrison recalled the U.S. minister to Italy and denounced the lynchings. (Tensions remained high for much of the spring and summer, but eventually relations between Italy and the United States normalized during the fall and early winter.)

April–September: The president, First Lady Carrie, Postmaster General John Wanamaker, and a party of fifteen, including three press representatives and Harrison's brother Carter, left Washington on April 14 for the cross-country trip. In all, the president visited nineteen states and three territories. The many speeches given along the way covered various topics, but in the South Harrison decided against talking about Black voting rights.

October–December: The traveling party switched to water transportation in San Francisco Bay and Puget Sound. When the president reached Seattle, he heard about the trouble in Chile. On October 16, in Valparaiso, Chile, American sailors on shore leave got into a brawl at a local saloon and subsequently were attacked by a mob. Two Americans were stabbed to death, and eighteen were injured. Local police joined in the fray, attacking the American sailors instead of helping them. At the time, anti-American feeling in Chile was running high because of U.S. refusal to support revolutionary forces.

There was no apology from Chile over the deaths, and a long delay in resolving the incident upset the State Department. Harrison was exasperated at the way the Chileans conducted their criminal court. War talk heightened when the body of one sailor was displayed in Independence Hall, Philadelphia.

In his December message, the president told Congress he hoped the United States would get satisfaction from Chile and if not he would write a special message. He said the altercation in the saloon had been "savage, brutal, unprovoked." The United States wanted an apology and indemnity.

An angry Chilean foreign minister, M. A. Matta, was abusive in talking to Harrison and Secretary of the Navy Benjamin Franklin Tracy. Harrison considered Matta's remarks an "atrocious insult to the American government." Talk of war between the nations was heard all over the country and spilled into the next year.

Former Presidents

RUTHERFORD B. HAYES, retired in Ohio and, 69 years old in October, still managed to travel despite money concerns. He noted in his diary: "Debts large and increasing. I have said yes to appeals too often during the last ten years. The interest on my debt now exceeds my income."

He found his daughter Fanny a good traveling companion when they went to Bermuda. Hayes made a lecture tour of the South with Reverend J. L. M. Curry, manager of both the Peabody and Slater Funds. Hayes spoke in Memphis, Tennessee, Montgomery, Alabama, and Columbus, Georgia.

§∞⊗

GROVER CLEVELAND wrote "The Silver Letter" early in the year to clear the air on where he stood, which was solidly behind the gold standard. Many political observers felt that this stance, in light of silver's popularity in the South and West, crippled Cleveland's chance in the 1892 presidential race. Cleveland wrote to his friend Wilson Bissell that it was a relief to take a stand on the issue rather than remain silent. By year's end, Cleveland advised Bissell that the campaign for his renomination should begin. Cleveland's great concern was that Governor David Hill of New York, a silver advocate, might capture the Democratic nomination. They disliked each other.

February: Although Cleveland had been advised to avoid the silver–gold issue, on February 10 he penned his silver letter. On free coinage he wrote: "The greatest peril would be invited by the adoption of the scheme.… We enter upon the dangerous and reckless experiment of free, unlimited, and independent silver coinage."

Southern and western newspapers, in favor of silver, showed their wrath. Lamont was shocked and suggested that Cleveland needed to tone down his "ultra anti-silver sentiment."

Cleveland told Bissell that the letter "lifted off" a weight from him, and now, "No one can doubt where I stand."

July–August: By midsummer, silver as an issue had died down and Cleveland's chances for the nomination seemed on the rise. Earlier in the year Governor Hill was elected to the Senate. Cleveland had been prepared to go public with his choice of Bissell for the Senate seat. Many, including Cleveland, thought it was improper for Hill to remain governor while waiting to take his seat in the Senate in December. Most states prevented the practice, and the *New York Tribune* called Hill guilty of "misconduct." Cleveland wrote to Lamont on July 3: "We are great fools if we allow ourselves to be hauled about by Hill and his gang." Tammany and the protectionists were behind Hill, but Cleveland did not want him to get the presidential nomination in 1892.

October: Cleveland's first child, a daughter named Ruth, was born in New York City on October 3. The former president was a father for the first time at age 54.

December: By the end of the year, Hill was hostile to Cleveland and his stance favoring the gold standard. Still, as late as December 12, Cleveland, in a letter to Bissell, expressed "my complete lack of political ambition" while making suggestions on how to derail Hill.

Future Presidents

William McKinley aggressively sought the governorship of Ohio and won the office despite Republican losses elsewhere. The campaign drew national interest because McKinley mostly discussed the currency issue, rather than domestic Ohio issues.

In the spring McKinley, now 48, went to Cincinnati and asked former governor Joseph Foraker, now practicing law, to make the nominating speech for McKinley's gubernatorial run.

McKinley worried that another election loss would mean his political life was finished. When the Ohio Republican convention was held in June, however, Foraker gave a rousing nominating speech, and McKinley had the prize by acclamation.

During the campaign McKinley took a middle ground on the silver–gold issue but leaned toward silver. He had supported Sherman's Silver Purchase Act. He opened his campaign in Niles, his birthplace, where he said, "We cannot gamble with anything so sacred as money." McKinley was easily elected governor in the November elections.

ဆဝဓ

Theodore Roosevelt's next attack on spoilsmen came in Baltimore as rumors circled that President Harrison might fire him from the Civil Service Commission.

March–April: On March 24, Roosevelt learned of corruption in the post office in Baltimore. Roosevelt took no direct action but instead passed the information on to Post-master General John Wanamaker, who did nothing. Roosevelt decided to make a dramatic appearance in Baltimore on the morning of election day, March 30, where he walked around and witnessed graft everywhere with voters being paid.

The *Boston Post* on April 1 and the *Washington Post* on April 14 ripped Roosevelt and suggested his immediate removal from the Civil Service Commission. Frank Hatton's Washington newspaper ran the headline, "Teddy at the Polls—Helping to Hurt Mr. Harrison" and a story that said if anti-Harrison delegates from Baltimore went to the next Republican convention, "The President will have nobody to blame more than his Civil Service Commissioner."

Roosevelt made three trips to Baltimore for interviews. He said that twenty-five of Harrison's appointees needed to be removed at once, since "the view of the spoils politician is that politics is a dirty game." The Roosevelt report was a short 146-page work, but the other two commissioners talked him into delaying giving it to the president.

July–August: Roosevelt did not meet with Harrison about the Baltimore situation until July 1 and found the interview distasteful. He then wrote to Lodge that the president was "a genial little runt, isn't he?"

On August 4 Roosevelt sent a copy of his Baltimore report to the president, and an abridged version made newspaper headlines.

Edith gave birth to a daughter, Ethel Carow, on August 13.

October: On October 10, Roosevelt asked Lodge about rumors that he faced firing from the Civil Service Commission. The *New York Times* said, "the President will not dare" to ask Roosevelt to resign and advised against a resignation or removal. However, Wanamaker ordered an investigation, saying Roosevelt's material "so far is inconclusive." This caused Roosevelt to blow up at the messenger who brought this news from Wanamaker.

ဆဝဓ

William Howard Taft, 34 in September, saw a chance for an appointment to a new appeals court, the first federal court below the U.S. Supreme Court. In March, Congress created new U.S. courts of appeals in all nine circuits, and Taft was interested in pulling wires to get on the bench.

Taft's interest was the sixth circuit—Ohio, Kentucky, Michigan, and Tennessee—but his wife, Nellie, saw a judgeship as a dead end and thought her husband was capable of reaching higher plateaus. In any case, Taft's desire for an appointment to the appeals court would have to wait a year.

January: Taft was involved in a Bering Sea case concerning seal hunting. The United States was having problems getting Britain, Russia, and Japan to agree not to hunt and exter-minate seals. A British suit concerning the American takeover of a Canadian sailing vessel hunting in the Bering Sea reached the Supreme Court.

Taft wrote to his father, Alphonso, on January 23, "The case has aroused great public attention.... I look forward with trepidation ... in making the argument before the court." Taft won the case, saying that Britain could not review the conduct of a branch of the American government at the same time diplomatic negotiations were being held on the- same issue. (Later an international arbitration review concluded that the Bering Sea was not wholly American, but steps were taken to safeguard the seals.)

May: Taft learned that his father's health was quickly failing, and he hurried to San Diego to see him. His father was unconscious part of the time but once asked Taft how he liked the "old men" on the Supreme Court. On his deathbed Alphonso told his son, "Will, I love you beyond expression." Before he died, Alphonso told Will he could be president. The elder Taft died on May 21 at the age of 80.

August 1: Nellie gave birth to a girl, Helen Herron Taft.

WOODROW WILSON, 35 in December, was upset that no progress was being made in starting a law school for Princeton and decided to try to raise the money himself. The professor sensed that President Francis Patton's talk about a law school was just talk. Wilson hoped that speaking appearances before alumni groups would help make the law school a reality.

Wilson was also becoming a favorite professor among students, who would pack his classes. One of Wilson's classes had 160 male students. Students gave him rapt attention and one recalled later Wilson's "magnificent, resonant voice."

WARREN G. HARDING married a domineering woman, Florence "Flossie" Kling, 5 years his senior. He had met her for the first time at a piano in his father Tyron's parlor. Florence was giving piano lessons to Chat, Warren's sister.

Florence was born on August 15, 1860, in Marion, Ohio. Her father, Amos Kling, was the richest man in Marion. When he first settled there, he clerked at a hardware store. Later he became the town's top financier, banker, and builder of the Hotel Marion. Florence's mother was Louisa Bouton Kling. Florence was headstrong and stubborn like her father as well as a divorcée. She had eloped in 1880 with Henry "Pete" DeWolfe, a neighbor in Marion and an alcoholic drifter. A son was born 6 months later, and 6 years later she petitioned for divorce. Her son, at age 4, was given to her parents.

Despite DeWolfe's erratic behavior, Amos Kling considered Harding an even a worse match for his daughter, and he exploded when he heard gossip about the possibility of their marriage. When the rumor turned out to be true, Amos disowned Florence and told the rest of the Kling family to have nothing to do with her. For 7 years he would not even nod to her on the street, and he kept his distance for 15 years.

Harding was age 25 and Florence age 30 on July 8 when they married in a new Victorian home they had jointly financed and had built. They took a honeymoon trip to the Northwest via Chicago and St. Paul.

Warren and Florence's wedding was announced in the *Marion Star* on July 9 when the paper reported, "unusual notice ... nuptials of the editor. [Harding] and Florence M. Kling were happily married at their own home on Mount Vernon Avenue Wednesday evening July 8 at 8:30. Quite a pleasant company of friends were present to witness the ceremony."

In June, Harding was a delegate to the state Republican convention. He began to dress like a statesman.

CALVIN COOLIDGE, 19 in July, entered Amherst College in Massachusetts in September but disliked it mostly because of his own timid nature. No other Coolidge had ever attended college. Two other major events for Coolidge, 19, during this year: his widowed father remarried and also took him to Bennington, Vermont, to see President Harrison deliver a speech.

To become better prepared on this second attempt to pass Amherst's entrance examinations, Coolidge attended St. Johnsbury Academy in Vermont, 200 miles northeast of his Plymouth Notch home. Calvin wrote to his father on April 14 from St. Johnsbury that he was "very much pleased with the school ... my room is heated by hot air furnace.... I have met a number of the boys and they all seem very pleasant." At the end of 2 months at St. Johnsbury, Coolidge passed the entrance exam for Amherst.

September–October: On September 8, with Calvin in attendance, John Coolidge married a Plymouth schoolteacher, Carrie A. Brown. The couple honeymooned in Buffalo, New York. Carrie had attended Kimball Union Academy before teaching, and she filled a void for John after the loss of his wife and daughter.

Before going to Amherst, Calvin went with his father to see President Harrison, who was dedicating a 300-foot monument in Bennington marking the American victory there over Burgoyne in the Revolutionary War.

Coolidge arrived in Amherst in late September and lived in a brick house on South Pleasant Street. The private home was necessary because Amherst's dormitories, built in 1820, were falling down. There were 336 students, a third of them from outside New England. Most were the sons of professional people. Coolidge lived with Alfred Turner of Rutland, Vermont.

Coolidge tried to pledge to a fraternity but lacked the personality needed to be selected. This rejection and his inability to mix led to homesickness, and on October 15 he wrote home, "I don't seem to get acquainted very fast."

HERBERT HOOVER, 17, entered Stanford, a new college in the Santa Clara Valley, 30 miles south of San Francisco. The school was founded by wealthy Senator Leland Stanford and named after his son who died of typhoid fever in 1884 at the age of 16.

The school was opened with a large ceremony on October 1. There were 400 students to hear Senator Stanford say, "All that we can do for you is to place the opportunity within your reach. Remember that life is, above all, practical."

Stanford was offering entrance examinations in Portland, Oregon, and Hoover decided on his own to take them. He did poorly on the exams largely because his Quaker education was poor preparation. But a Quaker math teacher, Professor Joseph Swain, decided to take a chance on the youth because he liked the way he showed resolve in solving math problems. First Hoover needed more tutoring, and this study took place in earnest in Minthorn's barn in Salem, Oregon. Hoover himself made extra money by tutoring another Stanford prospect, Fred Williams.

On August 29, Hoover and Williams boarded a train for Stanford. They for a time lived in an unoccupied farmhouse converted into boarding for students, called Adelante Villa. To pay for his boarding, Hoover took care of the horses. He also did additional studying for more exams. Hoover had to work his way through school: he became a clerk in the registrar's office, delivered newspapers, distributed laundry, and worked as a janitor.

During his first semester at the school, Hoover's English test results were poor and he was told to make this up prior to graduation. He studied geometry, trigonometry, algebra, linear drawing, freehand drawing, and shop.

%⃝℞

FRANKLIN D. ROOSEVELT, 9, in May went to Bad Nauheim, Germany, where he completed 6 weeks of study in a public school. He was learning German and French. The German schoolmaster found Franklin a "bright young fellow ... engaging manner ... so polite."

Back in Hyde Park, New York, the youth began a stamp collection, studying stamps with a magnifying glass. Like cousin Theodore, Franklin also began a bird collection and over the next 2 years killed and stuffed 300 birds. He also collected nests and eggs.

%⃝℞

HARRY S TRUMAN, age 7, lived in Independence, Missouri, and had not yet started school.

%⃝℞

DWIGHT D. EISENHOWER, 1 year old, moved with his family from Denison, Texas, to Abilene, Kansas. The Eisenhowers moved into a white, two-story house at Southeast 4th Street on the less affluent side of the railroad tracks.

Dwight's father, David, began work at $380 per year as a refrigeration mechanic in a creamery, a job that required little skill.

1892
Benjamin Harrison

President Harrison was matched against Grover Cleveland in the presidential election for a second time. This time, however, the results were reversed. Harrison's fourth and last year in the White House also featured all of the political

maneuvering typical of presidential election years. In his personal life, Harrison was faced with the death of his wife, Caroline, just weeks before the election.

January: The year began with the cabinet prepared to go to war with Chile over the incident the previous year involving the death of American sailors in Chile (see **Benjamin Harrison**, page 391). On January 25, Harrison considered asking Congress for a declaration of war. When it became apparent that no European country would come to Chile's defense, however, Chile offered to pay an indemnity of $75,000 to settle the conflict. The United States accepted the offer and war was avoided.

Early in the year, Harrison balked at the idea of a second term. At the same time, many in the Republican Party began to look to Secretary of State James Blaine to lead the party to victory in November.

February–May: Tensions between Harrison and Blaine began to mount. In early February, Blaine repeatedly stated that he was not a candidate for the Republican nomination. At the same time, however, he did not go on record in support of Harrison.

In April both the *Chicago Post* and the *New York Sun* stated that Blaine wanted to run, yet Blaine continued to deny this.

On May 5 the Chinese Exclusion Act was extended for 10 years, and it was amended to require a certification of residence for Chinese already living in the United States.

On May 7 the president's son, Russell Harrison, was quoted in the *New York World*, a Democratic paper, as saying that Blaine's health "was broken.... Nomination is out of the question.... He cannot remember the simplest things ... all the work has been on my father's shoulders for over two years. [Blaine] can scarcely sign his name to documents." In response to these comments, Blaine wrote to the president, "I have seen no withdrawal of these statements or denial of their authenticity.... I have heard similar ... emanated from the White House, but have not deemed them worthy of notice."

The article suddenly put the spotlight on Blaine's health. A few days after the *New York World* article appeared, the funeral service for Senator James S. Barbour of Virginia took place. It seemed everyone at the funeral was looking at Blaine. A Democratic congressman from Wisconsin sitting near Blaine wrote a friend on May 17 that Blaine appeared "standing in the shadow of death ... [a] flabby ... broken down old man."

By this time, Harrison had decided to commit himself to run for a second term. On May 23, Harrison told a few close friends that he would be a candidate.

June: The *New York Sun* stated on June 1 that Blaine was a candidate, and the *Chicago Tribune* stated that trains carrying Blaine people were arriving in Minneapolis, the site of the Republican national convention. Another candidate emerging at this point was William McKinley (see **William McKinley**, page 396).

Harrison's cabinet met on June 4 with Blaine present. Blaine's son Emmons advised his father to resign from the cabinet, and Blaine did, on June 4, asking that his resignation "be accepted immediately." The president accepted the resignation 45 minutes later, and Blaine was replaced ad interim by Assistant Secretary of State William Wharton.

The Republican convention was held June 7 to 10 at the Industrial Exposition Building in Minneapolis, Minnesota. Harrison won the nomination on the first ballot, with 535-1/6 votes to Blaine's 182-1/6 votes and William McKinley's 182 votes.

At the Democratic national convention in Chicago Grover Cleve-land was nominated for president on June 23, and Adlai Ewing Stevenson of Illinois was nominated for vice pres-ident (see **Grover Cleveland**, opposite column).

On June 29, John Watson Foster of Indiana was named secretary of state.

July: A new party, the People's Party (Populists), held a national convention in Omaha, Nebraska. That party nominated James Baird Weaver of Iowa for president and James Gaven Field of Virginia for vice president.

Secretary of State James Blaine resigned from Harrison's cabinet to oppose him for the 1892 Republican nomination. (Library of Congress)

Striking miners in Coeur d'Alene, Idaho, clashed with guards at the Frisco mill on July 11. The strikers blew up a quartz mill and seized strikebreakers, taking them as prisoners and marching them to an old union hall. On July 23 federal troops broke up the strike, forcing strikers to go back to work or face arrest.

October: Caroline Harrison, suffering for most of the year with pulmonary tuberculosis, became very ill at the start of the month. She died at the White House on October 25 at the age of 60.

November: Grover Cleveland defeated Harrison to regain the White House on November 8. Cleveland polled 5,556,918 popular votes to Harrison's 5,176,108 votes. People's Party candidate James Baird Weaver earned 1,041,028 votes. In the electoral vote, Cleveland received 277 votes, Harrison received 145 votes, and Weaver received 22 votes.

Former Presidents

RUTHERFORD B. HAYES, in retirement in Fremont, Ohio, attended the January inauguration of William McKinley as governor of Ohio. McKinley was a good friend and had been an efficient, courageous aide to Hayes during the Civil War.

Hayes had become quite deaf, a family affliction. He was now forgetful and slower of foot, and his memory faded on recent events but he remained sharp on Civil War details and his White House years.

On his seventieth birthday on October 4, he noted in his diary, "Now my life is as happy as that of the people of the common standard; more so, I suspect, far more so. [I've] been kept busy the past ten years working for other people.... I don't deny that I enjoy it."

☙ ❧

GROVER CLEVELAND won an easy victory at the Democratic national convention in Chicago and then beat the incumbent Benjamin Harrison to become the first and only former president to retake the White House after losing it.

January–March: Cleveland faced a challenge for the Democratic nomination from the governor of his home state of New York, David Bennett Hill. Hill showed early strength in the South. Democrats in New York called for an early state convention, set for February 22, whereas in past years it had never been held before April 20. There was great indignation by many regulars that Hill was trying to steamroller New York Democrats.

New York Democrats nominated Hill at the convention on February 22. The *Atlanta Constitution* then predicted a Hill victory at the national convention in Chicago in June.

In a March 9 letter to Edmund S. Bragg, Cleveland indicated an interest in being the Democratic candidate.

April–May: Hill embarked on a successful tour of the South in April and early May, shoring up support for his nomination. Lucius Lamar warned Cleveland on April 3 that Hill was picking up steam in the South. Cleveland wrote to Lamar on May 1 that the presidency "has not ... a single allurement. I shrink from another canvass [or] dark depth of another defeat. [But] I shall be obedient to the cause ... no one shall say that I refused to serve in time of peril."

The Hill balloon collapsed in May as Cleveland men in Syracuse and Buffalo quickly organized a shadow delegation for the national convention, to show the country that Cleveland could carry New York. Soon Rhode Island and Massachusetts selected Cleveland also.

June: As the Democrats met in Chicago from June 21 to 23, the top contenders, aside from Cleveland and Hill, included Issac P. Gray of Indiana, John M. Palmer of Illinois, Horace Boies of Iowa, and Speaker of the House John G. Carlisle of Kentucky.

A vote was taken early on the morning of June 23. State after state showed little or no support for Hill. On that first ballot, Cleveland took the nomination with 617-1/3 votes; Hill followed with 114 votes, and Boies took 103 votes.

Adlai E. Stevenson of Illinois was the vice presidential nominee. The Democratic platform attacked the McKinley tariff, calling it "the culminating atrocity of class legislation."

July–October: Cleveland played a more active role in this campaign. Although his participation largely consisted of writing letters and attending strategy meetings, it was a greater effort than he had made in 1888. Many Republican papers said that Cleveland was weak because he had been beaten before. They also argued that he was an enemy of the Pop-ulists and that his tariff position was unpopular.

November: Cleveland defeated Harrison in the presidential election, becoming the first person to regain the White House after losing it for a term.

Future Presidents

WILLIAM MCKINLEY, 49, the new governor of Ohio, appeared headed straight for the White House in 1896 because Mark Hanna, an Ohio businessman, so willed it. McKinley made no effort to build a political machine in Ohio as Governor Joseph Foraker had done, but at the Republican national convention it was evident that many delegates were thinking McKinley even as Harrison was endorsed again and James Blaine rejected for the last time.

January–May: McKinley was inaugurated as governor of Ohio on January 11. In his inaugural address, McKinley discussed state problems, including public welfare, and condemned the Democrats for their gerrymandering.

McKinley wanted economy in government, and one of his first acts was to appoint a bipartisan commission to look into ways to increase revenues without raising property taxes. He proposed a franchise tax on corporations.

One problem facing McKinley early in his term was that the Ohio constitution limited the governor's power. McKinley did play a role in labor law, particularly protection for railroad and streetcar employees. A bill was passed in the spring that would fine employers for not allowing workers to join unions.

June: Although McKinley did not want his name presented to the Republican national convention in Minneapolis, Ohio businessman Mark Hanna had quietly established a headquarters in Ohio. Hanna had buttons and all the other accoutrements ready before closing the headquarters without fanfare when it became known that the cause was lost. Hanna had earlier been involved with the campaign of James Garfield in 1880. He latched on to McKinley during the governor's race the previous year, and now saw McKinley as ready for the presidency in 1896. At the convention in Minneapolis, McKinley earned 182 votes on the first and only ballot. The nomination went to Harrison.

July–December: Soon after the Republican national convention, Hanna launched plans to make McKinley the Republican choice in 1896. For increased exposure, Hanna arranged through the National Republican Committee a schedule of speaking engagements for McKinley that stretched from Iowa to Maine. Hanna found a reliable man, Charles Dick, to be chairman of the Ohio Republican Committee to ensure that over the next 4 years McKinley would always be the favorite in his home state.

As governor, McKinley's first year was marked by smooth sailing, as the Ohio legislature was controlled firmly by the Republicans.

§∞ Q

THEODORE ROOSEVELT scored the major political triumph of his 34 years when he excoriated Postmaster General John Wanamaker, an insider in the Harrison administration, on the Baltimore spoils issue. Roosevelt was on the road this year also, making trips to Paris, France, Texas, and South Dakota. He also continued his writing career.

January: Roosevelt left for Europe on January 9, the trip's purpose being to bring home his brother Elliott, who had become an alcoholic. The brothers sailed from Le Havre on January 27, and Elliott was placed in an alcohol treatment center in Dwight, Illinois.

February–May: On returning from his trip to Europe, Roosevelt learned that the twenty-five spoilsmen in Baltimore were still employed and that Wanamaker's report on the issue had not been given to the U.S. Civil Service Commission because it was an "internal" report.

In a closed-door meeting of the Civil Service Reform Association of New York City on March 8, Roosevelt said, "damn John Wanamaker!" Carl Schurz recommended to the reformers that a push for a House investigation would force Wanamaker's hand.

The House agreed to this on April 19, saying its committee on reform would look at the Baltimore evidence. Wanamaker agreed to testify provided that Roosevelt was not there. Wanamaker, testifying on April 25, said Roosevelt conducted an investigation in Baltimore in a hurried manner that did not justify firing anyone. Wanamaker concluded, "I consider myself the highest type of civil service man…. I am a law keeper."

Roosevelt testified on May 2. He said he stood by his Baltimore report, paragraph by paragraph. Wanamaker had stated that there were violations in civil service regulations under Cleveland, and Roosevelt said that if "not checked" the violations would be "just as great" at the end of the Harrison administration.

At this point the House committee let Roosevelt read Wanamaker's report for the first time. Wanamaker's investigators had been unable to challenge a single fact cited by Roosevelt; it only complained that the commissioner's report was "malicious" and "unfair" and was made for "some political purpose." Frustrated, Roosevelt fired off an angry registered letter to Wanamaker, with a copy to Harrison. There was no reply.

On May 25, Roosevelt presented a statement to the committee and read his letter to Wanamaker and Harrison. Roosevelt suggested there had been a cover-up, concluding that Wanamaker was not interested in reform and had a "dislike of the commission, and a willingness to hamper its work."

June: The House Investigating Committee made its report on June 22 and used stronger language against Wanamaker because he was "evasive." Still, nothing came of the report, and Wanamaker continued as postmaster general.

ꙮ

WILLIAM HOWARD TAFT resigned his post as U.S. solicitor general when he was appointed to the Federal Circuit Court of Appeals. The move from Washington back to Cincinnati was just what his wife dreaded.

March: Taft resigned as U.S. solicitor general on March 12 and was appointed U.S. circuit judge for the Sixth District Judicial Circuit and ex-officio member of the Circuit Court of Appeals for the Sixth District. The court met in Cincinnati, Cleveland, Toledo, Detroit, and Nashville.

June–August: In the summer, the Tafts took a trip to Murray Bay, Pointe au Pic, on the St. Lawrence River in Quebec, Canada—a location 75 miles northeast of Quebec City and 30 miles southwest of the Saguenay River. Henceforth the Taft family went to Canada almost every summer. They rented a cottage above a river where they could watch white whales frolic.

Taft played golf there, and many friends would come for lunch.

November–December: In the final 2 months of the year Taft, now 35, wrote seven opinions for the circuit court.

ꙮ

WOODROW WILSON, 35, professor of jurisprudence at Princeton University, was offered the presidency of the University of Illinois in May. Instead of accepting the position, Wilson used the offer to get what he wanted from Princeton. He was able to secure an assistant to do the instruction work in political economy at Princeton and get a raise to $3,500 a year. That made Wilson the highest-paid faculty member at Princeton. Only the university president made more.

At this time, aside from his lectures at Johns Hopkins University, Wilson began a lecture series in constitutional law at New York Law School. He also spearheaded the Madison Conference, held in December, on history, civil government, and political economics.

ꙮ

WARREN G. HARDING ran for city auditor of Marion, Ohio, and lost. Harding, the small-town editor and publisher, was 27 in November and was increasingly drawn to Republican politics. After his defeat in a political race he had been co-

erced into running, he made his first visit to Washington, D.C., to mix with Ohio's congressional delegates.

In Democratic Marion, the Republicans had asked Jerry Ellmaker seven times to run for city auditor, and he had lost each time. At the Marion Republican convention in September, George Crawford, editor of the rival newspaper, suggested that the city executive committee endorse the Democratic candidate, Upton R. Guthrie.

Harding challenged Crawford, demanding that the Republicans field a man for every office. Crawford then agreed, and Harding offered to replace Ellmaker as the Republican candidate. Harding wrote in the *Marion Star*, "It was necessary to round out the Republican ticket, and in a vein of humor, the editor of the *Star* was named."

Guthrie won easily, but Harding's loss left him the spokesman for young Republicans in the city, and he made the *Marion Star* their voice. Observers now saw Harding as having a political future.

ꙮ

CALVIN COOLIDGE, on his twentieth birthday, was called on to give the annual July 4 oration at his intimate little hometown of Plymouth Notch, Vermont. He took the occasion to refight the Revolutionary War, praising the winners and damning the British.

At Amherst College the sophomore marched in a torchlight parade in support of President Harrison. But the election of Cleveland left Coolidge surprised, perplexed, and disappointed. In his first six terms he took French, German, Italian, Latin, and Greek. His math included integral calculus. He particularly liked the teaching of George D. Olds (who became Amherst's president in the 1920s). Calvin also studied rhetoric and physics. His best mark was an A in rhetoric, but he received a D in physics.

Coolidge enjoyed a mock Republican national convention on campus on March 15. The candidates were Blaine and Harrison. Coolidge returned to the farm for the summer, where lightning had burned a barn.

ꙮ

HERBERT HOOVER, 18, a student at Stanford University, now showed an interest in geology as well as baseball and football.

In the fall session he switched his major from mechanical engineering to geology after spending a summer on a field trip in the Arkansas Ozarks as an assistant geologist. Dr. John C. Branner, a geology professor to whom Hoover had become an office assistant, arranged the trip.

The geology survey in Arkansas paid Hoover $40 per month. He worked for a graduate assistant, John F. Newsom. Hoover was often alone on foot or on a mule mapping outcrops. He located limestone deposits near Mt. Judea.

During the fall term, Hoover took paleontology, mineralogy, and chemistry and passed a course in elementary French. The first geology class at Stanford had only eleven students.

In November, Hoover went with Professor J. P. Smith to look for fossils.

&so;&cr;

FRANKLIN D. ROOSEVELT, 10, accompanied his father on a trip to Chicago.

&so;&cr;

HARRY S TRUMAN, at 8, finally started school but had other problems: he cut off part of a big toe while slamming a cellar door. A doctor reattached it. He also almost choked to death on a peach pit. Later in the year, he broke his collarbone in a fall from a chair.

&so;&cr;

DWIGHT D. EISENHOWER, 2 years old, lived in Abilene, Kansas. His father could speak German but declined to pass it on to his sons on purpose, wanting them to be "Americans."

August 9: Dwight's younger brother, Roy, was born.

1893
Benjamin Harrison

President Harrison completed his presidency by trying to expedite a Hawaii annexation bill through the Senate. The divided Senate, however, sat on the measure awaiting Cleveland's inauguration.

January–February: Queen Liliuokalani of Hawaii was overthrown in Honolulu on January 15. On January 17 the United States sent 165 bluejackets and marines ashore to "protect" American lives and property. The queen, without an army, gave way in the face of what she called intimidation by the United States.

Harrison regretted the timing of the revolution by annexationists, wishing it had happened 6 months earlier to give him more time to deal with the problem, or better still, 60 days later when it would be Grover Cleveland's problem.

The U.S. minister in Honolulu, John L. Stevens, and the provisional government's president, Sanford Dole, drew up a treaty for annexation and appointed a commission to take it to the White House. Stevens wrote to Harrison: "The Hawaiian pear is now fully ripe, and this is the golden hour for the United States to pluck it." Harrison, favoring annexation, welcomed the commissioners.

Harrison sent the treaty to the Senate on February 16, asking for "annexation full and complete." He said annexation "would best serve the interests of the Hawaiian people." Harrison warned against allowing any other foreign power to obtain a foothold in Hawaii.

The Senate refused to act on Hawaii until Cleveland reached the White House.

March–May: Harrison called Inauguration Day on March 4 "fearfully bad," due to the cold and snow in contrast with the rain that greeted him in 1889. -The outgoing cabinet escorted Harrison to the train station for the trip to Indianapo-

lis. Back home he was greeted with a cheering throng and hundreds of hands to shake.

Once back in Indianapolis, Harrison said he intended to write a memoir of his presidential years to be made public after his death, but he never did. He also set about fixing his house, neglected during his years in the White House. Soon there was a new front porch, a new stable, and fresh paint.

June–September: Harrison, 60 in August, spent part of the summer at Cape May, New Jersey.

&so;&cr;

GROVER CLEVELAND had a difficult 1st year in his unprecedented return to the White House. He was faced with a financial panic in May, confronted the issue of imperialism in connection with developments in Hawaii, and was diagnosed with mouth cancer.

March: It was a cold day for the inauguration on March 4 with snow on the ground. Sworn in first was Vice President Adlai Stevenson of Illinois. Chief Justice Melville Fuller, the man Cleveland had selected during his first administration, gave the oath of office to Cleveland.

Cleveland, 14 days short of his fifty-sixth birthday, in his address said, "Certain conditions and tendencies menace the integrity and usefulness of the government." He said there was a need to challenge "wild and reckless pension expenditure [and to] remove … the demoralizing madness for spoils.… Civil service reform has found a place in our public policy and laws."

Cleveland had a difficult time putting his cabinet together, but by March 6, it was firmly in place: appointed were Walter Quintin Gresham of Illinois as secretary of state, John Griffin Carlisle of Kentucky as secretary of Treasury, Daniel Scott Lamont of New York as secretary of war, Richard Olney of Massachusetts as attorney general, Wilson Bissell of New York as postmaster general, Hilary Abner Herbert of Alabama as secretary of the navy, Hoke Smith of Georgia as secretary of Interior, and Julius Sterling as secretary of agriculture.

April: Cleveland stepped in and tried to settle the situation in Hawaii. Cleveland ordered the occupying U.S. forces to withdraw and sent a new minister, Albert S. Willis, to Hawaii to restore Queen Liliuokalani to the throne.

May–June: A financial panic hit the United States during the first week of May. On May 5, there was a rush to draw gold from the U.S. Treasury as speculators began to unload stock, and the value of silver declined as well. The main causes of the panic had been brewing for months, if not years. The shaky international financial scene, the economic cycle, the erratic financial measures taken since the Civil War, excessive federal expenditures, legislation by the Harrison administration, an extravagant Congress, and the Sherman Silver Purchase Act were all causes of inflation.

A stock market crash on June 27 gripped the nation in further panic, causing Cleveland to call for a special session of Congress to deal with the financial crisis.

July: Cancer in the upper palate of Cleveland's mouth led to a secret operation on a yacht in waters off New York City. The operation took place on July 1 aboard Commodore E. C. Benedict's yacht *Oneida* on Long Island Sound. Much of Cleveland's upper jaw was removed, and the matter was kept secret for 25 years. Secrecy was key because of fear that the truth would be more than Wall Street could handle. A second operation took place on July 17 and involved removal of other parts of the jaw. Placement of vulcanized rubber in the upper cavity returned Cleveland's speech to normal, and his facial appearance remained the same.

September 9: Frances gave birth to a second daughter, Esther, in the White House.

October–November: In response to the financial panic, the 1890 Sherman Silver Purchase Act was repealed by Congress on October 30. Under the law, the Treasury was required to buy 4.5 million ounces of silver per month, paying with paper money redeemable in gold or silver at a ratio of 16 to 1. This meant that people could buy a dollar of gold for less than 60 cents-worth of silver. Cleveland believed that repealing the law would stop the run on Treasury gold.

Chief Justice Melville Fuller (Library of Congress)

Former Presidents

RUTHERFORD B. HAYES lived in retirement at Fremont, Ohio.

On January 8, Hayes visited his wife Lucy's grave, taking a sleigh ride to the site at Oakwood Cemetery. He wrote in his diary, "My feeling was one of longing to be quietly resting in a grave by her side."

In mid-January, Hayes attended a meeting of the board of trustees of Ohio State University in Columbus and visited Governor William McKinley. He took a train to Cleveland and caught a cold in the smoke car. He tended to some business connected with Western Reserve University and then took ill at the Cleveland train station.

Accompanied by his son Webb, Hayes insisted on returning home by train to Fremont. His doctor met their train on January 15 and put Hayes to bed. "I know that I am going where Lucy is," he told the doctor.

Hayes died at Fremont on January 17 at the age of 70. The funeral at his Spiegal Grove estate on a sunny day was attended by president-elect Grover Cleveland and McKinley, members of the Sixteenth Ohio Regiment, and a corps of cadets from West Point. Hayes was buried at Oakwood Cemetery next to Lucy. (Rutherford and Lucy Hayes were reburied at Spiegal Grove in 1915.)

Future Presidents

WILLIAM MCKINLEY'S political future, so encouraging and hopeful, suddenly dropped into the abyss of bankruptcy and ruin. The crash came when McKinley, the governor of Ohio, was about to visit his wife Ida, then under new medical treatment in New York City. McKinley had blissfully signed a series of notes for a boyhood friend who had financed McKinley's earlier campaigns but whose business failed. The debts totaled $130,000. McKinley did not have that much. Ida's assets were $70,000 and McKinley's were $20,000. To pay the debts, they mortgaged their property.

Mark Hanna came to the rescue, contacting Republican titans Andrew Carnegie, Charles P. Taft, John Hay, and others for money. Soon the debts were paid off, property was returned, and small donations from 5,000 common folk dribbled in. McKinley, at 50, returned all the money donated by citizens.

With his financial worries behind him, it was time to run for reelection. In his second campaign for governor, McKinley worked over the national issues, including the fight over silver. He praised the tariff of 1890 and blamed poor business conditions on the free trade principles of the Democrats. Despite the panic over the Treasury picture and business conditions, and what Cleveland was doing in remedy, McKinley said silver, "should not be discriminated against."

His shift in emphasis made him seem inconsistent and unsure about a major national issue, and yet his victory margin of 81,000 was the largest by a Republican in Ohio since the Civil War. His victory in the election put McKinley back on track for the White House in 1896.

THEODORE ROOSEVELT had a pleasant chat with President Grover Cleveland and remained on the U.S. Civil Service Commission. But by year's end, Roosevelt complained that civil service reform was "not the right career.... I am not at all sure as to what I shall do afterwards."

Roosevelt managed to get John R. Procter, a geologist from Kentucky, named to the commission and sought to groom Procter as an eventual replacement to lead the commission.

Roosevelt was very busy during this year as a man of letters as well. He wrote *What Americanism Means* and late in the year published *The Wilderness Hunter*, possibly his finest work. It discussed the life habits of grizzly bears. He continued working on *The Winning of the West*—not only working on volumes III and IV, but also planning volumes V and VI.

Roosevelt, 35 in October, was also a part-time lecturer, often in New York City or Boston, speaking about history, hunting, politics, and foreign policy.

❧

WILLIAM HOWARD TAFT, 36 in September, continued on the federal circuit court. Taft's home base was in his native Cincinnati, but his jurisdiction covered four states of the Midwest and South.

One of Taft's major cases for the year took place early in spring. Taft handed down an injunction on April 3 in a railroad dispute in which he claimed an act by the Railroad Brotherhood of Locomotive Engineers, in a dispute involving the Toledo, Ann Arbor, and Northern Michigan Railway Company, had violated the Interstate Commerce Act. Taft's language in the case was often verbose or unclear. He cited his own findings in the Cincinnati bricklayers' union dispute in 1890, saying that the engineers were guilty of malice.

❧

WOODROW WILSON, 37 at the end of December, continued as professor of jurisprudence and political economy at Princeton. Wilson's endless push for a law school at Princeton began to lose steam by this year. In addition to his routine campus lectures, Wilson was active as a guest speaker off campus and was a prolific writer.

In many of Wilson's campus lectures, he focused on current events such as the panic of 1893, Populism, and labor strife. He also talked about obedience and authority.

His book, *Division and Reunion*, a discussion of sectionalism and the impact of the Civil War, was published during the year. He wrote that the South was shaped by slavery, and the North was shaped by manufacturing and railroading. His description of the Old South was sympathetic to the "Lost Cause."

Another book, *A Calendar of Great Americans*, was published in the fall. Wilson was looking for a "type of greatness." He wrote that only Abraham Lincoln was the "supreme American of our history." John Adams lacked "national optimism," he said, and Thomas Jefferson was too influenced by French philosophy.

❧

WARREN G. HARDING was thrilled by the World's Columbian Exposition in Chicago. His *Marion Star* had received complimentary tickets to the exposition after the newspaper ran advertisements for the event.

Although only 28 in November, Harding suffered from heartburn and indigestion. He sought his father's medical help so often at night that at Tyron's suggestion he and Florence left their new house and moved into Tyron's home on Center Street for 6 months.

By the end of the year, Harding was nearing another breakdown. The publisher was the target of a nagging wife who often retreated to her bedroom. Florence also had a low opinion of Harding's business sense.

❧

CALVIN COOLIDGE, 21, a junior at Amherst College in Massachusetts in the fall, joined classmates in an excursion to New Hampshire to see the Dartmouth football game. More important, Coolidge made his first visit to Boston in June to attend the traditional sophomore supper at Tremont House.

Coolidge was impressed with the best-known teacher at Amherst, Charles E. Garman, a professor of philosophy. Garman emphasized morality and the need to serve. During the fall term, Calvin's closest friend was John P. Deering. When Deering was asked to join an Amherst society, he said he would join if Coolidge could be included. They both were kept out.

❧

HERBERT HOOVER, at 19, found that the science courses at Stanford University—including geology, chemistry, and physics—came easily to him.

Hoover helped his geology professor, John Branner, prepare a large topographic relief map of Arkansas for display at the world's exposition in Chicago. He accompanied Branner to Oregon during the summer to look for fossils and in November gave a lecture on the rocks of western Oregon.

❧

FRANKLIN D. ROOSEVELT, now 11 years old, accompanied his parents in their private railroad car to the World's Columbian Exposition in Chicago. He also went to London and then impressed his parents when he insisted on taking a train alone to Nottinghamshire to see a celebrated bird collection. Franklin started keeping a diary on bird sightings and wrote an essay on the birds of the Hudson River valley.

❧

HARRY S TRUMAN, 9, lived in Independence, Missouri, near Kansas City.

❧

DWIGHT D. EISENHOWER, 3 years old, lived in Abilene, Kansas.

1894
Grover Cleveland

President Cleveland, in his sixth year in the White House, was confronted with the violent Pullman strike and ordered soldiers to the scene in Chicago against the wishes of the Illinois governor. Many newspapers depicted Cleveland as a hero, but his standing with the laboring man was now very low. The monetary crisis, a problem throughout 1893, became worse as the recession stifled business, particularly in the South and West, during the winter of 1894 to 1895. The drain of gold toward Europe continued as many Americans began hoarding it. Europe worried that the U.S. economy might collapse.

March–April: Cleveland and labor had a tough year starting with Jacob Coxey's army and a soft coal mine strike affecting 160,000 men from Pennsylvania to Colorado.

In Massillon, Ohio, on March 25, Jacob Coxey's army began its march on Washington. Coxey, a horse breeder and quarry owner, hoped to lead an "army" of 100,000 jobless people to the Capitol. Coxey's motive was to demand the issuance of $500 million in paper money, but his army numbered only about 1,000 at its peak and about 300 when it reached Washington on April 28. Many, including Coxey, were arrested for walking on the grass.

On March 30, Cleveland vetoed the Bland bill, which favored silver coinage. This bill on silver coinage was seen as a threat to the gold standard, and New England in particular had regarded Cleveland as the last hope for a stand on principle against the silver interests.

May–July: The Pullman strike in Chicago began on May 11 when George Pullman, head of the Pullman Palace Car Company, fired three members of a union grievance committee. The local union then voted to strike. Employees asked for a wage increase or a reduction in rent for company housing.

On June 26, the Railway Brotherhood, under Eugene Debs, took up the Pullman dispute and called for a strike and boycott of Pullman cars. The boycott and strike affected twenty-four lines and over 41,000 miles of track, all controlled by the

George Pullman, head of the Pullman Palace Car Company.

General Managers Association. By July 2, transport out of Chicago was down 75 percent. In Chicago, 20,000 men were out on the picket lines, and Debs said that farther west the figure was 40,000. The post office said that the mail was not getting through.

Cleveland was determined to keep the mail, as well as other interstate commerce, moving. Attorney General Richard Olney, a former railroad lawyer, wanted the president to use troops "without waiting for action by the courts." Olney appointed a special counsel to the U.S. attorney in Chicago and instructed him that the strike should be broken and its spread prevented by getting warrants and injunctions against those obstructing the mails. Olney based his case for an injunction on the Sherman Anti-Trust Act, which protected interstate trade.

An injunction against Debs was granted on July 2. The cabinet met on July 3. Olney was anxious to jail Debs to prevent "anarchy" and wanted to send in federal troops. Cleveland accepted Olney's version of events and dispatched troops to Chicago.

When the troops arrived on July 4, mob violence began—much of it believed started by foreigners, adventurers, youths, and criminals roaming the area rather than the strikers themselves. From July 5 to 10, buildings at the Chicago World's Fair were burned, boxcars were burned, and switches were smashed. Over several days, thirteen people were killed and fifty-three were injured. On July 10, Debs was arrested, effectively ending the strike. In all, seventy-one men were indicted.

Labor and states' rights proponents criticized Cleveland's action; however, many newspapers supported Cleveland. Governor John Altgeld of Illinois wrote the president to protest the haste of sending in troops while the strike was in progress and later said the matter should have been left to the state to handle.

Half a world away, things were coming to a head in Hawaii, where a republic was proclaimed on July 4 after the monarchy was ousted. A new constitution named Judge Sanford B. Dole as president. Queen Liliuokalani appealed to London and Washington, but to no avail.

August: The United States recognized the new nation of Hawaii on August 9.

The Wilson–Gorman Tariff Act, which became law on August 27, used an income tax to balance losses the government suffered because of the financial panic.

December 14: Eugene Debs received a 6-month sentence for contempt and ignoring an injunction to end the Pullman strike.

Former Presidents

BENJAMIN HARRISON was making $50,000 per year in his law practice. That, plus investments and selling magazine articles, made him feel wealthy. Offers to make him a bank president or a professor at the University of Chicago he turned down. He gave lectures at Stanford in the spring, enjoyed sightseeing on the Pacific Coast, and took his daughter and grandchildren along.

Now 61 years old, he spent the summer at Monmouth Beach, New Jersey. The subject of the 1896 campaign came up, especially after big Republican victories in November. Even John Philip Sousa wrote to suggest another presidential bid, but Harrison discouraged talk about running in 1896.

Harrison wrote to Frank Hiscock on May 17, "I do not see anything but labor and worry and distress in another campaign or in another term in the White House."

Future Presidents

WILLIAM MCKINLEY, the governor of Ohio, spent considerable time trying to counter strikes that crippled the state in a recession year. Pushing arbitration, McKinley had more success than Cleveland did. His positive reputation with miners helped even when he called out the National Guard to prevent violence. McKinley, 51, often worked secretly with labor leaders with success, while avoiding the limelight.

In the spring there was trouble in Stark County when Massillon, Ohio, miners sidetracked coal from West Virginia and tore up rail lines. The sheriff of Massillon appealed to McKinley. Wanting peace, McKinley called in John McBride, president of the United Mine Workers. McKinley told McBride that his men had gone too far and called out the National Guard to keep the railroads running.

McKinley sent many regiments to different areas of violence. He had learned in the Civil War that the use of massive force can prevent bloodshed, but he warned the guardsmen to avoid conflicts with the miners. With the presence of the guardsmen, further damage by Massillon miners was prevented, and McKinley earned a great deal of praise for his response to the crisis.

He also had a reputation as an excellent orator, and Republicans demanded his help. He made a sixteen-state speaking tour, traveling as far south as New Orleans. Of his 371 speeches during this off-year election, he made 23 in one day in Iowa. His speeches started softly, then would rise with a clenched fist to a thunderous climax.

80 CR

THEODORE ROOSEVELT had a second shot at being the Republican candidate for mayor of New York City, but he turned it down. William L. Strong, a political novice who accepted the nomination and then won, offered Roosevelt the job of keeping the streets clean. Roosevelt declined. Roosevelt continued his work on the U.S. Civil Service Commission. He remained aggressive in his investigations but complained about the need for a larger budget and staff.

April 9: A son, Archibald Bulloch, was born.

August: Congressman Lemuel E. Quigg of New York said that the party wanted Roosevelt in the mayor's race because he had the best chance of winning. Earlier Quigg had said that the party could not nominate Roosevelt again because he was burdened by a "variety of indiscretions, fads and animosities."

Roosevelt's prime feeling was "I have run once." He talked his decision over with Edith, who was against it, pointing out that they had little money. In the end Roosevelt turned Quigg down but felt he was a political failure. He wrote to Henry Cabot Lodge, "I simply had not the funds to run."

On August 13, Roosevelt received a telegram saying that his brother Elliott had been drinking heavily and was very ill. Elliott and his mistress were living under assumed names at 313 West 102nd Street in New York City. The next day Elliott tried to jump out of a window, had an epileptic fit, and died. He was 34 years old.

November: When a businessman, William L. Strong, was elected mayor, he offered Roosevelt a job as street cleaning commissioner. Roosevelt usually enjoyed civil service work and added that he got on "beautifully with the President." But Roosevelt turned down the offer.

80 CR

WILLIAM HOWARD TAFT, 37 in September, was involved in the Pullman strike by presiding over the trial of Frank M. Phelan, an associate of Eugene Debs. Publicly Taft was careful to say nothing, but privately he was antilabor.

At the height of the Pullman strike in July, Phelan had gone to Cincinnati to tell the railroad workers there that they had to stand behind their fellow workers in Chicago. At Cincinnati and elsewhere, the sequence of events was the same: an embargo on Pullman cars, workers fired, then a general walkout by all railroad workers. Phelan was arrested.

In court Phelan denied that he urged a walkout, but Taft did not believe him. Taft met with the mayor and police chief, who feared that jailing Phelan would cause a riot. On July 11, Taft informed his wife, Nellie, that he would find Phelan guilty of contempt. Taft ruled on July 13 that Phelan sought to "obstruct the operation" of the railroad and sentenced him to 6 months in jail. He said that a boycott against Pullman was illegal, but he defended labor's right to strike and to organize "in their common interest."

80 CR

WOODROW WILSON, 38 in December, continued as a professor at Princeton University in New Jersey.

During the year, he gave a series of lectures at other schools. In July he gave several lectures before the School of Applied Ethics meeting in Plymouth, Massachusetts. He said political morality "has no other standard than that of expediency," and added, "The standard cannot be the same for the state as for the individual … it must depend upon average judgments and follow an utilitarian ethic."

Speaking before the American Bar Association on August 23, he said: "We devote our instruction to the preparation of attorneys … and neglect to provide ourselves, in any systematic way, with barristers, who handle the principles of the law in argument."

80 CR

WARREN G. HARDING spent part of the year at the Kellogg Sanitarium in Battle Creek, Michigan, trying to avert a nervous breakdown. Harding entered the sanitarium on January 7 and returned home in February. By May he returned to Battle Creek and remained until the fall.

The circulation manager quit the first time Harding went to Michigan. With Harding in Michigan, Florence rode her bicycle to the *Marion Star*, took over the circulation department with a steel grip, quickly bringing order out of chaos and making the newsboys snap to. She wrote later, "I went down there intending to help out for a few days and I stayed fourteen years."

She was a rarity in the newspaper business—blunt, forceful, and tactless. Harding began calling her "Duchess."

ഇൻൽ

CALVIN COOLIDGE showed promise as a debater and orator at Amherst College. By finally entering a fraternity, the shy Vermonter found a needed sense of acceptance. The new fraternity man was often in the house and attended business meetings and social functions, but Calvin avoided the drinking, dancing, smoking, and cards that came with Greek life.

Coolidge took three semesters of public speaking. At the end of his junior year, he shared the J. Wesley Ladd Prize for oration. In September, Coolidge was elected the Grove Orator by a vote of 53 to 18, which meant he would speak to classmates and alumni on Class Day.

He also liked literature and read Shakespeare, Longfellow, Whittier, Kipling, Milton, Scott, Field, and Riley. Coolidge wrote "Margaret's Mist," a romantic tale based on a legend he heard on a visit to New York, for the school's *Literary Monthly* published in October.

ഇൻൽ

HERBERT HOOVER, now 20, spent the summer doing fieldwork in the high Sierras near Lake Tahoe for the U.S. Geological Survey. He was suddenly a federal employee. The experience was his major exposure to the rough life of working in a primitive, isolated environment far removed from campus or other conveniences.

The Stanford University junior also took over financial responsibility for the school's football team coached by Walter Camp. Hoover did not get to see the Thanksgiving Day game with California in San Francisco because he was too busy counting $30,000 cash in gate receipts along with his Berkeley counterpart all night long in a hotel room.

In a geology lab one day, Hoover met Lou Henry, like himself a geology student. A geology major was a rarity for any woman of this era.

In June, Hoover and other students drove a team of horses 300 miles from Palo Alto to Yosemite Valley, where Hoover was notified about the Sierra job. Without money for transportation, he walked from Yosemite to Stockton to board a boat. The 80-mile walk took him 3 days. Dr. Waldemar Lindgren, a top national geologist, who was impressed with Hoover's eagerness to learn, headed the Sierra survey work. Hoover's pay started at $20 per month but was later raised to $30.

ഇൻൽ

FRANKLIN D. ROOSEVELT, 12, when not at Hyde Park, New York, often was at the Delano estate on the Hudson River, 2 miles north of Newburgh. Called Algonac, the house had 40 rooms and was set on 60 acres. Franklin and friend Edmund Rogers built a raft, but it sank in the Hudson.

ഇൻൽ

HARRY S TRUMAN, 10, caught diphtheria and was paralyzed for a time in the arms and legs. His brother Vivian was also sick with the disease but recovered quickly.

Harry attended the Columbia grade school in Independence, Missouri. He began piano lessons with his mother and would play from 5 to 7 A.M. before breakfast.

ഇൻൽ

DWIGHT D. EISENHOWER, 4 years old, lived in Abilene, Kansas.

May 12: A brother, Paul, was born.

1895
Grover Cleveland

The president, isolated from his party with no confidants in the Senate, battled the unending financial crisis in another difficult year. So politically lonely was the president that he could rejoice only privately in the pleasures of a young family, which added another daughter during this year.

January–February: Cleveland sent a special message to Congress in January on the financial situation, as gold reserves fell when another $45 million flowed out of the Treasury. The reserve was down to $68 million on January 24 and reached $45 million by the end of the month. Cleveland foresaw disaster. There was a run on the banks in January, with near-panic conditions.

Cleveland's special message to Congress on January 28 said that the "emergency now appears so threatening" that different legislation was needed. He asked for a 3 percent bond payable in gold and also advised redeeming and canceling greenbacks and requiring payment of major duties in gold.

On January 31, Assistant Secretary of Treasury William E. Curtis met with bankers J. P. Morgan and August Belmont and agreed on a deal in which the banking houses would sign a contract with the government for $100 million. News of the deal returned confidence to Wall Street but produced wrath in the South and West.

On February 3, Cleveland notified Morgan and Belmont that he was against the deal. The two went to Washington the next day, and there was a White House meeting on February 5. Morgan said gold imported from Europe provided the only way to avoid a panic and that the public sale of bonds could take place later.

On February 7, Morgan returned to the White House, where Lamont met him and said that the president was still undecided. Morgan, disgusted, talked of returning to New York and letting the government go bankrupt.

The next day, a deal was finally struck. The banking syndicate would give $65 million in gold to the government in return for bonds. The deal increased gold reserves to $107

Millionaire financier J.P. Morgan strikes a photographer with his cane. Morgan helped bail the United States out of financial crisis in 1895. (Library of Congress)

million, and the export of gold to Europe was stopped. Despite the claim of profiteering by Morgan, the *New York Evening Post* on February 21 backed the president, saying that the country was close to a crash in January.

March: Nebraska Democratic Senator William Jennings Bryan, a staunch opponent of Cleveland's deal with Morgan and eastern bankers in general, resigned from the Senate on March 3 to begin a speaking tour in favor of silver. Bryan was now seen as a top candidate for the 1896 Democratic presidential nomination.

May 20: The Supreme Court ruled that the new income tax, part of the Wilson–Gorman Tariff Act passed the previous year, was unconstitutional.

June: Cleveland, 58, called on American citizens to avoid any direct involvement with the rebellion against Spain in Cuba. The rebellion, which broke out in February, garnered a great deal of support in the United States, especially by the two leading newspaper publishers in the country, William Randolph Hearst and Joseph Pulitzer.

July 7: A third daughter, Marion, was born while the president and Frances were in Buzzards Bay, Massachusetts.

December 17: In his message to Congress, Cleveland denounced Great Britain for its refusal to arbitrate with Venezuela in their territorial dispute over the Venezuela–British Guiana border dispute. The dispute between the two countries had been dragging on for the better part of the 19th century but had intensified with the discovery of gold in the area.

Former Presidents

BENJAMIN HARRISON, 62 in August, announced in December his engagement to Mary Scott Lord Dimmick, a young widow and daughter of his first wife's sister. Mrs. Dimmick had been with Carrie in the Adirondacks and at the White House during the First Lady's final months.

Harrison's children did not offer support, but he told them he did not want to live out his life in solitude. He wrote a friend on December 3, "It is natural that a man's former children should not be pleased … with a second marriage. It would not have been possible for me to marry one I did not very highly respect and very warmly love. But my life now [and] as I grow older, is and will be a very lonely one and I cannot go on as now."

Harrison continued his law practice throughout the year. A high-fee litigation case over a will occupied Harrison from January until May in Richmond, Indiana.

Governor Claude Mathews on June 10 asked Harrison to serve on the Purdue University board. In accepting, Harrison wrote Mathews on June 14, "I have felt a real interest in the school, growing out of a visit to one of their recent commencements." Minutes showed that over the next 5 years he attended most of the meetings, offered constructive advice, was often in demand for university functions, and often spoke to students.

Future Presidents

WILLIAM MCKINLEY, the governor of Ohio, moved ever closer to the Republican nomination in 1896 as Mark Hanna set up a headquarters at a house in Georgia and invited prominent Republicans to come and smoke cigars with McKinley. Even though Joseph Foraker seized control of the Ohio state Republican convention when Hanna wasn't watching, the convention endorsed McKinley's presidential aspirations.

It was at Thomasville, Georgia, early in the year that Hanna rented a house and established a sort of strategy school for Republicans leaning toward McKinley's nomination. Much of the work was done socially with McKinley, 52 in January, invited south in March. McKinley, however, described the trip as a "rest and outing."

June: Foraker, endorsed for the Senate race in 1895, seized the party apparatus in Ohio although a rival faction had the power to split the Ohio delegation to the national convention. Enthusiasm for McKinley was everywhere, and he backed Foraker's man, Asa S. Bushnell, as the next governor of Ohio

November: Hanna went to New York to discuss McKinley's prospects. The powers there wanted cabinet posts in return for support.

෨෬

THEODORE ROOSEVELT became a powerful force. Running the New York City Board of Police Commissioners he fired the police chief and quickly shook up the city while hunting graft, often in an entertaining way.

January–March: Roosevelt remained at his federal Civil Service Commission post for the first few months of the year. At the end of March, Roosevelt told Congressman Lemuel Quigg, a city powerbroker, that he would like to be on the New York City Board of Police Commissioners.

April–May: Roosevelt was nominated for president of the New York City Board of Police Commissioners at the beginning of April and confirmed on April 17. The other members on the four-member commission were Frederick D. Grant, son of the former president; Avery D. Andrews; and Andrew D. Parker.

After being sworn in at City Hall on May 6, Roosevelt ran up the street to police headquarters and greeted newsman Jacob Riis of the *New York Evening Sun* with enthusiasm. After ceremonies at police headquarters Roosevelt took Riis and Lincoln Steffens, a reporter for the *New York Evening Post*, into his office and said, "Now, then, what'll we do?"

Police Chief Thomas F. Byrnes was powerful, and corruption was rampant. "Taxation" was charged on everyone from storekeepers to brothel owners on various beats. Buying one's way into the police force was also common. Roosevelt later wrote, "From top to bottom, the New York police force was utterly demoralized by the gangrene."

On May 18 he wrote to Henry Cabot Lodge that he was ready to take on the chief. Any such action "will break you," the chief had warned. Nine days later Police Chief Byrnes was out, at full pension.

June–August: It was common for Roosevelt to walk a beat himself, often with Riis or Steffens. On June 7 at 2 A.M., Roosevelt and Riis walked several beats and quickly had the names of six policemen not doing their jobs. Large newspaper stories followed on how Roosevelt caught patrolmen sleeping on the job.

ജോ

WILLIAM HOWARD TAFT, 38, was based in Cincinnati but also held court in Detroit, Nashville, Cleveland, and Toledo.

When Supreme Court Justice H. E. Jackson died in August, his widow wrote President Cleveland that her husband had said Taft was the best qualified to replace him.

His brother, Charles P. Taft, publisher of the *Cincinnati Times-Star,* was elected to Congress.

Taft wrote to Nellie on December 18 that he disagreed with Cleveland's stance on Venezuela. He believed Cleveland's message to Congress was "phrased in such a way as to make it difficult for the country to avoid war with England without a backdown that will be humiliating."

ജോ

WOODROW WILSON, 39 in December, started writing a short history of the United States until *Harper's Magazine* offered $1,800 for six essays on Washington. Wilson took the money. The Princeton University professor continued on the lecture circuit.

February: Wilson spoke at Johns Hopkins University, where he outlined what eventually became the commission form of city government, and at Columbian University in Washington, D.C.

June: In a June 17 lecture on the "Writing of History," he said that telling the truth was half the battle and making it interesting and communicating the lessons of history was the other half. But as a historian he tended not to disappear in the archives but rather relied on the monographs of others. He said a historian needed to be a "sort of prophet."

October: Hard work during the previous months led to a near collapse during an intestinal attack.

ജോ

WARREN G. HARDING took a winter vacation in Florida from his Ohio newspaper labors despite bad weather, as a cold snap reached 6 degrees below freezing and the citrus crop was ruined. More exciting than black oranges was a battle between in-laws: Harding's father knocked down Harding's father-in-law, Amos Kling when the rich industrialist called Tyron a "nigger" outside the Kling house.

The Hardings made the Florida trip in January and stayed in Indianola House on Merritt Island, 50 miles south of Daytona Beach. Florence's brothers Clifford and Vetallis were close by. The boys were friendly with the Hardings and went to beach parties with them.

Harding left Florida in April to attend the county Republican convention. Meanwhile, the *Democratic Mirror* changed hands and stopped feuding with Harding.

Once back in Ohio, Harding began work on an industrial edition of his newspaper only to have another attack of "nerves." He checked into Kellogg Sanitarium in Battle Creek again on May 12. Still the new edition ran on June 15 as a 32-page supplement, and the *Marion Star* received congratulations from around the state.

The mayor of Milford Center requested Harding to be its Fourth of July orator. The mayor said he wanted an "up-to-date young man" as the speaker. Harding would turn 30 in November.

ജോ

CALVIN COOLIDGE began the study of law in Massachusetts rather than Vermont because a former governor of Vermont was unavailable to answer a letter of inquiry about employment from Calvin. Years later, Coolidge wrote that this stroke of fate, a simple matter of timing really, changed the course of his life.

Coolidge did well prior to departing Amherst College. He had been awarded the Class Day Grove Oration assignment, second only in importance to the Class Oration, given at commencement by Dwight Morrow, considered the outstanding member of the class of 1895. In addition, Coolidge won a national essay contest worth a gold medal and $150.

In a January letter, Calvin wrote to his father to say that he would either work at the store or go to law school in New

York City or Boston. He added that he wanted to "be of some use to the world" and "get a few dollars together." But the young man was uncertain if his father could afford law school.

When summer came, Coolidge worked on the farm again and discussed matters further with his father. They decided against store clerking or going to law school. Instead, Calvin would read law in a firm, the customary route for Vermont lawyers. It was less expensive.

Coolidge wrote to former governor William P. Dillingham on August 30, but classmate Ernest W. Hardy, reading law in Northampton with Richard W. Irwin, invited Coolidge to the small city near Amherst. Later Hardy escorted Coolidge to the law offices of John C. Hammond and Henry P. Field. Field said he could not give Coolidge much time, but he was welcomed to sit in the office, read, and learn. Coolidge accepted the conditions.

80 03

HERBERT HOOVER, 21, graduated from Stanford University and landed another backbreaking job in the high Sierras pushing ore carts in a mine for $2 per day. He had now decided to become a mining geologist, although he let friends know that he did not get a college education just to sweat the life of a miner.

Hoover almost did not earn his degree. He was warned early in the year by an English professor that he had not completed his English requirements. Hoover took 18 hours his final semester to remedy the problem and received his bachelor's degree on May 29. Hoover had no class standing at the school with 1,000 students because Stanford had a simple pass/fail system.

Hoover and Lou Henry were a twosome. He took her to the junior hop, but for the senior ball had to borrow $7.50 from his brother Theodore, now living in Oakland.

In the summer Hoover resumed work in the Sierra for the U.S. Geological Survey. He mapped the gold belt and climbed an 11,000-foot peak for a view of Lake Tahoe.

Hoover hoped for a fellowship to Johns Hopkins or Columbia or a job at the University of Oregon that he heard about. He quit his government job on October 15 and headed for a hotel in Nevada City to look for work. Finally he pushed ore carts at the Reward mine in Grass Valley, Nevada, for 10 hours per day, seven days per week. Then he moved to the Mayflower mine where he learned from Cornish miners how to use a drill.

80 03

FRANKLIN D. ROOSEVELT, age 13, lived in upstate New York and liked to read. He was once found reading the dictionary. He liked Mark Twain and read Francis Parkman and Admiral Alfred Mahan on naval power. He often accompanied his father on railroad or boat trips, once as far as Superior, Wisconsin.

80 03

HARRY S TRUMAN, 11, lived in Independence, Missouri. He was a good escort for his younger sister Mary Jane and could braid her hair.

80 03

DWIGHT D. EISENHOWER, 5, lived in Abilene, Kansas, and later said he and his brothers had no idea how poor the family was. His mother baked nine loaves of bread every other day.

March 16: Baby brother Paul died of diphtheria, a few months shy of his first birthday.

1896
Grover Cleveland

President Cleveland was disappointed and disgusted that the Democratic Party, by favoring silver, thoroughly repudiated its incumbent leader. The Democratic candidate, William Jennings Bryan, told the national Democratic convention in Chicago that he would not be "crucified on a cross of gold." To Cleveland, 59 years old in March, Bryan was a Populist, not a Democrat.

January: Congress voted on January 1 to fund a three-man commission to help determine the border in the dispute between Venezuela and Great Britain.

Utah was admitted to the Union on January 4.

The financial crisis lingered on early in the year as well, with J. Pierpont Morgan making new offers and proposing ideas to Cleveland. On January 6, Cleveland authorized a fourth bond issue, this time public, to raise $100 million.

April–June: Early in spring, there was strong talk in the Senate that Spain must shape up in Cuba or get out. Cleveland suggested home rule for Cuba and hinted that the United States might tire of Spanish ineptitude in getting the insurrection stopped. Congress suggested that Cleveland be an arbitrator to settle the Cuba rebellion.

By April, Cleveland was receiving letters from friends asking that he seek a third term. Several times Cleveland was on the edge of seeking it, but he always backed away. His failure to make an announcement early may have been a tactical error and led to his decision not to run.

The Supreme Court handed down its decision in *Plessy v. Ferguson* on May 6. The Supreme Court supported Louisiana's segregation law and the principle of "separate but equal."

On May 22, Spain rejected any offer for Cleveland to mediate the crisis between Spain and Cuba. This rejection caused a great anger among Americans toward Spain and increased their sympathy for the Cuban rebels.

Meanwhile, the tide in the Democratic Party was shifting away from gold and more and more toward silver. At state Democratic conventions across the country, silver candidates were winning support and platforms supporting silver were winning the day. Cleveland's name was hissed at many of the state conventions. At first Cleveland stood on the sidelines and said nothing.

Cleveland finally decided to speak out after gold supporters pressured him to make some kind of statement. On June 16, Cleveland issued a statement to the *New York Herald* that he was making a last appeal to the old party organization. He said he could not believe Democrats at the convention would go to silver. "I cannot believe this … such a course will inflict a very great injury. [There is] little hope [that] silver will attract a majority of the voters."

July: The national Democratic convention was held in the Coliseum in Chicago from July 7 to 11. The silverites controlled events, and the platform repudiated Cleveland and insulted him. When William Jennings Bryan spoke on July 9, he did not mention Cleveland. Bryan said, "We will answer demands for a gold standard by saying to them: 'You shall not press down upon the brow of labor this crown of thorns. You shall not crucify mankind upon a cross of gold!'" The roar that followed for 35 minutes was the signal that Cleveland no longer headed the Democratic Party.

The next day as the roll call began, the gold men retired from the hall to pack and leave the hotel. Bryan was nominated on the fifth ballot, and Arthur Sewall of Maine was the vice presidential choice.

Many sound moneymen on July 14 called for abandoning the Democratic platform and creating a third party.

August–September: The gold Democrats met in Indianapolis on August 7 and set a convention for September 2. At the convention, also held in Indianapolis, John McAuley Palmer was nominated for president and former confederate general Simon Bolivar Buckner was nominated for vice president.

Cleveland wrote to Senator William Vilas on September 5, "I feel grateful to those who have relieved the political atmosphere." The feeling was that Cleveland could have won the gold convention nomination by acclamation. But he declined in a letter on September 3 to Daniel G. Griffin, chairman of the New York delegation to the gold convention.

Cleveland disliked important federal officeholders siding with Bryan, which is what Secretary of the Interior Hoke Smith did. Cleveland wanted him out, and Smith resigned effective September 1. David R. Francis of Missouri replaced Smith on September 4.

October–November: The president was looking good on October 9 when he returned to the White House from a vacation, convinced Bryan would not win.

On Election Day on November 3, William McKinley defeated Bryan (see **William McKinley**, page 408).

Former Presidents

BENJAMIN HARRISON gave his last-hurrah speech, a splendid one for McKinley at Carnegie Hall, New York City, at Mark

Hanna's pleading. Harrison's own preference for the nomination was Senator William B. Allison of Iowa, but he did not make this public for fear it would draw him into convention conflicts.

February: Concerning the Republican nomination for president, Harrison wrote a public letter on February 3 to John Gowdy, chairman of the Indiana Republican Committee, declining to be a candidate at the national convention set for St. Louis. "There never has been an hour since I left the White House that I have felt a wish to return to it," he wrote. Others felt otherwise about him, but he wrote to R. S. Robertson on February 15, "A fresh pilot might steer the ship more satisfactorily than I."

April: Harrison married Mary Scott Dimmick on April 6 at St. Thomas Episcopal Church in New York City. Harrison was 62 and Mary was 37. Levi Morton and other former cabinet members were on hand, although attendance was limited to forty. The Harrison children did not attend the service.

Mary was born in Honesdale, Pennsylvania, on April 30, 1858. Her father was manager of the Delaware and Hudson Canal Company. She was the widow of Walter E. Dimmick, who had died in January 1882. She had lived in the White House for 2 years as social secretary.

Harrison was the first president since Millard Fillmore to remarry after his presidency.

July: When Harrison was in New York from July 28 to 30, he reported "Mr. Hanna pressed upon me with great urgency [to] make a speech in New York City in August." Hanna followed his appeal with a letter in an effort to keep the campaign off the silver issue. Clayton Powell, chairman of the speakers' bureau, wrote to Harrison on August 7: "The consensus of opinion, not only of the National Committee, but of all prominent Republicans [is that the] 'keynote' of the campaign should be sounded [in New York]. You … are the one man all agree best able to perform it."

Harrison said acoustics were poor at Madison Square Garden and instead recommended Carnegie Hall, which was selected on August 27. Harrison, now 63 years old, spoke without a script, his new wife in the audience. John Hay called the speech a "splendor of diction, master of method."

September–December: Harrison at first declined to do more for the McKinley campaign, explaining that if he were to talk one hundred times "it would be only a reiteration."

As he closed his summer camp in the Adirondacks, Harrison wrote to W. J. Steele on September 18 that he thought Bryan was dead, "We shall win easily."

Harrison turned down an appeal from Hanna to speak to Polish voters in Chicago and wrote to him on October 22 that he would give forty speeches, mostly in Indiana, "I think this ought to be accepted as my contribution to the campaign."

McKinley was elected on November 3, but Harrison retired from any continued association with the new president.

Future Presidents

WILLIAM MCKINLEY, 53 in January, won the Republican nomination with ease as expected and scored a smashing victory over William Jennings Bryan with the largest plurality since Grant.

January–May: Early in the year McKinley believed Matthew Quay and Senator Thomas C. Platt were stringing him along concerning support, because House Speaker Thomas Brackett Reed was expecting the backing of both. Platt said he favored Levi Morton for president. By February it appeared Reed was McKinley's only serious challenger.

The Ohio state convention endorsed McKinley in March, and he got Joseph Foraker to head the delegation to the national Republican convention. Before long McKinley was endorsed in Wisconsin, Nebraska, South Dakota, and Oregon.

When Illinois and Vermont conventions went for McKinley, the *Brooklyn Eagle* said on May 1 that nothing could stop McKinley from receiving the nomination.

June: At the Republican convention in St Louis, Missouri, June 16 to June 18, it was clear that McKinley was going to be the choice. McKinley enjoyed an easy first ballot triumph over scattered opposition, including Reed, Morton, and Quay. Garret A. Hobart of New Jersey was the choice for vice president. The Republican platform favored sound money.

The 1896 Democratic presidential nominee William Jennings Bryan. (Library of Congress)

July–October: McKinley had campaigned prior to the Bryan nomination in July as the "advance agent of prosperity" whose tariff views would bring about good times. And as a midwestern man he challenged the Republican powers in the East. Surprised by the Bryan nomination, McKinley resisted making an issue of the gold standard.

Although Hanna established headquarters in New York and Chicago, the McKinley campaign was largely a mid-western effort. The campaign heated up as fall arrived: On the last Saturday of September, special trains from morning until night brought 20,000 people from thirty cities and six states to Canton to hear the Republican nominee. In the week following, there were sixteen speeches to 30,000 people.

Ida sat in the parlor and gave out interviews on girlhood, romance with "the Major," and her love of children. McKinley made about 300 set speeches from his porch while Bryan was constantly on the move.

By October it looked as though the Republican would win despite Bryan's popular orations, evangelicalism, and large crowds. Bryan had little pull in the East. By October 28, Hanna told friends, "It is all over. Reports are satisfactory."

November: The election turnout on November 3 was the largest ever. In the North, 78 percent of those eligible voted. McKinley's winning coalition included the urban North, the prosperous farmers, industrial workers, and most of the ethnic minorities. The popular vote was McKinley 7,102,246 votes and Bryan 6,492,559 votes. In the Electoral College, McKinley took 271 votes to Bryan's 176 votes.

ഇരുള

THEODORE ROOSEVELT had a rough year at police headquarters; this time there was an internal fight with a rival member of the board. Republican power brokers in the state wanted Roosevelt ousted from the police post. Roosevelt, however, had already decided he wanted out of the job and into a top position with the Navy Department in Washington, provided William McKinley could win the presidency.

January–February: Roosevelt's hope for a navy job was clouded somewhat when he learned that McKinley was cool to the idea. In addition, New York's political boss, Thomas Platt, was against Roosevelt's landing in Washington. On January 19 in a meeting at the Fifth Avenue Hotel, Platt told Roosevelt that, as a result of a reorganization plan for the city, Roosevelt would be out of work in 60 days. Roosevelt called the meeting "entirely pleasant and cold-blooded."

The next day Roosevelt gave a speech before the New York Methodist Ministers Association, in which he stated that by February the city would be again wallowing "in vice, many politicians [are] bent on seeing this…. It is for you decent people to say whether or not they shall succeed." Some ministers around the state voiced the same warning. Mayor William Strong said he liked the speech and would oppose any effort to oust Roosevelt from the New York City Board of Police Commissioners.

Roosevelt had always been friendly toward Andrew D. Parker of the police board, even boxed with him; but now he heard that Parker was not to be trusted. On a promotion question discussed by the police board on February 28, Parker refused to go along and did not vote. Roosevelt turned to Chief Conlin, who also would not go along, saying such matters should go through his office.

Parker complained privately to Joseph B. Bishop, an editor at the *New York Evening Post*, that something needed to be done to stop Roosevelt from talking all the time, especially to newspapers, "The public is getting tired of it. It injures our work." The next day Bishop told Roosevelt that Parker was a "snake in the grass," although it took Roosevelt a long time to believe this.

March: The yellow press now claimed that Roosevelt was losing power and that Parker controlled the police board. Parker slowly had seized control of parts of the police force. If the Democrats gained power, the police board could become a one-man show with Parker in control.

Lincoln Steffens wrote in the *New York Evening Post* on March 24 that it was a clash of personalities, not something sinister, like a deal between Platt and Parker to get at Roosevelt. "Mr. Parker fights secretively, by choice, while Roosevelt seeks the open," Steffens wrote. The writer called events a "war" at police headquarters. Another police board member, Frederick Grant, went to Platt to try to break the police deadlock. Platt refused, hoping Roosevelt would resign.

Roosevelt wrote on March 30, "Though I have the constitution of a bull moose it is beginning to wear on me a little."

April: Roosevelt, together with Grant and Avery Andrews, got the New York legislature to consider a bill that would enable a majority of three to override a minimum of two (Parker and Conlin) on the police board. The measure passed the New York House, but Parker worked to stop the bill in the Senate, telling Platt that Roosevelt had the habit of promoting only Democratic policemen. On April 9, Roosevelt told the Senate Committee on Cities that it was "unqualifiedly false" and that he promoted without knowing what party policemen supported. Still, the Senate committee voted down Roosevelt's police bill.

May: At a meeting at city hall, Roosevelt got into a shouting match with the city comptroller, Ashbel P. Fitch, and there was talk of a duel. Fitch said, "You're always looking for a fight," and Mayor Strong threatened to have both men arrested. Newspapers had a field day, and the public wanted a real duel, although the *New York Evening Post* suggested fire hoses at 30 paces.

June–July: The annual police parade took place on Fifth Avenue on June 1. Roosevelt had canceled the 1895 parade until such time as "we have something to boast about." There were 2,000 men marching and wearing white gloves. At the end well-wishers mobbed Roosevelt and the mayor beamed.

When the police board met on June 3, Grant suggested new rules to break the deadlock while Roosevelt and Parker engaged in a tense debate. Finally Roosevelt picked up a new police Colt .32 off a desk and shook it in Parker's face. Parker, exhausted, agreed to the new rules.

Strong then drew up five charges of "malfeasance" against Parker. A public hearing was held in Strong's office on June 11 with Elihu Root as prosecutor and Tracy defending Parker. The hearing was dull, the evidence inconclusive, and the business dragged on until July 8. Parker was smooth, and the mayor realized he could not make the charges stick.

லை ૭

WILLIAM HOWARD TAFT, 39 in September, was confident that he could remain a judge for the rest of his career. On a trip to Washington he again heard talk that a Supreme Court nomination might be in the works.

Taft called on President Cleveland and wrote his wife, Nellie, on March 22, "We found his Royal Nibs in excellent humor and we had a very pleasant interview of some fifteen or twenty minutes." Taft later wrote here that "almost every person" he talked to seemed to think he could reach the top court. Some justices thought his appointment "very probable."

As for the political scene, he wrote Nellie on March 18, "I do not think … anything can prevent the nomination of McKinley. He seems to have a popular ground swell in his favor." As a U.S. federal circuit judge, he remained clear of partisan politics. But he was an observer, predicting that the Democratic convention would be a "wild affair … anarchistic, socialist, free silverite, and everything pleasing to the Populists."

With McKinley's election in November, Taft thought his chances of a Supreme Court appointment had been reduced, although his opinion was based on no real facts.

During the year, Taft became a dean and professor of property at the Cincinnati Law School. His commitment there, lecturing to both first- and second-year classes, took only 2 hours per week.

லை ૭

WOODROW WILSON, not 40 until the end of December, suffered a stroke and went to England and Scotland to recover. Wilson then gave the sesquicentennial celebration speech at Princeton University, which his wife termed "dazzling" and which was later printed in a magazine. Wilson also met Theodore Roosevelt and Henry Cabot Lodge in this year.

May–June: Wilson suffered a small stroke in May that left his right arm useless. His father, Joseph, thought Woodrow would die. Doctors diagnosed the problem as "neuritis." The need for a rest led to the trip to England. Wilson quickly taught himself to write left-handed, but Ellen wrote to him in England on June 18, "Tell me the truth," wanting to learn his real condition.

Wilson enjoyed England. He visited the graves of Adam Smith, Edmund Burke, and Walter Bagehot; was impressed with Oxford and Cambridge; visited Robert Burns's birthplace; and went to Stratford, the Wordsworth lake country, and London.

July: The sesquicentennial speech, given on his return from England, was titled "Princeton in the Nation's Service." Wilson defended a liberal education and was critical of science. "I am much mistaken if the scientific spirit of the age is not doing us a great disservice, working in us a certain great degeneracy. Science has bred in us a spirit of experiment and a contempt for the past." The speech integrated religious and political thought, and Wilson called for religion in the Princeton curriculum. At the end he talked about a scholars' paradise and asked, "Who shall show us the way to this place?"

෨෬

WARREN G. HARDING, editor of the *Marion Star* in Ohio, faced new competition when his father-in-law launched the *Republican Transcript*.

George Crawford quit the news business on December 8, ending 34 years as editor. His newspaper, the *Dollar Democrat*, collapsed. Harding's father-in-law, Amos Kling, then took over the Marion Publishing Company with $20,000 and started the new daily. Kling's editor, George E. Kelley, fresh from Washington, D.C. immediately charged the *Marion Star* with being a "traitor" to the Republican cause in north-central Ohio.

Harding charged that his father-in-law was out to sink the *Marion Star.*

෨෬

CALVIN COOLIDGE not only made a modest written attack on William Jennings Bryan's campaign against gold, but also attended the Massachusetts state republican convention as an alternate. The 24-year-old law student had joined Republican political activity in Northampton, Massachusetts.

On August 5, and urged on by Henry Field, Coolidge wrote an article for Northampton's *Daily Hampshire Gazette* to answer a defense of Bryan's position on silver that had been made by the former Democratic mayor of Northampton, John B. O'Donnell.

Coolidge also visited Plymouth Notch, Vermont, for a week in the summer and in a debate at Plymouth Union defended the gold standard.

෨෬

HERBERT HOOVER, 22, made geological field trips all over the Rockies from Wyoming to New Mexico, and by the end of the year was recommenced for a job in Western Australia. Hoover also published his first scientific article in a trade journal and was earning $2,000 per year.

A mining engineer recommended Hoover to an experienced professional, Louis Janin, of San Francisco. Janin was born in Los Angeles, was educated in Freiburg, Germany, and was known for helping young engineering prospects. Janin had no openings except as a copyist, but Hoover quickly took that job.

Janin was often an expert witness in litigation between mines. Hoover helped prepare maps and slides because he knew the western terrain from his work for Dr. Waldemar Lindgren.

Janin sent Hoover to New Mexico as assistant to the manager of the new Steeple Rock Development Company. The mine, near the Arizona border, was in a rough environment with Mexican miners, saloons, gambling, and violence. Hoover's job was to inspect and sample the properties.

Lindgren now offered Hoover a job with the U.S. Geological Survey. The decision of whether to be a mining engineer

or a geologist marked the turning point in Hoover's career. He turned to Dr. John C. Branner at Stanford University for advice. Branner said that large companies were "run like big machines … [people were] often promoted rapidly." Branner said government work was more "glory" than good pay. Hoover decided to remain with Janin.

Hoover traveled from mine to mine and after 9 months had also written several essays for mining and engineering journals concerning Cripple Creek, the California Mother Lode, the Routt project, and mining near the Sacramento River.

At the end of the year, Janin talked to a man about a London firm that needed a man in Western Australia. Bewick, Moreing and Company was operating gold mines at Coolgardie and Kalgoorlie. Janin recommended Hoover.

෨෬

FRANKLIN D. ROOSEVELT, 14, entered the Groton preparatory school in Massachusetts in September. But first he had a glorious time bicycling around Germany with his tutor.

The parting for Groton was difficult for Roosevelt's mother, who wrote, "It is hard to leave our darling boy.… James and I feel this parting very much."

Groton was near the Nashua River, 10 miles south of the New Hampshire border. The school had an enrollment of 110 boys, and Franklin went with his neighbor and friend Edmund Rogers. The first report from Headmaster Endicott Peabody to Franklin's parents in New York called Franklin "an intelligent and faithful scholar and a good boy."

Franklin was 2 years older than most classmates. He was sometimes ridiculed for speaking English with either a German or French accent. He wrote home on September 18, "I am getting on finely, both mentally and physically."

෨෬

HARRY S TRUMAN, 12, moved for the fifth time, from Chrysler Street to Waldo Street in Independence, Missouri. A neighbor was Bess Wallace at 608 North Delaware Street, only two-and-a-half blocks away.

Harry fished in the Missouri River and had a pond nearby for both swimming and ice-skating. His early heroes from his reading were Hannibal and Robert E. Lee.

෨෬

DWIGHT D. EISENHOWER, 6, lived in Abilene, Kansas, and wore hand-me-downs from his older brothers. The brothers, who were good fighters, usually stuck together. Dwight attended Lincoln school. During the year, Dwight's father was arrested for assault on a neighbor boy, put in jail, fined, and then let out.

1897
Grover Cleveland

Preseident Cleveland, prior to leaving the White House, expressed the opinion to McKinley that war with Spain was imminent. Upon retiring, he settled in with comfort near

410

Princeton University. He purchased a home that he called Westland after his closest friend at Princeton, classics scholar Professor Andrew F. West.

January–March: An arbitration treaty with Great Britain was negotiated early in the year to settle the sharp differences between the two countries—differences that had shocked and surprised the British public. Cleveland sent the treaty to the Senate on January 11 with a message that it would be a positive signal to the world that problems could be solved by arbitration. The press supported the treaty and so did Bryan's newspaper in Omaha. A National Arbitration Committee began a propaganda campaign favoring the treaty and sent out 50,000 circulars. (Despite all this, the treaty failed in the Senate on May 5: 43 in favor, 26 opposed, and short of the necessary two-thirds majority.)

One of Cleveland's last acts as president was to veto the Lodge bill on immigration on March 2. Conservatives were alarmed by all the newcomers from southern and eastern Europe, feeling that the United States was not getting what it considered "desirable" Europeans. The Lodge bill, which would have required a literacy test and some knowledge of English for new immigrants, passed the House and the Senate. But Cleveland believed the bill to be harsh and oppressive, and so he vetoed it.

Once out of the White House, the first thing Cleveland did was to go fishing off Cape Hatteras, North Carolina.

April–July: The Clevelands settled in Princeton, where Frances Cleveland selected a stone and stucco mansion built in 1854, which they now called Westland. They paid $30,915 for it. Cleveland liked the idea that Princeton was off the beaten path, with no close railroad connection.

In early summer, Cleveland bought a small farm 3 miles from the campus to use when hunting. He liked to shoot rabbit and quail.

October: A son, Richard, was born on October 28 at Princeton, and students posted a note that Richard would enter the freshman class of 1919 and play center on the football team.

୫୦ ଓଇ

WILLIAM MCKINLEY entered the White House and raised the tariff, sought international help on the monetary problem, and offered Spain help in ending the Cuban rebellion.

January–February: McKinley spent the first 2 months of

When William McKinley entered the White House in 1897, he sought an increase in tariffs. Eventually Congress passed the highest tariff increase in U.S. history.

the year contemplating his cabinet. He had decided to name 73-year-old John Sherman his secretary of state in order to free up Sherman's Senate seat for Mark Hanna. Hanna was appointed to the Senate seat on February 21.

March: A private Pullman car took the McKinleys to Washington. McKinley made a tearful farewell in Canton, Ohio: "I reluctantly take leave. [I have] sweetest memories of my old home." The traveling party included McKinley's mother, age 87, his sisters Helen and Sarah, and his brother Abner.

On March 3, McKinley dined with Cleveland and discussed Cuba with him. McKinley and Cleveland got along very well during the meeting, each having a great deal of respect for the other despite their political party differences.

Inauguration Day on March 4 was clear and crisp. McKinley, 54, took the oath as the twenty-fifth president from Chief Justice Melville Fuller, with Cleveland, his foot wrapped because of gout, nearby.

In his inaugural address, McKinley said he would confront "the prevailing business condition, entailing idleness upon willing labor and loss to useful enterprises … the country is suffering from industrial disturbances from which speedy relief must be had." He wanted a commission to review banking and currency laws. McKinley asked for patience in awaiting a return of prosperity.

On Cuba, the original draft of his address showed sympathy for Cubans, but the final version said nonintervention was best: "We want no wars of conquest; we must avoid the temptation of territorial aggression."

The remainder of McKinley's cabinet was in place by March 5: Lyman Judson of Illinois as secretary of Treasury, Russell A. Alger of Michigan as secretary of war, Joseph McKenna of California as attorney general, James Gary of Maryland as postmaster general, Cornelius Newton of New York as secretary of the Interior, and James Wilson of Iowa as secretary of agriculture.

May 22: Congress voted to allot $50,000 for relief of Americans living in Cuba.

June–July: Debate in both houses of Congress centered on tariffs. Republicans dominated both houses, and McKinley favored an increase in tariffs. On July 7, Congress passed the Dingley Tariff Act, raising duties on imports by an average of 57 percent. It was the highest tariff increase in U.S. history.

December 12: McKinley's mother died at the age of 88.

Former Presidents

BENJAMIN HARRISON became a father again at age 63, the baby younger than the former president's four grandchildren. Harrison, 64 in August, was the first president after Tyler to have children after leaving the White House.

The baby, a girl named Elizabeth, was born on February 21 in Indianapolis. She was named after Harrison's mother and grandmother.

Harrison appeared to enjoy his new responsibilities and hated to be away from Indianapolis. He declined several invitations to speak and turned down business opportunities that would have meant traveling to Europe, South America, and Japan. He told all that he was out of circulation and cut off from national politics.

Future Presidents

THEODORE ROOSEVELT returned to Washington as assistant secretary of the navy and before long was in the White House outlining to McKinley a strategy for defeating Spain by thrusts at Cuba and Manila.

January–April: At the start of the year, Roosevelt assumed that an appointment to the navy post would come from McKinley. To get in a nautical mood, Roosevelt worked on a revision of his book, *The Naval War of 1812*, adding a plea for a strong navy to the text. He was also invited to speak at the United States naval academy on January 23.

In Washington, however, there was a big debate about Roosevelt's appointment. Henry Cabot Lodge led the pro-Roosevelt forces, which included William Howard Taft, Speaker of the House Thomas Reed, and vice president–elect Garret Hobart.

McKinley believed that Roosevelt would try to get the United States into a war as soon as he took office. Secretary of the navy designate John D. Long was reportedly nervous about Roosevelt, believing that the young upstart would dominate the department within 6 months. Meanwhile, in New York, Thomas Platt had been nominated for the Senate and elected on January 20. Platt was at first against Roosevelt's appointment, but by April had backed away from his opposition to Roosevelt. Platt decided that having Roosevelt in Washington might be preferable to having Roosevelt in New York City.

Roosevelt was nominated on April 6 with Senate confirmation following on April 8. Roosevelt took office on April 19.

May–August: Roosevelt quickly flowed toward the expansionist group that had formed under Harrison and turned dormant under Cleveland.

Roosevelt's first address of this new career came before the Naval War College in June. In the address, Roosevelt repeated the word *war* sixty-two times. He said a stronger navy would promote peace by keeping others out of the hemisphere. "All the great masterful races have been fighting races," he said, adding that Japan, having beaten China, now had a cruiser in Hawaiian waters. He warned about the lengthy lead time needed to produce ships and munitions. He said Congress had to get moving. "Diplomacy is utterly useless when there is no force behind it," he said. The speech was printed in full in newspapers coast to coast, and expansionists praised it.

As the summer rolled on, strategic planning followed concerning Cuba and Hawaii. Cleveland's naval secretary had prevented any strident war plans from being developed at the Naval War College. Roosevelt wrote to Admiral Alfred Mahan: "If I had my way [I] would annex those islands [Hawaii] tomorrow." He added that he would build a Nicaragua canal at once, along with twelve new battleships, and put half the fleet in the Pacific.

☙❧

WILLIAM HOWARD TAFT, 40 in September and still working on the U.S. Federal Circuit Court, called on President McKinley at the White House on behalf of Theodore Roosevelt. Henry Cabot Lodge noted, "Judge Taft, one of the best fellows going, plunged in" to urge a political plum for Roosevelt.

A third child and second son, Charles P. Taft, was born on September 20.

In November, John A. Porter, a classmate at Yale University and secretary to McKinley, asked Taft if he would consider being attorney general, the job his father, Alphonso, once held briefly. In the end, nothing came of this "informal" question.

☙❧

WOODROW WILSON, 41 in December and a professor at Princeton University, was selected by the faculty to be its spokesman when raising issues before the board of trustees. Looking ahead, Wilson told Stockton Axson that if he were president of the school he would reorganize the social life so that freshmen could mix with older students.

Wilson served on many other committees, including the discipline committee and the committee on delinquent students. He was also involved in outdoor sports, the library, and the graduate school; coached the debate team; and defended the students' right to write songs poking fun at the faculty.

Wilson had recommended Frederick J. Turner for a history professorship, but President Francis Patton objected to Turner's Unitarianism. On January 29, Wilson told his wife that he might resign over the issue.

In May the Wilsons joined the Second Presbyterian Church because they remained loyal to Azel W. Hazen of Middletown, Connecticut, the minister of the second church they had met at while Woodrow was at Wesleyan University. Wilson was quickly elected an elder of the church. He gave time to the church and served on several committees.

WARREN G. HARDING, 32 in November, again made trips to Florida and Battle Creek, Michigan, as well as to Lake Huron's Georgian Bay in Ontario. While he was gone, George H. Van Fleet, a more aggressive newsman, took over the daily running of the *Marion Star*.

Harding went to Indianola House in Florida again, riding on a free pass from the Florida East Coast Railroad. He came down with a case of grippe, then moved to Daytona Beach and its yacht club. His return to Battle Creek was brief, and he was back to work in May.

Harding's mother, Phoebe, on July 18 treated a 10-month-old child with pepsin for cholera. The father of the child, Thomas Jefferson Osborne, charged Phoebe with negligence because she had used morphine that put the baby into a coma. The *Marion Star* defended Harding's mother, suggesting that Osborne's mother drugged the child. Osborne denied this in a rival newspaper. The Hardings thought their medical practice was in jeopardy, but the matter soon blew over.

CALVIN COOLIDGE passed the bar examination and decided to remain in Northampton, Massachusetts, to practice law.

It was June 29 when Coolidge appeared with Henry Field before two judges, William C. Bassett and William P. Strickland, to answer questions. He was admitted to the bar. Coolidge turned 25 on July 4. His law preparation had taken 20 months, and only then did he notify his father that he had been certified.

Now the question was where to practice. He considered Great Barrington, Lee, and Pittsfield in western Massachusetts, as well as Boston. He visited Lee on August 23 but felt the community was too small, the people there too slow moving. He decided to remain in Northampton.

He wrote that he was a very happy man as he entered the adult world, school preparation behind him.

HERBERT HOOVER, 23 before the year ended, was earning an astounding $10,000 as a mining engineer in the goldfields of Western Australia working for the firm of Bewick, Moreing and Company. He traveled 4,886 miles over the barren, hostile Outback landscape, going from mine to mine and sending recommendations to his employers in London on which mines to sell and which to buy or seek options. Hoover traveled by camel, horse-drawn buggies, and bicycle.

He started as the number-four man in the firm's western Australian branch office. By November he was number two and a junior partner in the company, which housed him in a bungalow that included a cook and valet. By the end of the year, miners called Hoover "the Chief," and he demanded management powers from London and got them.

FRANKLIN D. ROOSEVELT, 15, spent the July 4 holiday with cousin Theodore Roosevelt at Oyster Bay. In June, Theodore

had been a speaker at the Groton preparatory school in Massachusetts. Franklin wrote home that Theodore "kept the whole room in uproar for an hour," with tales about his New York police board days.

At Groton, Franklin was the only Democrat. He maintained a C average the first year. Franklin sang boy soprano in the choir, played intramural football, and cheered the varsity football team. He was the worst baseball player on the team but was also active in tennis, golf, and military drills.

HARRY S TRUMAN, now 13, lived in Independence, Missouri.

DWIGHT D. EISENHOWER, age 7, lived in Abilene, Kansas, about 130 miles due west of Independence.

1898
William McKinley

President McKinley, 55, directed the short Spanish-American War, which made this year a watershed in American history because it made the United States a world power. In a few months, the nation jumped the Pacific from Hawaii to the Philippines, creating complicated and difficult decisions for the president never imagined at the start of the year.

January: When liberal Praxedes Sagasta took power in Spain during the fall of 1897, he adopted a more conciliatory policy toward Cuba, offering home rule to Cuba under the Spanish flag.

Spain's new autonomy policy for Cuba took effect on January 1, but by this time Cuban insurgents would not be satisfied unless they were granted full independence. On January 12, mobs in Havana attacked the offices of several newspapers that had editorialized in favor of home rule.

To protect Americans in Cuba, on January 25 McKinley sent the battleship USS *Maine* to Havana. Meanwhile, the war of words in the circulation battle between the *New York Journal* and *New York World* escalated, as each tried to outdo the other with stories of atrocity from Cuba.

February: At 9:40 P.M. on February 15, an explosion occurred on the USS *Maine* in Havana harbor. Shortly after the first explosion came a second explosion. Within minutes, the *Maine* sank to the bottom of the harbor, killing 264 U.S. sailors.

Supporters of Cuban insurgents immediately viewed the explosion as Spain's doing. A court of inquiry, which convened shortly after the sinking, ruled that a submerged mine had destroyed the ship. Although there was some doubt as to the cause of the explosion, yellow newspapers where quick to blame Spain. The Hearst press cried, "Remember the Maine" and called for a war with Spain. (In 1911, the hulk of the *Maine* was raised, and an investigation came to the same conclusion as the 1898 inquiry. However, a 1976 investigation involving elaborate computer models indicated that an internal explosion due to spontaneous combustion from poorly ventilated bunkers using bituminous coal caused the accident.)

McKinley told Senator Charles W. Fairbanks of Indiana, "I don't propose to be swept off my feet by the catastrophe."

March–April: McKinley awaited word from naval investigators as to the cause of the *Maine* explosion. Spain's queen regent talked of selling Cuba to the United States, but the Spanish army would not accept any humiliation. The Sagasta government spoke out against negotiating with Cuban rebels.

After hearing that Spain planned to buy two Brazilian cruisers, McKinley called congressional leaders to the White House and asked Joseph G. Cannon of Illinois to introduce a $50 million national defense bill. McKinley took the $50 million from Congress and purchased the same two Brazilian ships for the United States. News of how quickly the pur-chase was made "stunned" Madrid, and the U.S. minister to Spain, Stewart Woodford, informed McKinley on March 8.

The naval inquiry into the explosion of the *Maine* relayed its findings to McKinley on March 25. McKinley used the findings to increase diplomatic pressure on Spain. At first McKinley demanded an immediate cease-fire between Spanish troops and Cuban rebels. Then he delivered an ultimatum: full independence for Cuba and a complete Spanish withdrawal from the island.

McKinley submitted his ultimatum to Spain to Congress on April 11 and called for Congress to recognize the independence of Cuba. On April 19, a joint resolution passed both the House and the Senate, calling for Spanish withdrawal from Cuba and recognizing Cuba's independence. The resolution also authorized McKinley to use the U.S. military to end the war in Cuba.

McKinley signed the resolution on April 20, and diplomatic relations between the United States and Spain were broken the next day. McKinley then ordered a blockade of Cuban ports.

On April 25, Congress passed another joint resolution that formally declared war on Spain.

May: The first battles of the Spanish-American War actually took place in the Philippines, where Spanish rule had also been challenged by Filipino insurgents.

Assistant Secretary of the Navy Theodore Roosevelt had told U.S. Commodore George Dewey to be prepared to attack the Spanish fleet in the Philippines should war be declared. On May 1, Dewey's fleet of seven ships attacked the Spanish fleet stationed at Manila. In a daylong battle, the American fleet virtually destroyed the fleet of ten Spanish ships stationed in Manila.

June: U.S. troops began landing in Cuba on June 22, on a deserted stretch of beach near Daiquiri, approximately 15 miles east of Santiago. The Americans, including Theodore Roosevelt and the Rough Riders, began their march to Santiago. On June 23, they advanced through the deserted town of Siboney, halting near Las Guasimas where the Spanish had entrenched troops. On June 24, the Americans encountered their first Spanish forces at Las Guasimas. The Rough Riders advanced toward the Spanish, who eventually pulled away under American fire. The American costs of the battle numbered sixteen dead and fifty-two wounded. The Spanish suffered ten dead and twenty-five wounded. Newspaper reports made heroes out of the Rough Riders, especially highlighting Lieutenant Colonel Theodore Roosevelt (see **Theodore Roosevelt**, page 415).

For the remainder of the month, U.S. troops consolidated their positions and made provisions for the attack on Santiago. In the meantime, the Spanish took the time to fortify Santiago and strengthen defenses around the high ground of the city known as San Juan Hill.

July–August: On July 1, General William Rufus Shafter ordered the assault on San Juan Hill. In a costly daylong battle, U.S. troops took the hill. In that frontal attack, more than 200 Americans were killed and nearly 1,200 were wounded, whereas the Spanish suffered 215 dead and approximately 400 wounded. The American troops sealed off all landward approaches into Santiago and established positions overlooking the city. This began a 16-day siege of the city, involving minor skirmishes between U.S. and Spanish troops as American leaders negotiated with the Spanish commanders to surrender the city.

On July 3, the American fleet in Santiago Harbor defeated the Spanish fleet, which all but assured the fall of Santiago. After several days of negotiations between General Jose Toral of Spain and General Shafter, as well as several minor skirmishes, the two commanders met for the official surrender of the city to the United States on July 17.

Operations shifted to the island of Puerto Rico, where U.S. troops landed at Guanica on July 25. The United States faced little opposition from Spanish troops there, although several small encounters took place during early August. In all, American casualties numbered seven dead and thirty-six wounded during the Puerto Rico campaign.

On August 12, Spain agreed to U.S. terms for peace, which called for ceding control of Cuba and Puerto Rico to the United States and the immediate evacuation of Spanish troops from both islands. The terms also called for the American occupation of the city of Manila, which would fall to American and Filipino insurgents the following day.

September: McKinley sent the American Peace Commission to France, with Judge William R. Day in charge, to negotiate a formal treaty with Spain.

October–December: Peace negotiations in Paris opened on October 1 and continued for several weeks. The largest sticking point over the course the negotiations was what to do about the Philippines. By the end of October, McKinley directed the peace commissioners to demand all of the Philippines in exchange for peace. The Spanish at first rejected this demand, and in fact there was growing opposition to the annexation of the Philippines in the United States.

Finally, on December 10, the American peace commissioners and the Spanish signed the Treaty of Paris. The issue of the Philippines was resolved when the United States agreed to pay Spain $20 million for the islands. The treaty also ceded Cuba, Puerto Rico, and Guam to the United States. Now, the treaty would face a hard road to ratification in the Senate (see **William McKinley**, page 418).

Former Presidents

GROVER CLEVELAND predicted that the imminent Spanish-American War would be regarded in hindsight as "unprofitable and avoidable" and without justification. He and many of his old Democratic Party colleagues opposed annexation of the Philippines.

Cleveland did not rest in retirement at Princeton. He spent the summer at Gray Gables and in the winter hunted ducks in South Carolina and Florida. On the yacht *Oneida* he sailed to Maine, South Carolina, and once to Bermuda. When not hunting or fishing, he concentrated on inside sports such as billiards and cribbage.

ℰᏣ

BENJAMIN HARRISON, at 65, tackled the largest law case of his career, representing Venezuela in its border dispute with Great Britain over its British Guiana (now Guyana) colony's western boundary.

Retired in Indianapolis, Harrison spent 2 years researching the issues with the assistance of three other lawyers. He turned his entire home into a giant law office to save the time it otherwise would have taken to ride by carriage downtown to his regular offices. His fee was $80,000.

In his preparation, Harrison had to sift through 4 centuries of documents, many of them in Spanish and in need of translation. He started out with very little knowledge on the subject but in 2 years' time became an expert.

The boundary was tentatively set when Venezuela gained independence in 1821. A British agent mapped the area between 1835 and 1844, giving most of the disputed territory to Great Britain. Venezuela protested in 1844 but was unable to obtain arbitration; and when England fortified the mouth of the Orinoco River in 1886, Venezuela broke off diplomatic relations.

In 1895 the United States sent a strong note to London, effectively invoking the Monroe Doctrine. In 1897, Venezuela and England signed an arbitration treaty, under U.S. pressure. The issue became an international law case, and Cleveland's Secretary of State Olney had to push Venezuela to accept this route to end the dispute.

Harrison and the Venezuela representatives reached an agreement to have the printed case done by March and the counter-case ready by December. Oral arguments would begin in 1899.

In addition to making his home a law office, Harrison set up workrooms at his retreats in the Adirondacks and on the New Jersey coast, and even on the top floor of the Fifth Avenue Hotel in New York City. He took responsibility for mastering the entire case and handled no other legal work over the course of 15 months.

All of the deadlines were met. The case was scheduled to be heard before a five-man world court in the summer of 1899 in Paris.

Future Presidents

THEODORE ROOSEVELT charged up San Juan Hill in Cuba to become a national legend. Combat with the Rough Riders made Roosevelt the most famous man in the United States, more so than Commodore George Dewey, and was a major factor leading to his presidency.

January–March: Before leaving Washington for the front, Roosevelt played a large role in naval war preparations, again making snap decisions when his boss, Navy Secretary John D. Long, was out of sight.

Roosevelt met with Long on January 13 and expressed his desire to go to Cuba if trouble came. Long told him to calm down. On January 14, Roosevelt wrote out battle plans for Long that sounded like orders and urged preparations. Long disliked Roosevelt's "fierceness," but did order naval ships in the South Atlantic to head north and those in the North Atlantic to go to Key West. Other units were ordered to Lisbon to monitor Spanish ship movements.

When the USS *Maine* blew up on February 15, Roosevelt wrote to Benjamin J. Diblec on February 16, "[The ship was] sunk by an act of dirty treachery on the part of the Spaniards."

At this point, Roosevelt cabled Dewey in Hong Kong to prepare for action against the Spanish fleet in the Philippines. He also ordered ships everywhere to fill up with coal.

When Long finally returned to his office, he found that Roosevelt was "causing more of an explosion than [the *Maine*]." Long vowed never again to leave the office in Roosevelt's hands and said that the orders fired off by the assistant navy secretary were an "action most discourteous to me, because it suggests that there had been a lack of attention." Yet the secretary never countermanded any of Roosevelt's cables, not even the one to Dewey.

At a dinner on March 26, Roosevelt told Mark Hanna, "We will have this war for the freedom of Cuba," and warned the Ohio power broker that American business interests could not stand in the way of the American people.

April–May: As Congress and McKinley waited in early April for a response to McKinley's ultimatum (see **William McKinley**, page 414), Roosevelt renewed his efforts to get an army commission. On hearing rumors that Roosevelt was anxious to fight, Henry Adams responded, "Is he quite mad?"

When McKinley called for 125,000 volunteers on April 23, including horsemen and marksmen, Roosevelt received an offer from Secretary of War Russell Alger to command the First Regiment. Roosevelt turned this down, saying that he lacked hard military experience. He told Alger that he would serve as a lieutenant colonel if a regular, namely Roosevelt's friend Leonard Wood, served as colonel. Alger approved even though he had planned to give Wood another command.

While Roosevelt was chairman of the Naval War Board, responsible for executing war plans, he also had to assist Wood in recruiting and equipping the First U.S. Volunteer Cavalry. All kinds of nicknames were suggested for this outfit, but it was Roosevelt's name, Rough Riders, that was finally accepted.

May: After Dewey's victory on May 1, Roosevelt wrote to him the following day, "You have made a name for the nation, and the Navy, and yourself … how pleased I am to think that I had any share in getting you the opportunity."

Roosevelt then took out a life insurance policy, gave Edith a drive through the countryside, and wrote a resignation letter to Long, in which he said he enjoyed working under the secretary. "I hate to leave you more than I can say," he wrote.

Roosevelt left for San Antonio to join the new Rough Riders on May 12 and arrived in Texas on May 15. The Rough Riders included many Ivy Leaguers, polo players, yachtsmen, a former Harvard quarterback, and plenty of cowboys.

June–July: Roosevelt and the Rough Riders arrived on the Cuban coast off Daiquiri on June 22. Soon after landing, they were on the march to Santiago. On June 23, they advanced through the deserted town of Siboney, halting near Las Guasimas where the Spanish had entrenched troops. On June 24, the Rough Riders advanced toward the Spanish. Colonel Wood halted the advance as the Spanish began to fire. The American troops fanned out through the surrounding woods, firing blindly on the Spanish troops. The Rough Riders suffered heavy losses early on, but eventually the Spanish troops pulled away under American fire. The American casualties numbered sixteen dead and fifty-two wounded, while the Spanish casualties numbered ten dead and twenty-five wounded. The victory opened the road as far as San Juan Hill, just east of Santiago.

Soon after the victory, the Rough Riders, along with the other U.S. forces, began their advance to San Juan Hill and Santiago. The attack on San Juan Hill took place on July 1. The American assault on the heavily defended hill proved costly. Eventually, the Americans overran the Spanish, with the Rough Riders and Roosevelt getting much of the credit for the victory. In fact it was a joint effort, with the African American soldiers of the Ninth and Tenth Cavalries proving just as instrumental in securing San Juan Hill.

Over the next 16 days, Roosevelt and the Rough Riders were involved with the siege on Santiago as American and Spanish commanders negotiated the surrender of the city, which finally took place on July 17 (see **William McKinley**, page 414).

On July 11, shortly after Wood was promoted, Roosevelt was promoted to colonel.

September–December: Roosevelt returned to the United States a national hero. He was mustered out of the army on September 15, and talk of his running for governor of New York began almost immediately. New York Republican boss

A painting of Theodore Roosevelt leading his Rough Riders into battle during the Spanish-American War in 1898. (Library of Congress)

Thomas C. Platt did not want Roosevelt to be the Republican nominee, but Roosevelt's popularity proved to be too strong and he was nominated against Platt's wishes.

Roosevelt used his military experience to the fullest in his campaign for governor. He often rode in uniform escorted by Rough Riders. Despite his popularity, only a small majority elected Roosevelt governor.

೫೦೦೩

WILLIAM HOWARD TAFT, 41 in September, had no interest in going to war and initially had little sympathy for war hawks.

On February 8, Taft gave a ruling in the Addystone Pipe case, the most important of his judicial career on the circuit court. The Supreme Court later upheld his ruling, which specifically revived the Sherman Anti-Trust Act.

Addystone was a Cincinnati firm. A lower court had dismissed a federal suit against six corporations selling iron pipe. Taft reversed this and ordered dissolution of the combinations on the basis that the Sherman Anti-Trust Act gave congressional power to regulate interstate commerce.

The government had found Addystone guilty of controlling prices in the Ohio and Mississippi River valleys and of crippling competition. Taft asserted that price-fixing was obviously going on. He struck directly at an earlier Supreme Court decision in a sugar trust case that had approved of combinations. Taft denied that the sugar case applied to the pipe case.

೫೦೦೩

WOODROW WILSON, 41, a professor at Princeton, had reservations about the Spanish-American War at first but later believed the United States had justice on its side and as much right to new territory as any other nation.

It didn't take long for Wilson to concede that the United States was going to win the war and that the cause was just. He felt that the war prevented Germany and Russia from gaining territory and that, if anyone received territory out of the war, it ought to be the United States.

೫೦೦೩

WARREN G. HARDING steered the Marion, Ohio *Star* through the turbulent waters of the Spanish-American War by urging readers to remain calm, in contrast to the war-fever push of the Hearst and Pulitzer press. The war caused a jump in circulation to 3,350 copies, large for a town of just under 10,000 people, but the paper was being read in rural, neighboring towns.

Harding, 33 in November, advised readers that it was "not a time for nervous excitement." As for the USS *Maine* explosion, Harding felt that it might have been an accident.

೫೦೦೩

CALVIN COOLIDGE had opened his own law office in Northampton, Massachusetts, on February 1. By the end of the year, he was elected to the city council.

September–December: When the Spanish-American War ended and soldiers began returning home from Santiago,

Calvin wrote to his father on September 9, "I am sorry I did not go."

October: Coolidge, now 26, was the ward two delegate from Northampton to the Republican convention. Calvin himself was nominated as one of three city councilmen from ward two.

December: Coolidge was elected to the city council from ward two. There was no pay for serving on the common council.

೫೦೦೩

HERBERT HOOVER quickly became a prominent mining engineer in Western Australia for a British company. At the end of the year, London decided to transfer him to China in 1899.

On Hoover's say-so, London invested $500,000 in the Sons of Gwalia gold mine. He managed the mine and a workforce of 250 men. He was still only 23. Hoover now was making so much money that he quietly financed the education of relatives and friends back in California who never knew their benefactor's identity.

In 7 months he submitted 600 letters to London, mostly blunt, brief recommendations on what new equipment would gain the company a technological edge.

The China assignment that Hoover accepted contained a proviso that he could first detour to California to marry fellow Stanford geologist, Lou Henry. At the end of the year, Hoover cabled a marriage proposal from the Perth office to Lou in California. Lou had graduated and was living with her parents in Monterey. Lou accepted, and an early 1899 marriage was planned.

೫೦೦೩

FRANKLIN D. ROOSEVELT, 16, was a student at Groton, a preparatory school in northern Massachusetts. Scarlet fever caused his mother, Sara, to rush to Groton where she found him "dreadfully wan." Franklin was excited by the Spanish-American War and was especially interested in the exploits of his cousin Theodore.

೫೦೦೩

HARRY S TRUMAN, 14, began work at the Clinton Drug Store in Independence, Missouri, for $3 per week. At Independence High School, Harry found history to be his favorite subject, but he also liked Latin. A voracious reader, Truman later claimed he read every book in the Independence public library.

೫೦೦೩

DWIGHT D. EISENHOWER, 8, and family moved from 2nd Street to 201 Southeast 4th Street in Abilene, Kansas. The house was a two-story frame house owned by Dwight's veterinarian uncle, Abraham Lincoln Eisenhower. He sold his house to Dwight's father for $1,000. There was a barn in back and room to grow vegetables.

February 1: A brother, Earl, was born shortly before the move to the new house.

1899
William McKinley

For much of the year, President McKinley was concerned over events in the Philippines. McKinley fought the Filipinos with regret in his third year in office but said that the United States would have been the laughing stock of the world if it hadn't taken over the Philippines. Politically, a thinly disguised campaign swing through the Midwest in the fall pretty much ended McKinley's private feelings that one term would be enough. He made 100 speeches, largely on the Philippines, and emphasized that America had become a world power.

January: McKinley sent the Treaty of Paris to the Senate for ratification on January 4. The debate on the treaty lasted for just over a month.

On January 20, McKinley named Jacob G. Schurman to head a commission to come up with recommendations on how to administer the Philippine islands. Schurman was charged with coming to an agreement with Filipino insurgent leader Emilio Aguinaldo.

February: Two days before the Senate was to vote on the Treaty of Paris, the first fighting broke out between the U.S. Army and Aguinaldo's Filipino insurgents on February 4. Fighting coincided with the failure of McKinley's Philippine commission members in Manila to reach a settlement with Aguinaldo. Aguinaldo's rebels attacked several key U.S. positions, but all were repulsed by American troops. The United States suffered more than 175 casualties in the attacks.

The Senate ratified the Treaty of Paris on February 6 by a vote of 57 to 27, getting the necessary two-thirds majority by just 1 vote.

March: Congress called for 35,000 volunteers to put down the insurgents in the Philippines and authorized an additional 65,000 troops for the regular army.

Without waiting for reinforcements, General Arthur MacArthur drove Filipino rebels from the city of Malolos on March 30, forcing the rebels into the jungle and triggering the start of guerilla warfare against American troops.

April: Although the fighting in the Philippines continued, those islands, along with Puerto Rico and Guam, were officially acquired from Spain.

On April 28, Aguinaldo offered to begin peace negotiations with the United States, but the United States demanded an unconditional surrender.

June: McKinley's wife, Ida, suffered a major epileptic seizure. Although she survived, her mental state continued to deteriorate, as she turned more possessive of the president's time.

July–August: Secretary of War Russell Alger resigned on July 19 after increasing criticism over the way he was doing his job. Alger was especially criticized for the way he conducted the war in Cuba, where sanitary conditions were so inadequate that for every soldier killed in action, thirteen died of disease. Elihu Root of New York took over the War Department on August 1.

September: Secretary of State John Hay introduced the Open Door policy for China. On September 6, Hay sent a message to Germany, France, Great Britain, Italy, Russia, and Japan in which he urged each nation to declare that it would respect China's territorial integrity and pursue a policy of free trade.

November–December: Vice President Garret Augustus Hobart died on November 21 at 55.

U.S. troops under General Elwell S. Otis captured the Philippine island of Luzon on November 24. The fighting continued in the other Philippine islands, however, where by the end of the year, U.S. troops numbered more than 56,000.

On December 2, the United States, Germany, and Great Britain signed a treaty that divided the Samoan Islands between the United States and Germany. The United States took the smaller eastern islands, totaling only about 75 square miles, whereas Germany took the larger western islands, of over 1,100 square miles.

Former Presidents

GROVER CLEVELAND, 62, was retired and living in Princeton, New Jersey. He hoped for Senate defeat of the Treaty of Paris that gave the United States Puerto Rico and jurisdiction in Cuba.

ဆ

BENJAMIN HARRISON, 66, made his only European trip; talked for 25 hours over 5 days in front of a five-man panel of arbiters in Paris in the Venezuela border dispute; and lost the decision.

January–February: At the start of the year, Harrison and his fellow attorneys wrapped up their preparatory work on the Guiana border dispute between Great Britain and Venezuela. The harder he worked on the case, the more anxious he got. With all paperwork done and exchanged, Harrison wrote to the Venezuelan minister to Washington, Jose Andrade, on February 27, "I have given myself so absolutely [to the Venezuela case,] I have felt I was on the verge of a breakdown. For one year now I have taken no rest. I hope Venequela is satisfied with the work." The case would not be heard until late summer.

May–July: Harrison sailed for Paris, where the border dispute case would be heard, on May 17 aboard the *St. Paul*. He took with him his wife, Mary, 2-year-old child, three servants, and Frank Tibbott, his secretary.

On July 4 he was the speaker before the American Chamber of Commerce meeting in Paris. He said that the United States "let it be known that she reprobated cruelty and persecution, but she has not felt that she had a commission to police the world."

August–October: The border dispute hearing began in late August before a panel that included U.S. Chief Justice Melville Fuller, the Cleveland appointee who had sworn in Harrison as president.

The British opened, and their presentation took 52 hours. Harrison's time didn't come until September. On September 28, Harrison wrote to William H. H. Killer, "At last the agony is over. I made a very strong effort to put the hearing upon an impartial judicial basis."

On October 3 the verdict was announced by the president of the tribunal, a Russian, who confirmed nine-tenths of the British claim—everything but a small bit of land near the mouth of the Orinoco River. The decision was unanimous, but no reasons were given. Harrison's wife wrote to her sister Elizabeth Parker on October 3, "We are all furious.... I never did believe in arbitration."

Harrison wrote to Miller on October 7, "The British Judges [on the tribunal] were as always aggressive advocates rather than judges. Law is nothing to a British judge it seems when it is a matter of extending British domain."

Harrison was back in Indianapolis when his legal associate, Mallet-Prevost, returned to New York and alleged that a deal between Great Britain and Russia had put pressure on the two Americans on the tribunal to seal a verdict for Great Britain. He continued to make this charge for the next 47 years. At first Harrison was indignant with the verdict and wanted the two Americans to file a dissenting opinion, but later he cooled down. (A United Nations debate in 1962 led to disclosure that Russia and the Great Britain indeed had worked out a deal.)

Future Presidents

THEODORE ROOSEVELT took office as the new governor of New York, and Henry Cabot Lodge soon advised him to seek the vice presidency on a McKinley ticket in 1900.

January–February: Roosevelt took office on January 2 and marched in an inaugural parade despite zero-degree weather. He was the first New York chief executive to conduct business in the new $22 million capitol building.

Soon after Roosevelt took office, Thomas C. Platt made a power play to test the new governor. Platt tried to force the appointment of a superintendent of public works and handed Roosevelt the telegram of acceptance. Roosevelt reacted firmly, saying he would pick his own people. Platt ex-

ploded at Roosevelt's arrogance. Roosevelt had trouble finding a superintendent, however, so he offered Platt four names from which to select. Roosevelt would use this method of compromise for other appointments, offering lists of nominees for Platt to make a choice. Roosevelt was soon regularly going to New York City on Saturday mornings to breakfast with Platt.

March–May: On March 18, Roosevelt announced to the press that he would like to see corporations taxed on public franchises they controlled. There were four bills in the New York Assembly regarding franchising.

A bill supported by Democratic state senator John Ford angered Platt, who said it would hurt business and was a concession to "Bryanism." Roosevelt caved in and sent a message to the legislature on March 27 recommending tax reform committee hearings as suggested by Platt.

Oddly, Roosevelt continued to speak kindly of the Ford bill and told the press on April 7 that he would "gladly" sign it. On April 12, the Ford bill passed the Senate by a 33-to-11 vote. On April 14, Roosevelt said the bill would benefit the community, but Platt managed to have it pigeon-holed in the house tax committee.

Roosevelt now decided to use the special emergency message rule to force the bill out of committee. On the next-to-last day of the session, Roosevelt sent a message to Assembly Speaker S. Fred Nixon, who tore it up, on Platt's orders.

Roosevelt felt challenged. He wrote another message to urge passage and mention that his earlier message had not been read. If it were not read, Roosevelt warned, he would come to the assembly himself and read it. Subsequently, the message was read and the bill was passed, 109 to 35. Adjourn-ment followed. Platt sent a letter to Roosevelt on May

A painting of a battle between U.S. troops and rebels during the Philippine Insurrection in 1899.

6 suggesting that it not be signed, that business would approve, and that Populist ideas were not popular in New York.

Roosevelt said he was willing to hold a special session to correct flaws in the Ford bill. "Of course it must be understood … that I will sign the present bill, if the [amended] bill … fails to pass."

The special session began on May 22. Roosevelt recruited legal experts to look at the bill, and Platt's men could do little. In 3 days the measure passed both houses, and Roosevelt signed it on May 27.

℘ℂℛ

WILLIAM HOWARD TAFT, in January, learned he was being considered for the presidency of Yale. He turned it down for religious reasons. A meeting in October with President William McKinley would soon show that an entirely different career move was taking shape.

January: Taft's brother Henry wrote him that the "liberal element" at Yale wanted him to be president at $10,000 per year. Taft declined on January 14 for two reasons: "The first is my religious views. The second is that I am not qualified." Yale support, he wrote, came from "Orthodox evangelical churches." To pick him "would shock the large conservative" group that gave the most money to Yale. To pick a president not of the Congregational Church of New England could "provoke a bitterness of feeling and a suspicion of his [Taft's] every act [as president]."

October: President McKinley met with Taft, 42, in Canton, Ohio. It is unclear whether Taft realized that the president was sizing him up for a possible Philippine assignment, which would come in 1900 (see **William Howard Taft**, page 422).

℘ℂℛ

WOODROW WILSON wrote his autobiography and, fatigued by his academic load at Princeton, made a second trip to Europe at the urging of his wife, Ellen. His companion was her brother Stockton Axson, who lived with them. They walked and bicycled everywhere, visiting many of the same places in England he had seen in 1896.

November: Wilson began his autobiography, *When a Man Comes to Himself*. It was published in *Century Magazine* 2 years later. Wilson wrote that early in life he was preoccupied with himself but later saw "the world as it is." To reach maturity, he said, Christian faith was essential for self-realization.

In a lecture to the Philosophical Society on November 2, Wilson said that men loved power and greatness because it was "an exercise of spirit so various and refreshing."

℘ℂℛ

WARREN G. HARDING, 34 in November, won election to the Ohio senate by 1,667 votes after narrowly winning the Republican caucus. His father-in-law's newspaper, the *Republican Transcript*, naturally opposed his candidacy.

July: On July 5, a week before the Republican county convention, Harding announced in the *Marion Star* that he was in the race. Newspapers in Kenton, Mt. Gilead, Bellefontaine, Cardington, Mansfield, and Fostoria supported Harding. Amos Kling persuaded Grant E. L. Mouser, a Marion lawyer, to enter the contest even though Mouser had offered to support Harding before the editor's candidacy was announced.

The Republican caucus was held on July 15, and Harding won in every precinct except Mouser's but the vote was close.

Harding was friendly with his Democratic opponent, John P. Bower of Logan County, a lawyer in Rushsylvania.

November: In the election Bower took Marion County, 3,677 votes to 3,413 votes, but Harding had enough strength in the other counties to edge out a victory.

℘ℂℛ

CALVIN COOLIDGE, the 27-year-old Northampton, Massachusetts, city councilman, was also a hard-working, diligent attorney who managed to settle many cases out of court. Coolidge's business included contracts, mortgages, titles, estates, real estate, and collection work.

As a councilman, Coolidge was a junior member of the lower chamber of the city's political structure. His input was insignificant. He offered two ideas: to build an armory for the veterans of the Spanish-American War and a resolution of respect for an Irish-American Democratic councilman who had died.

On November 16 the *Daily Hampshire Gazette* announced that Coolidge had filed "his declination of the Republican nomination" for reelection.

℘ℂℛ

HERBERT HOOVER, less than 4 years out of Stanford, headed a retinue of fifty mules, twenty Chinese soldiers (to guard against bandits), and dozens of others on a mine inspection trip that carried him over the Great Wall of China and into Inner Mongolia. Before heading to China, Hoover married Lou Henry.

Herbert and Lou married in Monterey, California, on February 10 and immediately began their honeymoon by taking a slow boat to China via Honolulu and Yokohama. Herbert and Lou were both 24 years old when they married. Lou was 4 months older; she was born in Waterloo, Iowa, on March 29, 1874.

Lou's father, Charles D. Henry, was a banker in Monterey. He had served in the Union army. Her mother was Florence Weed Henry. The Henry family came from Connecticut and had migrated to Whittier, California, in 1884 when it was feared that Florence had tuberculosis. Lou's family settled in Monterey in 1890.

℘ℂℛ

FRANKLIN D. ROOSEVELT, 17, was a student at Groton in Massachusetts. He was interested in Annapolis, but his father, James, was more interested in his becoming a lawyer.

HARRY S TRUMAN, 15, was a high school student in Missouri.

ᔆᘉᘓᔆ

DWIGHT D. EISENHOWER, 9, lived in Abilene, Kansas.
September 15: Another brother, Milton, was born.

1900
William McKinley

President McKinley won reelection with ease, increasing his 1896 margin over William Jennings Bryan. Fighting faded in the Philippines, where McKinley turned against the idea of sanctioning Philippine independence because it might encourage the insurrectionists. More important was the Boxer Rebellion and combat in Peking that challenged Secretary of State John Hay's Open Door policy. The war in China took up much of McKinley's campaign time as an American Army of 2,500 joined four other nations in marching on Peking to end the threat against the foreign legations in the city.

February 5: Great Britain, preoccupied with the Boer War, signed a treaty granting the United States a free hand for sole ownership of a canal in Central America.

March: Secretary of State John Hay announced on March 5 that Germany, Great Britain, Italy, Japan, and Russia had agreed to an Open Door policy in China.

The United States went back on the gold standard when McKinley signed the Currency Act on March 14.

April: The assumption was that the November election would be a McKinley–Bryan rerun, but Admiral George Dewey then told the New York press that he would like to be president. People were mostly amused by his remarks, and McKinley believed Dewey's only political strength came during the early days of his return home from the Philippines.

May: In China, the Boxers, a secret society opposed to any kind of foreign influence, began a campaign of terror against any Chinese suspected of being Christian. The attacks then spread to foreigners.

June: Congress established the territory of Hawaii on June 14, and McKinley appointed Sanford B. Dole as the first territorial governor of Hawaii.

The Republican National Convention was held in Exposition Hall, Philadelphia, June 19 to June 21. On June 21, McKinley, now 57, was unanimously renominated.

The contest for a new running mate for McKinley was spirited. With Garrett Hobart's death the previous November, many lined up seeking the job. McKinley preferred Secretary of War Elihu Root, but Root was unwilling to leave the War Department to become vice president. There were arguments put forth favoring Cornelius N. Bliss, Seth Low, Andrew D. White, and William B. Allison. McKinley's secret favorite was Allison. Soon, Theodore Roosevelt's name was put forward. Both McKinley and Mark Hanna disliked this choice, but Roosevelt carried the day and was nominated.

Meanwhile, in China, foreign diplomats and some 3,000 Christians barricaded themselves in buildings in Beijing in order to escape Boxer attacks.

July: The Democrats met in Convention Hall, Kansas City, July 4 to 6 and nominated William Jennings Bryan and Adlai E. Stevenson on a unanimous first ballot.

August: Bryan said on August 8 that, if elected, he would call a special session of Congress to grant Philippine independence. In this speech in Indianapolis, Bryan said that American corporations were prepared to despoil the Philippines.

A force of 19,000 American, British, French, Japanese, and Russian soldiers crushed the Boxers in Beijing on August 14, rescuing foreign legations and Chinese Christians who had been barricaded in the city for nearly 2 months.

September–November: McKinley's acceptance letter, dated September 8, served as the Republican platform and included an attack on the trusts. McKinley also rejected the idea of Philippine independence.

Hanna and Roosevelt made most of the Republican speeches. The vice presidential nominee was especially strong in denouncing trusts, and he traveled to the Midwest, the West, and New York.

On November 6, McKinley polled 7,218,491 votes to Bryan's 6,356,734 votes. The electoral margin was 292 to 155 for McKinley.

Former Presidents

BENJAMIN HARRISON, 67, skipped the Republican National Convention by taking a western trip in the spring through Yellowstone to the Pacific Northwest. Then from June until September, he holed up in his retreat in the Adirondacks and continued to remain aloof from the political scene.

ᔆᘉᘓᔆ

GROVER CLEVELAND refused to support William Jennings Bryan or be "dragged behind the chariot of Bryanism." Cleveland, 63, lectured at Princeton and wrote many magazine articles that appeared in the *Saturday Evening Post, Collier's*, and other periodicals.

Future Presidents

THEODORE ROOSEVELT, despite the frantic objections of Mark Hanna, became vice president. The office came with Roosevelt himself often in opposition to the idea, amid reports that President William McKinley also privately didn't want him on the ticket. Meanwhile, while still serving as governor of New York, the power plays continued between Roosevelt and U.S. Senator Thomas Platt early in the year, with the vice presidency issue a major part of the conflict between Republican factions in New York.

February: On February 1 the *New York Sun* carried a story that the Republican National Committee came to Albany to tell Roosevelt that he was wanted for the vice presidency. On the same day a Washington press report said that most Republicans in Congress felt the same way.

Henry Cabot Lodge was pressing Roosevelt for a decision on the vice presidency when the governor wrote to his friend on February 2 that, with reluctance, he did not agree with Lodge's judgment in the matter. Roosevelt said there would be nothing to do as vice president: "I am a comparatively young man yet and I like to work. I do not like to be a figurehead.... I have not sufficient means to run the social side of the Vice Presidency.... So, old man, I am going to declare decisively that I want to be governor and do not want to be Vice President."

Platt, on the other hand, saw the advantage of having Roosevelt out of New York and out of his hair. Platt asked Roosevelt on February 10 what he would do if the convention nominated him by unanimous vote. "I would not accept," Roosevelt answered.

April: Nicholas Murray Butler told Roosevelt that neither McKinley nor Hanna wanted him for vice president. The governor was also upset as Lodge went ahead with plans to nominate him for the job.

June: At the Republican National Convention in Philadelphia, June 19 to 21, Roosevelt was nominated for vice president (see **William McKinley**, page 421).

August–November: Roosevelt did much of the campaigning for the McKinley–Roosevelt ticket. The vice presidential nominee traveled to the Midwest, the West, and New York.

Roosevelt was elected vice president with McKinley's victory on November 6.

ഇറ

WILLIAM HOWARD TAFT was sent to the Philippines in an attempt to bring order out of the chaos caused by the American occupation and ensuing resistance by insurgents. To get Taft to agree to head the Philippines Commission, President McKinley said that the task would be of short duration and that a new judicial post would await Taft on his return to the United States.

January–March: In late January, Taft received a telegram from McKinley requesting a meeting. McKinley was naming a new Philippines Commission, and because Dr. Jacob Schurman was not free to return, the president needed a new commission chairman. McKinley consulted Joseph Foraker about Taft.

Taft told McKinley that he had opposed taking the Philippines, but now that the United States was there it had a sacred duty to provide good government to the people. Taft did not think the Filipinos were capable of self-government; nonetheless, he would work toward achieving self-government in the islands.

Taft asked for a week to think about the new assignment and returned to Cincinnati to talk to Nellie and his bro-

thers, Horace and Henry. Nellie was all for accepting the post. Taft decided he would go, provided that he led the commission.

Taft was formally named the president of the Philippines Commission on March 13. In that capacity, Taft had to master tariffs, public improvements, finance, and currencies.

June–December: Taft was determined to treat the Filipinos as equals and wrote on June 2, before reaching Manila, "We expect to do considerable entertaining ... especially of Filipinos, both ladies and gentlemen. [The U.S.] Army has alienated a good many [and] regard the Filipino ladies and men as 'niggers.' We propose ... to banish this idea."

Before long Taft was at war with General Arthur MacArthur. The general saw his role as one of conquering the Philippines. Taft warned Secretary of War Elihu Root on October 10 that the commissioners would resign unless cooperation with MacArthur could be achieved and gave Root a sort of either/or decision to make. Taft wrote to Root on November 14 that MacArthur "lacked any vigorous initiative ... naturally timid ...very set in his opinions."

ഇറ

WOODROW WILSON, 43, a professor at Princeton, had given close to 100 speeches around the country between 1890 and 1899. He continued to give more lectures throughout 1900.

ഇറ

WARREN G. HARDING, now an Ohio senator, increased his travel mileage, because as a newspaper publisher, he received complimentary passes from both railroad and shipping lines. Warren and Florence returned to Florida for the winter months and took up golf. In the summer the couple shipped out of Boston to Nova Scotia.

Harding moved ever upward in the world of Republican politics. During the presidential campaign, vice presidential candidate Theodore Roosevelt came to Marion for a speech. Alas, Roosevelt took no notice of Harding. For the first time there surfaced talk of putting Harding in Congress or in the governor's chair. Harding, now 35, actually took little part in McKinley's campaign aside from a few speeches.

ഇറ

CALVIN COOLIDGE was appointed the new city solicitor for Northampton, Massachusetts. Coolidge, age 28, had asked the city's aldermen for the job, and the city's councilmen promptly elected him. There was no opposition. The job paid $600 per year and provided a lift in prestige, yet left him time to expand his own law practice. His feeling was that the job of city solicitor would make him a better lawyer.

HERBERT HOOVER, 26, and his wife were caught up in war and chaos caused by the Boxer attack on Tientsin. Hoover's house was hit five times by artillery shells. Only because the Boxer force lacked a cohesive strategy was the foreign settlement, where the Hoovers lived, spared from the prospect of looting, rape, and death by gunfire.

The Russian army saved the settlement, and the Japanese army raised the siege of the city. For a few anxious moments, Hoover was armed by a group of American Marines who needed his familiarity with the locale. He acted as their scout. One American newsman and others said that Hoover showed courage during the excitement.

Before and after the Boxer Rebellion, Hoover had his own private disputes with Chinese mine officials in trying to inject new life into production at the Kaiping coal fields, 90 miles northeast of Tientsin. The mines had 9,000 employees. Hoover didn't want to waste time traveling as a mine scout; he wanted to concentrate on obtaining financing to increase production at Kaiping. In this effort the frustrations were endless.

In New York two reporters interviewed him on the Boxer aftermath, and the young engineer made his first political thoughts public. Hoover said that the United States needed to pursue a more aggressive policy to protect American interests in north China and that China faced the prospect of further revolution and chaos.

∞∞

FRANKLIN D. ROOSEVELT was 18 when his father died of heart disease on December 7 at the age of 72. Franklin and his half-brother Rosey were at the bedside in the family apartment in the Renaissance Hotel in New York City. Franklin's mother, Sara, 46, now concentrated all of her affection on her only child.

Roosevelt entered Harvard for the fall term with history and political science as a major, English literature and composition as a minor. Roosevelt roomed with Lathrop Brown at Westmorely Court, number 27, on Mt. Auburn Street in Cambridge. Roosevelt went out for football as an end. He was soon cut from the squad but went to New Haven on November 24 to attend the Yale game.

At Harvard the faculty included George Santayana, William James, George Palmer, George Baker, and George Kittridge. Roosevelt's teachers included Hiram Bingham Jr. and Frederick Jackson Turner.

∞∞

HARRY S TRUMAN, 16, attended the Democratic National Convention in Kansas City with his father, who had a box seat as the guest of William T. Kemper, an insurance man. Harry sat in the balcony. There were 17,000 in the hall. Truman always considered William Jennings Bryan a hero.

∞∞

DWIGHT D. EISENHOWER, 10, worked at a creamery in Abilene, Kansas, hauling ice and shoveling coal. He wanted to be a railroad engineer.

1901
William McKinley

The president made a triumphant swing though the South, Southwest, and Pacific Coast in his fifth year in the White House, and the press was impressed with his popularity. This led to talk of a third term. But all of this changed dramatically when an assassin shot down McKinley late in the summer.

January–March: Cuba and the Philippines occupied much of Congress and McKinley's time early in the year. The Spooner bill, which would authorize the president to govern the Philippines, had been introduced in January 1900 but was not brought to a vote all year.

McKinley gave Congress the Taft Commission report on the Philippines on January 25. Amendments were added to the Spooner bill on February 8 based on the commission's report, and 4 days later McKinley said that once the Spooner measure was passed be would make Taft the governor general of the islands. McKinley's adept handling of the measure brought about passage of the Spooner amendments, and he signed the measure at the end of February.

The Platt Amendment, introduced on January 11, dealt with the question of whether Cuba would recognize American rights of intervention in order to preserve Cuban independence. In addition, the amendment would not permit a Cuban treaty with any outside power. Senators Orville H. Platt and John C. Spooner worked out the agreement with Secretary of War Elihu Root and presented it to McKinley on February 8. He responded, "That is exactly what I want." The treaty made five points: (1) Cuba could make a treaty with a foreign power, (2) Cuba could not assume more debt than it could pay, (3) the United States had the right of intervention, (4) acts by military governor General Leonard Wood's government were to be approved, and (5) the United States wanted a naval base.

The Senate favored the measures of the Platt Amendment on February 27 by a vote of 43 to 20. The House did likewise on March 1, by a vote of 161 to 137, and the president signed it. The Cubans disliked the Platt Amendment.

Chief Justice Melville Fuller swore in McKinley for a second term on March 4. In his second inaugural address, McKinley rejoiced in the new prosperity of the United States. He also recommended reciprocity with other nations, as a policy that would eventually reduce the protectionism that McKinley had supported for years. And he suggested that the Philippines move toward self-government. McKinley said the "purpose" of his policy for the Philippines was "self-government as fast as they are ready for it."

American forces captured Philippine insurrection leader Emilio Aguinaldo on March 23.

April–August: The capture of Aguinaldo nearly ended the insurrection. On April 19, Aguinaldo took an oath of allegiance to the United States and urged his fellow rebels to do the same. However, pockets of rebels remained to fight on against the Americans.

McKinley's western trip began on April 29 and took 6 weeks. The touring party of forty-three people included cabinet members and the press. Along the way, McKinley often spoke about reciprocity and reducing the protective tariff in order to open foreign markets. The president was warmly received in the South, and there were large crowds in Los Angeles. The press was impressed with the president's obvious popularity.

On reaching San Francisco, an infected finger almost killed Ida and caused cancellation of plans to see the Northwest. At one point, Ida became unconscious and death appeared imminent. But she slowly recovered in a house in San Francisco. It was later determined that Ida had suffered a blood infection that led to acute endocarditis, an inflammation of the lining of the heart.

On May 27, the Supreme Court resolved the question of whether or not the Constitution had jurisdiction over Puerto Rico and the Philippines. In what was called the Insular Cases, the Court ruled that the two places were under U.S. protection even though the people were not U.S. citizens. In essence, the Court ruled that Puerto Rico and the Philippines were colonies of the United States.

The president left for Canton, Ohio, on July 5 for a 3-month stay, his longest rest in his own home during his presidency. In August, McKinley prepared his speech to be given in Buffalo, New York, at the upcoming Pan-American Exposition in September.

September: McKinley left Canton for Buffalo on September 4. The plan was for him to stay at the home of John L. Milburn, president of the exposition, at his Delaware Avenue home.

McKinley delivered his speech before 50,000 people at the Pan-Exposition on September 5. He then visited the exposition exhibits and marveled like a child at new gadgets.

McKinley visited the Temple of Music on Friday, September 6. For this visit the president had three secret service agents and four special guards and soldiers. The plan called for a long receiving line. At 4:07 P.M. in the receiving line, Leon Czolgosz, a 28-year-old anarchist, fired two shots into McKinley from close quarters with a .32-calibre revolver. Czolgosz fired through a bandage, wrapping his right hand, which hid the revolver. The first bullet bounced off a button on the president's coat; the other entered the stomach and was never located.

McKinley was taken to the emergency hospital at the exposition, still conscious but in shock. A Buffalo surgeon, Dr. Matthew D. Mann, decided to operate immediately but could not find the bullet. McKinley was then taken to an upstairs bedroom at the Milburn home.

George Cortelyou, McKinley's private secretary, issued a statement that the president was resting comfortably. Cortelyou also notified Vice President Theodore Roosevelt, who was on an island in Lake Champlain in Vermont.

A medical statement on Tuesday, September 10, said that McKinley was improving and recovery was expected. Optimism spread; and even the major surgeon in the case, Dr.

Charles McBurney of New York City, went sightseeing at Niagara Falls while Ida was taken for rides.

By September 12 gangrene had set in, and McKinley collapsed the next day. The vice president and cabinet were now warned that McKinley was dying. McKinley recovered enough the next day to tell the doctors, "It is useless, gentlemen.... I think we ought to have prayer." Ida was led in and held his hand. In a feeble voice he said, "Goodbye—goodbye, all.... It is God's way." Then he whispered, "Nearer, my God to Thee."

McKinley died at approximately 2 A.M. on September 14. The national grief for McKinley continued through a state funeral in Washington, a formal service in Canton, Ohio, and burial there on September 19.

(Czolgosz was diagnosed as schizophrenic. The Czolgosz trial was held on September 23. He was found guilty and was electrocuted on October 29 at Auburn Prison outside Syracuse, New York.)

ℰℭ

THEODORE ROOSEVELT became president at 42 with the death of President McKinley, thus climaxing an amazingly rapid political rise that embellished his legend and was unprecedented in American presidential history. Roosevelt brought to the presidency an exciting personality, an innovative, feisty leadership style, talent as an author and a scientist, and an enthusiasm not seen before at the top level of American leadership.

January–February: Roosevelt began the year as the governor of New York and as vice president–elect. To prepare himself to be vice president, Roosevelt studied the *Congressional Record* to see how to oversee Senate debate. On January 7 he went to Colorado to hunt cougars and returned to Sagamore Hill on February 23.

March–August: Roosevelt was sworn in as vice president on March 4.

As vice president, Roosevelt presided over Senate proceedings for a total of 4 days. From inauguration until McKinley's assassination, he had little to do, a condition he had dreaded when nominated. He spent his 6 months as vice president often playing with his children at Sagamore Hill.

September: On September 6, Roosevelt was attending a luncheon of the Vermont Fish and Game League on Isle La Motte, Lake Champlain. Roosevelt, chatting on the lawn, was motioned by the host, former governor Nelson W. Fisk, to come inside the Fisk home for a telephone call. When he got off the phone, Roosevelt had Senator Redfield Proctor tell the crowd outside that McKinley had been shot. Then Roosevelt left for Buffalo.

With McKinley improving on September 10, Roosevelt was advised to leave Buffalo. He left his itinerary with his host, Ansley Wilcox. Roosevelt went to the Adirondacks, where Edith and the children were in a mountain cabin at Camp Tahawus on the slopes of Mt. Marcy, the highest point in New York.

Roosevelt received a message from Elihu Root on September 13 that McKinley's condition had worsened: "The President appears to be dying and members of the cabinet in Buffalo think you should lose no time in coming."

In coming down off Mt. Marcy, Roosevelt took a wild ride in a buckboard for 50 miles to a special train awaiting him at North Creek. He reached the station at dawn on September 14 and learned from William Loeb Jr. of the White House staff that McKinley had died.

Roosevelt arrived in Buffalo at 1:30 P.M. and at 3:32 P.M. was sworn in by U.S. District Court Judge John R. Hazel. At 42, Roosevelt was the youngest man to hold the office of president of the United States.

Roosevelt said he would "continue absolutely unbroken the policy of President McKinley." Senator Nathan B. Scott, a West Virginia Republican, told the *New York Tribune* on September 22, "That simple declaration immediately restored confidence in the business world."

Roosevelt's first day in the White House was September 20. He met with McKinley's cabinet and asked them to stay. All said they would.

October: Roosevelt announced that the Executive Mansion would henceforth be called the White House.

December 3: In his first message to Congress, Roosevelt discussed the growing problem of trusts. He called for federal supervision of interstate trusts and for the creation of a new cabinet position of secretary of commerce. Roosevelt also said that the 8-hour workday was a must and that women and children in the workplace needed extra protection.

Former Presidents

BENJAMIN HARRISON, retired in Indianapolis, wrote to Supreme Court Justice John Marshall Harlan on February 8 that the "grip" that had been in Washington, D.C., was now in Indiana "and has been knocking at my door a little."

In March, Harrison had a severe cold that turned to pneumonia. When he didn't improve, telegrams of inquiry came to the house. On March 9, Harrison had a chill and a fever of 102 degrees. Two days later, his condition was worse and attending doctors gave up hope.

Mrs. Harrison watched him over the next couple of days. She took him in her arms, and he died quietly on March 13 at 4:45 P.M. at the age of 67.

Harrison's body was placed in the Indiana State House on March 16, and there was a demonstration by Indiana soldiers and survivors of the Seventieth Regiment. The funeral took place on March 17 at the First Presbyterian Church, and President McKinley attended. Harrison was buried at Crown Hill Cemetery in Indianapolis.

80C8

GROVER CLEVELAND, 64 in March, was elected a trustee of Princeton University on October 15. He never missed a meeting, was interested in detail, often spoke, and was known to rebuke idlers on the board for failing to show up for meetings. Cleveland also began to receive invitations to speak at sites across the country: at the Carnegie Institute in Pittsburgh, at the inauguration of President John Finley of City College of New York, and at Old Home Week in Norwich, Connecticut.

Future Presidents

WILLIAM HOWARD TAFT took over as governor-general in Manila on July 4 amid talk back home that he would make a good president some time in the future. But health problems later in the year would return Taft to the United States to recover.

Taft's appointment as governor-general became official on July 4. His days as the president of the Philippines Commission had endeared him to many of the Filipino people. When Taft took over in Manila, he received a cable from President McKinley with, "my full confidence and best wishes."

Taft, 44, became sick on October 2, the day after his wife left for a tour of China. Taft was in bed for 8 days, then had severe intestinal pains. On October 25 he wired his wife at the Hotel Astor in Shanghai: "Come dear am sick." The next day he told her not to come. That same day, he had a fistula operation.

The rectal abscess broke on October 27, and Taft was taken on a stretcher to the hospital, where surgeons found the abscess in the perineum. The doctors worried about gangrene, and an incision was made. His condition was grave, but he slowly returned to health. On recovery he was told to do no work for a month. A second operation was performed on Thanksgiving Day, and Taft made plans to recuperate in the United States. The family departed the Philippines on December 24.

80C8

WOODROW WILSON, 44, was a well-known and popular professor at Princeton.

In this year, he wrote *History of the American People* with the first sections serialized in *Harper's Magazine*. He had written his new book in some haste, and some errors in facts and dates resulted. Wilson replied to critics: "I am not an historian: I am only a writer of history."

Joseph Wilson's poor health caused him to move from Wilmington, North Carolina, to Princeton in the spring. This caused Wilson to reserve his evenings for his father rather than for his family.

80C8

WARREN G. HARDING rapidly became one of the most popular men in the state legislature. According to one newsman, he was a congenial good mixer, remembered names, and was a good poker player and drinker.

No state senator had been reelected in Harding's district in 57 years, owing to the policy of rotating senators to give different counties periodic representation within the senatorial district. It was Logan County's turn to name a man, but Harding begged to be reelected, saying he was still learning "the ropes." He was returned to Columbus by 3,563 votes, double his margin in 1899.

Harding, now 36, was appointed to committees on finance, ditches and drains, medical schools and universities, elections, and public printing. Of the hundreds of bills passed, Harding had introduced fifteen, most of them vanity measures for folks back home. One protected publishers from libel.

CALVIN COOLIDGE, 29 in July, won reelection as city solicitor of Northampton, Massachusetts, despite a spirited contest mounted by two Democrats.

HERBERT HOOVER, 27, spent most of the year trying to unsnarl management and control confusion at the Kaiping coal mines in China in the wake of the Boxer Rebellion. The Russian army occupied most of the property, and soldiers from Japan, Germany, and France controlled the rest. By the end of the year, Hoover was back in London where he had been made a partner in the growing Berwick, Moreing Company. At 27, he was the youngest partner.

Berwick, Moreing had offices in London, Johannesburg, Tientsin, Kalgoorlie, Auckland, and Tarkwan on the Gold Coast. It also had interests in Nevada, Canada, the Transvaal, Cornwall, and Egypt.

On leaving China, his annual salary had reached $33,000, and he wrote to his brother Theodore that he was now worth about $250,000.

Misunderstandings were frequent as Chinese officials sought to regain a hold on the Kaiping mines while accepting a transfusion of European money. Sometimes Chinese officials were suspicious of Hoover's dealings.

By September, Hoover sailed for San Francisco. He later told the *San Francisco Chronicle* that he was reputed to be the highest salaried man of his years in the world. He bought property in Monterey, California. At the end of the year, he returned to Australia.

FRANKLIN D. ROOSEVELT, 19, suddenly became a bigger man on the campus at Harvard after the McKinley assassination and Theodore Roosevelt became president.

When Theodore Roosevelt visited Harvard in April, Franklin called on him at Professor A. Lawrence Lowell's home. The interview that followed led to a scoop for the *Crimson*, the campus newspaper. Now Franklin became one of five *Crimson* editors.

While at Harvard, Roosevelt led a lively social life, with dinners and dances in Boston and New York. He tried out for the Harvard crew, and as happened in football, he failed.

In July, Franklin sailed for Europe with his mother, a cousin, a nephew, and Theodore's sister Corinne. Their itinerary included Norway, Germany, Switzerland, Italy and France.

HARRY S TRUMAN, 17, graduated from Independence (Missouri) High School on May 30 and soon took his first trips away from home, first to southern Illinois and later to Texas. Truman was not a standout student, his teacher Tillie Brown said, but he was hardworking.

Truman's train ride to Murphysboro, Illinois, near Carbondale and the Mississippi River, was to visit his favorite aunt, Ada. Returning home he visited cousins in St. Louis.

In September, Truman was off to Texas with his cousin Ralph, a Spanish-American War veteran. Truman was in Lone Oak, Texas, east of Dallas, when he heard of the McKinley assassination. Truman stopped in Wilmer, Texas, before returning to Kansas City to enroll in Spaulding Commercial College, which would soon prove too expensive.

DWIGHT EISENHOWER, 11, lived in Abilene, Kansas.

1902
Theodore Roosevelt

President Roosevelt settled a coal strike and launched antitrust actions that upset J. P. Morgan. Roosevelt also had a close call in a serious traffic accident in Massachusetts.

January: The Walker Commission recommended that a canal be built across the Isthmus of Panama.

March: Attorney General Philander Knox, under orders from Roosevelt, filed an antitrust suit against J. P. Morgan's Northern Securities firm on March 10. Morgan was upset that Roosevelt ordered Knox to file the lawsuit.

May: An anthracite coal strike hit Pennsylvania on May 12. Henry Cabot Lodge warned Roosevelt that if coal supplies were short when winter approached, Republicans would be hurt in the November elections. Several railroad presidents, who also happened to own several of the Pennsylvania mines where workers were striking, advised Roosevelt against taking any immediate action.

On May 20, Cuba officially became a republic when Tomas Estrada Palma became Cuba's first president.

August–September: In mid-August, Roosevelt began a tour of New England states, where his speeches focused on the dangers and evils of trusts. While visiting Pittsfield, Massachusetts, on September 3, his carriage was hit by a streetcar. All of the passengers were thrown from the open carriage. Roosevelt suffered minor injuries, but a secret service agent was crushed under the car and died.

October: When the price of coal doubled, Roosevelt decided he must act because the public expected action. The president invited the railroad presidents and miners to Washington on October 3. They met in Roosevelt's temporary residence, Jackson Place, because the White House was being renovated. First, Roosevelt said he had no right or duty to intervene. But "urgency" and "catastrophe impending" meant that he needed to apply his influence to end the strike. He asked for the immediate resumption of mining to "meet the crying needs of the people."

The president of the United Mine Workers (UMW), John Mitchell, suggested that Roosevelt name a tribunal to determine the issues. Mitchell said that if the mine operators accepted a tribunal's findings, so would the miners. But the mine operators asked the president to dissolve the UMW as a "trust" and use troops against "anarchistic conditions." Roosevelt was impressed with Mitchell and angry with the mine operators. Unlike Grover Cleveland in the 1894 Pullman strike, Roosevelt regarded the two sides as equals.

Roosevelt decided to form an investigative commission, which included Cleveland, Judge William R. Day, and others from business and labor. If such negotiations failed, then Roosevelt planned to have retired General John M. Schofield head a U.S. army contingent that would open the mines. Roosevelt informed Knox and Root of his plans and realized that he was setting a precedent.

Roosevelt, meanwhile, approved of a plan for Root to work through J. P. Morgan to sway the operators. Root and Morgan met on a yacht on October 11 and worked out a plan that did not recognize unions but would have a commission look at the issues. The owners wanted no union men on the commission, but Roosevelt used the ruse of having an "eminent sociologist" and a Catholic clergyman on the commission. The "sociologist" was also a railroad conductor union leader. With this plan in place, the miners returned to work on October 23, but the commission reached no decision until March 1903.

The *Review of Reviews* magazine called Roosevelt's handling of the strike "the greatest event affecting the relations of capital and labor in the history of America."

December 4: Roosevelt appointed Oliver Wendell Holmes to the Supreme Court.

Former Presidents

GROVER CLEVELAND was the speaker when Woodrow Wilson was installed as president of Princeton University on October 26. Cleveland reviewed the historic obligations of the school. He said that he was against the elective system in education, saying, "We of Princeton [are] better able to determine [the] most advantageous course of instruction."

When the United Mine Workers went on strike in May, Cleveland offered President Roosevelt some ideas on how the dispute might be settled. Roosevelt then asked Cleveland to head an arbitration commission, but the retired president did not participate because the operators objected. Roosevelt apologized to Cleveland for getting him involved.

Future Presidents

WILLIAM HOWARD TAFT, the governor-general of the Philippines, completed a sea voyage around the world in 1902 primarily to talk to the Pope at the Vatican. Taft twice turned down a seat on the Supreme Court and heard that the president thought Taft would be an early favorite for the 1908 presidential nomination. By the end of the year, Taft was back in the Philippines to face serious deterioration in overall conditions on the archipelago.

January: On returning to the United States after his illness in Manila, Taft received a warm welcome at the White House. As Taft wrote his wife, Nellie, on January 30, Roosevelt "was just the same as ever … very difficult to realize that he is the President."

February: Roosevelt, Elihu Root, and Taft met with American Archbishop John Ireland at the White House to discuss the problem of buying lands owned by the Roman Catholic Church in the Philippines and the removal of Spanish friars from the land. A decision was reached to send Taft to Rome. Root emphasized that it should be a business negotiation rather than a diplomatic mission.

May–August: Taft reached Naples on May 29. He saw Cardinal Rampolla, the papal secretary of state, in Rome on June 2 and then met with Pope Leo XIII. Taft felt that $5 million would be adequate payment for the land. The Pope seemed agreeable to the American mission, but after a week Taft began to have doubts and wrote to his wife on June 12, "These Italians are such liars."

On June 21 the church answered that it agreed to the sale but not to withdrawing the friars. Root ordered Taft to stand by the proposals, then later ordered the negotiations canceled. Taft sailed from Rome in July and arrived in Philadelphia on August 22.

October–December: Roosevelt cabled Taft in Manila on October 26 that George Shiras Jr. was retiring from the Supreme Court at the end of the year and that he wanted Taft to fill the post. At the same time, Taft worried that Washington believed he was doing a poor job in Manila and therefore asked his brother Henry on October 27 to see Root and "tell him my withdrawal now [would be a] great political mistake from the Philippine standpoint." Taft sent a message to Roosevelt on October 27, in which he said that some time in the future he would take a job on the bench, but not now.

Still, Roosevelt urged Taft to accept and asked his opinion of Lloyd Bowers, a Yale classmate. Taft urged Bowers for the vacant seat.

When he returned to the Philippines, Taft found the island in terrible shape. In a speech upon his arrival, Taft recited the problems but said the good news was that an "era of prosperity" would soon dawn in the islands.

More than 100,000 died of cholera during the year. By November, Taft learned that the rice crop was poor and that water buffalo were dying of disease. Taft asked Roosevelt for $2 million in relief funds.

෩෬

WOODROW WILSON became president of Princeton University as the first public suggestions were being made that he would also make a fine president of the United States. Wilson, 45, was the first Princeton president without theological training in the 156-year history of the Presbyterian school. He was the school's thirteenth president.

The board of trustees had been upset by President Francis Patton's lack of leadership. There was a feeling that Patton had let academic standards drop and had lost faculty confidence. Finally, the trustees offered Patton a $31,500 settlement plus the promotion of his son George S. Patton to professor of philosophy. When President Patton resigned on June 1, he took over the Princeton Theological Seminary. Wilson, elected within hours after Patton's resignation, told alumni on June 14, "This [was a] thunderbolt out of a clear sky." Wil-son's election reflected greater alumni influence, in contrast with earlier control of the school by Presbyterian ministers.

When the new president placed his ambitious $12.5 million improvement program before the board of trustees, Grover Cleveland moved that the plan be approved.

Wilson was officially inaugurated as Princeton's president in October. Cleveland, J. P. Morgan, Mark Twain, Robert T. Lincoln, and William Dean Howells were among those attending. In his inaugural address, Wilson expressed more concern with teaching undergraduates than with producing graduate scholars. Wilson pushed science and wanted students to have a broad education rather than to focus on narrow specialization.

෩෬

WARREN G. HARDING, an Ohio state senator, decided to go for the governorship with the blessing of retiring Governor Nash. During the year, Harding also made time for more trips, one to New England and another to Norfolk, Virginia.

The Marion, Ohio newspaper publisher now was a force in Ohio politics, consulting with Mark Hanna and putting Joseph Foraker's name in nomination for reelection to the U.S. Senate in a speech that was widely praised. Hanna and Foraker, long-time enemies, agreed to step aside if Harding made a bid for governor in 1903. But during the summer Myron Herrick, a Cleveland banker, announced his own plans to run. A Republican convention in Marion near the end of the year endorsed Harding, 37, for governor, as did Nash at a banquet in Columbus in December.

෩෬

CALVIN COOLIDGE, 30, lost his bid for a third term as city solicitor of Northampton, Massachusetts, when Theobald M. Connor defeated him in January. Coolidge then returned to his law practice full time.

෩෬

HERBERT HOOVER, 28, in the last days of December, struggled with the trauma of a massive embezzlement scandal caused by one of Berwick, Moreing's four partners. The financial disaster followed a long year on the road for Hoover, now considered a world-class mine "surgeon."

In January he was back in western Australia for more dusty field trips to mines in the Outback that Berwick, Moreing was managing. Herbert and his wife, Lou, traveled 3,500 miles in horse-drawn buggies or by camel.

After returning to London, Hoover was off to Colorado and British Columbia to inspect more mines. He covered 16,000 miles in 6 weeks. Berwick, Moreing now managed a dozen mines, and Hoover was often in a position to hire Stanford graduates or other American engineers.

෩෬

FRANKLIN D. ROOSEVELT, the 20-year-old Harvard junior, had tea at the White House with Alice Roosevelt. His cousin Eleanor was staying with Alice at the time. While in Washington for Christmas, Roosevelt stayed with his cousin Corinne, the president's sister. When Franklin accidentally saw Eleanor on a train in New York City going home to Tivoli, he took her off to meet his mother.

Sara took a place on Commonwealth Boulevard in Boston to be closer to her son, then gave lavish parties for Boston's elite. She always involved Franklin in these, but signs of her control over him put off many young ladies who viewed Roosevelt as a "featherduster."

෩෬

HARRY S TRUMAN'S hopes for a college education evaporated when his father, 51 and hoping to get rich quick, took a major financial loss by speculating in commodity futures. Instead he lost $40,000 in cash, stock, and land. As a result the family had to move from their Waldo Avenue house to North Liberty Street in Kansas City, taking a loss on the sale.

Harry, 18, after learning some bookkeeping, Pitman shorthand, and typing at Spaulding Commercial College, had to drop out as a result of his father's debacle. Harry took a job with the *Kansas City Star* as a mailroom clerk for $7 per week. Later he became timekeeper for L. J. Smith Construction, a railroad contractor, at $30 per month—working 6 days per week, 10 hours per day. There he learned to pump a handcar.

෩෬

DWIGHT D. EISENHOWER, 12, attended the Garfield school in the fall. The school was north of the Union Pacific tracks in Abilene, Kansas.

1903
Theodore Roosevelt

President Roosevelt rapidly became seen as a strong and dynamic leader. Washington had seen nothing like Roosevelt's bold presidential decisions since Andrew Jackson. In large part, this reputation came about as a result of Roosevelt's actions regarding Panama.

January–March: Secretary of State John Hay issued an ultimatum to Colombia on January 21 to negotiate a canal deal or the United States would turn to Nicaragua. The next day Colombia approved the Hay–Herran Treaty, pending the approval of its congress. The pact set forth that the French canal company would be sold to the United States without compensation to Colombia, but that Colombia would receive $10 million in gold plus an annual payment of $250,000 for the use of the land.

On February 14, the Department of Commerce and Labor was created. Two days later, George Bruce Cortelyou of New York was appointed the first secretary.

The U.S. Senate approved the Hay–Herran Treaty on March 17 by a vote of 73 to 5. A week later, Roosevelt sent the Isthmian Canal Commission to Panama to inspect the earlier French work done there.

June–August: President Maroquin of Colombia informed his congress in Bogotá of the Hay–Herran Treaty without making a recommendation. Colombia's senate began debating the treaty in June, and the debate lasted for 2 months. The Colombian senate then voted down the treaty on August 12 by a vote of 24 to 0.

On August 16, Hay told Roosevelt that it might be best to go back to the Nicaraguan plan, or "the far more difficult … scheme …" of building the canal without Bogotá's approval. Hay and Roosevelt discussed the matter further at Oyster Bay on August 28, and the *New York Herald* reported that their plan was to exert U.S. rights under the treaty of 1846 with New Grenada (now Colombia).

September–December: The United States was aware that chances were good for a revolt in Panama. William N. Cromwell, lawyer for the French effort, planted a story in the *New York World* that said Panama was ready to secede and do business unilaterally with the United States. Panama at the time was part of Colombia.

In September Phillipe Bunau-Varilla and Panamanian rebels planned an attack but decided to first talk to Roosevelt personally. The meeting took place in the White House on October 10. The president asked Bunau-Varilla what he thought was going to happen. Bunau-Varilla answered, "Revolution." Roosevelt privately wrote to editor Albert Shaw the same day, saying

John Hay, appointed secretary of state by William McKinley, was instrumental in political preparations for the building of the Panama Canal. (Library of Congress)

that the United States could not play any role in a secession but would "be delighted" if Panama were independent.

On October 15, U.S. naval forces were directed to move toward Acapulco in the Pacific and toward the Caribbean in the Atlantic. The next day, Roosevelt, now 45, met with two army officers who had been on an intelligence survey in Colombia and Panama, who said that a revolt was probable. The naval units were told to prevent any landing of any armed force in Panama.

The Panama revolt occurred on November 3 to 4. Roosevelt sent the U.S. cruiser *Nashville* to the Panama coast, effectively to keep Colombian forces from bombarding the city. More U.S. ships arrived at the scene, and the United States quickly recognized the rebels on November 6. Hay issued a statement that free transit over the isthmus was assured and that the United States would try to bring permanent peace to the Panamanians. On November 13, Roosevelt accepted Bunau-Varilla as minister plenipotentiary of Panama. European countries, Peru, and Costa Rica followed suit and recognized Panama.

The United States then rewrote the Hay–Herran Treaty, making a perpetual grant of a canal zone 10 miles wide. Other provisions put Panama at a disadvantage. The United States proposed a guarantee of Panama independence but not sovereignty over the canal. French interests wrote the $10 million back into the treaty and added language limiting Panamanian sovereignty. Bunau-Varilla signed the treaty on November 18 before the Panamanian delegation had even arrived in Washington. He told delegates that he had signed, and he declared that the "Republic of Panama is henceforth under the protection of the United States." The new Panamanian government agreed to this on December 2.

The American people wanted a canal, but Roosevelt's diplomacy caused the *New York Evening Post* to say: "This mad plunge of ours is simply and solely a vulgar and mercenary venture, without a rag to cover its sordidness and shame."

Roosevelt told Congress on December 7 that Colombia had forced his hand.

Former Presidents

Grover Cleveland held the belief that there was a chance he might be pressured into being the Democratic nominee in

1904 for a fourth run at the White House. On February 6 he wrote to Joseph Garretson, editor of the *Cincinnati Times-Star*, that he did not see enough support to make him run again. On November 25, Cleveland, 66, wrote to Dr. St. Clair McKelway of the *Brooklyn Eagle* that he would not be a candidate for president. "My determination not to [become a candidate] is unalterable and conclusive," the retired President wrote.

Future Presidents

WILLIAM HOWARD TAFT, the governor-general of the Philippines, was the indispensable man. First, Roosevelt told Taft that he was going to the Supreme Court. Later Roosevelt switched and told Taft he would become secretary of war, replacing Elihu Root. Meanwhile, in Manila the Filipino people, alarmed by these possibilities seemed now to appreciate Taft's administration and wanted him to remain. However, an attack of amoebic dysentery did much to persuade Taft that perhaps he had had enough of the tropics.

It was Taft's ambitious wife—as well as his mother, aunt, and brother Henry—who visualized bigger things in Taft's future than the seat he long coveted on the top bench. They all envisioned the cabinet post as putting him on track to the White House. The court, they argued, was a dead end.

January–February: On January 6, Roosevelt wrote to Taft, "I am awfully sorry, old man … I find that I shall have to bring you home and put you on the Supreme Court." It was the president's plan to put General Wright in charge of Philippine administration, but Roosevelt told Taft he could remain in Manila until August.

Taft replied on January 8: "Recognize soldier's duty to obey orders." He added that he hated to "leave work of intense interest half done. No man is indispensable, my death would little interfere with progress." He said the Filipinos would not understand the change.

Most of Taft's family was against a Supreme Court appointment. Only Will's brother Charles favored his taking the Court post. The others saw larger things in Taft's future. Brother Henry wrote to Taft on January 10 that he wouldn't want Taft to suffer a political disappointment. "without belittling … your ability to be a great judge, I really think you have the capacity to be a greater politician (or statesman, if you please)."

The Supreme Court post never came about, as Roosevelt appointed William Rufus Day to the Court on February 23.

September–December: Roosevelt ordered Taft to Washington to become secretary of war when it became clear that Elihu Root would be leaving the post. Taft liked his work in Manila and wrote to H. C. Hollister on September 21, "It seems strange that with an effort to keep out of politics and with my real dislike for it, I should thus be pitched into the middle of it." The president pointed out that as war secretary, Taft would be the overall administrator of Philippine affairs. Roosevelt told him to keep the news to himself, because the appointment would not become official until the new year.

෴

WOODROW WILSON, the president of Princeton University, while seeking educational changes at the school, lectured off campus to raise funds, or to pound home his ideals for the new Princeton: order, wholeness, coherence, direction, authority. Warned that he was working too hard, Wilson made his third trip to Europe during the summer, this time taking Ellen along. They visited France and Italy. Wilson's father Joseph, 80, died on January 21 in his son's home at Princeton.

Wilson, 47 in December, made a fundraising plea to his classmate Cyrus McCormick and also outlined his needs to Andrew Carnegie, attempting to use their mutual Scottish heritage as a lever. When instead Carnegie gave the school a lake, Wilson grumbled, "We needed bread and you gave us cake."

A tougher academic policy came in with a new academic dean, Henry B. Fine. Fine expelled seventy-five students in strictly enforcing established rules of scholarship. He reorganized the faculty into eleven departments, with each department chairman reporting annually to Wilson.

෴

WARREN G. HARDING, an Ohio state senator, announced in January his candidacy for governor. Harding made gubernatorial hopes known in the columns of the *Marion Star*. But by November the 38-year-old publisher was willing to accept that which kingmaker Mark Hanna approved—the lieutenant governor's position.

The *Columbus Dispatch* backed Myron Herrick for governor and on April 23 backed Harding for lieutenant governor. The *Ohio State Journal*, owned by Robert E. Wolfe, a power broker, floated a slogan: "Herrick, Harding and Harmony."

In June, Ohio Republicans met in Columbus. The 900 delegates in the Columbus Auditorium nominated Herrick by acclamation, but his speech was not rousing. Harding was nominated for lieutenant governor.

In November, Herrick and Harding were elected by the largest plurality ever in a race in Ohio. Exhausted from campaigning, Harding went to Battle Creek, Michigan, on November 19, taking along his mother who suffered from paralysis problems. Harding returned to Marion, Ohio, in a week and never again went to Battle Creek.

෴

CALVIN COOLIDGE in the spring was appointed clerk of the courts for Hampshire County in Northampton, Massachusetts. The office paid $2,300 per year and was open because the prior occupant, William H. Clapp, had died. Coolidge's law practice was a continued success; he wrote to his father about winning eleven cases before various courts.

The bachelor was 31 years old when, under strange circumstances, he first met Grace Goodhue, a vivacious type and good counterbalance to Calvin's dour nature. One day Grace was watering plants, looked up, and saw Coolidge at the window next door shaving, wearing underwear and a hat. She broke out laughing and then was embarrassed. He heard her laughter. He later explained that he had a lock of hair that didn't stay in place so he used the hat.

Grace was a lip-reading instructor at the Clarke Institute for the Deaf. She lived in Baker Hall, a residence for the Clarke staff on Round Hill, which was just below Rob Weir's house where Calvin rented. Weir introduced them and soon they were dating. They appeared to be opposites: he was straight, thin, and silent; she sailed, skated, sang, danced, acted in plays, played cards, and could be humorous.

Grace was the only child of a Burlington, Vermont, mechanical engineer, and a Democrat. She graduated from the University of Vermont in 1902 and came to Northampton to study in preparation for teaching at the Clarke Institute.

෨◌ඎ

HERBERT HOOVER, 29, faced bankruptcy in the wake of embezzlement. The loss to Berwick, Moreing and affiliates originally was estimated at approximately $700,000. In addition, two lawsuits threatened to strip Hoover of all his money, and return him to the struggling $2-a-day world he had known in the High Sierra 8 years earlier.

But he rebounded, became a 33-percent shareholder in Berwick, Moreing, and returned to West Australia for a third time. This time he also inspected a mine in Victoria near Melbourne, took a side trip to a New Zealand property, and returned to the United States with his son Herbert Jr., born on August 4 in London.

(A. Stanley Rowe, the Berwick, Moreing embezzler, was located in Toronto and later received a 10-year sentence.)

෨◌ඎ

FRANKLIN D. ROOSEVELT, 21, proposed to Eleanor Roosevelt in November, greatly upsetting his mother. His mother, Sara, stalled for time by planning a trip to Europe that would separate the romantic cousins. Eleanor confessed later to Franklin about the difficult experience of having an intimate talk on December 1 with Sara, which Sara described as a "long talk with the dear child."

Roosevelt had proposed at Groton when Eleanor was visiting the preparatory school. Then he broke the news to his mother at the Delano home, Fairhaven. Franklin later wrote to his mother from Harvard, "I know what pain I must have caused you.… I am the happiest man just now in the world," but added that the great love between himself and his mother would never change.

That summer Franklin went to Europe again to get some time away from his mother. He traveled with a Harvard classmate, Charles B. Bradley. They toured France, Switzerland, and England, often with wealthy Americans or Englishmen.

On his return from Europe in August, Franklin invited Eleanor to Campobello. Later he invited her to the Harvard–Yale football game in Cambridge and showed her his room. A maid or other chaperone always accompanied Eleanor.

On December 18, Roosevelt was elected chairman of the 1904 class committee. He received 168 of 253 votes.

෨◌ඎ

HARRY S TRUMAN, now 19, landed a job in Kansas City as a bank clerk, usually working in the vault below street level. His pay was $20 per month, later raised to $40. Truman spent Saturday afternoons as an usher at the Orpheum Theater, where he saw the Cohans and Sarah Bernhardt.

෨◌ඎ

DWIGHT D. EISENHOWER, 13, lived in Abilene, Kansas. Eisenhower attended the Garfield school where "tradition" called for the boys from the south side of the railroad tracks to fight boys from the north side. Dwight's brother Edgar had fought in 1902, and now it was Dwight's turn. His lengthy battle with Wes Merrifield left them both bloody. It was a draw because neither knew anything about boxing. Eisenhower, weighing about 115 pounds, could not go to school for 2 days after the fight.

1904
Theodore Roosevelt

President Roosevelt easily won a full term in the White House with his victory over Elton B. Parker, the Democratic nominee. It was the crowning achievement of his political career. This was also the year that the president developed the Roosevelt Corollary to the Monroe Doctrine, which suggested that the United States could intervene if a country threatened Latin America. Roosevelt also watched with interest the Japanese–Russian conflict in Northeast Asia. Roosevelt silently supported the Japanese.

January–February: Roosevelt's popular appeal with the public and inside the Republican Party made his nomination almost automatic. In January the White House staff started an organization to support a Roosevelt nomination.

On February 20 the United States sent a circular note to Russia and Japan. The two countries were at war, and the U.S. note asked them to respect the Open Door policy in the disputed territory of Manchuria.

The United States formally acquired the Panama Canal Zone. Construction of the canal would begin during the summer of 1905.

March 14: The Supreme Court dissolved J. P. Morgan's Northern Securities Company railroad trust under the Sherman Anti-Trust Act, upholding lower court rulings and giving Roosevelt a big victory over a giant trust.

April 30: Roosevelt was on hand to officially open the World's Fair in St. Louis, Missouri.

June: The Republican convention was held in Chicago from June 21 to 23 but lacked excitement. Roosevelt wanted to avoid tariff revision as an issue. The party choice for vice president was Charles Warren Fairbanks of Indiana, the idea being to balance the ticket. Roosevelt himself preferred Representative Robert R. Hitt of Illinois. Fairbanks was picked by a voice vote after the Illinois delegation withdrew Hitt's name.

July: The Democrats met in St. Louis from July 6 to 9 and nominated Judge Elton B. Parker, 52, of New York for president and former Senator Henry G. Davis of West Virginia for vice president. At 81, Davis was the oldest man ever nominated. Parker, born in Cortland, New York, was chief justice of the New York Appeals Court.

The tradition against campaigning upset Roosevelt. He wrote to Henry Cabot Lodge on July 14: "I wish I were where I could fight more offensively."

September: Roosevelt's official acceptance letter of the Republican nomination came on September 12. He wrote: "We base our appeal upon what we have done and are doing.... We intend to carry on in the same way that we have in the past." He justified his Panama policy, his antitrust actions, and the coal strike settlement, and he criticized the Democrats for calling for Philippine independence.

November: Roosevelt was easily elected to a full term on November 8. On election night, he walked back and forth as clerks brought in the results. "How they are voting for me!" he said. Then he later told the press, "Under no circumstances will I be a candidate for or accept another nomination."

Roosevelt polled 7,623,486 votes to Parker's 5,077,911, and he took 336 electoral votes to Parker's 140.

December: In his annual message to Congress on December 6, Roosevelt, 46, outlined his corollary to the Monroe Doctrine. The corollary, soon referred to as the Roosevelt Corollary, defended American intervention in Latin America in order to stop European aggression.

Former Presidents

GROVER CLEVELAND preferred that his old Secretary of State Richard Olney be the Democratic nominee for president. But Cleveland also had a high opinion of Elton B. Parker as a conservative Democratic and ended up supporting and speaking for Parker. There was also a fleeting interest in Cleveland becoming the candidate, but he said he would not accept the honor if offered.

Future Presidents

WILLIAM HOWARD TAFT officially became the secretary of war and was sent to Panama as a troubleshooter to get the monumental engineering project of the Panama Canal going. Roosevelt made Taft chairman of the Isthmian Canal Com-

mission, effectively putting him in charge of the entire Panama Canal Zone adventure.

January–February: Before Taft became secretary of war, Roosevelt sent him to Japan to discuss with Japan's leaders the tense situation between Russia and Japan. After Taft's visit with the emperor of Japan, he cabled Roosevelt on January 7 that war was probable between Japan and Russia but that Japan wished to remain friendly with the United States.

On February 1, Taft became secretary of war.

March–April: Taft met with the Isthmian Canal Commission on March 22. Soon after, Roosevelt announced that Taft would be in charge of the commission, placing him over the first chairman, Rear Admiral John G. Walker. Friction soon developed on the commission, in part because neither Roosevelt nor Taft had any engineering know-how.

Taft had advised against making the $4 million payment to start the canal. The others agreed with the president to make the payment, but they later supported Taft's position to delay.

July–August: Much of the talk about Taft during the summer concerned his future—whether he would become a member of the Supreme Court or be the Republican presidential nominee in 1908. Taft seemed to doubt his chances for either in letters to his wife and brothers.

September–December: Roosevelt decided in September to send Taft to Panama to squash uncertainty developing in the new country and said on October 18, "We have not the slightest intention of establishing an independent colony in the middle of the state." He said that failure of the United States to show "real sympathy" for Panama would "create distrust of the American government."

Taft arrived in the Panama Canal Zone on November 27 and saw President Dr. Manuel Amador. Taft said that American machinery was to be admitted free, that imports would go through Panama ports for duties, and that the Panamanian postal system would be used. Food and clothing would be bought from local merchants, but he warned against profiteering.

Taft talked to the chief engineer, John F. Wallace, and told Roosevelt on December 19 that the dig would mean the excavation of a mass greater than ever before made in the history of the world.

Taft was against locks for the canal and thought it should be built at sea level, but Roosevelt decided it would be cheaper and faster to build with locks.

જી જી

WOODROW WILSON, the 47-year-old president of Princeton, achieved the curriculum reform he wanted but confessed that he disliked the fundraising aspects of his job. He told trustee Alexander Van Rensselaer on January 13 that he loved the administration of Princeton, but "if only I did not have to beg for money." Board member David B. Jones soon became Wilson's financial adviser, as Wilson was not interested in money questions. Jones suggested finding ten men to give

$5,000 per year and twenty men to give $2,500 per year. Soon the pledges totaled $100,000 and the group became known as the Committee of Fifty.

ಶಿಂಖ

WARREN G. HARDING persisted in his plans to run for governor of Ohio in 1905, especially after Governor Myron Herrick's term ran afoul of angry farmers and every other special interest group. In November, Lieutenant Governor Harding promised Herrick a contest the next year. Harding's skills as an orator led to a contract during the summer to join the Chautauqua circuit that traveled to small Ohio towns. The pay was $100 per week plus expenses. Under the big tent, Harding talked about Alexander Hamilton. His one-hour talk was sandwiched between yodelers, singing quartets, and a Native American princess.

January–March: For the 1904 Ohio General Assembly meeting in Columbus on January 4, Republicans enjoyed a 7-to-1 margin in the senate and a 4-to-1 margin in the house.

Herrick and Harding were sworn in on January 11. Normally the office of lieutenant governor was a reward to one of the elderly faithful in the ranks. It was not seen as a steppingstone to the top. But Harding, being only 38, saw things differently.

Herrick's problems mounted quickly. Anger toward the new governor came from the farmers, insurance companies, schools, and religious groups, who claimed he had sold out to the liquor industry.

April: Frederick N. McMillin, president of the Dayton City Ministerial Association, wrote to Harding: "[The party] cannot afford to renominate Herrick…. I hear that you will go for the nomination…. There is no question about your election."-

June–September: Hearing about Harding's reputation as an orator, Harry P. Harrison of the Chautauqua circuit signed Harding to a contract. Harding was to talk about an early American statesman, and he selected Hamilton after reading Gertrude Atherton's *The Conqueror*, a book about Hamilton. Harding called his effort "Alexander Hamilton—Prophet of American Destiny." Harding would say Caesar, Napoleon, and Hamilton built the three great republics in history, with Hamilton the most accomplished. "Without Hamilton there would be no American Republic today, to astonish the world with its resources and its progress," he said.

October: Harding spent some time campaigning for Roosevelt. For the presidential campaign, Harding began in

Woodrow Wilson's official portrait as president of Princeton University.

central Ohio, then made his first out-of-state tour, traveling to Union City, Dunkirk, and Peru in Indiana.

CALVIN COOLIDGE was selected chairman of the Northampton (Massachusetts) Republican City Committee for the presidential campaign. The city went Republican in the November election as expected, but a Democrat was the surprise winner for mayor, by only 8 votes. The Republican loss in the mayor's race, Coolidge later wrote in his *Autobiography*, came about because the Republicans "made the mistake of talking too much about the deficiencies of our opponents and not enough about the merits of our own candidate. I have never again fallen into that error."

Northampton celebrated its two hundredth and fiftieth year, and Coolidge, 32, took Grace Goodhue to a reception for the governor and his council in a program sponsored by the Daughters of the American Revolution (DAR). Coolidge wrote in his *Autobiography* that he often took Grace to "places of entertainment." By that he may have meant that she pushed him into attending picnics, which he disliked, buggy rides, trolley rides, and church socials.

ಶಿಂಖ

HERBERT HOOVER, 30, took his first vacation in 5 years with a leisurely trip without his family to South Africa to inspect mines in the Transvaal. His doctor ordered it. Hoover said he had been "working like a dog." His Berwick, Moreing firm now controlled thirty-two mines around the world and employed 9,000 miners. The company's mines accounted for 50 percent of the gold production in western Australia.

Hoover continued to write engineering articles, anonymously. On long ocean voyages, he read many books and smoked his pipe.

FRANKLIN D. ROOSEVELT graduated from Harvard and remained in Cambridge in the fall to act as editor-in-chief of the *Crimson* and take graduate courses in history and economics. He never received a master's degree. Meanwhile, his secret fiancée, Eleanor Roosevelt, dined with the president at the White House and enjoyed visits with the Roosevelts at Sagamore.

Roosevelt sailed his yacht *Half Moon* to Oyster Bay when Eleanor was there. She tried to disguise her feelings, the pending wedding still not a public matter. Later, she asked President Theodore Roosevelt to give her away at her wedding, planned for sometime in 1905. The president wrote to Franklin on November 29, "I am as fond of Eleanor as if she were my daughter; and I like you and trust you and believe in you."

Sara, however, worked tirelessly to break up the romance. One move to stop the wedding was a Caribbean cruise in February. Harvard classmate Lathrop Brown joined them. Then Sara tried to have FDR assigned to the embassy in London as a secretary. But the ambassador felt that the 22-year-old Roosevelt was too young for such an assignment.

Franklin bought an engagement ring at Tiffany's for Eleanor's twentieth birthday, October 11. Their engagement was made public in November. After the engagement, Sara took to writing Franklin or friends about plans involving "We three."

෨෬

HARRY S TRUMAN, 20, was a bookkeeper at the Union National Bank in Kansas City making $100 per month. His superior, A. D. Flintom, wrote about him on April 14: "He is an exceptionally bright young man. He is a willing worker, almost always here, and tries hard to please everybody … [his] habits and character are of the best."

෨෬

DWIGHT D. EISENHOWER, at 14, faced amputation of a leg after blood poisoning developed from a scrape on the knee. When the doctors recommended amputation, Eisenhower argued that he would rather be dead than crippled. He received less radical treatment instead, and the leg was saved. The leg was black and swollen for several months.

Eisenhower started high school, which was temporarily several rooms at city hall in Abilene, Kansas. The students shared a floor with the fire department. Meanwhile a new high school was under construction. If there were a fire, the students would have to volunteer to help. Eisenhower started in September but missed much of the school year because of his leg.

1905
Theodore Roosevelt

The president helped Japan and Russia settle their war, and the peace negotiations, held in Portsmouth, New Hampshire, would lead to a Nobel Prize for the president in 1906.

January: A U.S. naval officer was sent to Santo Domingo on January 5 to negotiate a deal whereby the United States would help with the Dominican debt problem. Democrats in the Senate were hostile and wanted the Senate involved in this Latin American issue. On January 20, Roosevelt began managing the Dominican Republic's internal and foreign debts without congressional approval. Roosevelt said either the Monroe Doctrine would be utilized, or "we must submit to the likelihood of infringement of the Monroe Doctrine" by others.

In early January, Japan took Port Arthur, a Russian fortress. The United States warned neutrals on January 13 not to seek concessions from China at this crucial time. Roosevelt believed that Japan should keep Port Arthur, have influence in Korea, and guarantee China that it would stay out of Manchuria. Japan did not accept the third point.

On January 30, the Supreme Court ruled against the "beef trust" when it decided that Swift and Company was operating an illegal monopoly in violation of the Sherman Anti-Trust Act.

March–May: Roosevelt was sworn in for his first full term on March 4. In his inaugural address, Roosevelt stressed America's duties to the world and itself and lauded America's "self-reliance and individual initiative."

In March, Japan won the battle of Mukden but was nearing military exhaustion and wanted Russia to ask for peace. On April 18, Japan decided to seek Roosevelt's help in ending the war. Roosevelt was hunting in Oklahoma and Texas but when Japan sent messages to Roosevelt at his hunting site, he returned to Washington a week earlier than planned. Japan was ready to talk, but Russia was not.

The one-sided Battle of the Sea of Japan was fought on May 27 to May 28, and the Russian fleet was sunk.

June: Roosevelt believed that if the Russians did not come to the peace table it could lose all of its possessions in the Far East. Pressure was put on the czar in June. Even the kaiser urged a settlement and said Roosevelt might be able to soften Japan's terms.

On June 5, Roosevelt cabled his friend George Meyer to inquire if the Russians might negotiate directly with Japan. Meyer later met with Czar Nicholas II, who was talked into seeking terms by his generals. No Russian territory was yet occupied by Japan, but the czar worried about a possible Japanese attack on Sakhalin Island. Meyer wired Roosevelt on June 7 that Russia was willing to talk. Roosevelt then told both sides he would be willing to help, although he first advised direct negotiations with each other. Then he advised the press of developments.

July–September: Secretary of State John Hay, ill for some time, died on July 1. Elihu Root became the new secretary of state on July 7.

The Navy Yard at Portsmouth, New Hampshire, was selected for the Russian–Japanese peace sessions in August. As a prelude to the New Hampshire talks, delegations from Japan and Russia met first at Oyster Bay on August 5 and drank a toast on the yacht *Mayflower* to the "welfare and prosperity" of the two nations. Roosevelt sought a balance of power in Asia and was unaware of Japan's desperate need for money.

Many of the issues were resolved in the first 10 days at Portsmouth, but talks then stalled on August 18. The parties reached a final settlement on August 29 and signed a final treaty on September 5. Russia gave up its position in Korea, agreed to withdraw its troops from Manchuria, and handed over to Japan part of the island of Sakhalin.

Former Presidents

GROVER CLEVELAND, retired in Princeton, New Jersey, in this year went into the insurance business both as a trustee and as a referee in a dispute concerning fraud.

June 10: Cleveland was one of three trustees to hold stock and supervise the reorganization of Equitable Life Insurance. Joining Cleveland were George Westinghouse and Justice Morgan J. O'Brien. Their job was to pick a new board.

December 19: Cleveland accepted the position of referee in the dispute between New York Life, Mutual Life, and Equitable Life, and he was paid another $12,000.

Cleveland, 68, still thought about the subject of an autobiography when S. S. McClure of *McClure's Magazine* offered the retired president $10,000 to write twelve articles. Cleveland instead suggested a series of interviews of him to be done by a trained writer for the magazine. McClure was not interested in this.

Future Presidents

WILLIAM HOWARD TAFT found little time to run the War Department as he moved ever closer to the president and the presidency. As secretary of war, he supervised affairs in the Philippines; and with John Hay ill, Taft became practically an acting secretary of state. And he was still running things in Panama as construction of the canal began.

Taft's correspondence during the year showed little concern about War Department matters. He complained once that he had so much work outside his department that he left things to the chief of staff. He wrote to his brother Charles that in 1906 he hoped "to take a little more part in the administration of the War Department than heretofore."

April: When Roosevelt went to the Rockies in the spring, he told the *New York Times* on April 4 that all was well in Washington because he "left Taft sitting on the lid."

With Roosevelt out of Washington, Taft received a visit from Baron Kogoro Takahira, the Japanese minister to the United States. Takahira said Japan would demand indemnity from Russia, and all of Sakhalin. Taft wrote on April 25 that Japan was "quite anxious for peace but … determined … not to lose the fruits of a successful war, and in this they are entirely right."

May–August: Taft and an entourage of eighty, including Alice Roosevelt, left for a Far East trip in May. Their first stop was Hawaii, and their ship docked in Honolulu on July 15. The party took a trip to Nuuanu Pali, visited Pearl Harbor, saw a sugar plantation in Aiea, and attended a luncheon for 350 people at the Royal Hawaiian Hotel.

On July 27, in Japan, Taft talked to Count Katsura, the Japanese premier. Taft's talk with Katsura struck the terms for a secret understanding in which Roosevelt agreed with Japanese policy regarding Korea. Katsura said Korea was the cause of the war with Russia, and that Japan would not concede it to the Russians. Taft said that Korea should enter no treaties without the consent of Japan. Katsura assured Taft that Japan had no interest in the Philippines. He said that Japan's fundamental interest was for peace in the Far East.

Taft cabled Elihu Root on July 29 that he hoped he did not speak "too freely or inaccurately or unwisely" in his talks with Katsura. Roosevelt cabled Taft on July 31 that everything said to Katsura was "absolutely correct in every respect."

Taft then traveled to the Philippines, where there were banquets and speeches. Taft addressed a large crowd outside Malacanan Palace on August 5, saying, "Always in my heart the Philippines have had the first place." He also added that the time was not yet ripe for Philippine independence.

ಹಿ ಲ

WOODROW WILSON, 49 in December, inaugurated a tutorial system based on Oxford and Cambridge models that many supporters believed would impact education everywhere in the United States.

In the spring, Wilson made his first appointments of preceptors, men who would guide a student in his reading and

Baron Kogaro Takahira (center), Japanese minister to the United States, rides in a carriage during his visit to Portsmouth, New Hampshire, for the Japanese-Russian peace conference. (Library of Congress)

writing, He wanted to hire "gentlemen" committed to Princeton. One interviewee later recalled, "I had never before talked face to face with so compelling a person." Within 6 months, Wilson had recruited fifty young instructors for the fall term. The *Nassau Literary Magazine* and others fell in line supporting the preceptorial system. Many believed it was a revolution in education. For the most part, the preceptor system worked well and some students became lifelong friends with their teachers.

Ellen Wilson's brother Edward Axson, his wife, and son drowned in northwest Georgia in April while trying to cross a swollen creek. Wilson regarded Edward as a "son," and both Wilsons were grief-stricken.

୫୦୧୫

WARREN G. HARDING, still eager to obtain the Republican nomination for governor of Ohio, went to Washington, D.C., to plead his case with Senator Joseph Foraker, who turned him down. Harding now decided to turn his back on politics by not seeking reelection as lieutenant governor and sitting out Myron Herrick's expected defeat in November.

January–February: Harding's ambitions for the governorship surfaced on January 2 when he leaked to the *Ohio State Journal* that he was available for the Republican nomination, and "of course I'd accept." Four days later he told reporters he would not be a candidate for reelection as lieutenant governor.

The state convention was scheduled for May, and Herrick appeared to be in trouble. Harding received many letters urging his candidacy and newspapers in Richwood, St. Paris, and Van Wert came out for him.

Harding then decided he had to see Foraker in Washington. But the senator turned cool and said that the Harding boom was over. Harding never forgave Foraker for his blunt assessment.

Frustrated with politics, Harding then booked a Caribbean cruise in February for 3 weeks to Cuba. One week before sailing for Cuba, Florence was bedridden in Grant Hospital in Columbus by a serious kidney ailment. The kidney was removed on February 24, and the trip canceled.

May–November: On the eve of the state Republican convention in Columbus on May 25, the *Cincinnati Enquirer* said, "Harding is more than a considerable man. He has dignified a position [formerly] held in contempt." But Harding did not consider running again for lieutenant governor.

The convention was short and sweet. Harding was not there. Herrick was renominated, and Andrew L. Harris was nominated for lieutenant governor.

With Florence ill, Harding, 40 in November, took on a lover, the beautiful Carrie Fulton Phillips, age 30, wife of one of Harding's friends, James E. Phillips. Harding for a long time had entertained the idea of leaving Florence. But he was comfortable with having her around although bothered by her endless illnesses.

When James Phillips took sick with "nerves" in the spring, Harding suggested the sanitarium at Battle Creek, Michigan. At the same time, Florence was in Florida recovering from her kidney ailment. With Jim and Florence gone, Harding and Carrie became lovers; it was his first extramarital affair.

Politically, Harding, 40, remained friendly with Governor Herrick and even campaigned for him during the summer and early fall, making about twenty-five speeches.

In the election in November, Herrick lost to Democrat John Pattison, yet Harris was elected lieutenant governor.

୫୦୧୫

CALVIN COOLIDGE was married and lost an election to be a member of the Northampton, Massachusetts, school committee.

Coolidge married Grace Goodhue on October 4 in Burlington, Vermont. He was 33 and she was 26. The wedding took place in the parlor of the Goodhue home, and only fifteen friends attended. There was no best man or maid of honor. They went to Montreal for their honeymoon, but Montreal proved boring and they canceled the second week.

In his autobiography, Coolidge wrote of Grace, "We thought we were made for each other." He also admitted that they needed to live frugally after their marriage: "I know very well what it means to awake in the night and realize that the rent is coming due, wondering where the money is coming from with which to pay it."

On their return to Northampton, they lived in the Norwood Hotel for 3 weeks, then moved to a small, furnished house owned by a Smith College professor.

୫୦୧୫

HERBERT HOOVER, 31, logged 32,800 miles during this year. Twice he was in Australia, and he made side trips to New Zealand and Egypt's Sinai Peninsula. He also checked in at his tenth Stanford reunion.

London took great interest in the Kaiping mines lawsuit brought by the Chinese for restoration of ownership and tried in London. At issue was Berwick, Moreing management and financial dealings. Both Hoover personally and his company came under sharp criticism by the English judge, who saw "fraud" in their practices. Hoover felt his reputation was on the line.

The verdict went against Berwick, Moreing. Hoover was highly critical of the Labor Party in West Australia, but threats by Berwick, Moreing to withdrawn from its project were dropped when the Conservatives won the next election. Hoover and Berwick, Moreing now concentrated on the zinc potential at Broken Hill in Victoria, Australia, and at the same time considered a venture in Burma.

୫୦୧୫

FRANKLIN D. ROOSEVELT, 23, began law school at Columbia and married Anna Eleanor Roosevelt, 20, a fifth cousin once removed.

Franklin and Eleanor married on St. Patrick's Day, March

436

17, in the townhouse of her aunt, Mrs. E. Livingston Ludlow, on East 76th Street, New York. Star of the show was President Roosevelt. He gave the bride away and turned the wedding into a national news event.

The honeymoon was 3 months in Europe: Liverpool, London, Paris, Venice, St. Moritz, Black Forest, and Cortina. Both had been to these places before. On their return to New York, Eleanor, now pregnant, moved into the rented Draper House, 125 East 36th Street, three blocks from Sara. Sara picked the place, hired three servants, and selected the furnishings. Eleanor was left with nothing to do but defer to her mother-in-law.

Eleanor was the daughter of Elliott Roosevelt, Theodore's brother. Her mother was Anna Hall Roosevelt, who had died when Eleanor was 8, and Theodore had put her alcoholic father in a sanitarium in Dwight, Illinois, before his death. A grandmother raised Eleanor. She had private tutoring and attended Allenswood, a finishing school outside of London for 3 years.

℘℘

HARRY S TRUMAN, 21, began the year as a bank teller in Kansas City. He joined the National Guard in May to earn extra money and began drills with an artillery unit. He boarded with his Aunt Emma, but later moved to a regular rooming house at $5 per week. He roomed with Arthur Eisenhower of Abilene, Kansas.

Truman's father John moved to a small farm in Clinton, Missouri, 70 miles southeast of Kansas City. A flood soon wiped out his corn crop. Now John took over the Young family's Blue Ridge farm, because his father-in-law, Harrison Young, was too old to work the large farm of 600 acres himself. The Youngs had built a large, impressive house and barn in 1868. When the house burned down in 1893, a smaller house replaced it.

Harry's father and Harry's brother Vivian soon found it was too much for them, and Harry was told to quit his bank job and help work the farm. The place had no running water or electricity. If he was resentful about his new situation, he never let it be known.

℘℘

DWIGHT D. EISENHOWER, 15, entered the new high school in Abilene, Kansas, in the fall. It had a faculty of five. Eisenhower's class consisted of nine boys and twenty-two girls. He was interested in military history and admired George Washington and Hannibal.

1906
Theodore Roosevelt

President Roosevelt traveled to Panama to check the progress of work on the canal, the first time a president had ever left the country while holding office. He also sent troops into Cuba to quiet a revolt that threatened to turn into chaos. Roosevelt's strong executive style in this, his sixth year in the White House, included a major effort to regulate railroads, an attack on the meat packing industry, and a push for safe food and drug legislation.

January–June: It was a busy year in establishing regulatory controls over industry and fighting the trusts. The Dolliver–Hepburn bill, a railroad control measure, was introduced in the House on January 24 with overwhelming support. In the Senate, members had to fend off amendments between February 9 and 25. The bill was finally passed and signed into law on June 29 as the Hepburn Act. The new law empowered the Interstate Commerce Commission to investigate railroads and to set rates.

The move toward regulation of food and drugs had been in the making for several years, and the American Medical Association and *Ladies Home Journal* were among those questioning "soothing syrups" that turned out to contain mostly alcohol. The Senate opened debate in January when a pure-food bill was introduced. A pure-food bill passed the Senate on February 21 by a vote of 63 to 4. In the House, there were attacks on the patent medicine industry, but Speaker of the House Joe Cannon dragged his feet on a vote. Finally, on June 23 the House passed by a 241-to-17 vote a pure-food bill, and Roosevelt signed the measure on June 30.

A meat inspection bill was introduced in the Senate on May 21. The House was resistant to the bill, and Representative James W. Wadsworth, a New York Republican, sought to water down the bill with amendments. On June 4, Roosevelt released a stockyards report, saying conditions were "revolting," and that in the "interest of health and of decency," changes were necessary. The issue in the House was who would pay for meat inspections—the meat industry or the government.

A compromise bill quickly passed the House on June 19, and the Senate accepted the House version since the session was almost over. Roosevelt signed the measure on June 30.

In June, the White House announced that Roosevelt would go to Panama in November. Roosevelt wanted to see for himself what was going on, despite the lack of any precedent for a sitting president to leave the country.

Roosevelt's daughter, Alice, 22, married Ohio Republican Representative Nicholas Longworth, 36, in a White House ceremony on February 16. Much of the preparations for the wedding were handled by Edith Roosevelt.

August–October: Roosevelt and Taft were left to handle the crisis in Cuba because Secretary of State Elihu Root was making a swing through South America.

In August, Cuban President Tomas Estrada Palma asked the United States for help in putting down a rebellion led by Jose Miguel Gomez and Alfredo Zayas. The rebel leaders also asked for intervention by U.S. Army troops under the Platt Amendment.

In late August, Roosevelt allowed the Cuban government to purchase ammunition from the War Department but on September 1 sent three army officers to Cuba to size up the situation. Seven days later, two Navy ships were sent at Palma's request.

Roosevelt then wrote to British historian George O. Trevelyan on September 9 that the United States could not allow "misrule and anarchy" in Cuba, but that that did not mean the United States would assume "control" as it had in Puerto Rico and the Philippines. On September 13, Palma resigned and offered the government to the United States.

Roosevelt then sent Taft to Havana on September 14 to talk with Palma about staying on. When Taft warned Palma about avoiding "anarchy," Palma rejected Taft's recommendations. Taft wanted American troops landed but Roosevelt asked the secretary of war to make another last-ditch effort to end the chaos. Four days later, Roosevelt gave permission to land army units on September 28. The next day, Taft was made provisional governor, replacing the elected Palma. On October 13, Roosevelt appointed Charles Edward Magoon, a Nebraska lawyer, as governor of Cuba, replacing Taft. Roosevelt acted again under the Platt Amendment, which permitted Washington to intervene in Cuba to maintain order (see **William Howard Taft**, opposite column).

November–December: Roosevelt's 3-day visit in Panama was marred by heavy rains. He was satisfied with the work of the chief engineer, John Stevens, and gave Stevens absolute control of the endeavor on November 17. There was heavy press coverage, and a photograph of Roosevelt, now 48, at the controls of a huge shovel, was soon printed in newspapers around the world.

First Lady Edith Roosevelt and daughter Ethel. (Library of Congress)

On December 10, Roosevelt was awarded the Nobel Peace Prize for his efforts in bringing about peace between Russia and Japan.

On December 12, the Senate confirmed Roosevelt's choice of William Henry Moody to the Supreme Court. Roosevelt had offered the seat to William Howard Taft earlier in the year (see **William Howard Taft**, opposite column).

Former Presidents

Grover Cleveland, the Princeton University trustee, was appreciated by the school's president, Woodrow Wilson. Wilson penned a note on March 5: "Strong [is] the admiration and affection of those of us in Princeton who know you best."

Cleveland spoke at the remodeling of Nassau Hall, declaring that he favored the educational course then being pursued at Princeton. Cleveland wanted good professors for the school and said every professor should be a scholar but that scholars did not always make good teachers.

When his sixty-ninth birthday came around, Cleveland was hunting in Florida. He received so many messages of good cheer from various friends that he could hardly hold back the tears. Mark Twain wrote to say that he put Cleveland right at the presidential summit with Washington.

Cleveland's brother William died at the age of 74 on January 15.

Future Presidents

William Howard Taft remained a presidential prospect after Roosevelt, for the third time, offered him a Supreme Court seat but was again turned down. This time wife Nellie marched to the White House to privately protest the idea. Elihu Root agreed it was not apropos to join the court at a time when Taft appeared the favorite for a presidential nomination in 1908. Taft also found time to write a book in this year, *Four Aspects of Civic Duty*.

January: Taft was visiting a friend in New Jersey when he received a call from the president offering a seat on the Supreme Court, but not the position of chief justice. Mrs. Taft expressed strong disapproval.

March: At a March 9 meeting between Roosevelt, Taft, William Henry Moody, and Root, Taft said that his wife was "bitterly opposed to my accepting" a Court appointment. Nellie made her White House visit alone to express her feelings about the Supreme Court, and Roosevelt wrote to Taft on March 15 about their meeting. Still in support of the plan to put Taft on the Court, Roosevelt said he did not like the looks of the general conditions in the nation, that there was too much "greed and arrogance" among men, "corruption in business," and an "enormous increase in the socialistic propaganda."

August–October: Taft was resting at Murray Bay in Quebec when trouble developed in Cuba. A revolt threatened the regime of President Tomas Estrada Palma, which caused Taft to advise the chief of staff to prepare an invasion plan "promptly and efficiently." Americans had invested $200 million in the island republic since the Spanish-American War ended. But the Platt Amendment of 1901 had practically ended Cuban self-government.

Roosevelt did not wish to interfere in Cuban affairs and sympathized with Palma's regime. Palma asked for U.S. naval protection on September 8. But by September 13 Palma threatened to resign and offered the government to the United States. As an alternative to military action, Roosevelt sent Taft and acting Secretary of State Robert Bacon to Havana on September 14.

Taft was embarrassed by how little he knew about the island and wrote to Root on September 15, which was also Taft's forty-ninth birthday, "You know the Cuban situation … the Cuban government has proven to be nothing but a house of cards."

Taft's 3 weeks in Havana were difficult and hectic. He arrived on September 19 and cabled Roosevelt 2 days later that there was anarchy in the countryside. He suggested letting Palma and his moderates resign, finding a temporary chief, and then revising the election laws. But by September 22 Taft decided it would be better to keep Palma in office.

Taft wrote to his wife on September 27 that he was worried, could not sleep or eat, and did not know how his Cuban sojourn was playing in the American press. Two days later, Taft became provisional governor of Cuba.

He wrote to Roosevelt on October 3, "My theory … we are simply carrying Cuba under the Platt Amendment as a receiver carries on the business of a corporation." The insurgents turned in their guns and a crisis was averted. Taft was anxious to get out of Havana, and Charles E. Magoon replaced him on October 13.

∞

Woodrow Wilson, 49, suffered a severe stroke in May and spent a lengthy recovery period in England's Lake District. Late in the year, he took an additional rest in Bermuda on doctor's orders and there met Mary Hulbert Allen Peck, a vivacious lady in her forties. Wilson was also appointed to his first public office in this year, as a member of the New Jersey commission on the unification of state laws.

February: Publisher George B. X. Harvey, at a Lotus Club dinner in New York on February 3 that honored Wilson, said Wilson was well qualified to become president in 1908. Wilson's response: "It seems to me that the only method of guiding ourselves in life is by determining fixed points and steering by them.… Other wires taller than mine will attract the lightning."

Harvey said Wilson was "by instinct a statesman." Harvey then ran Wilson's picture on the cover of *Harper's Weekly* with Harvey's Lotus Club speech inside the magazine. Harvey's speech ran under the headline: "For President: Woodrow Wilson."

May–June: Wilson woke up on May 28 blind in one eye from a ruptured blood vessel. Ellen later reported, "Of course we had a dreadful week. Doctors said he must stop all work

at once…. He is very nervous." A month later, Ellen thought her husband was dying from hardening of the arteries. The problem actually was a severe stroke with permanent eye damage.

July–September: Three months in England during the summer brought recovery, although a Scottish doctor recommended that he ease up on his workload. In Wilson's absence, Dean Henry B. Fine was made acting president of Princeton.

While Wilson was in England, Harvey worked up a plan with Newark party boss James Smith Jr. to run Wilson for the Senate in 1907. Wilson expressed surprise at the idea on his return from Europe.

November–December: By November, Wilson was overworking again. He wrote, "I did not take a long breath for two weeks." Doctors now suggested Bermuda. While on the island, he preached at the church, played croquet or miniature golf with Mark Twain, and walked the beach with Mrs. Peck while reading from the *Oxford Book of Verse*.

∞

Warren G. Harding, out of politics for 6 months, had to wonder at the strange workings of fate when his successor as lieutenant governor suddenly became governor. Harding's work for the Republican Party in this year was minor: He was on the resolution committee at the state convention, and he made a few speeches in the fall campaign.

It was on January 8 that Lieutenant Governor Harding greeted incoming Governor John Pattison, badly ailing. A reception in the Senate chamber was the only event Pattison could attend. Because Pattison was unable to work, relatives in February urged him to resign. He died on June 19. The GOP lieutenant governor, Andrew L. Harris, became governor.

The "nerves" problem that had sent Harding to Battle Creek's Kellogg sanitarium many times seemed to be in the Harding blood. His brother, Deacon, left Columbus early in the year to be a superintendent of a sanitarium in Washington, D.C. Within 6 months, he wrote Warren that he needed a year's leave for rest and that he had resigned the job.

Harding's sister Daisy had a breakdown. Deacon wrote on December 18, that it was "advisable that she take a year's rest."

Harding, 41 in November, continued to see Carrie Phillips when her husband Jim was away.

∞

Calvin Coolidge, 34 in July, was elected to the Massachusetts House of Representatives. The Republicans nominated him for the statehouse, and he was elected in November by a margin of 264 votes.

Grace was pregnant in the spring, and the couple decided they needed a larger place. They rented a duplex at 21 Massasoit Street for $28 per month. Two weeks after moving, their son John was born on September 7.

439

Coolidge cultivated political friends, and he helped his landlord, Rob Weir, get elected as an alderman in Northampton's second ward.

§○○§

HERBERT HOOVER, the mining engineer in London, was now making $75,000 per year, enough to make him wealthy by the standard of the times. Hoover told a friend he hoped to retire from engineering soon, live at Stanford, and do something for the school. The friend was amazed that a 32-year-old man had a retirement plan.

Hoover's brother Theodore, tired of his mining job in California, moved to London and joined Berwick, Moreing.

§○○§

FRANKLIN D. ROOSEVELT, 24, was still wrestling with the Columbia Law School routine. His mother had made him study on the ship returning him from his honeymoon. When his grades arrived by mail in Paris he had two F's.

Daughter Anna was born on May 3, and after the temporary nurse left, Eleanor was at a loss as to how to do things for the baby. Sara resolved the crisis by hiring a nurse. Now the newlyweds had four servants.

Recovering from a difficult birth, Eleanor and Franklin went to Campobello. He introduced her to outside sports, and she failed in all: sailing, golf, tennis, and later ice-skating. Franklin loved these activities, and Eleanor became a sideline observer.

§○○§

HARRY S TRUMAN, 22, quickly learned how to farm. The Grandview, Missouri, farm, about 15 miles south of Kansas City, required his father, brother, and hired hands to work it. Harry learned how to plow with a team of four horses. He could work 5 acres in 10 hours. He learned how to operate corn planters and wheat drills, fix fences, hoe, hay, and make repairs.

In the summer he went on his first tour of National Guard duty. The Kansas City outfit took a train to St. Louis and then a steamboat to Cape Girardeau in the southeastern corner of the state.

§○○§

DWIGHT D. EISENHOWER, 16, lived in Abilene, Kansas, and did chores around the house by day and worked at the creamery by night.

1907
Theodore Roosevelt

President Roosevelt briefly faced a similar financial crisis to the one Cleveland had experienced in 1895 when panic hit Wall Street on October 22. Inflationary pressures increased throughout the year. There was a pinch in credit, the banking industry was shaky, the stock market was uncertain—and George Cortelyou, the new secretary of Treasury, had to shore

things up quickly. The financial crisis in October followed a buildup of ill feelings between the White House and Wall Street.

January–February: Roosevelt pressured the governor of California not to support anti-Japanese legislation after meeting with California's congressional delegates on January 30. No solution was found. Meanwhile, the San Francisco school board issued an order segregating Asian students.

In response to California's laws, Secretary of State Elihu Root and Senator Henry Cabot Lodge came up with a plan to amend an immigration bill to prevent laborers from coming to the United States. This bill passed the Senate on February 15 and the House 3 days later. Roosevelt signed the bill on February 20. The new law barred immigrants with a non-U.S. passport entry into the United States if such entry would be detrimental to U.S. labor conditions.

March: George Cortelyou became secretary of Treasury on March 4.

As a financial crisis loomed, Roosevelt met on March 11 with J. P. Morgan, who suggested that the president talk to four major railroads about cooling "public anxiety" over the relationship between the government and the railroads. Then, on March 13, stock prices on Wall Street plummeted. Large railroad companies led the decline in stock prices. Many business leaders pointed to Roosevelt's trust-busting efforts as a prime cause of the stock market drop.

On March 14, Roosevelt issued an executive order directing Japanese and Korean laborers who received passports to go to Mexico, Hawaii, or Canada, be refused entry into the United States. In response to the order, San Francisco rescinded its school segregation order.

May–June: Anti-Japanese riots broke out in San Francisco on May 20 to May 21. Several Asians were hurt during the rioting, and Roosevelt wrote to a friend on May 23: "Nothing during my presidency has given me more concern than these troubles."

Newspaper sensationalism over the next few weeks helped to lead some people to talk seriously about war with Japan. When Roosevelt went to Oyster Bay for the summer he asked the joint Army–Navy Board to send him their plans in case of war.

October–November: The financial crisis worsened when a run on the Knickerbocker Trust Company took place on October 16. The Knickerbocker failure coupled with the drop in copper prices in mid-October led to a panic on October 22. For the next 3 weeks, there was a run on banks as investors sought to get their money out.

On October 23, Roosevelt held an emergency meeting with his cabinet. Cortelyou transferred $37 million to New York banks, then soon added another $31 million, but by this point, banks had to suspend payments to depositors.

Things turned around when U.S. Steel bought a Tennessee coal company after Henry C. Frick and Elbert Gary met with Roosevelt for 20 minutes. They said they would not make the buy if the government were to take anti-trust action against them. Roosevelt then made a public announcement that U.S. Steel was not violating the Sherman Act.

In late November, Cortelyou issued $150 million in government bonds, which slowly bolstered confidence.

December: Roosevelt decided to send the U.S. fleet on a globe-circling tour. The "Great White Fleet" included sixteen American battleships under the command of Rear Admiral Robley D. "Fighting Bob" Evans. Roosevelt sent the ships first to the Pacific, mostly to demonstrate to the Japanese the strength of the U.S. Navy. Roosevelt wanted the publicity to increase naval appropriations. The sixteen battleships left Hampton Roads, Virginia, on December 16 with Roosevelt watching from the yacht *Mayflower*.

In his December message to Congress, Roosevelt asked for four more battleships because, "It would be most unwise for us to stop the building of our Navy." Meanwhile, *McClure's Magazine* ran a story on December 21 that outlined naval needs and criticized battleship armor and other flaws, the number of elderly admirals in the ranks, and other organizational problems with the U.S. Navy.

U.S. Senator from Massachusetts Henry Cabot Lodge (Library of Congress)

Former Presidents

GROVER CLEVELAND had difficulties with President Woodrow Wilson of Princeton when they differed on how undergraduates should be housed on campus. Wilson wanted things patterned after the British system; Cleveland preferred having things "American."

March: On Cleveland's seventieth birthday March 18, students gave him a loving cup, and he replied, "I feel young … because I have here breathed the atmosphere of vigorous youth and of hopeful aspiring young manhood."

June: Wilson surprised the trustees with the "quadrangle" (or quad) plan for undergraduate resident life—a plan that would be expensive to implement. Cleveland not only opposed the quad plan but also said that Wilson was not keeping faith with earlier assurances about what he wanted to do.

October: The trustees asked Wilson to withdraw the quad plan, and he did. Opponents of the scheme did not think it would profit American boys, but rather that it would cause a delay in building the graduate college.

Future Presidents

WILLIAM HOWARD TAFT kept the presidential nomination of 1908 within sight despite another extraordinary trip around the world that took him to familiar Tokyo and Manila and then on the Trans-Siberian Railroad across Russia from Vladivostok to Moscow. He interviewed the Japanese foreign minister regarding Japan's intentions in Asia and later interviewed the czar.

August: Some insiders suggested to Taft that he resign as secretary of war and keep his distance from Roosevelt. Taft wrote to E. G. Lowry on August 6: "I very much enjoy being in his cabinet and shall be quite content if the nomination goes elsewhere."

September–December: With all of the agitation in San Francisco over Japanese immigrants, Roosevelt decided to send Taft, 50, to Tokyo again to show U.S. goodwill. Taft would then travel on to the Philippines to open the Philippine Assembly, a move toward self-government for the islands.

The trip began in Seattle in September, with Taft headed for Yokohama. After traveling to Japan and the Philippines, he continued on to Europe, traveling across Russia by rail. Eventually, the trip ended when Taft shipped out of Hamburg, Germany, for New York in the beginning of December.

Taft's mother Louise died on December 8 at the age of 80. Soon after her death, Taft went to Cincinnati to put a wreath on her grave, then wrote to Mrs. Samuel Carr on December 24: "She was a remarkable woman."

ഇറയ

WOODROW WILSON, 51 in December, suffered the major defeat of his academic career when the board of trustees voted down his quadrangle plan. Wilson was devastated and wrote a letter of resignation, then thought better about mailing it. Grover Cleveland, Dean West, and best friend Hibben joined the opposition.

February–June: In February, Wilson told a colleague that he had "made a mistake" in putting the quad plan before the board in such a sudden manner in late 1906.

As Cleveland's criticism surfaced, it was apparent that Wilson had failed to consult either the faculty or the alumni on his quad idea. On April 15, Wilson invited a few faculty friends to his house to discuss the issue. At the same time there were additional problems for the club system, then a standard aspect of campus life.

441

Wilson supported his ideas before the board on June 10 and said that its club system, which separated the student's social life from his intellectual life, had to be changed in order for the university to develop its intellectual life. The board supported the idea, with only one member in dissent.

July–August: As opposition to his quad plan began to appear, Wilson wrote to M. W. Jacobus on July 1, "The fight for the quads is on very merrily." Wilson then went to the Adirondacks to consider his strategy.

West, Cleveland, and Hibben asked Wilson to soften his stance on quads. Hibben said that Wilson did not know the trustees well enough. Alumni opposition grew, and financial support from the Committee of Fifty began to dry up, in contrast to the generous donations that greeted his preceptorial plan (see **Woodrow Wilson**, page 432).

September–October: A faculty meeting revolt led by Hibben took place on September 26. Yet put to a vote, the faculty supported Wilson's quad idea, 80 to 26. The *Daily Princeton* said on October 2, "Never before has any movement excited such interest."

At a second faculty meeting on October 7, Wilson made an eloquent plea. He said that the clubs were outside the purpose of a university. "I beg of you to follow me in this hazardous, but splendid adventure."

On October 17 the trustees called on Wilson to withdraw his plan. The trustees recognized Wilson's right to free speech, and Cleveland proposed that something be done about the clubs. That night Wilson considered resignation, but overnight changed his mind. Then he told the *New York Sun* that the board might reconsider its position later and he predicted "ultimate acceptance." The board then turned down quadrangles for good a few days later.

❧☙

WARREN G. HARDING, 42 in November, went to Europe with his father-in-law Amos Kling, an amazing attitude turnaround for the Marion, Ohio, millionaire. Florence and Kling's new bride made it a foursome. Kling paid for everything.

In February the Hardings returned to Daytona, Florida's Marion colony. Kling and his new bride were there riding bicycles on the beach. Slowly Kling accepted Florence and Warren. When Harding returned to Marion, he mailed a batch of *Marion Star* newspapers to Kling, who wrote his first letter ever to his son-in-law: "This is a duty as well as a pleasure on which I ought to have realized long ago … answering your nice letter."

Kling later suggested that the two couples travel to Europe. The four sailed on August 1 from New York for Liverpool. From Liverpool, the group saw Chester, Stratford-on-Avon, Oxford, Windsor, London, and Canterbury, before continuing on to Germany, Austria, and Switzerland, and ending the trip with 10 days in Paris. They sailed for New York on September 19 with a trunk load of souvenirs.

On the political front, Harding wrote a piece for *Ohio Maga-*

zine in January supporting Joseph Foraker for president: "In the Senate [Foraker] has won his spurs and stands today the most eminent legislator of the great American Republic."

❧☙

CALVIN COOLIDGE, the new Republican member of the Massachusetts General Court, as the state legislature was called, was unknown and quiet for much of the session. Coolidge's pay was $5 per day, and his room at the Adams House was $1 per day. On weekends he took the train to Northampton to be with his family. Coolidge was reelected in November.

Coolidge arrived in Boston in January. Republicans were in the majority, but the progressive movement affected the situation as reformers were on the rise. Governor Curtis Guild Jr., a Republican, had won in 1905. He supported most progressive concerns, but Coolidge liked his program for reducing the size of government and the state debt. The Republican kingmaker in Massachusetts was National Committeeman Winthrop M. Crane, governor of the state from 1900 to 1903 and elected to the U.S. Senate in 1904. For the next 13 years, Coolidge was identified as a Crane man.

In his first year on the Massachusetts General Court, Coolidge served on two minor committees: mercantile affairs and constitutional amendments.

The general court adjourned on June 28. In the fall, the 35-year-old Coolidge was nominated again and elected for a second term.

❧☙

HERBERT HOOVER, 33, and his wife went to Burma, where they contracted malaria. Hoover left his wife, small boys, and sister-in-law in Rangoon while he inspected a lead mine in the jungles of the northern interior that had been worked by Chinese labor for hundreds of years. He was separated from Lou in January for the first 6 months of the year when he made his fourth trip to Australia, this time to the zinc mines at Broken Hill. He returned to London in July, just 1 day before the birth of his second son, Allan Henry, on July 17.

Hoover now sat on ten mining boards and wrote to President David Starr Jordan of Stanford that he was making about $100,000 per year. On the down side, the profit picture in Victoria was dark. On top of that, Hoover was getting tired of his association with Berwick, Moreing. Moreing thought that the Burma illness was a ruse by Hoover to try to get out of his contract with Berwick, Moreing.

❧☙

FRANKLIN D. ROOSEVELT, 25, dropped out of Columbia Law School without a law degree but later in the year passed the bar exam.

In September he joined a Wall Street law firm, Carter, Ledyard, Milburn. The firm dealt with corporate and admiralty law. John G. Milburn was the senior partner, and it was in his Buffalo home that President William McKinley had died. Roosevelt was a clerk in the firm and received no salary for a year. He wrote to his mother, Sara, that he was now a "full-fledged office boy." His major challenge was to look up things in the library.

Without consulting Eleanor, Sara planned a new living arrangement. She bought a lot at 125 East 36th Street, hired an architect to plan two interconnected houses, one for Franklin and Eleanor and one for her. Each house would be five stories. Sara would have title to both of them.

A son, James, was born on December 23.

ഇൻ

HARRY S TRUMAN, 23, was a farmer in western Missouri. He had very little spare time for reading or playing the piano. His reading consisted mostly of magazines such as *Everybody's* and *Adventure*.

ഇൻ

DWIGHT D. EISENHOWER, 17, was interested in high school athletics in Abilene, Kansas. He made the football team during the first year in which the forward pass was permitted. Abilene was unbeaten, winning seven straight and scoring 127 points to 9 for the opponents. In the spring, Eisenhower also made the baseball team.

1908
Theodore Roosevelt

President Roosevelt struggled with a stubborn Congress in his final year in office, as Speaker of the House Joe Cannon and the conservative caucus was less impressed by the president than the American people were. Roosevelt continued his attacks on those corporate leaders he felt were corrupt. He also declared American expansionism at an end and said the United States did not wish to digest any more territory.

January–February: Congressional debate over the future size of the navy began in January and soon turned into a referendum more on Roosevelt than on how many new battleships were needed. Senator Eugene Hale, head of the Naval Affairs Committee, held an investigation in February airing criticism of the navy. He opposed building more battleships.

Roosevelt was gun-shy about getting involved in the investigation for fear it would develop into a larger debate over the navy and his leadership. He then met with House Democrats who supported his hopes for a bigger navy.

In February the Naval Affairs Committee authorized two new battleships instead of the four that Roosevelt wanted. It also cut the fortification request from $38 million to $15 million but did agree to a base at Pearl Harbor.

April: Roosevelt sent Congress a special message on April 14 saying that a strong Navy was the "surest guaranty and safeguard of peace." The House turned down the request for four battleships, voting 199 to 83. Roosevelt wrote on April 16 that the House showed "an infinite capacity to go wrong." Senator Albert J. Beveridge agreed to lead Roosevelt's fight in the Senate.

There was a heated debate in the Senate, and the key vote on April 27 cut battleship construction from four to two.

May: Roosevelt and Gifford Pinchot, who was head of the forestry division in the Department of Agriculture, decided on a conference of governors to discuss conservation. The White House meeting on May 13 to 15 marked the first time governors were assembled as a group. Out of this meeting came an annual governors' conference on all manner of subjects, although initially Roosevelt hoped that future presidents would call the governors together only rarely.

On May 13, Roosevelt spoke for 50 minutes in the East Room, saying conservation was so important that there had to be plans and not "haphazard" or "piecemeal" efforts. He called conservation "the chief material question that confronts us," second only to "morality."

Pinchot kept a tight hold on the agenda. A resolution called for an inventory of the nation's resources. Roosevelt had warned earlier that the United States could not waste its resources and said Congress could not make resources decisions on its own because of special interests.

The declaration of the governors supported points the president made and received a favorable press. Within a year, forty-one states had formed state conservation commissions.

June: As an outgrowth of the governors' conference, Roosevelt announced on June 8 the establishment of the National Conservation Commission.

Republicans met in Chicago and nominated William Howard Taft for president and James Schoolcraft Sherman of New York for vice president (see **William Howard Taft**, page 444).

August: Roosevelt announced the creation of the federal Country Life Commission on August 10. The new commission would take a look at rural life in America as it existed in the new century.

November: With the support of Roosevelt and the country in good shape, Republicans swept the national elections. Taft defeated William Jennings Bryan, and the Republicans retained control of both houses of Congress (see **William Howard Taft**, page 444).

Former Presidents

GROVER CLEVELAND, in retirement in Princeton, New Jersey, wrote to a friend in March that he hoped John A. Johnson of Minnesota would be the Democratic nominee for president.

Cleveland's health had been poor for several years. He suffered from gastrointestinal disease complicated by a bad heart, kidney ailments, and arthritis. Following a gastritis attack in the spring he was taken to Lakewood, closer to the Atlantic, to recuperate.

He celebrated his seventy-first birthday on March 18 at a hotel in Lakewood. Cleveland was brought back to Princeton by automobile in secrecy; and William Sinclair, the old boss of the White House staff, was brought in to help nurse him. Several gastritis attacks followed.

Cleveland died at his Princeton home at 8:40 A.M. on June 24, probably from coronary thrombosis. He was 71. Cleveland's last words were: "I have tried so hard to do right."

He was buried at Princeton on June 26. Attending his funeral were President Roosevelt, Chief Justice Fuller, six former members of his cabinets, other prominent people, and friends.

Future Presidents

WILLIAM HOWARD TAFT was somewhat bedazzled by his nomination and election as president when for much of his life all he really wanted was a seat on the Supreme Court. Taft was no Roosevelt on the campaign trail, but his good nature helped him with the electorate while his certified conservatism helped him on Wall Street.

January–May: In the preconvention maneuvering, Taft wrote on January 18 to W. R. Nelson, publisher of the *Kansas City Star*, that the South was a problem for any Republican candidate but "[we] cannot afford to ignore the southern vote.... In the past it has been secured too frequently by pure purchase.... Of course I would never stoop to that method."

Frank H. Hitchcock, an assistant postmaster, resigned his position on February 15 to help with Taft's campaign. In May, Hitchcock reported that Taft had 563 delegates lined up ready to vote for him at the upcoming Republican convention.

William Jennings Bryan, the likely Democratic candidate for president, asked Taft on May 25 to join in asking Congress to publish the names of all campaign contributors prior to the election. Taft, however, suggested doing so after the election.

June–July: Taft took the following positions heading into the Republican convention: (1) labor had the right to organize and strike; (2) he was against boycotts and the closed shop; (3) trusts must obey the law, but capitalism should be preserved; (4) a change in the Sherman Anti-Trust Act was needed; and (5) hoarding upset currency reform. He believed in railroad controls and was against socialism and tariff reduction.

The Republican national convention began in Chicago on June 16. The Ohio delegation marched into the hall amid cheers and holding a large portrait of Taft. Nominations began on June 18 with Joseph Cannon, Charles Warren Fairbanks, and Charles Evans Hughes the first to be nominated. Later, Joseph Foraker and Robert LaFollette were nominated.

On the first ballot, Taft received the nomination, earning 702 votes. Far behind were Philander Knox with 68 votes, Hughes with 67 votes, Cannon with 58 votes, and the rest of the votes scattered among several other candidates.

For vice president, Taft favored Senator J. P. Dolliver of Iowa. Senator William E. Borah of Idaho made a plea for Governor A. B. Cummins of Iowa as a gesture toward the new progressives. Taft also approached Hughes. In the end, James "Sunny Jim" Sherman, a New York conservative and friend of Cannon, was nominated. Sherman's choice was a disappointment to Taft.

In the flush of victory at Chicago, Taft told Roosevelt that if elected he would retain the cabinet, and Roosevelt told the cabinet members that they would keep their jobs. In the end, this did not happen.

Taft resigned as secretary of war on June 30 to concentrate on the presidential campaign. He then took a rest at Hot Springs, Virginia.

The Democratic convention was held in Denver in July. Again, William Jennings Bryan dominated the proceedings, and he was nominated on the first ballot. For vice president, John Worth of Indiana was nominated.

In accepting the nomination at Cincinnati on July 28, Taft pointed out that he was the first Republican nominee since Lincoln that had not put his life on the line in battle, and hoped the veterans could overlook this want. He pledged full publicity of his campaign fund sources. New York already had such a law. He also promised a quiet administration after the tumult of the Roosevelt years.

The *Wall Street Journal* said of the Cincinnati speech that Taft was "really mapping out a policy of his own.... His task will be to finish ... work already done by Mr. Roosevelt."

August–December: Roosevelt wanted La Follette to campaign for the party, but Taft wrote to E. J. Hill on August 10 that, "La Follette and Bryan are not very far apart." At one campaign stop, La Follette actually praised Bryan.

Many Republicans felt that Taft was not being tough enough in his campaigning. Taft wrote to E. N. Higgins on August 11, "I am sorry but I cannot be more aggressive than my nature makes me. That is the advantage and the disadvantage of having been on the bench.... If the people don't like that kind of a man, then they have got to take another."

In September, Roosevelt told Taft, "Do not answer Bryan; attack him! Don't let him make the issues."

At first Taft thought he could stay in Cincinnati and not campaign. Beginning in September, he took a tour from Indiana westward to Colorado. People were warm and friendly, but Taft's speeches tended to run for too long.

Taft, 51, spent Election Day, November 3, at his brother Charles P. Taft's mansion in Cincinnati. By midnight it was clear that Taft had won New York and therefore the election. There was a band playing outside the home and the Citizens for Taft Club gathered. He went outside for brief remarks.

Taft received 7,679,006 votes to Bryan's 6,409,106 votes. In the electoral vote, Taft took 321 votes to Bryan's 162 votes.

Taft returned to Hot Springs, Virginia, for another rest after the election. He wrote to H. A. Morrill on December 2, "I pinch myself to make myself realize that it is all true." For the remainder of the year, Taft contemplated cabinet choices.

೩೦೦೩

WOODROW WILSON, 52 in December, flirted with national Democratic politics from the sidelines and made several speeches across the country.

January: Wilson made another trip to Bermuda in January. Mary Peck and her mother were there. On January 26, Wilson wrote to his wife, Ellen, that he had seen Mrs. Peck twice, and "she is very fine ... I know that you would like her so." He walked the beach with Mrs. Peck and told her that politicians were saying he could be elected governor and then president. Wilson wrote to a friend on January 26 that he always returned from Bermuda "more sane about everything."

March–April: As the political conventions approached, Wilson kept suggesting in speeches that his own style of leadership was what was needed. He told the Commercial Club of Chicago on March 14, "The only way you get honest business is from honest men."

On April 14, Wilson addressed the National Democratic Club in an affair William Jennings Bryan did not attend because Jennings would not have been given the lectern. Wilson told the club, "Both political parties [are] in the hands of receivers ... we have lost our principles."

June–August: Wilson traveled to Britain for the summer. Trustees offered to pay for his summer vacation trip, but he declined on the grounds that he might have to oppose some of them on certain issues.

September–November: Wilson talked to the American Bankers Association on September 30 in a speech entitled "The Banker and the Nation." He said that bankers had "lost the ideal of serving the public welfare."

In October, Wilson and Ellen visited Mary Peck in Pittsfield. Over the years, Ellen had encouraged Wilson to meet new women, and he did so and then would write to his wife about them. In a speech at Pittsfield on October 9, Wilson said, "If there is a place where we must adjourn our morals that place should be in what we call private life. It is better to be unfaithful to a few people than to a considerable number of people."

On November 2, the day after Bryan's defeat in the presidential election, Wilson wrote to Mary Peck and said that to combat Bryan, the Democratic Party needed "a man with a cause, not a candidacy." He said he would help to rehabilitate the party.

President-elect William Howard Taft was surprised at his nomination and election in 1908. (Library of Congress)

೩೦೦೩

WARREN G. HARDING, only briefly, was in the contest to replace a bitter, retiring Joseph Foraker as a U.S. Senator from Ohio. The winner was eventually Congressman Theodore Burton.

Initially, Harding editorially backed Foraker for president, then he swung to Taft when he saw that the Foraker cause was hopeless. Harding's switch cooled Foraker toward him.

The *Marion Star* announced on January 22: "Foraker is defeated and Ohio is for Taft!... This is not a bandwagon climb ... it is the calm recording of the trend.... The Buckeye State is for Taft."

೩೦೦೩

CALVIN COOLIDGE finished his second term in the Massachusetts General Court on June 13 and then retired from the political scene, as his Northampton district had a tradition of a two-term limit on public service. Coolidge returned to his law practice and made no secret of his willingness to accept any political office that might need a candidate.

January–June: Coolidge was appointed to the judiciary committee of the general court in January and drafted a bill to prevent injunctions in labor disputes. He was also on the banks and banking committee, where he helped to codify banking laws.

Later Coolidge acted as counsel to argue before the judiciary committee for legislation against undercutting price practices. Coolidge had guided such a bill through the legislature, but it died later in the Massachusetts senate.

A second Coolidge son, Calvin, was born on April 13.

July–December: Back home, Coolidge, 36, resumed the same type of law practice as always, adding a few small corporations, like the Springfield Brewery, to his list of clients.

೩೦೦೩

HERBERT HOOVER, 34, retired from Berwick, Moreing on June 30 after more then 6 years with the London mining and engineering firm. On leaving he was forced to sign a restrictive covenant that aimed to prevent him from becoming competitive with Berwick, Moreing while on any mining company operation within the British Empire for 10 years.

Now a free man for the first time since graduating from Stanford, the wealthy Hoover decided to concentrate on mining for profit rather than mine management. Earlier the Zinc Corporation in Victoria had become a highly successful venture. At the end of the year, the Hoovers, traveling separately on different ships, departed London for Monterey. Hoover was aboard the *Lusitania*.

Hoover leased an eight-room, two-story house at Campden Hill in Kensington called the Red House. But he opened an office in the same building where Berwick, Moreing was located.

Stanford wanted Hoover on its board of trustees, but Hoover told them he would be restricted to London for another year.

𝕊ℂ

FRANKLIN D. ROOSEVELT, 26, was a small cases lawyer in a big cases New York City firm, but his prospects were good. He often worked on municipal suits in which common people sued corporate giants that Roosevelt had to defend.

As at times FDR seemed bored with student life at Harvard, he now he seemed bored with the law. But he certainly had big dreams. One of the firm's clerks, Grenville Clark, later told how Roosevelt told several clerks, while sitting around, that eventually he would enter politics and become president of the United States. He said he would follow Theodore Roosevelt's path: the assembly in Albany, assistant secretary of the navy, and governor of New York.

While Roosevelt dreamed of the future, Eleanor wept over her present status, second fiddle to Franklin's mother, Sara. Sara never consulted her daughter-in-law about any family decisions, and FDR seemed to have no problem with his mother dominating the scene. He told the agitated Eleanor once that she was the victim of temporary insanity to complain so loudly.

Part of Eleanor's problem concerned son James's poor health during the spring. The child nearly died of pneumonia, and his recovery was slow.

𝕊ℂ

HARRY S TRUMAN, 24, was a farmer in Grandview, Missouri.

𝕊ℂ

DWIGHT D. EISENHOWER, 18, became president of the newly formed Abilene High School Athletic Association that aimed to get better football uniforms for the Kansas school. The junior played end and weighed 140 pounds.

Eisenhower was a good student, getting A's in English, history, and geometry. His grades were lower in algebra, geography, and German.

𝕊ℂ

LYNDON BAINES JOHNSON was born on the morning of August 27 in a three-bedroom farmhouse on the Pedernales River between Stonewall and Johnson City, Texas, in the hill country 40 miles west of Austin. His father was Sam Ealy Johnson Jr., 29; his mother was Rebekah Baines Johnson, 26. Lyndon was their first child and was nameless for 3 months. He finally was named after W. C. Linden, a family friend and lawyer. Rebekah selected the name and changed the spelling.

Sam Johnson was born in Buda, Texas, 20 miles south of Austin. A high school graduate, he taught school in Sandy and Hye, Texas, between 1896 and 1898, then turned to farming. Sam was elected to the Texas house in 1904 at the age of

27 and reelected the next year. He decided against a third term in 1908 and went into real estate.

Rebekah was born in McKinney, Texas, and raised in Blanco. Her father was an attorney. She worked her way through Baylor as a journalism major. Her grandfather, the Reverend George Washington Baines, was president of Baylor University during the Civil War.

Rebekah interviewed Sam in 1907 in connection with her schoolwork. She said that a "whirlwind courtship" followed, and he escorted her to hear William Jennings Bryan. The two married on August 20, 1907.

Great-great grandfather John Johnson lived in Oglethorpe County, Georgia, and was a veteran of the Revolutionary War. Great-grandfather Jesse Johnson moved to Lockhart, Texas, in 1846, and soon owned 332 acres. Grandfather Sam Ealy Johnson Sr. was a cattleman and Confederate veteran. He founded Johnson City, Texas, and built a ranch along the river. Grandfather Joseph W. Baines, a Confederate veteran, was a lawyer, publisher, member of the Texas house from 1903 to 1905 and Texas secretary of state from 1883 to 1887.

1909
Theodore Roosevelt

President Roosevelt was an executive whirlwind during his final days in the White House. He then did what no predecessor would have considered: He traveled to Africa to shoot lions, a hippo, and other game. In the last 2 months of his term, he pulled the army out of Cuba, welcomed the "Great White Fleet" back home from the oceans, bickered with Congress over numerous issues, proposed a National Archives, and again chastised California for its racist treatment of Japanese immigrants.

January–March: Roosevelt vetoed several bills in his last weeks as president, including a Census Bureau bill that would have given Congress 4,000 patronage plums. The *San Francisco Bulletin* said, "When Roosevelt attacks Congress the people feel that he is making their fight."

The California legislature on February 4 approved school segregation for Japanese students. Roosevelt called this "the most offensive bill of all" and wrote to the speaker of the California Assembly, "This school bill accomplishes literally nothing." The assembly then reconsidered and voted it down on February 10. Roosevelt wrote to his son Ted Jr., "I think I have won out as regard the Japanese–California trouble."

The "Great White Fleet" returned to Hampton Roads and Norfolk, Virginia, on February 22. Roosevelt viewed the naval parade from the yacht *Mayflower*. He told an admiral, "Isn't it magnificent? Nobody after this will forget that the American coast is on the Pacific as well as on the Atlantic."

Roosevelt's last words for Taft, who spent March 3 in the White House, were, "Everything will surely turn out all right, old man." The inaugural ceremony the next day was the first held indoors since Madison's first inaugural (see **William Howard Taft**, opposite column).

When Roosevelt left Washington, he shook hands on the train going to Jersey City, and it wasn't until 1:30 A.M. that he reached Oyster Bay, where several hundred people waited at the station to greet him.

Roosevelt left for Africa aboard the ship *Hamburg* on March 23 and reached the Azores on March 30. Edith Roosevelt did not travel to Africa with her husband, but son Kermit, 20, a freshman at Harvard, made the trip. Roosevelt agreed to receive $50,000 from *Scribner's* magazine in exchange for writing about his adventures in Africa.

April–December: Roosevelt arrived in Gibraltar on April 3 and Naples on April 5. From there, the traveling party went on to Africa. The ship docked at Mombasa in a downpour on April 21. The next day Roosevelt and company started inland on a British railroad. Their first camp was set in the Kapiti Plains.

Going eastward from the Kapiti Plains on April 24, the party saw zebra, wildebeest, hartebeest, gazelles, and many antelope. By the end of April, Roosevelt had shot his first lion at a range of 60 yards. Within 3 days Roosevelt had shot four lions. The natives would strip the meat and sort the bones.

First Lady Helen "Nellie" Taft *(Library of Congress)*

At the end of each day, Roosevelt would write for *Scribner's*. The magazine did little editing and ran his articles as they arrived. By June 1, Roosevelt had finished six articles of 5,000 to 15,000 words that the magazine ran between October 1909 and September 1910.

A 60-mile safari through the desert south of Nairobi in early June brought the party to Sotik on the border with German East Africa. There were many kills over the next 5 weeks. Evenings were cool, and the group would sit around the fire while Kermit played the mandolin.

From Sotik the party moved north to Lake Nairasha. Most of August was spent hunting elephant near Mt. Kenya, a peak of 17,000 feet, about 80 miles north of Nairobi.

Another American hunter, Carl Akeley, joined up with Roosevelt near Mt. Elgon so they could go elephant hunting together.

Roosevelt turned 51 while in the wild. On December 18 the small party took a railroad to Lake Victoria and then a steamer from Kisumu to Entebbe.

∞CR

WILLIAM HOWARD TAFT entered the White House in the shadow of Theodore Roosevelt, one of the most energetic presidents in history. Before the inauguration, Taft confessed to Roosevelt a sense of hesitancy and doubt about the job ahead. His wife, Nellie, suffered a cerebral hemorrhage while aboard a yacht on the Potomac, and Taft had to teach her how to speak again. Mrs. Taft kept her illness a secret from the public. She made almost a complete recovery by 1911, although some people thought she was never quite the same again.

March: The inauguration on March 4 was marred by a blizzard, forcing the oath of office to be administered indoors in the Senate Chamber. Chief Justice Melville Fuller administered the oath. Most of the inaugural parade was disbanded because of the blizzard.

Within a few days of the inaugural, the new cabinet was in place. Only Secretary of Agriculture James Wilson continued on from the Roosevelt administration. Other appointments included Philander Knox of Pennsylvania as secretary of state, Franklin MacVeagh of Illinois as secretary of Treasury, Jacob McGavock Dickinson of Tennessee as secretary of war, George Wickersham of New York as attorney general, Frank Hitchcock of Massachusetts as postmaster general, George von Lengerke Meyer of Massachusetts as secretary of the navy, Richard Ballinger of Washington as secretary of the Interior, and Charles Nagel of Missouri as secretary of commerce and labor.

April: Taft's first battle in Congress had to do with a new tariff bill. Roosevelt had avoided the tariff conflict but Taft was willing to explore new tariff options. The Dingley Tariff Act, which had set tariffs to their highest levels in U.S. history, had been the law for 12 years. Congress wrestled with a formula on what goods cost to produce in order to establish a tariff schedule. Taft was willing to consider a cut in tariffs, which the House favored in a bill passed in early April. But on the Senate floor, Senators Nelson Aldrich and Henry Cabot Lodge said that the Senate had no obligation to slash tariffs.

When the Senate took out the House cuts, Taft was unable and unwilling to make a fight of it. The Payne–Aldrich Act passed the Senate, and Taft signed it on April 9. The new act raised tariffs significantly over the previous levels found in the Dingley Tariff Act. One newspaper editor called the Payne–Aldrich Act the "most thoroughly high-protection measure that has ever been enacted in this country or in any other land."

July 12: Congress passed the Sixteenth Amendment to the Constitution, giving the federal government income tax power. The amendment was passed on to the states for ratification.

August: The government bought its first airplane on August 2, paying the Wright brothers $25,000 for it.

November: A rebellion in Nicaragua against President José Santos Zelaya forced Taft to send American troops to that country to protect American citizens there. Having already provided financial support to the rebels, upon hearing reports that Zelaya had executed 500 rebels, including 2 Americans, Taft decided to send troops to rebel strongholds in the city of Miskito. Miskito was one of Nicaragua's business centers, and many American companies were operating there.

Future Presidents

WOODROW WILSON, 53 in December, grew bitter, tired, and irritated by a lengthy struggle with Princeton school trustees over the proposed location of the graduate school. Wilson sensed board members no longer accepted his leadership. Much of his emotional turmoil was released through his letters to Mrs. Mary Hulbert Peck. Meanwhile publisher George Harvey was nonstop in his praise of Wilson, and Harvey's *Harper's Weekly* predicted that Wilson would be elected governor of New Jersey in 1910 and president of the United States in 1912.

February: Princeton's trustees met in New York on February 5 and criticized Dean West's graduate school plans as a "great big upper class club." The graduate school battle left Wilson drained by the bickering and tensions.

April–June: West announced in the spring that William C. Procter, the soap magnate, would put $500,000 into the graduate school if the site was other than Prospect, Wilson's home, and if other donors matched his funds. Wilson was cautious. Wilson, West, and Procter met in June, and the new golf course became a potential site for the project.

October: The trustees rejected a central campus location for the graduate school but accepted Procter's gift. Wilson was bitter about the victory by "that arch-intriguer West," coming as it did after Wilson's defeat in the quadrangle matter.

Wilson wrote to Mrs. Peck on October 24, "Twice, on two questions as important as can arise in my administration, they have refused to follow my leadership because money talked louder than I did. I am too angry … too disgusted, to think straight."

        ∞○∞

WARREN G. HARDING and Florence went to Europe with the Phillipses, a trip that Carrie Phillips had been encouraging for some time. Carrie was enamored with Germany and wanted to experience living there. The lovers managed to be discreet throughout. The four traveled from February to April. The voyage was possible because Harding was out of Ohio politics, the *Marion Star* was running smoothly, and he had the money, as did Jim Phillips.

        ∞○∞

CALVIN COOLIDGE, now 37, in the fall was elected mayor of Northampton, Massachusetts, by 187 votes in a friendly contest with his Democratic opponent.

In June, Coolidge's law practice led to his attending a corporate meeting in Phoenix, Arizona, his first trip west of Massachusetts.

        ∞○∞

HERBERT HOOVER, 35, opened an office on Broadway, took the Trans-Siberian Railroad to Korea, and attended the inauguration of President Taft. Hoover made a new friend in New York, A. Chester Beatty, both a mining engineer and a wealthy financier, and the two men quickly undertook numerous deals together. They jumped into Russia, first with a gigantic mining property in the southern Urals, then into wildcat oil on the Black Sea.

Hoover was in New York City twice during the year, the first time to repeat at Columbia a series of lectures on mine evaluation and administration given first at Stanford. The second stop put him in business at 71 Broadway.

After sailing from New York to London, Hoover had only 9 days before he was off to Korea, where eventually he sailed on a junk on the Yalu River. In London, Hoover entertained often, and dinner guests included Joseph Conrad and H. G. Wells.

        ∞○∞

FRANKLIN D. ROOSEVELT's son Franklin D. Roosevelt Jr. was born on March 18, but died 7 months later on November 8. The baby was at Hyde Park when he came down with the flu and was moved to an intensive care unit in New York City. Eleanor fought moods of guilt for leaving the baby with nannies, nannies hired by Roosevelt's mother. Roosevelt, 27, was always hands off in child raising.

        ∞○∞

HARRY S TRUMAN, 25, was farming in Missouri. He was admitted to the Belton Masonic Lodge on January 30, and 9 months later was made a deacon in the lodge.

        ∞○∞

DWIGHT D. EISENHOWER, 19, flipped a coin with his brother Edgar to see who would go to college first. There wasn't money for both to go. Edgar won the toss and entered the University of Michigan on the recommendation of an Abilene, Kansas, high school teacher who was a graduate.

As a result of the coin-flip deal, Dwight worked for a year at the creamery as night foreman, doing heavy work such as pulling a 300-pound block of ice out of a tank using pulleys. He often put in 84-hour weeks. Eventually he sent $200 from his earnings to his brother in Ann Arbor.

After a year, the deal was that they would switch, with Edgar working at the creamery.

In addition to doing well in history and math in high school, Dwight went on stage to give a speech critical of the Republican Party.

৪৩

LYNDON B. JOHNSON's father, Sam, thought his 6-month old baby was photogenic. He brought in a professional to take a picture, then ordered fifty prints to send to friends.

1910
William Howard Taft

President Taft and Theodore Roosevelt split over the direction they wanted the Republican Party to go, and Democratic victories in the November election were sobering to both men. Taft was convinced that Roosevelt had become radical and had lost touch with the Constitution. Taft's firing of Gifford Pinchot over a conservation issue had signaled the breakup of the Taft–Roosevelt friendship. As Taft drifted toward the conservative power base in Congress, the Progressives rallied around Roosevelt as their savior.

January: Taft fired U.S. Forest Service head Gifford Pinchot on January 7. In 1909, Pinchot had accused Secretary of the Interior Richard Ballinger with unfairly selling public lands to J. P. Morgan. Congress conducted an investigation and found the allegations without merit. Taft, who regarded Pinchot as a "radical and a crank," used this opportunity to fire Pinchot. Many saw Taft's action as a sign that he was in the pocket of big business. *Louisville Courier-Journal* editor Henry Watterson showed hostility to the president on January 22 by noting that the firing of Pinchot meant "For the first time in the history of the country [the] President … has openly proclaimed himself the friend of thieves."

April–May: Taft had old Cincinnati friends in for dinner at the White House in early April and said he thought Roosevelt would seek the nomination in 1912 and would "most certainly be elected."

Charles Evans Hughes was appointed to the Supreme Court on May 2.

U.S. Forest Service Chief Gifford Pinchot was fired by Taft in 1910. (Library of Congress)

Taft discussed his victories and defeats since taking charge in 1909 in a letter to Roosevelt on May 26. Taft said he had "had a hard time … thus far I have succeeded far less than have others trying to carry out your policies." He also told of his wife's continued struggles after her stroke the previous year.

June: Taft wrote Lyman Abbott on June 7 about Roosevelt's movements in Europe: "[He] has been a royal progress in courtesy … not been equaled since Grant made his tour." Meeting European leaders, Taft wrote, would make Roosevelt "more valuable to his country as a statesman."

On June 14, Taft wrote a letter to Roosevelt inviting him to the White House, adding that GOP chances for November now looked better. Roosevelt wrote to Taft saying it would be unwise for a former president to go to either Washington or the White House, even though former presidents had been returning to the capital for years.

On June 25, Taft signed the Mann Act into law. The new law, similar to bills that Roosevelt had championed during his presidency, barred the transportation of women across state lines for immoral purposes.

Taft was resting at his retreat in Beverly, Massachusetts, on June 30 when Roosevelt made a visit, bringing along Henry Cabot Lodge. Taft, exuberant, greeted Roosevelt warmly, "Ah, Theodore, it is good to see you." They exchanged small talk and the two were never alone. Both seemed to want it this way.

July–August: Taft spent a restless summer at Beverly. Playing golf with Henry C. Frick, the steel magnate, who lived at nearby Pride's Crossing, angered Republican insurgents. Taft also had a secret meeting with J. P. Morgan. Taft was now rapidly becoming alienated from Roosevelt, Robert La Follette, and the followers of William Jennings Bryan.

In August, Taft wrote that Republicans had to win the fall election, and that "differences should be forgotten." He warned that a Democratic majority in the House would reject protectionism.

Taft wrote to W. D. Bradley on August 10 about Roosevelt seeking the 1912 nomination: "I know nothing about [Roosevelt's plans.] I don't understand his conduct."

December: Two new members were appointed to the Supreme Court. On December 16, Willis Van Devanter was appointed to the Court, and on December 17, Joseph Rucker Lamar was appointed. On December 19, Associate Justice Edward Douglas White was elevated to Chief Justice of the Supreme Court.

Former Presidents

THEODORE ROOSEVELT ended his African adventure by sailing north on the Nile to Cairo, later meeting the crowned heads of Europe and vowing to keep out of political affairs at home—a vow he would soon break. He twice met with Taft, but the jollity of old was fleeting or largely missing as the two friends drifted apart politically.

January–June: Roosevelt continued with his African hunting trip into the new year, but still managed to keep up with the political happenings back in the United States. Roosevelt was especially upset about the firing of Gifford Pinchot. After Pinchot was fired, thirty newspapers in January suggested that Roosevelt seek the 1912 Republican nomination.

Roosevelt's final hunting scorecard in Africa was impressive: 296 animals killed, among them 9 lions, 8 elephants, 13 rhinos, 7 hippos, 6 buffaloes, 15 zebras, and 28 gazelles.

Before returning home, Roosevelt represented the United States at the funeral of Britain's Edward VII in May.

While in London, Roosevelt met with Elihu Root. Roosevelt said he had resolved to stay clear of any conflict with Taft. Yet, he told Pinchot: "It is a very ungracious thing for an ex-President to criticize his successor and yet I cannot as an honest man cease to battle for the principles for which you and I ... and the rest of our close associates stood."

A few weeks before returning to the United States, Roosevelt wrote to Lodge from Norway, saying, "Ugh! I do dread getting back to America, and having to plunge into this cauldron of politics."

When Roosevelt's ship docked in New York City on June 18, Roosevelt was greeted by about 2,500 people, including congressmen, senators, governors, and—keeping in the background—Franklin D. and Eleanor Roosevelt. Cornelius Vanderbilt, aboard the cutter *Manhattan*, headed the welcoming committee. Jacob Riis was there as were the Roosevelt boys, Ted, Archie, and Quentin. A parade up Broadway and

Former president Theodore Roosevelt, with hand outstretched, walks with New York City mayor William Gaynor (left) and Cornelius Vanderbilt during the parade welcoming Roosevelt back from his African hunting trip in 1910. (Library of Congress)

Fifth Avenue followed with Rough Riders escorting fourteen carriages. The crowd was estimated at 1 million.

Earlier at Battery Park, Roosevelt addressed about 100,000 in a brief speech in which he said was "eager to do my part" in solving the country's problems. "I am more glad than I can say to be back in my own country, back among the people I love.... I want to close up like a native oyster," he said.

Roosevelt met with Taft at the latter's retreat in Beverly, Massachusetts, on June 30. The two made small talk, with Roosevelt relating hunting stories. Outside the house waited 200 reporters, all hoping for words from both men.

August 31: Roosevelt dedicated John Brown Memorial Park in Oswatomie, Kansas. He carefully planned his Osawatomie speech, which was very political in nature. He said, "When I say that I am for the square deal, I mean not merely that I stand for fair play, under the present rules of the game, but that I stand for having those rules changed so as to work for a more substantial equality of opportunity."

September–November: Roosevelt campaigned hard for the Republican ticket for most of the fall, covering sixteen states and 5,000 miles. When the Democrats won in Congress, he was disconsolate.

Future Presidents

WOODROW WILSON, 54 in December, was elected governor of New Jersey in a very unorthodox switch in occupation. Political insiders believed Trenton was but a temporary stop en route to White House.

January–May: In January, longtime Wilson champion, publisher George Harvey, visited Princeton and told Wilson that he would receive the nomination for governor of New Jersey without lifting a finger.

Wilson was in Bermuda on February 12 when he wrote to his wife, "It would be rather jolly ... to start out on life anew together, to make a new career, would it not?" Ellen was all for rolling the political dice.

In March, Wilson wrote an article for George Harvey's magazine claiming that Roosevelt showed a distrust of "managing politicians." On March 29 he spoke to the Democratic Dollar Dinner in Elizabeth, New Jersey, but talked mostly in platitudes.

In April he advised Pennsylvania Democrats on what political stands to take, particularly with regard to the tariff. Then South Carolina Democrats asked him to write them a platform.

In a speech given to Princeton alumni in Pittsburgh, Wilson declared: "I believe that the churches of this country, at any rate the Protestant church, have dissociated themselves from the people of this country. They are serving the classes and they are not serving the masses." His conclusion: "If she loses her self possession, Americans will stagger like France through fields of blood before she again finds peace and prosperity under the leadership of men who understand her needs." Pittsburgh alumni were shocked at the speech and perhaps surprised by heavy press coverage. Wilson tried to soften the damage in a letter to the *New York Evening Post.*

In May, Wilson-for-governor backers organized a dinner at Elizabeth, where he refused to announce his intentions amid shouts, "Our next governor!" In an eloquent speech, he accused the Republicans of being aligned with vested interests.

June–August: By June, New Jersey political boss James Smith Jr. wanted to be sure Wilson was running. Smith and other leading Democrats went to Prospect to meet Wilson, but the president of Princeton didn't commit either way.

Wilson dined at Harvey's home in Deal, New Jersey, on June 26, and the governorship was offered as a step toward obtaining the 1912 presidential nomination. Wilson was given a week to think it over.

Wilson held off on a decision until early July. He met with Harvey and other New Jersey Democrats at the Lawyers' Club in New York. Wilson agreed not to dismantle the state machine, but otherwise he wanted no strings attached to his nomination. He then notified Princeton trustees of his decision and thanked them for their support over the years. He wrote, "I have all my life been preaching the duty of educated men to accept just such opportunities."

At Harvey's suggestion, Wilson went into seclusion at Old Griswold Place in Old Lyme, Connecticut. Harvey wrote to Wilson on August 12, advising him to keep silent: "The situation is well in hand. There are no breaches in the walls."

September: The New Jersey state Democratic convention was scheduled for Trenton on September 15, and Harvey wrote to Wilson on September 9 that there would be only one ballot. Therefore Wilson played golf that day. But the convention did not go smoothly, with Judge John W. Wescott, a Progressive, shouting against a "bargain sale and double cross." Forty Princeton men were seated on the stage and broke into a football cheer. Wescott bolted from the hall after the vote went for Wilson, who was then brought on stage for a speech. He was still wearing his golfing clothes.

November: Wilson defeated his Republican opponent, George Record, to become governor of New Jersey.

୫୦୯ଧ

WARREN G. HARDING, candidate for governor of Ohio, was defeated in a landslide by the Democratic incumbent Judson Harmon. Between January and the Republican nominating convention in June, Harding made 300 speeches around the state. He was well known, and the Chautauqua circuit experience helped boost his name recognition.

January: Five counties in Ohio endorsed Harding for gov-

ernor, and postcards were printed with his picture. Harding wrote to his sister Carolyn, traveling to Ohio from Burma on January 22, that he was busy writing speeches, the "penalty of trying to be in politics."

May: Harding's mother, Phoebe, died on May 20, a month before Harding's nomination.

June–July: With the support of Cincinnati's political boss, George B. Cox, Harding won the Republican nomination in June over Nicholas Longworth in a close contest. President Taft then endorsed Harding. Harding and Jim Phillips drove to Taft's summer retreat in Beverly, Massachusetts, in July to meet with the president.

Gossip now surfaced in Marion because Harding often was seen going to the Phillips house. Carrie Phillips asked him if he was prepared to leave Flossie and marry her. Otherwise she intended to leave Jim and move to Germany. Adding to this mix, possibly, was a high school girl, Nan Britton, 14, whose crush on Harding caused her father to warn the handsome politician and publisher about this strange situation. (Several Harding biographers call the Britton rumors false.)

November: On the eve of the voting, the Grand Opera House in Marion was filled to hear Harding. He denied that political bosses "put him over," and said that his only boss was his wife, Florence.

On election night, Democrat Judson Harmon won in a landslide by a margin of more than 100,000 votes. The Democrats also took over the state assembly. After the election, Harding, 45, wrote a friend that he was "serene and happy. [Now I] can go ahead and do other things which pleases me more." In the *Marion Star*, he wrote of his regret and the "debt of gratitude" that he owed friends.

୫୦୯ଧ

CALVIN COOLIDGE, 38, was reelected mayor of Northampton, Massachusetts, in November. Earlier in the year, his father, John Coolidge, had been elected to the Vermont state senate. In two terms as mayor, Coolidge increased teacher pay and made changes in the police and fire departments. Sidewalks and streets were improved and a beautification program started. He stepped in to stop an electric lighting contract under which the city would lose money. Coolidge also avoided scandal and strengthened his influence over the city's Republican organization.

Coolidge wrote to his father on June 25, "You will find the senate interesting, if not very profitable." Calvin said his sons were "pleased" to know that their grandfather would be in the Vermont senate.

୫୦୯ଧ

HERBERT HOOVER, 36, the eager mining engineer in London, with his friend A. Chester Beatty, put together endless mine combines and holding companies in elaborate financial packages. To put together financing for a mine deal in the Urals, Hoover talked to sixty financiers. He and Beatty now had a finger in mining operations in Korea, Nicaragua, Newfoundland, Siberia, the United States (California), Peru, Japan, Rumania, Burma, Madagascar, and Russia. Hoover also was thinking about the Klondike.

A friend, Scott Turner, later said, "That's the way he made his money—to get in quick enough" before a property came to the attention of the stock market and the public. Hoover was building a small staff, mostly American, and including old friends such as John Agnew and later Dean P. Mitchell. The Zinc Corporation, which Hoover had created at Broken Hill in Victoria, Australia, was a huge success and one of Hoover's greatest achievements.

Hoover remained a very patriotic American despite years in London. He wrote to one friend that he sympathized with Republican Progressives. At a railroad station in Russia, Hoover saw "a long line of intelligent, decent people brutally chained together," waiting to be shipped to Siberia. The scene was to give him nightmares. But Hoover wrote that American engineers got along well with the "progressive elements in the Czar's government."

℘ℂℛ

FRANKLIN D. ROOSEVELT, 28, in a surprise move ran for and won a seat in New York's senate in Albany. FDR and Eleanor were aboard the committee boat in New York Harbor to greet Theodore Roosevelt on his return from Europe and Africa on June 18. But once FDR considered his first political run, he worried about how Theodore Roosevelt would react. Theodore answered, "Franklin ought to go into politics without the least regard as to where I speak or don't speak." He added that FDR was "a fine fellow" and regretted he was not a Republican.

September: FDR's plunge into politics came about through the encouragement of Poughkeepsie District Attorney John E. Mack. He saw potential in a man with the name Roosevelt, as well as Franklin's wealth, good looks, and interest in public service. Mack went to New York City and asked FDR if he would like to make a run for a senate seat in Albany. Roosevelt's mother was opposed to the idea, but Franklin said he was interested.

Another son, Elliott, was born on September 23.

October–November: Franklin made his first political speech on October 6 at the Democratic Party nominating convention in Poughkeepsie, New York: "As you know, I accept this nomination with absolute independence. I am pledged to no man … no special interest."

In the campaign, FDR rented a red Maxwell and a driver to take him around the district, as his campaign was late in getting started. This had never been done in the district before.

Eleanor, busy following the birth of Elliott, could be of no help and viewed her husband as "high strung and nervous."

Roosevelt won in the November election by a vote of 15,708 to 14,568 for the Republican candidate.

℘ℂℛ

HARRY S TRUMAN, 26, the farmer in Missouri, began his courtship of Bess Wallace in December. Harry was visiting his cousins, the Nolands, on North Delaware Street in Independence, when Bess's mother sent over a cake to the Nolands across the street. Harry later grabbed the empty plate and took it back to the Wallace home. Bess answered the door. Harry had not kept in touch with her since their high school days.

Truman squeezed in a trip to Texas and New Mexico, as he was interested in land speculation. His National Guard service included trips to Fort Riley, Kansas, and Wisconsin. The family occasionally took the train from Grandview to Kansas City for shopping and entertainment. Truman spent $25 on a set of books by Mark Twain.

℘ℂℛ

DWIGHT D. EISENHOWER, 20, studied for the examination that would gain him entrance to West Point. He had pressed his U.S. senator for a chance to take the exam. The Eisenhower family could not afford to finance a college education for any of the boys, and the coin-flip arrangement with Eisenhower's brother Edgar was going to take too long for both of them to complete a four-year course. Eisenhower at first actually preferred the Naval Academy at Annapolis.

Dwight took the train to Topeka, Kansas, where he took the test for both military academies along with seven other candidates. Four young men were interested only in West Point, but Eisenhower joined the other two in expressing no preference. Eisenhower scored 87 out of 100, close to the highest. He ranked number 1 for Annapolis and number 2 for West Point. Senator J. L. Bristow then wrote to Eisenhower, saying that the man who scored the highest for West Point could not go. Eisenhower never learned why.

Now the track was cleared for Eisenhower to take the special examination for West Point the following January, and if he passed he would be Bristow's choice. Eisenhower decided that the way to prepare for future examinations was to enroll at Abilene High and study algebra, history, and English. As a "grad" he also played football, because there was a shortage of players.

℘ℂℛ

LYNDON B. JOHNSON, 2, liked to run away and hide so his mother, Rebekah, would have to hunt for him. The older he got, the farther he would wander. The Johnsons lived in the Texas Hill Country west of Austin.

1911
William Howard Taft

President Taft, in his third year in office traveled widely to talk about world peace but felt the general hostility to his administration on both coasts. Taft's effort to bring international disputes to arbitration received backing in Great Britain and France, joyful support from Andrew Carnegie, and cold water from Theodore Roosevelt. Meanwhile, Wall Street did not like the Justice Department's forceful anti-trust policy. On top of that, the Supreme Court ruled in favor of the breakup of gigantic Standard Oil.

January: Citing ill health, Secretary of the Interior Richard Ballinger submitted his resignation to Taft. The president asked Ballinger to remain in office for a few more weeks.

March: Ballinger resigned on March 5, and Walter Lowrie Fisher of Illinois replaced him as secretary of the Interior on March 7.

A revolution in Mexico caused Taft to order mobilization and send forces to the border as a few stray bullets killed two Americans and wounded twelve in Douglas, Arizona. On March 7, Taft ordered 20,000 U.S. troops to the Mexican border to protect American interests.

May–June: The Supreme Court decision that Standard Oil was a monopoly came down on May 15. Justice John Marshall Harlan was the only dissenter, although he acknowledged the oil giant's illegal acts. Chief Justice Edward White read the 20,000-word opinion.

Taft wrote to his wife the next day that it was a "good opinion—the Standard Oil Company will have to dissolve."

Two weeks later the Supreme Court gave a decision in the American Tobacco Company case, forcing the company to split into fourteen different companies. As with Standard Oil, restraint of trade was involved. Taft also agreed with this decision.

The *New York World* said that Attorney General George Wickersham would pursue another hundred corporations for violating the Sherman Anti-Trust Act and that guilty offenders would go to jail. Wickersham had included United States Steel in his remarks but later told Taft his quotes as published were "somewhat inaccurate," and besides, he didn't think he was speaking for publication. But Taft said that every corporation violating the law would "be brought into court."

July–August: Earlier in the year, Theodore Roosevelt had written an article for *Outlook*, in which he said that he doubted if arbitration would settle disputes between nations. However, Taft felt differently and sought to work out arbitration agreements with Great Britain, France, and Germany.

Secretary of State Philander Knox worked out treaties with Great Britain and France, but Germany dropped out of negotiations. Taft signed the measures on August 3. Andrew

Attorney General George Wickersham pursued corporations for violating the Sherman Anti-Trust Act. (Library of Congress)

Carnegie wrote to Taft on August 4 from his castle in Scotland: "You have reached the summit of human glory," he said. "Countless ages are to honor and bless your name." Taft thanked him profusely the next day.

The Senate, however, objected to many clauses in the treaty, especially the third clause, which called for a six-man Joint High Commission from each nation to decide whether questions should go to arbitration. It would take a 5-to-1 vote to send a matter to arbitration at The Hague.

September–October: Because the Senate was raising so many issues over the arbitration treaty, Taft decided to take the matter to the people. Taft's fall trip took 49 days, and he traveled from Wisconsin to Washington and gave 306 speeches in 115 cities.

At Marquette, Michigan, Taft said the War of 1812, Mexican War, and Spanish-American War could have been "settled without a fight and ought to have been." Taft avoided ever mentioning Roosevelt, although he knew Roosevelt would take offense at the president's opinions on the Spanish-American War. The president wrote to a friend on September 10, "The truth is that he [Roosevelt] believes in war and wishes to be a Napoleon and die on the battlefield."

At the University of Idaho on October 7, Taft said international peace was a possibility and told how dueling among individuals had stopped. War was no more rational than dueling, he said.

Former Presidents

THEODORE ROOSEVELT wavered all year on whether or not to seek the presidency in 1912. Roosevelt's uncertainty played havoc with Robert La Follette's plans to run as the champion of the Progressives.

January: When the National Progressive Republican League was formed in January, Roosevelt endorsed its objectives in an article in *Outlook*, but he didn't wish to participate because the obvious purpose of the group was to back La Follette for the 1912 race. Charter members included the Pinchot brothers, Gifford and Amos, and Editor William Allen White. Senator Jonathan Bourne of Oregon, president of the league, said that the 1912 race would be between La Follette and Wilson.

March–May: Using the *Outlook* as his sounding board, Roosevelt in the spring took several strong stands against President Taft's policies. Roosevelt attacked Taft's idea of an arbitration treaty with Great

Britain, France, and Germany as being anti-nationalist and contrary to national interest and independence. Roosevelt gave the Decoration Day speech at Grant's tomb on May 30 and used the occasion to oppose the arbitration treaties and those "mollycoddles" seeking "unrighteous peace."

June: When a newspaper reported on June 6 that Roosevelt endorsed Taft's renomination, Roosevelt issued a denial. He said he was not a candidate himself for 1912 and would not support any other man. La Follette immediately declared his own candidacy, which made Taft think that Roosevelt would back La Follette.

Roosevelt met Taft in Baltimore on June 6 at a function for Cardinal James Gibbons. And later Roosevelt sent the Tafts a silver wedding anniversary gift. Taft sent a thank-you note on June 18, but after that there were no more letters between the two.

September–December: Roosevelt assailed the arbitration treaty with Great Britain and France in the September 9 *Outlook*, calling it a "sham." He later claimed his break with Taft came over the arbitration policy.

When the Progressive League endorsed Robert La Follette in October, Roosevelt wrote that he expected his friends to do everything "to prevent any movement looking toward my nomination." Two emissaries from La Follette tried to get Roosevelt to say he would not run, and La Follette considered but rejected, writing a public letter to force Roosevelt to respond.

On October 27, Roosevelt indicated to Governor Hiram Johnson of California that he might run in 1912 but added that he would be a "weak" candidate in the East. Yet Roosevelt seemed to encourage those then starting a "Roosevelt for President" movement.

In a December article in *Outlook*, Roosevelt discussed why there was such a "strong undercurrent to come to the surface in the shape of talk about my nomination for President." Much of this had to do with a general disappointment in Taft's presidency.

Future Presidents

Woodrow Wilson, 55 in December, pushed an impressive menu of legislation at the statehouse in Trenton, then took a tour of the West Coast and South to show off his "presidential" style and possibilities. There was little doubt from the time of Wilson's inauguration as New Jersey's governor in January that his campaign to capture the Democratic presidential nomination in 1912 was underway. Wilson met with William Jennings Bryan and received his important support in a sort of "Christian" bonding. Wilson also picked up a new confidant and adviser in "Colonel" Edward House.

Wilson began the year in combat with New Jersey Democratic "Boss" James Smith. In a speech on January 5 in Jersey City, Wilson damned the machine politics of Smith. He said that the bosses had been "trashed" in the recent election and asked Martine, winner of the most votes for a U.S. Senate seat, upon the stage and told him never to withdraw in the face of Smith's maneuvers to have someone else appointed to the Senate. Wilson's pitch for Martine sounded like an evangelical sermon.

Wilson was inaugurated on January 17 in Trenton. Four horses pulled Wilson's landau from the statehouse to the opera house. After "Hail to the Chief" and a seventeen-gun salute, Wilson was presented to the legislature.

Speaking without notes, Wilson said, "We have never seen a day when duty was more plain, the task to be performed more obvious." The serious speech was well received.

The legislature met in mid-January with Wilson adviser Joseph Tumulty deftly working on members to isolate James Smith. On January 25 the legislature elected Martine to be senator by a large majority. Newsmen loved the drama of the contest. Wilson's triumph was reminiscent of his early successes at Princeton.

Wilson's legislative program for New Jersey featured direct primary, honest elections, workmen's compensation, and the regulation of utilities. Later reforms involved schools, food storage and inspection, and working conditions for women and children. Some legislators thought he was too strong willed and stepped on too many toes. But the *New York Times* at the end of the legislative session considered his work "really very great," and the *Washington Post* termed Wilson a "national" figure.

Managers who believed the people of the West needed to see the man they had been reading about plotted the western tour in May. Wilson covered nine states and gave thirty-three speeches. A second trip in the fall covered the Midwest and Texas, where he met "Colonel" House.

෪෬

Warren G. Harding and Florence, for a small-town Ohio couple, experienced the apex of their social careers when they were invited to the White House on June 19 to attend President Taft's silver wedding anniversary. There were 3,400 guests, and the Hardings met many diplomats, military officers, and top politicians.

The Hardings also resumed their overseas travel, first to Bermuda with Jim and Carrie Phillips and later to Europe for a vacation with Warren's old friend Ed Scobey of Texas.

Later Jim Phillips let Carrie go to Berlin with their daughter Isabelle. Harding was in a state of panic over her departure and was obviously concerned that she would attract admirers. She had told Jim she wanted an indefinite separation.

Meanwhile Harding's father, Tyron, 68, married Eudora K. Luvisi, a 43-year-old widow. After the death of his wife Phoebe in 1910, Tyron became rather slovenly, sold his farm in Caledonia, then suddenly cleaned up to romance Eudora. They married on November 23 in Anderson, Indiana. The marriage for Tyron came 47 years after his first marriage.

Eudora returned to Indiana, and Tyron bought a farm there. Before long, Tyron and Eudora moved back to Marion.

Harding turned 46 on November 2.

୫୦୧୫

CALVIN COOLIDGE, 39 and the mayor of Northampton, Massachusetts, now the most prominent Republican in his county, won election in November to the Massachusetts senate.

Coolidge's second term as mayor began on January 2. He wrote to his father, "I was inaugurated again this morning. I shall not run again."

It was Hampshire County's turn to seek a state senate seat for the district that included Hampshire, Hampden, and Berkshire Counties. Coolidge was the logical man. He was well known now in Hampshire and Hampden counties. The Republican organizations in all three counties endorsed him, and he won easily in the Republican district, besting the Democratic candidate, Alfred J. Preece, 5,451 to 4,061.

The *Daily Hampshire Gazette* said on November 8 that "Coolidge is the Republican strong man. It is he who gets the votes and not only in his own town but everywhere else."

୫୦୧୫

HERBERT HOOVER, 37, was a wheeler-dealer mining tycoon in London financing various packages when the man who practically bankrupted him in 1902 asked for a meeting. A. Stanley Rowe, the former Berwick, Moreing partner who had embezzled from the firm and allied companies, was released from prison after serving 8 years. Hoover declined a meeting and wrote to Rowe, "Your actions caused me five years of absolutely fruitless work in the best portion of my life." Hoover said he wasn't being vindictive.

Hoover and Beatty put together a $1 million loan to work a prospective site in the Klondike and together made a quick trip to Russia to visit the Kyshtin mines, the largest copper producer in Russia. Hoover wrote a Stanford friend that London financial circles were going through a 25-month depression. He wrote another friend that he hoped to return to the United States for good in another year.

୫୦୧୫

FRANKLIN D. ROOSEVELT, 29, in his first work in the senate in Albany tried to twist the Tammany tiger's tail. Roosevelt and his supporters were against the "boss rule system." Roosevelt told a Buffalo audience on December 23 that progressivism was winning over "bossism." He said, "Murphy [Charles P., Tammany chief] and his kind must, like the noxious weed, be plucked out, root and branch." One Tammany man said that Roosevelt was an "awfully arrogant fellow."

Roosevelt was made chairman of the Forest, Fish and Game Committee. In January, Roosevelt joined in the plot to cut down Tammany and defeat Tammany's choice for a U.S. Senate seat, William F. Sheehan, an old foe of Grover Cleveland. Soon Roosevelt's home became the home of the anti-Tammany reformers.

When Murphy put over New York Supreme Court Justice James A. O'Gormon as the Democratic U.S. Senate candidate, FDR held out against the selection. But he and his followers were hooted and laughed at on their arrival on the floor of the New York Senate. FDR then voted for O'Gormon, who beat the Republican candidate, Chauncey M. Depew, the incumbent, 112 votes to 80 votes.

Alfred E. Smith, 37, leader of the assembly; Robert F. Wagner, 33, president pro tempore in the senate; and Frances Perkins of the National Consumers League, all took a dislike to Roosevelt and his haughty manner. Tammany's Tim Sullivan said, "So we've got another Roosevelt ... wouldn't it be better to drown him before he grows up?"

୫୦୧୫

HARRY S TRUMAN, 27, proposed to Bess Wallace in June, but she turned him down. He thanked her for taking him seriously: "I never was fool enough to think that a girl like you could ever care for a fellow like me but I couldn't help telling you how I felt." She answered all of his letters (then destroyed them all in her old age). Truman, when dating Bess, walked a mile to Grandview, took the train to Sheffield, and then took a streetcar to Independence.

Truman quit the National Guard and joined the Kansas City Athletic Club and the Grandview Community Club. He also established the Masonic Lodge at Grandview and became a first master.

୫୦୧୫

DWIGHT D. EISENHOWER, 21, arrived at West Point on June 14. At the top of a hill, the upperclassmen jumped the new arrivals. One plebe fled the scene immediately. "I thought they were crazy," Eisenhower said. Hazing eliminated five plebes during the first 3 weeks.

Eisenhower was assigned to room 2644. His roommate, Paul A. Hodgson, also from Kansas, was a football player too. He listed his previous occupation as "refrigerator engineer." On the first Sunday, the class was marched around the grounds above the Hudson River. In these grey ranks were Omar N. Bradley, James A. Van Fleet, Hubert R. Harmon, and Joseph T. McNarney.

୫୦୧୫

LYNDON B. JOHNSON, 3, lived in Texas.

୫୦୧୫

RONALD REAGAN was born on February 6 in a rented five-room flat above a bakery in Tampico, Illinois, about 105 miles west of Chicago. His father was John "Jack" Edward Reagan, age 28; his mother was Nellie Wilson Reagan, age 26.

Reagan's father was a shoe salesman, born in Fulton, Illinois. Jack had been orphaned at age 6 when his parents died of tuberculosis a week apart. An aunt in Bennett, Iowa, and a grandmother in Fulton raised him. He had a sixth grade education, was Roman Catholic and an alcoholic. Reagan's mother, also born in Fulton, was Protestant.

Ronald's older brother Neil, known as "Moon," was born on September 3, 1909. The Reagans came from Ballyporeen

County, Tipperary, Ireland. Ronald's great-grandfather fled the potato famine, lived in London for 10 years, and immigrated to the United States via Canada in 1856.

Ronald's was a difficult birth, and Dr. Harry Terry advised the couple against any more children. When Nellie first saw her boy she said, "For such a little bit of a fat Dutchman he makes a hell of a lot of noise, doesn't he?" His nickname was "Dutch" from then on.

1912
William Howard Taft

President Taft suffered the worst defeat of any incumbent president running for reelection in U.S. history. The Progressives, Woodrow Wilson, and Theodore Roosevelt, plus Eugene Debs, earned a combined 11.5 million votes to Taft's 3.4 million votes. The man who never sought the job in the first place was relieved to walk away from it. By the end of his 4 years in office, Taft had moved with more anti-trust vigor against corporations than Roosevelt did in 7 years.

January: Taft's rocky relationship with Roosevelt began, in this year, on January 2 when the president wrote to Andrew Carnegie that he was deeply "hurt" by Roosevelt's attacks on peace arbitration in *Outlook* magazine. Taft told Archie Butt that there was pressure to answer Roosevelt's attacks: "I don't understand Roosevelt. I don't know what he is driving at except to make my way more difficult." The *New York World* said that Taft's peace talk was the "greatest ever presented in practical form for the betterment of the world." The *New York Times* also praised Taft and said Roosevelt's reply was "ill-natured and ill-mannered."

February: There was little doubt by early February that Roosevelt was going to be a candidate for president. Taft believed he could take the high road and asked friends not to attack Roosevelt. Aside from Roosevelt, Taft also faced opposition from Robert La Follette until February 2, when La Follette damaged himself with endless repetitions in an after-dinner speech that put people to sleep.

Roosevelt entered the race on February 21 in a speech in Columbus, Ohio, and 2 days later in Cleveland said, "My hat is in the ring" (see **Theodore Roosevelt**, page 457).

March: The Senate tacked amendments on the arbitration treaties before finally confirming the treaties by a 76-to-3 vote on March 7. The amendments disappointed foreign governments, Taft, and Carnegie.

Socialist presidential candidate and noted union leader Eugene Debs (Library of Congress)

Republican delegate strength began to shift against Roosevelt. On March 26 the New York primary vote gave 83 delegates to Taft and only 7 delegates to Roosevelt, despite some corruption in the tally. And for the first time Roosevelt hinted that he might break with the party. Taft wrote to his aunt Delia Torrey on March 27 that he didn't think Roosevelt would walk out of the convention.

By the end of March, Taft had 274 delegates of the 540 needed for renomination.

June–July: When Republicans met in Chicago for their convention, it was clear that Roosevelt lacked the support needed for the nomination. Taft was renominated on the first ballot, receiving 561 votes to Roosevelt's 107. Vice President James Sherman was also renominated.

On July 2, the Democrats nominated Woodrow Wilson for president and Thomas Riley Marshall for vice president (see **Woodrow Wilson**, page 458).

August–November: Taft did little to no campaigning after his nomination. He left the campaigning to others while he concentrated on other issues.

The new Progressive Party held its convention August 5 to 7 in Chicago and nominated Theodore Roosevelt for president and Hiram Warren Johnson for vice president (see **Theodore Roosevelt**, page 457).

On August 14, Taft sent marines to Nicaragua to help the government threatened by a civil war.

On Election Day, November 5, Taft ran a distant third to Wilson and Roosevelt. Wilson won the presidency, earning 6,293,454 votes to Roosevelt's 4,119,538 votes and Taft's 3,484,980 votes. Socialist candidate Eugene Debs took 900,672 votes. In the electoral vote, Wilson earned 435 votes to Roosevelt's 88 votes and Taft's 8 votes.

Former Presidents

THEODORE ROOSEVELT, his popularity mostly intact, was unable to control the Republican national convention but beat President William Howard Taft for second place in the election as a third-party candidate. As the campaign developed into a contest between Wilson and Roosevelt, Wilson's progressive "New Freedom!" and Roosevelt's "New Nationalism!" became only vaguely different. Some historians suspect that had Roosevelt wrested the nomination from Taft at the Republican showdown, Roosevelt might have beaten Wilson.

January–February: Secretary of War Henry Lewis Stimson visited Roosevelt early in the year to determine his feelings about Taft. Stimson reported back that there was animosity between Roosevelt and Taft. Roosevelt wrote to William L. Ward, a New York national committeeman, on January 9, that he did not want the Republican nomination "as a result of artificial stimulus."

In mid-January, Roosevelt decided that his uncertainty about seeking the Republican nomination was hurting him. He wrote to publisher Frank Munsey that he needed "some tangible evidence" of "a real popular movement."

This letter led to a series of letters in February signed by seven Republican governors, endorsing Roosevelt and offering him evidence that "a large majority" of Republican voters wanted Roosevelt. Now Roosevelt said, "The sentiment among the people is two or three to one in my favor."

Roosevelt had decided to speak to the Ohio Constitutional Convention meeting in Columbus in February "to put out my platform," but otherwise he would not lift a finger for the nomination. Roosevelt discussed his "platform" in Ohio on February 21. He asked for the recall of judges, offered opinions involving constitutional interpretations at the state level, and scored inaction on social and economic reform. He called legalistic justice "a dead thing ... never forget that the judge is as much a servant of the people as any other official."

On leaving Columbus, Roosevelt told news reporters, "My hat is in the ring. The fight is on and I am stripped to the buff." On February 24 he notified the governors that he would accept the nomination "if it is tendered to me." Publisher George W. Perkins, a major financial backer, hastily organized a group of men without much political experience.

April–June: During the spring, things heated up as the Republican convention neared. Taft called Roosevelt a "demagogue" and a "dangerous egotist." Roosevelt called Taft a "puzzlewit," a "fathead," with "brains less than a guinea pig."

In mid-April, replying to a questions about a third-party effort, Roosevelt said, "We will have to consider it" if "political thugs" exploit the Republican convention. County results were ignored in Colorado and Washington, where Taft delegates were picked.

On the eve of the convention in June, Roosevelt was contesting 252 delegates. On June 4, Roosevelt wrote to a British editor: "My own belief is that I shall probably not be nominated at Chicago but they will have to steal the delegates outright ... to prevent my nomination, and if the stealing is flagrant no one can tell what the result will be."

On the second day of the Republican convention on June 19, the Progressives in the party met and talked of bolting. That night, Hiram Johnson said, "We are frittering away our time." Munsey and George Perkins met in the corner of a crowded room at the Congress Hotel and made a financial commitment, then put their hands on Roosevelt's shoulder and said "Colonel, we will see you through."

The next day Roosevelt said a rump convention was likely. Roosevelt advised supporters not to vote when the GOP roll

call began and called the voting "this successful fraud." In the end, Taft was nominated by a wide majority on the first ballot.

August: The first Progressive Party convention was held August 5 to 7 in Chicago. Roosevelt was nominated for president, and Hiram Warren Johnson of California was nominated for vice president. The "Bull Moose" Party adopted several progressive reforms in its platform, including regulation of trusts, unemployment pay, old-age pensions, and female suffrage.

October 15: During a campaign stop in Milwaukee, Wisconsin, Roosevelt was shot while leaving his hotel en route to giving a speech. John Nepomuk Schrank, a saloon-keeper, shot Roosevelt in the chest. Roosevelt, bleeding from the bullet wound, insisted on continuing on to the auditorium to deliver his speech. Roosevelt delivered a 50-minute speech before finally going to the hospital. He soon made a full recovery, lucky that his heavy overcoat, an eyeglass case, and a folded copy of his speech had slowed the bullet.

November 5: Roosevelt, 54, lost the election to Woodrow Wilson but earned nearly a million more votes than William Howard Taft (see **William Howard Taft**, page 456).

Future Presidents

WOODROW WILSON, 56 in December, the scholar and visionary, was elected president in a three-way race in which he defeated the incumbent William Howard Taft and the popular Theodore Roosevelt. The election returned the Democrats to the White House for the first time since Cleveland's second victory 20 years earlier and was the broadest Democratic win since 1852. Wilson was the only Ph.D. to attain the presidency in American history and the first elected southerner since Taylor.

January–May: Wilson adviser Joseph Tumulty called the first months of the year the "dark days" for Wilson. Wilson attacked the Republican tariff plan in January, attacked protection, and vowed to take the tariff out of politics.

Wilson's final months in Trenton as governor found him stifled by a new Republican legislature whose work prompted fifty-seven Wilson vetoes. He proposed reorganizing the administration and more legislation in public health and labor, but the Republicans were uninterested in promoting Wilson's hopes for the 1912 presidential nomination.

Long before the election, Wilson had lost the friendship of George Harvey, the publisher who had been Wilson's earliest and most enthusiastic promoter. Harvey's friends now told the publisher that Wilson was a "dangerous man." Wilson was hurt by Harvey's actions, and he told Hiram Woods, "I just do not understand Harvey." William Jennings Bryan, however, was pleased with Wilson's break with Harvey.

William Randolph Hearst and others tried to show that Wilson was an arch reactionary instead of a Progressive, citing Wilson's book *History of the American People* as showing contempt for Populists, Unionists, and many other interests. In addition, the foreign-born feared that Wilson would restrict immigration. The foreign language press was against Wilson.

In February, Hearst ran front-page stories calling Wilson a Tory, Judas, "a perfect jackrabbit of politics." Wilson refused to stoop to Hearst's level.

On February 11 a Missouri primary picked delegates for its native son, Speaker of the House Champ Clark. In April, Hearst announced his support for Clark and then Nebraska followed suit.

A western swing by train in the spring to demonstrate Wilson's charm was successful and helpful in humanizing Wilson's public image. Wilson kept a notebook with data on each state and the names of the key people in that state.

June–July: Democrats met in Maryland June 25 to 29 and July 1 to 2 to choose their presidential candidate. Heading into the convention, Clark looked like the frontrunner, along with Judson Harmon of Ohio and Oscar Underwood on Alabama. By most counts, Clark had just over 500 delegates going into the convention, a few short of the necessary 545 for the nomination. On the first ballot, however, Clark received just 440½ votes, whereas Wilson came in with 324 votes. Ballot after ballot came and went with no candidate receiving the needed 545 votes. Finally, on the 46th ballot, Wilson was nominated, earning 990 votes to Clark's 84 votes. Thomas Riley Marshall of Indiana was nominated for vice president.

August–November: Wilson campaigned under the banner of his "New Freedom" philosophy. Wilson said that he "wanted to restore our politics to their full spiritual vigor again, and our national life … to its pristine strength and freedom." Wilson often spoke about the dangers of a too-powerful national state.

In speeches during the closing weeks of the campaign in October, Wilson characterized the election as a "second struggle for emancipation" and said that if Roosevelt were to win, America "can have no freedom of no sort whatever."

On November 5, Wilson easily beat Roosevelt and Taft, although he only received 41 percent of the vote. But it was enough to beat Roosevelt by more than 2 million popular votes and Taft by nearly 3 million votes.

୫୭ ଓଃ

WARREN G. HARDING became a national political figure when he put Taft's name in nomination for reelection at the Republican national convention in Chicago. In Harding's oratory, marred by abuse from hecklers, he described Taft as the "greatest progressive of all time." Republican officials later asked Harding to campaign for Taft for 20 days in the Midwest, between Kansas City and Michigan. After the election, in editorials, Harding suggested to Woodrow Wilson that Taft be put on the Supreme Court.

Harding favored Joseph Foraker for governor of Ohio in the columns of the *Marion Star* early in the year, but by March people again talked about running Harding. He said he was not running.

Harding had an understanding with the White House that he would place Taft's name in nomination. In June, Harding was made a delegate-at-large to the national convention, and Taft wrote him, "It is a good deal of a task … but I know your earnest support of me."

Ohio's delegates met in Columbus on June 3 and voted 34 for Roosevelt and 8 for Taft. In a battle over the six delegates-at-large, Taft got all of them including Harding's. Taft was disappointed that his home state went for Roosevelt.

When Harding got up at the Republican convention in Chicago on June 19 to speak, he was soundly booed before he had said a word. His nomination speech for Taft was scarcely heard.

After the election, Harding, now 47, left for Texas to hunt with Scobey and Henry H. Timken, a "Bull Moose" supporter. Florence did not go along, as kidney and heart trouble caused doctors to tell Warren that she might not live through the year.

୫୭ ଓଃ

CALVIN COOLIDGE was loyal to Taft in the presidential contest. In a letter to his father after the election, he said that many Democrats voted for Taft and many Republicans voted for Wilson to make sure that Roosevelt lost. Coolidge himself was reelected to the Massachusetts senate.

In the senate, he made almost every session and committee meeting but said little in public. The highlight of his year in the state senate was his appointment as chairman of a special legislative committee to seek a settlement of a textile strike in Lawrence. Coolidge was seen as being even-handed in dealing with labor issues.

On November 5, Coolidge, 40, received 6,211 votes to 4,222 votes for his Democrat opponent, Herbert C. Joyner.

୫୭ ଓଃ

HERBERT HOOVER, 38, became increasingly interested in mining properties in the Ural Mountains, where prospects appeared reasonable. But Hoover told his partner A. Chester Beatty that caution was advisable in Russia, where sometimes it was better to get in on the second floor than on the ground floor. Even more caution was needed in the Klondike, where a secretive promoter made Hoover feel "absolutely helpless" to know what to do about his investment there.

T. A. Rickard, writing in *Mining Magazine*, said, "Hoover and Beatty represent an amount of technical knowledge and financial astuteness not to be matched by any other two men now prominent in mining affairs."

Hoover returned to California in August and stayed 6 months, his longest U.S. sojourn since 1897. He also made two trips to New York and landed a seat on the Stanford University board of trustees.

ဆုၢ

FRANKLIN D. ROOSEVELT, 30, actively backed the Wilson candidacy at the Democratic national convention in Baltimore, and in November was reelected to the New York senate even though he had been sick in bed for weeks. Wilson's election in November, however, put FDR's political future in limbo amid great expectations.

In New York, the political battle pitted Tammany against Wilson and the young reformers led by Roosevelt. Initially, Roosevelt thought Wilson could not get the nomination and that Roosevelt's own chances of reelection were not bright. Roosevelt attended the national convention, met for the first time Josephus Daniels, Henry Morgenthau Sr., Joseph E. Davies, and Cordell Hull. Earlier he had huddled with William G. McAdoo in New York City to discuss strategy. Roosevelt became chairman of the Wilson group for the state. But Tammany controlled 90 New York votes. Roosevelt headed 150 men favoring Wilson. After Wilson's nomination, Roosevelt went to Sea Girt, New Jersey, to confer with Wilson on campaign plans.

In Roosevelt's own campaign for the New York senate, he was sick in bed for weeks with typhoid fever picked up from drinking water aboard a boat taking him to Campobello. Eleanor was sick also. Roosevelt was unable to run a campaign of his own. His opponents were Republican Jacob Southard and Progressive George A. Vossler. In desperation Roosevelt sent for Louis M. Howe, a former newsman who was seeking a campaign job, and paid him $50 per week to campaign.

With Roosevelt in bed, Howe campaigned everywhere, mapping strategy, appealing to farm elements, and running full-page newspaper ads. On November 5, Howe phoned Roosevelt to tell him that he had won with a greater margin than in 1910. Roosevelt received 15,590 votes; Southard received 13,889 votes, and Vossler received only 2,628 votes.

ဆုၢ

HARRY S TRUMAN, 28, was a farmer in Missouri and interested in Wilson's chances of heading the Democratic ticket. His father John favored Champ Clark. Truman lost most of his ninety hogs to cholera before he could get them to market. When not plowing, Harry was noted as a good dresser with a winning personality.

ဆုၢ

DWIGHT D. EISENHOWER'S promising football career came to a sudden end, and he was so despondent that he considered dropping out of West Point. Eisenhower, 22, sat on the bench for the opening game of his sophomore year but played in the next five. The *New York Times* predicted Eisenhower would become "one of the best backs in the East."

In a game against Jim Thorpe and the Carlisle Indians, Eisenhower twisted his knee. He re-injured it the next week against Tufts University and spent 5 days in the dispensary. There followed a cavalry drill, and he tried to tough it out. He jumped from his horse to scale a wall. On hitting the ground his knee buckled. In the hospital he was put in traction for 30 days.

Eisenhower had been an average student during his plebe year, ranking 57 out of 212. He had forty-three demerits by the end of the spring term on May 31. His grades dropped after the football injury; He ranked 81 out of 177 by the end of his 2nd year.

ဆုၢ

LYNDON B. JOHNSON, now 4, was taught to read and spell by his mother. She read to him from the Bible, mythology, history, and even poems by Tennyson and Longfellow. Life was difficult in the Texas Hill Country, and later Johnson recalled seeing his mother crying at the water pump.

ဆုၢ

RONALD REAGAN was a baby in Illinois.

1913
William Howard Taft

President Taft left the White House with a friendly respect for the incoming Wilson. Taft first went to Augusta, Georgia, for golf, then received a rousing welcome at Yale University when he arrived to make New Haven his new home. Taft taught 4 hours of constitutional law per week but was out of Connecticut half the time, often to lecture.

February–March: Early in the year, the situation in Mexico troubled Taft. When General Victoriano Huerta overthrew President Francisco Madero in February, Taft and Secretary of State Philander Knox were willing to recognize Huerta but wanted American property claims there settled first. But this was left to Wilson to deal with later (see **Woodrow Wilson**, page 463).

The Sixteenth Amendment became law when Delaware became the thirty-eighth state to ratify it on February 25. The new amendment gave Congress the power to collect taxes on individual income.

On March 3, the day before Wilson's inauguration, Taft exchanged greetings with the president-elect at both the Shoreham Hotel and the White House. Later that day, Taft discussed his administration with news reporters. He seemed to be most proud that he had appointed six out of the nine Supreme Court justices. That evening he signed autographs for several hours, then got up in the middle of the night to sign more of them for another hour and a half.

One of the last things to happen under Taft's administration was the reorganization of the Department of Commerce and Labor into separate departments on March 4.

After Wilson's inauguration on March 4, the two men rode in a carriage back to the White House. Taft wished Wilson success, saying, "We will all be behind you." Taft decided neither to ask Wilson for any favors nor to make any suggestions unless asked.

❧❧

WOODROW WILSON, quickly lowered tariff rates, instituted an income tax, and established the Federal Reserve Board to end the frequent financial panics and government money problems of the past. He took an historic step in guiding this legislation personally by appearing before Congress to sell his program. No president had addressed Congress since John Adams. Jefferson had no liking for public oratory, which led to a century of clerks droning presidential messages to Congress. When the first year of the Wilson administration ended, the *New York World* said it had been "a year of achievement [with] few, if any, parallels in American history."

March: Wilson was inaugurated on a cold March 4. Chief Justice Douglas White swore him in. Wilson gave a brief but moving inaugural address, concentrating solely on domestic issues.

By March 5, Wilson's cabinet was in place. As a result of his support during the presidential campaign, William Jennings Bryan was appointed secretary of state. Another friend and supporter of Wilson, William Gibbs McAdoo of New York, was named secretary of Treasury. Other cabinet members included Lindley Garrison of New Jersey as secretary of war, James Clark McReynolds of Tennessee as attorney general, Albert Burleson as postmaster general, Josephus Daniels as secretary of the navy, Franklin Knight Lane of California as secretary of the Interior, David Houston of Missouri as secretary of agriculture, William Redfield of New York as secretary of commerce, and William Wilson of Pennsylvania as secretary of labor.

April–May: On April 8, Wilson decided to address Congress directly on the tariff issue. Congress was cool to the idea of Wilson's appearance, especially Speaker of the House Champ Clark.

In his opening remarks, Wilson said he that was "a human being trying to cooperate with other human beings in a common service [and not coming] from some isolated island of jealous power, sending messages, not speaking naturally with his own voice." He said "semblance of privilege" had to be abolished, and that "new principles" would save the nation from monopolies. There was great applause at the end of Wilson's 10-minute address.

Oscar Underwood, chairman of the Ways and Means Committee, reported a tariff bill on April 22 that was tied to the new income tax amendment. It passed the House on May 8 by a 281-to-139 vote. However, the bill would be tied up in debate between the Senate and the House for the next 6 months.

On May 31, the Seventeenth Amendment was ratified. It called for the direct election of senators by the voters, instead of by state legislatures.

June–September: Wilson decided to tackle currency reform next. The National Monetary Commission had studied the matter in 1911 and 1912. Paul M. Warburg drew up plans endorsed by the American Banking Association for a central institution with fifteen regional branches.

Wilson hoped for a plan under which the United States would control the currency through the Federal Reserve. The debate went on through the summer, as variations of the plan were discussed.

October: The tariff measure, now known as the Underwood–Simmons Bill, passed the Senate, and Wilson signed it on October 3. Fifty Democrats were on hand for the celebration. The idea of the legislation was that an income tax would supplement import duties. The tariff was lowered on 900 items.

December: Debate on the Federal Reserve plan continued as Congress neared its break for Christmas. Wilson threatened to keep Congress in session until something was worked out. Finally, on December 23, Congress passed the Federal Reserve Bank Act drafted by Representative Carter Glass of Virginia. Under the new law, the United States would be divided into twelve districts, each with a Federal Reserve Bank. The banks, privately owned and overseen by a Federal Reserve Board, would not deal with the public. Instead, they would deal with public banks, both national and state banks. National banks were required to join the system, whereas state banks could join if they qualified.

After signing the banking act in December, Wilson took his family by train to Pass Christian, Mississippi, where they stayed in a house built before the Civil War.

Former Presidents

THEODORE ROOSEVELT, the most prolific writer in American political history, wrote his *Autobiography* and then took a hike in the Grand Canyon as a warm-up for an adventurous and dangerous trip up an unknown river in the Amazon basin. In his *Autobiography*, there was not a word about Taft and the 1908 campaign. With his "Bull Moose" run history, Roosevelt indicated an unwillingness to do any legwork to keep the new party going.

April 4: Roosevelt's daughter Ethel, 21, married Richard Derby at Oyster Bay. Derby, as a Harvard student in 1901, had attended a seminar put on by then Vice President Roosevelt at Sagamore Hill.

May: Roosevelt brought a libel suit against George Newett, an Ishpeming, Michigan, magazine publisher for a story about Roosevelt's "drunkenness" in the October 1912 issue of his magazine. The case was tried in Marquette at the end of May. Many witnesses said they never saw Roosevelt drunk. His aide of 15 years, William Loeb Jr., said he never saw Roosevelt intoxicated. Roosevelt himself told the court: "I have never drunk a cocktail or highball in my life.... I never drank whisky or brandy except under the advice of a physician.... I don't smoke and I don't drink beer." Newett retracted his comments and apologized.

July–August: Roosevelt went cougar hunting in the Grand Canyon with sons Archibald, 19, and Quentin, 15, along with Nicholas Roosevelt. They took the Bright Angel Trail to the Colorado River and in August crossed the Painted Desert. On August 10 they took a 6-day pack trip to the Rainbow National Bridge, which had been discovered by explorers only 4 years earlier.

October–December: The idea for a South American trip came from a Catholic priest, John A. Zahn, who first met Roosevelt in 1908. Zahn had crossed the Andes to the Amazon and now wanted to explore the Paraguay River. Roosevelt put him off for several years. During the summer Roosevelt received invitations to speak in Brazil, Argentina, and Chile. He accepted and planned the trip, in part, to show that he was not yet an old man. Unlike his sojourn in Africa, Roosevelt said this trip would have "no hunting and no adventure."

The party, including wife Edith and two scientists, George K. Cherries and Anthony Fiala, sailed from Brooklyn on October 5. After a stop at Bridgetown, Barbados, the ship reached Bahia, where son Kermit joined them. He had postponed his marriage to make the trip. Roosevelt reached Rio de Janeiro on October 21. He was in Sao Paulo for his fifty-fifth birthday on October 27. Roosevelt's speeches on progressive doctrines drew large crowds. After Montevideo, Buenos Aires, and Santiago, they reached Valparaiso, from which Edith then sailed home for New York. Roosevelt was back in Buenos Aires by early December.

It was in South America that Roosevelt first heard about the uncharted River of Doubt, which flowed northward from the Brazilian plateau to the Amazon. Candido Rondon had discovered this river 4 years earlier. The River of Doubt was the largest uncharted river on the continent.

Roosevelt and Kermit were in Ascunción on December 7, and 2 days later they started upriver aboard a gunboat-yacht supplied by the president of Paraguay. At the Brazilian border Roosevelt met Rondon aboard a steamer. For 3 weeks, Roosevelt made side trips to various ranches and, contrary to what he said earlier, hunted jaguar. He ended 1913 in the wilds of South America.

Future Presidents

WARREN G. HARDING, Republican and publisher of the *Marion Star*, spent a quiet year outside the political arena with Democrat James Cox the governor of Ohio and Democrat Woodrow Wilson in the White House. Harding played more golf and signed up again with the Chautauqua speaking circuit.

October–November: Florence's father, Amos Kling, came back from Florida due to homesickness and died of a kidney ailment on October 20.

Harding's sister Mary died of a stroke on October 29.

Harding turned 48 in November.

❦❧

CALVIN COOLIDGE showed political resourcefulness and support to win the presidency of the Massachusetts senate for 1914. The job was second in political importance only to the governorship. Boston and other newspapers had praise for Coolidge's ambition. One paper saw a future for Coolidge as a judge. Political observers believed Coolidge succeeded because of the support of W. Murray Crane, the Republican powerhouse in the state.

In the fall the president of the senate, Levi Greenwood, decided to seek the office of lieutenant governor, as the Democratic incumbent wanted to run for governor. Coolidge, now 41, then won endorsement for a third term in the senate in the hope that he might become president of the senate. Greenwood then switched, deciding that there was too much competition for lieutenant governor and that he wanted to remain in the senate. Greenwood, however, was defeated in his senate race, thus leaving the senate office open to Coolidge after all.

Coolidge hurried by train to Boston and began rounding up support. Within 5 days he had the votes needed. Coolidge said he wanted to be senate president because it would give him "a chance to emerge from being a purely local figure to a place of state-wide distinction and authority."

❦❧

HERBERT HOOVER, 39, knew that the life of a mining engineer was one of peaks and valleys. During this year, things picked up in Burma while they dipped in the Klondike. Hoover and A. Chester Beatty had put up $4.5 million in loans to develop the Klondike venture, but they found the promoter a burden.

Stress over the Klondike caused Hoover to fear for his reputation and wonder if the promotion there would end in scandal. But Hoover's men found huge reserves of silver, lead, and zinc buried under ancient Chinese diggings in Burma. Hoover even shipped large samples of ore to Europe for smelting experiments at his own expense.

Hoover wrapped up his stay at Stanford University by getting deeply involved with school plans and politics. Hoover's wish list to trustees included a new gym, new libraries, a medical school, a stadium, and more attractive grounds. Hoover wrote a memo on January 2 in which he said that Stanford was falling behind in hiring good faculty members because the pay scale was too low.

❦❧

FRANKLIN D. ROOSEVELT, 31, became assistant secretary of the navy, the youngest in history.

Navy Secretary Josephus Daniels, who wanted Roosevelt as his assistant, immediately considered Roosevelt a prospect to run the same route to the White House that Theodore Roosevelt had taken prior to the Spanish-American War.

Roosevelt had been called to Trenton, New Jersey, to discuss New York patronage with president-elect Woodrow

Wilson. He also attended the inauguration on March 4 and bumped into Secretary of the Navy Daniels the night before. Daniels told Wilson he wanted FDR at his side. The idea was approved, and Roosevelt was sworn in on March 17. New York newspapers soon said gossip suggested that Roosevelt might become governor or senator.

Roosevelt enjoyed navy ritual and once reviewed a parade of battleships at Hampton Roads prior to their deployment to the Mediterranean.

Meanwhile, Eleanor hired Lucy Mercer, 22, as a social secretary. Lucy, a Roman Catholic, came from a broken home and until 1912 lived in a convent in Melk, Austria.

Josephus Daniels, secretary of the navy under Woodrow Wilson, appointed Franklin D. Roosevelt as assistant secretary of the navy in 1913. (Library of Congress)

৪০৫৪

HARRY S TRUMAN, 29, romanced Bess Wallace and made a trip to Montana to look at land, then decided against buying.

September: Truman made the train trip to Glasgow, Montana, to take part in a land lottery. He drew a claim, joined the Fort Peck Settlers Association, but then backed out of buying any land.

November: Bess finally got off the fence and said she would think about marrying Truman. He replied by letter, "Let's get engaged anyway to see how it feels" and keep it a secret.

৪০৫৪

DWIGHT D. EISENHOWER, 23, and a West Point cadet, returned to Abilene, Kansas, for a 10-week leave at the end of his second year. At home he dated, went for all-night walks alone, and had a fight with a bully. He was keenly disappointed that his football career was over due to his knee injury and that he also had to give up playing baseball.

His grades improved, and after 2 years he was ranked 81 out of 177. He tied Omar Bradley in sharp shooting with a score of 245.

৪০৫৪

LYNDON B. JOHNSON, 5, attended a public school near his birthplace until the family moved into a three-bedroom, white frame house in Johnson City. Johnson's mother, Rebekah, had the only college degree in town.

৪০৫৪

RICHARD MILHOUS NIXON was born at 9:35 in the evening of January 9, in a small Sears kit house his father had built in Yorba Linda, California. His father was Francis "Frank" Anthony Nixon, age 33; his mother was Hannah Milhous Nixon, age 27. They were married on June 25, 1908, in Whittier, when he was 29 and she was 22.

The family lived at the poverty level. There was no running water, electricity, refrigeration, or telephone. They used oil lamps and a wood stove. Frank, with a sixth-grade education, was a school dropout who was for a time a farm hand, house painter, telephone installer, oxen driver, bricklayer, potter, tractor operator, glass blower, and finally gas station and grocery store manager. His brother Ernest had a Ph.D. and taught at Penn State.

Frank lost his mother when he was 8, hated his stepfather, and ran away from home at 13. Born in Vinton County, Ohio, about 20 miles east of Chillicothe, frostbitten toes one day literally drove him to try California in 1904. He returned to Ohio, then moved back to California in 1907.

Hannah was born near Butlerville, Jennings County, in southeast Indiana. She was a Republican and student in Whittier prior to her marriage. Her family was Quaker, and she converted Nixon from Methodism in 1909. Richard was their second child; Harold Nixon had been born in 1909.

The Nixons moved from Scotland to Ireland in the 17th century. James Nixon emigrated from Ireland to New Castle County, Delaware, in 1731 and died in 1773. George Nixon crossed the Delaware with George Washington, settled in Washington, Pennsylvania, later moved to Ohio and Illinois; George Nixon III was killed at Gettysburg.

The Milhous family was German Quaker, yet Franklin Milhous was descended from King Edward III of England (1312–1377). The Milhous family emigrated from England to Pennsylvania in 1729, later moved to Butlerville, Indiana, then to Whittier. Hannah was one of six sisters. Her family opposed the marriage to Nixon, feeling it was a step down for her. Their romance lasted only 4 months. Two years after the marriage, Hannah's father advanced $3,000 to the couple.

At birth Richard was described by the nurse as "roly-poly." He was named after Richard the Lionhearted. Nixon was a distant cousin of Taft and Hoover and author Jessamyn West.

৪০৫৪

GERALD R. FORD JR. was born on July 14 in Omaha, Nebraska. He was named Leslie Lynch King Jr. His father was Leslie Lynch King, age 31; his mother was Dorothy Ayer Gardner, age 21.

The couple had been married at the Christian Episcopal Church in her hometown of Harvard, Illinois, on September 7, 1912. Within weeks the marriage turned into an unending disaster during a lengthy, expensive honeymoon. King beat her, and lied about his income.

Dorothy met King, born in Chadron, Nebraska, through his sister Mariette. King came to visit Mariette and met her close friend Dorothy. He told her parents later that he had $35,000 in the bank and earned $150 per month running a wool storage company. Other investments brought his income to $6,000 annually, he claimed.

The honeymoon began with a Pullman to Minneapolis. The luxury trip, paid for by King's wealthy father, continued to Seattle, Los Angeles, Denver, and back to Omaha.

Fifteen days after the wedding, in the Multnomah Hotel in Portland, Oregon, King struck Dorothy in the face, claiming she was flirting. In the Pullman going to Los Angeles, he hit and kicked her. More abuse followed. He had promised a cottage in Omaha but on their arrival there 7 weeks after the wedding, they moved in with his parents who had a large fourteen-room house.

During the first week in Omaha, King kicked his bride out, and she returned to Harvard in shock, keeping developments a secret within the family. Then King showed up and begged her to return to Omaha. He promised they would not live at the Woolworth Avenue house. She acquiesced. They moved into a basement apartment, and she then learned he was in debt, his money boasts just hot air.

Dorothy went to a movie one night with Mariette and on returning to the apartment was kicked out by her furious husband. Now she was reduced to going to her husband's office to ask for food and rent money.

Following the birth of his son, King began threatening Dorothy and the doctor. When lawyer Arthur C. Pamcost advised Dorothy to leave, she did not even pack but grabbed the 16-day-old baby and fled Omaha. She joined her parents, and they took a train to Chicago on July 30. Dorothy moved in with her married sister, Tannisse, in Oak Park, Illinois. Pamcost filed divorce papers as King went to court claiming desertion. An Omaha court on December 19 found King "guilty of extreme cruelty" and ended the marriage.

The assassination of Austrian Archduke Franz Ferdinand was one of the sparks that ignited World War I. *(Library of Congress)*

RONALD REAGAN, now 2, moved with his family to the south side of Chicago.

1914
Woodrow Wilson

President Wilson, 58 in December, was put under tremendous strain as the start of World War I coincided with the death of his wife.

January–May: Early in the year, Wilson had great difficulty preventing a second war with Mexico. Wilson failed to persuade President Victoriano Huerta of Mexico to resign. Wilson then gave his support to General Alvaro Obregon, Huerta's main rival. He allowed arms to flow to Obregon, but Huerta remained in power.

In April, a motorboat from the American warship *Dolphin* landed in the southern Mexican port of Vera Cruz. Huerta's soldiers arrested the crew, but soon afterward Huerta's commandant in the city apologized. With Wilson's backing, the apology was not accepted by Admiral Henry T. Mayo. Instead, on April 22, American troops were landed in Vera Cruz and took the city. American losses totaled nineteen killed and seventy-one wounded.

Wilson's wife, Ellen, had taken a fall in her bedroom on March 1. She had been bothered by a kidney ailment for a long time, and now she remained in bed for 2 weeks. In late May specialists were called in, and Ellen was diagnosed with Bright's disease.

In the meantime, doctors also discovered that Wilson had hardening of the arteries.

June–August: Austrian Archduke Francis Ferdinand was assassinated on June 28. Soon, European countries were preparing for war.

Although President Huerta of Mexico had threatened to invade Texas and arm blacks against the U.S. government, his forces surrendered to General Obregon on July 10.

Tensions in Europe increased as July came to an end. The Austro-Hungarian Empire declared war on Serbia on July 28. The New York Stock Exchange closed on July 31 in response to the declaration of war. On August 1, Germany declared war on Russia, and Russia in turn declared war on Germany. This was followed by France declaring war on Germany on August 3, and Great Britain doing the same on August 4.

Wilson talked to news reporters on August 3 and warned against hysteria, saying, "America ... stands ready to help the rest of the world." Wilson then proclaimed American neutrality on August 4.

Ellen Wilson died on August 6. Her death from Bright's disease left a void in Wilson's life.

To emphasize U.S. neutrality, Wilson sent a message to the Senate: "The United States must be neutral in fact as well as in name."

September 26: With the passage of the Federal Trade Commission Act, the Federal Trade Commission was established.

October 15: Congress, strengthening the Sherman Anti-Trust Act of 1890, passed the Clayton Anti-Trust Act.

Former Presidents

THEODORE ROOSEVELT almost died during a harrowing adventure of endless close calls in the darkest Amazon wilds of Brazil while exploring an uncharted river.

January–May: Roosevelt's Brazilian expedition traveled northward on the River of Doubt. The aim of the expedition was to map this unknown tributary of the Amazon.

On January 16 the party moved into the unexplored area after Roosevelt wrote Frank M. Chapman, "We are now about to go into the real wilderness, where we shall have to travel light, and can hardly collect any big animals." The party, moving by packhorse and mule, started through the highlands of the Mato Grosso on January 21. The Roosevelt party now included 40 people and 200 animals.

They reached the headwaters of the River of Doubt on February 26. On March 2, Roosevelt said it was "delightful to drift and paddle slowly down the beautiful tropical river." Soon, however, the party faced rapids, and the broad river was now squeezed down to only 2 yards between exposed rocks. It took 2½ days to portage this spot. One damaged and two older canoes sank, and the party had to stop for 4 days to build new canoes.

On March 15, son Kermit's canoe overturned in white water and one paddler vanished. Kermit, exhausted, barely made shore by grabbing an overhanging branch. The next day they found worse rapids ahead, and a blinding rain discouraged all.

On March 19 they stopped for 3 days to build more dugouts. The expedition now had covered 140 kilometers.

Endless downpours kept the men wet. By the end of March, they were working through a mountain range and down to the bare essentials as they faced more rapids. Two paddlers came down with jungle fever.

Roosevelt's knee was pinched trying to prevent two capsized canoes from hitting the rocks. Badly hurt, Roosevelt had to be carried. Fever followed in the first week of April, and Roosevelt could not be moved. After his fever broke, Roosevelt asked to be abandoned. There were abscesses and much pain in his leg. Roosevelt even considered suicide but felt that Kermit, in such a case, would insist on trying to bring the body out of the jungle.

There were more rapids, more hardship, terrible insect bites, and a relentless sun. On April 15 they spotted a marking on a tree, put there perhaps by a rubber plantation employee. Then they reached an unoccupied house, then another house, and finally civilization, in the form of the hamlet of Sao Joao, on April 27.

Roosevelt had explored a river 1,500 kilometers in length but at a high cost. Historian William Roscoe Thayer wrote

that the Brazilian trip "stole away ten years of his life." Roosevelt's sister Corinne said he never recovered from his jungle fever.

Roosevelt reached New York on May 19.

October–November: Roosevelt jumped into the fall campaign on behalf of the Progressive cause, speaking in the South, Midwest, and East. But he confessed to a newsman that this was his last political hurrah, that he was finished promoting the Progressive program, and after election day he would be a "free" man.

ഇരു

WILLIAM HOWARD TAFT, professor of law at Yale University, toyed with the idea of running for president in 1916, or, following the John Quincy Adams precedent, trying for a seat in the House of Representatives. He dismissed both ideas before the year ended. Taft thought it wise to remain silent publicly on all aspects of the war in Europe. Taft also predicted he would never get the Supreme Court appointment he had cherished for so long.

March: Taft returned to the White House for a delightful lunch with President Wilson and Elihu Root.

June–August: Two Republican leaders in New Haven, Max Pam and Isaac Ullman, asked Taft for his recommendation for a congressional candidate from that district. Taft answered in a jocular manner, suggesting "the wisdom of my coming to Congress." Taft said his only motive for seeking a congressional seat would be for "promoting the cause of judicial procedure … if I could get on the Judiciary Committee in the House, I believe I might make a fuss on the subject." A House seat also would keep him before the public eye in order to possibly make the presidential race in 1916.

Taft believed some voters were open minded regarding a second term and believed his treatment by Roosevelt was unjust, "because they think I have proved to be a good loser and have conducted myself sensibly since the election." By mid-August he decided against making another run.

Taft was at Murray Bay in Quebec when World War I started. News reporters on July 29 asked him for a statement and he replied, "All good people [were] hoping that the sentiment in favor of peace was growing. [I] hope [the] foreign policy of Russia and Germany will localize the trouble, so that we shall not have a general European war."

As the war widened, Taft wrote, "Nothing like it has occurred since the great Napoleonic wars.… Nothing like it since the world began.… It is a cataclysm."

Future Presidents

WARREN G. HARDING defeated his former mentor, Joseph Foraker, in the new primary system for the Republican nomination for the U.S. Senate, then won the election in November over both the Democrat and Progressive candidates. The outbreak of war forced Carrie Phillips to leave Berlin and return to Marion. She and Harding now were lovers again but with a difference. She ridiculed his seeking political honors, and their relationship turned stormy largely due to her strong pro-German attitude.

January–May: Republicans and Progressives held a banquet on January 14 in Columbus to resolve differences. Although there was harmony, the effort failed. And although the Progressives were outnumbered at the dinner by the time of the Lincoln's Birthday celebration, Garford announced his candidacy for the Senate on the Progressive ticket.

By April 8, Senator Theodore Burton was tired of it all, and after losing newspaper support, said in a statement that someone uninvolved in the recent factionalism would be more favorably regarded.

Burton and Maurice Maschke decided that Harding would be a good man to inject harmony into the Republican problem. Harding agreed but only if Dan Hanna would support him. "I am not seeking any nomination," Harding wrote, but said he would accept a draft.

Harding went to Cincinnati and told Foraker that reluctantly he would enter the primary against him. Foraker had expected Harding's support but wished him well. Harding announced his candidacy on May 27.

August: The primary was held on August 11. Harding won by 12,000 votes. He had 88,540 votes to 76,181 votes for Foraker and 52,237 votes for Congressman Ralph D. Cole. Congressman Frank B. Willis won the Republican nomination for governor. Willis had campaigned with vigor during Harding's gubernatorial campaign in 1910.

Harding wrote to Foraker on August 20: "[I] regret that you are not to go back to the Senate.... I would have rejoiced [in] your return to the Senate ... my admiration [for you] has not waned."

September–November: The Republicans opened their campaign in Akron on September 26, as Harding and Willis reviewed a giant parade. Anti-Catholic and anti-Irish feeling worked against the Democratic candidate, Attorney General Tim-othy Hogan, who was attacked by Ohio's fundamentalists.

It was a big victory for Harding, now 49, with 526,115 votes to Hogan's 423,748 votes and Garford's 67,509 votes. Willis defeated James Cox to become governor.

"This is the zenith of my political ambition," Harding told a Marion crowd at his home.

ৎেCৎ

CALVIN COOLIDGE, president of the Massachusetts senate, was now a major power and the best vote-getter in Republican politics in the state.

When the Massachusetts senate met in January, Coolidge was the unanimous choice in the Republican caucus to be president of the senate, as he had lined up the necessary support in the last days of 1913. The senate president was second in power only to the governor. The president named committees, assigned bills, and selected conference committees.

In his speech to open the session, he said: "Laws must rest on the eternal foundation of righteousness.... The people cannot look to legislation generally for success." The speech underlined Coolidge's philosophy and served notice on Governor David Walsh that he was not going to rush the Senate into anything.

Coolidge was chairman of a committee that framed the Republican platform for the Republican gubernatorial candidate in the November election. But Congressman Samuel W. McCall lost to incumbent Democrat Walsh. Coolidge, however, won for the fourth time.

ৎেCৎ

HERBERT HOOVER, 40, took charge of feeding 7 million starving Belgians isolated by the German advance into northern France. He rose to sudden prominence first by his administration of efforts to help rescue 125,000 Americans, many of them tourists, caught by the war on the continent and anxious to reach London. By the time feeding Belgium became his major mission, he was often at meetings with British political leaders. Hoover, a volunteer, took no pay.

Early in the year, Hoover was in California, and he returned to London on the *Lusitania* in March. Active in Stanford politics, some saw him as a future university president. His policy as a trustee was to clear away deadwood, including unproductive professors. Some observers thought he ought to be governor of California. His preference was for a seat in the U.S. Senate.

Hoover was negotiating to purchase the *Sacramento Union*, but the outbreak of the war ended his interest in buying the newspaper.

World War I caught Hoover by complete surprise. His wealth made it easy for him to put aside his mining investments and development business to help in Belgium. He later said that Germany's war declaration against Great Britain on August 4 sent him moving on a slippery slide toward a career in public service.

At the war's onset, Hoover had 100,000 men working at his various mines around the world. He had earned $5 million in just a few years. The Belgian relief effort followed the arrival in London of 100,000 Belgian refugees. The Germans had no plans to feed the Belgians but agreed to allow Hoover's group, the Committee for Belgian Relief (CBR) to do its work. Hoover took charge of Belgian relief on October 19, causing the American press to raise the question, "Who is Herbert Hoover?"

Hoover appealed to thirty-one governors in the United States to collect food supplies for shipment. He traveled to Brussels twice near the end of the year to check on his organization.

ৎেCৎ

FRANKLIN D. ROOSEVELT, 32, took a beating in a Democratic primary contest for a U.S. Senate seat from New York.

Tammany's choice, James W. Gerard, ambassador to Berlin, won in September, 210,765 votes to 76,888. FDR's loss margin in New York City was four to one.

On August 17, Franklin Roosevelt Jr. was born.

The war in Europe found Roosevelt, the assistant secretary of the navy, siding with Theodore Roosevelt's belligerent stance. Franklin was often at odds with Secretary of the Navy Josephus Daniels over policy. Roosevelt worked to make the U.S. fleet ready for war once Europe became engulfed in it. His positions on preparation mimicked Theodore Roosevelt's anxieties in 1898.

        ᔥ◌ᔤ

HARRY S TRUMAN, 30, lost his father and, in turn, lost interest in continuing to farm. In letters to Bess Wallace, he never mentioned the war. He was appointed postmaster of Grandview, Missouri, for 7 months, and he became president of the Washington Township chapter of the Farm Bureau.

Truman's father strained his shoulder moving a boulder. Later X-rays revealed a tumor in the intestines near a hernia. John Truman postponed surgery for months and tried Chinese medicines. Operated on in October, he died on November 2 with Harry at his bedside.

        ᔥ◌ᔤ

DWIGHT D. EISENHOWER, 24, at the end of his third year at West Point stood 65th in a class of 170.

Now he was coaching the junior varsity football team.

        ᔥ◌ᔤ

LYNDON B. JOHNSON, 6, was a first grader in Texas, in the Hill Country west of Austin.

January 31: Lyndon's brother Sam Houston Johnson was born.

        ᔥ◌ᔤ

RICHARD M. NIXON was a baby in Yorba Linda, California.

        ᔥ◌ᔤ

GERALD R. FORD, a baby, was moved from Oak Park, Illinois, to Grand Rapids, Michigan. The move was an adjustment for his grandfather, Levi Gardner, who, for the sake of propriety, decided it was best for his daughter Dorothy to move from their hometown of Harvard, Illinois, and make a new start. Gardner owned property in Grand Rapids.

Gardner bought a nice new house at 457 Lafayette Street and invited his daughter to start a new life with her boy, now called "Junie."

        ᔥ◌ᔤ

RONALD REAGAN was a 3-year-old living outside Chicago.

1915
Woodrow Wilson

President Wilson, 59 in December, struggled to maintain U.S. neutrality in the face of the nation's outrage over the sinking of the passenger liner *Lusitania* near Ireland, with the loss of

128 Americans. However, through much of the summer and fall of his third year in Washington, Wilson appeared unable to keep his mind on the flow of complex problems caused by World War I because he was in love. Wilson was infatuated with a widow, Edith Bolling Galt, and some White House business was left undone as the president penned love letters of up to forty pages in longhand. By the end of the year, they would be married.

January–April: Early in the year, Congress was tied up dealing with a new immigration bill and a shipping bill. The immigration bill would have required immigrants to pass a literacy test. The bill passed the House and Senate on January 28, but Wilson vetoed it that same day.

The Senate debate on a shipping bill dealing with how to maintain commerce with Europe in times of submarine warfare caused Senator Henry Cabot Lodge to reveal how much he disliked Wilson. The shipping bill was left over from before the November 1914 election, and it soon became bogged down in Congress.

Charles W. Eliot of Harvard cautioned Wilson that the shipping bill was antagonizing all businessmen and making possible a Republican victory in 1916. The bill passed the House on February 16. When Democrats in the Senate refused to consider amendments to it, Lodge blamed Wilson and indicated that the president was an egoist and dictator.

Lodge wrote to Roosevelt, "I never expected to hate anyone in politics with the hatred I feel towards Wilson. I was opposed to our good friend Grover Cleveland, but never in any such way as this."

Congress adjourned on March 4 without acting on the shipping bill.

On February 4, Germany proclaimed the waters around the British Isles a war zone. Every ship would be destroyed without guaranteeing safety for passengers and crew. This meant that noncombatant ships risked sinking due to mistakes in identity. There were no guarantees against error.

On February 10, Wilson told the German government that he would hold it to "strict accountability" if German submarines fired upon and sank American ships.

On March 11 the British Order in Council directed the Royal Navy to stop all traffic to Germany. The United States protested.

The Germans sank the *Falaba* on March 28 with several Americans aboard. The newspapers responded, "Barbarism run mad." Robert Lansing, a close adviser to Wilson, wrote a protest, asking Germany to punish the officers responsible. Secretary of State William Jennings Bryan wanted to soften this message, and Wilson tended to agree with Bryan. Wilson avoided taking any action. He told Southern Methodist University students on March 25, "Wars will never have any ending until men cease to hate one another."

Wilson was still depressed by the death of his wife, Ellen, when in the spring he met Edith Bolling Galt. Wilson was introduced to Galt through his close friend, Dr. Gary Grayson. Soon, Wilson and Galt developed a friendship that quickly turned to love.

Galt was a 42-year-old widow born in Wytheville, Virginia. Her husband, Norman Galt, had died in 1908.

May–July: On May 1, the German embassy warned that Americans traveling into war zones around Great Britain did so at their own risk.

On May 7, the British Cunard liner *Lusitania* was sunk. Of the 1,200 passengers who died, 128 were Americans. The sinking was just what Wilson dreaded and turned American sentiment against Germany. Wilson did not want to be hasty. If he went to Congress, he would get authority for war, but he thought about the long casualty lists that would come later. He felt he owed it to the world to avoid getting embroiled.

Wilson addressed new citizen immigrants in Philadelphia on May 10: "Once a citizen, then your nationality has changed.... America was created to unite mankind.... There is such a thing as a man being too proud to fight. There is such a thing as a nation being so right that it does not need to convince others by force that it is right." Peace-loving people loved the speech, but partisans of Great Britain were angry, and the next day at a press conference, Wilson said these were merely his views, and not a comment on the *Lusitania*.

Soon after the speech, the German ambassador to the United States apologized for the sinking.

On May 13, Secretary of State William Jennings Bryan sent a letter to Germany demanding complete disavowal of the sinking of the *Lusitania*. At the same time, he told the Austrian ambassador to the United States that the strong language used in the letter was there only to "pacify excited public opinion." Soon, word of Bryan's remarks was leaked.

Wilson was upset and soon asked Bryan to sign his name to a second, strongly worded note to Germany. Bryan refused, and under increasing pressure, he resigned on June 8. Robert Lansing replaced him.

On June 9, Wilson sent the second letter to Germany, this time demanding reparations for the sinking of the *Lusitania*. Germany ignored this letter. On July 21, Wilson sent a third note to Germany, which was also ignored. In the end, Germany made no reparations for the sinking of the *Lusitania*, and Wilson let the matter fade away.

December: In his message to Congress on December 7, Wilson presented a plan to Congress that would increase the size of the army and the navy.

Wilson and Edith were married on December 18 in a small ceremony in Washington, D.C. The couple honeymooned in Hot Springs, Virginia.

Former Presidents

WILLIAM HOWARD TAFT expressed willingness early in the year to be the Republican nominee again in 1916. But by October he thought this could never happen. Taft supported Wilson's neutrality policy before and after the *Lusitania* disaster. He said that Henry Cabot Lodge and Theodore Roosevelt would have pulled the United States into the war.

February 9: Taft wrote to Felix Agnus, "I would not decline [the presidential nomination. If] it does come, it must be because the convention can find no one else."

May: After the *Lusitania* sinking on May 7, Taft felt compelled to write to Wilson. On May 10 he wrote to "express … my appreciation of the difficult situation which you face … every patriotic citizen [ought] to avoid embarrassing you in your judgment. [War should be] avoided."

Wilson responded on May 13 that the nation admired Taft's generous spirit in putting aside party differences to lend his support.

October 9: Taft, now 58 years old, wrote, "My candidacy is resting in the tomb where it ought to be."

☙❧

THEODORE ROOSEVELT thought that the United States needed to enter the war and told a newspaper friend after the *Lusitania* sinking that he wished he were in the White House. As for Woodrow Wilson, Roosevelt said he was the worst president with the possible exception of James Buchanan and Andrew Johnson. Roosevelt's truculence irritated pacifists but did much to condition the American people to the inevitability of participating in the carnage of World War I. Roosevelt even

The Lusitania *leaves New York on its final voyage. The Germans sunk the British liner on May 7, 1915, killing some 1,200 passengers, including 128 Americans.* (National Archives)

sketched out a plan to head a cavalry outfit into battle—a rebirth of the Rough Riders.

In the wake of the *Lusitania* sinking, Roosevelt said that the United States would receive "scorn and contempt if we follow … those who exalt peace above righteousness, if we heed the voice of feeble folk who bleat peace when there is no peace." The government's failure to act against Germany, Roosevelt said, was "literally inexcusable and inexplicable." Roosevelt was critical of pacifists and believed they worked with German Americans hoping for victory by Germany.

Future Presidents

WARREN G. HARDING traveled to Texas, Hawaii, and Quebec between his first session in the U.S. Senate in March and his second in December. Harding was a frequent speaker even while off the campaign trail, making speeches in San Antonio, Honolulu, and New York City.

February: In Honolulu, Harding addressed the Ad Club, the Bar Association, and the Buckeye Club and was a guest at a Chamber of Commerce banquet. In Hawaii, Charlie Forbes, who was directing construction of the Pearl Harbor Naval Base for the Wilson administration, befriended the Hardings.

May: The *New York Times* ran a "favorite son" article about the 1916 presidential election and from Ohio mentioned Theodore Burton, Myron Herrick, and Harding.

On May 27, Harding joined Taft to speak in New York. Harding termed World War I a commercial rivalry, even though he was a big fan of economic development. He "heartily favored" preparedness, which was Theodore Roosevelt's theme, but added, "It is not wise to rush militarism and we will not do it. We do need an army double the present force."

June–August: In June and July, Harding was back on the Chautauqua speaking circuit in Ohio, with Florence accompanying him.

In August he took a fishing trip to Quebec.

November–December: Harding went alone to Washington in November. Florence Harding was never comfortable in Washington society. She always preferred Marion, Ohio, where she was seen as Amos Kling's daughter.

The Sixty-fourth Congress opened on December 6.

ഇൻ

CALVIN COOLIDGE was elected lieutenant governor of Massachusetts as Northampton's *Daily Hampshire Gazette* made a prediction that he would eventually become governor. Meanwhile, a Boston dry goods tycoon, Frank W. Stearns, took a personal interest in Coolidge and began promoting his political career and prospects without expecting anything in return. Stearns amused Boston friends by saying Coolidge would be president some day.

In the beginning of the year, presiding over the Massachusetts senate as president, Coolidge dispatched business quickly, limited the introduction of laws, made sure reports were made on time, stressed conservatism, and amused all with his dry wit.

Coolidge campaigned for lieutenant governor by auto with Republican candidate for governor, Samuel McCall, in the fall. McCall was elected governor in November over the popular David Walsh, but Coolidge received more votes than McCall.

ഇൻ

HERBERT HOOVER, 41, kept the Belgian relief movement functioning as he worked his considerable powers of persuasion on British, German, and French officials, with uneven results.

He discussed the complex relief situation with President Wilson in the White House. Wilson wrote to Hoover on September 20 that his was "a work wonderfully done."

The Belgian relief program built in 4 months was the largest such effort in history. There were 240 warehouses holding food for Belgian distribution through 4,700 communes. One million tons arrived in the first year of operation, some of it from Australia and Argentina.

ഇൻ

FRANKLIN D. ROOSEVELT's difficulties with Secretary of the Navy Josephus Daniels regarding methods for getting the U.S. fleet ready for war dominated politics within the Navy Department. Daniels awaited congressional action on preparedness. Roosevelt, 33, sided with hawkish admirals.

Roosevelt was glad to see William Jennings Bryan depart the cabinet in June. Roosevelt called Bryan a "hillbilly."

ഇൻ

HARRY S TRUMAN, 31, took over his father's job as county road overseer but lost money in lead and zinc mines in Commerce, Oklahoma. Because of this involvement in the mining business, the county court fired Truman. Angered, he ran for Democratic township committeeman but lost.

When a judge criticized Truman for his neglect of the roadwork, Truman wrote a scathing response, then decided not to mail it. Instead he invited the judge to dinner and smoothed out their differences.

ഇൻ

DWIGHT D. EISENHOWER, 25 in October, graduated from West Point with a ranking of 61 out of 164 seniors. Offered a post in coast artillery, Eisenhower objected; he wanted the infantry.

Eisenhower wanted to get married. Returning to Abilene, Kansas, after graduation, he proposed to Gladys Harding on August 5. She delayed giving Eisenhower an answer and later left for a piano concert tour in the East. When she returned to Abilene, she married a widower instead of Eisenhower.

The army assigned Eisenhower to the Nineteenth Infantry, Fort Sam Houston, San Antonio, Texas. In October he met Mamie Doud, an 18-year-old high school girl from Denver. She was popular at Sam Houston, dating many officers.

Mamie's family spent the winter months in San Antonio to get away from Denver's severe weather. Her father, John, had made a fortune in meatpacking, retired at age 36, and earned a degree in math from the University of Chicago. Her mother, Elivera, was the daughter of Swedish immigrants.

৪০০৪

LYNDON B. JOHNSON, 7, the Texas schoolboy, studied little and often misbehaved. People remembered him hanging around on the fringe of men discussing politics, listening to what was being said.

৪০০৪

RICHARD M. NIXON, now 2, lived in California.

৪০০৪

GERALD R. FORD, 2 years old, lived in Grand Rapids, Michigan. Gerald's mother, Dorothy, age 23, met Gerald R. Ford, age 24, at an Episcopal church social. Ford had been born in Grand Rapids, and his father was killed in a train accident when he was 14. Ford had to quit school to support his mother and sisters. He sold varnish and paint to furniture factories.

৪০০৪

RONALD REAGAN, 4, lived in Illinois.

1916
Woodrow Wilson

The president, 60 in December, moved ever closer to war as he won a razor-thin election over Supreme Court Justice Charles Evans Hughes in part due to the slogan, "He kept us out of war."

January: When the British liner *Fersla* was sunk, Wilson told adviser Joseph Tumulty, "I am more interested in the opinion [the] country will have of me ten years from now than the opinion [expressed] today.... I understand that the country wants action but I will not be rushed into war."

Wilson hit the road for twelve speeches in New York and the Midwest in January, saying, "All the rest of the world is on fire, and our own house is not fireproof." He said that the future "does not depend upon what I say. It depends upon what foreign governments do." There was a general feeling that his speeches went over the head of the average voter, who only wanted to know how close to war with Germany the United States was at that moment.

On January 28, Wilson nominated Louis Brandeis to the Supreme Court. When he was confirmed by the Senate in June, he became the first Jewish Supreme Court justice.

March: Mexican rebel leader

Louis D. Brandeis was appointed to the Supreme Court in 1916, becoming the first Jewish associate justice. (Harris and Ewing, Collection of the Supreme Court of the United States)

Pancho Villa led 1,500 men on a raid into Columbus, New Mexico, killing 17 Americans. Wilson ordered U.S. troops to Mexico to capture Villa. On March 15, General John Pershing led a force of 6,000 troops across the Mexican border to search for Villa—a search that would last for almost a year before being abandoned without success.

April: Wilson again threatened to break diplomatic relations with Germany after the Germans sank the French ship *Sussex* in March. In what became known as the "*Sussex* pledge," on April 18, Germany agreed to "visit and search" a ship to establish whether it was carrying war material before it attacked.

June: Congress passed the National Defense Act on June 3. The new law would more than double the size of the regular army from 105,000 to 220,000. In addition, the National Guard would be increased to 450,000.

Democrats met in St. Louis on June 14 to 16 and renominated Wilson and Vice President Thomas Riley Marshall.

July: Meeting in Chicago, Republicans nominated Supreme Court Justice Charles Evans Hughes for president and Charles Warren Fairbanks of Indiana for vice president.

September: Wilson signed the Keating–Owen Act in September 1, banning interstate commerce in products made by children under age 14. The law also banned children under 16 from working in mines and from working more then 8 hours per day.

November: In a close election on November 7, Wilson defeated Charles Evans Hughes. In the popular vote, Wilson polled 9,129,606 votes to Hughes's 8,538,221 votes. The electoral vote gave Wilson 277 votes and Hughes 254 votes. Earlier, thinking that he might lose, Wilson prepared for a dramatic change in the American transitional routine. Favoring the British system, Wilson would have resigned immediately after the election along with the vice president and the secretary of state, so that Hughes could be made a temporary secretary of state and head of government until his inauguration in March. Wilson's cabinet talked him out of the idea.

Former Presidents

THEODORE ROOSEVELT was nominated again at a Progressive Party convention, but the Bull Moosers were deeply shocked when Roosevelt suggested that they endorse his old friend Henry Cabot Lodge. Roosevelt also made peace with the Republican Party and, although he wasn't an early supporter, campaigned for

Hughes. Roosevelt had said before the Republican convention that if the American people wanted something of the "heroic" in a leader, then he was available for the nomination.

In his campaign effort against Wilson, Roosevelt came close to calling the president a coward for not leading America into the European war.

January: Roosevelt set his personal strategy for the presidential campaign by asking the Progressive National Committee to issue a statement calling on its members to return to the Republican fold. He had faint hopes for the Republican nomination himself.

February–March: Roosevelt and Edith started a Caribbean tour on February 11 and after 6 weeks ended it at Port of Spain.

&)C&

WILLIAM HOWARD TAFT, the Yale University law professor, supported the Hughes candidacy but was inactive in the campaign. He met briefly with Theodore Roosevelt when Republican strategy managers felt it absolutely essential to get them on the same platform.

By 1916, Taft believed both the need to demonstrate partisanship and a feeling that Wilson was no longer leading the way in the nation's near encounter with the European conflict.

January: An opening on the Supreme Court found some supporting Taft. When Wilson turned instead to Louis Brandeis, Taft was upset by the choice.

April–May: By spring Taft was unhappy with Wilson's war policies and regarded the administration as a whole as a terrible failure. The Wilson program was far too radical, Taft thought. He believed that Wilson had surrendered to labor's agenda and had bungled things in Mexico.

June: After the Hughes nomination, Taft wrote to Gordon McCabe on June 19 that he wasn't sure of Hughes's judgment of men but that he knew "the wisdom of keeping on good terms with Congress."

Future Presidents

WARREN G. HARDING, the U.S. Senator from Ohio, made the keynote speech at the Republican National Convention that endorsed Hughes, but many critics said that the speech was too long and dull. Some delegates even walked out during it.

Harding was discouraged that his speech did not thrill delegates because he fancied himself as an accomplished orator. He did complain that continuous tampering with the speech by Old Guard Republicans made the final product a "rag carpet."

For months before the Republican convention voting, Harding's name surfaced as a potential dark horse candidate. In the end, Harding received one vote for the nomination on the second ballot.

After Wilson's reelection, Harding corresponded frequently with Theodore Roosevelt about ways to revitalize the Republican Party.

&)C&

CALVIN COOLIDGE campaigned for Hughes and easily won re-election as lieutenant governor of Massachusetts. His new friend, Boston merchant Frank W. Stearns, took Coolidge to Washington to meet Henry Cabot Lodge and other political powers. At the Republican National Convention, Stearns worked the lobby of the Congress Hotel, talking up Coolidge for president.

As lieutenant governor, Coolidge, 44, did not preside over the Massachusetts senate; his role was to chair the governor's council, an advisory group. The governor's council had the power to veto pardons. Coolidge also was chair of a committee on nominations to state offices and also had to inspect public institutions. Many times, he also had to fill in for Governor Samuel McCall at many speaking engagements. His load was so heavy that Coolidge hired Ralph W. Hemenway to keep his law practice going.

&)C&

HERBERT HOOVER, 42, was worn out by all the bickering between himself and some Belgian officials over how to administer the massive relief effort. He threatened to quit the thankless task more than once.

His reputation continued to soar. *Harper's Weekly* saw Hoover as having vice presidential potential. Interior Secretary Franklin K. Lane, in June at Brown University, called Hoover "the incarnation of the spirit of American desire to help the world." Six months later, Lane asked Hoover to become assistant secretary with control over the Bureau of Mines, Indian Affairs, Reclamation, and the Alaska Engineering Commission.

At one low point in his dispute over the internal management of Belgian aid, the discouraged Hoover favored letting the Belgians handle the entire operation.

&)C&

FRANKLIN D. ROOSEVELT, the 34-year-old assistant secretary of the navy, campaigned for Wilson in New York, Maine, and Rhode Island. All went to Hughes. Roosevelt, obsessed with lagging war preparations under Josephus Daniels, found himself too often in agreement with Republican campaigners on this issue. After the election a movement took shape to oust Daniels as secretary of the navy in favor of Roosevelt. But Roosevelt wrote that he had no use for anyone who would be "disloyal" to his navy "chief." Yet Roosevelt persisted in telling Daniels that the United States had to get into the war.

Roosevelt sent a steady stream of letters to Eleanor, either in Hyde Park or Campobello, with inside information on cabinet and congressional decisions. She was never in the dark on sensitive policy matters.

In this year, son Elliott, 5, was very ill for months, and son John was born in Washington on March 13.

୨୦୧୪

HARRY S TRUMAN, 32, lost money speculating on a zinc mine in Commerce, Oklahoma, but he showed endless enthusiasm for trying to strike it rich. Once he boasted to Bess Wallace that he would make $400 per week from zinc and would have "a Pierce-Arrow to ride in." But by May 19 he was down in spirits over delays and reverses at the mine. He confessed to Bess, "You would do better perhaps if you pitch me into the ash heap and pick someone with more sense and ability."

Truman had joined T. C. H. Mining Company in Commerce on May 4 and put up $5,000 with $500 down. For a while, for security reasons, Truman slept close to the mine. Before long Truman resumed farming in Missouri, and the mine closed in early May, a bust, or so it seemed. But the relentless Truman made changes in mine operations and his hopes rose again. He was shuffling between the farm in Missouri and the struggling mine in Oklahoma.

By September he could no longer meet the payment schedule and the mine closed again. Truman paid the workers and took a personal loss of $2,000. He wrote to Bess that all he needed was some luck. On September 25 he invested in Morgan and Company, an oil investment firm in Oklahoma.

୨୦୧୪

DWIGHT D. EISENHOWER, age 25, married Marie "Mamie" Geneva Doud, age 19, in Denver after a 4-month engagement. He was promoted to first lieutenant on his wedding day, July 1.

From a life of plenty in Denver, Mamie adjusted quickly to very small quarters at Fort Sam Houston in San Antonio. Mamie Doud was born on November 14, 1896, in Boone, Iowa. Her father, the rich meatpacker, was born in Rome, New York. The Doud clan came from Guilford, England, and founded Guilford, Connecticut, in 1639. Mamie's mother was Elvira Carlson Doud.

Eisenhower wanted to get his career jump-started and applied for the infant aviation section of the signal corps, which would include a 50-percent pay hike. His father-in-law, John S. Doud, objected, saying flying was too dangerous. The transfer was approved, but Dwight had to turn it down—he preferred Mamie.

Eisenhower received a 10-day leave to get married. The wedding was at the Doud home. Then the couple went to Manhattan, Kansas, to visit Dwight's brother Milton, a Kansas State student.

୨୦୧୪

LYNDON B. JOHNSON, 8, lived in Texas where he did household chores. His mother became a newspaper stringer for papers in Austin and Fredericksburg.

June 20: A sister, Lucia, was born.

୨୦୧୪

RICHARD M. NIXON, now 3, fell out of a buggy, gashed his scalp on a wagon wheel, and bled profusely on the 25-mile ride to the hospital.

୨୦୧୪

GERALD R. FORD, 3, had a new stepfather, although he was too young to know it, when Gerald R. Ford Sr. married the child's mother, Dorothy, on February 1 at the Grace Church in Grand Rapids, Michigan, where they had met.

୨୦୧୪

RONALD REAGAN, 5, lived in Illinois.

1917
Woodrow Wilson

President Wilson took the nation to war in response to the resumption of unrestricted German submarine warfare. The country had to make a rapid adjustment to dozens of unfamiliar war measures. War came after Wilson failed to convince Europe's belligerents to consider a peace conference.

January–March: In a prewar address to the Senate on January 22, Wilson spoke of the need for a "just" peace, a peace "between equals" to prevent revenge from becoming the overriding motive driving a future settlement. Robert La Follette called Wilson's remarks, "The greatest message of a century."

On February 1, Germany resumed unrestricted submarine warfare. In response to this, the United States broke diplomatic relations with Germany on February 3. Wilson said, however, that the United States would remain friends with the German "people."

On March 1, the "Zimmerman note" was published publicly for the first time. Intercepted by the British in January, the note was a telegram written by German foreign minister Arthur Zimmerman to the German ambassador in Mexico. Zimmerman suggested that Mexicans take up arms against the United States. Zimmerman promised a German alliance with Mexico and help to regain Texas, Arizona, and New Mexico. The public was outraged by the telegram.

Wilson was inaugurated for a second time on March 5, because March 4 fell on a Sunday. Wilson's inaugural address focused mostly on the war and spent little time on domestic issues.

From March 18 to 21, German submarines sank four U.S. merchant ships. Pressure was mounting on Wilson to act, and on March 20 the cabinet unanimously advised him to ask Congress for a declaration of war.

April: On April 2, Wilson asked Congress to recognize that a state of war existed between the United States and Germany. In his speech, Wilson said, "The world must be made safe for democracy."

On April 4, the Senate voted 82 to 6 in favor of war, and the House followed suit on April 6 by voting 373 to 50 in support of the Senate's declaration of war.

May–June: Congress passed the Selective Service Act on May 18. The act, which Wilson had proposed, required all able-bodied men between ages 21 and 30 to register for active duty. Registration was set to begin on June 5.

On May 26, Brigadier General John Pershing was named commander of the American Expedition Force (AEF).

On June 5, nearly 10 million men registered for the draft. Wilson, who had been worried about how the public would react to the new law, was relieved that the first day went so smoothly.

The first U.S. infantry troops, 14,000 total, arrived in France on June 26. Most were untrained and many were still unarmed.

July–August: Congress passed the Espionage Act on July 15. The new law imposed fines and prison terms of up to 20 years for anyone found guilty of supporting insubordination or disloyalty in the military.

U.S. troops cross the Westminster Bridge in London on September 5, 1917. These troops were among the first U.S. forces sent to fight in Europe during World War I. (Library of Congress)

On August 10, the United States Food Administration was officially created under the Lever Food and Fuel Act. Although technically in existence since May, the Lever Food and Fuel Act gave the U.S. Food Administration legitimacy as an official government bureau.

September: The first American casualties of the war were recorded on September 4 after a German air raid on a British hospital. Four Americans were killed.

November: When the Communists in Russia took control of the Russian government on November 7, Wilson feared that this would mean the withdrawal of Russia from the war.

Former Presidents

THEODORE ROOSEVELT was angered by Wilson's refusal to let him lead troops in France. Roosevelt was also willing to serve in the ranks as a private and said that his volunteer division could fight under British or French direction if necessary. Roosevelt even considered asking Canada to sponsor his legions. When these hopes dimmed, Roosevelt settled for a self-appointed role as Wilson's greatest critic.

ॐ

WILLIAM HOWARD TAFT, a lecturer in law at Yale University, was humored by Roosevelt's desire for heroism in France. Taft visited the White House, where an idea to send him to London to explain U.S. war aims was shelved after discussion.

The call to the White House came on December 12 to discuss a possible trip to London. Taft, now 60, was willing to go, but Wilson eventually dropped the idea. Taft wanted an invitation from the British first. The president said it was not desirable to get involved in British policy.

Taft's daughter Helen became a dean at Bryn Mawr College. Son Robert sought military service but was rejected for poor eyesight. Son Charles left Yale on May 21 to enlist in the artillery as a first lieutenant. In June he became engaged to Eleanor Chase. The couple was married in Waterbury, Connecticut, on October 6.

Future Presidents

WARREN G. HARDING, 52 in November, supported Wilson in the war effort and told the *New York Times* that the president might as well be given dictatorial powers, and the title supreme dictator. Harding told the newspaper that Alexander Hamilton had seen the need for a dictator in times of crisis.

Harding's lover, Carrie Phillips, was openly pro-German and warned the U.S. Senator from Ohio that if he voted for war she would expose their relationship. Despite the threat, Harding still voted for war.

ॐ

CALVIN COOLIDGE was elected to a third term as lieutenant governor of Massachusetts and soon after the election wrote to his father in Vermont, predicting that he would be nominated for governor in 1918. Whenever Governor Samuel McCall was out of state, Coolidge was acting governor and gained more experience.

During the year, Coolidge was often asked to give speeches on war measures and needs and war loans. Coolidge often spoke at charity drives.

In the fall election, McCall's plurality was 90,000 over his Democratic foe, Frederick W. Mansfield. Coolidge, now 45, won reelection by defeating the Democrat, Matthew Hale, by slightly more than 102,000 votes.

〆〇

HERBERT HOOVER, 42, as U.S. food czar, rallied housewives to join his "clean plate" movement aimed at reducing waste in food consumption. He made two trips between England and New York City dodging German mines, and met several times with President Wilson, congressional leaders, Britain's Lloyd George, and the war cabinet in London.

Wilson selected Hoover for the job of U.S. food administrator on May 13. Hoover fought price fixing, had many solutions for how to save on food, and even employed Hollywood techniques and talent to propagate his views.

〆〇

FRANKLIN D. ROOSEVELT, 35, a hawk, found his boss Navy Secretary Josephus Daniels continuing to procrastinate on crucial decisions concerning beefing up the navy for wartime readiness. FDR was occasionally ushered into the White House to discuss pet projects with President Wilson, such as stringing a line of mines across the North Sea and English Channel to thwart the German U-boats.

Roosevelt's activist manner often nettled Daniels, who criticized Navy League lobbying. The league often belittled Daniels for his slow pace and alleged bumbling. On the other hand, the league regarded FDR as cool and efficient. Sometimes FDR would pen a criticism to Daniels about how ship construction was behind schedule, and then send a copy to Wilson.

Roosevelt early in the year made trips to Haiti and Cuba. In Haiti he spoke French, took long horseback rides in the heat, and climbed mountains.

During the summer, Roosevelt was seen escorting Lucy Mercer around on the presidential yacht on the Potomac. FDR's letters to Eleanor at Campobello sometimes mentioned Lucy. Alice Roosevelt would often invite FDR and Lucy to dinner.

〆〇

HARRY S TRUMAN, 33, entered the army, became an officer in charge of a canteen in Oklahoma and, by December, was ticketed for France. He became engaged to Bess Wallace, who opposed his serving in the army. He could have received a deferment to continue working on the farm, but he felt the tug of patriotism when the United States entered the war. He supported Wilson's war message.

May–July: Truman rejoined his Missouri National Guard unit in May. Truman worked hard enlisting members, which led to his selection to be an officer.

When Truman went to Bess's house wearing his uniform on July 4, she cried on his shoulder and wanted to get married. Truman, not long after, wrote to her that he was "dead crazy" to marry her before leaving for camp, but he said it wouldn't be fair to her if later he returned home a cripple.

August–September: On August 5, Truman was transferred into the regular army's One Hundred Twenty-Ninth Field Artillery.

On September 26 he started basic training at Camp Doniphan, Fort Sill, Oklahoma. He soon became the regular canteen officer working in tandem with enlisted man Eddy Jacobson. Truman kept the books.

Life was tough in Oklahoma for soldiers. Sand blew into the tents, and the water was contaminated. When the wind kicked up, Truman wrote Bess, he couldn't see another tent 50 yards away.

There were 6 batteries in the Second Missouri Field Artillery regiment—about 1,300 men, almost all of them from Missouri and Kansas. He was surprised to be selected a first lieutenant for Battery F.

〆〇

DWIGHT D. EISENHOWER, 27, was sent to Texas, Georgia, Maryland, and Kansas by the army. But he asked for duty in France too often, and the army had to rebuke him for sounding like a broken record. His problem: The army found out he was an excellent teacher.

Ike expected to go to France with the Fifty-Seventh Infantry. He received target practice at Leon Springs, Texas, only 30 miles from San Antonio. Made captain in May, Eisenhower next took command of 6,000 men at Fort Oglethorpe, Georgia, on September 20, for tank training. Yet he had only one French tank on base and was expected to show that many men how to operate it. This led to his being an instructor in the officer training school at Oglethorpe, because the army had a serious shortage of capable teachers.

Lieutenant Colonel Ira Welborn, a Medal of Honor winner in the Spanish-American War, was impressed with Eisenhower and had him moved to Camp Meade, Maryland, to organize the Sixty-fifth Battalion Engineers. By year's end, Eisenhower was at Fort Leavenworth, Kansas, as an instructor in the army service school.

Mamie returned home to Denver and on September 24 gave birth to a boy they named Dwight Doud Eisenhower.

〆〇

JOHN F. KENNEDY was born at 3 P.M. on May 29, in a two-and-a-half story clapboard house at 83 Beals Street in Brookline, Massachusetts. His father was Joseph Patrick Kennedy, age 29; his mother was Rose Fitzgerald Kennedy, age 27. John was their second son; Joseph P. Kennedy Jr. had been born on July 28, 1915.

Rose's father, John "Honey Fitz" Fitzgerald, tried his best to prevent the marriage. The Fitzgeralds and Kennedys were rival Irish political enemies of long standing. John Fitzgerald, a graduate of Boston College, was a member of Congress from 1895 to 1901 and Boston's mayor from 1906 to 1907 and 1910 to 1914. To prevent the match, Rose's father took her to Europe in 1911, then to Panama, then across the country to meet President Taft, then to Baltimore for the Democratic National Convention of 1912.

Joseph Kennedy, born in Boston in 1888, graduated from Harvard in 1912 and at age 25 was the youngest bank president in the state. Rose Kennedy was born in Boston in 1890, educated at the Sacred Heart convent in Boston and the Blumenthal Academy convent in Valls, Netherlands. She also studied piano at the New England Conservatory of Music and spoke French and German. The couple married on October 7, 1914.

෨෬

LYNDON B. JOHNSON, at 9, was a shoeshine boy at a small town barbershop in Texas. In November, his father, Sam, a Democrat, ran unopposed for his old seat in the Texas house. His mother, Rebekah, experienced a slow recovery from two minor operations and gave up her newspaper stringer job and started writing poetry. Sam would hold spelling bees for the children at the dinner table and quiz them on other matters; he became a member of the draft board.

෨෬

RICHARD M. NIXON, 4, almost died of pneumonia. He lived in Yorba Linda, California, where his mother taught him to read before he went to school.

෨෬

GERALD R. FORD, 4, lived in Grand Rapids, Michigan.

෨෬

RONALD REAGAN, 6, entered the Willard School in Galesburg, Illinois.

1918
Woodrow Wilson

President Wilson, 62 in December, saw the United States become an even greater world power as its army helped the Allies defeat the Central Powers in World War I. With the war over in November, Wilson became the first president to go overseas while still holding office when he traveled to Paris in December to take part in the Paris Peace Conference. At the end of the year, Wilson's major interest was in establishing a League of Nations.

January: In a speech before Congress on January 8, Wilson presented his vision for international peace. Wilson's Fourteen Points plan was designed to demonstrate to the Central Powers that they would be treated fairly at the end of the war. Among some of the Fourteen Points were a call for no secret treaties, freedom of the seas, worldwide arms reductions, and the removal trade barriers and establishment of equal trade conditions. Several of the points dealt with specific countries and boundary disputes. The fourteenth point called for the creation of the League of Nations.

March–April: Germany and Russia signed the Treaty of Brest–Litovsk on March 3, ending Russia's involvement in World War I.

On March 4, Wilson established the War Industries Board to lead with war production. Wilson appointed Bernard Baruch to head the board, which would give the U.S. gov-

ernment increased power over free enterprise in mobilizing for the war effort.

The Germans opened up the Somme Offensive on March 21, attacking poorly prepared British and French forces and pushing them back to the Somme River in a week. But reinforced by fresh U.S. troops by the end of March, the Allies held their ground against an increasingly exhausted German army.

During this time, the U.S. troops remained a separate fighting unit and did not fight with the British and French. From the beginning of U.S. involvement in the war, the U.S. commander, John J. Pershing, had been adamant to keep U.S. troops under the separate command of U.S. officers. On April 2, Wilson ordered Pershing to assign some U.S. units to fight with French and British units. Pershing did but kept the majority under his command and that of other U.S. officers.

May–June: Congress passed the Sedition Act on May 16, making it a crime to utter "disloyal or abusive language" about the government, the Constitution, the draft, or the U.S. flag.

U.S. Marines went on the offensive on June 6 at Belleau Wood in France. The offensive was started with the objective of quickly clearing Belleau Wood of Germans, but the Germans were determined not to let the U.S. achieve a quick, morale-boosting victory. The Germans sent in reinforcements, forcing the United States to do the same. By June 26, the Americans had achieved their goal but at a heavy cost, suffering more than 5,000 casualties.

September–November: General Pershing was finally allowed to command an American offensive. He decided to take the St. Mihiel salient south of Verdun, France. The Germans had held this territory for much of the war. On September 12, American troops numbering 200,000 and nearly 50,000 French soldiers attacked. Nearly 1,500 Allied planes supported the ground troops from the air. The St. Mihiel salient fell in 4 days.

On September 26, the Meuse–Argonne Offensive began, with the goal of a general Allied offensive along the entire western front. U.S. troops were to clear the Argonne Forest of German troops. Early success by American troops was soon curtailed by reinforced German troops. It took 5 weeks for the Americans to clear the Germans out of the Argonne.

On November 1, American and French troops launched a new offensive along the Meuse River. More than 1 million Allied troops, most of them American, attacked and sent the Germans into retreat. By November 10, the Allies had taken Sedan and Mezieres, two valuable rail centers, and had fought in what would be the last major battle of the war. An armistice was signed at 11 A.M. on November 11 between Germany and France, bringing the Great War to an end.

December: Wilson sailed for France on December 4 for the Paris Peace Conference, determined to sell his Fourteen Points to the Allies, in particular the idea of the League of Nations.

German prisoners, captured during the first day of the attack on Saint Mihiel in France, are marched to the rear by U.S. troops in September 1918. (Library of Congress)

Former Presidents

THEODORE ROOSEVELT, although his health was poor during the year, expressed an interest in being the Republican candidate in 1920. He had some support from party leaders.

February: Roosevelt suffered from malaria, a consequence of his Cuban days. Abscesses on both his thigh and an ear compounded his condition.

July 14: Roosevelt's youngest son, Quentin, 20, was killed when his plane was shot down in an aerial dogfight on the western front over France.

November–December: Roosevelt suffered more health problems. He spent 7 weeks hospitalized with rheumatism that threatened to put him in a wheelchair for life, even though he was only 60.

ක⟩ග

WILLIAM HOWARD TAFT moved back to Washington to be co-chairman of the National War Labor Board. Wilson, on April 8, created the board by proclamation, with Taft and Frank Walsh of Massachusetts as co-chairman. The board had five members from each of two sides: employer and employee. Taft was seen as representing the employers and received leave from Yale to take the job. The work of the National War Labor Board involved settling disputes between employers and workers in war industries. It gave Taft a new understanding of the needs of working people.

Taft supported the League of Nations, as he had been active earlier as president of the League to Enforce Peace. But the former president was disappointed that Wilson did not take him to Paris in December for the peace conference. Despite Taft's growing disillusionment with Wilson as a leader, Taft was always the patriot, making speeches at Liberty Bond rallies and lecturing soldiers at army camps.

Future Presidents

WARREN G. HARDING said little during U.S. Senate debates over war bills, yet voted for the Sedition Act, food control, and the war revenue bill. Personal dilemmas plagued him, as Carrie Phillips continued to demand that he get a divorce and marry her, while his wife, Florence, continued to have kidney problems.

Some began to see Harding, 53 in November, as a strong candidate for the Republican presidential nominee in 1920. To close friends he expressed the feeling that presidential responsibility would be too much for him and that another term or two in the Senate would satisfy his political ambition.

ක⟩ග

CALVIN COOLIDGE won the close Massachusetts gubernatorial race by a slim margin while most of the Republicans in the state dominated their political contests.

January–February: By the start of the year, it was no secret that Lieutenant Governor Coolidge wanted a promotion but did not want to appear to be seeking the office. Governor Samuel McCall's decision to try for a U.S. Senate seat led him to ask Coolidge to run for governor.

November: Coolidge defeated Democratic nominee Richard H. Long, a wealthy shoemaker but political amateur from Framingham, by more than 17,000 votes. Long earlier had lost a bid for lieutenant governor.

Coolidge's mentor, Frank W. Stearns, wanted the new governor to move into a historic home on Beacon Hill in Boston. Instead Coolidge added one room to his living quarters at Adams House.

ක⟩ග

HERBERT HOOVER, 44, a household name all over America, resigned as food czar and returned to Europe again to combat starvation on a staggering scale. He wanted the European rehabilitation task and recommended to Wilson that it was a job that needed to be done.

Hoover sailed for Europe 6 days after the armistice was signed. His job title was director of American Relief Administration. As peace was discussed in Paris, it was Hoover's hope to "save life and prevent anarchy." He later claimed that the American effort in Europe "saved civilization" and more than 100 million lives.

Hoover insisted on setting prices on commodities even though some corporate suppliers made huge profits. Farmers were often upset with Hoover's guidelines, even though he needed their cooperation in managing food production.

৪০০৪

FRANKLIN D. ROOSEVELT, 36, went to the western front, met the major players in the war drama, and almost died of double pneumonia caused by his hectic inspection schedule.

Soon after he returned to New York City from France on a stretcher, Eleanor unpacked his luggage and discovered love letters between her husband and Lucy Mercer. Eleanor offered a divorce in a showdown meeting of the triangle. She issued an ultimatum: If Roosevelt still wanted eventually to become president, then she would stick with him and be a part of the deal. Roosevelt and Lucy backed off, but the Roosevelt marriage was never the same again. Eleanor much later wrote, "The bottom dropped out of my particular world … I really grew up that year."

July–September: Roosevelt sailed for Europe on July 9 aboard a new U.S. Navy destroyer via the Azores. In Great Britain, Roosevelt shared German schooling experiences with King George V at a private session on July 28. He spoke at a dinner attended by war leaders including Winston Churchill and lunched with Lloyd George at the American embassy.

In the war zone starting August 4, FDR rejected security precautions and went to French headquarters at Chateau-Thierry, Verdun, and Belleau Wood. He just missed a German shelling near Fort Douaumont, experienced the dangers of air raids, and saw a clash between a U-boat and a destroyer in the English Channel. Roosevelt saw the debacle of the western front—all of the destruction, death, and chaos. On the go from 6 A.M. to midnight day after day finally affected his health, and he was rushed back to the United States on September 19.

October–December: Theodore Roosevelt wrote to Franklin: "[I] trust you will soon be well. We are very proud of you." After his recovery, Franklin sought active duty with the navy, but Wilson issued a firm denial, pointing out in mid-October that it was "too late," and that the fighting was almost over.

With his health recovered, Roosevelt made a second trip to Europe in December. Eleanor accompanied him this time on her first trip abroad since their honeymoon.

৪০০৪

HARRY S TRUMAN, 34, saw rough fighting on the western front and showed leadership abilities in bringing his motley artillery unit of tough Kansas City Irishmen through virtually unscathed. Truman had several close calls from German artillery strikes, particularly at Mount Herrenberg in the Vosges Mountains.

March–June: Truman, a first lieutenant with the One Hundred Twenty-ninth Field Artillery, sailed for Europe aboard the *George Washington* on March 30. From April to early June, he was trained at the Second Corps Artillery School in France at Chantillon-sur-Seine. Truman graduated from the school on June 8 and was promoted to captain.

July–August: Truman rejoined his regiment, and on July 5 the regiment was sent to artillery school at Coatquidan. On August 5, the regiment was ordered to the front.

September–November: Truman's regiment took part in the major battles at St. Mihiel in September, Meuse-Argonne in October, and the final assault along the Meuse River in November. When panic set in when first under attack, Truman bravely rallied his men and later brought them through many tight situations.

৪০০৪

DWIGHT D. EISENHOWER, 28, never reached France and forever regretted it. A record with no combat upset and disgusted him. On the other hand, by August he commanded 10,000 men at a camp near the Gettysburg, Pennsylvania, battlefield, and by October he was a lieutenant colonel. His promotions put him on a faster track than almost anyone else in the class of 1915.

On November 11 he told Captain Norman Randolph that he would spend the rest of his life explaining how he never saw the western front. Most of Eisenhower's friends were in France. His leadership ability kept him in the United States. He was assigned to Camp Colt, Pennsylvania, on March 23 to organize tank crews as commander of the Tank Corps Training Center. Because Eisenhower had no tanks at Camp Colt, he trained his men to become good truck drivers.

By October he was one of the youngest lieutenant colonels in the army. While at Colt, Dwight and Mamie lived in an empty fraternity house at Gettysburg College. It was their first time together at a base since San Antonio. Eisenhower's work with the tank training led to a Distinguished Service Cross 4 years later.

৪০০৪

JOHN F. KENNEDY, 1, was a baby in Brookline, Massachusetts. His father was drafted but avoided service by holding on to his job as a shipyard executive.

September 13: A sister, Rosemary, was born.

৪০০৪

LYNDON B. JOHNSON, now 10, joined his father on the campaign trail for a seat in the Texas statehouse. They rode in a Model T. Sam, 41, who never lost an election, defeated August Benner, a farmer and neighbor in Johnson City.

৪০০৪

RICHARD M. NIXON, at 5, was disappointed when the family, including brother Don, made a trip from California to Ohio, and he was left behind in Yorba Linda.

May 26: Nixon's brother Arthur was born.

৪০০৪

GERALD R. FORD, 5, lived in Grand Rapids, Michigan.

July 15: Gerald's half-brother Tom was born.

৪০০৪

RONALD REAGAN, 7 years old, moved for the fifth time—from Galesburg, Illinois, to Monmouth, 17 miles to the west. Ronald entered the second grade at Central School on September 9.

He received a grade of 97 percent by getting A's in reading and math, and B's in other subjects.

1919
Woodrow Wilson

President Wilson's dogged persistence led Allied leaders to accept the League of Nations as the crown of the World War I peace settlement. But back home in the United States, Senate objections led by Henry Cabot Lodge prevented ratification. A determined Wilson took the league's cause on the road, a campaign that led to a breakdown and to his wife, Edith, virtually acting as president for the ailing Wilson.

January–March: Wilson began the year in Paris, still working to iron out the details of the peace treaty between the Central Powers and the Allies. During this time, Wilson presented to the Allied European leaders his outline for the League of Nations, presenting his final plan on February 14.

The Eighteenth Amendment to the Constitution—prohibiting the manufacture, sale, and transportation of liquor—became law when Missouri, Nebraska, and Wyoming ratified it on January 16. It would take effect on January 16, 1920.

Wilson returned to the United States on February 24 to explain the league and the treaty to congressional leaders and the American people. At this point, it appeared that Wilson had the general support of the Congress, the newspapers, and the public on the issue of the League of Nations.

On March 5, Wilson departed the United States for Europe again to take part in the final peace treaty talks. Wilson's return to Paris in March engendered none of the public enthusiasm that had greeted his first arrival in Paris in Decem-

ber 1918. By now Allied leaders and newspapers were becoming critical of Wilson's performance and his headstrong approach to making the league the cornerstone of the peace agreement.

April–June: Friction developed between the Big Four negotiators in Paris. The Big Four consisted of Wilson, David Lloyd George of Great Britain, Georges Clemenceau of France, and Vittorio Orlando of Italy. Each man came to the table with an agenda specifically to promote the interests of his country, and the European leaders sought high reparations from Germany and the other Central Powers. Wilson, who largely opposed the severity of the reparations, openly predicted another fight to the finish in 25 years.

Signing of the Treaty of Versailles between Germany and the Allies finally took place on June 28. The treaty limited Germany's military strength and forced it to give up much of its territory as well as pay a reparations bill to the Allies of $33 billion.

Congress passed the Nineteenth Amendment to the Constitution, granting women suffrage. It would be ratified on August 18, 1920.

July–September: Wilson returned to the United States on July 8 to find that support for his League of Nations had dwindled, especially in the Senate. Senator Henry Cabot Lodge of Massachusetts announced that he would not support the league.

Wilson decided to take the league issue directly to the American people. He was convinced that he could go over Lodge and the Senate's head and woo the American people into pressuring the Senate to endorse the league.

Wilson's tour of the Midwest and West began on September 3 and featured thirty-four speeches made at a whirlwind, frenetic pace over 3 weeks and 8,000 miles.

Toward the end of the tour, on September 25 in Denver, Wilson suffered a paralytic attack and nervous breakdown, forcing the cancellation of the scheduled stops between Colorado and Washington, D.C. A week later, Wilson suffered a cerebral hemorrhage that paralyzed his left side and nearly killed him. The public was never informed just how seriously Wilson was crippled by the attack.

October–December: While Wilson remained in his sickbed for much of the remainder of the year, Edith Wilson controlled all access to the president. The news blackout on Wilson's condition spawned various rumors, including that Wilson was insane and that he had syphilis. Edith maintained that Wilson's mental state was fine, yet no document was passed on to the president unless first shown to Edith.

To appease some of the doubters in Congress, Republican Senator Albert Fall was brought into

The "Big Four" in a public show of unity during their peace talks in Paris. From left to right are Britain's Lloyd George, Italy's Vittorio Orlando, France's Georges Clemenceau, and Woodrow Wilson.
(National Archives)

Wilson's sick room to see not only that the president could talk but also that his mind was sharp. Fall was satisfied with what he saw.

Owing in large part to Wilson's illness and his inability to campaign for it, the Senate rejected the Treaty of Versailles on November 19, effectively crushing any chance of U.S. participation in the League of Nations.

Former Presidents

THEODORE ROOSEVELT lived for only 6 days in 1919. During those 6 days, he was still railing against President Woodrow Wilson.

On January 1, he told Ogden Reid of the *New York Tribune*: "I never allude to Wilson as an idealist. He is a doctrinaire; he is always utterly and coldly selfish. He hasn't a touch of idealism in him." On January 3,

The interior of a New York City bar minutes before prohibition went into effect in 1920. (Library of Congress)

he dictated several letters, including one in which he told a man in Iowa that his only error in the war years was to have supported Wilson's neutrality for the first 60 days.

On January 4, Edith called James Amos, their former valet, and asked him to come help. Amos found Roosevelt looking weary and later said, "It was perfectly plain that he had suffered deeply."

The next day Roosevelt and Edith read to each other. Later that night, Dr. George W. Faller, a family physician, visited and found Roosevelt having trouble breathing. "James, will you please put out the light," Roosevelt asked Amos that night. Amos sat in a chair next to Roosevelt in the dark and noted that his breathing was regular.

At 4 A.M. on January 6, Amos noticed irregular breathing, and he rushed out to get the nurse. When they returned, Roosevelt was dead. The cause was pulmonary embolism—a blood clot on the lung. Roosevelt was 60 years old.

The funeral was held on January 8 at the Oyster Bay Episcopal Church. There were approximately 450 mourners, but no music and no eulogy. Roosevelt's estate was estimated at $500,000, with a $60,000 trust divided among the children.

୨୦ଔ

WILLIAM HOWARD TAFT made a fifteen-city speaking tour for the League of Nations and was angered by Republican opposition to the league. Taft supported the Wilson strategy of keeping the league in the peace treaty.

February–March: Taft wrote on February 22 about the "narrowness" of Senator James A. Reed of Missouri, the "ignorance" of Senator Miles Poindexter of Washington, and the "vanity" of Henry Cabot Lodge for their refusal to support the league.

When Wilson returned to Washington, Taft wrote to his son Robert on March 17 that he would "vote for the cov-

enant as it is, without hesitation, because I don't think it contains any of the dangers [that opposition senators claimed]."

October–December: At the beginning of October, Taft, 62, went to Washington to lobby for the league and found Senator Frank Billings Kellogg of Minnesota, "in a state of great nervousness ... damning the President.... He said he wished the treaty was in Hell."

Taft wrote to W. A. Edwards on October 27 about Wilson's health: "The truth is, he has [so] insisted on hogging all the authority.... trusting no one ... he has broken himself down."

He wrote to Senator Gilbert M. Hitchcock of Nebraska on November 15: "I beg of you to consider the consequences if you defeat the treaty [which] represents enormous progress toward better conditions as to peace and war."

The Senate defeated the treaty, and Taft later said it was a "stunning blow."

Future Presidents

WARREN G. HARDING moved closer to becoming a presidential candidate in 1920 as campaign manager Harry Daugherty worked out the details. All through the year, Harding expressed to friends and family that he had doubts about his ability to govern the country. Daugherty, however, scoffed, and told him alleged presidential greatness was a thing of the past, an "illusion" for most people. Harding also opposed the League of Nations and was one of fifteen U.S. senators who went to the White House to question Wilson on certain provisions.

January: The year began with the sudden death of Theodore Roosevelt. Vice President Thomas Marshall assigned Harding as a member of a congressional committee to attend the funeral, where about fifty politicians were present. In late January, Harding gave a Roosevelt memorial address to the Ohio General Assembly in Columbus. He said Roosevelt was "less radical than he often times appeared."

February: At a Lincoln Day dinner in Toledo, Ohio, the state central committee endorsed Harding for president. Harding, however, was emphatic about the other good candidates available for 1920.

৪০৫৪

CALVIN COOLIDGE, the governor of Massachusetts, became front-page news across the nation when he ended the violent Boston police strike in September. Coolidge said: "There is no right to strike against the public safety by anybody, anywhere, any time!" Coolidge later won reelection as governor by a landslide, and his promoter, Frank W. Stearns, beat the presidential drums at an accelerated pace. Coolidge was now a national political figure.

The police strike began on September 9, and for a time Boston was defenseless against looting and other crime in the streets. Boston police were disgruntled with their low pay during the war when war industry workers made big money. In May, Police Commissioner Edwin U. Curtis, a former Boston mayor, managed a $200 raise to a maximum salary of $1,600 per year for police officers. After this raise, there was a move for police to join the American Federation of Labor (AFL). Curtis was against this and would not budge on this issue, saying that police officers couldn't do their duty and be in a union at the same time.

However, the Boston police received an AFL charter on August 15, and Curtis charged nineteen men with violating his orders against the union. Curtis announced on September 8 that the nineteen police officers had been suspended. Police voted 1,134 to 2 to strike on September 9. Coolidge made contradictory statements concerning the strike, saying he was against a strike but was sympathetic with police and hoped that the suspended officers would be reinstated.

On the evening of September 9, the strike began. Some 1,117 of 1,544 men in uniform walked out. Those who stayed put were mostly superiors and senior officers worried about their pensions. In response, Mayor Andrew J. Peters of Boston fired the striking officers. Soon, rioting and looting began in the streets of Boston.

On September 10, Coolidge called out the National Guard to bring peace to Boston. There was pressure on Coolidge to intervene, and Curtis went to him for help. There were worries that the young Peters would make poor decisions under stress. Coolidge decided arbitration was out of the question, that the issue was authority of law and obedience to the orders of the police commissioner.

Disorder continued while Coolidge considered his options. In South Boston, the National Guard troops fired into a crowd killing two. More looting and assaults followed, but by September 11 order was restored in the city.

Coolidge wrote a proclamation on September 11 and issued an executive order. He called out more National Guard troops and ordered loyal police to obey him. Soon after the order, the police decided against continuing the strike.

Less then two weeks after the strike ended, Coolidge was renominated on September 23 to run for another term. His opponent was Democrat Richard H. Long.

In the November election, Coolidge easily beat Long, receiving 317,774 votes to Long's 192,673.

৪০৫৪

HERBERT HOOVER, 45, witnessed negotiation of the Versailles Treaty from up close and later organized the American Relief Association to feed the starving in twenty-one nations. In the final assessment, the United States delivered $5 billion-worth of American food to starving areas of Europe. Hoover's European Children's Fund helped 6 million children.

In April, Hoover agreed to help 15 million Russians avoid famine. He drove across Central Europe by car from Austria to Poland, where he was honored by a parade of 50,000 Polish children, some of whom sang the "Star Spangled Banner" for him.

More than $24 million in profit from the Committee for Relief of Belgium was given to the country to rebuild libraries and establish a Belgian–American student exchange program. In working on Europe's economic recovery problems, Hoover headed a staff of 1,500 U.S. Army officials. Throughout most of the year, Hoover served the War Trade Council, the Sugar Equalization Board, the European Coal Council, and the Economic Council. He was economic adviser to Wilson until June. By then Hoover was too critical of the president to remain on the inner-circle team.

Hoover told Wilson he opposed recognizing the new revolutionary regime in Russia because of its use of murder and terror. He wrote to Wilson on March 28: "We cannot even remotely recognize this murderous Bolshevik tyranny without stimulating actionist radicalism" everywhere in Europe. Hoover advised patience in dealing with the Bolsheviks because he expected them to collapse quickly.

Hoover opposed the Versailles Treaty's treatment of the Germans. On June 5, Hoover wrote to Wilson that if Germany were treated harshly, "she will turn either to Communism or reaction, and will thereby become either militarily or politically on the offensive." The Versailles Treaty, Hoover told Wilson, would destroy any seeds of democracy growing in the country.

In Palo Alto, Lou Hoover supervised the construction of their new home, which started June 1 on land leased from Stanford. It was completed on November 20. Hoover returned to New York on September 13, wishing to never see Europe again. Then he continued on to Palo Alto.

৪০৫৪

FRANKLIN D. ROOSEVELT, 37 in January, made a 35-day inspection tour of Europe, saw the trenches, and later took the stump in Chicago and elsewhere to preach for the League of Nations. It was his second European trip as assistant secretary of the navy.

January–February: Eleanor accompanied Franklin on the trip to Europe, leaving New York City on January 2 and returning with President Wilson on February 24. FDR was the major negotiator in Europe for the disposal of navy property in France. Eleanor remained in Paris when FDR went to Belgium and into the Rhineland. Together they visited battlefields on the Somme, and the Amiens and Cambrai sectors. Roosevelt was not privy to Wilson's League of Nations negotiations with France and Great Britain.

May 29: At a Democratic National Committee banquet in Chicago, Roosevelt discussed the difference between liberals and conservatives. He said that the GOP was busy with "Americanism and jingo bluff, to the old hypocrisy of Penrose, Mark Hanna and Blaine." FDR said Republicans wanted to reduce taxes for the rich. He also criticized Henry Cabot Lodge's foreign policy views. Newspapers gave wide coverage to what was considered a "fighting" speech.

June 9: A bomb blast at the home of Attorney General A. Mitchell Palmer across the street from the Roosevelt home shattered windows in the bedroom of Roosevelt's son, James, age 11. Roosevelt himself was busy parking a car after a party when the blast narrowly missed injuring him.

HARRY S TRUMAN, 35, had been romancing Elizabeth Bess Wallace for 8 years, and the two finally married in Independence, Missouri, on June 28. She was 34.

The marriage was at the Trinity Episcopal Church. The brief honeymoon included the Blackstone Hotel in Chicago, Detroit, and the beach near Port Huron, where Harry visited his cousin, Mary Colgan Romine. Later the couple moved into 219 North Delaware, the home of her grandparents. In total, five people lived in the house: the newlyweds and her sister, brother, and mother Madge.

Bess was born on February 13, 1885. Her father, David Wallace, was a public official and a suicide in 1903. Her mother was Madge Gates Wallace. She attended Barstow's finishing school for girls in Kansas City.

Truman met her at church when he was 6—they were classmates from the fifth grade on—and she was his only sweetheart. The shy Harry wrote her 1,600 letters over the years.

Truman and old army buddy Eddy Jacobson opened a haberdashery in November. It was on the corner of 12th Street and Baltimore in Kansas City. They sold only shirts and underwear, no suits. They operated from 8 A.M. to 9 P.M., 6 days per week. The store was in a five-story brick building that also housed the Glennon Hotel.

DWIGHT D. EISENHOWER, 29, while commanding a tank battalion in Maryland, took a cross-country trip in a truck convoy—a publicity stunt thought up by a captain to boost the army's image. Eisenhower was selected as an observer. The convoy of 72 vehicles and 280 men moved at a snail's pace, 6 miles per hour, over 3,200 miles of terrible roads. It was estimated that 3.2 million Americans saw the convoy. The trucks started outside the White House on July 7, and Eisenhower joined the caravan at Frederick, Maryland. The trip was later credited with inspiring Eisenhower's interest in creating an interstate highway system during his presidency.

At Boone, Iowa, Eisenhower met Mamie's aunt and uncle. At North Platte, Nebraska, Mamie and her parents joined the parade and tagged along as far as Laramie, Wyoming. There was royal treatment in Salt Lake City and Stockton and a banquet in Oakland.

JOHN F. KENNEDY, 2, lived in Brookline, Massachusetts. His father Joe became a stockbroker at Hayden Stone in downtown Boston.

LYNDON B. JOHNSON, 11, took to imitating his father by getting close to people when he was talking to them. The Johnson City, Texas, youth also tried to dress like his father.

RICHARD M. NIXON, 6, entered the first grade on September 19 in Yorba Linda, California. His teacher, Miss Mary George, found the boy quiet, studious, and able to remember facts.

GERALD R. FORD, 6, started school in Grand Rapids, Michigan.

RONALD REAGAN, age 8, and family, moved back to his birthplace in Tampico, Illinois, when his father once again went to work for H. C. Pitney. An elderly couple next door to the Reagans gave Ronald 10 cents a week to read to them.

1920
Woodrow Wilson

The president, 64 in December, still in extremely poor health and barely able to walk, made no effort to prevent a minor push to give him a third term. But reason prevailed among Democratic Party managers at the Democratic National Convention.

January–February: In January the servants in the White House were getting edgy with Edith Wilson, who was stung by newspaper criticism of her role in the White House.

Wilson began to regain control of his paralyzed leg and arm. One day in February, Ray Stannard Baker came to the White House and watched Wilson make his first faltering steps.

March: The Treaty of Versailles met a final defeat in the U.S. Senate on March 19 when it failed to receive the necessary two-thirds approval of the Senate.

April: Wilson talked to Dr. Grayson about resigning the presidency and letting Vice President Thomas Marshall take over. Wilson said the "country cannot afford to wait for me" to regain his health. Grayson replied that Wilson was keeping abreast of events and should not resign.

May–July: As Wilson's health improved, he began to think about a third term. At the end of May, when some Democrats learned this, they were horrified. Joseph Tumulty asked Wilson to reject the idea publicly, but Wilson refused.

Late in the spring, Tumulty arranged an interview for Wilson with Louis Seibold of the *New York World*. The story indicated that Wilson's health was improving and concluded that Wilson was capable of handling a third term.

Dr. Grayson privately went to many Democratic leaders in June, asking that Wilson not be considered for another term. "He couldn't survive the campaign. He is permanently incapacitated and gradually weakening mentally," he told one Democratic leader.

Wilson wanted Bainbridge Colby to be convention chairman. On July 2, Colby sent Wilson a coded message that unless instructed otherwise, Wilson would be nominated by acclamation. But a telephone call from the White House said this would not be acceptable to Wilson.

At the Democratic convention in San Francisco in July, James Middleton Cox of Ohio was nominated for president on the forty-fourth ballot. Franklin D. Roosevelt was nominated for vice president (see **Franklin D. Roosevelt**, page 483).

August–November: Wilson was of little help in the Democratic campaign and wrote to Edward Bok that he didn't want to interfere. Cox and Roosevelt visited the White House shortly after the convention and found Wilson weak, a shawl over his left shoulder. Cox said to Wilson that he would go all out for the League of Nations.

Wilson broke his silence on October 3 when he said that the election would be a national referendum on the League of Nations. The week before the election, Wilson sat in his wheelchair to talk to fifteen pro-league Republicans: "The nation was never called upon to make a more solemn determination than it must now make. The whole future moral force of right in the world depends upon the United States."

On Election Day, November 2, Wilson told the cabinet, "The American people will not turn Cox down and elect Harding. A great moral issue is involved." Many cabinet members tried to prepare Wilson for a Harding victory, but he would not listen. Hurt and bewildered by Harding's victory, Wilson made no statement.

December: With Wilson's term coming to an end, Woodrow and Edith had to confront their future. They sketched out their needs, considering friends, climate, library, and amusements. New York City rated the highest with them, aside from Washington. They also considered moving to Baltimore, Richmond, and Boston. Edith went house hunting in both Virginia and the District of Columbia. In the end, the couple bought a house in Washington, D.C.

On December 10, Wilson was awarded the Nobel Peace Prize for his efforts in bringing an end to World War I.

Former Presidents

WILLIAM HOWARD TAFT campaigned for Warren G. Harding despite having reservations about the nominee. After the election, Harding offered Taft a seat on the Supreme Court.

Taft, the Yale professor of law, made many speeches for Harding. But Taft was not enthusiastic about him. He wrote to W. Murray Crane on August 14 that Harding was "certainly talking too much … and allowing himself to say things about the league that are embarrassing."

In December, Taft was concerned about meeting the president-elect: "I really don't know how to deal with Harding when I see him because I haven't known him personally very well." On December 24, Taft went to Marion, Ohio, for breakfast with Harding. He talked social protocol with the Hardings—of the necessity to insist that all of his friends, except the family, should call him Mr. President instead of Warren.

Then Harding asked Taft to serve on the Supreme Court. Taft explained how he had declined two offers earlier, then said that he could not accept anything but the top post. Taft wrote to his wife Helen on December 26, "He said nothing more about it."

Future Presidents

WARREN G. HARDING, a dark horse nominee, won the presidential election in a landslide as the American people sought to turn away from Europe's problems. Harding won the nomination in a hot "smoke-filled" Chicago hotel room, a decision reached by fifteen Republican power brokers. The intimate caucus was made necessary because the three favorites (Leonard Wood, Frank Lowden, and Hiram Johnson) could not muster enough delegates to win. Harding was the first standing U.S. senator to be elected president.

January–June: In January a split in the Wood camp caused Harry Daugherty to foresee a Wood–Lowden impasse that could possibly lead to a compromise candidate. Daughtery now traveled the country at his own expense and met with Republicans while trying to obtain second, third, and fourth choices for Harding. He later said this strategy won the nomination. In mid-January, Harding said he wanted the support of only those delegates who would stick with him.

Twenty states had primaries between March and June. Harding lacked the funds to enter most primaries. Wood and Johnson were the major players in the primaries. Johnson won in Michigan and Nebraska. Lowden beat Wood in Illinois. Wood barely beat Johnson in New Jersey, a surprise.

The contest in Ohio was on April 27, and Harding barely beat Wood.

Howard D. Mannington, Harding's campaign secretary, wrote on April 29, "The fact still remains that Ohio is a doubtful state [in] November. There is not within the state any Republican stronger than Senator Harding."

In mid-May, Harding and Senator Irving L. Lenroot of Wisconsin went to Boston for speeches at the Home Market Club. On the train to Boston, Harding told Lenroot that he considered himself out of the race, and in his speech he predicted that Coolidge might be nominated.

It was in Boston that Harding first used the word "normalcy." He said, "America's need is not heroics but healing; not nostrums but normalcy; not revolution but restoration." Reporters claimed he mispronounced "normality" and said "normalty," and news reporters changed the gaffe to "normalcy."

Three weeks before the June convention, Harding wrote that he expected to have 115 votes on the first ballot.

When the Republican convention in the Coliseum opened on June 11, Chicago's temperature skied into the 90s.

Willis nominated Harding as the senator had requested. Willis gave the briefest talk, saying, "The record of Ohio's candidate is the record of the Republican party for the past fifteen years....We want safe and sane seamanship by a captain who knows the way." He then cited Harding's similarity to McKinley, and the way he could get along with Congress.

On the first ballot, Wood garnered 287½ votes, followed by Lowden with 233½ votes and Johnson with 133½ votes. Harding polled 65½ votes on the first ballot. On the second ballot, Harding dropped to 59 votes.

After several more ballots without a candidate, old guard insiders met on the thirteenth floor of the Blackstone Hotel. Delegates wandered in and out from 8 P.M. to 2 A.M., pouring drinks. Lowden's manager told a reporter before midnight that it would be "Lowden or a darkhorse." Someone suggested Henry Cabot Lodge, who replied that he was too old. Calvin Coolidge was discussed. As the bosses suggested names, Harding's was always on the table, and Lodge discussed the need to carry Ohio to win. At 1 A.M. those in the "smoke-filled room" decided by a standing vote that it would be "wise" to vote Harding on the next ballot.

On June 12, on the tenth and final ballot, Harding received 692-1/5 votes to Wood's 156 votes and a smattering of votes for others. His nomination was then made unanimous.

Senator Lenroot of Wisconsin, a Bull Mooser, was the choice of the power brokers for vice president, but a demonstration from the galleries, coupled with an Oregon delegate's getting the attention of the chair, led to a landslide Coolidge victory over Lenroot (see **Calvin Coolidge**, below).

July–November: Harding campaigned on the pledge of a return to normalcy. He was elected president on November 2, his fifty-fifth birthday. He easily defeated Democrat James Middleton Cox, earning 16,152,200 votes to 9,147,353 votes for Cox. In the Electoral College, Harding received 404 votes to Cox's 127.

℠℟

CALVIN COOLIDGE began the year as the governor of Massachusetts but became a surprise nominee for vice president and was elected in the Republican sweep. Warren Harding did almost no consulting or coordination with Coolidge during the campaign.

Early in the year, the Coolidge-for-President movement was never a serious factor, although many Massachusetts delegates were pledged to Coolidge. In January, James B. Reynolds, secretary of the Republican National Committee since 1912, resigned to manage the Coolidge movement for president, and offices were opened in Chicago and Washington.

Democratic presidential candidate James Cox greets voters at a campaign stop. (Library of Congress)

However, Coolidge announced on January 26 that he was not a candidate and would not enter any primaries. Reynolds then closed the offices but continued seeking funds.

At the convention, Coolidge received 34 votes on the first ballot but lost ground thereafter. Senator Lenroot of Wisconsin, a former Bull Mooser, was the choice of many for vice president. However, a demonstration from the galleries led to a Coolidge landslide victory over Lenroot in balloting for the vice presidential nomination.

∞Q

HERBERT HOOVER, 46, had widespread backing for president from prominent people and publications but received only 10½ votes from delegates at the Republican National Convention in Chicago. Going into the Republican contest, Hoover was far better known nationally than major contenders Governor Frank Lowden of Illinois or General Leonard Wood. Harding, the dark horse nominee, had little name recognition in the streets of America compared with Hoover.

Prior to the summer conventions in Chicago, there was a major problem identifying Hoover's political position and preferences. Initially he said he was not a party man. Then he reiterated his earlier preference for Theodore Roosevelt's progressive wing of the GOP, yet Democrats sought to claim him, and Hoover backed the League of Nations throughout the Harding campaign.

In California, Hoover let enthusiasts pit him against Hiram Johnson in the Republican primary. In the April vote, Johnson received 370,000 votes to Hoover's 210,000 votes, a good enough showing by Hoover to virtually eliminate Johnson from the presidential contest.

In other primaries Hoover won a few districts in New Hampshire, and in Michigan both parties entered him on the ballot. Hoover beat McAdoo on the Democratic side, and he ran fourth on the Republican side. In a *Literary Digest* poll in June, Hoover ran third with 260,000 votes behind 277,000 for Wood and 263,000 for Johnson.

The party affiliation question was a puzzler. On February 8, Hoover told the *New York Times* that he would support the party that backed the league. He officially became available for the Republican run in March. On March 30, Hoover said he would be the nominee if drafted but would want to run on a liberal, constructive platform on the treaty. Hoover's positions: higher taxes on the rich, support for collective bargaining, and the League of Nations.

After the election, Hoover was one of many making the pilgrimage to Marion, Ohio, to speak with the president-elect.

∞Q

FRANKLIN D. ROOSEVELT, 38, was the Democratic candidate for vice president of the United States and with Governor James M. Cox went down to defeat in November. It was a stunning rejection of the party by voters. Early in the year, an old friend from *Harvard Crimson* days, Louis B. Wehle, had recommended a Hoover–Roosevelt ticket.

January–June: That Roosevelt achieved the number-two slot at all is a wonder because he made a political blunder on February 1 by criticizing his boss, Secretary of the Navy Josephus Daniels, in a speech in Brooklyn. Roosevelt was seen as repeating and supporting the contention that Daniels's lack of naval preparedness in the pre-1917 period flirted with disaster. Criticizing Daniels was a miscalculation that hurt Daniels personally and cooled the Wilson White House toward Roosevelt. Daniels, who considered firing Roosevelt, wrote in his diary, "FDR persona non grata with Wilson. Better let speech pass."

Roosevelt quickly realized that he had misspoken but didn't know how to correct the matter. When Congress held hearings to investigate whether Daniels was ill prepared prior to the war, FDR was fearful about being asked to testify because it would be ready-made ammunition for the Republican cause. However, when Roosevelt gave a speech before the hearings backing Daniels, the *Journal* story clearly suggested that FDR could be two-faced.

July–December: By July, when Roosevelt boarded a train for the Democratic convention in San Francisco, he wanted to be vice president. On the train he buttered up old Tammany enemies and remained friendly with Governor Al Smith.

Smith received New York's favored-son nomination, and Roosevelt went striding down the aisle to give a seconding speech that was interrupted five times by applause, especially when he said that Democrats would not make their presidential choice at 2 A.M. in a hotel room.

When Smith withdrew after seven ballots, Roosevelt switched his attention to William McAdoo. James Middleton Cox won on the forty-fourth ballot. His campaign manager wanted Agriculture Secretary Edwin T. Meredith of Des Moines as vice president. Cox wanted Roosevelt, just 38, though the two had never met. Cox liked FDR's name recognition and the geographic balance he would provide to the ticket (Midwest and East Coast).

Judge Timothy T. Ansberry of Ohio nominated Roosevelt, and Smith offered a second. When three other vice presidential hopefuls withdrew, among them oil tycoon Edward L. Doheny, FDR received the honor by acclamation.

Roosevelt's candidacy lifted the spirits of Eleanor, who was beginning to turn political herself. Eleanor was in Campobello when she received the news from Daniels via telegram. She immediately wrote to Franklin's mother, Sara, "This certainly is a world of surprises." During the campaign, Eleanor told a Poughkeepsie, New York, reporter, "I was brought up a staunch Republican—and turned Democrat."

On the train ride back east, Roosevelt met Cox for the first time in Columbus, Ohio, and together they went to the White House on July 18 to meet Wilson. They were shocked by Wilson's wan appearance.

Roosevelt gave up his Washington residence and resigned from his navy position on August 6. Some 2,000 navy employees presented him with a silver loving cup.

Roosevelt campaigned in New England, the Midwest, and twice in the West, but not in the South. At Hyde Park on Election Day, November 2, Roosevelt expected defeat but the landslide surprised him.

∞Q

HARRY S TRUMAN, at 36, was in the men's clothing business in downtown Kansas City. Store business totaled $70,000 in the first year.

❧

DWIGHT D. EISENHOWER, now 30, lived next door to George S. Patton at Fort Meade, Maryland, and they became fast friends.

With the war over, Eisenhower was reduced in rank to major, which dropped his pay from $290 per month to $220. Eisenhower's father-in-law helped out by giving the young couple $100 per month.

❧

JOHN F. KENNEDY, 3, was very ill with scarlet fever that required hospitalization in Boston. A 3-month recovery period in a sanitarium in Maine followed. After John returned home with a nurse, the Kennedy clan moved from Beals Street to a larger home in Brookline, at 51 Abbotsford Road on the corner of Naples Road.

February 20: John's sister Kathleen was born.

❧

LYNDON B. JOHNSON, 12, moved into his grandfather's house in Johnson City, Texas, in January. His paternal grandfather and grandmother had died in 1915 and 1917, respectively, and in 1919, his father, Sam, made a bid of $19,500 for the family farm to keep it from being sold to strangers.

The house badly needed work. To do the repairs, Sam sold his hotel in Johnson City, a store, and all of the property he owned. He received a mortgage of $15,000 that put him in debt to three banks. He would ultimately invest $40,000 in the place.

Lyndon transferred from the Junction School to the Stonewall and Albert School.

❧

RICHARD M. NIXON, 7, was promoted from first grade to third grade, as his teacher detected his interest in things beyond his age group.

❧

GERALD R. FORD, 7, moved from Madison Elementary School to East Grand Rapids Elementary in Michigan. His mother was a very energetic person active in the garden club, a book club, and church functions.

❧

RONALD REAGAN, 9, made his seventh move in his 9 years when his father moved the family in September to Dixon, Illinois. Jack Reagan now ran the H. C. Pitney store.

1921
Woodrow Wilson

President Wilson, 65 in December, finished out his second term as president and began a quiet retirement on S Street, less than a mile and a half northwest of the White House. He was swamped with laudatory mail, hate mail, and requests to undertake numerous writing projects. He surprised everyone by joining his last secretary of state, Bainbridge Colby,

in a new law firm; however, Wilson's enfeebled condition prevented any real participation in the firm.

Wilson made a dignified appearance at Warren G. Harding's inaugural and later at Arlington in the parade connected with the burial of the Unknown Soldier. Prior to the inaugural, when someone suggested that Wilson do something to put Harding and the Republican Party "in a hole," Wilson replied, "I do not wish to put Mr. Harding in a hole.... I should like to help Mr. Harding and I hope every good citizen will try to help him."

For much of the year after his retirement, Wilson was seldom seen by the public despite frequent automobile rides through Washington's suburbs. Edith took over all housekeeping chores and was at his side almost constantly.

❧

WARREN G. HARDING, upon entering the White House, was popular with the American people and the press. By the end of the year, however, he confessed to friends that he hated the job and even suggested to Congress in December that the presidency be limited to one 6-year term. During the year, he initiated arms reduction with a popular multinational naval conference in Washington, which aimed at stopping battleship construction and developing a formula that would maintain a naval parity that Great Britain could accept. Late in the year, the country faced a postwar economic slump.

March: Harding's inauguration on March 4 drew a smaller crowd than inaugurations in past years. The American flag on the Capitol was at half-mast for Speaker Champ Clark, who had died on March 2. Chief Justice Edward Douglas White administered the oath of office to Harding, who rode to the Capitol in an automobile, the first president to do so for an inauguration.

Harding, 55, opened his inaugural address by talking about the great destruction that World War had caused: "Our supreme task is the resumption of our onward normal reconstruction, readjustment, restoration.... We do not hate; do not covet.... We must strive for normalcy to reach stability." He said that the United States wanted "no part in directing the destinies of the world."

Harding's cabinet consisted of Charles Evans Hughes of New York as secretary of state, Andrew Mellon of Pennsylvania as secretary of Treasury, John Wingate Weeks of Massachusetts as secretary of war, Harry Daugherty as attorney general, William Hays of Indiana as postmaster general, Edwin Denby of Michigan as secretary of the navy, Albert Bacon Fall of New Mexico as secretary of the Interior, Henry Wallace of Iowa as secretary of agriculture, Herbert Hoover as secretary of commerce, and James John Davis of Pennsylvania as secretary of labor.

April–September: Harding told Congress on April 12 that he wanted "less of government in business as well as more business in government." The Senate then passed the McCormick bill, creating a national budget system. The House approved its version of the bill, and Harding signed it on June 10.

Idaho Senator William Borah, in 1920, had pushed for a naval conference with considerable popular support. He liked being seen as the champion of peace. In May, Borah amended a naval appropriations bill to authorize the president to hold a conference on naval disarmament with Japan and Great Britain. The Senate was unanimously in favor, and the House approved the conference by a vote of 330 to 4. The conference was scheduled for November.

Harding appointed former president William Howard Taft chief justice of the Supreme Court on June 30 (see **William Howard Taft**, opposite column).

Hoover, speaking in Chicago on July 21, said that the business slump in the country was not an evil but rather was "the result of influence and disasters from the war" and "the necessary reaction from the foolish post-war boom."

Harding told union leader Samuel Gompers that the workingman must accept wage cuts to "give an opportunity for a revival of industry." During the war years, railway workers had received numerous raises. Now the Railroad Labor Board decreed a cut of 12 percent, and the workers accepted it.

President Warren G. Harding (National Archives)

November: The naval conference began on November 12 with Great Britain, France, China, Belgium, the Netherlands, India, Australia, and Portugal invited. Harding selected Charles Evans Hughes, Elihu Root, Henry Cabot Lodge, and Oscar Underwood to represent the United States. The Chinese delegation included Wellington Koo. India and Australia also took part. Mrs. Harding, Calvin Coolidge, Oliver Wendell Holmes, and Louis Brandeis attended the opening session held at Continental Memorial Hall in Washington, D.C.

Harding made brief welcoming remarks before leaving the main negotiations up to Hughes and the other U.S. representatives. Hughes proposed major naval cuts and advised eliminating 1.8 million tons, accompanied by a 10-year "construction holiday." The conference lasted 12 weeks, and its main consequence was the scrapping of obsolete battleships. The conference did not address air power or land armies.

December: In his message to Congress on December 5, Harding offered the first government budget. He also told Congress he wanted it to set up tribunals to mediate strikes.

Former Presidents

WILLIAM HOWARD TAFT finally realized his lifelong dream when he was appointed chief justice of the Supreme Court. But he had to wait until the summer for the appointment to come through.

Taft visited President Harding on March 26, then went to visit Chief Justice Edward White. Taft later expressed to friends his disappointment when White made no mention of retiring. Taft wrote to C. S. Shepard on April 11, "As a man comes to the actual retirement, after he is seventy … he seems to regard it as an admission of weakness.… If the position, which I would rather have than any other in the world, is not to come to me, I have no right to complain, for the Lord has been very good to me."

On May 19, Chief Justice White died. Taft wrote to a friend the same day, "The unexpected has happened.… What is to be done? I observe in the Associated Press dispatches opposition to me based on my age." Taft would turn 64 in September. Taft was kept in suspense for 40 days before being appointed chief justice by Harding on June 30.

Future Presidents

CALVIN COOLIDGE held the innocuous office of vice president of the United States, a position that kept him in the shadows except for the need to make routine speeches on the banquet circuit and at the dedication of statues. Coolidge's words in the Senate in support of administration legislation usually fell on deaf ears.

On arriving in Washington, Coolidge was met by outgoing Vice President Thomas Marshall. Later Coolidge was at the Union Street station for Harding's arrival from Marion. In taking over the number-two office, Coolidge inherited Marshall's Cadillac, chauffeur, and clerk. Coolidge often had to unveil statues or lay wreaths, and he even represented Harding in some speaking engagements.

୫୦ର

HERBERT HOOVER, 47, as commerce secretary in the Harding administration, had wide control over economic matters. He held many meetings with industrial leaders and put out fact sheets with great regularity to assist business leaders in making decisions. He added 3,000 employees to the department and allowed business leaders access to Census Bureau information. His department added three divisions: radio, aeronautics, and housing. In 1921 there were only two radio stations in the country.

Through public conferences, Hoover obtained cooperation with business. His regulatory powers were wide: The Commerce Department concerned itself with mine safety, studied the over commercialization of scenic sites such as Niagara Falls, settled disputes between states on the use of Colorado River water, and sent explorers to South America to seek sources of rubber.

ഇൗരു

FRANKLIN D. ROOSEVELT, 39, was stricken by infantile paralysis at Campobello Island in August. His life, physically, would never be the same again. Privately he entered a period of utter despair, he later told Frances Perkins. But outwardly he was upbeat, as were Eleanor and Sara.

Roosevelt was tired before arriving at Campobello by yacht. While fishing on August 9 he fell overboard and found the water very cold. The next day Roosevelt played baseball and tennis, went sailing, fought a forest fire with neighbors, and then went swimming in the icy waters of the Bay of Fundy. Later Roosevelt sat around in a wet suit to read his mail. Chills and aches followed, and he went to bed.

On August 11 he got up with a pain in his legs that he thought was lumbago. He went back to bed and soon ran a fever of 102 degrees Fahrenheit. Dr. W. W. Keen, who had played a role in President Grover Cleveland's secret jaw operation, diagnosed temporary paralysis; but Dr. Robert W. Lovett, an orthopedic doctor from Newport, arrived and immediately diagnosed polio.

Roosevelt's mother, Sara, arrived at Campobello on September 1. Roosevelt wrote to Langdon Marvin on September 3: "I am almost wholly out of commission … but the doctors say that there is no question that I will get their [legs] use back." Roosevelt took the train to New York City on September 13 and checked into the hospital.

Roosevelt was out of the hospital by October 28 and moved in with his mother on 65th Street. He could now swing himself with a hanging strap from his bed into a wheelchair. Leg pain returned on November 19, then mysteriously vanished a few days later. He began to exercise his upper body using a trapeze above his bed.

Prior to his illness, Roosevelt had joined a New York City law firm as vice president at $25,000 per year, his largest income ever. His friend Van Lear Black also made him vice president of Fidelity and Deposit Company of Maryland.

ഇൗരു

HARRY S TRUMAN, 37, as his business failed, came under the influence of Kansas City boss Tom Pendergast. The city machine suggested Truman consider becoming a city commissioner for eastern Kansas City. The recession caused falling prices. Truman and Eddy Jacobson financed their stock

with credit and now were stuck with an inventory of $30,000 and customers unable to buy.

Late in the year, Mike Pendergast and son Jim came into the store to talk. Jim had been with the One Hundred Twenty-Ninth Field Artillery unit during the war. They asked Truman to consider running as eastern judge of Jackson County, which was not a court job, in 1922. The eastern district included Independence, whereas most of Kansas City was in the western district. Tom Pendergast, Mike's father, was one of the most successful city bosses in the country.

ഇൗരു

DWIGHT D. EISENHOWER, 31, lost his son Ikky (Dwight) on January 2 to scarlet fever at the age of 3 years, 3 months. The grief was great, and he later called it the "greatest disappointment and disaster of my life."

ഇൗരു

JOHN F. KENNEDY, though only 4 years old, entered Betsy Bean's kindergarten class at the Edward Devotion School in Brookline, but illness may have cut his attendance to 10 weeks out of 34.

July 10: John's sister Eunice was born.

ഇൗരു

LYNDON B. JOHNSON, 13, on entering Johnson City High School in Texas, became arrogant and hostile, largely due to his father's failure as a farmer. Lyndon, no longer on good terms with his father, was sent to his Uncle Tom and Aunt Kitty's home to board while at school. They later complained that he was failing.

ഇൗരു

RICHARD M. NIXON, 8, was a serious, hardworking student in Yorba Linda, California.

ഇൗരു

GERALD R. FORD, 8, had to move to a cheaper, rented house at 649 Union Avenue in Grand Rapids, Michigan, because the country's economic slump hurt his father's business and caused the foreclosure on their home.

ഇൗരു

RONALD REAGAN, 10, lived in Dixon, Illinois, where his father opened a new shoe store, Pitney & Reagan, on March 19.

1922
Warren G. Harding

President Harding thought the success of the naval disarmament conference might be seen later as the crowning accomplishment of his administration. Instead, shortly after the conference ended, there was the slow, evolving Teapot Dome scandal involving Secretary of the Interior Albert Fall.

January–February: The naval disarmament conference continued into the new year. Harding kept a close watch on the sessions and the strategy of Secretary of State Charles Evans Hughes. The conference ended in February with England, the United States, and Japan agreeing to a naval ratio of 5:5:3 for 15 years. The French and Italian navies would be limited to about half the size of Japan's.

The Four Power Treaty (United States, Great Britain, Japan, and France) replaced the Anglo-Japan Alliance. In his speech ending the conference on February 6, Harding said that all hoped "the torches of understanding have been lighted and they ought to glow and encircle the globe" over the next decade.

The Senate ratified the Four Power document, 67 to 27, despite the opposition of many, including Robert La Follette and William Borah. Before the Senate vote, Harding told H. H. Kohlsaat, "The success or failure of this administration depends on the ratification of these treaties. If these treaties are ratified … this administration's name is secure in history."

April–September: Fall, on April 7, granted a 20-year lease of Teapot Dome oil reserves (20 miles north of Casper, Wyoming) to Harry F. Sinclair, head of Sinclair Consolidated Oil, which would pay 50-percent royalties to the government. There were no other bids, and Fall kept the contract a secret. By an earlier executive order, the Teapot Dome oil reserves had been reserved for the navy. However, Fall revised the order so that the reserves could be leased without the approval of the secretary of the navy.

On April 15, Fall opened proposals for the construction of storage tanks at Pearl Harbor along with channel dredging. The job went to oilman Edward Doheny with the proviso that Doheny get a preferential future lease on the Elk Hills oil reserves in California. The deal was signed on April 25.

Rumors began to spread that Fall had taken illegal loans from Sinclair and Doheny to make these two deals. Soon after these dealings, Fall began making improvements to his ranch in New Mexico, including building a $35,000 hydroelectric plant. By the end of the year, over $170,000-worth of improvements had been made to Fall's ranch. Fall's annual salary was only $12,000.

Sensing a scandal, Senator Robert La Follette asked for a Senate investigation of all oil leases on April 28. The investigation would last for more than a year.

A coal strike hit in April as 600,000 took to the picket line,

Secretary of State Charles Evans Hughes, seated and holding his grandson, and his son, Charles Evans Hughes Jr. (Library of Congress)

the largest such protest in American history. Coal operators refused to meet with the miners' union.

Harding wrote to the president of U.S. Steel in April that the 12-hour workday should be reduced to 8 and the 7-day workweek should be reduced to 6. He wrote to a businessman: "Nothing will contribute to American industrial stability as abolition of the 12-hour working day." It wasn't until August 1923 that U.S. Steel announced an 8-hour day.

Trouble in the railroads began in May when the Railroad Labor Board ordered pay cuts amounting to $108 million. The strike began on July 1 and did not end until September 13.

Former Presidents

WILLIAM HOWARD TAFT, the chief justice of the Supreme Court, worked diligently on Court reform and took abuse from old progressive opponents in Congress such as Robert La Follette and George Norris, but stayed the course as twenty-four new judgeships were created along with an innovative Conference of Senior Circuit Court Judges with Taft as its head.

Because the Supreme Court was often under fire, Taft countered the critics by becoming a banquet circuit regular in order to explain Court policy and its decision-making processes. Taft also agitated for a new building to house the Court. The judges had shared space at the Capitol for decades.

Taft went to Great Britain during the summer for two reasons: to receive an honorary degree from Oxford and to review "the much simpler procedure" of the British court system with the idea of suggesting legislation to Congress. Taft also received honorary degrees from Cambridge and Aberdeen. Taft met the king and queen, as well as all of the important judges and lawyers in the country.

☙❧

WOODROW WILSON, 66 in December, lived in relative obscurity in Washington. His health did not improve over the course of the year.

His law firm with Bainbridge Colby dissolved as Wilson was unable to perform any work, even though potential clients inundated Wilson & Colby with requests. Wilson went to the law offices in Washington only once.

The disabled retired president received visits from Lord Robert Cecil, Lord Balfour, Clemenceau, and Franklin and

Eleanor Roosevelt. FDR, disabled by polio, would kid Wilson about who was going to be the first to get back on the golf course.

Future Presidents

CALVIN COOLIDGE, in his private letters, talked about the "barren life" of being vice president. But later he claimed that watching the Senate at work was fascinating. He was presiding over the Senate when Robert La Follette demanded an investigation of Albert Fall's Teapot Dome dealings.

There was some talk in GOP ranks of easing Coolidge out of the 1924 race in order to have him run for the Senate against Massachusetts Senator David Walsh.

Coolidge was 50 years old on July 4.

HERBERT HOOVER, 48, as commerce secretary, chaired conferences, offered new ideas to stimulate the economy, showed charts at a White House dinner, and wrote *American Individualism*. He drew closer to Secretary of State Charles Evans Hughes and Secretary of the Interior Albert Fall but had conflicts with Secretary of Agriculture Henry Wallace, who saw Hoover as an empire builder. Hoover saw Wallace's price-fixing as fascist in nature.

Hoover was busy on many different projects during the year. He wrote a building code, became president of Better Homes for America, and wrote a homeowners' manual. He presided over four conferences on wireless telephone regulations. He monitored the building of 1,000 miles of airport runways. His bureau of fisheries helped save the salmon industry in Alaska.

Meanwhile Hoover's library at Stanford was being filled with World War I documents from European governments. For instance, President Fritz Ebert of Germany had no interest in papers from the 1914–1918 War Council. As a result, 8,000 volumes of manuscripts filled fifteen railroad cars and ended up in Palo Alto. The Soviets permitted twenty-five carloads of documents to be shipped to Palo Alto on policy dating to the czars and the Bolshevik government.

FRANKLIN D. ROOSEVELT, 40, and Eleanor both promoted Al Smith for governor of New York. Smith won by 400,000 votes, the largest margin in state history. But later, on December 20, FDR wrote to Byron R. Newton that the boomlet for Smith for president in 1924 was premature and that New York Democrats needed a moratorium on such talk.

FDR's battle with polio had ups and downs. By January his legs had atrophied and were pulling back. He needed plaster casts to straighten them, which was like being stretched on a rack. By March he was fitted with steel braces but hated them. Roosevelt predicted complete recovery for himself and on April 30 made a bet with Wilson about who would be the first to get back on the golf course.

In June, Roosevelt became president of the American Construction Council, an organization that Hoover promoted; and on September 14, Roosevelt became president of a new concern, United European Investors, Ltd., with the objective of investing in Germany. Meanwhile he worked at the parallel bars to strengthen his shoulders and enjoyed swimming in a heated pool in Rhinebeck.

HARRY S TRUMAN, 38, was elected political administrator for the eastern side of Kansas City at a salary of $3,465 per year, thanks to support from the city's political machine boss, Thomas J. Pendergast. Harry needed the job because the 1921 recession had forced his haberdashery into closing in April. The business had lost $28,000. Truman also spent his nights at the Kansas City School of Law, taking a 4-year course taught by prominent lawyers. He earned A's and B's.

Shortly after announcing his candidacy in March, a group of backers pressured Truman into joining the Ku Klux Klan, saying that it was a good political move. The KKK was gaining strength in western Missouri at this time. Truman paid $10 for a membership fee, but soon the money was returned when he would not promise to prevent public appointments of Roman Catholics.

With Pendergast's support, Truman beat off three Democratic contenders in the contest for presiding judge before defeating the Republican in the general election. The job had the title of judge of Jackson County, Eastern District. In reality there was no court-of-law work involved. The job was comparable to that of a city administrator: He levied taxes, approved public works, and managed charitable institutions.

DWIGHT D. EISENHOWER, 32, was transferred to Panama and came under the influence of General Fox Connor, who pushed Eisenhower to prepare himself for command. Eisenhower was assigned to the 20th Infantry Brigade, consisting mostly of soldiers from Puerto Rico, at Camp Gaillard. Connor believed, as did others, that another war would result from the Treaty of Versailles. Connor talked by the hour to his young protégé about global geopolitics, flash points, and the impact of colonies. Eisenhower's understanding of war strategy and of the strengths and weaknesses of the United States came from these sessions with Connor.

The Eisenhowers sailed for Panama on January 7 aboard an army transport, the *St. Mihiel*. In Panama, Mamie was disappointed by their quarters, a little house on a hill once used by French engineers. She thought the house nothing more than a shanty. Eisenhower soon made improvements to the place, including the addition of an upstairs porch.

In June, Mamie returned to Denver for the birth of son John on August 3.

JOHN F. KENNEDY, 5, entered the first grade at the Edward Devotion School near Boston.

John's father Joe was busy manipulating the stock market and making money without ever telling his wife where it was coming from or how. He bought a chain of movie theaters in New England and made more money. His father-in-law ran for governor of Massachusetts and lost.

৪৩৫

LYNDON B. JOHNSON, at 14, spent the summer attending the San Marcos Normal School, 30 miles from home, which resulted in better grades when he returned to Johnson City High School for the fall term. But the farm scene was one of quiet desperation. Sam Johnson lost his farm and had to move to Johnson City deeply in debt. If Sam's brothers, George and Tom, hadn't cosigned on Sam's mortgage, the family would have had no place to live.

With cotton prices down, Sam sold his farm in September for $10,000. The money went to the Fredericksburg Loan Company. Sam still owed merchants for seed, farm equipment, and horses. When he moved off his property, he still owed about $35,000.

৪৩৫

RICHARD M. NIXON, now 9, moved to Whittier, California, as his father left the lemon growing business to run a gas and grocery store. That meant that at 4:30 each morning, Richard went to Los Angeles with his father to help load produce to take back to the grocery store in Whittier.

৪৩৫

GERALD R. FORD, 9, lived in Grand Rapids, Michigan.

৪৩৫

RONALD REAGAN, 11 years old, came home one afternoon in February and found his father dead drunk on his back in a snowbank. The boy dragged Jack Reagan up on the porch, into the house, and got him into bed. Jack would sometimes disappear from home in Dixon, Illinois, for days at a time.

1923
Warren G. Harding

President Harding's administration began to implode before he left on a trip to Alaska somewhat reminiscent of Woodrow Wilson's West Coast swing in 1919 to sell the League of Nations. In this case Harding wished to recharge the American people with enthusiasm for his administration, now plagued by scandal. Harding hoped to achieve a curative personal triumph to offset growing public doubt and to show that he was ready for the 1924 race. However, Harding died just as the trip came to an end.

January–March: In January, Secretary of the Interior Albert Fall received another quiet $25,000 payment from Harry Sinclair. The Senate investigation into the Teapot Dome leasing continued. Pressure continued to mount on Fall, and he finally resigned on March 4. Hubert Work of Colorado replaced him. (After several indictments and trials, Fall was

convicted in 1929 of taking a bribe and sentenced to a year in prison.)

In March, Harding and Florence returned to Florida for a vacation, which included a cruise on the Indian River, golf, and fishing. Many noticed that Harding tired easily.

Despite all of his problems, it appeared that Harding wanted a second term. By March most Republicans were behind Harding despite talk of a challenge from Robert La Follette or Hiram Johnson.

June–August: Harding, his wife Florence, and a large traveling party set off on a transcontinental trip that included a stop in Alaska. Harding hoped to rejuvenate his administration's reputation in the eyes of the public. When Harding and Florence returned from Alaska, they made a stop in San Francisco at the end of July. Harding soon became ill but seemed to improve on August 1. Harry Daugherty had arrived in San Francisco on August 1 but did not see Harding immediately because he didn't want to burden him.

On Thursday, August 2, Harding made plans to return to Washington. Later that night, as Harding sat up in his bed, Florence read the president an article in the *Saturday Evening Post* by Sam Blythe, entitled "A Calm View of a Calm Man." The article called Harding a strong leader and a "captain of a steady course despite the howls of critics."

As Florence read the article, Harding said, "That's good. Go on, read some more." Suddenly Florence saw his face twitch and his mouth drop open. His head slumped into his pillow, and his head rolled to the right. Florence called for a doctor, but it was too late. Harding was dead at age 57. The official cause of death was listed as apoplexy, although there was some disagreement. Books published later claimed that Harding was poisoned by his wife, but there is no concrete evidence to support this theory.

৪৩৫

CALVIN COOLIDGE stood in a Vermont farmhouse living room illuminated by oil lanterns at 2:47 in the morning of August 3 and took the oath of office to become president of the United States. Coolidge's father, a notary public and justice of the peace, administered the oath. Amazingly, just a few weeks earlier, Republican insiders were discussing the possibility of replacing Coolidge on the 1924 ticket. In 2 years and 5 months as vice president, Harding had never consulted Coolidge about any serious issue.

January–August: With Harding down with the flu, Coolidge gave the budget message to Congress.

For Coolidge, the first 6 months of 1923 were as laconic and dull as the prior 2 years had been for the ignored vice president. In March, Coolidge and Grace took a short vacation at Hot Springs, Virginia, and then went to their Northampton, Massachusetts, house and stayed there for several months. In July they went to Vermont to help Coolidge's father with the farming while the Coolidge boys worked in the area as hired hands.

On August 2, Coolidge helped a neighbor in Plymouth Notch with the haying and went to bed at 9 P.M. Coolidge's father did not have telephone in his house. The message for Coolidge reporting the death of President Harding came through the telegraph office at Bridgewater, Vermont, a few miles north of Plymouth.

The telegrapher sought out two Coolidge staffers in town. They, along with a newsman, drove through the night to Plymouth Notch. They awoke Coolidge's father, who slept downstairs and told him what had happened.

The vice president woke up and read the telegram. Coolidge and Grace dressed, then knelt to pray. He dictated a message to Mrs. Harding and to the nation before taking the oath of office at 2:47 A.M. Coolidge reached Washington by 9 P.M. the next day.

On convening the cabinet after Harding's funeral on August 10, Coolidge said he wanted it to remain intact. Secretary of Treasury Andrew Mellon tried to resign, but Coolidge said, "Forget it."

Herbert Hoover later said that Coolidge got along well with the cabinet and that they liked him. Secretary of State Charles Evans Hughes stood above and separate from all the others and served as Coolidge's prime adviser.

Calvin Coolidge became president in 1923 after the sudden death of Warren G. Harding. (Library of Congress)

September–December: When Coolidge hired C. Bascom Slemp, a millionaire and former Virginia congressman as his personal secretary, there was an understanding that he would work toward getting Coolidge the Republican nomination in 1924. Slemp was a wheeler-dealer good at rounding up delegates. He was especially effective at fund-raising in the South. With Slemp's hiring, *The Brooklyn Eagle* said, "Washington today knows that Coolidge is a candidate."

Coolidge was not a leader in the GOP or even well known by many of the faithful. Any doubts about Coolidge's plans were put to rest on December 8, when he announced that he was a candidate for the 1924 nomination.

Former Presidents

WILLIAM HOWARD TAFT became an adviser to Coolidge, suggesting that the president do nothing, be passive, and let the government and country run itself. Chief Justice Taft wrote his brother Horace on September 29 concerning Coolidge: "He is very self-contained, very simple, very direct and very shrewd."

₭ʠ

WOODROW WILSON, 67 in December, made a final salute to the American people on the fifth anniversary of Armistice Day, November 11, with a halting radio address that reached 3 million homes on a Saturday night. It was the biggest radio audience up to that time. Afterward he went outside his home where thousands had gathered in a festive mood and Wilson gave a last public statement.

The idea of the former president addressing the nation came from Bernard Baruch's daughter, Belle, an activist for American entry into the League of Nations. She begged Wilson to go on the radio, even though it was a new medium and he didn't like it. Wilson and his wife, Edith, worked on a 10-minute radio speech that was broadcast nationwide from the Wilson library.

He gave the talk standing up, faltered in his opening sentences, and was often unintelligible. Wilson said, "Memories of that happy time [when the shooting stopped] are forever marred and embittered for us by the shameful fact that when the victory was won we withdrew into a sullen and selfish isolation which is manifestly ignoble because [it is] manifestly dishonorable." For the most part, there was a positive reaction to the speech from around the country.

Future Presidents

HERBERT HOOVER, 49, was close to the dying president during the trip to Alaska. Harding tried to tell Hoover what annoyed him about certain cabinet members. Their communications were inexact. Harding talked of betrayal and asked Hoover for advice.

With Harding failing, it was Hoover who alerted his close Stanford friend, Dr. Wilbur, to come to San Francisco to consult on Harding's condition. On August 3, it was Wilbur who signed the death certificate. Hoover had earlier phoned Hughes to alert Coolidge to Harding's condition.

Hoover supported the Dawes Plan to ease German reparations. Hoover also supported a dam for the Colorado River and development of a St. Lawrence Seaway. He drew up blueprints for a new Commerce Department building and received a scroll from the Soviets for helping avert starvation in Russia in the wake of that nation's 1917 trauma.

₭ʠ

FRANKLIN D. ROOSEVELT, 41, and Governor Al Smith shared concern over how Prohibition was causing division in Democratic ranks everywhere. Smith was against Prohibition, as was Roosevelt for the most part. FDR warned William

Jennings Bryan on June 20 that Prohibition was becoming a problem for the party and suggested exempting light wine and beer as a compromise. FDR said a national referendum might be the way to gauge the public's sentiment on this diverse issue.

Roosevelt's incapacity gave him more time for his hobbies: He abandoned a plan to write a biography on John Paul Jones but did take time to work on his stamp collection, make model sailboats, and write features for the New York Historical Society on Hudson River homes and towns.

In July, FDR published an article in the magazine *Asia* on relations with Japan. To the question, "Shall We Trust Japan?" Roosevelt answered yes, a change of heart from his views of 10 years earlier.

℘

HARRY S TRUMAN, 39, took over his new job in Kansas City on January 1. People called him Judge when he entered the courthouse. Truman learned about political power from the ground up.

Truman, as Tom Pendergast's man, had to work as a team with Judge Henry F. McElroy against the forces backing a rival political power, Joseph B. Shannon, who controlled Judge Miles J. Bulger. Truman moved against the city engineer, Les Koehler, who let his friends joyride in a fleet of county automobiles. When Bulger was elected to the Missouri legislature, he offered a bill that would prevent county judges such as Truman from appointing road overseers. Republican Governor Arthur M. Hyde vetoed the bill.

Truman and McElroy cut many pork barrel spending items in the county budget, such as charity lists. They were often critical of Shannon's new judge, Elihu W. Hayes. Truman worked to cut waste, reduce county debt, and improve the roads.

℘

DWIGHT EISENHOWER, 33 and serving in Panama, took an interest in how the Panama Canal worked. His mentor, General Fox Connor, had plans to get Eisenhower assigned to the Command and General Staff School at Fort Leavenworth, Kansas. The school was seen as the place where future generals either made it or dropped back into in the faceless officer ranks.

℘

JOHN F. KENNEDY, 6, was a second-grade student under Miss Bicknell in Massachusetts. Meanwhile, his father made his first million. Joe Kennedy put up $24,000 on credit on insider information and made $675,000 on Pond Creek Coal Company shares.

℘

LYNDON B. JOHNSON, 15, was still getting occasional whippings from his father, Sam, who was broke and could not afford to run for reelection to the Texas legislature. Sam was sick in bed much of the time, the cause not certain. Eventually he returned to real estate and selling insurance.

Sam lost his credit and owed money to several people in town.

℘

RICHARD M. NIXON, 10, took the bus to school each morning after helping his father set up supplies in the family grocery store in Whittier, California.

Richard's brother Harold was a Boy Scout, but the Nixons could not afford to let Richard join in scouting.

℘

GERALD R. FORD, 10, was a schoolboy in Grand Rapids, Michigan. Later he said his childhood was a happy experience because his stepfather was a good and fair man.

℘

RONALD REAGAN, 12, attended school in Dixon, Illinois.

1924
Calvin Coolidge

President Coolidge easily swept aside feeble challenges to his Republican presidential nomination and then routed the Democrats' little-known candidate, John William Davis, in the November elections.

January–March: Early in the year, Coolidge's presidential team was quietly at work. Massachusetts National Committeeman William M. Butler worked in New England, while National Committee Chairman John T. Adams of Iowa watched over the western states. Hiram Johnson appeared to be Coolidge's biggest challenger. In March, Johnson narrowly defeated Coolidge in the South Dakota primary.

April–July: Despite the loss to Johnson in South Dakota, by mid-April, Coolidge was well on his way to the Republican nomination. By the end of the month, Coolidge could count on at least 530 of the necessary 555 delegates for the nomination.

In an effort to solve the reparations problem plaguing postwar Europe, Chicago banker Charles G. Dawes, head of the Committee of Experts of the Allied Reparations Commission, formulated the Dawes Plan in April. The plan set up a new payment schedule and called for the reorganization of the German Reichsbank under the supervision of the Allies. As part of the plan, Allied troops would leave the Ruhr Valley, which they occupied in 1923 to force the Germans to make their payments.

On May 15, Coolidge vetoed the Soldiers' Bonus Bill. However, on May 19, the Senate voted to override Coolidge's veto. The new law allocated $2 billion in 20-year annuities for Americans who served in World War I.

On May 26, Coolidge signed the Johnson–Reed Act. The act set new restrictions on immigration based on ethnicity, cutting the number of Europeans allowed into the United States by half and completely barring the immigration of Asians.

Republicans met on June 10 to 12 in Cleveland, Ohio, to nominate their presidential candidate. They nominated Coolidge on the first ballot and Charles G. Dawes as the vice presidential candidate.

Democrats met in New York City on June 24 to 30, July 1 to 5, and July 7 to 9. Choosing a presidential nominee proved to be an exhausting feat. The names of more than sixty men were put into nomination before Wall Street lawyer John William Davis was nominated on the 103rd ballot. Davis was a former U.S. ambassador to Great Britain.

November 4: Coolidge easily defeated Davis to win a full term in the White House. In the popular vote, Coolidge earned 15,725,016 votes, whereas Davis polled 8,386,503 votes. In the electoral vote, Coolidge took 382 votes to Davis's 136. Progressive Party candidate Robert La Follette earned 4,822,856 votes and took 13 electoral votes, winning only his home state of Wisconsin.

Former Presidents

WILLIAM HOWARD TAFT took more interest in purely political matters than any Supreme Court chief justice since Salmon Chase. Taft made many suggestions to Coolidge about appointments and other issues. In this presidential year, Taft even did the unexpected and attended the Democratic National Convention just for pleasure. In the end, however, Taft was more than satisfied with Coolidge's victory.

John William Davis, the little-known 1924 Democratic Presidential nominee. (Library of Congress)

&

WOODROW WILSON, very weak and still incapacitated by his stroke in 1919, lived quietly on a residential street in Washington. Wilson was having trouble seeing and could scarcely hold a pen to sign letters.

January–February: On January 16, Wilson asked Cordell Hull, chairman, and members of the Democratic National Committee, to visit. The 125 members arrived during a cold rain. Wilson sat by the fireplace, and Hull introduced each man quietly. Wilson said nothing, his head often drooping, but he shook hands with each man, as did Edith. The audience lasted an hour, and Wilson was very tired at its completion.

On January 20, Wilson, although very weak, met with young Raymond Fosdick, a League of Nations officer based in Geneva even though Fosdick was American. Wilson talked about the waste of the 1914 war. "It must never happen again," he said. Fosdick was later to write, "My last impression of him was of a tear-stained face, a set, indomitable jaw, a faint voice whispering 'God bless you.'"

Wilson seemed very tired on January 27 and January 29. On January 29, the night nurse was alarmed, causing Edith to send a telegram to Dr. Grayson. Grayson responded that he would catch a train and reach Washington by January 31. On his arrival, Edith asked him if Wilson's daughters should be notified about his condition. He said there was no use alarming them. But Edith, fearing that her husband was at death's door, had the daughters notified. Margaret was in New York, Nellie in California, and Jessie in Bangkok, where her husband was an adviser to the government of Siam.

Word leaked out, and soon reporters arrived at the Wilson residence. Grayson met with them and was honest about Wilson's condition.

At dawn on Saturday, February 2, people gathered outside the Wilson house. Cars would come by and drop off cards from William Howard Taft, Herbert Hoover, Oscar W. Underwood, Florence Harding, and others.

On Sunday morning, February 3, Wilson opened his eyes for about 10 minutes, and both Edith and Margaret spoke to him. Each of the two women held one of his hands. At 11:15 A.M. Wilson died. The cause of death was a massive infarction of the brain. He was 67 years old.

Future Presidents

HERBERT HOOVER, 50, was a candidate for vice president but lost the nomination at the Republican National Convention in Cleveland on June 10 to Charles Dawes. Delegates voted for Dawes on the third ballot by a margin of 682 to 334½.

Hoover campaigned for Coolidge in California. When Coolidge appointed Hoover to head the St. Lawrence Commission to study the feasibility of creating a waterway, Hoover wrote to a friend that the project "meant more to me than almost anything else in the world." He toured the river for a look at the possibilities for improved commerce.

In an October 1 speech to the American Dairy Federation, Hoover complained about the production of certain farm commodities. He wrote to Coolidge about the need to practice conservation in the fishing industry and said that some stocks, such as Alaskan salmon, were disappearing.

&

FRANKLIN D. ROOSEVELT, 42, held the spotlight at the Democratic National Convention at Madison Square Garden in June when he supported Al Smith for the presidential nomination with a ringing speech for the "Happy Warrior." But when Smith deadlocked with Woodrow Wilson's son-in-law, William McAdoo, the convention dragged on for 16 days and 103 ballots before John Davis won as a compromise candidate. The convention was a disaster, but FDR was a star in an otherwise bleak experience for the Democrats. The *New York Times* called FDR and Senator Thomas Walsh of Montana the outstanding personalities at the convention.

Roosevelt took a fancy to Warm Springs, Georgia, during the fall campaign. He had first heard about Warm Springs from George F. Peabody, a New York City philanthropist, and in October took a look and was stunned by the poverty in this region. The terrible condition of the hotel and guesthouses on the property shocked Eleanor. Warm Springs was a large pool of water naturally warmed to 89 degrees. FDR had heard swimming might be beneficial, tried it for more than an hour, and loved it. He found he could move his toes afterward.

FDR returned to New York City on November 4 to vote for Davis for president and Smith for governor. Smith won by 140,000 votes, but in the presidential race Coolidge carried New York by 700,000.

೮೦೧೪

HARRY S TRUMAN, 40, lost his job as city manager of eastern Kansas City to a Republican, only the second GOP victory in Jackson County since the Civil War. Both the *Kansas City Star* and the *Independence Sentinel* backed Truman. The KKK tried to work a deal with him at a rally one dark night, but instead Truman gave a speech critical of it. Truman didn't get any support from the NAACP either.

Truman was accused of not supplying equipment for the impressive Industrial Home for Negro Boys. African Americans accounted for about 10 percent of the vote in Kansas City at this time. Both county presiding judges were also accused of trying to take control of county homes away from circuit court judges. The election went to Henry W. Rummell, 8,791 to 7,932.

Truman then switched to selling memberships in the Kansas City Auto Club and earned $5,000 the first year, although he had to pay sales commissions on 1,000 memberships. Truman and former business partner Eddie Jacobson paid off their $2,800 loan from the Baltimore Bank.

Truman's daughter Mary Margaret was born on February 17. Bess, 39, had two prior miscarriages.

೮೦೧೪

DWIGHT D. EISENHOWER, at 34, was sent to Fort Logan, Colorado, as a recruiter. He was bored and disgusted, but his Panama mentor, General Fox Connor, now deputy chief of staff, tipped him off that a high profile assignment to the General Staff College at Leavenworth, Kansas, probably would be forthcoming. Eisenhower's preference had been the infantry school at Fort Benning, Georgia.

General Connor's fitness report on Eisenhower said, "One of most capable I have ever met." Eisenhower had gone to Washington to ask Frank L. Sheets, head of the infantry school, to send him to Benning, but Sheets turned him down. Then Eisenhower saw Connor, who later sent him a telegram saying to make no protest whatsoever about his next orders. Fort Logan it was, but then Connor followed with a letter saying there would be an opening at the Leavenworth school and that it would be more beneficial than Benning.

೮೦೧೪

JOHN F. KENNEDY, 7, now scored higher on intelligence scores than his brother Joe Jr., which surprised their mother.

John was in the third grade when he was abruptly transferred on October 22 to the new private school Joe Jr. was attending—Noble and Greenough Lower School in Brookline, Massachusetts.

The $400-per-year school was almost totally non-Irish; the parents were largely anti-Catholic and anti-Joe Kennedy.

May 6: John's sister, Pat, was born.

೮೦೧೪

LYNDON B. JOHNSON, 16, graduated from Johnson City High School, the youngest in the six-member senior class. The other five went to college, the most ever for the school, but not LBJ. He didn't want to.

One night Johnson was driving Sam's car with several older boys headed for a rendezvous with a bootlegger. Johnson went into a ditch, smashed the car, and told the others that he could not face his father. The passengers took up a collection for Johnson, who slept in the car that night. Then he hitched to Austin, took the bus to Robstown, 160 miles to the south near Corpus Christi, where his cousin Roper lived.

The only job available there was in a cotton gin. It was an 11-hour day in a dangerous working environment. Johnson's father sent a man to fetch him, and Lyndon agreed to go home, provided that his father sought no retaliation for his wrecking the car.

In July, Johnson ran off to California with four older boys in a $25 Model T. He asked Sam if he could make the long joyride, but Sam refused. Lyndon said he would go anyway and escaped when his father was busy looking at a farm for sale in Blanco. Sam, on returning home, called the sheriff's office plus another in El Paso, asking them to arrest Lyndon.

El Paso, with 74,000 people, was the largest place Lyndon had ever seen. Later the boys picked grapes at Tehachapi in the San Joaquin Valley. Here the story gets murky. Johnson later claimed that when the money ran out, the boys separated and Lyndon went job hunting up and down the Pacific Coast—washing dishes, waiting tables, and doing farm work.

The reality, according to biographer Robert Caro, was that he visited his cousin Tom Martin in San Bernardino, asked for a job, and received work as a clerk in a law office. Martin bought Lyndon two new suits, and the teenager settled down in Clarence's nice ranch house. Clarence suggested LBJ study law, pass the bar in Nevada, and then get admitted to the

California bar. At that point Martin would hire him, but Nevada would license no lawyer younger than 21.

ᔥᔥ

RICHARD M. NIXON, 11 years old, and his brothers living in Whittier, California, became sick from drinking unpasteurized milk. Richard's father believed in raw milk, and the family had their own cow. One by one the children became sick, starting with Arthur. Richard lost 20 pounds from undulant fever. In addition, Harold came down with tuberculosis. A doctor had warned Frank Nixon against unpasteurized milk, but he would not listen.

ᔥᔥ

GERALD R. FORD, 11, lived in Michigan. The family would vacation at Ottawa Beach and fish the Little South Branch of the Pere Marquette River.

June 3: Gerald's brother Dick was born.

ᔥᔥ

JAMES EARL CARTER JR. was born on October 1 at the Wise Hospital in Plains, Georgia, the first future chief executive to be born in a public facility rather than at home or in a log cabin.

His father was James Earl Carter, age 30; his mother was Bessie Lillian Gordy Carter, age 26.

Earl was born in Calhoun County, Georgia, on September 12, 1894. He was a peanut farmer, the founder of a peanut warehouse business, a broker, and a local public official. Lillian was a registered nurse and a native of Richland, Georgia—born there on August 15, 1898.

Earl's farm would expand in time to 4,000 acres worked by 200 African American tenant farmers. Earl was a lieutenant in the army's quartermaster corps during World War I. He never joined the Ku Klux Klan but did not share his wife's tolerant views toward blacks. The couple married on September 27, 1923.

Thomas Carter Sr., left England for Isle of Wight County, Virginia, on the James River in 1637. Great-grandfather Kindred Carter, who died in 1800, settled in Georgia. Great-great-grandfather Littleberry W. Carter, a Confederate war veteran, was murdered by a business partner in a dispute over earnings from a merry-go-round. Grandfather Jim Jack Gordy, a Confederate veteran, was active in Democratic politics and postmaster for Richland.

ᔥᔥ

RONALD REAGAN, 11, lived in Dixon, Illinois, where he caddied at the Dixon Country Club. He often went to the library to read Mark Twain and Zane Grey.

ᔥᔥ

GEORGE HERBERT WALKER BUSH was born on June 12 in the family's Victorian home in Milton, Massachusetts. His father was Prescott S. Bush, age 29; his mother was Dorothy Walker Bush, age 23.

Prescott was a businessman born in Columbus, Ohio. He entered Yale in 1913, left with National Guard forces for the

Mexican border campaign against Pancho Villa, and then returned to Yale and graduated in 1917. He was a captain in the One Hundred Fifty-Eighth Field Artillery Brigade in the Meuse–Argonne offensive in France in 1918 and then served in the army of the occupation in Germany.

In 1920, Prescott worked for the Simmons Hardware Company in St. Louis as a salesman, then rebuilt a failing floor-covering firm that was to merge with the U.S. Rubber Company, and the company moved him to the U.S. Rubber office in Braintree, Massachusetts. Later, in 1924, Prescott was transferred to the New York City office and bought a home in Greenwich, Connecticut, a nine-bed Victorian house on a 2-acre wooded lot on Grove Lane.

Bush's mother was born near Walker's Point, Kennebunkport (York County), Maine, the daughter of a dry goods wholesaler who later went into investment banking. She was raised in St. Louis. She married Prescott on August 6, 1921 at Kennebunkport. George was their second child. Prescott Bush Jr., was born in 1922.

The Bush ancestors had reached Cape Cod, Massachusetts, about 1650. Great-great grandfather Obadiah Newcomb Bush was a forty-niner in California and died at sea on his return to the East Coast. He was an Episcopalian minister. His grandfather, Samuel P. Bush, was a mechanical engineer. Grandfather George Herbert Walker founded the investment firm, G. H. Walker and Company. He became president of the United States Golf Association, 1921 to 1923, and established the Walker Cup as the prize in the U.S.–British golf competition.

Bush is a distant cousin of Benedict Arnold, Franklin Pierce, Theodore Roosevelt, William Howard Taft, Abraham Lincoln, and Winston Churchill.

1925
Calvin Coolidge

President Coolidge, this cool, quiet man, seemed in many ways a radical contrast with the life and times of the Roaring Twenties. It was a good time for Americans, as they enjoyed peace and prosperity.

January–March: Secretary of State Charles Evans Hughes resigned on January 5, effective March 5. Hughes expected Coolidge to ask him to stay on, but the president did not. In response to the retirement notice, Coolidge wrote a nice letter on January 10, calling Hughes a man "so well qualified" to fill the job. Former U.S. senator from Minnesota Frank Billings Kellogg was selected on February 16 to replace Hughes.

Clear skies greeted viewers on Inauguration Day, March 4, as the first elected New Englander since Franklin Pierce took the oath of office. Chief Justice William Howard Taft administered the oath, the first time a former president administered the oath to a president-elect.

494

Coolidge was the first president to deliver his inaugural address to a radio audience, as twenty-five radio stations took his voice to approximately 22.8 million listeners. Coolidge said, "Here stands our country, an example of tranquility at home, a patron of tranquility abroad. … Here it will continue to stand, seeking peace and prosperity."

Soon after his inauguration, Coolidge named Charles B. Warren as attorney general. Warren, former president of the Michigan Sugar Company, was under indictment for illegal marketing of sugar pulp. Coolidge had never consulted Republican leaders about the arrogant Warren, who had been a floor leader for Coolidge at the 1924 Republican National Convention and had been ambassador to Japan and Mexico.

The House Judiciary Committee approved Warren's nomination on March 6. The next day the Progressives joined the Democrats to ask pointed questions from the Senate floor. James Reed, a Missouri senator, called Warren a criminal and scoundrel and said the nomination would make it appear as though the trusts were naming the attorney general.

When the nomination went to the full Senate for a vote, it was defeated by 1 vote. Coolidge, angry, said he would submit Warren's name again. The president felt that the rejection was an insult to him and unfair to Warren. On resubmission, Coolidge said he hoped an "unbroken practice of three generations of permitting the President to choose his own cabinet will not now be changed." On March 18, Warren was rejected again, this time by 7 votes.

After this defeat, Coolidge nominated former Vermont attorney general John G. Sargent, who was quickly confirmed by the Senate.

July: The Scopes "Monkey Trial" came to an end in Dayton, Tennessee on July 21. The trial of teacher John Scopes for teaching the theory of evolution had gained national attention. Scopes, whom Clarence Darrow defended and former presidential candidate William Jennings Bryan prosecuted, was convicted of breaking Tennessee's law that prohibited teaching evolution. Just 5 days after the trial ended, Bryan died.

August: More than 40,000 members of the Ku Klux Klan marched through the streets of Washington, D.C., on August 8. As many as 200,000 spectators lined the streets on a rainy day to watch the parade of Klansmen. Coolidge was said to be embarrassed about the march and support shown to the Klan.

October: Secretary of War John W. Weeks became ill, and Dwight F. Davis, who had donated the Davis Cup to international tennis, replaced him on October 14.

Former Presidents

WILLIAM HOWARD TAFT became the first former president to swear in the president-elect when he administered the oath of office to Calvin Coolidge on March 4. Now a true supporter of Coolidge, Taft thought the president ought to run for another term in 1928.

Future Presidents

HERBERT HOOVER, 51, the secretary of commerce, created the National Academy of Science and became its chairman. The

The crowded courtroom in Dayton, Tennessee, during the Scopes Monkey Trial in 1925. Clarence Darrow is seated at the far right. (Library of Congress)

idea behind the academy was to have industry support university research ideas.

November: *Time* magazine put Hoover on the cover of its November 16 issue. In the accompanying article, Hoover was called "the brains" of the Coolidge administration, with his fingers in a number of pies. In truth, Hoover was not as close to Coolidge as he had been to Warren Harding.

⃞⃟

FRANKLIN D. ROOSEVELT, 43, wanted a national conference of Democrats to determine party aims, but he didn't get far with the idea. He rode a train to Florida in February with Senator Thomas Walsh of Montana and tried to get him to call the conference. Roosevelt was enjoying Warm Springs when he learned his project would not fly.

⃞⃟

HARRY S TRUMAN, 41, became manager for stock sales of Community Savings and Loan of Independence, Missouri, in September. Old artillery battery friend, Spencer Salisbury, helped him land the job. Truman wrote the advertising for the sales effort and, to solicit business, formed a partnership with Arthur Metzger.

Truman remained active in the Army Reserve. He went to camp at Fort Riley, Kansas, each summer, and was promoted to lieutenant colonel in 1925.

⃞⃟

DWIGHT EISENHOWER, 35, in August entered the General Staff College at Leavenworth, Kansas. George S. Patton had graduated at the top of the 1924 class, and Eisenhower had Patton's notes on how to tackle major combat situations. Early tests ranked Eisenhower fourteenth out of 244 students. He prepared for college in part while in Denver recuperating from having his appendix removed.

⃞⃟

JOHN F. KENNEDY, 8, lived near Boston.

November 20: John's brother Robert was born.

⃞⃟

LYNDON B. JOHNSON, 17, studied law books in a nice ranch house owned by his cousin Clarence Martin near San Bernardino, California. Lyndon wanted to become a lawyer, as did his roommate Fritz Koeniger. The two youths practically ran Martin's law business whenever Martin went on a drinking binge, but they ran out of money for filing fees and realized if anyone found out that they were practicing law without a license they would be in trouble. In November, Martin gave Lyndon a ride back home to Texas.

⃞⃟

RICHARD M. NIXON, 12, experienced the great shock of his youth when his brother Arthur, 7, died from tuberculosis.

January–May: Nixon transferred to Lindsey Elementary some distance from home so that he could take piano lessons from his mother's sister, Jane Beeson. Nixon was unhappy and homesick during his months there, mostly because of a stricter household atmosphere.

June–August: In June, Nixon's parents picked him up for the return trip to Whittier. Arthur Nixon was gleeful about seeing his brother again and hugged and kissed him, a behavior atypical in the Nixon family.

Arthur became sick in July and died on August 11 after a spinal tap. The death caused a new evangelical fervor in Frank Nixon, and he saw Arthur's death as the work of a punishing God. Frank became the revivalist at subsequent Quaker meetings.

September–December: Richard, the eighth grader, wrote his autobiography as a school essay. He looked ahead and said he would take postgraduate work at Columbia after high school and college, and then travel to Europe. He would then study law and enter politics for an occupation "so that I might be of some good to the people."

⃞⃟

GERALD R. FORD, 12, joined Troop 15 of the Boy Scouts at Trinity Methodist Church in Grand Rapids, Michigan.

⃞⃟

JIMMY CARTER, 1, was a baby in Plains, Georgia.

⃞⃟

RONALD REAGAN, 14, lived in Dixon, Illinois, and the family moved yet again, to 318 West Everett, which was close to the railroad tracks. The move made it possible for the Reagan boys to attend a better school.

Ronald spent the summer in hard labor, digging foundations for houses at 35 cents per hour. Clearing weeds from building sites was part of the job. In November, as a high school sophomore, he began writing what would become a long series of fictional stories.

⃞⃟

GEORGE H. W. BUSH, 1, was a baby in Greenwich, Connecticut.

1926
Calvin Coolidge

President Coolidge once again boasted of a land of peace and prosperity, but received the first warnings that trouble loomed on the horizon. Poor banking controls and increased speculation in the stock market worried many observers, but the president felt there was no justification for federal intervention under the circumstances.

January–March: Reflecting on his role, Coolidge wrote to his father, John, on New Year's Day: "I suppose I am the most powerful man in the world, but [it means] great limitations. I cannot have any freedom even to go and come. I am only in the clutch of forces greater than I am. Thousands are waiting to shake my hand today."

In February, Congress passed a new bill reducing the income and inheritance taxes. Coolidge signed the Revenue Act into law on February 26.

In March, John Coolidge was dying, and the president sped by train and automobile to the family homestead in Plymouth, Vermont. Coolidge arrived too late. John Coolidge died at 10:41 P.M. on March 18, and the president's train arrived in Vermont at 6:45 the next morning.

May: Congress passed the Air Commerce Act on May 5. The new law assigned air routes across the country from coast-to-coast and gave the Commerce Department control over licensing of aircrafts and pilots (see **Herbert Hoover**, opposite column).

September–October: Coolidge believed arms limitations to be his best card to play, as there was public support, and in the fall he decided the time had come to push for them. Other nations reacted favorably. Coolidge worked to hold down military appropriations and the construction of new ships, although newspapers criticized him for letting the army and navy slip into a sorry condition.

November: In the midterm elections, the Republican margin in the House fell from 60 to 39. In the Senate, the margin declined from 16 to 2. During the fall campaign, Coolidge, 54, did very little to help fellow Republican candidates.

December: In his annual message to Congress, Coolidge said: "I find it impossible to characterize [the state of the union] other than one of general peace and prosperity." He asked for new highways, inland waterways, land reclamation, railroad consolidation, and regulation of radio.

Problems in Nicaragua followed the ouster of two presidents. Coolidge supported President Adolfo Diaz, saying his election was legal. But Vice President Juan Sacasa, ousted in 1925, established a rebel government in December, and a civil war began. In December, Coolidge decided to send U.S. Marines to Nicaragua. He told the press that whenever a revolution in Central American occurs, "it means trouble for our citizens."

Former Presidents

WILLIAM HOWARD TAFT was criticized for writing an article for *Collier's* magazine about America's crime wave and later admitted that perhaps it had not been a good idea.

At the time of the *Collier's* piece, the press was playing up a national crime wave. Readers were told that mobsters were in action everywhere. Chief Justice Taft granted an interview on the subject to *Collier's* entitled, "Stop Helping the Criminal," an outburst against poor police work. Later he was questioned on the propriety of granting the in-

Franklin D. Roosevelt in Warm Springs, Georgia, during the mid-1920s. *(National Archives)*

terview. He wrote to *Collier's* editors on December 13 that he consented because "the circumstances are exceptional." A month later, Taft expressed doubts to the editor, saying perhaps he should not have sounded off.

In a letter to a Yale classmate, Taft lamented that the majority of their old college friends were now dead. Taft turned 69 on September 15.

Future Presidents

HERBERT HOOVER, 52, secretary of commerce, often dealt with the growing needs of the aviation industry, which had captured the interest and imagination of the general public. The Commerce Department gained passage in Congress of the Air Commerce Act to deal with matters such as lighted runways, navigation, and weather equipment. Hoover proposed that airlines fly from New York to Los Angeles and from Chicago to Texas.

Hoover was also working on waterway matters. He wrote to Senator Arthur Capper of Kansas that what the country needed was inland waterways, but President Coolidge saw these ideas as costly dreams. Hoover made a 2-day tour of the Columbia River basin to study irrigation plans. He was also involved in the Railroad Labor Mediation Board. His opposition to foreign cartel control of resources meant, he said, that "the public's interest as consumers against the monstrous imposition [from abroad and] growth of foreign monopolies directed against consuming countries can be halted [causing] international friction."

෨෬

FRANKLIN D. ROOSEVELT, 44, was receiving pressure to run for the U. S. Senate. However, he decided not to run because he did not want to be tied down for 6 years. FDR and his strategist, Louis Howe, thought that rejecting a bid for the Senate would free him to focus on the White House and give him more leisure time at his Warm Springs estate, which he finally bought for $200,000. His wife and mother were against the deal.

April–July: Warms Springs was directly tied to Roosevelt's determination to cast off his braces and walk again. Eleanor felt that the Warm Springs property was too far away from New York City to be manageable; but on April 29, Roosevelt made the plunge, buying 1,200 acres, the old hotel, and many cottages.

FDR immediately poured money into improvements and hired doctors and physical therapists. In July the Georgia Warm Springs Foundation was established with Roosevelt as president. He was always enthusiastic when in the water and moving with other polio-afflicted swimmers.

In May, FDR wrote a commencement address he delivered at Milton Academy and then had it published as a thin book that sold about 350 copies. In it he prophesized rapid changes in technology, reciting the changes in the nineteenth century.

September: Al Smith asked Roosevelt to deliver the keynote address at the New York State Democratic Convention. Roosevelt jotted down hints on how Smith could capture the Democratic nomination in 1928. Political personalities were constantly making visits to the Roosevelt residence in New York City.

ᔆᥩᶜᶳ

HARRY S TRUMAN, 42, was elected presiding judge of Jackson County, Kansas City, becoming the chief administrator for the city. The job had nothing to do with judges or lawyers. He owed his sudden success to Kansas City political powerbroker Thomas J. Pendergast, even though Truman had never met Pendergast until this year. Mike Pendergast, Tom's younger brother, had engineered Truman's earlier political victory in 1922 as presiding judge for the Eastern District of Kansas City. Truman's current term began on January 1, 1927.

As chief executive, Truman was responsible for obtaining bonds to build roads, construct hospitals for the elderly, and finance buildings (including a new county courthouse), and for handling competitive bids for construction projects. Mike Pendergast had believed Truman would make a good county collector. At $10,000 per year, the salary could have retired Truman's debts, but conflicts between political insiders brought about Truman's surprise run for the larger job.

ᔆᥩᶜᶳ

DWIGHT D. EISENHOWER, 36, graduated first in his class of 275 at the General Staff College at Leavenworth, Kansas, in June and was promoted to major. One instructor was George S. Patton Jr. When congratulating Eisenhower on his class standing, Patton added, "Major, some day I'll be working for you."

Eisenhower had risen to third in class standing by May and the next month edged West Point classmate Charles M. Busbee for first. The commandant at Leavenworth wanted Eisenhower to remain as an instructor, but Eisenhower rejected the offer. Then a second offer came to teach military science at Northwestern University and coach football at the same time for an extra $3,500 per year. He turned that down too.

His next assignment was Fort Benning, Georgia, where he commanded an infantry battalion. The job bored him. Matters were made worse when he was asked to be the head coach of a poor football team. He was unhappy with the request but reached a compromise—he would handle the backfield only. When the season ended, Eisenhower applied to the Army War College in Washington. The Fort Benning commandant wrote a supporting memo: "Major Eisenhower has force, character and energy as well as knowledge." The problem was that the next college class wouldn't begin until September 1927.

Then came a surprise question from army headquarters in Washington—would he consider going to France to write a guidebook to American battlefields? Eisenhower's big booster, General Fox Connor, interviewed Eisenhower in Washington on this matter, saying that the book would be for the American Battlefield Monument Commission and that Pershing himself wanted it because large numbers of American tourists were now visiting graves. Eisenhower would start work on the book the following year.

ᔆᥩᶜᶳ

JOHN F. KENNEDY, 9, entered the new Dexter School because the Noble-Greenough School in Brookline, Massachusetts, was operating close to bankruptcy. John's father put together a group of nine parents and $110,000 to start the Dexter School.

John's father, Joe, was so busy in the movie business that he was traveling constantly between Hollywood and New York City. Now he wanted the family moved to New York, but Rose dug in and refused to leave Brookline, saying she didn't

This cartoon from a popular magazine depicts the frivolous and fun times of the "Roaring 20s."

want to uproot her family every time Joe negotiated a different business deal.

LYNDON B. JOHNSON, 18, worked in a road building gang around Johnson City, Texas. It was pick and shovel work. He walked with a scoop behind a mule, trying to break up the hard ground. Roads were built by hand using a composite of rocks, not blacktop. The pay was $2 per day. His father, Sam, was convinced Lyndon faced a lifetime of manual labor.

When not working, Lyndon ran around with a wild bunch of older men getting into trouble and drinking moonshine before taking farm cars and drag racing on the roads.

RICHARD M. NIXON, 13, entered Fullerton High School and faced setbacks in both debating and football. Tuberculosis caused removal of his brother Harold from the family home to a sanatorium in Prescott, Arizona, at 5,000 feet elevation in mountain country. Nixon's mother, Hannah, stayed with Harold and rented a house in nearby Pinecrest for $25 per month. She was absent from California for long periods to nurse Harold as well as gassed war veterans at the facility. This development further depleted the Nixon family funds.

Nixon's father would drive to Prescott—a 15-hour, 750-mile trip—almost every month.

The boys in Pinecrest slept in the back bedroom, and Richard worked at part-time jobs.

Richard became a regular on the Fullerton debate team and won a competition his first year, but that came after he lost a debate, struck dumb on his feet and walked off the stage humiliated. After that, he temporarily quit debating until his parents talked him into trying it again. Then his English teacher, H. Lynn Sheller, advised him to drop his wooden, formal approach to debating in favor of a more conversational style, which worked.

GERALD R. FORD, 13, lived in Grand Rapids, Michigan, a city of 169,000 that called itself the Furniture Capital of the World.

JIMMY CARTER, 2, lived in Plains, Georgia.

October 22: Jimmy's sister Gloria was born.

RONALD REAGAN, 15, enjoyed sports at Dixon High School and began work during the summer months as a lifeguard at Lowell Park on the Rock River in northwest Illinois. The pay was $15 per week plus all the food he needed from the manager of a concession stand. He worked 12 hours per day, 7 days per week. To prepare for this, Ronald took a lifesaving course held at the YMCA and was certified by the Red Cross.

Reagan played right guard on the football team and also participated in basketball and track.

GEORGE H. W. BUSH, age 2, was a child in Greenwich, Connecticut. His father, Prescott, was named a vice president of W. A. Harriman and Company in New York City, a Wall Street investment house.

1927
Calvin Coolidge

President Coolidge succinctly startled the country by removing himself from the 1928 presidential race. Many thought he was playing a trick to stretch his incumbency to an unprecedented 10 years. Herbert Hoover advised Coolidge's renomination but, more actively than others, positioned himself to be the Republican nominee.

January: Coolidge sent a special message to Congress on January 10 to justify the sending of marines to Nicaragua the previous December. He said that American property and canal rights had been in jeopardy.

February: Coolidge, on February 10, proposed a naval arms limitation meeting to supplement Warren Harding's earlier Washington conference. Coolidge told Congress that "deliberate self-denial ... by the great naval powers [would help to] guarantee peace." The meeting was scheduled for June in Geneva, Switzerland. Coolidge picked Charles Evans Hughes to head the U.S. delegation, but Hughes declined the offer. When a team consisting of Secretary of State Frank Kellogg, Secretary of Treasury Andrew Mellon, and Senator Claude Swanson of Virginia was proposed, Kellogg thought such a delegation would appear too "heavyweight" in character and give the impression of being "overanxious to have an agreement." Instead, Admiral Hilary Jones and Hugh Gibson, the U.S. ambassador to Belgium, were chosen to represent the United States.

April–August: Since the end of the war, France had caused constant difficulties for the United States over peace plans, arms limits, and reparations. Now surfaced James T. Shotwell, a Columbia University professor, who talked French foreign minister Aristide Briand into considering his position in favor of outlawing war. Briand, on April 6, pledged France's cooperation to outlaw war as a means to settle disputes.

With Charles Lindbergh's flight across the Atlantic from New York to Paris May 21 to May 22, goodwill between the United States and France was heightened. With all the excitement that the Lindbergh flight caused, Coolidge believed he could not afford to ignore Briand's peace feelers.

On May 31, Coolidge told the press that he would be pleased if a way could be found to put "into a practical form" the ideas that Briand had discussed. Kellogg, on June 11, had Ambassador Myron T. Herrick tell Briand that the United States was willing to discuss the matter. Briand proposed, on June 21, that the two nations "condemn recourse to war and renounce it.... All disputes [shall be settled] by pacific means."

Charles Lindbergh stands in front of his plane, the **Spirit of St. Louis,** *shortly before his historic transatlantic flight in 1927. (The Lindbergh Foundation)*

There was renewed interest in Briand's peace efforts in the fall. Still, some members of Congress worried that the peace Briand was proposing would take away Congress's ability ever to declare war on France.

In November, Senator Capper said he would offer a resolution asking other nations to join in renouncing war. When Kellogg appeared before the Senate Foreign Relations Committee on December 22, Senator William Borah suggested that "outlawry of war" be made multilateral and not confined to France only, but would include "all nations."

On December 28, Kellogg suggested to Briand that the proposal be broadened to include "all the principal powers of the world to a declaration renouncing war as an instrument of national policy."

Still, Coolidge and Kellogg were not satisfied, believing France was only interested in pulling the two nations together to contain Germany.

In the meantime, the General Naval Conference opened in Geneva on June 20. France and Italy, however, refused to participate. Great Britain, Japan, and the United States could not find agreement during the 2 months of meeting. The main sticking point between Great Britain and the United States was over "tonnage." When the conference collapsed in August, Coolidge was embarrassed.

Coolidge then decided to stall Briand's peace efforts, suggesting that the Senate might not confirm any agreement because such an agreement might be unconstitutional.

In the summer, Coolidge selected the Black Hills of South Dakota for his vacation. He stayed at a lodge near Rapid City. On August 2, the fourth anniversary of Harding's death, Coolidge went to the Rapid City High School for a routine press conference, accompanied by Senator Arthur Capper. As newsmen filed into a mathematics room they found slips of paper piled up. Coolidge himself handed each newsman the statement: "I do not choose to run for President in 1928."

The national reaction was either to accept the statement at face value or to assume it was a trick to obtain another term in office. Returning to Washington from South Dakota with Capper, Coolidge told the senator that if he took another term he would remain in Washington until 1933, saying, "Ten years is longer than any other man has had it—too long!"

September–December: In September, Herbert Hoover went to the White House and told the president that he wanted Coolidge to run for another term. Coolidge made no direct reply. Hoover then told the press he wanted to see Coolidge renominated.

In December, Coolidge told the Republican National Committee that he would not run in 1928.

Former Presidents

WILLIAM HOWARD TAFT was convinced Coolidge had to be renominated because he was the "safe" choice but by midyear resigned himself to the prospect that Herbert Hoover was headed for the Republican nomination.

Taft also began to express concern over his health and the load his weight had put on his heart over the years. He enjoyed a seventieth birthday party in September with friends and neighbors at his Murray Bay, Quebec, retreat.

Taft had nothing but contempt for the worldwide clamor to save Nicola Sacco and Bartolomeo Vanzetti from execution. The two Italian radicals were convicted in 1921 for the 1920 murder of two men during an attempted robbery at a Massachusetts shoe factory. The case had received international attention over the years, with many believing that the two men were innocent. Asleep at Murray Bay at 2 A.M. on August 22, Taft was awakened by a telegram messenger from defense lawyers asking for a stay pending appeal to the Supreme Court. To do so would have meant a long trip for the chief justice to the Canadian–Vermont border in order to sign the papers on American territory. He refused, and Sacco and Vanzetti were executed on August 23.

Future Presidents

HERBERT HOOVER, 53, as secretary of commerce, was preoccupied from April on with one of the greatest floods in the history of the Mississippi River. The disaster made 350,000 homeless and turned 600,000 people to a life of desperation. Hoover jumped into action much as he had in the Belgian calamity of 1914 and established a headquarters for relief at Memphis. (Some observers later claimed Hoover's response to public needs along the Mississippi made possible his election in 1928.)

Hoover quickly was on the scene and put together an armada of 600 ships, received food shipments from Chicago, requisitioned supplies, and organized and created 150 tent cities. President Coolidge made him commerce secretary chairman of the Mississippi Flood Commission. Hoover called the situation the greatest peacetime calamity ever and asked for a special session of Congress to meet the crisis, but Coolidge vetoed the idea.

In August, with Coolidge's public announcement that he wouldn't run for another term, Hoover emerged as the likely Republican nominee in 1928. Still, during the fall, Hoover was trying to convince Coolidge to change his mind.

ഇരുത

FRANKLIN D. ROOSEVELT, 45, announced in the spring that he backed Al Smith for the 1928 presidential run, but wrote to Josephus Daniels in June that prosperity might cripple the Democratic Party effort. Another possible hindrance to a Smith nomination would be his Catholicism. *Atlantic Magazine* ran articles that to elect a Catholic would mean a candidate such as Smith would hold beliefs irreconcilable with the Constitution. Smith strenuously objected, and Roosevelt attacked the magazine's reasoning as ridiculous.

Roosevelt expanded his Warm Springs, Georgia, holdings by buying a 1,750-acre farm at Pine Mountain and hiring the farmer who had sold him the property to manage it. Roosevelt also published a pamphlet on the wonders of Warm Springs.

In 1926, Roosevelt rushed to an American Orthopedic Association (AOA) meeting in Atlanta, hoping to speak on Warm Springs, but he was turned away on the grounds that he was not a doctor. Some members of the AOA were engaged by his Warm Springs development ideas, however; and in January 1927, an AOA committee did a study which found that 23 percent of patients at Warm Springs responded favorably to 5 to 17 weeks of treatment. The committee recommended the establishment of a hydrotherapeutic center at the site.

Roosevelt's law partner, Basil O'Conner, had established the Warm Springs Foundation, and now, after revisions, it was made into a nonprofit operation that could accept donations. Many friends, including Henry Morganthau Jr., put money into Warm Springs.

On May 7, Roosevelt's half-brother James died at age 73.

ഇരുത

HARRY S TRUMAN, 43, as presiding judge for Kansas City, ran a $7 million operation with 700 employees. He was soon adept at political back-scratching with Kansas City boss Tom Pendergast. Truman was clever enough to avoid what had

brought down several predecessors: women, graft, and gambling. This led Pendergast to point to Truman as proof that the machine ran an honest operation in Kansas City. Truman in return made sure he found jobs for Pendergast's men. But Truman showed early independence and later awarded roadwork contracts to the lowest bidder, even when that bidder, in one case, came from South Dakota. The locals howled and took their complaints to Pendergast.

Truman had control of a wide range of employees, from surveyors and purchasing agents to sheriffs. He developed the habit of going from town to town to explain exactly what was going to happen in road construction.

ഇരുത

DWIGHT D. EISENHOWER, 37, was given 6 months by the U.S. Army to write a guidebook for tourists visiting French battlefields, then entered the Army War College in Washington, D.C., in September.

Eisenhower reported to the Battle Monuments Commission in January and immediately had to sort through maps, photos, and reams of information, including personal accounts of fighting in France submitted by soldiers. Because this was General John J. Pershing's project, his approval would be needed on the finished product. As it turned out, Eisenhower wrote the book first and went to France later for a final update of the material. The guidebook had two goals: to satisfy the tourist and to satisfy the army's administration. *Encyclopedia Britannica* called Eisenhower's effort an excellent reference work.

Eisenhower was one of the youngest students at the Army War College. He wrote a paper entitled "An Enlisted Reserve for the Regular Army." The college commandant called it a work of exceptional merit.

ഇരുത

JOHN F. KENNEDY, now 10, was moved from Massachusetts to New York because a polio epidemic caused his mother Rose to panic. On September 26, she took a rented mansion on 252nd Street at Independence Avenue in Riverdale, New York, on the Hudson northwest of the Bronx. The boys were pulled out of the Dexter School in Brookline and placed in the equally exclusive Riverside Country Day School. Rose was pregnant for the eighth time.

John's father, Joe, was very busy: He purchased a Hyannis residence on Cape Cod for $25,000, and he took over Hollywood star Gloria Swanson's movie company. The Hyannis property had fourteen rooms and nine baths.

On November 11, Joe met Swanson at the Savoy Palace on 5th Avenue in New York. She asked him for a loan to do her own production of Sadie Thompson, a story to which both the Roman Catholic Church and Joe objected. Quickly Joe's next objective was to take over her production career as a silent partner.

In December, he followed her back to Hollywood, bringing along three of his own accountants and soon took over her company. He fired her production people and replaced them with his own.

&⊗℞

LYNDON B. JOHNSON, 19, ended more than 2 years of hard labor with a road gang and entered a third-rate college, Southwest Texas State Teachers College at San Marcos. The small school had been a normal school until 1927 and had only recently been accredited.

Johnson was dirt poor, which made every week a challenge to find enough food. The San Marco tuition was only $400 per year, and thus the school was a favorite among students with meager means. In no time, LBJ wrangled free housing above the president's garage and shared this space with the football captain. Johnson was now chatting politics with school president Cecil Evans and running errands for him.

Johnson organized the Blanco County Club for students from his area. He wrote for the *College Star* and quickly became editor-in-chief. He wrote complimentary stories about faculty members and was agreeable to everything they said at meetings. Other students sized up Johnson as an expert at kowtowing.

&⊗℞

RICHARD M. NIXON, 14, was a student at Fullerton High School in California.

&⊗℞

GERALD R. FORD, 14, became a football player during his first year at South High in Grand Rapids, Michigan. In the fall, Ford played every freshman game as a center and linebacker. The coach called him Whitey because of his blond hair.

August 11: Gerald's brother James was born.

&⊗℞

JIMMY CARTER, 3, lived in Plains, Georgia, in a rural district called Archery, 3 miles west of town. His parents were strict in his upbringing. Jimmy began memorizing verses from the Bible.

&⊗℞

RONALD REAGAN, 16, was elected president of Dixon High's student body. His girlfriend, Margaret Mugs Cleaver, was elected president of the senior class. They were a twosome, and friends predicted they would marry. Both were in school theatricals and played opposite each other in *You and I*. They were also officers in the dramatic society. On the school paper, she was a reporter and Reagan was art director.

&⊗℞

GEORGE H. W. BUSH, 3, lived in Greenwich, Connecticut.

1928
Calvin Coolidge

President Coolidge continued to talk about prosperity and good times, but privately he expressed reservations about the country's economic future. During the year, some were still pressuring him to try for another term in office.

January: On January 6 a reporter asked Coolidge if brokers' margin loans had expanded too fast. The president said that he felt loans were not excessive, that bank deposits were up and more securities were now being offered on Wall Street.

This contradicted what he privately told H. Parker Willis, editor of the *New York Journal of Commerce*. Parker later said Coolidge questioned the gambling going on in the stock market, which caused Willis to tell him that he wished the president had added that point to his January 6 statement to cut the growing trend in speculation. Coolidge told Willis that his economic statement was made as a representative of the people, but that he, as an individual, was allowed to take a dim personal view on speculation.

Coolidge traveled to Havana, Cuba, to take part in the Sixth Conference of American States. Coolidge and his wife, Grace, boarded a special train for Key West, Florida, on January 13, then transferred to the battleship *Texas*. Cuban president Gerardo Machado greeted them, and the streets were lined with cheering Cuban citizens.

In his speech to the conference on January 16, Coolidge showered praise on Central American countries and said that the United States would help with highway construction and aviation facilities.

Coolidge left Havana aboard the cruiser *Memphis* on January 17. Despite hostilities between many delegates, the visit was an overall success.

March–June: In March the Wyoming State Republican Committee asked Coolidge about the possibility of his accepting a draft to run for another term. Coolidge replied that he was unavailable.

The *New York Evening Post* reported on April 21 that Coolidge would run if it appeared that either Frank Lowden or Charles Dawes might be gaining the lead in the GOP sweepstakes. Herbert Hoover had lined up 400 delegates by May but told the president that he would release them if Coolidge entered the race. The president told Hoover to keep his delegates.

In June, Hoover won the Republican nomination (see **Herbert Hoover**, page 503).

July–August: Negotiations on the Kellogg–Briand Pact continued. Coolidge still had some reservations but allowed Secretary of State Frank Kellogg to go to Paris in July to take part in the final negotiations.

In Wausau, Wisconsin, on August 15, Coolidge publicly supported the Paris pact. He said it was the kind of work that might have prevented the World War. Coolidge called it "one of the greatest blessings ever bestowed upon humanity. It is a fitting consummation of the first decade of peace." The president's speech was highly praised.

On August 27, fifteen nations including the United States signed the Kellogg–Briand Pact in Paris, France.

Secretary of State Frank Kellogg (right) walks with President Calvin Coolidge at the White House. (Library of Congress)

When Hoover visited Coolidge in Wisconsin during the campaign, the two men posed for photographs without talking. Although many sensed a certain coolness between them, Coolidge wrote many friendly letters to Hoover during the fall campaign.

September–December: In September, Coolidge was upbeat with the press, saying that he was only "a candidate for retirement and apparently I am going to be successful in that."

Speaking on the tenth anniversary of the Armistice on November 11, Coolidge said he was disappointed in efforts to reach a naval arms agreement and directed his criticism at Great Britain and France. He called for U.S. naval construction for defensive purposes only.

In the annual message to Congress given December 4, Coolidge said, "No Congress has met a more pleasing prospect than that which appears at the present time. [There is] domestic tranquility and contentment … there is peace … mutual understanding … the country can regard the present with satisfaction and anticipate the future with optimism."

Coolidge also said that the Kellogg–Briand Pact was one of the most important treaties ever laid before the Senate: "It is the most solemn declaration against war [but] does not supercede our inalienable sovereign right and duty of national defense. [The treaty] promises more than any other agreement ever negotiated."

Former Presidents

WILLIAM HOWARD TAFT complained that the Coolidge White House paid no attention to him anymore. Taft was happy with Hoover's victory in November but was thoroughly upset that his daughter Helen had openly supported Democratic nominee Al Smith.

The chief justice complained to his son Charles P. Taft on August 11 that Coolidge ignored him. But with the presidential campaign in full swing, Taft was enthusiastic about Hoover, saying he was "really one of our great men.… He has the highest ideals … and courage to follow them."

Taft wrote his son Robert on June 3 that in disposing of cases, the Supreme Court made "far and away the best showing" of any court since the Civil War.

Taft was very impatient with lawyers who argued poorly before the Court. In such cases Taft might ask loudly, "What I want to know.…" With more dissents, Taft asked his associates to write opinions "so as to be dignified at least."

Future Presidents

HERBERT HOOVER, 54, was elected president—capping an extraordinary career as an ocean-crossing mining engineer and humanitarian involved in feeding millions of hungry children while refusing to taking any pay.

January–May: With Coolidge bowing out of the race the year before, Hoover began the year as the leading Republican candidate for the nomination. By the end of the primary season in May, Hoover had more than 400 delegates.

June: At the Republican National Convention in Kansas City on June 12, John S. McNab nominated Hoover, "He sweeps the horizon of every subject. Nothing escapes his view."

Outside the hall, 500 farmers registered their protests against Republican policy. Although Hoover entered the Kansas City show as a big favorite, he was not the only candidate. At the eleventh hour a "Stop Hoover" movement sought the nomination of either Calvin Coolidge or Charles Curtis of Kansas. These efforts soon failed. Various Republicans also wanted General John J. Pershing, Governor Frank Lowden of Illinois, Senator George Norris of Nebraska, or even Charles Evans Hughes again.

On the first ballot, Hoover received 837 votes to 72 votes for Lowden, 64 for Curtis, and small totals for several others. Curtis, part Kaw Indian, was the choice for vice president.

The Democrats met in Houston on June 24 and nominated Al Smith on the first ballot. Senator Joseph T. Robinson of Arkansas became the first southerner to make a presidential ticket since the Civil War, when he was chosen as the vice presidential candidate.

August: Hoover accepted the Republican nomination on August 11 before 70,000 cheering people in the Stanford football stadium. This victory marked the first time Hoover ever ran for elective office. In his acceptance speech, he recited his accomplishments in radio, aviation, highways, and other fast-moving changes in the American scene as commerce secretary, saying, "We are erecting a structure of idealism." Continuing the Coolidge prosperity, Hoover promised, "We shall soon ... be in sight of the day when poverty will be banished from this nation."

September–December: Hoover had problems with some of his supporters who targeted Smith because of his Catholicism. When a Republican committeewoman from Virginia cautioned against "Rome and rum," a replay of the combination that helped defeat James Blaine in 1884, Hoover reacted by saying, "I resent and repudiate it."

Democratic presidential nominee Al Smith during a campaign stop in Chicago. (Library of Congress)

Hoover spoke at Madison Square Garden on October 22: "We have steadily reduced the sweat in human labor ... our leisure has increased." After 1920, he said, the United States turned against Europe's "paternalism and state socialism."

Hoover easily defeated Smith in both the popular and electoral votes on November 6. Hoover won 444 electoral votes to Smith's 87. In the popular vote, Hoover polled 21,392,190 votes, whereas Smith earned 15,016,443 votes. Approximately 67.5 percent of eligible voters took part in the balloting, the highest percentage ever.

Three days after the election, Hoover announced that he would visit eleven Latin American states before his inauguration. He left on November 19 aboard the battleship *Maryland* and made stops in Honduras, Salvador, Nicaragua, Costa Rica, Ecuador, Peru, Chile, Argentina, and Brazil. Lou's ability in Spanish helped during this cruise.

෨෬

FRANKLIN D. ROOSEVELT, 46, a very reluctant candidate, was elected governor of New York by a paper-thin margin, and although both Franklin and Eleanor were enthusiastic workers for Al Smith's presidential run, by the end of the year a split between Roosevelt and Smith loomed. Smith, 55, thought Roosevelt's career was tied to Smith's; Roosevelt thought he owed Al Smith nothing.

June: Going into the Democratic convention in Houston, everything favored Smith. Roosevelt made the nominating speech for Smith, walking carefully to the podium on his own. He knew that an awkward flop or misstep could damage his political future. His speech reached out to an estimated 15 million radio listeners. Roosevelt said that Hoover lacked the "quality of soul," that the United States needed a man who

"understands the human side of life." Newspapers liked the speech. Will Durant wrote in the *New York World* that Roosevelt was "the finest man" to appear at either convention.

July–August: Now Smith's problem was to get Roosevelt to run for governor. The New York gubernatorial picture offered FDR few positive options. He had a hunch that Hoover would win and thought it too early to make a run at Albany. If he lost, Roosevelt felt his White House hopes might be delayed until 1936. But Smith and his handlers, huddling in Albany, decided a strong candidate for governor was needed to carry New York for Smith. Roosevelt was clearly the strongest candidate.

Smith had FDR's friend Edward J. Flynn call Warm Springs to get an answer. FDR played hard to get. Finally Smith pressed Eleanor, but she suggested that he make the call to Roosevelt himself. He did and Roosevelt caved in, later writing to his mother that the pressure was too great.

The New York State Democratic Convention was held in Rochester on October 1. Smith wanted John J. Raskob, a businessman, to be his campaign manager, even though Roosevelt objected. Raskob was a wealthy member of General Motors's financial team and a vice president at DuPont. He could find large donors.

On October 2 the convention nominated Roosevelt for governor by acclamation. The Republicans picked Albert Ottinger, the state's attorney general and a reformer, the first Jew ever nominated in New York. The Republican press played up Roosevelt's physical problems; Smith replied that being governor of New York did not require "an acrobat."

Joining FDR's campaign team were James A. Farley, Samuel I. Rosenman, Raymond Moley of Columbia University, Henry Morganthau Jr., William H. Woodin, and Flynn. The campaign swept through Binghamton and the Finger Lakes. At Buffalo on October 20, Rosenman made his first effort at speech writing. Roosevelt urged Smith's election everywhere.

November: Roosevelt spent election night, November 6, at the Biltmore in New York City with Rosenman, Frances Perkins, and Farley. Smith dropped in, already a loser, and walked out at midnight. Roosevelt went to bed that night unsure if he had won or lost the election.

The morning editions named Ottinger the winner, but FDR had gained the lead when he left for Warm Springs on November 9. Ottinger conceded that day. FDR won by 25,564 votes, with 4.2 million total votes cast.

December: On December 11, FDR was back in New York City and talked to Smith for 4 hours. Then Smith had Mrs. Belle Moskowitz write FDR's inauguration address, but FDR told Smith the speech was finished already. Smith wanted Moskowitz to be secretary to the governor; Roosevelt picked Guernsey Cross. On December 31 an FDR motorcade traveled from Hyde Park to Smith's Albany mansion, where Roosevelt was sworn in as governor.

෨ඏ

Harry S Truman, 44, a county administrator in Kansas City, made a lengthy drive across the country to gaze at courthouses and statues. He wanted ideas to incorporate into projects planned for Jackson County, Kansas City, especially for a county courthouse. Fred Canfil, a burly tough guy, did the driving. Truman had hired him as a tax investigator. They drove to Denver, then Brooklyn, Charlottesville, Nashville, Shreveport, and Baton Rouge.

Truman had trees planted along roads, the sort of thing he saw in France, but farmers would mow down the small seedlings. Truman also made his first visit to Washington, D.C., to give a report to the Daughters of the American Revolution (DAR) on the National Old Trails Association.

On May 8, his forty-fourth birthday, a county bond issue passed by a 3-to-1 margin, the money needed to build roads and a county hospital. A South Dakota firm won the first bid for $400,000. The bids were honest, and Truman had $75,000 left over.

෨ඏ

Dwight D. Eisenhower, 38, did it again—he finished number one in his class at the Army War College in Washington, graduating on June 30. Then he set out for France on the best duty he ever received from the army, he said years later. Eisenhower was given a choice: the General Staff in Washington or France. He took France, either because Mamie had pushed him or because he had learned that the chief of the General Staff, General Charles Summerall, was a reactionary, narrow-minded soldier.

The family, with John now 6, settled down at Rue d'Auteuil in Paris. The stay would last 14 months. Eisenhower hired a French-speaking driver and began studying the language himself. He crisscrossed the Western Front, mostly on foot, while Mamie enjoyed Paris, a contrast to the string of colorless army camps of the past.

Visiting the battle sites starting in July enabled him to rework the tourist guidebook to cemeteries and to take note of logistic questions such as favorable terrain for tank warfare. He also studied the French army.

෨ඏ

John F. Kennedy, 11, living in Riverdale above the northern tip of Manhattan, was improving in school and won a Riverside School commencement prize for writing the best composition.

His sister Jean was born on February 28. His mother, Rose, left New York months before the birth to be near her parents in Boston. When Joe arrived at the hospital in Boston after the birth, he offered her a choice of three bracelets. After the birth, Rose left for Paris. She later was to say that she made her husband pay for his infidelities by making demands on him for clothes and trips.

The *New York Journal* called Joe Kennedy the "coming Napoleon of the movies" after he merged his Film Booking Office with Pathe. A later merger with First National Pictures failed. Joe went to Europe, returned to make a merger of FBO with RCA to create RKO with assets of $80 million. By year's end, Joe was $5 million richer and no longer in the film business.

Early in the year, Joe practically owned star Gloria Swanson, 27. "My whole life was in his hands," she said later. By January he had lent her $750,000. He took over her film company, hired her husband, along with director-actor Erich Von Stroheim. But the failure of Von Stroheim's *Queen Kelly* helped Joe decide to abandon his Hollywood hopes.

Gloria was always at Kennedy's rented home on Rodeo Drive in Hollywood, and each night a flunky would drive her home. She even flew to Hyannis, Massachusetts, and once in a seaplane. Gloria felt that Rose was naïve about the affair.

෨ඏ

Lyndon B. Johnson, 20, always short of money, took a job in September teaching Mexican children at Cotulla, southeast of Uvalde on the Nueces River and 60 miles from Mexico. He liked the work, the children looked up to him, and he showed signs of leadership ability.

While going to college at Southwest Texas State Teachers College in San Marcos, in the spring, Lyndon began dating Carol Davis, daughter of the richest man in the region. With his new girlfriend and her uncle, he "crashed" the Democratic National Convention in Houston, accredited as a reporter for a college newspaper. He temporarily quit college because he needed money.

W. T. Donaho, superintendent for Cotulla, immediately made LBJ the principal of Welhausen School, the so-called "Mexican school." About three-quarters of the residents in the area were Mexicans working for slave wages on ranches. Johnson slept in a small room at the Shelby House near the railroad tracks.

The first thing Lyndon thought up was for the teachers to run a series of games during the lunch recess for students who carried no lunch to school. He set up track meets, arranged volleyball, softball, and baseball. He talked a few parents with cars into taking the athletes to track meets out of town. What other teachers liked was the way Johnson took over without hesitation. A good showing on his part could lead to a recommendation to a better school. While working he took extension courses from San Marcos.

Johnson wrote to Boody Johnson and admitted being "very lonely." His diversion was to drive 33 miles to Pearsall, where Carol Davis was teaching. He took her to San Antonio to see opera performances, although he was not interested. Carol was 2 years older and had graduated before his arrival in San Marcos. Her father had a large wholesale grocery business in San Marcos, had been mayor of the town, and opposed the KKK.

Before the year ended, Harold Smith took an interest in Carol. Her father sent her to California to think things over. Later, Lyndon learned she was engaged to Smith.

∞♢∞

RICHARD M. NIXON, 15, transferred to Whittier High School in California for his junior year and became a superior scholar and budding actor. He won the Harvard Club of California award as the "best all around student" in the state.

Nixon worked at his studies with such diligence that he was trying to get by on 4 hours of sleep a night. He earned high marks in Latin (the classics of Cicero and Virgil), was good in French literature and equally strong in math, physics, and chemistry. He favored literature and history, however.

∞♢∞

GERALD R. FORD, 15, was shaping up as a very good football player for South High School in Grand Rapids, Michigan. Although only a sophomore when the varsity center was injured, Ford filled in and was the regular for the rest of the season, making the All-City team. South High won a championship. He was very aggressive on the field, but quiet and shy in class.

∞♢∞

JIMMY CARTER, 4, and family moved to a farm in Archery, not far from Plains, Georgia, a community largely made up of African-American sharecroppers who ate two meals a day. The Carter home had sand and chickens all around the house, kerosene for light, an outdoor toilet, a well for water, pigs, and cows. The house was on a dirt road close to the Seaboard Airline Railroad tracks with no warning light at the intersection of the road and the tracks.

∞♢∞

RONALD REAGAN, 17, was a football player for Eureka College in central Illinois who, though he sat on the bench for every game, covered the game story for his college newspaper, the *Pegasus*.

Also on the paper was his girlfriend, Margaret Cleaver, who was elected vice president of the freshman class. She followed him to Eureka after their graduation from Dixon High.

He also took part in a student strike against college president Bert Wilson, who wanted to make cuts in the curriculum to save money. Wilson, in November, asked the students, "Can Eureka, a small church college in a small town, survive at all in the face of the present trend of education and civilization?" Then he resigned and left town. Reagan was one of the speakers at a student rally.

Reagan had a partial football scholarship to the Disciples of Christ–affiliated college in a town of 1,500. There were 50 in the freshman class and only 227 students in the college. Reagan's major was sociology and minor was economics. To get by, Reagan washed dishes at Tau Kappa Epsilon fraternity or a girls' dormitory.

On August 3 lifeguard Reagan received press coverage when he saved a life just before dark in the Rock River, pulling out a man who needed resuscitation to survive.

∞♢∞

GEORGE H. W. BUSH, 4 years old, lived in Greenwich, Connecticut. His brother Prescott was 6, his sister Nancy was 2.

1929
Calvin Coolidge

President Coolidge retired from the Washington scene while fielding innumerable suggestions on what he should do with himself in the Hoover era. Ideas ranged from being governor of Massachusetts again to going into railroading or advertising. His best offer was to take over as czar of the petroleum industry, but he settled instead on writing his *Autobiography*.

January–March: Before leaving the White House, Coolidge said it was best to leave unfinished business for Herbert Hoover the "wonder boy" to solve. In January, Supreme Court Justice Harlan Stone dropped by to chat and recommended that Coolidge consider a new career in the Senate. Coolidge told Stone that running for the Senate would be an embarrassment.

On January 15, the Senate ratified the Kellogg–Briand Pact.

By the middle of February, Coolidge and his wife, Grace, had more than 100 boxes packed and ready to be moved back to Northampton, Massachusetts, including many gifts to the president. He told a press conference that he was having "more trouble in getting out of the White House than I had getting in."

As March drew closer, he had fewer visitors. People were more eager to wait and visit with Hoover.

April–December: Coolidge returned to Northampton and the duplex at 21 Massasoit Street, where he often sat on his porch to watch the traffic pass by.

Chief Justice William Howard Taft administers the oath of office to Herbert Hoover on March 4, 1929. (Library of Congress)

first object must be to provide security from poverty and want. We want to see their [the public] savings protected." He said America consisted of "happy homes, blessed with comfort ... [a] government worthy of respect.... I have no fears for the future of our country. It is bright with hope." The Inaugural Ball later at the Washington Auditorium was the largest ever.

Hoover's cabinet retained two members from the Coolidge administration. Andrew Mellon continued as secretary of Treasury, and James Davis stayed on as secretary of labor. The rest of his cabinet was made up of Henry Lewis Stimson of New York as secretary of state, James Willing Good of Illinois as secretary of war, William DeWitt Mitchell of Minnesota as attorney general, Walter Folger Brown of Ohio as postmaster general, Charles Francis Adams of Massachusetts as secretary of the navy, Ray Lyman Wilbur of California as secretary of the Interior, Arthur Hyde of Missouri as secretary of agriculture, and Robert Lamont of Illinois as secretary of commerce.

The job suggestions kept flowing in, including offers to enter a brokerage house or get into banking, manufacturing, or utilities. In turning them all down, he said that to trade on his influence would lack "propriety."

Coolidge's major income after leaving Washington came from writing. Before leaving office, he assembled notes for a book on his career. It ran as a serial beginning in the spring in *Cosmopolitan*. Later it was made into a book. The work lacked literary merit but doubled his estate. He also wrote articles for *Collier's*, *Ladies Home Journal*, and the *Saturday Evening Post*, among other periodicals.

Coolidge's only return to Washington later in the year came in July to attend a White House luncheon to celebrate the Kellogg–Briand Pact. Coolidge was unescorted coming and going but was surrounded by old staffers and reporters.

ಸಂ ಲ

HERBERT HOOVER, 55, staggered under the weight of the greatest economic collapse the country had ever seen. By the end of the year, the bottom had yet to be reached as the Dow Jones industrial average dropped from 469.5 in September to 220.1 in November. By the end of November, the loss in paper profits had reached $30 billion. Causes for the crash were many: too much buying of stock on margin; depressed farm prices; a high tariff; and an increase in corporate profit without an increase in wages.

January: Bruce Barton, a successful advertising man, said to Hoover, "People expect more of you than they have of any other president."

March: Hoover, the first president born west of the Mississippi, took the oath of office from Chief Justice William Howard Taft on March 4. In his inaugural address, Hoover said: "Our

In one of the administration's first reports, the Commission on Recent Economic Changes said there was "dynamic equilibrium" and that "our situation is fortunate, our momentum remarkable."

April–May: In April, Hoover expanded civil service protection, canceled private oil leases on government lands, made tax refunds, asked law enforcement to concentrate on crime conditions in Al Capone's Chicago, sought new immigration policies, and started a Commission on Conservation. The *New Republic* said Hoover's list of proposed reforms was the longest since Woodrow Wilson's in 1913.

In May, Roy Roberts of the *Kansas City Star* said, "The White House has become a positive force." Hoover recommended reorganization of all government departments and named a commission to analyze social trends. The Bureau of Reclamation made plans to build dams in the valley of the Tennessee River and in central California.

June: Congress passed the Agricultural Marketing Bill, which Hoover signed into law on June 15. The new law established the Farm Board, set up to encourage cooperatives and to dispose of surpluses to increase farm prices.

September–November: By early September, the Dow Jones industrial average was 82 points above its January level, but then radio stocks dropped 40 percent on October 24 while retailer Montgomery-Ward had dropped 33 points. The next day Hoover said, "The fundamental business ... production and distribution is on a sound and prosperous basis." Then, on Black Tuesday, October 29, the stock market collapsed. Losses on that day were the worst in the history of the New York Stock Exchange in terms of total losses and the number of investors ruined by the crash. Total losses for the day came to $9 billion dollars, bringing the total losses for October to $16 billion. The next day, the stock market gained 31 points, easing some fears, but overall, the stock market crash had badly shaken American confidence.

Hoover called a conference of business, labor, and farm leaders on November 21 and said that the crash was more serious than a mere market adjustment. He said that neither the depth nor the duration of the slump was known. Hoover used the word "depression" for the first time and predicted lengthy hard times. He sought to hold the line on wages and wanted voluntary pledges of assistance from business and a government increase in public works spending. Industry and labor promised to support the program Hoover outlined.

In late November, Randolph Hearst pushed Hoover to make a reassuring public statement. Hoover met with Secretary of Treasury Mellon and Roy A. Young, the president of the Federal Reserve Board, and said a tax cut was needed immediately, later adding, "Any lack of confidence in the economic future of the United States is foolish." He signed into law a $160 million tax cut, hoping that consumers would pump the extra money back into the economy.

December: In his December message to Congress, Hoover asked for more prisons, a program for county health units, civil service protection, reform in railroad rates and banking, and a rural child health program. He also said that confidence in the country's business affairs had been restored.

Former Presidents

WILLIAM HOWARD TAFT, as he completed his eighth year as chief justice of the Supreme Court, was in failing health by year's end. Taft now weighed 244 pounds, about the same as his weight as a Yale senior in 1878, and almost 100 pounds less than in his White House days.

Taft, 72 in September, had written approximately 250 opinions since 1921 and hoped Hoover would succeed in maintaining the Court's conservative majority.

In the spring, rumors spread that Taft would retire. Taft knew that Harlan Stone, Hoover's favorite, would become chief justice.

Taft's half-brother Charles P. Taft died in Cincinnati on the final day of the year. Charles had been an important adviser and much-needed financial supporter for Taft from the time he had first arrived in Washington.

Future Presidents

FRANKLIN D. ROOSEVELT, 47, the new governor of New York, selected Tammany's new clubhouse for a July 4 speech that humorist Will Rogers said put Roosevelt on track for the 1932 Democratic presidential nomination. The thrust of Roosevelt's speech in the Tammany setting was to separate business from government.

January–April: Roosevelt took office on January 1 standing on the spot Theodore Roosevelt once occupied. Al Smith talked first, then Roosevelt, who asked for an Era of Good Feelings and no "partisan politics" in his inaugural address. The next day Roosevelt asked the general assembly, "Come to me with your problems."

During the legislative session, Roosevelt and the general assembly clashed often. Most FDR measures were killed, and the Republicans claimed victory on adjournment. FDR protested that the legislature was trying to run the executive branch but signed a compromise Republican budget bill. During the session, Roosevelt vetoed more bills than Al Smith had.

To explain his program for the state, Roosevelt initiated the Fireside Radio Chat, the first of many, on April 3. His emphasis was that special interests controlled Republican policy in Albany.

July–September: Roosevelt attended a governor's conference in July at New London, Connecticut, that was dominated by talk for and against prohibition.

Eleanor had a miserable summer trying to show her two youngest sons Europe, specifically the battlefields of France. She didn't want to make the trip but FDR insisted, and instead of camping out occasionally as Eleanor desired, Sara insisted that there be no informality, that the governor's sons must look nice and stay at first class hotels. But the boys fought each other often in unrestricted roughhousing. Franklin Jr. was 15 and John was 13. They returned to Albany in September.

At the same time FDR made a long boat trip himself in July and August. He took a cruise boat from Albany to Buffalo on inland waterways, then on to Lake Ontario, the St. Lawrence, and down the East Coast to the Hudson and back to Albany.

℮ℤ

HARRY S TRUMAN, 45, would make a good governor of Missouri, the small *Clinton Eye* suggested. The Kansas City political figure, however, lost an important mentor on September 2 when Mike Pendergast died.

On April 30, Truman signed road contracts worth $6 million. He also made enough from a default judgment to cover his haberdashery debt. When the business folded in 1922, the loss had been $28,000.

℮ℤ

DWIGHT D. EISENHOWER, 39, spent most of the year in France and by November had become special assistant to the secretary of war in Washington. General John J. Pershing was impressed with Eisenhower's writing about the French battlefields. He said it showed an "exercise of unusual intelligence and devotion to duty." Pershing now asked Eisenhower to read the general's own memoirs. Instead of saying that Pershing's was a great work, Eisenhower was critical of the general's diary style for the two major American battles—those of St. Mihiel and Meuse-Argonne. The general replied, "Write me something."

After the rewrite, Pershing said he wanted to show the material first to Colonel George Catlett Marshall. Eisenhower met Marshall for the first time outside Pershing's office, and Marshall was against any change in the rhythm of Pershing's prose. "My idea is different," Eisenhower answered. If not for Marshall, Eisenhower would have ghosted the two chapters.

The Eisenhowers arrived back in New York on September 24 and soon moved back into the Wyoming Apartments in Washington. His new job was to study army procurement needs as well as those of the air force. The army had created an Army Industrial College in 1924 to study procurement, which had been a problem in 1917.

৪০৫৪

JOHN F. KENNEDY, 12, moved into a twelve-room house on Pondfield Road in Bronxville, New York. His brother Joe Jr. entered Choate, a preparatory school in Wallingford, Connecticut, in September. John's father, Joe, made a fortune on the stock market and then pulled out just before the crash. Joe Kennedy now turned to real estate, buying the Merchandise Mart in Chicago.

৪০৫৪

LYNDON B. JOHNSON, 21, finished his teaching career in Cotulla, Texas, in June and resumed his studies at Southwest Texas State Teachers College in San Marcos, where his interest was in joining a new secret society that did not want him. Members of White Star society figured Lyndon would be unable to keep secrets.

Shortly, however, LBJ was admitted to White Star and suggested the club run Bill Deason for school president. Johnson ran the campaign, went everywhere appealing for votes, and helped make Deason the surprise winner.

Johnson wrote editorials for the school newspaper, the *College Star*, and became a member of the student council. He was also president of the press club, a member of the Harris Blair Literary Society, and worked with the debating team.

Lyndon's brother Sam later claimed that LBJ was engaged this year to the daughter of a Ku Klux Klan member who disliked the Johnson family. When Lyndon heard about her father's attitudes toward the Johnsons, he dropped the girl.

৪০৫৪

RICHARD M. NIXON, at 16 a senior at Whittier High School, could have gone to Harvard on a tuition-free scholarship, but his father lacked the money to meet his son's costs for food and lodging. Thus Nixon was unable to capitalize on winning Harvard's "best student" award. The disappointment for Nixon was directly attributed to the family's high

expenses in supporting his brother Harold's tuberculosis treatment in Prescott, Arizona. Nixon's father had to sell off farmlands to meet nursing costs.

Nixon had a second disappointment, a political one. He had been the favorite in the election for student body president, but Bob Logue, with a sports background, was a late addition to the field as a third candidate and won the election. It was to be Nixon's lone political loss in 3 decades.

Nixon had a diversion from the two disappointments. He began dating Ola Florence Welch, a vivacious student and daughter of Whittier's police chief. In March, at the time of the school election, Ola wrote, "Oh, how I hate Richard Nixon." Before long, however, the two had the leading roles in the classic *The Aeneid* by Virgil, put on by the Latin club. The play was a disaster. Nixon called the play's climax "sheer torture."

Later Nixon introduced Ola to his parents and on May 2 wrote her, "I'm so cracked about you," and signed it "love." Now they were a steady couple taking walks, visiting the beach, playing miniature golf, and going to movies.

৪০৫৪

GERALD R. FORD, 16, typical of many of the nation's top high school scholars, earned a trip to Washington, D.C., with thirty others from schools in the Midwest. He also had a traumatic first meeting with his birth father, Leslie Lynch King Jr.

Ford, on his trip east, went to the White House, stood in the gallery of the House of Representatives, and decided he would become a lawyer. Ford had joined the high school debating club but was not good at it. By the end of his junior year at South High in Grand Rapids, Michigan, Ford was in the top 5 percent of his class and was a member of the National Honor Society.

Ford worked at Bill Skougis's restaurant across the street from the high school. He was working one day when Leslie Lynch King Jr. drove up in a new Lincoln with his second wife, Margaret, and small daughter. King asked Ford if he would like to live with him in Riverton, Wyoming, and boasted about all the land he owned. King gave him $25, then drove off. Ford was left in tears. Gerald was stunned by the event and was fearful about how to break the news at home. Back home, the Fords were sympathetic to the teenager's confusion.

Three weeks before the Wall Street crash in October, Ford's stepfather bought a paint company and named it the Ford Paint and Varnish Company. He had ten employees. After October he told them he would pay each $5 per week to buy groceries, with only $5 for himself until times improved.

Ford's grandfather King in Omaha lost his fortune in the stock market crash and died, ending child support payments for Gerald. His mother asked the court in Nebraska to make her first husband pay $100 per month for child support after she heard that he had inherited $50,000 from his father. She won the judgment, but King refused to pay anything.

৪০৫৪

JIMMY CARTER, 5, was a barefoot boy selling boiled peanuts on the main street in tiny Plains, Georgia, but inspired by his mother's brother, dreamed of life as a sailor. Uncle Tom W. Gordy had been in the Pacific with the navy, and the family followed his adventures by mail. From this early age, Jimmy thought of Annapolis and a navy career even though no Carter had ever finished even high school.

Despite rather primitive conditions, the Carters were fairly well off by Georgia standards of the times. Earl built a dirt tennis court near the house, a rarity in the area, and introduced the boy to the sport.

August 7: Jimmy's sister Ruth was born.

∞ ℃

RONALD REAGAN, 18, a student at Eureka College in central Illinois, was joined by his older brother John, who quit his job at a cement factory to try college. When John joined the Tau Kappa Epsilon fraternity, Ronald, at the initiation ceremony, had the opportunity to paddle his older brother with enthusiasm.

Ronald made the football team but was disgusted with the coach, who considered Reagan too slow afoot. If he couldn't play football, Reagan talked of going to the University of Wisconsin to try making the rowing

First Lady Lou Hoover (Library of Congress)

team. At Eureka basketball games, Ronald took the floor to lead the cheers. His girlfriend, Margaret Cleaver, was elected class president.

∞ ℃

GEORGE H. W. BUSH, 5, lived in Greenwich, Connecticut.

1930
Herbert Hoover

President Hoover, 56, kept trying to be optimistic as the Great Depression deepened. No one worked harder than Hoover. He canceled a vacation in Palo Alto and virtually remained in the White House for the next 2 years, working 16-hour days, including Sundays.

January–May: In January, for the first time, the administration talked of pump priming through government work projects.

A conference in January also recommended that people build houses. Yet, before long, new construction dropped by 25 percent.

Chief Justice William Howard Taft resigned on February 3,

and Charles Evans Hughes replaced him on February 13 (see **William Howard Taft**, page 511).

On February 18, Hoover said that the initial shock to the economy was over. In March he said, "We have now passed the worst" and that the crisis would abate in 60 days.

By April, Hoover had approved $150 million in public works projects, which caused the market to rally briefly. The Dow Jones industrials hit a high of 257.3 in April.

In May, Hoover told a congressional committee, "I am convinced that we have now passed the worst and with continued unity of effort we shall rapidly recover."

June: Hoover signed the Hawley–Smoot Tariff Bill on June 17. The new act set tariffs at the highest level in U.S. history and upset many European countries, which relied heavily on exporting goods to the United States. In the long run, the higher tariffs reduced the number of European exports and eventually forced European countries to raise their own tariffs on imported goods from the United States.

Bankers and religious leaders came to the White House on June 19 to warn of growing unemployment, which by this point was estimated at over 4 million people. Hoover replied, "You have come six weeks too late," because the economy was recovering. William Green, head of the American Federation of Labor (AFL), agreed, but men selling apples began to appear on city streets.

July–August: On July 21, the Senate ratified the London Naval Treaty that the United States, Great Britain, and Japan had signed in April. The new pact set building limits on all types of warships, with a ratio of 5:5:3 for the United States, Great Britain, and Japan.

An August drought added to the woe of the already ailing farm communities across the United States.

September: Work began on the Boulder Dam in Colorado. The dam would later be renamed the Hoover Dam.

October: Hoover told the American Bankers Association that he was against those "economic fatalists" who believed the Great Depression was beyond the "genius of modern business" to overcome and that he refused to believe in "perpetual unemployment." Bernard Baruch refused, however, to join the optimists.

November: With the midterm elections, Hoover quickly saw how the American people felt about his presidency and the Republican Party. The Democrats made major gains, with the Republicans losing fifty-two seats in the House. Losses in the Senate cut the Republican majority to just one seat.

December: Hoover sought some sort of emergency job program to help solve the unemployment problem in the country. On December 21, Congress passed a $116 million appropriations bill for emergency construction projects for unemployed workers. Many felt that the amount of money appropriated was too small, yet Hoover combated this criticism by saying that public works alone was not the answer to solving the economic crisis, because "prosperity cannot be restored by raids upon the public treasury."

On December 30, Congress allocated $45 million in farm relief. Much of the money would go to farmers who had suffered through the summer drought.

Former Presidents

WILLIAM HOWARD TAFT went to Cincinnati during the first week of January for the funeral of his half-brother and long-time benefactor, Charles.

January–February: Soon after his half-brother's funeral, Taft's health took a turn for the worse. On his return to Washington, Taft was hospitalized briefly, and doctors ordered an 8-week vacation. Taft and his wife, Nellie, went to the Grove Park Inn in Asheville, North Carolina, with a view of the Great Smokies. He informed the Court that he would not return to work until February 24.

Taft's condition worsened toward the end of January. Mischler, his secretary for 26 years, wrote to Horace Taft on January 11 and said that Taft was having hallucinations.

Taft's resignation as chief justice went to Hoover on February 3, and Taft returned to Washington. He was helpless on his arrival as he was lifted off the train at Union Station. Doctors told Nellie that his death was now just a matter of time.

March: By the beginning of the month, Taft could not eat and could no longer recognize anyone. He died on Saturday night, March 8, at the age of 72.

The funeral and burial at Arlington took place on March 11. He was given military honors even though he had never worn a uniform. He had, of course, been secretary of war. He was buried near Robert Todd Lincoln.

೮ා೮ಌ

CALVIN COOLIDGE made a trip to Florida and California but was irritated by curious citizens and never took a similar trip. Too many curiosity-seekers outside the small duplex on Massasoit Street in Northampton, Massachusetts, also drove Coolidge to a larger, more sumptuous home on the Connecticut River that was owned by the president of Smith College.

January–March: The Coolidges started the year with a January trip to Florida for 4 weeks, then stopped in New Orleans en route to the West Coast. In Hollywood film czar Will Hays arranged a tour of the film colony. Coolidge also visited William Randolph Hearst's San Simeon castle. On the return east, the couple stopped for the formal opening of Coolidge Dam near Globe, Arizona.

April: In the spring, the Coolidges moved to the Beeches, a 9-acre estate with twelve rooms, a swimming pool, a tennis court, a forest of trees, and all the privacy that Massasoit Street did not provide.

May–December: Coolidge did not revive his law practice because he believed that to go back to writing wills and collecting debts, as he did in his early law years, would be undignified for a former president.

The McClure Syndicate hired Coolidge to write a few paragraphs of news commentary. Nearly 100 papers carried his column, "Thinking Things Over with Calvin Coolidge." He wrote it only it for a year, and many news critics found his style dull and "turgid."

In general, as criticism of his administration mounted during the Great Depression, Coolidge became withdrawn. He wrote that the causes of it were over-borrowing, too much credit in Europe, and cheap Russian farm products dumped on world markets. In looking for causes, Coolidge used the same points that Hoover raised, as together they worked to blunt charges that both men were responsible for the Great Depression.

Future Presidents

FRANKLIN D. ROOSEVELT, 48, was easily reelected governor of New York, recording the most smashing victory in New York gubernatorial history. Endorsements for the 1932 Democratic presidential nomination were also starting to come his way by the end of the year.

January–March: In Roosevelt's address to the New York General Assembly on January 1, he did not even mention the October crash or the economic crisis facing the United States. Instead his speech underscored the need for state-owned power sources.

Roosevelt first touched on the Great Depression on March 29, saying that growing unemployment in the state meant, "The situation is serious." He appointed a Commission on Stabilization of Industry.

June–August: On June 30 at the annual governors' conference, in Salt Lake City, Utah, Roosevelt said that Hoover "juggles figures" and "distorts facts." He also told governors that old-age pensions and unemployment insurance were national needs.

In the summer, Roosevelt wrote to Robert F. Wagner that repeal of Prohibition would be best for the country.

November: In his reelection campaign, Roosevelt spoke on November 1 at Carnegie Hall in New York City. He said that the problem in New York City was corruption, pointing to flamboyant Mayor Jimmy Walker and the problem of corrupt judges, including Republican judges in upstate New York.

Roosevelt defeated Republican Charles H. Tuttle in the gubernatorial election, receiving almost 1.8 million votes to Tuttle's 1 million votes.

ℰᏜ

HARRY S TRUMAN, 46, although reelected presiding judge of Jackson County, Missouri, by 58,000 votes over his Republican opponent, often experienced deep anguish over the foul nature of the people with whom he had to deal. Sometimes business in Kansas City caused him to remain in a downtown hotel for the night.

The other two presiding judges disgusted him, Truman wrote, by chasing women and taking bribes: "I have believed in honor, ethics and right … a very small minority agree with me."

Tom J. Pendergast, boss of Kansas City, called Truman into his office one day, where Pendergast had three angry contractors who were not getting work. Truman said they were not the low bidders. Alone later with Pendergast, Truman later claimed "the boss" told him to go ahead and do things his way.

Times were tough with many farm and business failures. Low-paying jobs were important to people. Once Truman had to fire 200 people, and then he went home and threw up.

Truman outlined a 10-year plan for Independence, Missouri, dealing largely with roads and zoning.

ℰᏜ

DWIGHT D. EISENHOWER, 40, special assistant to the secretary of war, continued to work on war mobilization plans and had many conferences with Bernard Baruch, who had run the War Industries Board in 1917 to 1918.

In the spring, Eisenhower traveled to Texas and northern Mexico looking for a synthetic rubber source, guayule, to supplement the Southeast Asia rubber supply. His companion was an engineer, Major Gilbert Wilkens.

In the meantime, Congress created the War Policies Commission, which aimed at taking the profit out of war. There was a backlash in the country at this time aimed at World War I profiteers.

Wilkens, Eisenhower, and his commanding officer, Brigadier General Moseley, wrote *Industrial Mobilization Plan– 1930*, and Eisenhower published an article on the subject in *Army Ordinance.*

ℰᏜ

JOHN F. KENNEDY, 13, was headed for Choate to join Joe Jr., until his mother opted for Canterbury, a small Roman Catholic school in New Milford, Connecticut.

John wrote to a relative that he was homesick from the first night. "The swimming pool is great even though the football team looks pretty bad," he added. He wrote about his plans to attend the Harvard–Yale and Army–Yale football games.

ℰᏜ

LYNDON B. JOHNSON, now 22, graduated from Southwest Texas State Teachers College in San Marcos in August and landed a teaching job in Houston, although his mind was made up to launch a political career at the first opportunity.

In July, LBJ accompanied his parents to Henly to hear political speeches, particularly by former Governor Pat Neff, a celebrated orator who was now the state's railroad commissioner. When Neff's name was called to deliver his speech, there was no response, and LBJ volunteered on the spot to talk in Neff's place. Judge Stubbs of Johnson City told the gathering they would now hear from Sam Johnson's "boy." Johnson talked for 5 to 10 minutes, his first political speech.

Representative Welly K. Hopkins, who was running for state senate, was a witness. He asked for Johnson's help in the upcoming campaign. Now Johnson talked several San Marcos College friends into piling into his Model A and delivering campaign literature, especially in Blanco County. The San Marcos graduate arranged a rally in San Marcos that managed to attract a large crowd. Hopkins won by 2,000 votes and gave credit to Johnson.

In another political race, Edgar Witt, campaigning for lieutenant governor, turned over his Hill Country effort to Johnson. Witt carried the region. Then and there LBJ turned from a career of teaching to one of politics. But first he needed a teaching post in order to eat, and that was difficult to find. Finally he landed one in Pearsall, a town smaller than Cotulla.

In October he found a better job, at Sam Houston High School in Houston. Johnson would teach speech and handle the debate team. He lived with relatives, sharing a room with an uncle.

ℰᏜ

RICHARD M. NIXON, 17, graduated first in his class at Whittier High and at Whittier College was elected president of the freshman class. He not only was in the fast lane as a scholar, but also showed promise as an actor while participating in all sorts of extracurricular activities. He found time for football, basketball, glee club, drama, debate, orchestra, politics, weekend skiing, picnics, and Gilbert and Sullivan performances.

Nixon finished his high school work with the California Interscholastic Federation Gold Seal Award for excellence. His high school debating coach said Nixon could easily take either side in a debate.

On entering Whittier College, Nixon and Dean Triggs quickly founded the Orthogonians, an alternative to the Franklins, an elite group that sought to separate itself from the college's Quaker roots.

ℰᏜ

GERALD R. FORD, 17, made the all-state football team while helping South High win the state championship. He was elected captain for his senior year, then not only made all-state but also was selected as the all-state team captain. His coach said he was hard working and dependable, never made a mistake on the field, and was a great tackler as a linebacker.

Football was a good diversion for Ford, because all around him factories were closing in Grand Rapids, Michigan, a city in the grip of the Great Depression. Ford made Eagle Scout with the Boy Scouts, which led to his becoming assistant counselor at Camp Shawondossee, as well as swimming coach, and a guide at Fort Mackinac.

෫෨෬

Jimmy Carter, only 6, went to school at the high school because that was the only school in Plains, Georgia. Each day started with a half-hour of chapel. His first grade teacher thought he was a model student.

෫෨෬

Ronald Reagan, 19, looked like an actor-to-be, according to one Eureka College professor.

Ronald was selected as one of the six best actors seen in a one-act play competition sponsored by Northwestern University. Reagan played the shepherd boy in *Aria de Capo* by Edna St. Vincent Millay performed near Lake Michigan on the Northwestern campus. The Eureka junior also played right guard on the Eureka Tornadoes football team and competed in varsity swimming and track.

The Great Depression had considerable impact on the Reagan family. After Jack Reagan's Fashion Boot Shop went broke in 1929, he was unemployed for months until hired in January by the Red Wing Shoe Company as a traveling salesman at $260 per month. Ronald's mother became a seamstress at a dress shop and also worked as a sales clerk.

෫෨෬

George H. W. Bush, 6, was a student at the Greenwich County Day School in Connecticut near New York's Westchester country. His father Prescott's investment firm was merged with Brown Bros., Harriman and Company, which made him one of twelve partners.

In May, the Bush family could always be found at Kennebunkport, Maine. At Christmas, the family settled in Aiken, South Carolina, near Augusta, Georgia.

1931
Herbert Hoover

The president, 57, resisted handouts as a way to cure the Great Depression, which continued to cripple American industry and cause private desperation. There were now 10 million Americans unemployed, and banks were collapsing everywhere. Food riots gripped New York City and Minnesota; the homeless filled Grant Park in Chicago. Cardboard shacks housing the poor and helpless were sprouting everywhere and soon were called "Hoovervilles." By the end of 1931, the Dow Jones industrials had fallen to 116.6. Hoover's critics increased as the year went on.

Hoover resisted many relief suggestions, but the administration made numerous innovations to improve conditions. Taxes on the rich were increased from 24 percent to 55 percent. Hoover and Mellon hatched the National Credit Finance Corporation, which later became the Reconstruction Finance Corporation. Finally, by December, Hoover's annual message to Congress called for a Public Works Administration. He also cut federal salaries by 15 percent.

February: Concerning the clamor over handouts, Hoover told the press in February that people did not accuse him of a "lack of human sympathy ... but [the] foundation [of his past work] has been to summon the maximum of self-help." Hoover believed that putting people on the public dole would "endow the slacker." The president felt that his efforts to help were akin to sticking his finger in the dike only to find problems mounting.

In a February radio address, Hoover said that when a community shifted responsibility to Washington, it would lose "a large part of its voice in the control of its own destiny." The banking industry was in a shambles. The National Credit Association was created with $500,000 and aimed at shoring up weak banks. When 522 banks went under in the first month, the program was scrapped.

Another major issue involved veterans' bonuses. In February, Hoover vetoed a bill that would have allowed veterans to borrow half of the bonus they were scheduled to receive in 1945. He said that the country should not make loans "to those who can by their own efforts support themselves."

June–August: In part because of the Smoot–Hawley Tariff, European economies were in a shambles. On June 20, Hoover advocated a 1-year moratorium on collecting war reparations and debt payments from European countries. Congress passed the legislation on July 6, and on August 11 eighteen other countries accepted Hoover's moratorium.

Democrats in Congress shot down a sales tax idea in August. When Democrats began calling for payments to the unemployed, even Republican Senator William Borah agreed.

September–October: In September, Hoover's committee on employment reorganization under the chairmanship of Walter Gifford of AT&T called for "great spiritual experience" of donations to the cause from private sources. The average family in New York City was now receiving $2.39 per week in assistance. The National Association of Social Workers voted against a system of handouts.

On October 7, Hoover announced a plan to mobilize banking resources after a run on banks by customers removing their money forced the failure of hundreds of banks.

In the fall, the Agriculture Department gave seed to farmers and diverted Lake Michigan waters to combat erosion. Hoover created a federal land bank to stop foreclosures, had the Interstate Commerce Commission reduce railroad rates on supplies going to farmers and launched a program to build 37,000 miles of highways.

December: In his message to Congress on December 8, Hoover still said that he opposed "any direct or indirect dole" for the needy, which would only cause further unemployment. He said businesses needed to be helped, however, and called for a $500-million emergency reconstruction program, with the bulk of the money going to help businesses and railroads.

Former Presidents

CALVIN COOLIDGE, while president, had refused several times to dedicate the ornate marble Warren G. Harding Memorial in Marion, Ohio. Now, as honorary president of the Harding Memorial Association, Coolidge, with reluctance, joined President Hoover at the dedication in June.

Coolidge continued to resist anything that might put him before the public eye. For instance, he offered excuses to stay in his Northampton, Massachusetts, retirement retreat while his wife, Grace, went to Newport News, Virginia, in February to christen the new Dollar Line passenger ship, the *President Coolidge*.

Late in the year, his secretary noted that Coolidge was wearier, taking two naps a day, and had stomach trouble and hay fever.

Coolidge was 59 on July 4.

Future Presidents

FRANKLIN D. ROOSEVELT, 49, as governor of New York, worked on a relief program to counter the Great Depression and put more heat on New York City Mayor Jimmy Walker as a "corrupt" figure in Empire State politics. As Roosevelt worked to help New Yorkers struggling with the depression, the groundwork was being laid to nominate FDR for president in 1932. Jim Farley was a key player, and Colonel Edward House, from the Wilson team, boarded the FDR express.

January: A Roosevelt-for-president New York City headquarters was established in mid-January at Madison and 43rd Street, and newsman Ernest K. Lindley was hired to write a campaign biography.

March–April: A group that included Rabbi Stephen S. Wise gave Roosevelt a petition on March 17 which outlined

ten charges of gross negligence and incompetence concerning Mayor Walker. Roosevelt forwarded the charges to Walker, who gave a meandering reply. Republicans also jumped on Walker and passed a resolution calling for an investigation of the mayor. A special session of the legislature in Albany in August granted immunity to witnesses willing to confront Walker.

June: Farley and Louis Howe, the key men in the FDR campaign organization, decided to bring in Colonel House to help the Roosevelt-for-president movement. House announced his support for Roosevelt in an interview on June 4.

Farley, starting June 29, took a cross-country trip through seventeen states and met thousands while promoting Roosevelt's candidacy.

October–November: On October 15, Al Smith criticized Roosevelt's program to plant trees on marginal land, calling the idea socialistic and warning it would put the State of New York in the lumber business. Roosevelt met with Smith on November 17 to sooth feelings, but later Smith told a Roosevelt booster that the governor had never consulted with him about anything.

Roosevelt saw his Temporary Emergency Relief Administration as a 7-month effort that could cost $20 million. He said that relief "must be extended by government, not as a matter of charity, but as a matter of social duty." Roosevelt put Jesse Straus in charge of the effort that began on November 1.

෴

HARRY S TRUMAN, 47, was hurt by the depression like everyone else, but still managed to get the highways built. As presiding judge for Kansas City, a nonjudicial, county manager type post, he received approval for a second bond issue for highway construction. When he was through, only two counties in the country had more roads than Jackson County.

By the end of 1930, Truman's operation had run $1.1 million into the red. Thus, in January, he announced a 15-percent cut in expenditures and cut the number of road overseers from fifty-one men to sixteen. By the end of 1931, his operational deficit stood at $460,000 with overall work projects cut by 22 percent. Meanwhile, three banks closed in Independence, Missouri, and approximately 2,800 people were on the relief rolls.

෴

DWIGHT D. EISENHOWER, 41, doing staff work in Washington, wrote a report on his study of industrial mobilization during World War I called *War Policies*

This lithograph by Reginald Marsh depicts a bread line, a common scene across the United States during the Great Depression. (Library of Congress)

for *Cavalry Journal* and enrolled in the Army Industrial College. Eisenhower's job title was special assistant to the secretary of war. Frederick Payne, an industrialist and assistant secretary of war, asked Eisenhower to write speeches for him, and General Douglas MacArthur had Eisenhower write the annual report of the chief of staff. MacArthur wrote a commendation for Eisenhower in November, acknowledging his "outstanding talents."

∞ ∞

JOHN F. KENNEDY, 14, missed considerable school time because he was sick for much of the year. When he was not ill, John was unfocused, always a special problem for the harassed headmaster. John did not enter Choate, a private school in Wallingford, Connecticut, until October 2 due to his health problems. He spent the spring months still at Canterbury. To get into Choate, headmaster Wardell St. John said John would have to study Latin and forgo the usual family frivolity at Hyannis, Massachusetts, and its idle summer of sailing.

At Choate, John was popular but was poorly matched with his roommate, the son of the owner of the *Washington Star*. The headmaster wrote that John was often at odds with school rules and had "natural ability, but is careless in applying it."

∞ ∞

LYNDON B. JOHNSON, 23, an effective debating club coach at a high school in Houston, suddenly went to Washington, D.C., to begin a political career. On November 25, Johnson was sitting around talking to other high school faculty members when he received a phone call and job offer from new Congressman Richard Kleberg, who needed an assistant. Welly Hopkins, a new state senator whose own campaign Johnson had helped, had recommended Johnson to him.

Kleberg won a special election for Texas's Fourteenth District seat because of the death of its GOP incumbent. The district stretched across southeast Texas from Blanco to the Gulf. Five days after Kleberg interviewed Johnson in Corpus Christi, Johnson was hired and Washington-bound aboard a train with Kleberg.

Lyndon's introduction to the nation's capital came on December 7 with the opening session of the Seventy-Second Congress. He watched from the balcony. Kleberg was rich and uninterested in politics. He liked to golf and drink and was at the bottom of the seniority pyramid in the House.

Johnson was Kleberg's secretary. Sam Houston High gave Johnson a leave of absence, and soon he was sharing a room at the Mayflower Hotel with Kleberg. Johnson moved the next day into a basement apartment in a cheap hotel. The hotel was close to the Capitol, and Johnson literally ran to work. Kleberg took his secretary around to meet the major political players from Texas. Quickly Johnson returned home for Christmas and later, on the return trip to Washington, met his new assistant, Estelle Harbin, 28, at the San Antonio train station.

∞ ∞

RICHARD M. NIXON, 18, was a sophomore majoring in constitutional history at Whittier College.

A retentive memory led to the lead role in a number of stage performances. He showed good technique in debate. When the subject once was "free trade versus protectionism," Nixon took the free trade side and supported that position for decades after.

History professor Paul S. Smith was an influence. Nixon corresponded with Smith for years despite Smith's liberal slant on political affairs. Later Smith claimed Nixon was "a liberal in a conservative sort of way."

∞ ∞

GERALD R. FORD, 18, graduated from South High in Grand Rapids and entered the University of Michigan in the fall to play football. He had no money but landed jobs waiting tables at the university hospital and Delta Kappa Epsilon dining rooms. He slept on a cot in a third-floor backroom along with a basketball player. Ford later said football at Michigan was the "luckiest break I ever had."

The star Grand Rapids South High center became the outstanding member on the Michigan freshman team. Principal Arthur Krause at South High had wanted to help Ford, who was both an honor student and a standout football player. Krause wrote to Harry Kipke, the University of Michigan football coach. Michigan offered no football scholarships in those days. Kipke visited the family, then took Ford to Ann Arbor for a look around and lined up the job at the hospital. The annual tuition was $100, which Ford did not have. After the visit, Ford wrote to Kipke on June 8 thanking him "for entertaining me so wonderfully during my visit to Ann Arbor.... I desire to attend school at Michigan. I've always wanted to be a student [there]." To help Ford, Krause gave him the profits from the South High bookstore. Ford arrived in Ann Arbor in September with one suit and $25. His stepfather's sister sent him $2 every Monday for spending money.

∞ ∞

JIMMY CARTER, 7, lived in Plains, Georgia, where his father, Earl, employed 200 laborers and sharecroppers on his farmland.

∞ ∞

RONALD REAGAN, 20, was a fair student at Eureka College in Illinois but nothing like his brother John, nicknamed "Moon." Ronald received two B's, five C's and two D's, one of them in a course on the life of Christ. Moon made A's, but Ronald was president of his class. Ronald was also a reporter for the school newspaper, the *Pegasus*.

In July at his summer job at Lowell Beach, lifeguard Reagan recorded his fiftieth save of a person who ran into trouble while swimming in the Rock River.

Reagan was very upset by the death in a plane crash of famed football coach Knute Rockne of Notre Dame. His father was also upset. Working in a store in Springfield, Illinois, he received his dismissal notice on Christmas Eve.

ॐ QՁ

GEORGE H. W. BUSH, 7, moved into an eight-room house on Grove Lane in Greenwich, Connecticut. The Bush children had a governess, and other family employees included two maids, a cook, and a chauffeur.

While George and his brother Prescott attended Greenwich County Day School, sister Nancy entered Rosemary School.

1932
Herbert Hoover

President Hoover, 58, suffered a resounding defeat at the polls as the bitter climax of another frustrating year of seeking solutions to the grief caused by the Great Depression. By year's end, the Dow dropped further, sinking to 84.81 compared with 469.5 in September 1929. The steel industry was working at 19 percent of capacity. A growing problem was unemployed drifters; the Southern Pacific Railroad reported that it removed 683,000 drifters riding its rails, and California ordered border guards to stop drifters from entering the state.

January: The Reconstruction Finance Corporation (RFC) was officially created on January 22, with Charles Dawes named as the head. The RFC was set up to dispense $500 million in loans to failing farms, banks, and railroads. Critics of the program, such as Representative Fiorello La Guardia of New York, called the RFC a "millionaire's dole."

March 14: Hoover appointed Benjamin N. Cardoza to the Supreme Court to replace Justice Oliver Wendell Holmes, who had resigned from the bench in January.

May–July: As the Republican National Convention neared, there were no serious challengers to Hoover for the nomination. Republicans met in Chicago June 14 to June 16 and renominated Hoover on the first ballot. Vice President Charles Curtis was also renominated, although some moved to get Calvin Coolidge the nomination (see **Calvin Coolidge**, opposite column). The convention was a dispirited affair, as the GOP was $200,000 in debt and had little support from business or farmers. H. L. Mencken called the convention "the stupidest and most boresome ever."

Democrats met in Chicago June 27 to July 2 and nominated Franklin D. Roosevelt for president and John Nance Garner of Texas for vice president (see **Franklin D. Roosevelt**, page 517).

In late July, Hoover suffered a major public relations nightmare when he ordered federal troops to forcibly remove the "Bonus Army" from the streets of Washington, D.C. The "Bonus Army," made up of World War I veterans, began to gather in Washington in January to urge Congress to pro-

vide them with their promised bonuses for serving in the army during the war. The bonuses were not set to be paid out until 1945, but the veterans demanded the money sooner because many were unemployed and desperate.

The "Bonus Army," which in May numbered approximately 1,500 men, grew to nearly 20,000 men by mid-July. Many set up shacks and shanties, nicknamed "Hooverville," across the Potomac River. Hoover at first supported their right to express their views and even provided tents, cots, and field kitchens to some. When a bill to pay the bonuses earlier was defeated in Congress on July 17, most of the men began to leave Washington, but more than 2,000 remained in the "Hooverville" shanties and in abandoned buildings.

Hoover ordered the evacuation of the buildings. When a fight broke out between police and the veterans at one building, the police fired on the veterans, killing two. Hoover then ordered army units to help the police clear the veterans. General Douglas MacArthur, using tanks, machine guns, and tear gas, carried out Hoover's orders. The shanties were burned and the veterans driven from the city. Although no one was killed, the images of burning shanties and bullying army soldiers further damaged Hoover's reputation.

August–October: Although Hoover felt that he would lose the election, he still embarked on the campaign trail. In campaign speeches, Hoover said Democrats would create a "rubber dollar" and said, "Let no man tell you it could not be worse." He called Roosevelt "a chameleon on plaid." Hoover drew 30,000 supporters in an Akron, Ohio, campaign stop and received help from Calvin Coolidge, Henry Ford, and Alice Longworth. The *Literary Digest* said on October 16 that Hoover was gaining on Roosevelt, but in Detroit, Hoover heard crowds loudly chanting "Down with Hoover."

November–December: On November 8, Franklin Roosevelt easily defeated Hoover in the presidential election. Roosevelt polled 22,821,857 votes to Hoover's 15,761,845 votes. In the Electoral College, Roosevelt earned 472 votes to Hoover's 59 votes.

On Hoover's defeat, Arthur Krock summed things up in the *New York Times* by writing that Hoover was the first president turned out of office after one term by the "the American people, not the party leaders."

Hoover had two brief meetings with Roosevelt after the election. Once they were alone for 17 minutes to talk about war debt issues. The meeting was cool. Hoover thought Roosevelt "amiable, pleasant, anxious to be of service, very badly informed and of comparatively little vision."

Former Presidents

CALVIN COOLIDGE was upset that a serious effort was made at the Republican National Convention to name him vice president for a second time in order to dump Vice President Charles Curtis, considered a ticket liability. Even more startling was a minor movement to remove the incumbent and make Coolidge president again. Coolidge urged party insiders to abandon this nonsense as the retired president continued to suffer ill health.

At that, the reluctant Coolidge did join the Hoover campaign effort with a speech at Madison Square Garden and an election-eve radio address from his Beeches home in Northampton, Massachusetts. This was despite Coolidge's claim that he was completely out of touch with Hoover's policy to fight the depression and did not know what was going on in Washington.

At Madison Square Garden on October 11, Coolidge said he was making the appearance to "reiterate my support of the President [and] faith in the Republican Party." He blamed the Democrats for obstructionism, said "things were much worse in other parts of the world," and praised Hoover's efforts to correct economic conditions.

Future Presidents

FRANKLIN D. ROOSEVELT, 50, won a resounding victory in the November election and promised a New Deal for the American people. The Great Depression was the overriding issue in the campaign, as the economic crisis was unparalleled in American history. The only greater threat to the country's stability was the outcome and impact of the election of 1860.

January: Columnist Walter Lippmann said that Roosevelt was a "highly impressionable person without a firm grasp of public affairs and without very strong convictions.… He is too eager to please … without any important qualification for the office."

June–July: Heading into the Democratic National Convention is Chicago, Roosevelt's main competition for the nomination would be Al Smith and Speaker of the House John Nance Garner. Jim Farley and Louis Howe set the strategy for Roosevelt's nomination drive.

The convention opened on June 27. Judge John E. Mack of New York, who first convinced Roosevelt to seeking a life in politics, gave Roosevelt's nominating speech. On the first ballot, Roosevelt had 666¼ votes to Smith's 201¾ and Garner's 90¼, with a scattering of votes to others. The number of votes necessary for the nomination was 766. By the third ballot, when Roosevelt was 87 votes short of the nomination, Garner withdrew and threw his support to Roosevelt. FDR was then nominated on the fourth ballot with 945 votes. Smith, bitter, refused to give up his votes to make the nomination unanimous.

Roosevelt selected Garner for vice president and then dramatically took the rostrum and announced: "I pledge myself to a new deal for the American people. … This is more than a political campaign, it is a call to arms [to win] this crusade to restore America to its own people."

August–November: Roosevelt assembled a brain trust, a "kitchen cabinet" à la Andrew Jackson, consisting of Rexford

G. Tugwell, Raymond Moley, A. A. Berle, and Sam Rosenman—all focused on policy issues. Jim Farley was the brains of the campaign itself. In blaming the Republicans for the depression, Roosevelt's team favored a 20-percent cut in federal expenses, a balanced budget, unemployment and old age insurance, regulation in the securities and utilities industry, banking restrictions, free trade, sound currency, aid to farmers, stronger antitrust laws, public works projects, and repeal of Prohibition. Skeptics wondered how he would pay for the laundry list of reforms he promised and keep his word to balance the budget, but Roosevelt drew the large crowds and projected nonstop optimism with a "we can do it" attitude.

On November 8, Roosevelt defeated Hoover in the presidential election (see **Herbert Hoover**, page 516).

സോൽ

HARRY S TRUMAN, 48, the administrative chief of Jackson County, (Kansas City), now decided he wanted to be a congressman. If he ran, it would be from a reorganized congressional district including eastern Kansas City. He told Bess that if they went to Washington she would "see all the greats and near greats in action." Bess, however, told Truman to take the county collector's job, which paid $10,000. Congressmen made $7,500. Truman told his wife he need not make a decision on the offer until 1933.

Meanwhile, Truman sponsored a booklet entitled "Jackson County: Results of County Planning," which described the road improvements he had achieved. He sent copies to other counties in the state.

സോൽ

DWIGHT D. EISENHOWER, 42, was in the front lines, finally, but the contest was the army against the "Bonus Army" of World War I veterans. He was at MacArthur's side throughout the one-sided contest in July.

Eisenhower's diary at the time was uncritical of events. Years later he claimed to oppose MacArthur's decisions. His diary entry for August 10 declared, "A lot of furor has been stirred up [for] political capital" and noted that his report to MacArthur was "as accurate as I could make it."

Eisenhower was tired of his boring job as assistant to Secretary of War Patrick Hurley, and he wanted to return to working with soldiers. He was eligible and due to receive troop command duty. MacArthur told him he would get command of Fort Washington in September 1933, if he would stick it out. Mamie had other ideas. She wanted her husband returned to San Antonio, where her parents wintered. Eisenhower's job in Washington was a combination of writing reports and speeches.

സോൽ

JOHN F. KENNEDY, 15, a prep student at Choate, "lacks stability" and is not "growing up," the administration complained to his mother. John was again often sick, spending time in the infirmary in November and again after Christmas.

He failed French and Latin, but Rose did not want him to be tutored at home during the summer. Again, instead of a fun time at Hyannis, he was back in Choate on August 7 to make up the missed material. For the fall term, he was moved to East Cottage but complained that he wanted to return to his former house, as he couldn't get away with anything at East Cottage.

John's father boarded Franklin Roosevelt's campaign train for a swing through the West after visiting the candidate at Warm Springs. Joe liked to claim later that he took care of the details aboard Roosevelt's train.

John's youngest brother, Edward, was born on February 22, the last Kennedy child.

ഇ൱

LYNDON B. JOHNSON, 24, quickly took charge in Representative Richard Kleberg's congressional office in Washington. He learned how things worked and enjoyed helping Texans with special problems. Johnson and his assistant, Estelle Harbin, would open the mail together and make decisions on what to do with every letter Kleberg received.

Lyndon and Estelle inherited bags and bags of unopened letters sent to the dying Republican representative who had been Kleberg's predecessor. Much of this old mail, as well as the daily load, came from people wanting jobs such as postmaster slots.

Initially Johnson was buried by the mail, unsure of how to get things done or where to turn. For one thing, Kleberg didn't answer mail, and in fact made little effort to do anything. Soon Lyndon did everything. He was a quick study and soon wrote longhand replies to letters for Estelle to turn into typed letters. Johnson made an effort to get an answer to every problem.

ഇ൱

RICHARD M. NIXON, 19, was a student at Whittier College in California.

ഇ൱

GERALD R. FORD, 19, a sophomore center on the University of Michigan football team, sat on the bench because Michigan had an all-American, Charley Bernard, a junior, playing center. Ford played very little on this unbeaten, national championship team. In spring practice earlier, Ford won the Morton Trophy, given annually to the "most improved" player who showed the "greatest promise for the varsity."

ഇ൱

JIMMY CARTER, age 8, lived on a farm in southwest Georgia where the crops, mainly cotton and peanuts, also included corn, okra, wheat, rye, oats, peas, and watermelon. His father was a teacher and a deacon of the Plains Baptist Church.

ഇ൱

RONALD REAGAN, 21, became a college football radio announcer for a small station in Davenport, Iowa. He graduated from Eureka College in Illinois in June as his grades improved: A in public speaking, four B's, and a C in philosophy. His romance with Margaret "Mugs" Cleaver was on hold after graduation.

Ronald's dreams included acting. Even while doing lifeguard duty on the Rock River outside Dixon, he would sit up on his stand and imagine acting situations. Reagan later admitted, "I was crazy about acting."

Ronald was still engaged to Mugs, but she wanted him to land a job before they married. She took up teaching. In September he hitched a ride to Chicago to look for work in radio. He lacked experience, they all said, but WOC in Davenport offered him a shot at football broadcasting on a trial, freelance basis. His first game was on October 1 at Iowa Stadium, the largest stadium he had ever seen, for the Iowa–Bradley game. A staff announcer and two engineers assisted him. WOC paid him $10 per game plus bus fare, weekends only, and he seemed to manage as he handled four games.

ഇ൱

GEORGE H. W. BUSH, 8, was a schoolboy in Greenwich, Connecticut.

INDEX

Note: Italicized page numbers refer to artwork. With the exception of Theodore and Franklin Roosevelt, in instances in which two presidents are related, entries for relatives are indexed by their relationship to the elder president.